Part Two

The National Experience

Fourth Edition

*A History of the United States
since 1865*

Part Two

The National

John M. Blum
Yale University

Edmund S. Morgan
Yale University

Willie Lee Rose
The Johns Hopkins University

Arthur M. Schlesinger, Jr.
The City University of New York

Kenneth M. Stampp
University of California, Berkeley

C. Vann Woodward
Yale University

Experience

Fourth Edition

A History of the United States since 1865

HARCOURT BRACE JOVANOVICH, INC.

New York / Chicago / San Francisco / Atlanta

The National Experience, Fourth Edition

John M. Blum
Edmund S. Morgan
Willie Lee Rose
Arthur M. Schlesinger, Jr.
Kenneth M. Stampp
C. Vann Woodward

Hardbound ISBN: 0-15-565680-5

Paperbound ISBN, Part One: 0-15-565681-3

Paperbound ISBN, Part Two: 0-15-565682-1

Library of Congress Catalog Card Number: 76-13664

Printed in the United States of America

Cover illustrations:
Hardbound: Aerial view of a Nebraska wheatfield by Georg Gerster from Rapho/Photo Researchers
Paperbound, Part One: Keystone from Photoworld
Paperbound, Part Two: NASA

A note on the paperbound edition

This volume is part of a variant printing, not a new or revised edition, of *The National Experience*, Fourth Edition. Many of the users of the Third Edition found the two-volume paperbound version of that edition useful because it enabled them to fit the text into the particular patterns of their teaching and scheduling. The publishers have continued that format in preparing this printing, which exactly reproduces the text of the one-volume version of *The National Experience*, Fourth Edition. The first of these volumes begins with the discovery of America and continues through Reconstruction. The second volume, repeating the chapter on Reconstruction (Chapter 15, "The Aftermath of War"), carries the account forward to the present day. The variant printing, then, is intended as a convenience to those instructors and students who have occasion to use either one part or the other of *The National Experience*. Consequently, the pagination and index of the one-volume version, as well as its illustrations, maps, and other related materials, are retained in the new printing. The difference between the one-volume and the two-volume versions of the book is a difference only in form.

Preface

Men and women make history. Their ideas and their hopes, their goals and contrivances for reaching those goals, shape all experience, past and present. The Indians, the first Americans, had to decide, by deliberation or by default, how to use the continent and its extraordinary resources. So have the successors of the Indians and the children of those successors—the early European settlers, the English colonists, the men and women of the new United States, and the generations that have followed them. Each generation has committed the nation to a complex of policies, some the product of thought and debate, others of habit or inadvertence, still others of calculated or undiscerning indifference. As the nation has grown, as its population has diversified, its economy matured, and its responsibilities multiplied, questions of national policy have become more difficult to understand but no more troubling. It took long thought and hard debate to settle the issues of independence, of democratic reform, of expansion, of slavery, of union itself, of control of private economic power, of resistance to totalitarianism across two oceans. All those issues and many more have made up the national experience.

This book endeavors to recount and explain that experience. It examines both the aspirations (often contradictory among themselves) and the achievements (often less grand than the best hopes) of the American people. It examines, too, the ideas, the institutions, and the processes that fed hope and af-

fected achievement. It focuses on the decisions, positive and negative, that reflected national goals and directed national purposes, and consequently it focuses continually on the men and women who made those decisions, on those who made history. The book emphasizes public policy, but the history of public policy perforce demands continuing discussion of the whole culture that influenced it.

The authors of this book believe that a history emphasizing public policy, so conceived, reveals the fabric and experience of the past more completely than does any other kind of history. They believe, too, that an emphasis on questions of public policy provides the most useful introduction to the history of the United States. In the light of those convictions they have agreed on the focus of this book, on its organization, and on the selection and interpretation of the data it contains. The structure of the separate parts and chapters is now chronological, now topical, depending on the form that seemed most suitable for the explanation of the period or the subject under discussion. The increasing complexity of public issues in the recent past, moreover, has persuaded the authors to devote half of this volume to the period since Reconstruction, indeed more than a third to the twentieth century.

The authors have elected, furthermore, to confine their work to one volume so as to permit instructors to make generous supplementary assignments from the abundance of excellent monographs, biographies, and "problems" books now readily and inexpensively available. Just as there are clear interpretations of the past in those books, so are there in this, for the authors without exception find meaning in history and feel obliged to say what they see. The authors also believe that, especially for the beginning student of history, literature is better read than read about. Consequently, in commenting on belles-lettres and the other arts, they have consciously stressed those expressions and aspects of the arts relevant to an understanding of public policy. Finally, they have arranged to choose the illustrations and the boxed selections from contemporary and other sources in order to enhance and supplement not only the text but its particular focus.

This is a collaborative book in which each of the six contributors has ordinarily written about a period in which he or she is a specialist. Yet each has also executed the general purpose of the whole book. Each section of the book has been read and criticized by several of the contributors. This revision has profited from the assistance of many historians who were kind enough to review portions of the book before it was revised. These include: David Brion Davis, Yale University; Sidney Fine, University of Michigan; Michael Holt, University of Virginia; Howard R. Lamar, Yale University; Robert Middlekauff, University of California, Berkeley; James T. Patterson, Brown University; Bradford Perkins, University of Michigan; Edward Pessen, Baruch College; and Morton Rothstein, University of Wisconsin. As in all previous editions of this text, so in this one, Everett M. Sims has assisted all the authors with his perceptive and gentle criticisms.

Not even a collaboration as easy and agreeable as this one has been can erase the individuality of the collaborators. Each section of this book displays the particular intellectual and literary style of its contributor; all the contribtors have been permitted, indeed urged, to remain themselves. The ultimate as well as the original responsibility for prose, for historical accuracy, and for interpretation remains that of the author of each section of this book: Edmund S. Morgan, Chapters 1–6; Kenneth M. Stampp, Chapters 7–12; Willie Lee Rose, Chapters 13–15; C. Vann Woodward, Chapters 16–21; John M. Blum, Chapters 22–26; Arthur M. Schlesinger, Jr., Chapters 27–29, revised for this edition by John M. Blum; and Arthur M. Schlesinger, Jr., Chapters 30–33 and Epilogue.

JOHN M. BLUM, *Editor*
New Haven, Connecticut

A note

On the suggestions for additional readings

The lists of suggested readings that follow the chapters of this book are obviously and intentionally selective. They are obviously so because a reasonably complete bibliography of American history would fill a volume larger than this one. They are intentionally so because the authors of the various chapters have tried to suggest to students only those stimulating and useful works that they might profitably and enjoyably explore while studying this text. Consequently each list of suggested readings points to a relatively few significant and well-written books, and each list attempts to emphasize, in so far as possible, books available in inexpensive, paperback editions—books whose titles are marked by an asterisk.

Use of the suggested readings, then, permits a student to begin to range through the rich literature of American history, but interested and energetic students will want to go beyond the lists. They will profit from the bibliographies in many of the works listed. They should also consult the card catalogs in the libraries of their colleges and the invaluable bibliography in the *Harvard Guide to American History*, rev. ed. (Belknap). For critical comments about the titles they find, they should go on, when they can, to the reviews in such learned journals as the *American Historical Review*, the *Journal of American History*, the *Journal of Southern History*, and the *William and Mary Quarterly*.

Those students who want to acquire libraries of their own and who want also to economize by purchasing paperback editions will find the availability of titles in paperbacks at best uncertain. Every few months new titles are published and other titles go out of print. For the most recent information about paperbacks, students should consult *Paperbound Books in Print* (Bowker), which appears quarterly.

The reading lists refer to very few articles, not because articles are unimportant, but because they are often rather inaccessible to undergraduates. There are, however, many useful collections of important selected articles, often available in inexpensive editions. So, too, students will have no difficulty in finding collections of contemporary historical documents that add depth and excitement to the study of history. A growing number of thoughtful books organize both contemporary and scholarly materials in units designed to facilitate the investigation of historical problems.

The problems books, documents books, and collections of articles will whet the appetite of engaged students for further reading in the fields of their interest. They can serve in their way, then, as can the lists of suggested readings in this volume, as avenues leading to the adventures of the mind and the development of the understanding that American history affords.

Contents

CHAPTER **15**

The aftermath of war   356

Into the third century   826

849   Appendix

Maps

Part Two

The National Experience

Fourth Edition

*A History of the United States
since 1865*

The aftermath of war

Charleston, South Carolina: the ruins of war

The long war was over. Now the nation, still divided in spirit, plunged into a decade of political and social turmoil. Northern victory had preserved the Union and had ended slavery; the constitutional right of states to secede would never be argued again. But all else was confusion. The Constitution was as silent on how states could be readmitted to the Union as it was on their right to secede. Indeed if Lincoln was correct in holding that states could not secede, then the Southern states had not seceded. They would simply resume their former responsibilities and enjoy their old privileges. The Southern states hoped for just such a simple restoration, even though the bitterness of the war made it unlikely that the North would at once embrace them again.

Uncertainty too marked the future of the blacks emancipated by war. Would the Southern states relegate the freedmen to peonage, handicap them legally as they had handicapped free blacks before the war, or grant them full citizenship? That question would have to be resolved by the Southern people, ill equipped to do so, because they had been devastated materially and emotionally by the war. And, although many Southerners were slow to realize it, their answer would have to satisfy the Northern people.

Northerners faced dramatic changes of their own. Since the 1840s the North had been moving rapidly toward an industrial economy. The war had only diverted the demographic and social changes that accompany industrialism, and with the return of peace those changes sped forward once again. In 1863 immigration resumed its prewar pace, and after the war, for approximately ten years, an average of three hundred thousand new Americans arrived each year at the nation's ports. Every year more workers moved to the city, where they became increasingly dependent on industrial employment, and more vulnerable to cycles of trade. Unprecedented opportunities for wealth opened for businessmen. The distractions posed by a dynamic economy prevented Northerners from concentrating steadily on the problems of Southern Reconstruction. Then, too, the passions of war were slow to subside, and few politicians of either section could rise above partisanship to disinterested statesmanship. The war lasted four years; winning the peace required twelve.

The problems of recovery

The new nation. The South had seceded from a union of states. It returned to a nation forged by war and vindicated by victory. Although the new spirit of nationalism was evident in many ways, especially in the powers exercised by the President and Congress, it revealed itself most clearly in economic legislation enacted during the war years. The absence of traditional Southern opposition in Congress during the war had made it easy for Republicans to adopt a protective tariff and reduce foreign competition in industry, to create a national banking system, to put through a homestead act, and to start funding a transcontinental railroad. Those measures signaled a new era of expansion in industry, agriculture, and transportation—all under the favoring hand of the national government.

Prosperity fed a mood of confident materialism. Seizing the opportunities of wartime economic expansion and inflation, entrepreneurs concentrated in their own hands new wealth that they now sought to invest. They had not far to look. Technological advances, many inspired by the demands of war, opened thousands of new opportunities to put capital to work. The natural resources of the country, seemingly inexhaustible, were more available than ever; industrialists exploited them fully, often ruthlessly and wastefully. Such vital indexes of industrial growth as the production of pig iron and bituminous coal and the extent of railroad mileage climbed sharply.

The iron horse symbolized the age of energy. The forty thousand miles of railroad track laid in the decade after 1865 stimulated heavy industry and opened the further West to agriculture, supplying the food for an expanding army of industrial workers. Federal loans and land grants had sped the construction of the Central Pacific eastward from California and the Union Pacific westward across the plains. For every mile of track laid the railway company received 6,400 acres of free land. Congress made generous loans on second-mortgage bonds: $16,000 for each mile of level ground covered, $48,000 in the mountains, and $32,000 in the high plains. As the two roads raced for their share of the federal subsidies, they sacrificed quality to speed. Still their accomplishment was spectacular. The Union Pacific built 1,089 miles of track; the Central Pacific, 689. They met at Promontory Point, northwest of Ogden, Utah. At ceremonies there on May 10, 1869, the blows of a silver sledge drove in the golden spikes connecting the rails. Now only a week's journey separated the Atlantic Ocean from the Pacific.

Demobilization posed problems for the Northern economy. Eight hundred thousand Union veterans were released in six months, and the abrupt cancellation of war contracts threw a million men out of work. Secretary of the Treasury Hugh McCulloch picked this inopportune time to withdraw from circulation nearly $100 million of the greenbacks that had been issued during the war. Constricting the currency when so many were unemployed intensified a brief but sharp economic slump in 1867. Within a year, however, railroad construction and expansion of the industries that supplied railroads with essential equipment created new jobs for the unemployed. Until 1873, when a new depression struck, most Americans were optimistic about the future.

The devastated South. In the South there was no such boisterous return to civilian pursuits. Agriculture, the region's economic bulwark, had been ruined wherever armies had clashed and passed. "The country between Washington and Richmond was . . . like a desert," wrote one observer. Another described the path of Sherman's march as "a broad black streak of ruin and desolation." Houses and outbuildings had been burned, crops destroyed, and livestock killed. Seed to plant new crops was often unavailable, and many farmers could not afford to buy it when they found it. Horses and mules to plow the land were even harder to find. Credit was almost unobtainable, and labor was scarce. A quarter of a million soldiers had lost their lives, and many freedmen were reluctant to work for their former masters. They believed, not without reason, that one-time masters would never treat one-time slaves as free people. The freedmen had other problems. Seeking relatives lost in slavery, returning to old homes, and looking for land and jobs, they were much on the road. They long remained a disorganized element in the work force the South required for economic recovery.

The cities fared no better than the countryside. Industry had been crippled or abandoned, financial institutions ruined, and resources for credit wiped out. At one stroke, emancipation had destroyed a credit base made up of billions of dollars invested in slaves. Land values slumped in response to the general devastation and lack of labor. The appearance of cities in the path of the armies was as dreary as the real condition of their industry and commerce. Charleston, South Carolina, was "a city of ruins, of desolation, of vacant houses, of widowed women, of rotting wharves." Columbia lay in ashes, as did most of Richmond.

Most Southerners, accepting defeat with fortitude and resignation, set about rebuilding their land. Many Southern whites expressed relief that slavery had come to an end but were at the same time uneasy about how the races would live together in the future. Long conditioned to rely on slavery as a means of controlling blacks, they were afraid of insurrections in the first year after the war, especially in regions where there were many freedmen. They could not even imagine political equality between the races. The freedmen had to face their own emotional hurdles. Learning to accept the responsibilities of family and self-support was not easy for men who had no land, no money, no education. When freedmen did manage to win some success, few understood the effort success required; when they failed, friend and foe alike were apt to explain it on grounds of inferiority.

The Northerners proved to be generous conquerors, as conquerors go. They executed no one for treason and briefly imprisoned only a few Confederates, one of them Jefferson Davis. They volunteered indispensable relief for the destitute of both races. In the last year of the war they had created the Bureau of Refugees, Freedmen, and Abandoned Lands, commonly known as the Freedmen's Bureau, to aid emancipated slaves. The Bureau frequently aided whites as well. After the war was over the Bureau sent supplies, seed, and rations to planters so farming could begin anew and freedmen could get work. It protected freedmen from exploitative planters and provided them with transportation to reach their families.

But poverty and daily reminders of defeat were hard for white Southerners to bear, and Northern bounty was not always graciously received. Women expressed their bitterness by shunning the army of occupation and by wearing on their gowns the insignia of the Confederacy in the form of buttons taken from the uniforms of husbands and sweethearts. Many young people of the defeated planter class had little hope for the future. "For the first time in my life I feel the pressure of want," wrote one young veteran, struggling vainly to conquer bitterness. "I have no country, no flag, no emblems, no public spirit. . . . I live now simply to live, and for my family." Experienced Southern leaders, however, were eager to reorganize their state governments and regain their lost political rights. They anxiously awaited reassuring signals from the North.

The dilemma of Reconstruction. Southerners aware of Lincoln's course during the war had reason to be optimistic. Although Lincoln had used military might to reestablish state governments, his plan was generous, its workings swift. As the Northern armies occupied Tennessee, Louisiana, and Arkansas, Lincoln had installed military governors and had sought the support of the loyal minority of citizens in establishing governments loyal to the Union. He had generously pardoned former Confederates who would take an oath of loyalty to the Constitution and the Union. In December 1863, by presidential proclamation, Lincoln outlined a plan for the full restoration of the Southern states to the Union. When in any state one-tenth of the citizens who had voted in the presidential election of 1860 had taken that oath, they could establish a government, without slavery, and the President would recognize it as the "true government." In 1864 Tennessee, Louisiana, and Arkansas had reorganized under Lincoln's "10 percent plan."

The Radical Republicans in Congress had challenged Lincoln's plan by passing the Wade-Davis bill. Moreover, Congress refused to seat congressional delegations from the states Lincoln had reorganized under his plan. In these actions the Radicals had strong support from moderate Republicans who agreed that Lincoln had usurped Congress' authority by taking over Reconstruction and who distrusted the loyalty of the Southern citizenry almost as deeply as the Radicals did (see p. 351). The harsh Wade-Davis bill provided that only after a majority of citizens in a state had taken an oath of loyalty to the United States could their state be reorganized. But only citizens able to take an ironclad oath of past loyalty could vote for representatives to the constitutional conventions. To deny former Confederate officials any role in the new governments, the bill provided that they could not be representatives to the conventions, and that new constitutions must disqualify them from voting and holding office. Lincoln vetoed the Wade-Davis bill, but Congress adamantly refused to seat delegates from the states Lincoln had reorganized. In the Wade-Davis Manifesto the Radicals rebuked Lincoln publicly, instructing him to execute the law and leave the making of it to Congress. The war ended with this conflict unresolved.

The Republicans in Congress faced a serious political problem. By an ironic twist, the late Confederate states stood to gain in defeat more representatives in Congress than they had had before the war. The elimination of slavery meant that blacks, only three-fifths of whom had been counted for purposes of congressional representation while they were slaves, would now be counted to their full number as freedmen. If the freedmen were enfranchised, Republicans might hope they would vote for the party that had emancipated them. To insist that the Southern states enfranchise freedmen before being readmitted to the

Camp for freedmen

The problems of recovery

Union was politically dangerous, however, because even in the North only a few states (those with the fewest blacks) allowed blacks to vote. There was also the danger that Southern planters might use their economic power to influence the votes of their former slaves, thus strengthening the Democrats rather than the Republicans. Beyond these immediate concerns was the Constitution's guarantee that states had the right to regulate their own suffrage requirements, and no one supposed that any Southern state would voluntarily grant the vote to freedmen. Republicans saw no way around their problem. On one point they were firm, however: they had no intention of giving the Democrats the Southern votes they needed to win back their power in Congress. Lincoln himself had hoped to build Republican support among Southern whites, but even he had wavered when he saw Louisiana electing conservatives unwilling to compromise on the race issue.

Republicans seldom spoke openly about the dilemma posed by Southern congressional representation. They stressed instead their distrust of the former rebels and what they pictured as the disloyal behavior of Northern Democrats during the war. Many Republicans, perhaps a majority, believed that the safety of the Union rested on their party's staying in power. They suspected that a combination of former rebels and Northern "Copperheads"—their name for pro-Southern Democrats—might even persuade the federal government to assume the Confederate war debt. For these reasons the Republicans were determined to bar Southern representatives from Congress until the government of the Southern states rested securely in the hands of loyal Unionists, preferably Republicans.

Johnson takes charge. Lincoln might have untangled the political snarl in which his party was caught. He was a superb politician, deft in maneuver. But before he could devise a workable plan, an assassin's bullet put Andrew Johnson in the White House.

Born to poverty in North Carolina, Johnson moved to Tennessee as a young man and earned his living as a tailor. After he was married, his wife taught him to read and write. By dint of determination and hard work he overcame his background and rose in the politics of his adopted state, serving before the war in both houses of Congress. Johnson never outgrew the attitudes shaped by his harsh past. A belligerent man, he hated aristocrats and special privilege. And yet he had little regard for the freedmen, who in his view were instruments of planter privilege rather than oppressed chattels. Only the destruction of the planter class would, he believed, give power to the poor whites and yeoman farmers, the classes best equipped, in Johnson's mind, to make the South democratic and loyal. Johnson's struggle upward through the rough

politics of Tennessee had not taught him the need to compromise. A rigid man, devoted to the Constitution, he was unable to reconcile his literal interpretation of that document with the revolutionary demands of the times. He showed none of Lincoln's flexibility or capacity for growth.

With Congress in recess when the war ended, Johnson seized the initiative. On May 29 he issued two proclamations. The first granted amnesty to former Confederates who would take an oath of loyalty to the Constitution and the federal laws. Their property was to be restored to them, except for slaves and any lands and goods that were already in the process of being confiscated by federal authorities. Fourteen classes of persons were excepted from the general amnesty, however, including the highest-ranking civil and military officers of the Confederacy, all those who had deserted judicial posts or seats in Congress to serve the Confederacy, and persons whose taxable property was worth more than $20,000. Those men were to make individual applications for amnesty, though the President promised to judge each case fairly. In denying automatic pardon to the rich, Johnson seemed as reluctant as the most ardent Radicals to trust Reconstruction to the "bloated aristocrats" he deemed responsible for secession. Still, no one knew what criteria he would use in judging their pleas for amnesty.

The second proclamation, in which Johnson outlined his requirements for the reconstruction of North Carolina, foreshadowed the policy he would follow in future proclamations to other states. He appointed William W. Holden, a well-known Unionist, as provisional governor and directed him to call a convention for the purpose of amending the state constitution "to restore said State to its constitutional relations to the Federal government." Johnson stipulated that only those who had taken the loyalty oath could vote for delegates or serve in that capacity at the convention. Although he did not include the "10 percent" provision, Johnson believed he was following Lincoln's plan of Reconstruction. Indeed, he accepted the governments already established in Arkansas, Louisiana, Tennessee, and Virginia under Lincoln's plan. Only after a public outcry against the leniency of his terms did Johnson require the returning states to disavow their ordinances of secession, repudiate the Southern war debt, and ratify the Thirteenth Amendment. That amendment, which would end slavery forever in the United States, had been approved by Congress in January 1865. Because there were now thirty-six states, approval by some of the former Confederate states was needed to reach the three-fourths that was required for ratification.

The easy terms that Johnson set for the restoration of Southern states to the Union bothered many

Northerners. Southerners heightened that concern by voting into public office popular former-Confederates. Johnson might have helped by being more chary of his pardons to Confederate leaders, for without pardons they were not qualified to hold public office. The pardoning process was extremely cumbersome, however, demanding his attention to every case, and the harassed President fell into the habit of approving all the pardons requested by the provisional governors. Since those governors were Unionists, he followed their advice. Some, like Governor B. F. Perry of South Carolina, forwarded every petition they received. Others requested pardons to reward or to win political friends and withheld them to destroy political foes. Johnson, inundated with petitions, pardoned freely. All too often those he pardoned soon turned up as duly elected congressmen and officers of the restored state governments. Among them was the former Vice President of the Confederacy, Alexander H. Stephens, who was elected senator from Georgia. The stubborn loyalty of the Southern voters to their former leaders alarmed the North.

There were other signs of Southern obstinacy. Some states refused to repudiate the Confederate war debt. South Carolina merely "repealed" its ordinance of secession, thus refusing to admit that it had been unconstitutional. The Thirteenth Amendment was ratified, but without Mississippi's approval. Southern Unionists and freedmen complained that they were not safe under the Johnson governments.

Clearly Johnson was failing in his plan to transfer leadership to the yeoman farmers. By late summer of 1865 Governor Holden of North Carolina was complaining to the President that there was "much of a rebellion spirit" left in the state. He feared that Johnson's "leniency" had "emboldened" the enemies of the government. Privately Johnson counseled Southern leaders to avoid antagonizing the Radicals in Congress, but he was too stubborn to admit publicly that his plan had misfired. Trapped by his own lavish pardoning policy, he had bestowed political power on the very leaders he had once distrusted most.

Reconstructing the South

Congress acts. When Congress reconvened in December 1865, only the Democrats and a few Republicans were willing to admit the Southern delegates. The majority of Republicans feared that if they seated former champions of the Confederacy they would surrender control over the course of Reconstruction. And yet many of those who voted against admitting the Southern delegates still hoped that Johnson might cooperate with the moderates in Congress by adopting a stronger Southern policy. The moderates were not, in the winter of 1865–66, ready to adopt a radical plan of Southern Reconstruction.

The Radicals, though only a small minority in Congress, had one advantage over the moderates: they held strong opinions on Reconstruction and they knew what they wanted. They believed that, beyond the freedmen, there were few true Unionists in the South. To ensure the future of the Republican party and the safety of the Union they worked for the rapid advancement of the freedmen and the exclusion of the old Southern leaders from politics. Some Radicals were bent mainly on humiliating the South. But others were truly concerned for the safety of the blacks, most of whom had supported the North during the war, some by serving in the army. All the Radicals, however, wanted to protect Southern Unionists from the ex-Confederate leaders whom Johnson was now restoring to power.

Thaddeus Stevens, a rancorous but able congressman from Pennsylvania, exemplified this mixture of vindictiveness and idealism. He opposed black suffrage (though he was later to endorse it), because he feared that the Southern planters would use their economic power to control the freedmen's votes. Instead of the vote, he proposed to give the freedmen land. He would confiscate the holdings of former Confederates and divide it into small freeholds. "Forty acres . . . and a hut," he declared, would "be more valuable . . . than the . . . right to vote." In the coastal areas of South Carolina and Georgia freedmen were already farming land, under "possessory titles," that had been assigned them by the government on estates confiscated during the war. Stevens wanted this policy extended throughout the South.

Charles Sumner, on the other hand, pinned his hopes on suffrage. He called first for votes only for educated blacks and black veterans but soon moved for general black suffrage. He argued that freedmen required the vote for their own protection. Other Radicals, including Salmon P. Chase and Ben Wade, agreed with Sumner. But the moderates, still the majority of Republicans, hoped to discover a middle road short of suffrage, between Johnson's simple restoration and the Radicals' more sweeping plans. The moderates dominated the Joint Committee on Reconstruction, which was created in December 1865 to formulate a plan for the South.

As the Joint Committee began its work, signs of Southern intransigence multiplied. Radical congressmen received countless letters from Southern Unionists complaining that they were at the mercy of former rebels. The deepest suspicions were aroused when the Southern states began to pass laws defining the status of blacks. These new "black codes," which

Thaddeus Stevens on black suffrage

There is more reason why colored voters should be admitted in the rebel States than in the Territories. In the States they form the great mass of the loyal men. Possibly with their aid loyal governments may be established in most of those States. Without it all are sure to be ruled by traitors; and loyal men, black and white, will be oppressed, exiled, or murdered. There are several good reasons for the passage of this bill. In the first place, it is just. I am now confining my argument to negro suffrage in the rebel States. Have not loyal blacks quite as good a right to choose rulers and make laws as rebel whites? In the second place, it is a necessity in order to protect the loyal white men in the seceded States. The white Union men are in a great minority in each of those States. With them the blacks would act in a body; and it is believed that in each of said States, except one, the two united would form a majority, control the States, and protect themselves. Now they are the victims of daily murder. They must suffer constant persecution or be exiled....

Another good reason is, it would insure the ascendency of the Union party.... I believe ... that on the continued ascendency of that party depends the safety of this great nation. If impartial suffrage is excluded in the rebel States, then every one of them is sure to send a solid rebel representative delegation to Congress, and cast a solid rebel electoral vote. They, with their kindred Copperheads of the North, would always elect the President and control Congress. While slavery sat upon her defiant throne, and insulted and intimidated the trembling North, the South frequently divided on questions of policy between Whigs and Democrats, and gave victory alternately to the sections. Now, you must divide them between loyalists, without regard to color, and disloyalists, or you will be the perpetual vassals of the free-trade, irritated, revengeful South.... I am for negro suffrage in every rebel State. If it be just, it should not be denied; if it be necessary, it should be adopted; if it be a punishment to traitors, they deserve it.

From Thaddeus Stevens, Speech to the United States House of Representatives, January 3, 1867.

looked like the old slave codes, were actually more like the laws governing free blacks in antebellum times. Blacks could now own property, witness, sue and be sued in court, and contract legal marriages. In some states they could even serve on juries. Despite these seemingly liberal provisions, the thrust of the new codes revealed Southern determination to keep blacks in a separate and inferior position. Blacks were segregated; intermarriage was forbidden; in Mississippi blacks could not own land; in several states they had to pay a special license fee in order to engage in certain trades. Everywhere special punishments were prescribed for black vagrants and for those who broke labor contracts. In some states blacks who could show no means of support could be bound out by the courts as labor apprentices. The most severe codes, drawn up by Mississippi and South Carolina in 1865, reflected the fears of whites during the social chaos of the first six months of peace. Those that followed in the winter of 1865–66 were little better. All were based on the assumption that freedmen would never be anything but dependent farm-workers. Both Radicals and moderates quickly agreed that the black codes must go.

The search for a middle course. In order to counteract the black codes, Congress soon enacted two bills reported by the Joint Committee on Reconstruction. The first, passed in February 1866, extended the life and expanded the powers of the Freedmen's Bureau; the second, passed in April, made a sweeping guarantee of civil rights.

Moderates regarded the Bureau of Refugees, Freedmen and Abandoned Lands as the perfect means of safeguarding Southern Unionists and blacks. Basically a paternalistic agency, the Bureau had been set up in March 1865 primarily to help thousands of displaced persons—refugee white Unionists, and freedmen—get homes, jobs, food, and transportation. The original Freedmen's Bureau Act had empowered the agency to administer lands abandoned by Confederates or confiscated from them and had committed the government to grant freedmen homestead rights to those lands. Under the benevolent administration of Commissioner Oliver Otis Howard, the Bureau provided housing and transportation to Northern schoolteachers who came to the South to teach illiterate freedmen. The Bureau had its faults.

The aftermath of war

*Southern freedmen:
objects of the black codes*

The military officers who served as bureau agents sometimes seemed friendlier to the planters than to the freedmen, and a few of them were cruel and even venal. Some of the agents leased farms for themselves and worked them with their charges; others used their power to "enforce contracts" more in the interest of the planters than the freedmen.

On the whole, however, those who were concerned for the safety of the freedmen knew that the Bureau was indispensable. Only those unsympathetic to the fate of blacks accused the Bureau of "coddling" them. Though Johnson had rendered the land provision in the original act void by returning confiscated property to its owners, the Bureau still had substantial power. The new bill, extending the life of the Bureau, would grant local agents authority to see that free labor contracts were just and that they were enforced, to defend freedmen against unscrupulous employers, and even to conduct courts when they found that freedmen were not receiving justice.

President Johnson held that those provisions would lead to "military jurisdiction," which was unconstitutional in time of peace. Accused persons tried in the Bureau courts would be tried and even convicted, he stated, without benefit of jury, rules of evidence, or right of appeal. And so Johnston vetoed the bill. He used his veto message to rebuke Congress for continuing to exclude the Southern delegates. Although Johnson's observations on the dubious constitutionality of the Freedmen's Bureau bill had some merit, they irritated congressmen who knew that freedmen were not getting justice in Southern courts. Four days after vetoing the bill Johnson harangued a

crowd gathered outside the White House to hear him deliver a Washington's Birthday greeting. In a rambling speech he denounced his opponents as traitors, suggested that they wanted to kill him, and compared himself to the crucified Christ. Johnson clearly saw himself as the martyred champion of the Southern states and constitutional liberty.

Furious, Congress turned to its civil-rights bill. That bill sought to grant freedmen the protection of federal citizenship, thus securing for them the same rights and protection as whites regardless of local statutes. Further, it authorized the use of troops to enforce its privileges and penalties. Again the President resorted to a veto. But this time Congress overrode him and voted the Civil Rights bill of 1866 into law. Heartened by their success, congressional leaders now put through a mildly amended version of the Freedmen's Bureau bill. Once again Johnson vetoed it, and once again Congress overrode his veto. Some Republican senators had sustained Johnson's veto of the first Freedmen's Bureau bill, but only three of them sustained his veto of the amended bill. The broad middle section of the Republican party had joined forces to guarantee civil rights for the freedmen. The President in his obstinacy had consolidated his adopted party in opposition.

The Fourteenth Amendment. In the case of Dred Scott (see p. 306) Chief Justice Roger B. Taney had given his opinion that no black, whether free or slave, could be regarded as a United States citizen or was entitled to the privileges the Constitution granted citizens. Many Republicans, remembering that decision, were afraid to depend on an act of Congress, which would be subject to Supreme Court review, to secure civil rights to the freedmen. They decided that

School for freedmen, Vicksburg, Mississippi

Reconstructing the South

only an amendment to the Constitution would safeguard the freedmen and secure a new electorate in the South loyal to the Union. The Fourteenth Amendment, proposed in April 1866 by the Joint Committee on Reconstruction, was subsequently passed by Congress on June 19. First it defined American citizenship: "All persons born or naturalized in the United States, and subject to the jurisdiction thereof, are citizens of the United States and of the State wherein they reside." The amendment then prohibited states from passing laws "which shall abridge the privileges or immunities of citizens of the United States," from depriving "any person of life, liberty, or property, without due process of law," and from denying "to any person within its jurisdiction the equal protection of the laws." Although the courts in time began to interpret the word "person" to include corporations (to protect them from state regulatory laws), the framers of the Fourteenth Amendment had only the freedmen in mind.

The second and third sections of the Fourteenth Amendment attempted to bring about a basic change in the Southern electorate. The second tried to force the states to grant Negro suffrage: either they enfranchised all male citizens or else they would lose seats in the House of Representatives proportionate to the number they excluded. Some Radicals would have preferred a specific guarantee of universal manhood suffrage. Practical politicians realized, however, that such a guarantee might have led to the defeat of the amendment in the North, for only a few New England states had enfranchised blacks. The third section disqualified from officeholding, state and federal, all who before the war had held public office requiring an oath to support the Constitution and who had subsequently supported the Confederacy. Only Congress could remove this disability. Other sections of the amendment disavowed the Confederate war debt, validated the United States war debt, and disallowed all claims for loss of property, including slaves.

The battle joined.   The upcoming congressional elections of 1866 caught the voters in a widening rift between President and Congress, with the Fourteenth Amendment as the central issue. The summer and fall witnessed the bitterest congressional election in national history. As with the Thirteenth Amendment, favorable action by some Southern legislatures was needed to secure ratification by the required three-fourths of the states. President Johnson opposed the Fourteenth Amendment and encouraged Southern legislatures to oppose it too. Of all the former Confederate states only Tennessee ratified the amendment. Vainly hoping to prompt other states to follow suit, Congress seated Tennessee's delegates.

Johnson continued to oppose Republican measures, especially the Civil Rights Act and the Freedman's Bureau Act, with all the weapons at his command. He used the patronage to reward his friends and hurt his enemies. As commander in chief he replaced military officers serving as agents in the Freedmen's Bureau who showed themselves too enthusiastic in the freedmen's cause. He interpreted acts of Congress passed over his veto so narrowly that he almost negated their intent. By cultivating the support of Democrats he angered all Republicans. Though Johnson claimed to be working for peace and reconciliation, he was actually trying to unite moderate and conservative Republicans with willing Democrats in a new National Union party. His purpose was to elect his own supporters to Congress in 1866.

The new party held a convention in Philadelphia in August, but the delegates could do no more than state grand principles. There was no real community of interest in the conglomeration of conservative Republicans, Democrats, and former Confederates who attended. Republicans grew skittish, moreover, at the reappearance of their old enemies, the "rebels" and the "Copperheads." At one point Governor Orr of South Carolina, a huge man, walked down the aisle arm-in-arm with Governor Couch of Massachusetts, a slight man. The scene symbolized the Republican fear that the Southerners were about to overpower the Unionists. The convention was a fiasco.

An even greater fiasco was the President's personal campaign to win support for conservative congressmen. In a "swing-around-the-circle" stump-speaking junket through the Middle West, he met hecklers on their own terms and sacrificed the dignity of his office at every whistlestop. The people grew angry, especially as the President revealed over and over his hostility to blacks. In recent outbreaks of racial violence in Memphis and New Orleans scores of blacks had been killed and hundreds wounded. The President deplored those events, as did most Southerners, but the voters could see nothing in Johnson's restoration policy to prevent them from recurring. In November the Democrats and most of Johnson's supporters were swept out of office. The Republican regulars had won a critical victory.

Congressional Reconstruction.   Although the election was more a rejection of Johnson than a mandate for extremists, the Radicals eventually gained most of their aims. The voters in calling for the Fourteenth Amendment as a basis of Reconstruction were endorsing a moderate measure, contemplating only essential changes. But securing enough Southern states to adopt so unpopular an amendment would require forcible measures. Thus a moderate victory

The aftermath of war

became the avenue for a Radical triumph. Even Thaddeus Stevens, though disappointed that Southern estates would not be confiscated and turned over to the freedmen, was pleased with the stringency of the legislation Congress now passed.

On March 2, 1867, in its final hours and after long debate, the outgoing Thirty-ninth Congress drove through a bill "to Provide for the more efficient Government of the Rebel States." This Reconstruction Act returned the South, two years after the war, to military rule. The severity of the act was partly owing to the determination of the Radicals, but even more to the unwitting aid of the Democrats who had joined with them to defeat less harsh proposals offered by moderate Republicans. Johnson's veto, not unexpected, condemned the bill as "utterly destructive" to the "principles of liberty," but his veto was promptly overridden.

The new law divided the ten Southern states (Tennessee had already been readmitted to Congress) into five military districts, each under the command of an army general backed by troops and armed with full authority over police and over judicial and civil functions. Each commander's immediate task was to secure a new (and verifiably loyal) electorate in his district, to enroll blacks, and to eliminate all persons excluded under the Fourteenth Amendment. Those voters were to elect a constitutional convention, which would draw up a document granting universal manhood suffrage and excluding "such as may be disfranchised for participation in the rebellion." Although the conventions interpreted that requirement variously, most new state constitutions excluded former Confederate leaders from voting and officeholding, and some excluded any who had sympathized with the Confederacy. An estimated 150,000 whites were thus disfranchised. The Reconstruction Act further declared that after a state had presented an acceptable constitution to Congress and had rati-fied the Fourteenth Amendment, Congress would then admit that state's delegates.

Even after this impressive victory, congressional leaders feared that Johnson might use his authority as commander in chief to subvert their intentions. Some even suspected that he might attempt a military coup. So they passed two more measures to trim his power. The Army Appropriations Act directed the President and the Secretary of State to issue military orders through the General of the Army, U. S. Grant, who was required to maintain his headquarters in Washington. The Tenure of Office Act provided that any officeholder appointed by the President with the Senate's consent was to serve until the Senate had approved a successor. If the President replaced a Cabinet member while the Senate was out of session, the replacement would serve after the Senate reconvened only with its consent; otherwise, the former incumbent would resume his duties. The Tenure of Office Act was designed in general to keep Johnson from using the patronage to destroy those who opposed his views on Reconstruction, in particular to prevent his replacing Edwin Stanton, Secretary of War. Stanton was the only member left in the Cabinet who was friendly to the Radicals, and many Radicals, including Stanton himself, believed that the safety of the nation depended on his remaining in office. The Tenure of Office Act further provided that, unless the Senate approved a change, Cabinet members were to hold office "during the term of the President by whom they may have been appointed, and for one month thereafter." These two acts, the second of dubious constitutionality, were passed on March 2, the day on which the Reconstruction Act was passed.

The Radical program of Reconstruction was now as airtight as its sponsors could make it. In the following months Johnson and the Southern leaders exploited loopholes in the new laws, but Congress promptly closed them by passing three supplementary

Reconstruction

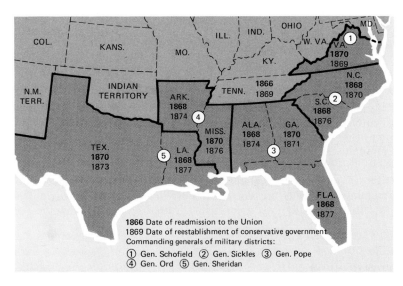

1866 Date of readmission to the Union
1869 Date of reestablishment of conservative government
Commanding generals of military districts:
① Gen. Schofield ② Gen. Sickles ③ Gen. Pope
④ Gen. Ord ⑤ Gen. Sheridan

acts. However unhappily, Johnson at last declared that he would execute the laws.

The Republican South. During the last half of 1867 most of the Southern states wrote acceptable constitutions under military supervision, called their new legislatures into session, and ratified the Fourteenth Amendment. All but three were readmitted to the Union in 1868. There was much foot-dragging over the disfranchisement of former Confederates, who were often the most popular leaders in their states. Endless discussions of this bitter point delayed the writing of constitutions in Virginia and Texas; in Mississippi the constitution was defeated because of it. It was 1870 before those three states won congressional approval of their constitutions and were permitted to reenter Congress. Georgia, admitted in 1868, was cast out again when its new legislature dismissed duly elected black delegates. Georgia, too, had to wait until 1870.

By this time one further requirement had been added for readmission: ratification of the Fifteenth Amendment, proposed by Congress in February 1869. This amendment forbade the states to deny the right to vote "on account of race, color, or previous condition of servitude." Its most immediate effect was to enfranchise Northern blacks; in the South, blacks were already enfranchised under the new state constitutions. Its sponsors hoped, however, that the amendment would prevent unfriendly legislatures from disfranchising freedmen in the future.

The new constitutions of the Southern states were in many respects better than their antebellum constitutions. The states now assumed responsibility for many social services that had formerly been left to local officials and private initiative. States without public-school systems now established them, along with institutions for the care of the indigent, homeless, and the physically handicapped. Tax systems were made more equitable, penal codes more humane, and the rights of women more comprehensive. For the first time in its history, South Carolina now had a divorce law. In states where planters had enjoyed advantages over upcountry farmers, districting for representation in the legislature was made fairer. The new constitutions also empowered state governments to undertake programs of economic recovery, especially for the rebuilding of the ruined railroads. Though not radical, the new constitutions were modern for their time, and they served the Southern states for several decades after the hated Republicans who initiated them had fallen from power.

Southern conservatives denounced the new governments, mainly because they detested the political coalition that had created them and that served in the first legislatures. They dubbed resident Northerners who held office in the new governments "carpetbaggers," suggesting that as transients they had no stake in Southern society. They denounced Southern whites who cooperated with the new regimes as "scalawags," a term suggesting at once disloyalty and a smallness of means and spirit. The spectacle of blacks

The power ... given to the commanding officer over all the people of each district is that of an absolute monarch. His mere will is to take the place of all law. The law of the States is now the only rule applicable to the subjects placed under his control, and that is completely displaced by the clause which declares all interference of State authority to be null and void....

It is plain that the authority here given to the military officer amounts to absolute despotism. But to make it still more unendurable, the bill provides that it may be delegated to as many subordinates as he chooses to appoint, for it declares that he shall "punish or cause to be punished." Such a power has not been wielded by any monarch in England for more than five hundred years. In all that time no people who speak the English language have borne such servitude. It reduces the whole population of the ten States—all persons, of every color, sex, and condition, and every stranger within their limits—to the most abject and degrading slavery.

From Andrew Johnson, Veto of the Reconstruction Act, 1867.

voting for public officers shocked the white South. Although blacks never held office in proportion to their numbers, their very presence in government fostered resentment and complaints of "Negro rule."

The assumption behind all this criticism was that none of these groups had any right to participate in the governing of the South. Actually there was little truth in the stereotypes the conservatives fastened on the Republican coalition. Many scalawags were prominent and affluent leaders who found Republican economic policies not unlike the old Whig program. Small farmers sensed that their interests would be better protected than they had been before the war, and they voted accordingly. The carpetbaggers included all sorts of people who had business in the South after the war. Some were military personnel; some were professionals—teachers, ministers, and lawyers; some were planters; and some, of course, were adventuring businessmen and speculators. There were fewer carpetbaggers than there were scalawags and blacks, but their undoubted loyalty to the Union and their connections with the federal government gave them great influence. Working through local groups called "Loyal Leagues," they organized the black Republican vote in the South.

The great weakness of this Republican coalition was that it had come to power as a result of revolutionary drives generated outside the South. Members of the once-powerful class of planters, now excluded from public office, would always regard the Republican governments as fraudulent and alien.

Yet idealism and high purpose marked the early stages of the Republican effort to rebuild the South. Whether the three groups comprising the coalition could stand together against the stresses of biracial politics was uncertain. Uncertain too was the strength of individual Republicans to resist the temptation for easy wealth presented by the rich spending and borrowing programs that were now launched for economic recovery. The Republican leaders, who professed commitment to more genuine democracy than the South had ever known, were under special obligation to conduct themselves as virtuous public servants.

The impeachment of Johnson. Congress had been right in suspecting that Johnson would use his control of the army to weaken the Reconstruction acts. His behavior was technically correct. But by instructing district commanders not to question the past behavior of those who took an oath of allegiance, he permitted Southerners of doubtful loyalty to regain the vote. He eventually removed three generals who were sympathetic to the Radical program, and he rashly challenged Congress in his December message of 1867 by declaring that he would maintain his rights as President, "regardless of consequences."

Several times the Radicals in Congress had contemplated impeaching Johnson, but they could find no legal ground for action. Their opening came when Johnson resolved to test the constitutionality of the Tenure of Office Act. While Congress was in the 1867 summer recess, he dismissed Edwin Stanton and appointed Grant as temporary Secretary of War. When Congress reconvened, the Senate refused to consent to Stanton's removal. Grant withdrew in confusion, protesting that he had never agreed to join the President in breaking the law. Grant had spoiled Johnson's plan, and his critics suggested that he had done so after a hint from the Radicals that he might himself become

367

... Those Union men who really maintained their integrity and devotion to the Federal Union through the war, and embraced the republican view at its close, were ... mostly of that class who are neither rich nor poor, who were land-owners, but not slave-owners. The few who were of the higher class had been so completely shut out from the intellectual movements of the North during those momentous years, that, as a rule, they were utterly confounded at the result which was before them. They had looked for the nation to come back to them, when its power was re-established, absolutely unchanged and unmodified. It came back, instead, with a new impetus, a new life, born of the stormy years that had intervened, putting under its feet the old issues which had divided parties, scornful of ancient statesmanship, and mocking the graybeards who had been venerated as sages in "the good old days of the Republic."

But for those Southern men, who, knowing and realizing all these changes, facing all these dangers and discomforts, recognizing the inexorable logic of events, and believing in and desiring to promote the ultimate good which must flow therefrom, in good faith accepted the arbitrament of war, and staked their "lives, fortunes, and sacred honor," in support of this new dispensation of liberty, words enough of praise can not be found! Nor yet words enough of scorn for their associates and affiliates of the North, who not only refused them the meed of due credit for their self-sacrifice and devotion, but also made haste to visit them with coolness, indignity, and discrediting contempt, because they did not perform the impossible task which the Wise men had imposed upon them.

From Albion W. Tourgée, A Fool's Errand; By One of the Fools, 1879.

a presidential candidate. Johnson, angry with Grant, now embarked on an *opéra-bouffe* search for a more cooperative general. As stand-in he finally produced General Lorenzo Thomas, but he had no success in installing his protégé in the War Department. Stanton, barricading himself in his office, cooked his own meals and regularly consulted with the Radical leaders. Removing Stanton was bad enough but trying to replace him with a pliable Secretary of War convinced even moderate Republicans that Johnson now intended to have a free hand in his use of the army to undo what the military Reconstruction Acts were bringing about in the South, and to do so in face of specific laws Congress had passed to prevent him. For moderate Republicans it was the last straw. Mindful of the fall elections when the voters had given the Radicals signs of displeasure over the extreme measures they had taken, the Republican moderates had in December blocked a vote of impeachment, but by February their patience was gone.

Confident that most citizens believed Johnson had broken the law, the Republican majority in the House of Representatives voted, unanimously, on February 24, 1868, to impeach Johnson for "high crimes and misdemeanors in office." The Radicals then drew up a list of specific charges, centering on his alleged violation of the Tenure of Office Act. The most significant was the charge that Johnson had been "unmindful of the high duties of his office . . . and of

the harmony and courtesies which ought to exist . . . between the executive and legislative branches." He had attempted to bring Congress into "contempt and reproach." Essentially the House, by this charge, was accusing Johnson of disagreement with congressional policies. A conviction on that charge would have established a precedent for the removal of any President who could not command a majority in the House of Representatives on an important issue. In that event, the American system of balance of powers in government might have given way to the parliamentary system.

To convict the President, two-thirds of the Senate sitting as a court presided over by the Chief Justice would have to agree that Johnson had broken the law (with the implication that he had no right to test the constitutionality of an act of Congress) and that he was not "fit" to hold his office. Johnson's able legal defense had no trouble disposing of the first point. Whatever Johnson had done, he had not broken the Tenure of Office Act, because Stanton had been appointed by Lincoln and not by Johnson and had served beyond the term of the President who appointed him. Cautious senators were troubled by the magnitude of the changes that might follow the removal of a President on the political charge that he had not worked for "harmony" with Congress. By a margin of only one vote, the Senate acquitted Johnson. Chief Justice Chase, who presided at the trial, was in sympathy with the President's arguments, and additional Republican senators would have voted for acquittal had their votes been needed. Many of those who voted to acquit the President did so because they distrusted the radicalism of Benjamin Wade, acting President of the Senate, who would have become President if Johnson had been convicted. Wade's views on public finance, labor, and woman suffrage were fully as radical as his views on civil rights for blacks, and they were far more shocking to the moderate Republicans. After Johnson's narrow escape, Stanton resigned and the Senate adjourned. The defeat of the impeachment was an ominous sign for the future of the new Republican governments in the Southern states.

The Supreme Court and Reconstruction.

During the war much of the power formerly held by the states had gravitated to the national government. It was not clear whether the executive or legislative branch would be the greater beneficiary of this shift. Then, after the war, the struggle over the military phase of Reconstruction severely upset the balance of powers within the federal government itself. Congressional power had reached a high point in the impeachment action against Johnson, but Johnson had won that contest. In another power struggle he failed: he never got a Supreme Court judgment on the Tenure of Office Act, which remained on the books for twenty years. Neither had he managed to get rulings on the two Reconstruction Acts. What was the role of the Supreme Court during this prolonged struggle between the President and the Congress?

The Court had started off boldly late in 1866. In the case of *Ex parte* Milligan it had ruled unanimously that neither Congress nor the President had the power to create military courts to try civilians in areas remote from war. That noteworthy decision liberated several men who had been condemned by such courts for military subversion in the North during the war. Still, the Milligan decision angered congressional Radicals because it cast doubt on the legality of the courts the Freedmen's Bureau was then sponsoring in Southern states. By passing the Reconstruction Acts in the spring of 1867, Congress delivered an overt challenge to the Court. Unsure of the Court's response, the Radicals began to talk of reducing its size, with some even urging that the Court be abolished. The Supreme Court grew cautious. By a five-to-four decision in the twin cases of *Cummings* v. *Missouri* and *Ex parte* Garland, heard in 1867, it invalidated the use of loyalty oaths, pronouncing them ex post facto and bills of attainder. In the same year, in the cases of *Georgia* v. *Stanton* and *Mississippi* v. *Johnson*, the Court was challenged to rule on the constitutionality of the Reconstruction Acts. In both instances it refused jurisdiction on technical grounds.

The Court's critics charged cowardice. The Justices, they suggested, were afraid that Congress would destroy the Court's power, if it ever elected to use that power, just as it had ridden over the President's prerogatives. But this was not the main reason for the Court's caution. The Court had not been popular in the years following the Dred Scott decision. But when Lincoln replaced the Southern Justices with staunch Unionists, it had grown much stronger in public esteem. By the time Congress and the President clashed, it had no reason to be fearful. Only a few Radicals wanted to destroy the Court. There were more compelling reasons for the Supreme Court's refusal to rule on the Reconstruction Acts: the Justices knew that the country was passing through a revolutionary period marked by questions on which the Constitution was either silent or not clear, and they realized that public opinion in the North demanded a rigorous Reconstruction of the South. Moreover, the Justices felt the public good would be best served by judicial restraint. After Radical Reconstruction waned, the Chase Supreme Court reemerged in the early 1870s with strong decisions that had a profound effect on American law for the rest of the century.

Foreign affairs under Johnson.

Although Johnson's Southern policy was a disaster, his conduct of foreign relations under the able direction of Secretary of State William Seward was a credit to his record. During the war the French under Napoleon III had affronted the Monroe Doctrine by setting up a puppet government in Mexico under the pliant and ambitious Austrian Archduke Maximilian. Fully occupied with fighting the Confederacy, Lincoln and Seward had denounced the French action but had been unable to challenge Napoleon's bid to restore French imperial power in the Western Hemisphere. Seward lost no time once the war was over. In 1866 President Johnson sent fifty thousand veteran troops to the Mexican border, and Seward demanded the withdrawal of French forces. The French complied, and the Mexicans reestablished their independence.

A vigorous expansionist, Seward believed that trade with other countries would help convince the world of the superiority of American democracy. In 1868 he signed a treaty of friendship and commerce with China. In 1867 he negotiated a treaty to buy the Virgin Islands from Denmark for $7,500,000. The Senate rejected that treaty but at the same time approved one that Seward had arranged with Russia for the purchase of Alaska for $7,200,000. Many Americans joked about Seward's "icebox," for it seemed no more than a frozen wasteland. Time was to demonstrate the strategic value and the richness of Alaska.

The election of 1868. Johnson's able conduct of foreign affairs was overshadowed by the turbulent issue of Southern Reconstruction, which dominated the presidential contest of 1868. The Republicans, rejecting Johnson's leadership, nominated Ulysses S. Grant as their presidential candidate, with Speaker of the House Schuyler Colfax as his running mate. Grant had no political experience, but moderates in the party had long favored the candidacy of the popular war hero. While the Radicals preferred Benjamin Wade, they came around to Grant as an "available" candidate who had listened to their advice during the struggle with Johnson and had broken with the President over the Tenure of Office Act. Who better than this popular war leader could inspire voter confidence in the safety of the military Reconstruction measures?

The Democrats were thoroughly demoralized. They had yet to rid their party of the taint of disloyalty, and they had no leaders capable of replacing their prewar spokesmen. For President they nominated Horatio Seymour, a wealthy conservative who as war governor of New York had gained an undeserved reputation for disloyalty. His running mate, Francis P. Blair, though recognized as a staunch Unionist, added little allure to the ticket. The Democratic platform declared the questions of slavery and secession to be settled forever and denounced Republican Reconstruction policies. The party called for amnesty for former Confederates and restoration of the Southern states. Negro suffrage, the Democrats urged, was a matter for the states to settle, not the federal government. This position gained less for the Democrats than it might have, because the Republicans themselves agreed that in the North the suffrage question should be left to the states, while maintaining that black suffrage was essential in the South. The Democratic platform opened the party to the charge that it was soft on the South.

The Democrats' only hope for victory was to focus public attention on the question of money and the repayment of the war debt, which was under hot debate. During the war the government had issued some $450 million in greenbacks. The value of that currency had fluctuated over the years, but it was always below the value of coins and gold-backed currency. Between 1866 and 1868 the Treasury Department had retired some $100 million of greenbacks from circulation. Now the Democrats adopted the "Ohio Idea," sponsored by George H. Pendleton, congressman from that state, who demanded that the notes be reissued to redeem outstanding war bonds not explicitly requiring redemption in gold. This demand for cheap money appealed to debtors, especially farmers with long-term mortgages who stood to benefit from inflation. It appealed also to critics of the "bloated bondholders," the war-profiteers. The Republicans, on the other hand, pledged themselves to the redemption of the national debt in gold. They knew that conservative financiers would approve this adherence to sound money, and they also understood that Western farmers, however much many of them might prefer cheap money, would, like other Northerners, still remember the passions of war vividly enough to distrust the Democrats' amnesty proposals for the South. The racial demagoguery of the Democratic campaign stirred that memory.

The Republicans worked to keep those passions alive. In the savage campaign of 1868, they concentrated on the alleged treason of the Democrats and waved the "bloody shirt" of war. They knew they could count on the support of the Southern states now dominated by carpetbaggers and on the backing of a multitude of federal officeholders. The Democrats lost whatever appeal they might have enjoyed from the Ohio Idea when their nominee, Horatio Seymour, repudiated that plank in the platform. Even with all their advantages, however, including the popularity of U. S. Grant, the Republicans just managed to win. Grant carried the Electoral College by 214 to 80 but received only 52.7 percent of the popular vote. Without the "bloody shirt" and the support of six Southern states safe in Republican hands, Grant would have lost the election. Of the former Confederate states, Seymour carried Louisiana and Georgia and showed strength in all the Border States. Mississippi, Virginia, and Texas had not been readmitted to the Congress, and their votes were not counted. The signs for future Republican victories were not auspicious, and it was plain that without the black votes of the South Grant's popular majority would have been a minority.

The Grant era

Government under Grant. No President had ever come to office so poorly equipped in temperament, intellect, or political experience as Ulysses S. Grant. And it was Grant's fate to come to that office in trying times. The white South, increasingly restive under Republican rule, began to express that restiveness in violence; in the West, farmers were beginning to feel the pinch of a long decline in commodity prices; in the North, a spirit of greedy materialism fostered graft inside the government and out. Grant did not create those problems, but he lacked the statesmanship to meet the first two and the strength of character to resist the third. He had been a great general, with the soldier's virtues of judgment, courage, and loyalty to subordinates. As President he was rudderless and confused by circumstances. His judgment was valueless because it was uninformed. When he found the courage induced by frustration, he often vented it in the malignant persecution of honest critics. He took everything personally. Loyalty to his subordinates proved his undoing, for he was duped at every turn. His mediocre Cabinet included several rascals who helped themselves to public funds. He was so obtuse in his choice of friends, so easily flattered, that he accepted expensive gifts from favor-seekers and appeared in public as the guest of such notorious stock-market swindlers as Jay Gould and Jim Fisk.

Grant, who had a fatal talent for falling out with the few able men who found themselves in his constantly shifting Cabinet, thereby lost the services of those who might have saved his Administration from shame. The one exception was Hamilton Fish, Secretary of State, an able and conscientious man who conducted foreign affairs with dignity and success.

Through the Treaty of Washington, signed in 1871, Fish opened a new era of friendly relations with Great Britain. Among the many problems that had exacerbated Anglo-American relations in recent years, the most serious had arisen over the extensive damage done to American shipping by the *Alabama* and other raiders that the British had built for the Confederacy. Violent speeches had been made in the Senate by irate patriots like Charles Sumner, who demanded that England be made to pay for indirect damage to American shipping as well as for the actual destruction of property. All those problems were referred, under the Treaty of Washington, to international arbitration. The British expressed "regret" about the *Alabama* and agreed to abide by the decision of the arbitration commission. That decision turned out to be favorable to the United States. Although the commission did not allow the indirect claims, it found that Britain had not exercised "due diligence" over her shipyards and awarded the United States $15,500,000. This successful arbitration of a sore dispute advanced both Anglo-American understanding and international peace.

The President's friends could be proud of little else. In his last annual message, Grant sadly acknowledged the faults of his Administration, blaming many of them on his own inexperience. But he pointed out that his political appointments, disastrous as many turned out to be, had been made "upon recommendations of the representatives chosen directly by the people." The patronage system had failed the President, because those representatives were on the whole true products of their age. The gaudy materialism symbolized by the brightly patterned waistcoats and florid oratory of Senator Roscoe Conkling, the flashy idol of New York, had its counterpart in the cheerful abandon with which Congress disposed of public goods. Politicians ignored the plight of the poor and showered their favors on the wealthy. In 1872, Congress abolished the wartime income tax. Like the wealthy, the lobbies of industrial interests, particularly those of copper and steel, found Congress receptive to their urgings. In spite of a 10 percent reduction of duties to placate farmers in 1872, many tariff rates that stood at 25 percent in Henry Clay's time had climbed to 500 percent by that year. Still the industrialists were not satisfied.

Neither were the railroad men, nor the congressmen themselves. In the fall of 1872 newspaper-reporters disclosed that prominent congressmen had accepted stock at "token" rates in return for a promise not to investigate the construction company of the Union Pacific Railroad. The Crédit Mobilier's relation to the Union Pacific was wholly fraudulent. Its purpose was to divert the profits from building the Union Pacific to the pockets of the road's promoters. In this way the Union Pacific was relieved of some $23 million in securities appropriated by Congress. Though many were involved in the chicanery—including Vice President Schuyler Colfax and future President James A. Garfield—only one, Oakes Ames, representative from Massachusetts and organizer of the scheme, was censured.

Corruption in Congress was tame compared to the colorful swindles that were taking place elsewhere. Grant's friends, Fisk and Gould, conspired with the President's brother-in-law to corner the available supply of gold in the New York stock market. Assuming they had convinced Grant not to sell government gold, they drove its market price to dizzying heights. Because many transactions had to be made in gold, the nation's business was thrown into panic. At last Secretary of the Treasury George Boutwell destroyed the scheme by selling $4 million of government gold, bringing the market suddenly down to earth. When the crash came on "Black Friday," September 24, 1869, many innocents were ruined but the principal culprits escaped. Gould, probably on the basis of inside information from government bankers, had started selling early; Fisk escaped by the simple expedient of repudiating his debts and then hiring thugs to threaten his creditors.

In New York City, "Boss" William Marcy Tweed of Tammany Hall relieved the city of an estimated $200 million. That figure included the proceeds from fraudulent bond issues and the sale of franchises as well as graft collected from corrupt contractors and merchants dealing directly with the city government. Since the governor of New York was a Tweed henchman, the "Boss," though a Democrat himself, had little trouble silencing the Republican legislature with bribes. Control of the police, the courts, and the district attorney made Tweed almost invulnerable. At last, when the city was nearly bankrupt, Samuel J. Tilden successfully challenged Tweed for control of the Democratic organization in the city. Tilden gained a perhaps inflated reputation for having "smashed" the ring. Tweed's was only the most notorious of the party machines. Others operated in Philadelphia, Chicago, and Washington. In their heyday they had little trouble winning the cooperation of reputable public figures.

The South experienced the same blight. The corruption of the reconstructed Southern legislatures was particularly disastrous. Governments organized for the first time on the basis of racial equality were hopelessly discredited by association with railroad and printing swindles and eventually fell into bankruptcy. The ideal of political equality suffered in public esteem because it was supported by corruptionists. Bold efforts to rebuild the South's transportation system dissolved in the wholesale theft of railroad stock. In South Carolina even the Land Commission founded to help blacks buy farms ended up as a device for transferring state funds to the private accounts of unscrupulous assessors and their friends in high places. Florida's bill for printing costs in 1869 was more than the entire cost of running the state government in 1860. The list of scandals was long and the crooks were blithe. "Damn it," expostulated Henry Clay Warmoth, carpetbag governor of Louisiana and one of the worst spoilers, "everybody is demoralizing down here. Corruption is the fashion." He had a point. It takes two to make a deal, and many of those who bribed the legislature for favors were native Southerners and Democrats.

Blacks, seldom the beneficiaries of these schemes, were frequently the dupes of those wiser in the ways of the world. Nevertheless the presence of blacks in the legislatures and their loyalty to the carpetbag Republicans enabled disfranchised whites to condemn "Negro rule" and to blame corruption on this experiment in political equality. Even the performance of the honest and efficient Radical government of Mississippi, and of remarkable black leaders like Senator Hiram Revels of that state and South Carolina's Secretary of State Francis Cardozo changed few opinions. Political association with blacks and carpetbaggers became more unpopular as scandals multiplied. Scalawags found themselves ostracized by their neighbors. As one former Whig planter explained when he withdrew from the Republican party, a man with four marriageable daughters could do no less.

White resentment took a vicious turn with the appearance and rapid growth of the Ku Klux Klan. First organized in 1866, the white-hooded nightriders contented themselves for a time with playing pranks on freedmen to frighten them into "good" behavior. But soon the Klan, with its Grand Dragon, "Dens," and "Cyclopses," had spread over the South. Now an instrument of political terror, it attacked the Loyal Leagues, intimidated black voters, and destroyed the effectiveness of local black organizers. Nor did the Klan shun murder. Many able black leaders, including Wyatt Outlaw of North Carolina, lost their lives to the fury of the Klansmen. When the organization was officially disbanded in 1869, it went underground. After an elaborate investigation Congress passed the Ku Klux Klan Act of 1871, empowering the President to suspend the writ of habeas corpus in order to cope with the violence that regularly erupted at elections. The Republican governors were often forced to call on federal troops to keep peace, but critics of the Administration, north and south, abhorred the practice of using soldiers to supervise elections. The North was growing tired of the "autumnal outbreaks," indeed of Southern Reconstruction in general. Before Grant's first term was over, the Republican governments in the South, steeped in corruption and torn by violence, were doomed.

The Liberal Republican movement. Few doubted that the Republicans would nominate Grant for a second term. In 1872, however, a revolt in the ranks of the party gave the regulars pause. Calling themselves "Liberal Republicans," the dissidents challenged the party regulars on three issues: corruption in government, Grant's financial policies (the high level of tariff protection and the continued use of greenback currency, which delayed resumption of specie payments), and the Radical Southern policy.

To eliminate corruption in government, they demanded a reform of the civil service. As early as 1870 Carl Schurz, a German immigrant and war hero, had led a Liberal Republican revolt in Missouri. There the Radical Republicans had all but proscribed party members who wanted to restore political rights to former Confederates in the state. The victorious Liberals took up the cause of the excluded faction and placed B. Gratz Brown in the governor's chair. Before 1872 the Missouri Liberals had merged with a group of prominent Eastern leaders to form a new party. A number of distinguished journalists who had had a hand in exposing scandal lent their talents; E. L. Godkin of the new reform paper, *The Nation*, and two young brothers, Boston patricians, Henry and Charles Francis Adams, were among them. Indeed many men of talent and idealism in the East were sympathetic to the movement, and many one-time abolitionists enrolled against Grant. Even Charles Sumner, who had fallen out with Grant over the President's stubborn but futile determination to annex Santo Domingo (see p. 491), joined the Liberals.

The party had its share of office-seekers, however, who at the 1872 convention in Cincinnati were able to kill the nomination of any of several men they

The aftermath of war

These men are not only armed, disciplined, oath-bound members of the Confederate army, but they work in disguise; and their instruments are terror and crime. Why, sir, we are already familiar, and perhaps too familiar, with the common description of these Ku-Klux Klans riding at night over a region of country, going from county to county, coming into a county town, and spreading terror all over a community; and not only that, but they endeavor to excite superstition. They pretended, I believe, in the outset to be the representative ghosts of the Confederate dead. That was the idea which they sought to give out; the ghosts of the Confederate dead were coming back to punish those who had been disloyal to the Confederate service; and they terrified men, women and children, white and black. They excited the superstition of the ignorant negroes of the South, endeavored to frighten them first by superstition, then by intimidation, by threats, by violence, and by murder.

Mr. President, I do not know anywhere an organization similar to this Ku-Klux Klan. I have thought of the Thugs of India. They murdered, and they murdered secretly; but they did not disguise themselves while they were in the act of murder. If any Senator now, in looking over the record of crime in all ages, can tell me of an association, a conspiracy, or a band of men who combined in their acts and in their purposes more that is diabolical than this Ku-Klux Klan I should like to know where it was. They are secret, oath-bound; they murder, rob, plunder, whip, and scourge; and they commit these crimes, not upon the high and lofty, but upon the lowly, upon the poor, upon feeble men and women who are utterly defenceless. They go out at night, armed and disguised, under color of superstitious forms, and commit their work. They go over vast regions of country, carrying terror wherever they go. In all the record of human crime—and God knows it is full enough—where is there an organization against which humanity revolts more than it does against this? I know there is not a Senator here but feels that this thing ought to be put down.

From John Sherman, Speech in the United States Senate, March 18, 1871.

feared might fight too well for reform. After a chaotic convention, the Liberals ended up nominating Horace Greeley, the quixotic editor of the New York *Tribune*. Though the Liberals opposed the tariff, Greeley was a protectionist. During his long, controversial career in journalism, the candidate had himself written the script for those who now attacked him for his contradictory statements on public issues. Greeley understood politics well, but not well enough to know that he was a poor candidate. With his wispy chin-whiskers and cherubic face, he looked anything but a President.

In short, the Liberals had failed to come up with an attractive alternative to Grant. The worst of the Grant Administration scandals were yet to be exposed, and the general's heroic image retained its luster. Few Republicans would abandon him to join hands with the hated Democrats. Moreover, the Democrats gave the kiss of death to the new party of dissident Republicans by weakly endorsing its candidates. Even so, the Democrats could not deliver all their party's potential votes to Horace Greeley, long-time Whig, staunch Republican, archfoe of Democrats in general, and anathema in the South. The "bloody shirt" was still a potent symbol, and Grant won a great victory. Greeley died a few weeks later, broken-hearted over his personal defeat and sad that corrupt government had won so thunderous an endorsement.

The collapse. Even though they had lost the election, the Liberals had redefined the goals of most of the concerned and best-informed Northern citizens. Most of them were tired of Southern Reconstruction and embarrassed by the Radical governments in the Southern states. To them reform now meant clean government. Civil-service reform took precedence over civil rights for blacks, and the nation became more interested in economic questions than in supporting regimes in the South that regularly sent delegates to Washington to vote with the Radicals.

Republican sensitivity to the Liberals' criticism was demonstrated just before the election of 1872, when Congress passed the Amnesty Act. By its terms political rights were restored to all former Confederates except about five hundred of the most prominent leaders. In the South, Liberal Republican factions charged party regulars with misgovernment and made a bid for white conservative support in a cleanup campaign. They seldom succeeded, because the white conservatives, now rehabilitated politically, preferred a new political coalition to any form of Republicanism. Defecting scalawags promptly joined ranks. Sometimes the new coalition called themselves Democrats, and sometimes simply "conservatives."

Thoroughly factionalized, the Republican state governments in the South fell, one by one, over the next four years. Now Grant sent troops at election time only when he thought there was a strong chance that the Republicans could win. The triumphant conservatives claimed that they had "redeemed" their states from the Radicals. By the time of the 1876 presidential election, only three (South Carolina, Louisiana, and Florida) were still in Republican control.

Less than a year after Grant's second election political scandals and economic distress had destroyed the brittle reputation of his Administration. A congressional committee revealed that the newspaper-reporters had been right about the affairs of Crédit Mobilier. Worse yet, five of Grant's Cabinet officers were exposed as corruptionists. The most notorious was William W. Belknap, Secretary of War, who had accepted bribes from traders at Indian posts. Benjamin Bristow, Grant's new Secretary of the Treasury, uncovered the Whiskey Ring, a conspiracy of hundreds of distillers who had bribed Treasury officials in order to evade federal taxes. Grant's private secretary, Orville E. Babcock, was implicated in that corrupt adventure. Grant declared, "Let no guilty man escape," but he provided Babcock with a deposition that helped him evade punishment.

Economic disaster followed in the wake of public scandal. In September 1873 a rash of financial failures in New York dragged the country into the deepest depression it had known. The sudden withdrawal of European investments, prompted by the Franco-Prussian War and vast railroad-building abroad, triggered the panic. But American investment in concerns that produced no immediate or real profits, such as the railroads, rendered bankers unable to cope with the crisis. The failure of Jay Cooke & Co., one of the most respected banking firms in the country, set off a chain reaction. Cooke's firm was deeply involved in financing the Northern Pacific Railroad. Eighty-nine railroads defaulted on their bonds, and eighteen thousand businesses failed in two years. Iron mills and furnaces fell idle, and by 1875 half a million men were out of work. Wages declined, and agricultural prices dropped so low that many farmers, unable to pay their mortgages, had to surrender their properties, their homes, their fondest dreams.

Hard times and scandal hurt the Republicans in the congressional elections of 1874. The Democrats elected a majority in the House of Representatives, improved their standing in the Senate, and won control in twenty-three states. Many dissatisfied groups were now blaming Republican financial measures for their problems. As exporters of agricultural products, the South and West disliked the protective tariff. In the West farmers wanted a freer circulation of paper money (the greenbacks issued as legal tender during the war) to ease their burden of debt and, so they presumed, to raise farm prices. But businessmen, with some exceptions, favored a retirement of greenbacks and a return to the gold standard, for they thought that these measures would stabilize the value of currency and thus reduce the uncertainty of commerce and exchange.

The legal status of greenbacks was in doubt. In 1870 the Supreme Court, under Chief Justice Chase, who had been, ironically, Secretary of the Treasury when greenbacks were issued, ruled that the Legal Tender Act was unconstitutional. Protesting that decision, Grant's advisers pointed out that it cast doubt on the validity of all contracts calling for payment in money that had been legal tender ever since 1862. They also feared that the abrupt removal of greenbacks would overly contract the supply of money. Grant, with the consent of the Senate, therefore expanded the Supreme Court by appointing two Justices whose views he knew in advance, and in 1871 the enlarged Court ruled that the government had been within its rights in issuing the paper currency. That opinion settled the legal question but left open the question whether the greenbacks should be kept in circulation.

In 1873, in order to relieve the deflation accompanying the panic, the Treasury Department reissued $26 million of the greenbacks it had retired earlier. But the Administration balked at a further expansion of the currency demanded by Congress the following year. It backed instead a bill designed by John Sherman to give the West and the South a a fairer share of the nation's banking facilities. That bill increased the number of national banks and allowed them to augment the amount of bank notes in circulation. It also provided that after January 1, 1879, the Treasury would, on demand, redeem all legal-tender notes in coin. The Specie Resumption Act became law in 1875. In the same year the Republicans, with the help of some Eastern Democrats, restored the protective-tariff duties that had been reduced three years earlier.

The Republicans were now adopting the twin principles of political economy that would become the party's articles of faith in the decades to come—

The aftermath of war

high tariffs and hard money. Those principles endeared the party to business and industry but rendered it increasingly suspect to farmers, debtors, and workers. Advocates of paper money severely criticized the Specie Resumption Act. Overlooking its constructive aspects, they predicted that resumption would precipitate a disastrous contraction. But nothing of the sort happened in 1879, when payments in specie were resumed, because of the coincidental return of prosperity. This accident convinced the Republicans of the merit of their "sound money" policy, but it was too late to mitigate the unpopularity the Grant regime had reaped from the depression, from corruption, and from its steady deference to the propertied interests of the country.

The twilight of Reconstruction.

Scandal and depression during Grant's second term diverted the attention of Congress from the South. Grant, sensing the disenchantment of the public, grew less willing every year to support the toppling carpetbag regimes with troops. Moreover, with most of the older states of the Middle West now safe for the Republicans, a Republican South was no longer essential to their control of the federal government. With federal support withdrawn, the carpetbag governments could no longer withstand the onslaught of the white South. Openly now, without hoods or robes, conservatives organized to intimidate blacks who showed interest in politics, and the few surviving scalawags.

Congress made a last pathetic gesture to the blacks whose fate was at stake. Senator Charles Sumner had introduced a civil-rights bill in 1872 that was passed in 1875, after his death, in a much denatured form. Sumner had intended to assure full equality for the freedmen, including political rights, all civil liberties, and the elimination of social segregation. His purpose was frustrated by the ambiguous racial views of Republican moderates and by Northern opinion. The act, as it was finally passed, guaranteed equal accommodations in such public places as inns and theaters and forbade the exclusion of blacks from jury duty, but it provided no practicable means of enforcement. Moreover, school integration, which Sumner had proposed, was quietly dropped from the final bill. What little force the act carried was destroyed in 1883 when the Supreme Court declared invalid those parts of it designed to secure social equality. The Court also ruled that, although the Fourteenth Amendment prohibited the invasion of civil rights by the states, it did not prohibit the invasion of civil rights by individuals unaided by state authority. Blacks might be driven from the polls or otherwise abused by individuals, and the federal government would have no power to intervene.

Although the emasculation of Sumner's program revealed that Republicans were no longer committed to protecting blacks in their citizenship, the Civil Rights Act of 1875 established a significant precedent. In the next century a new generation of crusaders would rediscover the Civil Rights Acts of 1866 and 1875 and in the Fourteenth and Fifteenth Amendments their original purpose. A new Supreme Court would restore their original meaning. But for two generations blacks were to face a lonely struggle. Deprived of legal recourse to defend their freedom and abandoned by Northern public opinion, they were largely ignored by the federal government.

Reconstruction was a story of lost opportunity. Victory in war had opened the grand prospect of a country reunited on the principles of liberty. Sometimes with the best intentions, but often with greed and venom, the nation's leaders allowed the principles of liberty to be smirched by corruption. In restoring the South, they scarred it. In developing the economy, they abandoned power and granted privilege to a grasping few. In dealing with civil rights, they inspired blacks to reach for high goals and then left them to the mercy of demagogues and embittered whites. The fruits of victory were lost in the aftermath of war.

Suggestions for reading

GENERAL

There is a concise analysis of Reconstruction and critical discussion of the bibliography on that subject in J. G. Randall and David Donald, *The Civil War and Reconstruction* (2nd ed., 1961). That volume also covers the Grant years. Three recent and indispensable studies in the rapidly growing scholarship on Reconstruction are W. R. Brock, *An American Crisis** (1963); David Donald, *The Politics of Reconstruction** (1965); and K. M. Stampp, *The Era of Reconstruction** (1965). See also J. H. Franklin, *Reconstruction After the Civil War** (1962); Avery Craven, *Reconstruction: The Ending of the Civil War* (1969); and R. W. Patrick, *The Reconstruction of the Nation* (1967). Another general treatment of the period 1865–78, stressing social and economic conditions, is Allan Nevins, *The Emergence of Modern America, 1865–1878** (1927). The national politics of the period receive detailed but sometimes jaundiced treatment in Matthew Josephson, *The Politicos, 1865–1896** (1938). The national mood

*Available in a paperback edition.

concerns P. H. Buck, *The Road to Reunion, 1865–1900** (1937). J. G. Randall, *Constitutional Problems under Lincoln* (rev. ed., 1951), discusses wartime legal decisions that had an impact on postwar reorganization. Clement Eaton, *The Waning of the Old South Civilization** (1968), traces Southern reactions to defeat in war.

Lincoln's views on Reconstruction are discussed in W. B. Hesseltine, *Lincoln's Plan of Reconstruction* (1960), and R. N. Current, *The Lincoln Nobody Knows** (1958). See also Benjamin Quarles, *Lincoln and the Negro* (1962).

JOHNSON, THE RADICALS, AND RECONSTRUCTION

H. K. Beale, *The Critical Year: A Study of Andrew Johnson and Reconstruction* (1930), provides a sympathetic treatment of the President, with an interpretation of the Radicals that emphasizes their economic motives. Johnson is criticized for his inept dealings with Congress in E. L. McKitrick, *Andrew Johnson and Reconstruction** (1960), an indispensable study. Two recent works of note on Johnson's impeachment are M. L. Benedict, *The Impeachment and Trial of Andrew Johnson** (1973), and H. L. Trefousse, *Impeachment of Andrew Johnson* (1975). W. A. Dunning's older study, *Reconstruction, Political and Economic, 1865–1877** (1907), is still useful for its concise account of events, though its interpretation is marred by the author's assumptions on race. E. M. Coulter, *The South During Reconstruction, 1865–1877* (1947), has been faulted on the same score, but it provides strong chapters on cultural life. W. E. B. DuBois, in his beautifully written *Black Reconstruction** (1935), imposes a Marxist interpretation on the period, without much success.

The two most famous Radical leaders have excellent biographies, in Fawn Brodie, *Thaddeus Stevens, Scourge of the South** (1959), and D. H. Donald, *Charles Sumner and the Rights of Man** (1970). More generally, H. L. Trefousse treats *The Radical Republicans** (1969). David Montgomery, *Beyond Equality: Labor and the Radical Republicans 1862–1872* (1967), discusses the relationship between Northern labor and the Radical goals for Southern blacks. A general survey is Robert Cruden, *The Negro in Reconstruction** (1969), as are the relevant chapters in J. H. Franklin, *From Slavery to Freedom* (3rd ed. rev., 1966), and August Meier and E. M. Rudwick, *From Plantation to Ghetto: An Interpretive History of American Negroes* (1966). Peggy Lamson, *The Glorious Failure: Black Congressman Robert Brown Elliott and the Reconstruction of South Carolina** (1973), and J. R. Lynch's own *Facts of Reconstruction** (1913), provide insights on the position of black leaders in the South.

Alone on its subject is J. E. Sefton, *The United States Army and Reconstruction, 1865–1877* (1967), but related, and of great significance, are two studies of the Freedmen's Bureau: G. F. Bentley, *A History of the Freedmen's Bureau* (1955), and W. S. McFeely, *Yankee Stepfather: General O. O. Howard and the Freedmen** (1968). What the Bureau was up against in the South may be overstated in Allen Trelease's powerful *White Terror: The Ku Klux Klan Conspiracy and Southern Reconstruction** (1971), but Otto Olsen's *Carpetbagger's Crusade: Albion Winegar Tourgeé** (1965) shows that the problems were great. John W. Blassingame, *Black New Orleans, 1860–1880* (1973), deals splendidly with a famous black community in transition, and Peter Kolchin, *First Freedom: The Responses of Alabama's Blacks to Emancipation and Reconstruction* (1972), ably treats a more typical world of farming freedmen. V. L. Wharton, *The Negro in Mississippi, 1865–1890** (1947), was a pathbreaking work, now a classic, while Joel Williamson, *After Slavery** (1965), records the South Carolina experience. An early contributor to the story of blacks in Reconstruction was A. A. Taylor, whose *Negro in South Carolina during Reconstruction* (1924), *The Negro in the Reconstruction of Virginia* (1926), and *The Negro in Tennessee* (1941) are still useful. W. L. Rose records the experience of blacks and their relationship with the federal government and Northern abolitionists in *Rehearsal for Reconstruction** (1964), also about South Carolina. Carol Bleser, *The Promised Land: The History of the South Carolina Land Commission, 1869–1890* (1969), writes of the use and abuse of the one state commission founded to gain for the freedmen what they most wanted. H. L. Swint, *The Northern Teacher in the South, 1862–1870* (1941), is a general treatment of its theme, still useful, and J. M. McPherson, *The Struggle for Equality: Abolitionists and the Negro in the Civil War and Reconstruction** (1964), stresses the humanitarian motivation of the abolitionist wing of the Republicans' support. LaWanda and J. H.

*Available in a paperback edition.

The aftermath of war

Cox, *Politics, Principle, and Prejudice, 1865–1866** (1963), also stress civil rights as the basic issue of political reconstruction, but a number of newer works have questioned the depth of the North's commitment to implementing civil equality for blacks. Louis Gerteis, *From Contraband to Freedman: Federal Policy Toward Southern Blacks* (1973), is illustrative of the trend in interpretation, as is C. V. Woodward, "Seeds of Failure in Radical Race Policy," from the *Proceedings* of the American Philosophical Society, 110(1966), 1. F. G. Wood, *Black Scare: The Racist Response to Emancipation and Reconstruction** (1968), also stresses limits. Michael Perman, *Reunion without Compromise* (1973), stresses Southern politicians' skill in resistance.

Among the many reliable state and local studies of Reconstruction in the South are: J. G. Taylor, *Louisiana Reconstructed* (1974); E. S. Nathans, *Losing the Peace: Georgia Republicans and Reconstruction (1865–1871)* (1968); W. M. Evans, *Ballots and Fence-Rails: Reconstruction on the Lower Cape Fear** (1967); F. B. Simkins and R. H. Woody, *South Carolina During Reconstruction* (1932); and T. B. Alexander, *Political Reconstruction of Tennessee* (1950). Also of interest on special topics are Richard Current, *Three Carpetbag Governors* (1967), O. A. Singletary, *The Negro Militia and Reconstruction* (1957), and J. W. DeForest's own account of his experiences, *A Union Officer in Reconstruction,* edited by J. W. Croushore and David Potter (1948).

On the Fourteenth Amendment, see J. B. James, *The Framing of the Fourteenth Amendment** (1956), and Jacobus ten Broek, *The Antislavery Origins of the 14th Amendment** (1951). On the Fifteenth Amendment, see W. R. Gillette, *The Right to Vote** (1969). On pardons, see J. T. Dorris, *Pardon and Amnesty under Lincoln and Johnson* (1953). On the role of the courts, see S. I. Kutler, *Judicial Power and Reconstruction Politics* (1968). For a broad general study of the judicial process in the period consult H. J. Hyman, *A More Perfect Union* (1973). For a very detailed history of the Supreme Court, see Charles Fairman, *Reconstruction and Reunion 1864–1888* (1971). Part One, which is Volume VI of the Oliver Wendell Holmes Devise *History of the Supreme Court of the United States.* For wartime thinking in Washington about the constitutional issues of Reconstruction, see Herman Belz, *Reconstructing the Union: Theory and Policy during the Civil War* (1969). (General and special literature on the South and its postwar problems through 1900 is listed in connection with Chapter 16; on American business, consult the listing following Chapter 18.)

THE GRANT ERA

There is a dearth of truly satisfactory books on this period. W. B. Hesseltine is best on Grant, *U. S. Grant, Politician* (1935). A good general study of business is contained in T. C. Cochran and William Miller, *The Age of Enterprise: A Social History of Industrial America** (1942), which also touches intelligently on public policy. Rendigs Fels, *American Business Cycles, 1865–1897* (1959), is authoritative on the Panic of 1873. Glenn Porter is helpful on *The Rise of Big Business 1860–1910** (1973). For the currency question, see Irwin Unger, *The Greenback Era* (1964), and for a balanced and significant analysis of public policy on money and the general economic picture of the period, see R. P. Sharkey, *Money, Class and Party* (1959). Postwar diplomacy has had able attention, especially in Dexter Perkins, *The Monroe Doctrine, 1876–1907** (1937), and Allan Nevins, *Hamilton Fish: The Inner History of the Grant Administration* (1936), which also provides the best account of the topic described by its subtitle. See specifically Adrian Cook's *The Alabama Claims: American Politics and Anglo-American Relations, 1865–1872* (1975). On the scandals of Grant's time and on the responses to them, three worthy studies are D. G. Loth, *Public Plunder: A History of Graft in America* (1938); C. R. Fish, *The Civil Service and the Patronage* (1904); and E. D. Ross, *The Liberal Republican Movement* (1919). There is a first-rate analysis of Grant and the Liberals in the beginning chapters of E. F. Goldman, *Rendezvous with Destiny** (1955). J. G. Sproat, *The Best Men** (1968), describes the liberal reformers of the Gilded Age. See also C. M. Fuess, *Carl Schurz: Reformer* (1932), and G. G. Van Deusen, *Horace Greeley: Nineteenth Century Crusader** (1952). For a delightful contemporary exposure of Grant era scandals, see C. F. Adams and Henry Adams, *Chapters from Erie (1866).* On the Tweed Ring see A. B. Callow, *The Tweed Ring** (1966), and Seymour Mandelbaum, *Boss Tweed's New York** (1965). For a cartoonist's observations of the Grant era's heroes and villains, see Morton Keller, *Art and Politics of Thomas Nast** (1968).

*Available in a paperback edition.

CHAPTER **16**

The New South: reunion and readjustment

The central theme of American history during the quarter-century following Reconstruction was laissez faire—"let alone." In this period control over public policy was surrendered very largely to private interests or state governments under their control. The six chapters that follow will reveal this philosophy at work in all sections of the country, in the city as in the countryside, in economics as in politics. Laissez faire profoundly affected the lot of black freedmen and red Indians, the fate of buffaloes, natural resources, and public lands, the course of railroad operations, industrial management, and labor relations. After 1877 the center of historical forces and the focus of historical interest shift away from Washington. The federal government and the major political parties followed an economic policy of promotional indulgence. Such exceptions to the rule of laissez faire as internal improvements, subsidies to railroads, and protective tariff were made in the name of speeding productivity. Regulation and restriction for public welfare would have lacked support from the highly democ-

ratized electorate, even if politicians had urged such policies.

White Southerners responded with fervor to the doctrine of laissez faire. Their enthusiasm sprang from a revolt against Reconstruction, an attempt to apply a philosophy that was in certain respects and for a limited period the opposite of laissez faire. Disillusionment with Reconstruction, in fact, was spreading in the North as well as in the South, and Southern conservatives were beginning to hope for support from their former enemies. The great experiment of the Radicals had failed to solve the two problems it was designed to solve: the status of the South in the nation and the status of the Negro in the South. These two problems had torn and agitated the country for more than a generation, and Reconstruction proved no more successful than the Civil War had been in finding a solution. "We have tried for eight years," wrote Joseph Medill, the influential Republican editor of the Chicago *Tribune*, "to uphold Negro rule in the South officered by carpetbaggers, but without exception it has resulted in failure." Patience was running out in

The cotton levee, New Orleans

1876, and the demand for some practical solution was growing more and more insistent.

The return to compromise

For sixteen years, ever since Fort Sumter, North and South had settled their differences by armed force—not only during the four years of war but during the twelve years that followed. If the country was ever to give up force and return to peaceful ways of settling sectional disputes, it would have to revive the neglected art of compromise. The opportunity for a drastic change in relations between North and South and a return to the tradition of compromise on the classic model of 1850 came unexpectedly with the presidential election of 1876.

Tilden versus Hayes. Economic depression, political scandal, and weariness with Grant's Southern policy clouded Republican prospects in 1876. The election of 1874 had returned the Democrats to control of the House of Representatives for the first time since the Civil War. During the next two years the depression that had started in 1873 deepened, and discontent increased. Throughout 1876 reformers filled the air with exposures of new scandals in the corrupt Grant Administration. Growing disgust with corruption, more than anything else, led to the elimination of the two leading contestants for the Republican nomination. One was President Grant himself, for, incredible as it may seem, the general had permitted the Stalwarts (see p. 466) to persuade him for a time that he would make a logical candidate for a third term. He withdrew, however, before the Republican convention met. The second candidate to be knocked out of the race for the nomination was Congressman James G. Blaine of Maine, formerly Speaker and currently minority leader in the House.

Blaine was known best as the leader of the Half-Breeds, who favored Hayes' Southern policy and civil-service reform, and for his personal enmity with Roscoe Conkling, the Stalwarts' leader. A master of florid oratory and dramatic political maneuver, he commanded a large personal following and an army of political dependents. Blaine's opening maneuver in 1876 was the very opposite of compromise. Taking the floor on January 10, he artfully revived wartime bitterness over the suffering of Northern troops in the South's Andersonville prison camp. He declared that "the thumbscrews and engines of torture of the Spanish Inquisition did not begin to compare in atrocity with the hideous crime of Andersonville," and charged that Jefferson Davis was "the man that organ-

Samuel J. Tilden: he deserved to win

ized that murder." Here was the classic example of "waving the bloody shirt"—of stirring up old war hatreds for partisan purposes. Southern congressmen responded heatedly in defense of Davis. Blaine thus succeeded in identifying the Democratic party anew with disloyalty and rebellion and in thereby diverting attention from the scandals of the Republican Administration. His strategy almost won him the Republican nomination and the Presidency.

On the eve of the nominating convention, however, a congressional investigating committee suddenly produced a witness named James Mulligan, who said he had evidence that Blaine, while Speaker of the House, had received secret and lucrative commissions for granting favors to a railroad company. Boldly seizing the "Mulligan Letters," which contained the alleged evidence, Blaine quoted selectively from them and claimed that he had cleared his name of the charges. In the ensuing convention, however, the Mulligan affair and the disfavor of President Grant and the Stalwarts finally eliminated Blaine from the race.

The Republicans nominated Rutherford B. Hayes, a comparatively obscure figure from the strategically important state of Ohio. Three times governor of his state, Hayes had a creditable war record, an unblemished reputation, and an association with mild civil-service reform. In short, he was the ideal nominee for a party bedeviled by smirched reputations and beset by scandal. Of Whig antecedents and puritanical conscience, Hayes was conservative in his economic and financial views, conciliatory toward

Southern whites, and philanthropic toward the freedmen. To balance the ticket, the Republicans chose Congressman William A. Wheeler of New York for Vice President.

Stressing the issue of reform, the Democrats nominated Samuel J. Tilden, governor of New York. Before his election to the governorship in 1874, Tilden had won fame by helping to smash the notorious ring of Boss Tweed, head of Tammany Hall, and by sending Tweed and others to jail; as governor, he had shattered a powerful organization of grafters known as the Canal Ring. Tilden had made a private fortune as a corporation lawyer serving railroads, and his conservative economic views and hard-money doctrines were more pleasing to the business community of the East than they were to the South and the West. Popular enthusiasm for Tilden's candidacy was further limited by his railroad associations, his secretive habits, and his poor health. In order to make up for these drawbacks, the Democrats named for Vice President Thomas A. Hendricks of Indiana, who had served his state as senator and governor and held soft-money views.

The campaign of 1876 was a struggle of exceptional bitterness and trickery. For the first time in twenty years the Democrats had a reasonable hope of winning a presidential election, and they bore down hard on Republican corruption in high places and misrule in the South. Their opponents countered with bloody-shirt oratory, charging that the Democrats were sympathetic to the rebels and attacking Tilden's personal integrity. When the returns came in, the Democrats seemed to have carried the day, for the majority of popular ballots were cast for Tilden with a quarter of a million to spare. And, while Tilden was conceded 184 electoral votes, only one vote short of the 185 required for election, Hayes was conceded only 165. But nineteen of the twenty contested electoral votes lay in the three Southern states that were still under Republican government—South Carolina, Louisiana, and Florida. The twentieth vote, from the Republican state of Oregon, was claimed by the Democrats on a technicality. Tilden needed only one of the twenty votes to assure his election, while Hayes had to have them all to win a bare majority of one vote. Republican managers promptly claimed all the votes and announced a Hayes victory. Charging that the Democrats had used intimidation and fraud against black voters, Republican returning boards in the three Southern states threw out enough Democratic popular votes to give those states to Hayes. Both parties had resorted to chicanery in the election, but modern scholars hold that Tilden deserved more than enough of the contested votes to win. On December 6 Republican electors met and cast the votes of the three states for Hayes, but on the same day a rival set of Democratic electors cast the votes of the same states solidly for Tilden.

Congress, with a Democratic House and a Republican Senate, now faced the problem of deciding which returns were authentic and which candidate had won. The Constitution was not explicit on who should count the electoral votes, and the law was silent. As the weeks passed an ominous deadlock ensued.

The solution proposed by moderate congressmen was to refer the disputed returns to an electoral commission created for the purpose, consisting of fifteen members drawn in equal numbers from the Senate, the House, and the Supreme Court. Seven were to be Republicans, seven Democrats, and one was expected to be Justice David Davis, an independent. Counting on Justice Davis to break the tie in their favor, Democrats supported the measure in greater numbers and

Rutherford B. Hayes: President by compromise

381

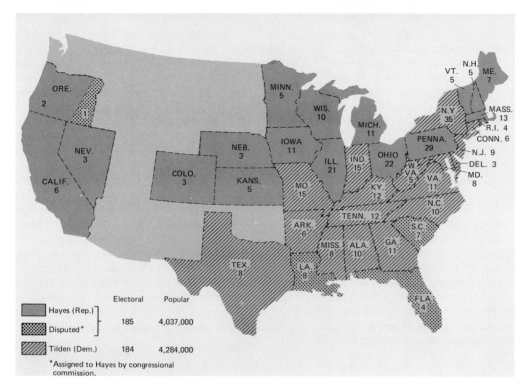

The election of 1876

	Electoral	Popular
Hayes (Rep.)	185	4,037,000
Disputed*		
Tilden (Dem.)	184	4,284,000

*Assigned to Hayes by congressional commission.

with more enthusiasm than Republicans. At the last moment, however, too late for the Democrats to renege, Davis was elected to the Senate from Illinois and his place on the commission was filled by a loyal Republican. The commission then decided in February by strictly partisan votes of eight Republicans to seven Democrats to accept the Republican returns for all twenty contested electoral votes. Tilden was thus in effect removed from the race, and it remained only to seat Hayes by formal action of the House. This met with determined opposition. Enraged by what they denounced as a "conspiracy" to defraud them of their victory, many Democrats refused to abide by the votes of the commission and launched a filibuster that threatened to prevent any election whatever and bring on anarchy.

The Compromise of 1877. At this point, with only three weeks before inauguration day, the electoral crisis made juncture with the settlement of old sectional and racial issues that were of more historical importance than the presidential election. This was the shaping of one of the great sectional compromises of American history, comparable with those of 1820, 1833, and 1850, but far more long-lasting. In December, conservative Southern Democrats, mainly former Whigs, approached like-minded friends of Hayes, himself a former Whig, with offers of political support in the disputed election and future political support in exchange for a firm Republican commitment to "home rule" in the Southern states. "Home rule"

meant many things, among them Republican abandonment of freedmen, carpetbaggers, scalawags, and radicals, and the virtual nullification of the Fourteenth and Fifteenth Amendments and the Civil Rights Act—in short, many of the hard-won fruits of the Civil War and Reconstruction and, some thought, the honor of the Republican party. Nevertheless, Hayes readily fell in with this policy. He hoped not only for immediate help in the electoral crisis but expected to make the Southern conservative whites the basis of a reconstituted Republican party in the South along old Whig lines.

While "home rule" was always the main objective of the ex-Confederates, Hayes and his friends found other means of attracting Southern Conservatives. War had destroyed Southern capital, depression had dried up sources of Northern investment, and carpetbaggers had exhausted the credit of the states. The only source of capital left was the federal Treasury, and Southern congressmen were knocking at its doors with hundreds of bills for internal improvements—for controlling floods along the Mississippi, for clearing harbors, river channels, and choked canals, for reconstructing depleted railroads, fallen bridges, broken levees, and public buildings. Southerners had already discovered that Republicans were consistently more sympathetic to such requests than were their fellow Democrats of the North, who lectured them sternly about "Grantism," public morals, and reform. Most powerful of the many lobbies promoting Southern measures was the one supporting the effort of Thomas A. Scott, president of the Pennsylvania Railroad, to get a subsidy of more than $200 million for the Texas & Pacific Railroad. General Grenville M. Dodge, the most astute railroad lobbyist of the Grant era, organized the forces behind the Scott bill. Persuaded by intermediaries that Hayes as President would be friendly to the Texas & Pacific, Scott added his powerful influence to that of others seeking to win Southern support for Hayes in the electoral crisis.

The deadlock continued. The Hayes forces intensified their efforts to win over Southern Democrats, thus enabling the latter to demand a higher price for their support. Not only did Hayes promise to withdraw federal troops from the South and leave the state governments in the control of Conservatives, but he agreed to appoint a Southern Democrat to his Cabinet and permit him to hand out patronage to his friends. The Republican candidate and his spokesmen emphasized that the new administration would take a conciliatory attitude toward Southern needs and wishes generally, and particularly toward bills for internal improvements.

These Republican concessions and promises undoubtedly helped persuade Southern Democrats to accept the electoral commission's decision for Hayes, and the South's capitulation influenced many Northern Democrats to abandon the filibuster and accept the loss of a prize they were convinced they had

rightfully won. Other influences worked toward the same end, including a patriotic urge to avoid anarchy and a yearning to return to traditional ways of peace and compromise. At last Hayes' dubious cause prevailed, and he was declared President only two days before he took office.

The politics of reconciliation. President Hayes, sincere in his role as the man of conciliation and faithful to his promises to the South, appointed a Democrat, ex-Confederate General David M. Key of Tennessee, to his Cabinet. After a few weeks of awkward hesitation Hayes withdrew the federal troops from South Carolina and Louisiana, and the last two carpetbagger governments promptly collapsed, never to be restored. (The compromise guarantee of "home rule" lasted eighty years, until troops were sent to Little Rock in 1957.) All the Southern states and the border states as well were now under Conservative control. In his courtship of the South's ex-Whig Democrats, Hayes appointed many of them to federal offices, even though it meant turning down Republican applicants. The Texas & Pacific bill failed in spite of repeated endorsements by the President, but generous internal improvements for the South were enacted. Admirers cheered Hayes with the rebel yell during his three visits to the South.

Hayes' policy of conciliation pleased Southern Conservatives and eased somewhat the old tensions

The "strong" government, 1869–77   *The "weak" government, 1877–81*

between North and South. But certain results of that policy disappointed the President. For one thing the ex-Whig Democrats of the South did not rally in numbers to the Republican standard as he had hoped they would. A ground swell of agrarian discontent and radicalism below the Potomac made it difficult for conservative Democratic leaders there to continue their cooperation with business-minded Republicans. Finally, congressmen of Hayes' own party resisted his policy of appeasing the South and appointing Democrats to office. And so the Republicans returned to the practice of bloody-shirt oratory and to charges of Southern disloyalty. Only a few Republicans seemed disturbed by their party's desertion of the carpetbaggers and the freedmen and its repudiation of the goals of Reconstruction policy.

Subordination of the freedmen

The abandonment of equality. By constitutional amendment and statutes, the United States was presumably committed to the principle of equal civil and political rights for the freedman and to the use of federal power to guarantee them. Yet after Reconstruction the country quickly broke this commitment and virtually forgot about it for two generations. That the North was also remiss was indicated by the conduct of federal troops in the South, the army's treatment of black soldiers, the policies of labor unions, and the discriminatory laws of Northern cities and states. Furthermore, the Radical promise of equality was an embarrassment to Hayes' effort to reconcile the estranged South and to put aside bitter war memories.

In short, the white people of the North and South were reconciled at the expense of Negroes. When Hayes visited Atlanta in the fall of 1877, he told the freedmen that their "rights and interests would be safer" if Southern whites were "let alone by the general government." This sentiment was greeted with "immense enthusiasm"—by the whites. "Let alone" became the watchword of government policy in race relations as well as in industrial and business affairs. Former champions of the freedmen in the North took up the new slogan and dropped their concern for the rights of the Negro. The *Nation* declared that the federal government should have "nothing more to do with him" and doubted that he could ever "be worked into a system of government for which you and I would have much respect."

The plea for reconciliation, the let-alone philosophy, and the prevailing disillusionment with high ideals and promises also had their effect on the Su-

Frederick Douglass: militant black

preme Court. In a long series of decisions the Court underwrote white supremacy, state rights, and laissez faire and virtually nullified the Fourteenth and Fifteenth Amendments insofar as they applied to the rights of freedmen. In 1876 Chief Justice Morrison R. Waite, in *United States* v. *Cruikshank,* decided that the Fourteenth Amendment "adds nothing to the rights of one citizen as against another" and does not extend federal protection to other rights except when they are infringed by a state. Applying the same interpretation in the *Civil Rights Cases* of 1883, the Court pronounced the Civil Rights Act of 1875 unconstitutional. This act had provided that all persons, regardless of race, were entitled to "the full and equal enjoyment" of all public facilities such as inns and railroads, as well as theaters and other places of amusement. In holding that the Fourteenth Amendment was a prohibition against states only, the Court said in effect that the federal government could not lawfully protect Negroes against discrimination by private individuals. The court joined the President in adhering to laissez faire.

Now, with the official approval of the federal courts, the acquiescence of many Northern liberals and Radicals, and the cooperation of the Republican party, blacks were relegated to an inferior grade of citizenship. Their freedom was not seriously challenged, but their equality most certainly was. There

The New South: reunion and readjustment

was little they could do about it. Even Frederick Douglass, once the militant leader of the blacks, accepted office under Hayes' Administration, and so did Carl Schurz, one of their most outspoken white liberal friends. The high hopes and fine promises of earlier days were shattered.

The road to segregation. The freedmen were not yet wholly abandoned to their worst enemies nor entirely without friends of a kind. Harder times were to come, but meanwhile they fell under the paternalistic regime of the Southern Conservatives. These men were not wholly insincere in their public pledge to protect the freedman's rights—as they conceived those rights. They thought of Negroes as subordinate and inferior but as having limited rights appropriate to their lower status. They did not feel the need for humiliating and persecuting Negroes, as did the men who were to gain control of race relations in the future. The Conservatives professed to feel a paternalistic responsibility for the underprivileged freedmen.

Deserted by many Northern friends and neglected by the federal government, the blacks not unnaturally turned to the Southern Conservatives. They did this, not out of love for their old masters, but out of a real need for protection against worse enemies. They had nowhere else to turn. For their part, the Conservatives partially tamed the antiblack passions they had helped to arouse in overthrowing the carpetbaggers. In politics they sometimes used

Carl Schurz: liberal reformer

black votes against agrarian whites who were antagonized by the Whiggish, probusiness policies of the Conservative governments. Such prominent Conservative leaders as Wade Hampton of South Carolina, L. Q. C. Lamar of Mississippi, and Alexander H. Stephens of Georgia invited freedmen's support. Although the Negroes were often coerced, intimidated, or defrauded, they nevertheless continued to vote in large numbers in many parts of the South for two decades after Reconstruction. What is more, they continued to hold minor offices and to keep at least one black congressman in Washington (in all but one term) until after the end of the century. To attract black support to the Democratic party, Governor Hampton of South Carolina appointed eighty-six Negroes to office during his Administration, and Governor Francis R. T. Nicholls of Louisiana also gave minor offices and political favors to blacks. A common device was the "fusion principle," by which the Conservatives helped the black against the white wing of the Republican party in return for Negro assistance in the Conservatives' struggle against discontented whites of their own party. By this means the Conservatives strengthened their control over the Democratic party and kept the Republican party divided along racial lines within the South.

For a time this balance of forces restrained extremists who advocated systematic disfranchisement and rigid segregation of the blacks. The idea of racial inferiority had struck roots long before the war, but rigid and universal segregation was incompatible with slavery even in cities and was rarely required under the system. After the Civil War, blacks withdrew from the white-dominated churches to found their own. Except in a few brief experiments, the Radicals did not mix races in the public schools of the South. In transportation and in some other public services, however, the races continued to mingle for two or more decades to an extent that would be unthinkable to a later era of Jim Crow (the popular name for segregation).

The Conservatives themselves were to blame for opening the way to segregation and disfranchisement. In order to defeat the Populists, a radical movement of the early nineties that sought black support (see p. 480), they once again lifted the cry of white supremacy as they had in their struggle to overthrow the carpetbaggers. But this time they could not tame the passions they aroused, and the extremists took over. By 1900 all the Southern states had Jim Crow railroad cars; three required or authorized segregation in railway stations; and one had Jim Crow streetcars. Eventually the harsh rule of segregation spread to all public services and institutions. Little protest came from the North, where the Negro also suffered increasing discrimination. And in 1896, in the case of *Plessy* v.

Subordination of the freedmen

Ferguson, the Supreme Court sanctioned segregation by declaring "separate but equal" facilities constitutional.

Two years later, in 1898, the Supreme Court took another step toward laissez faire in the case of *Williams* v. *Mississippi* by approving a Mississippi scheme for depriving the Negro of the ballot. This plan, which had been adopted in 1890, combined the poll tax, the literacy test, and residence requirements to reduce the number of black voters to a handful. South Carolina followed suit in 1895, and the rest of the Southern states during the next twelve years. Each state added minor variations to the Mississippi plan, but everywhere the result was the same. As the Negro disappeared from the polls, he also dropped out of the minor offices and public services on which he had

Virginia public school: the races were not mixed

managed to retain some hold. The last black congressman to be elected from the South left Washington in 1901.

By the end of the century, the great laissez-faire reaction had virtually undone the work of Reconstruction. The constitutional amendments guaranteeing equality before the law and at the ballot box had been practically nullified, and life itself was jeopardized by the spread of lynching. This crime reached its peak between 1889 and 1899, when an average of some 187 lynchings a year occurred in the United States as a whole. About four-fifths of the lynchings took place in the South, and the great majority of the victims of the lynch mobs were blacks.

Lynch mob, 1893

Who can picture the vast, illimitable future of this glorious sunny South?... Here is a land possessing in its matchless resources the combined advantages of almost every other country of the world without their most serious disadvantages.... It is beyond the power of the human mind to fully grasp the future that is in store for this country.... The more we contemplate these advantages and contrast them with those of other countries, the more deeply we will be impressed with the unquestionable truth that here in this glorious land, 'Creation's Garden Spot,' is to be the richest and greatest country upon which the sun ever shone.

From Richard H. Edmonds, in *Manufacturers' Record*, 1888.

The Atlanta Compromise. Freedom had not emancipated the blacks from labor in the cotton field, for they continued to till the white man's land. At the end of the century a little more than 75 percent of the black farmers in the South were croppers or tenants. Handicapped by prevailing agricultural depression and by their heritage of oppression, they contrived to live little better than they had under slavery. The great exodus of the Negro to the North did not begin for more than a half-century after emancipation, but many freedmen did move into the towns of the South and North. There they went into the trades and crafts and shortly after the war greatly outnumbered white artisans in the South. Employers increasingly discriminated against black workers, often at the insistence of all-white trade unions, which kept up a constant pressure to drive blacks out of the better-paid, more attractive work and confine them to "Negro jobs." Gradually, blacks disappeared from some skilled trades they had traditionally monopolized and were excluded almost entirely from certain of the newer industries, such as textiles. Generally barred from labor unions, black workers were sometimes used as strikebreakers, thereby earning additional ill will from the unions.

By the 1880s the freedmen had become stratified into social and economic classes. The new Negro middle class, consisting largely of professional people and businessmen, was proportionately smaller and commanded far less wealth and power than the corresponding class of white people. Within black society, however, its dominance was quite as strong. The Negro middle class, which reflected many of the attitudes, assumptions, and aspirations of the white middle class, found full expression in Booker T. Washington, the foremost leader of his race in the generation following Reconstruction.

Washington became head of an industrial school for blacks at Tuskegee, Alabama, in 1881 but soon attained influence and power that far transcended this modest post and contrasted strikingly with his habitual attitude of humility. The foremost spokesman for his own race, he was also a leader of white opinion on racial policy and a powerful influence in shaping national philanthropic and educational policies. He believed that education for the Negro in that era should stress industrial training rather than intellectual development. In a famous speech delivered in Atlanta in 1895, Washington set forth a philosophy of race relations that came to be known as the Atlanta Compromise.

Washington's compromise in race relations received the support of Southern whites, Northern whites, and many blacks. He conciliated the white South by abandoning the militant Reconstruction demand for equality, emphasizing economic opportunities instead of political rights, and identifying himself and his race with the industrial order established by the Conservatives. To his own race he preached patience, conservatism, and the primacy of material

Booker T. Washington: conciliator

The New South: reunion and readjustment

Twenty-odd years ago ... I fondly imagined a great era of prosperity for the South. Guided by history and by a knowledge of our people and our climatic and physical advantages, I saw in anticipation all her tribulations ended ... and I beheld the South greater, richer and mightier than when she molded the political policy of the whole country. But year by year these hopes, chastened by experience, have waned and faded, until now, instead of beholding the glorious South of my imagination, I see her sons poorer than when war ceased his ravages, weaker than when rehabilitated with her original rights, and with the bitter memories smoldering, if not rankling, in the bosoms of many.

From Lewis H. Blair, *The Prosperity of the South Dependent
on the Elevation of the Negro*, 1889.

progress. This submissive and compliant doctrine, widely accepted at the time, was rejected as "Uncle Tomism" by a later generation.

Anticipating the later militancy of black nationalism, Alexander Crummell, who was educated in England and had spent twenty years in Liberia, preached that American blacks should regard themselves as "a 'peculiar people' in this land," a distinct nation within a nation. And Bishop Henry M. Turner, a leading advocate of African colonization in the late nineteenth and early twentieth centuries, declared that "a man who loves a country that hates him" was beneath respect. His agitation produced some black identification with Africa but extremely few emigrants.

Politics in the New South

The Redeemers. The new rulers of the South, claiming that they had "redeemed" their section from the carpetbaggers, spoke of themselves as the Redeemers. We have already seen that ex-Whigs played a prominent part in this redemption and in the reconstituted Democratic party. It was partly out of regard for their feelings, in fact, that the Democratic party was often called the Conservative party in the South. It deserved that name, for the old Whigs had brought their philosophy with them into their new party.

With some exceptions, notably in South Carolina, the Redeemers were businessmen or industrialists rather than planters. In Tennessee, Kentucky, and Georgia the old planter element made a bid for power, but they were unsuccessful in each case. Mississippi, one-time principality of planter-statesmen, was in the hands of five corporation lawyers, two of whom held the governorship for two decades and three of whom

shared the state's Senate seats throughout the eighties. Redeemed Georgia was ruled by a triumvirate who speculated in railroads, coal- and iron-mining, and textiles. Virginia, still a countryman's state, was governed by city men for the benefit of bankers, bondholders, and railroad-operators. In Tennessee the leader of the Redeemers was also general counsel of the Tennessee Coal and Iron Company; the first Redeemer governor of the state was president of the company, and his two successors were directors and officials. All were former Whigs and all were industrialists. Similarly, the Redeemers of Alabama were closely associated with the Louisville & Nashville Railroad, which helped put the new regime in power and won many favors in return.

Although the Redeemers were often called Bourbons, they did not really represent the restoration of the old order or cling to its values. They represented instead a new phase of the revolution that had been touched off in the South by the overthrow of the Confederacy, and in that revolution they played a more important and lasting role than the carpetbaggers and the scalawags, who have received far more attention. The Cotton Kingdom of slavery and the Radical regime of equalitarianism proved ephemeral compared with the new order of race relations, economic institutions, and politics established by the Redeemers.

The new regime. The new state constitutions framed by the Redeemers embodied a strong reaction against the government interference so characteristic of Reconstruction. They revealed suspicion and distrust of legislatures and placed such hampering restrictions upon government that positive action of any sort became difficult. The constitutions were, above all, laissez-faire documents. The new Southern governments also reacted against Reconstruction through their policy of "retrenchment," which meant cutting taxes and starving or eliminating tax-supported public services. The chief beneficiaries of the tax policy were the railroads, the utilities, and the factories, whose burdens were lightened; and the chief victims were the public schools. The schools, which bore the stigma of carpetbagger support, were gravely crippled by the pinch of Redeemer retrenchment as well as by general poverty and depression. The Redeemers also cut appropriations for other public institutions, but none so drastically as those for prisons. The state governments actually turned prisoners into a source of revenue by leasing them as cheap labor to industrialists with the right political connections. The convict-lease system, often marked by brutal exploitation, became an ugly blot on the reputation of the new regime.

This was an era of corrupt government and lax public morals across the country, and it would be unfair to single out the Redeemers for special censure. They invited such censure, however, by the attack they made on graft and corruption in their campaigns to overthrow the carpetbaggers. Faced with no effective party of opposition, protected by long tenure of office, and consequently immune from criticism and exposure, the Redeemers fell into a laxity that eventually covered some of the state governments with disgrace. In the eighties one scandal after another came to light. Some were exposed only by the absconding of state treasurers, nine of whom were guilty of defalcation or embezzlement, and one of whom defrauded Louisiana of more than a million dollars. Such losses, as an Alabamian said, made a mockery of "niggardly economy in public expenditure."

In national affairs the Redeemers revealed their Whiggish heritage by lining up with Northerners of like mind on questions of currency, banks, and internal improvements. In so doing they reversed the sectional diplomacy of Southern Democrats, who traditionally allied themselves with the West, and tied the South instead to the policies of the conservative wing of the party centered in the Northeast. To overcome the unpopularity of this shift in alignment, the Redeemers hushed the discussion of economic issues and stressed issues of race and tradition.

Stirrings of revolt. The "Solid South" won its name prematurely. Hardly had "home rule" been restored when revolt began to stir against the Redeemer regime. Once the pressure of occupation was removed, ancient class, party, and sectional antagonisms within the South began to reassert themselves, and local parties calling themselves Independents, Greenbackers, or Readjusters organized for action. Poorly led, they were often cheated at elections and won only limited success, but they provide a clue to

what was seething beneath the surface solidarity of Southern politics.

The most disruptive issue of all was the "readjustment," or repudiation, of state debts. So disruptive was it, in fact, that it unseated the Redeemers in some states and threatened the security of the whole regime. By the end of Reconstruction, the Southern states had incurred a total debt of about $275 million, and in nine states there was talk of scaling the debts down or partially repudiating them. In one way or another these nine states contrived to reduce their total liabilities by $150 million. Naturally the states' creditors and bondholders protested bitterly, and in each state a faction of Redeemers fought the debt-readjusters. In Tennessee the fight brought the Republicans back to power, and in Virginia it led to the triumph of a third party calling itself the Readjusters. The advocates of repudiation argued that much of the debt was a heritage from carpetbagger looting, that the states themselves had derived little benefit from the sale of Reconstruction bonds, and that in any event the section was too impoverished and ravaged to carry the burden of Reconstruction debts.

Encouraged by the revolt against the Conservative Democrats, the Republicans began to dream of returning to power in the South through an alliance with local third parties. Even though the Republicans had little in common with these parties save their opposition to Democrats, they put aside President Hayes' commitment to the Southern Conservatives and threw their support to the reformers and debt-repudiators. "Anything to beat the Bourbons" was the Republican policy. The Conservatives responded by reviving the tactics of fraud and intimidation once used against the carpetbaggers, employing them so effectively that by 1883 they had beaten all but the last spark out of the Independent revolt and had shattered Republican hopes of exploiting it. Not for a decade was there to be further talk of insurgency in the South. This was the real period of the Solid South, of exclusively one-party politics, and of the most complete political torpor that ever settled over the region. It was not to be broken until the Populist revolt of 1892.

The doctrine of the New South. There had long been advocates of industrialism in the South, but before the Civil War they had looked on factories as a means of buttressing the existing social order. Propagandists of the New South, by contrast, sought to replace the old order with an economy like that of the North, a business civilization of cities, factories, and trade, with new values and new aims. This was what the "New South" meant to its champions in the 1880s. "As for Charleston," declared an editor from that city in 1882, "the importation of about five hun-

The New South: reunion and readjustment

dred Yankees of the right stripe would put a new face on affairs, and make the whole place throb with life and vivid force."

Propaganda for the New South point of view found full voice during the 1880s and 1890s in such journals as the Atlanta *Constitution*, edited by orator Henry W. Grady. Full of the bustle and salesmanship of business enterprise, Grady exuded optimism and good will. In an address on "The New South" delivered in 1886 to the New England Society of New York he proclaimed:

> We have sowed towns and cities in the place of theories and put business above politics. We have challenged your spinners in Massachusetts and your iron-makers in Pennsylvania. . . . We have fallen in love with work. . . . We have let economy take root and spread among us as rank as the crab grass which sprung from Sherman's cavalry camps, until we are ready to lay odds on the Georgia Yankee, as he manufactures relics of the battlefield in a one-story shanty and squeezes pure olive oil out of his cotton seed, against any Down-easter that ever swapped wooden nutmegs for flannel sausages in the valleys of Vermont.

As models for young Southerners, Grady held up the businessman, especially the self-made man, the millionaire. What Grady and his friends were preaching was laissez-faire capitalism freed of restraints, a new industrial way of life, and a businessman's scale of values.

One sign of the popularity of the New South doctrine was the Southerner's eagerness for Northern approval. "Beyond all question," declared a Richmond journal, "we have been on the wrong track and should take a new departure." And Henry Watterson, a Louisville editor and orator, thought that "the ambition of the South is to out-Yankee the Yankee." But the appeal of the New South doctrine would have been less compelling had it not been embellished by sentimental tribute to the past: a heritage "never to be equalled in its chivalric strength and grace," as Grady put it. The invention of a legendary Old South and the cult of the "lost cause" revealed the curiously divided mind and the conflicting impulses of the Southern people in the new era. They marched hopefully in one direction and looked back longingly in the other.

The inner tensions of the Southern mind were reflected in the career of the Georgia writer Joel Chandler Harris, author of *Uncle Remus* (1881). A gentle, rather wistful man of humble origins, Harris portrayed the old slave in quaint dialect with humor and affection, casting a spell of charm over memories of the antebellum plantation. But while he was writing his nostalgic stories about the Old South, Harris was also chief editorial-writer for Grady's Atlanta *Constitution*, doing his daily best to encourage the growth of the New South of business and industry. Both the admirers of the old order and the propagandists of the new advocated sectional "reconciliation," urging that the North abandon its reformist aims and accept the new order in the South. In political terms reconciliation was simply an alliance between conservatives of both regions.

The colonial economy

The agrarian pattern. The dream and design of the new men of the South was to build an urbanized, industrialized society like that of the Yankees. But the habits and economic realities of the Old South were slow to change and hard to shake off. Despite all the factories that were constructed, 96.1 percent of the North Carolinians and 94.1 percent of the Alabamians were still not classified "urban" by the census of 1890. Only 8.5 percent of the population of the South Atlantic states below Maryland was urban in 1890, as compared with 51.7 percent of the population of the North Atlantic states from Pennsylvania up. By 1900 the urban population of those Northern states had further increased by nearly 7 percent, that of the Southern states by only 1 percent. The New South was still the most rural and agrarian section of the country.

The increase of farm tenancy in the South

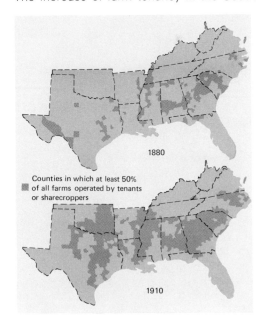

Counties in which at least 50% of all farms operated by tenants or sharecroppers

1880

1910

On the surface it would seem that deep changes had occurred in the distribution of land ownership in the South. The census of 1880 reported an amazing increase in the number of farms since 1860, and the average farm turned out to be less than half its former size. Optimists concluded that the Civil War had broken up the concentration of land in the hands of planters and had brought about "economic democracy." The truth was, however, that the old plantation lands had been parceled out in small plots among sharecroppers, each plot counting as a new "farm," and that large tracts of new land had been brought under cultivation. The sharecropper had replaced the slave, and his share of the crop depended largely on the tools, work animals, and feed the landlord furnished.

Ownership of the land tended to shift from the old planters into the hands of merchants or other townsmen. Moreover, whatever efficiency and planning, whatever virtues of proprietorship, had resided in the old plantation system were largely missing from the sharecropper system. The old evils of land monopoly, absentee ownership, soil-mining, and the one-crop system were not only retained but intensified. From a strictly economic point of view, cropping was probably worse for the agriculture of the region than slavery had been.

The most desperate need of the Southern farmer after the war was credit. With no cash in hand, and no banks from which to borrow it, the farmer was at the mercy of merchants who were willing to advance supplies in return for a mortgage or "lien" on his future crop. The farmer pledged an unplanted crop for a loan of unstipulated amount at an undesignated rate of interest. Trapped by the system, a man might continue year after oppressive year as a sort of peon, under lien to the same merchant and under the merchant's constant oversight. The lien system fostered the stubborn persistence of the one-crop system; for the merchant would advance credit only against such cash crops as cotton or tobacco. The one-crop system was more characteristic of the new agricultural order than it had ever been of the old, and more and more the South had to turn to other sections for supplies that it might have grown itself.

During the last quarter of the nineteenth century, farmers the country over were plagued by low prices and chronic depression. The Southern farmer shared these ills with farmers elsewhere, but he also suffered from a combination of burdens peculiar to the South. Among these was the heritage of military defeat, pillage, and occupation that had cost the section every third horse or mule and nearly half its agricultural machinery. On top of these burdens were

A Georgia plantation in 1860 and 1881

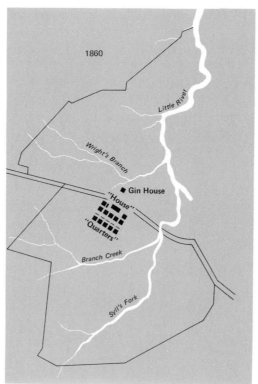

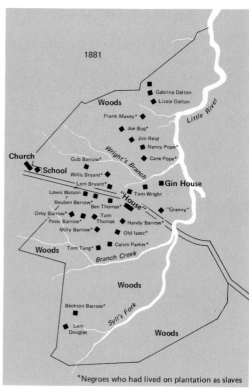

*Negroes who had lived on plantation as slaves

392

The New South: reunion and readjustment

Sharecroppers: often a grim peonage

heaped the ills of sharecropping, peonage, and the lien system. By the 1890s a spirit of grim desperation had settled on the farmers of the South, a spirit that long manifested itself in a suspicion of city folk and their ways and a resentment of wealth and its display. This spirit was to enter into the soul of the Populist movement in the years ahead (see p. 479).

Industrial stirrings. Toward the end of the 1870s the depression that had settled over the nation in 1873 started to lift. Once again Northern investors began to show interest in opportunities below the Potomac and freed the springs of capital. The propagandists of the New South boasted that the South, like the West, was an empire ripe for exploiting. "The way to clear and large profits is open," announced a Philadelphia editor in 1877. A book appeared in 1888 on *How to Get Rich in the South* and another in 1894 describing the South as *The Road to Wealth.* The Redeemers welcomed investors with open arms, tax exemptions, and promises of cheap and docile labor.

With the willing cooperation of Southern legislatures, speculators rounded up huge grants of public lands and mineral resources. Florida granted several million more acres than were in its public domain, and Texas surrendered an area larger than the state of Indiana. In 1877 the law reserving federal lands in five Southern states for homesteaders was scrapped, and the rich Southern empire of timber, coal, and iron was thrown open to unrestricted exploitation. In the next decade nearly 6 million acres of federal lands were sold, most of them to Northern speculators, who indulged in a reckless destruction of forests and a rifling of other resources.

Exploitation of this sort, as well as more laudable schemes of industrial development, would have been impossible without dramatic improvements in transportation. Between 1880 and 1890 railroad mileage in the South, starting from a low base, increased from 16,605 miles to 39,108, a growth of 135.5 percent, 50 percent greater than the national rate of growth in mileage in the same period. Railroad development

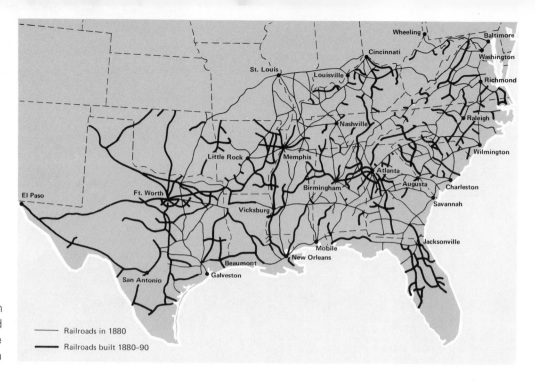

The growth
of the railroad
network in the
South

Railroads in 1880
Railroads built 1880-90

exposed to exploitation the landlocked mineral resources of the South, particularly the iron mines of
Tennessee, Virginia, and Alabama. Between 1876 and
1901 pig-iron production increased seventeen times in
the South, as compared with an eightfold increase in
the country at large. Alabama, with its unrivaled deposits of iron ore, coal, and limestone in unique proximity, quickly outstripped its Southern competitors,
and by 1898 Birmingham was the largest shipping
point for pig iron in the country and the third largest
in the world.

So long as the Southern economy stuck to its
traditional role of supplying raw materials of mine,
forest, and farm, it met with encouragement from
Northern bankers and investors. Production of lumber and forestry products soared sensationally, as did
the output of such fuels as coal and oil, and such ores
as iron, sulphur, bauxite, phosphate rock, and manga-
nese. Eastern capital entered each of these enterprises,
and Eastern control followed. The modern era of oil
production, for example, opened with an unprecedented gusher at Spindletop, near Beaumont, Texas,
in January 1901, and soon the newly opened fields of
the Southwest became the province of three nominally competing pipeline and refining companies presided over by Standard Oil. The story of the development and control of vast sulphur deposits in
Louisiana and bauxite deposits in Arkansas was similar to that of oil in Texas.

The tobacco industry, the oldest in the region,
discovered new markets and developed new techniques of manufacture during the new era. The genius of concentrated control was a tall, rugged, red-

headed North Carolinian named James Buchanan
Duke, called "Buck," whose rise paralleled that of the
industry. He started out in 1865 with two blind mules
and a load of tobacco, all the war had left on his
father's small farm. "Tobacco is the poor man's luxury," he observed, and on that insight he founded a
fortune. By 1889 his firm was producing half the
country's cigarettes, and the following year he absorbed his main competitors into the American Tobacco Company.

The true symbol of the New South, however, was
the cotton mill, and the zeal of its promoters stirred
up a veritable "cotton mill crusade." Actually, the
industry was confined largely to the Carolinas, Georgia, and Alabama. Cotton-manufacturing began in the
Old South and continued to grow through the Civil
War and Reconstruction, but between 1880 and 1900
the amount of capital invested in the Southern mills
increased sevenfold. The mill-building fever infected
whole communities. Much of the growth came at the
expense of New England, which was unable to compete with the vast Southern supply of unorganized
workers accustomed to long hours and low pay. The
chief textile products of the South were unfinished
goods that were sent north for final processing, and in
this, as in the use of cheap labor, the cotton mills were
typical of the South's new industries.

The colonial status. For all its boasts of industrial
progress, the New South lagged far behind the rest of
the country. So rapid was the expansion of the North
and West that by the end of the century the South
had a smaller percentage of the nation's factories and

The New South: reunion and readjustment

*North Carolina
cotton mill, 1895*

a slightly smaller percentage of the nation's capital than it had in 1860. With few exceptions, the industries that did take root in the South were low-wage industries that gave the first rough processing to the agricultural, forestry, and mining products of the region. Transportation costs made it more economical to do this processing near the source of raw material, and large supplies of cheap, unskilled labor were an even stronger attraction to such industries. Cotton yarn, cottonseed oil, cane sugar, polished rice, fertilizers, liquors, and tobacco, and such forestry products as turpentine, resin, and lumber constituted the bulk of the South's industrial output. The final processing of these products was usually done in the North, and from the final processing came the greatest profits.

There was no law relegating the South to a raw-material economy, no plot to exclude Southerners from the better-paying jobs and the more profitable industries. What, then, were the reasons for the persistent industrial backwardness of the section? A lost war, a late start, and a lack of capital were some of the reasons. These disadvantages might have been overcome more readily, however, had it not been for certain artificial barriers: a host of practices and rules adopted to suit the convenience of private interests in the North while the South was out of the Union or later when the section was without significant influence in national decisions.

One of these barriers was the system of regional freight-rate differentials adopted in the seventies and eighties by private railway associations and later given legal sanction by the Interstate Commerce Commis-

sion. These differentials meant that shippers of manufactured goods in the South and West were charged far higher rates than shippers in the privileged "Official Territory," north of the Ohio and Potomac and east of the Mississippi. The system discouraged the Southern producer from competing in the richest market area, the Northeast, but enabled the Northeastern producer to penetrate the Southern market. At the same time, favorable "commodity rates" were provided for Southern raw materials. Taken together, these rate differentials discouraged the South from developing manufactures of its own and encouraged it to concentrate on raw materials. A price differential imposed on Birmingham steel by the Pittsburgh steelmasters and their allied railroads had a similar effect. "Pittsburgh Plus" meant that buyers of Birmingham steel had to pay the Pittsburgh price *plus* the freight charge from Pittsburgh. Later, the "Birmingham Differential" replaced the freight charge with a straight additional charge of $3 a ton.

During these years the Northeast assumed something like an imperial power over the other sections, and the national economy fell into a neomercantilism reminiscent of colonial days. The Northeast discouraged the rise of competing manufactures, promoted ample supplies of raw materials for its own factories, monopolized the carrying trade by the combination of regionalized freight rates, steel-price differentials, and patent control, and reduced foreign competition in its domestic markets by the protective tariff. In brief, the Northeast became for a long time the workshop of the nation, reserving for its own coffers the profits of

"Poor whites" in Kentucky

processing, transporting, and distributing goods. The South was left to produce the raw materials for the new economic order, to serve as a tributary of industrial power.

Division of labor was, of course, natural in a national economy, and the South derived real benefits from its role in the form of increased job opportunities, payrolls, and taxable assets. On the other hand, this subordinate economic status imposed grave penalties on the South. As late as 1910 some 62 percent of its workers were engaged in the extractive industries—agriculture, forestry, animal husbandry, fishing, mining—as compared with 11 percent in New England and 14 percent in the Middle Atlantic states. Throughout the country, these industries paid the lowest wages of all, and the wages of Southern workers were even lower than the national average.

In wealth, living standards, and general welfare the Union was more a "house divided" now than when Lincoln first used the phrase. In 1880 the estimated per capita wealth in the South was $376 as compared with a national average of $870. No Southern state came within $300 of the national average nor within $550 of the average outside the South. In 1900 the national average in per capita wealth stood at $1,165, and in the South the average was $509. The earliest income estimates, those of 1919, indicate that per capita income in the South was about 40 percent lower than the national average. Little wonder that the region was noted for its "poor whites" and its "poor blacks" as well. Poverty was a characteristic of the regional economy. Closely related to that poverty was a lag in literacy, education, libraries, public health, and living standard.

The South of the New Order was humbled politically as well as economically. Its political abasement, in fact, represents the most striking shift in the geography of power that has ever occurred in American history. In the seventy-two years between Washington and Lincoln, southerners held the Presidency for fifty years and the title of Chief Justice of the Supreme Court for sixty years. They furnished more than half the Justices and diplomatic representatives to major powers, nearly half the men of Cabinet rank, and more than half the Speakers of the House of Representatives. During the next half-century, by contrast, no Southerner save Andrew Johnson served as President or Vice President, and the South furnished only 14 of the 133 Cabinet members, 7 of the 31 Justices of the Supreme Court, 2 of the 12 Speakers of the House, and fewer than one-tenth of the diplomatic representatives to major powers. From the power and glory of the eighteenth and early nineteenth centuries the South had fallen to a lowly state. In the process of reunion it had lost some of its old distinctiveness, along with much of its disproportionate power, and had become the frontier of a dynamic new order that was expanding southward as well as westward.

Suggestions for reading The best guide to books on the South is A. S. Link and R. W. Patrick, eds., *Writing Southern History** (2nd ed., 1967). C. V. Woodward, *Origins of the New South, 1877–1913** (1951), concentrates on the post-Reconstruction period. W. J. Cash, *The Mind of the South** (1941), contains provocative interpretations of uneven value. P. M. Gaston, *The New South Creed: A Study in Southern Mythmaking* (1970), is well described by its subtitle. The stresses and strains of sectional adjustment and reconciliation are the subject of P. H. Buck, *The Road to Reunion, 1865–1900** (1937). C. V. Woodward,

*Available in a paperback edition.

*Reunion and Reaction: The Compromise of 1877 and the End of Reconstruction** (1951), investigates the complex national crisis of 1876–77. The development of President Hayes' policy toward the South is traced in Harry Barnard, *Rutherford B. Hayes and His America* (1954), and in K. I. Polakoff, *The Politics of Inertia: The Election of 1876 and the End of Reconstruction* (1973). Republican efforts to revive their party in the South are pictured in V. P. De Santis, *Republicans Face the Southern Question: The New Departure Years, 1877–1897* (1959), and S. P. Hirshson, *Farewell to the Bloody Shirt: Northern Republicans and the Southern Negro, 1877–1893** (1962).

The struggles of the blacks after the abandonment of Reconstruction are illuminated in August Meier, *Negro Thought in America, 1880–1915** (1963); J. H. Franklin, *From Slavery to Freedom: A History of Negro Americans* (3rd ed., 1969); and E. F. Frazier, *The Negro in the United States* (rev. ed., 1957). G. M. Fredrickson, *Black Image in the White Mind** (1971), has much to say on this period of racism. Older views of the Negro are revised or discredited in V. L. Wharton, *The Negro in Mississippi, 1865–1890** (1947); G. B. Tindall, *South Carolina Negroes, 1877–1900** (1952); C. E. Wynes, *Race Relations in Virginia, 1870–1902* (1961); L. D. Rice, *The Negro in Texas, 1874–1900* (1971), R. A. Fischer, *The Segregation Struggle in Louisiana* (1974); and F. A. Logan, *The Negro in North Carolina, 1876–1894* (1964). C. V. Woodward, *The Strange Career of Jim Crow** (3rd rev. ed., 1974), traces the origins and rise of segregation, and R. W. Logan, *The Negro in American Life and Thought: The Nadir, 1877–1901* (1954), depicts the deterioration of Reconstruction ideals of racial equality. L. R. Harlan, *Booker T. Washington: The Making of a Negro Leader, 1856–1901* (1972), is first rate.

Insight into the politics of the New South is furnished by J. M. Kousser, *The Shaping of Southern Politics: Suffrage Restriction and the Establishment of the One-Party System, 1880–1910* (1974); and by biographies of popular leaders, such as F. B. Simkins, *Pitchfork Ben Tillman: South Carolinian** (1944); J. F. Wall, *Henry Watterson: Reconstructed Rebel* (1956); C. V. Woodward, *Tom Watson: Agrarian Rebel** (1938); and N. M. Blake, *William Mahone of Virginia: Soldier and Political Insurgent* (1935). J. P. Maddex, Jr., *The Virginia Conservatives, 1867–1879: A Study in Reconstruction Politics* (1970), and C. C. Pearson, *The Readjuster Movement in Virginia* (1917), are the best studies of the first breach in the Solid South; W. W. Rogers, *The One-Gallused Rebellion: Agrarianism in Alabama, 1865–1896* (1970); W. I. Hair, *Bourbonism and Agrarian Protest: Louisiana Politics, 1877–1900* (1969); and A. D. Kirwan, *Revolt of the Rednecks: Mississippi Politics, 1876–1925** (1951), are colorful accounts of poor-white revolts. Paul Lewinson, *Race, Class, and Party: A History of Negro Suffrage and White Politics in the South** (1932), shows how the race issue has been exploited. V. O. Key, Jr., *Southern Politics in State and Nation** (1949), treats of twentieth-century politics but sheds a bright light on earlier years.

Industrialization of the South is viewed critically and analytically by H. L. Herring, *Southern Industry and Regional Development* (1941), and from the New South viewpoint by Broadus Mitchell and G. S. Mitchell, *The Industrial Revolution in the South* (1930). N. M. Tilley, *The Bright Tobacco Industry, 1860–1929* (1948), recounts the revolutionary changes that overtook the South's oldest industry in this period. C. C. Rister, *Oil! Titan of the Southwest* (1949), tells of the boom period of a new industry. Broadus Mitchell, *The Rise of Cotton Mills in the South* (1921, 2nd ed., 1968), stresses the "crusading" aspects of the movement for textile-manufacturing. On the freight-rate discriminations W. H. Joubert, *Southern Freight Rates in Transition* (1949), is useful. R. B. Nixon, *Henry W. Grady: Spokesman of the New South* (1943), is an able portrayal of the industrial propagandist. The plight of the Southern farmer is investigated in F. A. Shannon, *The Farmer's Last Frontier: Agriculture 1860–1897** (1945).

Southern men of letters have furnished some of the most profound insights into the life and history of the South. Of special relevance to this period are some of the works of William Faulkner, foremost of the novelists, particularly *The Hamlet** (1940) and *Go Down, Moses** (1942).

*Available in a paperback edition.

The New West: empire within a nation

CHAPTER 17

After the Civil War the American people embarked on the conquest and exploitation of an area greater than all the territory that had been settled since the landing at Jamestown in 1607. Up to this time the settlers of the trans-Mississippi West had occupied only its eastern and western fringes, in one tier of states just beyond the Mississippi and in another tier half a continent beyond along the Pacific coast. Between these two frontiers, separated by fifteen hundred miles, stretched a vast and fabulous expanse of ocean-like plains, spired and towering mountain ranges, grassy plateaus, painted deserts, and breathtaking canyons. Of all the American wests, this was the one that captured the imagination of the world, the one that would be perpetuated in song and story.

Americans had conquered many frontiers in the past, but the New West was different from all the others. The experience of the pioneers there was less like that of their forefathers in taming the forested "wests" of the East and more like the imperialistic adventures of nineteenth-century Europeans in Africa and Asia. America was a nation with a built-in empire, an empire disguised as a nation. What Englishmen and western Europeans had to seek "somewhere east of Suez," their American contemporaries, until the region was tamed and settled, might find somewhere west of the wide Missouri. The impulse behind this late nineteenth-century quest was more than a desire for private gain. It partook of the strange drive that was sending Western man into all the remote corners of the world, mainly in the Southern Hemisphere, to impose his will upon people of color and to master exotic environments. If in Rudyard Kipling's Mandalay there were no Ten Commandments and the best was like the worst, so it was too in Deadwood Gulch and in a hundred mining towns, cow towns, and trading posts of the Wild West.

Subordination of the Indians

The Great Plains environment. The steady westward advance of the American frontier ground to a halt in the 1840s and then (except for Utah, p. 261) skipped all the way to the Pacific coast. What stopped the pioneer in his tracks was the forbidding new environment of the Great Plains. Abnormally dry, almost treeless, and mostly level, the plains had their

Santa Fe Trail

399

own peculiar soil, weather, plant life, animal life, and human life. The woodcraft and Indian craft that had enabled the frontiersman to master the humid, forested East were simply inadequate or useless on the treeless, arid plains, and so were his ax, his plow, his canoe, and his long rifle. And so, for that matter, were some of his laws and institutions. As Walter P. Webb writes: "East of the Mississippi civilization stood on three legs—land, water, and timber; west of the Mississippi not one but two of these legs were withdrawn—water and timber—and civilization was left on one leg—land. It is small wonder that it toppled over in temporary failure." Major John Wesley Powell, explorer of the region, wrote in 1879: "The physical conditions which exist in that land and which inexorably control the operations of men, are such that the industries of the West are necessarily unlike those of the East and their institutions must be adapted to their industrial wants."

So harsh and uninhabitable did the plains appear that the Easterner wrote them off as wasteland; in American atlases and geographies from 1820 to 1860 this vast stretch of land was labeled simply "The Great American Desert." Dry winds parched the Easterner's throat, cracked his lips, and made his eyes smart. Everything was different. There were chinooks, or warm mountain winds, northers, blizzards, and hailstorms. All but the chinook could bring distress

and disaster. Writing of the Texas plains, Colonel Richard I. Dodge warned: "Every bush had its thorn; every animal, reptile, or insect had its horn, tooth, or sting; every male human his revolver; and each was ready to use his weapon of defense on any unfortunate sojourner, on the smallest, or even without the smallest provocation."

The rivers dried up unexpectedly, and when they flowed, their unpalatable water concealed treacherous sands. The slight rainfall, usually under fifteen inches a year, made traditional methods of farming impracticable and demanded a new extensive agriculture to replace the old intensive type. Not for a generation after they reached the edge of the Great Plains did Americans begin to find satisfactory solutions to the problems posed by the new environment—the problems of water and wood, of fences and transportation, of agriculture and cattle-raising.

The animals native to the plains seemed to need little water—the jack rabbit and the prairie dog apparently none at all. The swift and elusive antelopes, coyotes, and wolves depended on speed for safety and were difficult to bag. The one exception was the most famous, the most numerous, and, for human life, the most important plains animal of all, the buffalo, or American bison. This great, shaggy, lumbering beast, neither swift of gait nor alert to danger, could be overtaken by any good horse and was easy prey to a

Sioux camp, South Dakota

hunter armed with either bow and arrow or rifle. Though they existed in small numbers far east of the Mississippi in colonial days, the buffaloes found their true home on the Great Plains, from Canada to the Gulf of Mexico. Estimates of the buffalo population around the end of the Civil War range up to 12 million.

Once the rebellious South had been put down, Americans turned anew to the conquest of the Great Plains. Here they encountered rebels of a different and even more difficult breed.

The plains Indians. Of some three hundred thousand Indians left in the United States in 1865, more than two-thirds lived on the Great Plains. The frontiersman called them "wild Indians"—and so they were, in comparison with their sedentary cousins of the Eastern forests. The only mounted Indians the white man ever encountered, most of them were nomadic and nonagricultural. Above all, they were fierce, skillful, and implacable warriors—"the most effectual barrier," according to Webb, "ever set up by a native American population against European invaders in a temperate zone." Against all comers—Spanish, French, English, and American—they had held their own as masters of the plains for two and a half centuries.

The Spaniards had introduced horses into Mexico in the sixteenth century and the animals had multiplied and spread northward over the plains in wild herds. Before then, the plains Indian had been a miserable, earthbound creature, hard pressed to earn a living and defend himself. The horse revolutionized the life of the tribesmen and brought on the golden era of the plains Indians—an era that had about reached its peak when the Anglo-Americans first encountered them. The horse made the Indians more mobile and hence more nomadic than ever, less agricultural, more warlike, and above all, far more effective buffalo-hunters. The buffalo was even more indispensable to the plains Indians than the horse, for it provided them with food, clothing, shelter, and even fuel. Necessities, luxuries, ornaments, tools, bedding, their very tepees—all were fashioned from the flesh, bone, and hide of the buffalo. The nomadic tribes moved back and forth across the plains with the great herds and organized their life and religion around the hunt. Whatever threatened the buffalo threatened their very existence.

The plains Indians were generally superior in physique to the Indians of other regions. Although their culture varied from that of the peaceful tribes of the pueblos to that of fierce nomadic tribes, all the plains Indians shared the culture of neolithic man, using stone knives, stone scrapers, and bone awls as tools. The warriors carried bows and arrows and four-teen-foot, stone-tipped lances for hunting and warfare. Yet in combat the stone-age man asked no quarter of early industrial man. With his short three-foot bow and a quiver of two-score arrows or more, the Comanche would ride three hundred yards and get off twenty arrows with startling force and accuracy while the Texan was firing one shot and reloading his long and cumbersome rifle. Even the Colt six-shooter, with which the white man began arming himself in the 1840s, did not entirely overcome the Indian's advantage. As armor he carried a loosely slung shield made of buffalo hide so tough that it could deflect a bullet. The arrows he used against an enemy, unlike those he used in the hunt, were fitted with heads that came off in the wound when the shaft was withdrawn.

The plains Indians lived on horseback, and in case of emergency even used their mounts as food. They could hang by a heel to one side of the horse and discharge arrows under its neck; they could execute intricate cavalry maneuvers controlled by a secret system of communications and signals that was the envy of white military experts.

Until the white man finally crushed the plains Indians, he was conscious of them mainly as warriors, as ruthless and dreaded enemies who held military supremacy in their own country. The Indian's conception of the conduct of war and the treatment of captives differed from that of the white man. "Cruelty is both an amusement and a study," wrote Colonel Dodge of the plains Indians. "So much pleasure is derived from it, that an Indian is constantly thinking out new devices of torture, and how to prolong to the utmost those already known. His anatomical knowledge of the most sensitive portions of the human frame is wonderfully accurate." The Indian's reputation for cruelty was probably as much deserved as the white man's reputation for ruthlessness. The military struggle between the two races on the Great Plains was marked by a peculiar ferocity and savagery.

White supremacy in the West. So long as Americans thought of the plains as the "Great American Desert" and as "one big reservation" for the red man, conflict as well as contact between the races was rare. But in the 1850s the situation changed. Mass migrations got under way across the plains to Oregon; miners began to beg for protection; the Kansas and Nebraska territories were organized; and politicians demanded that the Indians be pushed out to north and south to clear the way for transportation and settlement. In 1851 the federal government adopted a new Indian policy of "concentration," under which the chiefs of the plains tribes were persuaded to restrict their people to areas the white man solemnly promised he would never violate. Caught between the mining frontier that, as we shall see, was closing in

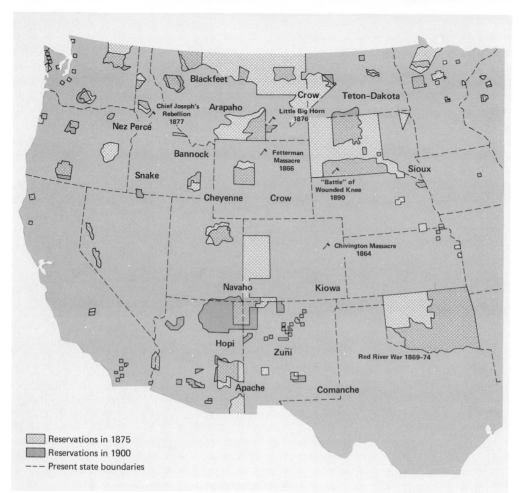

Blackfeet

Crow

Teton–Dakota

Chief Joseph's
Rebellion
1877

Arapaho

Little Big Horn
1876

Nez Percé

Bannock

Fetterman
Massacre
1866

Sioux

Snake

"Battle" of
Wounded Knee
1890

Cheyenne

Crow

Chivington Massacre
1864

Navaho

Kiowa

Hopi

Zuñi

Red River War 1869–74

Apache

Comanche

Reservations in 1875
Reservations in 1900
Present state boundaries

from the west, and an agricultural frontier advancing from the east, the plains Indian was soon to learn what the woods Indian had learned long before: that he could trust none of the white man's promises, however solemn. The red man was further embittered by the behavior of corrupt officials of the Indian Bureau of the Interior Department, who defrauded him of his land, cheated him in trade, and sold him liquor, and by the treachery of a reckless breed of beaver-trappers, gold-prospectors, hunters, and outlaws. Then in 1858 and 1859 the Pike's Peak Gold Rush sent tens of thousands hell-bent for Colorado and trouble, soon to be joined by deserters and draft-dodgers from the Union and Confederate armies.

Indian war broke out in Colorado about the time the Civil War was starting in the East. The immediate provocation was the effort of government officials to force the Arapaho and Cheyenne to abandon all claim to the area that had been granted them forever only ten years before. Many braves rejected the agreement made by their chiefs and took the warpath. After an intermittent warfare of pillaging, home-burning, and murdering that went on for more than three years, they sued for peace. Chief Black Kettle of the Chey-

enne, after being assured of protection, was surprised and trapped by a force led by Colonel John M. Chivington on the night of November 28, 1864. Ignoring Black Kettle's attempts to surrender, the militia shot, knifed, scalped, clubbed, and mutilated the Indians indiscriminately until the ground was littered with men, women, and children. Chief Black Kettle and a few warriors escaped, but before a year had passed the Cheyenne and Arapaho, as well as the Kiowa and Comanche, were compelled to surrender their claims and move on to more restricted areas assigned by the white masters.

Hardly had peace been restored to the Southwest in the fall of 1865 when Indian war broke out in the Northwest. The bloody Sioux War of 1865–67 was brought on by many forces, but it was triggered by the demands of miners who had invaded the Sioux Country. In response to their request, the federal government announced its intention to build a road through the foothills of the Big Horn Mountains to connect the mining towns of Bozeman and Virginia City with the East. Such a road would spoil one of the Sioux' favorite hunting grounds, and Chief Red Cloud warned that it would be resisted. Sioux warriors am-

The New West: empire within a nation

bushed a party of soldiers under Captain W. J. Fetterman near Fort Phil Kearny in December 1866 and slaughtered all eighty-two of its members.

The Chivington and Fetterman massacres, together with scores of minor battles and endless shooting scrapes, prompted the federal government to review its Indian policy in 1867. Easterners clashed with Westerners, humanitarian impulses with fire-and-sword military policies, and at last authority over the Indians was split between the Department of the Interior, which would placate them with gifts, annuities, and reservations, and the War Department, which was accustomed to punish with violence. The Westerner's disgust was reflected in a letter signed "Texas" in the Chicago *Tribune*: "Give us Phil Sheridan, and send Phil-anthropy to the devil." It is hard to say at times whether West or South was in fiercer revolt against the Eastern philanthropists. The East prevailed against the West as it had against the South, however, and sent out a Peace Commission of four civilians and three generals in the autumn of 1867 to end the Sioux War and to inaugurate a policy of "small reservations" to replace the old one of "concentration." The new policy meant that the Indians were to abandon their way of life, submit to segregation in small out-of-the-way reservations on land spurned by the white man, and accept government tutelage in learning "to walk the white man's road." The Black Hills section of the Dakota Territory was to be set aside for the northern tribes. Poor lands in the western part of what is now Oklahoma, of which the five civilized tribes of the Southeast had just been defrauded on false charges of treason because of their Confederate sympathies, were to be divided among the plains Indians of the Southwest.

The white man's policy toward the red man in these years contrasted strangely with his professed policy toward the black man, though both promised uplift by education. The same Congress that devised Radical Reconstruction to bring equality and integration to the Negro of the South approved strict segregation and inequality for the Indian of the West. General William T. Sherman, the deliverer of the Southern slaves, instructed General Winfield S. Hancock in 1867 that his principal mission to the Cheyenne and Kiowa was to "impress on them the imprudence of assuming an insolent manner and tone when they visit our posts."

But many Indians refused to renounce their way of life and enter meekly into the reservations. When they took the warpath in the summer of 1868, General Sherman unleashed his troopers and launched a decade of remorseless war against them. "I will urge General Sheridan to push his measures for the utter destruction and subjugation of all who are outside [the reservations] in a hostile attitude," Sherman

George A. Custer: rash and young

wrote. "I propose that [he] shall prosecute the war with vindictive earnestness against all hostile Indians, till they are obliterated or beg for mercy." It took more than two hundred battles from 1869 through 1874 to restore peace. Sometimes called a war of "extermination," this, like other Indian conflicts, was not one-sided. A recent study finds that during the entire nineteenth century no more than five thousand Indians were killed, while the Indians killed some seven thousand soldiers and civilians in the same period. These figures, however, do not include indirect casualties caused by starvation and disease.

President Grant was persuaded early in his Administration to place under a dozen religious denominations the control of Indians living on reservations. Supported by government funds, agents chosen by religious bodies sought to educate, "civilize," and assimilate their charges. These actions became known unofficially as "Grant's Peace Policy." Indians refusing to settle on the reservations, however, were mercilessly subjected to the very unpeaceful policy of the United States Army. Coordination of the two policies served to remove most Indians from the path of white settlers and developers.

By the end of 1874 all seemed calm. Then in 1875, when government authorities permitted tens of

*Chief Sitting Bull:
compelled to surrender*

when it was discovered that buffalo pelts and leather could be marketed at a profit, the slaughter was organized on a commercial basis. Now professional hunters and skinners working in teams stepped up the butchery. The advance of the railroads hastened the end of the herds as well as the subduing of the Indians. By 1878 the vast southern herd, the larger of the two main herds, had been wiped out. Five years later, when collectors tried to round up a few specimens of what had recently been the most numerous breed of large animals in the world, only remnants of the northern herd could be found in remote parts of Canada.

The slaughter of the buffalo is the classic example of the white man's heedless rapacity in the exploitation of nature; the United States' Indian policy is the classic instance of his racial, cultural, and religious bigotry. Reformers and humanitarians won their fight against the policy of physical extermination of the Indian only to substitute their own policy of relentless attack on Indian society, customs, religion, and tribal unity. This, they were convinced, was necessary if they were to "civilize" the red man, save his soul from "paganism," and integrate him into white civilization. In 1884 the Department of the Interior passed a criminal code forbidding and penalizing Indian religious practices, and in 1887 the Dawes Act struck at tribal authority and organization by breaking up reservation land into small family or individual holdings, often not suited to farming, with the best of the land usually sold to the whites. All Indians who received grants were to become citizens of the United States.

Thus the oldest residents of the land became the newest citizens. But their government simultaneously deprived them of the basic rights of citizens. Virtually imprisoned and pauperized on the reservations, they were constantly subjected to the withholding of rations—those still entitled to them—in an effort to compel them to abandon their tribal customs and loyalties. A government that guaranteed freedom of worship carried its religious persecution of the Indians to the point of espionage and armed violence. The sacred Sun Dance, the supreme expression of tribal unity, was outlawed as "pagan." The notorious corruption of the Indian Bureau and its agents was checked by civil-service reform in the 1880s, but this only meant that the misguided Indian policy was administered more efficiently and destructively than ever before. The real trouble, according to the twentieth-century reformer John Collier, was not corrupt agents but "collective corruption; corruption which did not know it was corrupt, and which reached deep into the intelligence of a nation. It was such a collective corruption that dominated the plains-Indian record and nearly the whole Indian record of the United States."

thousands of gold-prospectors to crowd into the Black Hills, the outraged Sioux and other northern Indians reacted violently. At the Battle of the Little Big Horn on June 25, 1876, the rash young General George A. Custer and 265 men were wiped out in the general's first, and last, stand in the new Sioux War. In spite of this victory, the Indians were compelled to surrender the following fall. Chief Sitting Bull and a few warriors fled to Canada, but, facing starvation, they were forced to sue for peace in 1881. The Nez Percé Indians of Oregon staged a rebellion that was repressed in 1877, and the survivors of this once-proud tribe were herded into a barren preserve in Indian Territory to be ravaged by disease and hunger. The last incident of the Indian wars was the sickening "Battle" of Wounded Knee in 1890, in which United States troops mowed down two hundred Dakota men, women, and children.

Long before the fighting ended, the near-extermination of the buffalo herds had hastened the collapse of Indian resistance. At first the indiscriminate shooting of buffalo was motivated by little more than the desire for "sport" or for the diversion of railroad hands and passengers, who might incidentally help to clear the tracks and curb a nuisance. But in 1871,

The New West: empire within a nation

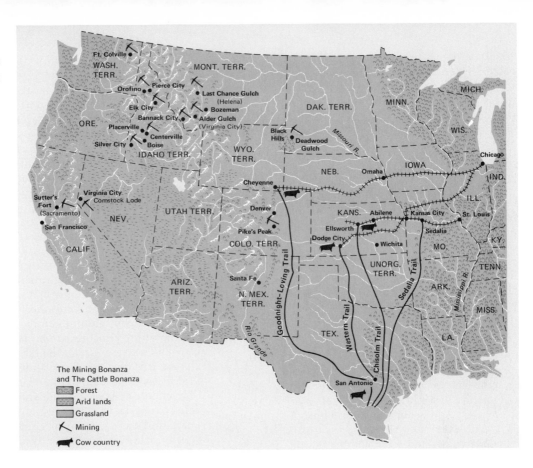

The Mining Bonanza
and The Cattle Bonanza

- Forest
- Arid lands
- Grassland
- ⚒ Mining
- 🐄 Cow country

The era of the bonanzas

Webb in *The Great Frontier* distinguishes between the "primary windfalls" and the "secondary windfalls" that are gleaned from any frontier. The primary windfalls are the first easy pickings—gold, silver, furs—that are gained with little investment of energy or time. The secondary windfalls require more patience and expense. Usually the primary windfalls are grabbed up early in the game. The Spanish mined the precious metals in their quarter of the New World or seized them from the Indians in the sixteenth and seventeenth centuries, and the French gathered their bales of furs in Canada a little later. Entering the continent north of the gold and south of the furs, the Anglo-Americans were obliged to concentrate on secondary windfalls. Then late in the nineteenth century, after the frontier had become a prosaic matter of timber, corn, and cotton, they belatedly entered upon a fabulous phase of frontier history that for the rest of the world had faded into the mists of legend with the conquistadors and the Spanish treasure ships. The beaver pelts had been gathered, and we have seen what happened to the buffalo. But there remained the bonanzas of gold and silver and the lush grass left by the bison.

The miner's bonanza. There had been gold rushes from time to time in the East, but from 1804 to 1866 the five-state Appalachian gold field had yielded only $19,375,890. An entirely new scale was set by the California yield of $555 million in a single decade, 1848–58. In the 1860s and 1870s the turbulent gold rush of the forty-niners (see p. 271) was to be repeated with variations time and again in the mountain areas of Nevada, Colorado, Arizona, Idaho, Montana, and Wyoming. Since the experienced Californians usually led the invasion of these areas, the mining frontier advanced eastward instead of westward. The Californians also developed the primitive technology of "placer" mining, by which "pay dirt" was washed in pans, "cradles," or sluice boxes. Armed with nothing more than a pick and shovel and a crude pan, the lucky prospector could gather up loose gold that had washed down through debris to bedrock. The richer deposits of gold, usually in deep-lying veins of quartz, could only be mined with machinery that was beyond the means of the prospector and had to await the corporation. It has been estimated that by 1868 placer miners, with their wasteful methods, had lost beyond recovery nearly $300 million in precious metals. During the sixties placer mining was more and more superseded by quartz mining.

The lure of the bonanza—even the hope of modest pay dirt—was enough to keep thousands of prospectors feverishly exploring gulches and canyons for three decades. Working in groups—the lone prospector is largely mythical—they crisscrossed the vast mountain area in their obsessive quest. Few of them were qualified to interpret the evidence they uncovered, and some of the richest lodes were discovered by chance. Prospectors were entitled by law to one claim by preemption and one by discovery; latecomers were entitled to only one claim. The typical claim ran from side to side of a gulch and was one hundred feet wide. Only the exceptional claim really paid off, but the promise of fabulous riches and the wild thrill of discovery seemed reward enough. After the discovery came the inevitable leak of the secret and the headlong scramble by other prospectors to stake a claim. One such rush in 1861 was described by a witness:

> On Friday morning last, when the news of the new diggings had been promulgated, the store of Miner and Arnold was literally besieged. As the news radiated—and it was not long in spreading—picks and shovels were thrown down, claims deserted and turn your eye where you would, you could see droves of people coming in "hot haste" to town, some packing one thing on their backs and some another, all intent on scaling the mountains through frost and snow, and taking up a claim in the new El Dorado. In town there was a perfect jam—a mass of human infatuation, jostling, shoving and elbowing each other.

The prospectors' invasion of the interior was touched off by discoveries in Colorado and Nevada. During the summer of 1858 prospectors made a number of small strikes in the vicinity of what was later to become Denver. Rumors of these finds, wildly and perhaps deliberately exaggerated, spread rapidly through the frontier region and started a rush for the Pike's Peak country that fall. A new discovery in May 1859, followed by several smaller ones, had offered some justification for the excitement, but the great majority of fortune-hunters were doomed to disappointment. The dejected horde returning from Pike's Peak symbolized the disillusioned gold-rusher of the period. Thousands of the unsuccessful miners, however, stayed on to become settlers and future citizens of Colorado.

In the meantime prospectors had struck it rich on the eastern slope of the Sierras in Nevada opposite the California fields on the western slope. Two Irishmen named Patrick McLaughlin and Peter O'Riley accidentally turned up a vein of bluish rock while digging a water reservoir for their modest placer operation. They were promptly bluffed out of a large share of their find by a loud-mouthed scamp named Henry Comstock, who sold out before he had more than an inkling of the treasure he had acquired: the incredibly rich Comstock Lode, the biggest bonanza of them all! At the first rumor, a thundering stampede of fifteen thousand claim-stakers blanketed the Washoe district. But most of the gold and silver was locked in veins of quartz, and little mining could be done until quartz mills and mining machinery were brought in. Not until 1873, after heroic tunneling operations and giant engineering feats under the direction of John W. Mackay and his partners, was the greatest lode of silver and gold struck. From 1859 to 1879 the total output of the Comstock mines was $350 million, of which 45 percent was in gold and 55 percent in silver. No deposits of equal richness have ever been recorded in ancient or modern mining history.

Perched on the roof of this subterranean treasure house on the steep side of Mount Davidson, seventy-two hundred feet above sea level, was Virginia City, the most celebrated of the Western mining towns.

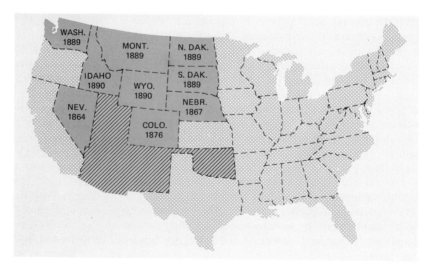

New states, 1864–90

The New West: empire within a nation

Last Chance Gulch, 1865

Mark Twain, who arrived at the diggings in the early days, described the town in *Roughing It:*

> Virginia [City] had grown to be the "livest" town, for its age and population, that America had ever produced. The sidewalks swarmed with people—to such an extent, indeed, that it was generally no easy matter to stem the human tide. The streets themselves were just as crowded with quartz wagons, freight teams and other vehicles. The procession was endless. So great was the pack, that buggies frequently had to wait half an hour for an opportunity to cross the principal street. Joy sat on every countenance, and there was a glad, almost fierce, intensity in every eye, that told of the money-getting schemes that were seething in every brain and the high hope that held sway in every heart . . . a dozen breweries and half a dozen jails and station-houses in full operation, and some talk of building a church. The "flush times" were in magnificent flower!

After Comstock one strike followed another in western Nevada. None was so rich as Comstock, but all served to attract an unstable population to the territory and to increase the demand for statehood. Eight days before the election of 1864 Nevada became a state and promptly furnished three electoral votes for Lincoln.

In the meantime the future states of Washington, Idaho, and Montana were the scene of gold rushes and flush times. During the tragic years from Bull Run to Appomattox "yonder-siders" from California joined "pilgrims" from the East and seasoned prospectors from Nevada in stampedes to Orofino, Pierce City, Elk City, Boise, Placerville, Centerville, and Silver City. Some remained in Idaho as permanent settlers, but only fifteen thousand were living there in 1870. Many joined the great Montana gold rush around Bannack City, then jumped on to the spectacular diggings in Alder Gulch that produced $30 million of gold in three years, and ended up at Last Chance Gulch, where Helena was first laid out as a mining camp. A few more strikes after the war turned up the last surface gold in Idaho and Montana; then the placer miners passed on, leaving scarred hills and ghost towns behind them. As in Nevada, the richest deposits lay in deep veins of quartz that could be reached only by expensive shafts and crushed only by heavy mills. Eastern capital moved in and opened up new mines in the seventies and eighties, one of which, the Bunker Hill and Sullivan Mine, discovered in 1885, yielded a quarter of a billion dollars in silver and lead.

During the early days of the gold rushes a motley and cosmopolitan assortment of humanity accumulated on the mining frontier. The population of one camp was somewhat unscientifically classified as "Saxon, Celt, Teuton, Gaul, Greaser, Celestial, and Indian." The 206 souls of another camp were more carefully tabulated as 73 American white citizens, 37 Chinese, 35 British subjects, 29 Mexicans and Spaniards, 8 Negroes, and the rest assorted Europeans. Every camp of any size attracted its share of lawless outcasts—jailbirds, gamblers, prostitutes, deserters, desperadoes, stagecoach-robbers. And every town had to decide whether or not to let the outcasts take over. As one observer described life in Last Chance Gulch in 1864: "Not a day or night passed which did not yield its full fruition of fights, quarrels, wounds, or murders. The crack of the revolver was often heard above the merry notes of the violin. . . . Pistols flashed, bowie knives flourished, and braggart oaths filled the air." The United States government was far off and preoccupied with other matters, and its arm was not always long enough to reach into Nevada and Idaho. As a result the miners developed their own informal codes of law and their own informal means of enforcement. Throughout the region there was a generous and sometimes loose resort to vigilantism, a more or less formalized lynch law intended to terrify the desperadoes.

The old mining frontier had its last mad fling in the Black Hills of what later became South Dakota. The army had finally given up as hopeless its effort to keep the insistent horde of prospectors out of the Sioux reservation, and in October 1875 it threw open the district to all who were willing to enter at their own risk. Thousands of prospectors, still hopeful after two decades of disappointments, rushed in for one last chance. In a grand finale at Deadwood Gulch the miners' frontier outdid itself in a lurid caricature of its reputation. The curtain was rung down on the rowdiest brawls, the wildest desperadoes, and the most vigilant vigilantes of them all. After the Black Hills rush the prospectors and their supporting casts trooped off the scene, leaving mining to heavy investors and engineers. The frontier's "primary windfall" of precious metals had been stripped off, though the serious business of mining had only begun.

The cattleman's bonanza. The windfall of the early cattlemen was almost as rich and free as that of the early miners. The cows harvested the free crop of grass, turned it into beef and hides, transported these commodities to market on the hoof, and dropped calves along the way as replacements.

For a brief interlude between the passing of the Indian and the buffalo and the entry of the farmer and the barbed-wire fence, the Great Plains witnessed the most picturesque industrial drama ever staged— the drama of the open range and the cattle ranch. If the southern planter could once claim that cotton was king, the Western cattleman could proclaim with equal fervor that grass was king. For the time being, at least, the plains were one limitless, fenceless, gateless pasture of rich, succulent, and ownerless grass that was his for the taking. Within an incredibly short period the red man's herds of bison had been replaced and outnumbered by the white man's herds of cattle.

The miner's invasion of the mountain and plains country came mainly from the Far West: the cattleman, his animals, and his ranch culture invaded from the South. Herdsmen had acquired some of the cowboy's arts and lingo on their long trek across the Gulf states and the antebellum Southwest, but it was not until they had reached Texas and had begun to handle Spanish cattle from horseback that the craft took on its Mexican flavor and exotic style. A diamond-shaped area of the tip of Texas, with San Antonio at its apex, was the cradle of the future cowboy and his long-horned charges. The bulk of the cattle, a Spanish stock, grew up wild and were said to be "fifty times more dangerous to footmen than the fiercest buffalo." A tough, stringy, durable breed, wonderfully adapted to the plains, they multiplied so rapidly that they became a pest. Within just one decade the cattle population of Texas increased over 1,000 percent, and by 1860 cattle were estimated at nearly 5 million in that state alone.

Even before the Civil War Texas cattlemen had made a few inconsequential drives to Northern markets, and after the war inducements multiplied. During the 1860s the population of the United States increased 22 percent, while the number of cattle in the country decreased about 7 percent. But industrialization was piling up big meat markets in the cities and pushing the railroad out to the plains. At the end of the war cattle that brought $3 to $5 a head in Texas could be sold for $30 to $50 a head in Northern markets. Fantastic profits had recently induced speculators to bring Confederate cotton through armed ranks of blue and gray to Yankee mills, and Texans were not to be daunted by the mere twelve or fifteen hundred miles that separated them from the fabulous meat markets in the North. In 1866 they set forth on the long drive north with more than a quarter of a million head. Taking the most direct route to the nearest railhead, Sedalia, Missouri, the cattlemen fell into the hands of thieves along the wooded parts of their route. Thereafter they kept to the open plains. The first town founded for the specific purpose of receiving cows for shipment was Abilene, Kansas, established by J. G. McCoy (single-handedly, he implied) on the Hannibal and St. Joe Railroad in 1867. Of Abilene and its reputation, Webb has written:

> Abilene was more than a point. It is a symbol. It stands for all that happened when two civilizations met for conflict, for disorder, for the clashing of great currents which carry on their crest the turbulent and disorderly elements of both civilizations—in this case the rough characters of the plain and of the forest. On the surface Abilene was corruption personified. Life was hectic, raw, lurid, awful. But . . . if Abilene excelled all later cow towns in wickedness, it also excelled

Roundup: eighteen hours a day

them in service—the service of bartering the beef of the South for the money of the North.

Other cow towns followed—Wichita, Ellsworth, Dodge City—pushing farther and farther westward and southward with the railroad, an indispensable adjunct to the cattle kingdom. The Texas trails themselves pushed in the same direction toward the Texas Panhandle and eastern New Mexico and Colorado. The trails shifted during the years of the long drive, to take advantage of the best grazing and water supplies. Some of them—the Goodnight-Loving Trail, the Western Trail, and the Chisholm Trail—left broad, brown, beaten tracks across hundreds of miles of grasslands. Riders of the long drive, beset by heartbreaking misfortunes, watched helplessly as the weight of their droves dwindled on the way to market. Nevertheless, the cowboys drove more than 5 million head of cattle northward over these trails between 1866 and 1888.

Not all the Texas cattle were sold directly for beef. Of the record drive of six hundred thousand in 1871 only half could find buyers and the rest spent the winter as "feeders" in the neighboring areas and corn states. It was mainly from this surplus of the Texas drives, many of them crossed with Hereford bulls to produce the white-faced hybrid, that the Great Plains area was stocked. Many herds were driven directly to the ranges of New Mexico, Arizona, Colorado, Wyoming, Montana, and the Dakotas to feed mining camps and railroad-builders and to supply the ranchers' demand for fresh stock. Some Eastern cattle, called "pilgrims" (as were the miners from the East), contributed slightly to the stocking of the plains. In the amazingly brief period of fifteen years, by 1880, the cattlemen and their ranches had spread over the whole vast grassland from the Rio Grande into Canada as well as up into the recesses of the Rockies.

With the boom of the 1880s, the monarchs of the cattle kingdom became intoxicated with the magnificence of their domain and its immediate prospects. The depression of the seventies had been rolled aside, the Indians had been driven into reservations, the railroads were coming on, and neither the homesteader nor barbed wire had yet arrived in menacing quantity. Beef prices were soaring and the grass was growing higher by the hour. No wonder the cow king got a wonderful feeling that everything was going his way. His optimism spread abroad, and investors from the four corners of the earth rushed to the plains to seek their fortunes, money hot in their pockets. Cheyenne, where a new cowman's club served caviar and rare wines, was described in 1882 by a local journalist:

> Sixteenth Street is a young Wall Street. Millions are talked of as lightly as nickels and all kinds of people are dabbling in steers. The chief justice of the Supreme Court has recently succumbed to the contagion and gone out to purchase a $40,000 herd. . . . A Cheyenne man who don't pretend to know a maverick from a mandamus has made a neat little margin of $15,000 this summer in small transactions and hasn't seen a cow yet that he has bought and sold.

As a symbol of this spectacular adventure, the public took to its heart not the cow king but his hired hand, and there the cowboy has remained enshrined, his cult faithfully tended by votaries of screen and television. Known sometimes as "cowpoke" or "cowpuncher," names derived from an early method of

The era of the bonanzas

prodding lagging critters with long poles, the cowboy is more popularly identified with the lariat and the branding iron. His picturesque accouterments—sombrero, spurs, long-heeled boots, chaps, gloves, and saddle, which he called his "workbench"—were strictly functional, not ornamental, and strictly adapted to life on horseback. There, indeed, much of his life was spent—eighteen hours or more a day during phases of the long drive or the roundup. Each cowboy had a "mount" of from eight to fourteen horses, depending on the work he was doing and the class of horses. Normally a hardworking man of Spartan and sober habits, the cowboy has come to share with the sailor a public image derived from his rare escapades of frantic recreation after long ordeals. The cowboy's two or three months in the saddle on the long drive built up as big a head of steam as a long voyage built up for the sailor. As for the cowboy's addiction to lethal six-guns, it was exaggerated.

Violence of the shooting-iron sort, however, was unavoidable in the open-range cattle kingdom. With millions of dollars' worth of property wandering at large on public lands, unfenced and poorly marked, rustlers found the temptation overwhelming. Since government was remote and undependable, cattlemen resorted to private associations for protection and self-government in matters of roundup, branding, and breeding. These associations sometimes furnished all the government there was. The sort of justice they dispensed and the methods they used are suggested by a laconic item in the obituary of John S. Chisum of New Mexico, who died in 1884. Annoyed by Indians who had stolen some of his sixty thousand cattle in 1877, he armed a hundred men, moved against the presumed offenders, and "killed 175."

Even with free pasturage and virgin grassland, cattle-raising on the open range was extravagant and uneconomical. It exposed the herds to weather hazards, made adequate care of animals impossible and improvement of breeds difficult, encouraged rough and wasteful handling of cattle, and provoked costly and sometimes bloody range disputes. The approaching doom of the free range was further hastened by the expanding railroads and their loads of settlers, who staked claims and ran fences, and by the sheepherders, who fouled the water holes and stripped the grazing land. But the cattlemen contributed to their own downfall. They resorted to land fraud, monopoly, and ruthless violence to protect their interests. They even adopted for their own use before homesteaders arrived that concrete denial of the open range, the barbed-wire fence: Charles Goodnight ran one all the way across the Texas Panhandle into New Mexico. Worse still, they overstocked and overgrazed the range.

The day of reckoning dawned in 1885, when beef prices started to tumble. On top of that, during the severe winter of 1885–86 up to 85 percent of the herds on the southern ranges either starved or froze to death. A bad drought the following summer scorched the grass and left the animals in poor condition. Then the legendary winter of 1886–87 fastened its cruel grip on the plains and brought panic to men as well as animals. When the thaw finally came, the emaciated corpses of enormous herds were left stacked up against fences or piled deep in coulees. A few grisly survivors staggered about on frozen legs.

The disaster spelled the end of the great beef bonanza. It ruined the larger corporations and many individual ranchers and took the heart out of the enterprise. There was little left of the reckless confidence with which cattlemen had greeted the great

410

The New West: empire within a nation

risks of the open range in its heyday. When nature smiled again and the public domain beckoned, some of the more hardy ranchers carried on in the old manner through the depressed nineties. But there was a steady and unmistakable retreat of investment to the security of privately owned pasturage and a deliberate avoidance of the wild gambles and risks of the old days. Ultimately it was sheep-herding that triumphed on the Great Plains. Cattle had become a sober business instead of a high, wide, and handsome adventure.

The farmer moves West

Ever since 1607 American farmers had been moving west to break new ground. But in the last three decades of the nineteenth century they occupied and brought under cultivation more land than in all the years before 1870. It might seem natural to attribute this rapid expansion to the free-homestead policy adopted in 1862 (see p. 358). Before we jump to such a conclusion, however, it would be well to review that policy.

American land policy. The number of farms in the United States increased from some 2,000,000 in 1860 to 5,737,000 in 1900. And yet fewer than 600,000 homesteads were patented in those years, and they accounted for only 80,000,000 acres out of the more than 430,000,000 acres that were added to the total land in farms. Thus even if all the farmers who filed claims had been bona fide homesteaders, they would have accounted for fewer than one-sixth of the new farms and a little more than one-sixth of the added acreage. Actually, a great number of the so-called homesteads fell into the hands of large landholders and did not become farms until they were sold to settlers by speculators.

Nothing could have been further from the intention of the framers of the Homestead Act than the promotion of land monopoly. On the contrary, by distributing the bounty of free land among needy people they had hoped to defeat land monopoly. In practice, however, the great American promise of free land—a promise that was published around the world—turned out to be pretty much a delusion. One trouble was that few prospective homesteaders could afford to take advantage of the opportunity, because they lacked the capital to transport their families and possessions to the public domain, stock up with expensive machinery, and stick it out for years until the farm became self-supporting. Fewer still understood the new type of agriculture required on the arid plains. Two-thirds of all homestead claimants before 1890 failed at the venture. Speculators hired men to stake out homesteads, falsely claim they had fulfilled the required conditions, and then turn over the land to their employer.

But the fundamental weakness of the Homestead Act was that it simply was not appropriate to the region where it applied. The law covered all public lands, of course, but by the time the act was passed the great bulk of public lands available for homesteading lay on the Great Plains and beyond. The Eastern congressmen who framed the law for the plains knew little about the needs of the people who were eventually going to live there. To the farmer back in the humid East a 160-acre tract seemed ideal for a family-sized farm—a good deal larger than the average, in fact. In the arid or semiarid West, however, land was useful only for intensive irrigated farming, extensive dry farming, or grazing. A 160-acre tract was too small for grazing or dry farming and too large for irrigated farming. Of the last there was little anyway, so the great Western complaint was against the smallness of holdings. If the East persisted in writing laws for the West that did not work, said the Westerners, then the West was justified in ignoring or violating them.

In land policy, as in Indian policy, it proved difficult to reconcile the views of East and West—particularly since the Eastern outcry was against land monopoly and the Western demand was for larger and larger units of land. One attempt to adjust land policy to Western needs was the Timber Culture Act of 1873, which permitted the homesteader to add another 160 acres of relatively treeless land to his holdings provided he would plant trees on one-quarter of it within four years. The law failed to increase rainfall, however, and nine out of ten claimants are said to have made no serious effort to forest their holdings.

A more absurd law was the Desert Land Act of 1877, which offered 640 acres to anyone who would pay 25 cents an acre down and promise to irrigate the land within three years. Upon presenting proof of irrigation and paying an additional dollar per acre the claimant could close the deal. The trouble here was that the law required irrigation where no water was to be had. Cattlemen seized on the Desert Land Act to enlarge their holdings, but at least 95 percent of the "proofs" of irrigation were estimated to be fraudulent.

The Timber and Stone Act of 1878 permitted any citizen, or any alien with first papers, to buy at $2.50 an acre 160 acres of land "unfit for cultivation" and valuable chiefly for timber and stone. This act was as enticing an invitation to the timber barons as the Desert Land Act had been to the cattlemen. Using dummy entrymen to claim quarter-sections and deed them promptly to the corporation that paid them,

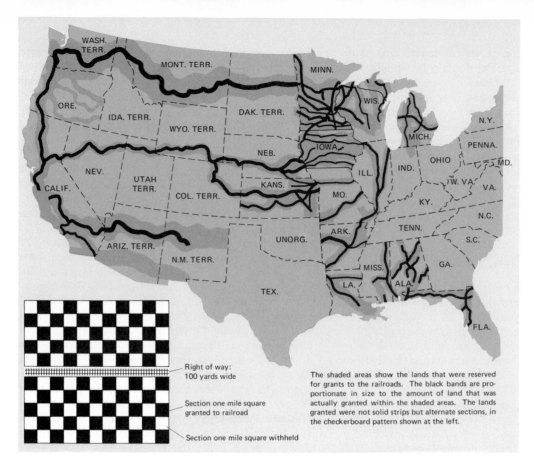

Right of way:
100 yards wide

Section one mile square
granted to railroad

Section one mile square withheld

The shaded areas show the lands that were reserved
for grants to the railroads. The black bands are proportionate in size to the amount of land that was
actually granted within the shaded areas. The lands
granted were not solid strips but alternate sections, in
the checkerboard pattern shown at the left.

lumber monopolists gobbled up vast empires of forest lands.

The laissez-faire philosophy of the period speeded the land-speculator to the more desirable lands and locations well ahead of the homesteader. Taking advantage of cash sale and public auction of government lands, the speculator moved in early and cornered the choice lands, the probable town sites, and lands along streams and roads to hold for high prices. When the bona fide homesteader finally arrived on the scene to stake out his claim, he usually had to choose from the least desirable and worst located tracts or else pay the speculator's price. In addition to about 100 million acres bought from the federal land office, the land-jobbers bought up another 100 million acres from shrinking Indian reservations that became available under the government's policy of concentration and 140 million acres from state land holdings. This accounted for some 340 million acres that were beyond the reach of homestead privileges.

Between 1850 and 1871 the federal government and the states had granted railroad corporations over 200 million acres of land to encourage construction (see p. 358), making the railroads the largest land-jobbers of the West. Not all of this land was patented. But the form of the federal grants meant that many millions of acres in addition to the actual land granted were withheld from settlement. The railroad lands lay on both sides of the track, from twenty to forty square miles for every mile of track laid in the territories and up to twenty for every mile laid in the states. This land was not arranged in solid strips, however, but in alternate sections, checkerboard fashion. But the whole solid strip was commonly withheld from settlement until the railroad chose its right-of-way and decided which alternate sections to keep. Great belts of land on either side of the tracks were placed beyond the homesteader's reach. At one time or another some three-tenths of the area of the country, and a much greater proportion of the West, was forbidden to use. Homesteaders were obliged either to accept areas remote from the rails or to pay the price the railroads asked. In 1887 this evil was alleviated by the Cleveland Administration (see p. 474), which threw open to settlement most of the land thus withheld.

The advance of settlement. The railroads became the principal colonizers as well as the biggest land-owners of the New West. Rapid settlement along their lines meant larger revenues from passenger fares and freight charges and bigger profits from land sales. Railroads and states sold settlers nearly six times as much land as the farmers were able to obtain by homesteading. Each Western road had its land department and its bureau of immigration, and each Western state its agency to advertise and exaggerate opportunities for settlers. Steamship companies with an eye to emigrant passengers joined in the campaign abroad; working with railroad agents, they plastered Europe with posters and literature calculated to attract settlers to the "Garden of the West." The railroads provided what the Homestead Act had neglected: credit terms, special passenger rates and agricultural guidance and assistance for prospective purchasers and settlers. The success of the railroad colonizers was striking, and their campaigns in Europe infected whole countries with the "American fever." From Norway, Sweden, and Denmark, which were especially susceptible, peasants by the millions emigrated to the Northwest. By 1890 Minnesota had four hundred towns bearing Swedish names. Irish and German colonies were sprinkled across Minnesota, Nebraska, and Dakota Territory.

As in the past, however, the states immediately to the east of the advancing frontier furnished a large proportion of the new settlers. In the 1870s some 190 million acres, an area equal to that of Great Britain and France combined, were added to the cultivated area of the country, mostly just to the west of the Minnesota-Louisiana tier of states. The line of settlement surged westward irregularly, first along the river valleys, rapidly along the growing railroad lines, and out over the rolling plains. A frontier in Kansas that had not budged perceptibly in two decades forged rapidly ahead in the seventies, and both Kansas and Nebraska had filled out to the edge of the semiarid plains by 1880. To the north the frontier advanced in a succession of three "Dakota Booms" roughly coinciding with three contemporaneous gold rushes. A demonstration of how to make a 100 percent profit in wheat-growing, put on by the Northern Pacific Railway after the Panic of 1873, started a rush that covered three hundred miles of the Red River Valley with "bonanza farms" ranging up to one hundred thousand acres in size, a remarkable commentary on the supposedly democratic land system. Farther north in Dakota Territory was the special province of James J. Hill, inspired colonizer of the Northwest and head of the Great Northern Railway. Hill planned and directed the settlement of thousands of pioneers along the tracks of his road to the Pacific. By 1885 all of Dakota east of the Missouri River was settled, and the population had increased 400 percent in five years. The mountainous territories to the west, except for the Mormon settlements of Utah, were slower in attracting settlers, but by the mid-eighties homesteaders in western Nebraska and Wyoming were challenging the cattlemen there.

In the meantime settlers of the Southwestern frontier were pushing ahead. The number of farms in Texas more than doubled during the seventies. As both the Texas and the Kansas frontiers approached the semiarid country to the west, avid land-seekers began to eye the tempting lands of the Indian Territory between the two states. Egged on by railroad companies with actual or projected lines in the territory, agitators defied the troops guarding the boundaries, repeatedly invaded the territory, and besieged Congress with demands to throw the cowed and defeated Indian tribes out of their last refuge. Congress yielded to their demands and on April 22, 1889, threw open some 2 million acres of the Oklahoma District in the heart of the territory. At the signal, a hundred

Guthrie, Oklahoma, 1889: holding down a claim

thousand "Boomers" and "Sooners," riding on every conceivable vehicle, including fifteen trains with passengers jamming the roofs, swarmed into the district, staked it off in claims, and founded two cities—all within a few hours. Congress yielded to pressure again and created the Oklahoma Territory on May 2, 1890. In succeeding years one strip after another was opened—the largest, the 6 million acres of the Cherokee Outlet, in 1893—until the entire area of Oklahoma had been settled.

The superintendent of the census of 1890 discovered after the returns were in that something was missing: the long-familiar frontier. "Up to and including 1880," he reported, "the country had a frontier of settlement, but at present the unsettled area has been so broken into by isolated bodies of settlement that there can hardly be said to be a frontier line." In 1893 Frederick Jackson Turner, a young historian from Wisconsin, undertook to interpret the meaning of this development in a paper entitled "The Significance of the Frontier in American History." A devoted son of the West, Turner maintained that contact with the frontier created the continuous rebirth and rejuvenation of democracy—a conclusion not easy to reconcile with the way land was distributed and the frontier advanced.

New farms and new methods. The tribulations of the new pioneers of prairie and plain rivaled those of the Jamestown settlers in the early seventeenth century. Like the plagues that the God of Moses sent against the Egyptians, new calamities visited Western farmers with each season. Hardly had the winter blizzards ceased when melting snow brought flash floods to menace man and beast. Summer temperatures soared to 118°; drought and hot winds seared corn to crisp blades and whitened men's faces with the salt of sweat. Worst of all were the grasshoppers, especially during the terrible plagues of the mid-seventies. The insects came in clouds that darkened the sun, cracked the limbs of trees with their weight, and covered the ground inches deep. After they had chewed the crops down to the roots, they stripped the few trees of leaves and tender bark and even consumed the curtains at the farmers' windows. Prairie fires, dust storms, marauding Indians, claim-jumpers, and rattlesnakes further chastened the spirit of the pioneers and discouraged all but the sturdiest.

Mrs. Abigail Scott Duniway, woman suffrage leader in the Northwest, never forgot the death of her mother, who was a victim of frontier hardship in Dakota. She described her own lot later in a pioneer community of Oregon: "To bear two children in two and a half years from my marriage . . . to sew and cook, and wash and iron; to bake and clean and stew and fry; to be, in short, a general pioneer drudge, with never a penny of my own, was not pleasant business for an erstwhile school teacher."

Gradually inventiveness and industry solved many of the problems of soil and climate and overcame the lack of wood and water. In his first few years the homesteader lived in a miserable sod house, half buried in the prairie and roofed with slabs of cut turf. But later, when the railroads brought down the cost of lumber, he built a frame house. The problem of how to fence his land in a woodless, railless, stoneless region was solved by the invention of barbed wire. Of the several types devised, the most successful was patented by Joseph F. Glidden, an Illinois farmer, in November 1874. Joining forces with a wire-manufacturer, Glidden began mass production two years later, and by 1883 the Glidden factory was turning out six hundred miles of barbed wire a day. Farmers and cattlemen strung it up as fast as it was produced.

The problem of water supply was harder to solve. The only reliable sources of supply lay far below the surface, too deep to reach by open, hand-dug wells. And even when a well was drilled, pumping the water up two hundred to eight hundred feet by hand was impractical. The obvious solution was to harness the free power of the winds that steadily swept the plains, and by 1880 scores of small firms were producing windmills adapted to this purpose.

To meet the problem of cultivating soil in semi-arid country without irrigation, Westerners developed the technique of "dry farming" where rainfall was at least ten inches per year. To break the tough soil of the plains and cultivate larger farms where labor was scarcer than ever, the farmer needed a new type of machinery. A revolution in farm machinery had started before 1860, and most of the basic patents had been granted by that year. But the mass production of machines came only after the Civil War.

The plow that most successfully broke the plains was devised by James Oliver of Indiana. After working on it for twenty-five years, by 1877 he had perfected the modern chilled-iron plow and smooth-surfaced moldboard. On bonanza farms in California before 1900 huge steam tractors were pulling sixteen plows, four harrows, and a seed drill, simultaneously breaking and planting as much as fifty acres a day.

Machine harvesting of wheat was improved in 1880 by a mechanical twine-binder that tied up the cut bundles. An even speedier device, used in drier

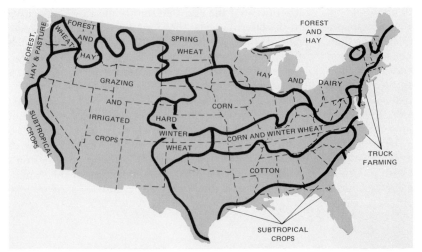

Agricultural regions of the United States

Homesteaders,
Nebraska, 1887

parts of the West, was the header, which cut off the heads of the grain and left the stalk for pasturage or plowing under. The threshing machine was improved over the years by refinements that increased its capacity and efficiency, and in 1884 a blowing device was developed for stacking straw.

The soft winter wheat of the East could not withstand the rigors of the new climate and was replaced by a new variety imported from northern Europe and by Turkey Red from the Crimea. To mill the hard grain of the new varieties, the basic idea of the roller mill was borrowed from Hungary, and chilled-iron rollers were added by 1879. By the early seventies the storage, loading, handling, and transporting of wheat had all been reduced to mechanical processes.

The most striking results of mechanized farming were achieved in wheat production. An acre that had required 61 hours to farm by hand took only 3 hours to farm by machine, and where one man could farm only 7½ acres by old methods he could take on 135 acres in the nineties. Mechanization released men from drudgery and stupefying toil. On the other hand, in the very states where mechanization was most prevalent there was a remarkable growth of tenancy in the last two decades of the century and a corresponding decline in the percentage of farmers working their own farms. The farmers, like the placer miners and the range cattlemen, were destined in the late eighties for trouble and disenchantment with the Golden West. They fell victims to their own illusions—the illusion of inexhaustible resources and the illusion of unlimited markets.

The illusions of the farmer were part of a great national illusion dating from the early years of the republic. This was what Henry Nash Smith in *Virgin Land* has called "The Myth of the Garden"—the myth that the West was a realizable utopia, an agrarian Eden where free land and honest toil would produce a virtuous yeomanry and the good life. According to the myth, the West was the true source of national regeneration, the means of realizing the ideals of democracy and equality, and it was celebrated by poets, novelists, and historians alike. "All of the associations called up by the spoken word, the West," wrote the Western novelist Hamlin Garland in 1891, "were fabulous, mythic, hopeful." To the frontier West Frederick Jackson Turner attributed "that buoyancy and exuberance which comes with freedom."

But the stark contrast between the hopes fostered by the myth and the harsh realities of experience could not escape even the dullest farmer. Far from utopian were the sod house, the dust storm, the grasshopper plague. "So this is the reality of the dream!" exclaims a character in a Garland novel. "A shanty on a barren plain, hot and lone as a desert. My God!" Far from equalitarian or democratic was a land system that fostered monopoly in the guise of distributing free land. It was a curious "safety valve" for the urban discontent of the East that sent homesteaders flocking to the city to escape the rural discontent of the West. The disillusionment with the Myth of the Garden that dates from these years helps explain the bitterness of the agrarian revolt that burst forth toward the end of the century.

Whether as myth or as reality, whether as the last stand of the first American or as the last frontier of miner, cattleman, and farmer, whether as man's last hope of equality or as a disillusioning experience with monopoly and inequality—this last of the nation's many wests left a profound imprint upon the American mind and the American legend.

416

The New West: empire within a nation

Suggestions for reading

Two readable and comprehensive surveys of Western history are R. A. Billington, *Westward Expansion: A History of the American Frontier* (1967), which stresses the Turner thesis, and T. D. Clark, *Frontier America: The Story of the Westward Movement* (2nd ed., 1969), which disclaims the thesis. The thesis itself appears in an essay by F. J. Turner, "The Significance of the Frontier in American History," in his *The Frontier in American History** (1920). R. A. Billington, *America's Frontier Heritage** (1967), is a synthesis of recent thought on the subject. W. P. Webb, *The Great Plains** (1931), is the most provocative study of regional culture and environmental influences in our literature; his *The Great Frontier** (1932, rev. ed., 1964), examines the world significance of the New World frontiers since the Age of Discovery. H. R. Lamar, *The Far Southwest, 1846–1912** (1966), is an excellent history of territories. J. C. Malin, *The Grassland of North America* (1947), brings agricultural and geographical science to the aid of historical understanding. Wayne Gard, *The Great Buffalo Hunt** (1959), is the best book on this dramatic subject, and R. G. Athearn *Union Pacific Country** (1976) is best on another. The West as symbol and myth in American thought is brilliantly analyzed in H. N. Smith, *Virgin Land** (1950).

Three general histories of the Indians are recommended: W. E. Washburn, *The Indian in America* (1975), W. T. Hagan, *American Indians** (1961), and J. R. Swanton, *The Indian Tribes of North America* (1953). F. G. Roe, *The Indian and the Horse* (1955), and Robert Utley, *Last Days of the Sioux Nation** (1963), are first rate. Two champions of the red man's rights have left moving accounts: H. H. Jackson, *A Century of Dishonor** (1881), a stirring indictment, and J. J. Collier, *The Indians of the Americas** (1947), by a leader of policy reform. On reform see R. W. Mardock, *Reformers and the American Indian* (1970). L. B. Priest, *Uncle Sam's Stepchildren: The Reformation of United States Indian Policy, 1865–1887** (1942), defends the reformers against their critics. H. L. Fritz, *The Movement for Indian Assimilation, 1860–1890* (1963), treats the philanthropists. Revealing books on military activities are R. G. Atherton, *William Tecumseh Sherman and the Settlement of the West* (1956); E. I. Stewart, *Custer's Luck* (1955); and C. C. Rister, *Border Command: General Phil Sheridan in the West* (1944).

On mining, the best reading on this period is R. W. Paul, *Mining Frontiers of the Far West, 1848–1880** (1963), D. A. Smith, *Rocky Mountain Mining Camps** (1967), and W. S. Greever, *The Bonanza West: The Story of the Western Mining Rushes, 1848–1900* (1963). C. H. Shinn, *The Story of the Mine* (1896) and *Mining Camps: A Study in American Frontier Government** (1885), are based on firsthand experience. For colorful reminiscences, see Mark Twain, *Roughing It** (1872), and Dan De Quille, *History of the Big Bonanza** (1876, reprinted 1947).

The cattleman's bonanza is briefly surveyed in E. S. Osgood, *The Day of the Cattleman** (1929, reprinted 1957), and more fully in E. E. Dale, *The Range Cattle Industry* (1930, reprinted 1969). Maurice Frank, W. T. Jackson, and A. W. Spring, *When Grass Was King* (1957), is a roundup of scholarship. Lewis Atherton, *The Cattle Kings** (1961), is thoughtful and sympathetic. Also helpful are J. M. Skaggs, *The Cattle Trailing Industry: Between Supply and Demand, 1865–1890* (1973), G. M. Gressley, *Bankers and Cattlemen** (1966), and R. R. Dykstra, *The Cattle Towns** (1970). Of the vast cowboy literature, Andy Adams, *The Log of a Cowboy** (1927), and J. F. Dobie, ed., *A Texas Cowboy* (1950), contain firsthand experiences; J. B. Frantz and J. E. Choate, *The American Cowboy: The Myth and the Reality* (1955), is a realistic analysis.

The best histories of agriculture in this period, especially in the West, are F. A. Shannon, *The Farmer's Last Frontier: Agriculture, 1860–1897** (1945), and G. C. Fite, *The Farmer's Frontier, 1865–1900** (1966). On the history of American land policy and its administration, two works of value are P. W. Gates, *History of Public Land Development* (1968), and R. M. Robbins, *Our Landed Heritage: The Public Domain, 1776–1936** (1942). The history of the new farm machinery is found in Waldemar Kaempffert, *A Popular History of American Invention* (1924), and R. M. Wik, *Steam Power on the American Farm* (1953). The pioneer farm on the Western frontier is pictured in Everett Dick, *The Sod-House Frontier, 1854–1890* (1937). Vivid fictional accounts are Willa Cather, *O Pioneers!** (1913) and *My Antonia** (1918), O. E. Rølvaag, *Giants in the Earth** (1927), and Mari Sandoz, *Old Jules** (1935).

*Available in a paperback edition.

417

The return of peace in 1865 had stimulated magnificent expectations among fortune-builders, profit-makers, and industrial entrepreneurs. "The truth is," Senator John Sherman wrote his brother General William T. Sherman, "the close of the war with our resources unimpaired gives an elevation, a scope to the ideas of leading capitalists, far higher than anything ever undertaken in this country before. They talk of millions as confidently as formerly of thousands." Their high hopes and expectations seemed justified by all they surveyed: half a continent to be developed; a built-in empire rich in coal, iron, oil, waterpower, lumber—most of the resources essential for great industrial power; a responsive federal government eager to further business interests; the greatest free-trade market in the world surrounded by a high protective-tariff barrier; and European immigrants swarming in to provide cheap labor. Surely the stage appeared to be set for the "heroic age" of industrial enterprise that has been glorified in history and legend.

Long disposed to believe in the uniqueness of their society and its superiority to any in Europe, Americans believed then and have continued to believe that their economy set the pace and outstripped all others in its rapid rate of industrial growth in the late nineteenth century and after. Furthermore, those on the victorious side of the Civil War chose to believe that it not only achieved moral aims but material wonders as well and played an important part in stimulating what they believed to be the unequaled speed and efficiency of American industrial progress. This faith still has many followers and defenders. In recent years, however, close students of comparative growth have questioned the validity of that faith. They point out that because of rapid population growth in the United States its gross national product increased faster than in nations of Europe, but that in growth measured by product per capita the American economy did not take the lead. And production and distribution per capita are more closely related to

Kansas Pacific roundhouse

The ordeal
of industrialization

individual welfare than is gross production. The legend of American economic superiority needs to be revised in some respects.

However unavoidable the Civil War may have been, it was more devastating and exhausting than any European war between 1815 and 1914. On balance it probably did more to retard than to stimulate growth in the national economy. The same may be said of some of the very natural endowments once thought to have been unique American advantages. The high rate of natural increase in population, for example, produced a larger percentage of nonworkers, higher investment in child-rearing and new households, as well as retarded savings and lower per capita income. The hordes of immigrants provided cheap labor (and again, low per capita income), but not well-adjusted, educated, or geographically distributed labor—or labor highly endowed with "the Protestant work ethic." The very size of the country, whose vast expanse was the pride of patriots, was the most consistent handicap to rapid economic growth. Contrasts with the compact location of factories, resources, and markets in Europe point up American disadvantages. Where a one-hundred-mile railroad was adequate there, it took one thousand miles of rails to do the job here. Far-flung raw materials and settlements deprived manufacturers of usable capital, slowed the movement of capital, created problems of management, curbed technological innovation, and produced conflict and frustration with local jurisdictions, jealousies, and corrupt governments.

Whether because of these or other deterrents and handicaps, American economic growth in product per capita during the famous "heroic age" of enterprise lagged behind that of European leaders such as Germany, France, and Sweden, though it remained above that of Great Britain. It is the economic paradox of the period 1880–1914, when Americans were exploiting their fabulous natural resources and developing mass production and were assumed to be leading the world, that their country instead remained at about the average level of growth per capita maintained in northwestern European countries. Of course, it should be remembered that the leading countries had a very high rate and that Western Europe was increasing its industrial power enormously in those years. To have kept up with the average in such a race was a remarkable achievement.

Size and numbers and rate of population increase did tell in gross national product and sheer value of manufactured goods, and the United States looked better in comparative growth on those terms. In 1860 the United States was a second-rate industrial country, lagging behind the United Kingdom and perhaps France and Germany. But by 1890 the United States had stepped into first place, and the value of its man-ufactured goods almost equaled the combined production of all the three former leaders. Between the eve of the Civil War and First World War, American manufacturing production multiplied twelve times over. In sheer size there was surely something "heroic" about the scale, if nothing else.

The railroad empire

"The generation between 1865 and 1895 was already mortgaged to the railways," reflected Henry Adams, "and no one knew it better than the generation itself." This was the generation that planned, built, financed, and made the first attempts to control the most extensive railroad network in the world. The headlong haste and heedless ethics of its experience are caught in the national expression "railroaded through." No one, not even the enemies of the railroad, could be found in that age to deny its importance. Everyone believed it was the key to mass production and mass consumption, to the utilization of natural resources and the creation of a national market, and to the binding together and settlement of a two-ocean land mass. The railroad dominated the imagination, the politics, the economy, and the hopes of a generation, and the outsized cowcatcher and smokestack of the old-fashioned steam locomotive might well be taken as the symbol of the age. The poet William Ellery Leonard, who was born in 1876, entitled an autobiographical work *The Locomotive-God*, and the popular ballad-makers lavished a devotion on the iron horse they had formerly reserved for the flesh-and-blood steed and the sailing ship.

Most celebrated of the railroad achievements were the great transcontinentals. But as the historian Thomas C. Cochran has said, "it would have been far better for the economy if the Rocky Mountains had never existed" and the Great Plains had not been so wide.

Building the network. The laying of rails, which until the eighties were mainly iron rather than steel, went forward in fits and starts, impeded by panics and depression and spurred on by speculative booms and prosperity. Starting with only about 35,000 miles of railway at the end of the Civil War, during which less than 5,000 miles were laid, the country had doubled its mileage before the Panic of 1873. The next six years of depression added only some 16,000 miles. The 1880s, the great decade of railway expansion, opened with some 93,000 miles and ended with 166,000, an increase of more than 73,000 miles in ten years. By the end of the century the United States had

The ordeal of industrialization

The Union Pacific meets the Central Pacific, 1869

a total of nearly 200,000 miles, or more than all Europe including Russia. In the meantime the ungainly little "bullgine" with the disproportionate funnel had evolved into a giant that could master mountain and plain, a giant that dwarfed any foreign make of locomotive. Greatly improved by the Westinghouse air brake and other inventions, the trains carried more passengers in 1900 than they did in any year of the decade beginning in 1932.

To build this vast railway network was an undertaking comparable in magnitude to the construction of a navy, and for the United States it was even more costly and probably more essential to the national interest. European governments assumed responsibility for building and running their railroad establishments as readily as for their military establishments. In America, apart from a few state-owned roads of antebellum origin, initiative and management were left primarily in the hands of private enterprise. Even by 1880, before half the network was completed, an investment of more than $4,600 million had gone into the nation's railroads. By 1897 their stocks and bonds totaled $10,635 million as compared with a total national debt of less than $1,227 million. Economic historian Edward Kirkland concludes that the handling of railroad finances had "a greater effect upon the economy than the management of the national finances." Since such huge sums were far more than private American investors could supply, promoters turned to foreign investors and to local, state, and federal governments. Foreign investment reached its peak earlier, but in 1898 Europeans, mainly British, owned $3,100 million worth of American railroad securities, about one-third of the whole.

While public enthusiasm for railroad-building was at its height, government at all levels fairly thrust credit and resources upon the railroad-promoters. Villages, towns, cities, and states came forward with extravagant support in the form of bonds and other commitments. The federal government lent approximately $65 million to six Western railroads and extended even more important aid through grants of public land. In all, Congress committed 175,000,000 acres of the public domain, of which the railroads actually received more than 131,000,000 acres. In addition they received 49,000,000 acres from the states. These grants made a substantial contribution toward paying for the railroad investment. Their main value to the railroads was not the cash they brought from sales but the credit and security they supplied for bond issues. Although government subsidies were often obtained through bribery and were responsible for much corruption, the policy of subsidizing the railroads with grants of public land was probably justified in the long run. By attaching conditions to the land grants that obliged the railroads to furnish cheap transportation for mail and military shipments, the government has enjoyed substantial savings over the years. Actually, less than 10 percent of the railroad mileage of the country was built with federal land grants. And most of that mileage was on the roads built across the Great Plains, where investment was slow in yielding returns and where some form of public credit was essential.

The transcontinental lines called for the most heroic efforts and attracted some of the ablest—and some of the most unscrupulous—enterprisers. The completion of the Union Pacific-Central Pacific in 1869 (see p. 358) realized the antebellum dream of spanning the continent with rails, and within the next quarter of a century four more lines flanked the original one, two on either side: the Southern Pacific and the Santa Fe to the south and the Northern Pacific and the Great Northern to the north. Each line excited intense rivalries and ambitions in the cities they connected and the sections they served, as well as among the railroad-builders and promoters.

Collis P. Huntington, one of the Californians behind the Central Pacific, took the leading role in pushing through the Southern Pacific, the second and southernmost of the transcontinentals. Like many railroad barons of his generation, Huntington was tough and cynical about business and politics and ruthless in his methods. He talked about bribing and buying congressmen as he would about the purchase of so many cattle. The son of a large and unprosperous Connecticut family, he grew up with little schooling, became a peddler, and went west with the California gold rush of 1849. He did not strike gold, but he made money as a merchant and a fortune as a builder of the Central Pacific. His next ambition was to build the Southern Pacific southward from San Francisco through California and eastward across Arizona, New Mexico, and Texas. This enterprise brought a head-on clash with Thomas A. Scott, who was equally determined to build the Texas & Pacific over roughly the same route. Scott was president of the Pennsylvania Railroad and as powerful and ruthless a man as Huntington. The effect the Scott lobby had on the Compromise of 1877 has already been noted (see p. 382). But in spite of President Hayes' support of Scott's bill for a $200 million government subsidy for the Texas & Pacific, Congress failed to pass it. There were several reasons for the failure, but one important reason was Huntington, who once remarked, "It costs money to fix things so that I would know his bill would not pass." Huntington would stop at nothing, and nothing could stop him. In defiance of a War Department order he laid rails across an Indian reservation and then boasted to the President of his defiance. Scott continued to resist, but Huntington kept laying rails until at last he forced the Southern Pacific

The ordeal of industrialization

into El Paso, Texas, in 1881, and Scott decided to give up the struggle.

In the course of the contest with Scott, however, Huntington met his match in Jay Gould, the most notorious land pirate of all the railroad barons. Gould won control of the Texas & Pacific, forced his way into the Southern Pacific, and threatened to block Huntington's way through the state of Texas. He relented only after exacting a traffic-sharing agreement from Huntington and a large influence in the Southern Pacific. The Gould and Huntington lines joined near El Paso in 1882, and two years later the Southern Pacific reached New Orleans.

About the same time another major system, the Atchison, Topeka, & Santa Fe, usually known simply as the Santa Fe, entered the Southwest and threatened the Huntington-Gould monopoly. Financed by Boston capital, this road cut across Kansas and a corner of Colorado to reach Santa Fe, New Mexico. Huntington and Gould cleverly thwarted the Santa Fe's efforts to gain direct access to the coast by buying up its charter. In 1883 the Southern Pacific, on its own terms, permitted the Santa Fe to enter California on Southern Pacific lines. The competing Santa Fe was then subordinated to the monopoly, and by 1890 Gould was the virtual dictator of transportation in the Southwest.

The Northwest was somewhat more fortunate in its railroad pioneers and masters. The Northern Pacific had been chartered to build a line from Lake Superior to Puget Sound, but construction was halted in 1873 when Jay Cooke and Company as well as the

railroad it was financing went bankrupt. Reorganized in 1875, the Northern Pacific was acquired in 1881 by Henry Villard, a German-born capitalist with large holdings in Oregon. Villard completed the line to Tacoma, Washington, in 1883, but he was never able to enjoy a monopoly of transportation in the Northwest. In 1878 a competing line under the management of James J. Hill had begun to push westward from St. Paul, parallel to the Northern Pacific. A Canadian by birth, Hill had a long-cherished dream of colonizing the Northwest. First he had acquired the two-hundred-mile track of the bankrupt little St. Paul & Pacific, and then had started building westward through Minnesota, North Dakota, Idaho, and across Washington for 2,775 miles to the Pacific. The Great Northern, as he renamed this line, had no land grant such as the Northern Pacific enjoyed. Consequently, in order to build up traffic and revenue, Hill had to rely on Canadian and American capital and his own efforts to settle the country. "We consider ourselves and the people along our line as co-partners in the prosperity of the country we both occupy," said Hill. He completed his line to Puget Sound in 1893. Built more carefully and solidly than its competitor, financed more soundly, and integrated more thoroughly into the economy of the region it served, Hill's Great Northern was the only transcontinental road to pull through the Panic of 1893 and the depression that followed.

East of the Mississippi, railroads, with exceptions such as the New York Central, were built mainly to serve local needs and to promote the interests of particular cities. Hundreds of small lines using a variety of gauges were built after the Civil War, many without connections. The South alone had four hundred companies averaging not more than forty miles apiece. One task of the postwar generation was to fill in the gaps between lines and to weld them into an integrated national network. Through consolidation by lease, purchase, or merger, nearly two-thirds of the country's railroad companies were absorbed by the other one-third. In 1880 alone, 115 companies lost their identity, and between 1880 and 1888 some 425 companies were brought under the control of other roads. The Pennsylvania Railroad by 1890 was an amalgamation of 73 smaller companies and some five thousand miles of rail.

Consolidation sometimes, but not always, brought improvements: steel rails to replace iron rails, safety precautions such as double-tracking and the block signal, and cheaper, more reliable, and more punctual service. In the last half of the century, real passenger charges fell nearly 50 percent and freight rates much more. In 1883 the American Railway Association divided the country into four time zones with an hour's difference between each and, in spite of outraged advocates of "God's time," regularized their timetables. The standard gauge of 4 feet 8½ inches for rails became virtually nationwide in May 1886, when the Southern roads moved one rail three inches closer to the other.

Competition and disorder. In spite of all these improvements, the American railroads were in serious difficulties. They were under heavy criticism and attack from the public, and they were suffering from grave and uncontrolled disorders within the industry itself. The troubles of the railroads were inherent in the very nature of American industry in the age of unrestricted competition. The mania for construction in the seventies and eighties provided all the major transportation areas with an overdeveloped network of railroads, much greater than was needed at the time. Railroad-managers, faced with the need to make regular payments on swollen bonded indebtedness, with the demand to make profits on overcapitalized stock, and with the pressing need for traffic when there was not enough to go around, resorted to ruinous competitive wars of line against line. Between St. Louis and Atlanta, for example, shippers could choose between twenty competitive routes. Competitors and interlopers paralleled each other's lines for purposes of blackmailing or ruining rivals. Railroads offered fantastic "rebates," secret rates below the published tariffs, to secure the traffic of big shippers and overcharged outrageously to compensate where they had no competition. They often charged less per mile for a long haul than for a short haul, resorted to all kinds of

rate jugglery and deception, and trusted neither client nor competitor. "No wonder that railroad managers accused each other of fraud and deception," testified one manager before a Senate committee in 1885. "Men who in all other relations of life were blameless winked at falsehoods, and dallied with deception, not because they were morally debased, but actually because they knew not the way out of the toils."

Competition under such circumstances, instead of being "the life of trade" and benefiting enterprise as well as the public, proved a curse to both. The railroads themselves suffered heavily from the rate wars, for they were often driven to cut rates below the cost of handling the business and thereby imperiled the dividends, if not the solvency, of the firm. Obviously the railroads had to find some way to stop the piratical practices of rebate, rate-cutting, and blackmail. They sought solutions in treaties and solemn agreements—most of which proved unenforceable. A more formal device of railroad cooperation was the pool, an agreement to divide traffic on some proportional basis and charge uniform rates. But the pool

James J. Hill:
empire builder of the Northwest

The ordeal of industrialization

agreements were also difficult to enforce and were always breaking down. The temptation to gain advantage over competitors by violating agreements often proved irresistible. As Charles Francis Adams, Jr., a keen student as well as an executive of railroads, described the demoralization:

> Honesty and good faith are scarcely regarded. Certainly they are not tolerated at all if they interfere with a man's getting his "share of the business." Gradually, this demoralizing spirit of low cunning has pervaded the entire system. Its moral tone is deplorably low. . . . That healthy, mutual confidence which is the first essential to prosperity in all transactions between man and man, does not exist in the American railroad service taken as a whole.

If the railroad industry could not set its own house in order, then order would have to be imposed from outside. The problem was nationwide, but the federal government continued through the years of the worst railroad anarchy to practice laissez faire. The state governments took the initiative and made the first experiments in regulation and control. Their laws and commissions are often attributed to the "Granger movement," the work of a farmers' organization (see p. 478), and associated with the Middle West. But the movement to regulate railroads was limited to no one class or section. Massachusetts and New York made important contributions, and states in the Southeast, the Southwest, and the Far West also participated. Merchants, wholesale dealers, and manufacturers were more prominent and effective than farmers in pressing for regulation in several areas. Shippers of all kinds suffered from the abuses and disorders of the railroads. In particular they resented rate and service discrimination between persons and places, favoritism that gave unfair advantages to powerful shippers and to cities where railroads had competition. Small men resented bigness and the power it gave the railroads over legislatures, governors, and judges and correctly charged some roads with using bribes and free passes to corrupt or influence public officials.

Popular resentment of abuses found expression in numerous state laws. In 1869 Massachusetts established a commission to supervise railroad activities and investigate grievances and made Adams a member. Within the next ten years a dozen more states established commissions modeled on that of Massachusetts. Several state legislatures in the Middle West adopted more thoroughgoing measures of regulation. Illinois, for example, laid down explicit and detailed provisions against discrimination and went further to give its commission power to bring suit "against any railroad corporation which may violate the provisions of this act." The Supreme Court upheld the constitutionality of the legislation in the case of *Munn* v. *Illinois* (1877) and declared that when private property is "affected with a public interest" it "must submit to be controlled by the public for the common good" and that in the absence of federal policy states could act. Railroads nevertheless waged relentless war against such legislation, which in some states was carelessly drawn, and limited its effectiveness from the start. Then in the Wabash case of 1886 (*Wabash, St. Louis, & Pacific Railway Co.* v. *Illinois*) a more laissez-faire Supreme Court reversed earlier decisions and held an Illinois statute invalid on the ground that it was the exclusive power of Congress to regulate interstate commerce. With the states thus largely excluded, any effective regulatory action would have to be taken by the federal government.

A second spur to federal action in 1886 was the report of a Senate committee headed by Senator Shelby M. Cullom of Illinois, which denounced railroads sharply for the "reckless strife" of their competition and for "unjust discrimination between persons, places, commodities, or particular descriptions to traffic." Railroad-leaders themselves urged federal regulation, for they acknowledged the necessity for measures to end the anarchy in which they struggled. The Republican platform of 1884 had declared that "the principle of the public regulation of railroad corporations is a wise and salutory one." The Interstate Commerce Act, which eventually grew out of demands for regulation, was a milestone in American history, but it was not a triumph of radicals over conservatives or of the people over the corporation.

The Interstate Commerce Act, passed by large majorities in both houses of Congress and signed by President Grover Cleveland on February 4, 1887, forbade railroads to engage in discriminatory practices, required them to publish their rate schedules, prohibited them from entering pooling agreements for the purpose of maintaining high rates, and declared that rates should be "reasonable and just." The act placed enforcement in the hands of an Interstate Commerce Commission of five members, who were to hear complaints and issue orders to the railroads to "cease and desist." For enforcement of its orders, however, the commission had to appeal to the courts, and there the advantage was consistently with the railroads. During the first eighteen years after the act was passed the Supreme Court heard sixteen cases brought before it by the Interstate Commerce Commission and decided fifteen for the railroads and against the commission. As an assertion of the federal government's right to regulate private enterprise and as a precedent for more effective measures in the future, the Interstate Commerce Act was important. But it did not provide any immediate solution to the problem of cutthroat com-

The railroad empire

"The Farmer and the Railroad Monster"

petition. It was a conservative measure, based on the old belief that competition was beneficial rather than harmful and adopted mainly to alleviate the anxieties of the public.

Morgan and banker control. Within a year of the passage of the Interstate Commerce Act, the railroads began to return to the discriminatory practices that were now illegal. They were somewhat more secretive about rebates and blackmail competition, but it quickly became evident that the law had no teeth and that there was nothing to fear from the courts. With no effective government control, the industry appeared as anarchic as ever and management as quick to resort to speculative looting and stock-watering. After decades of waste, mismanagement, and folly,

The ordeal of industrialization

many railroads were in a shaky financial plight and in no condition to weather hard times. Railroad speculation and overexpansion had prepared the way for the panics of 1857 and 1873, and the first signal of the Panic of 1893 was the bankruptcy of the Philadelphia & Reading Railroad, on February 20. This panic was less closely connected with railroad overexpansion than the earlier panics. Railroad failures were not the only index of calamity, but by the middle of 1894 there were 192 railroads in the hands of the receivers. "Never in the history of transportation in the United States," reported the Interstate Commerce Commission at that time, "has such a large percentage of railway mileage been under the control of receiverships." There were 40,818 miles of railway insolvent then, and 67,000 miles, or about one-third of the total mileage of the country, were foreclosed by the middle of 1898. Among the failures were some of the greatest systems in the country, including the Erie, the B&O, the Union Pacific, and the Northern Pacific. To obtain the funds needed for reorganization, the distressed railroads turned to the bankers. The railroads received not only reorganization but a measure of control that neither they themselves nor the state and federal governments had so far been able to contrive.

Numerous bankers took part in the railway reorganizations of the nineties, but none took so prominent and conspicuous a part as J. Pierpont Morgan, the dominant investment banker of his time. For the quarter of a century ending with his death in 1913, this tall, massive figure with piercing eyes and fiery nose was the very symbol of American financial power. Morgan began life near the top of the economic and social ladder, the son of a rich merchant from Hartford, Connecticut, who established a bank in London during the Civil War. He grew up with all the advantages of wealth, including a good education, travel and residence abroad, and study at the University of Göttingen in Germany. He established his firm and his family in New York during the seventies in princely fashion and began to collect treasures of art and rare books. His elegant steam yacht, *Corsair* (165 feet long at the water line), or its successors, *Corsair II* (204 feet) and *Corsair III* (302 feet), always awaited his pleasure in the harbor. Aboard his yacht or in the library of his home at 219 Madison Avenue the titans of industry and finance met at his call and submitted to agreements that made history in the world of business and sometimes in the world of politics as well. At such meetings he brought to bear his passion for order and his interest as a seller of securities. Morgan enhanced his reputation as a masterful peacemaker among railroads when in 1885 he intervened in a reckless war of blackmail competition between the New York Central and the Pennsylvania and persuaded them to abandon the destructive operation of

J. P. Morgan:
the very symbol of financial power

parallel lines. It was natural that the managers of the sick railroads of the nineties should come to him, as to a famous surgeon, for the strong medicine and heroic surgery the bankrupt roads needed for recovery.

Other investment banking firms, such as Kuhn, Loeb & Company, employed the same methods as Morgan and charged huge fees for their services. First they ruthlessly pared down the fixed debt of the railroad, then assessed holders of the old stock for working funds, and next issued lavish amounts of new stock, heavily watered. To assure control along lines that suited them and to veto unwise expansion plans, the bankers usually installed a president of their own selection and placed members of their own houses on the boards of railroad directors. Between 1894 and 1898 the House of Morgan reorganized the lion's share of big railroads. Banker control was not the ideal solution or the final answer to the problems of competition and control, but it did curb prevailing anarchy, whether or not it improved the management and efficiency of railroad service.

427

The railroad empire

Industrial empire

Carnegie and steel. The new industrial order of America was based on steel, and by 1870 the techniques of production, the supply of raw materials, and the home market were sufficiently developed to make the United States the world's greatest steel-producer. A cheap and practical process of making steel by forcing a blast of cold air through molten iron to clean it of impurities had been invented by Henry Bessemer, an Englishman, in 1857. A rival patent for the same process was held by one William Kelly, a Kentucky ironmaster who claimed to have made the discovery before Bessemer. The two patents were merged in 1866, and the following year the first steel rails in the country were rolled for commercial use. In 1867 the United States made 1,643 tons of steel ingots; in 1897 it made 7,156,957. In the meantime new discoveries of ore deposits in the fabulous Lake Superior district opened exciting prospects for the ironmasters. Government surveyors in 1844 had discovered the Marquette Range in Michigan, including "a mountain of solid iron ore, 150 feet high." In 1868 the rich Vermilion Range in Minnesota was discovered, and in 1875 it was tapped by a railroad. Within the next decade the Menominee, the Gogebic, and the Mesabi mines—all within close proximity to Lake Superior and cheap water transportation—were opened up. Together they constituted the greatest iron-ore district in the world.

These opportunities brought a multitude of entrepreneurs into the field of iron and steel in quest of profits. By 1880 there were 1,005 iron companies in the nation, all of them subject to the competitive struggle under which the railroads labored, with all its uncertainties, anxieties, and ruthlessness. In fact, the spread of the railroads intensified the competitive struggle in iron and steel by breaking down the protection against competition provided by distance, creating a national market. Like railroad operators, the iron and steelmasters resorted to cutthroat tactics, price-slashing, and blackmail. Faced with large fixed costs, they sometimes ran their plants at a loss rather than let them remain idle. They sought rebates and unfair advantages and rushed into pools, combinations, and mergers to hedge against competition. Out of the melee emerged one dominant figure, Andrew Carnegie, the most articulate industrialist America ever had.

Quite untypical of industrial leaders of his day in several respects, Carnegie was of immigrant and working-class origin, a voluble speaker, a facile writer, and a religious skeptic. He came to the United States from Scotland with his family when he was thirteen years old and went to work immediately to earn a living. At eighteen he became a telegraph clerk in the office of Thomas A. Scott, then a rising official of the Pennsylvania Railroad, and won his employer's favor and confidence. His service with Scott, which lasted through the Civil War, not only brought valuable acquaintance with the foremost railroad and industrial leaders of the country but guided him in making shrewd and extremely profitable investments. With a salary of only $2,400 a year, he was receiving a millionaire's income from investments when he was twenty-eight years old. He was drawn into the iron business and then in 1872 into a venture for building a huge steel plant on the Monongahela River, twelve miles from Pittsburgh, a site with excellent river transportation and service from both the Pennsylvania and the B&O railroads. The new plant rolled its first rail in 1875.

Without pretense of engineering or technological skill, Carnegie was first of all a superb salesman with a genius for picking the right subordinates to supervise production. He was personally acquainted with all the railroad barons of the day and, as he said, simply "went out and persuaded them to give us orders." He did not have to remind them that steel rails lasted twenty times as long as iron. The supreme example of the industrial capitalist, Carnegie refused to permit his company to become a corporation, maintained it as a limited partnership, and retained a majority of the shares himself. Giving no hostages to the bankers, he used the firm's enormous profits to construct new plants, acquire raw materials, buy out competitors, and win fights with organized labor. His independent resources enabled him to go on building and spending even during depressions and thus to approach his goal of establishing an "integrated industry." After hesitation about entering the ore business, he bought ore deposits in the Mesabi Range and ore ships on the Great Lakes, and he acquired docks, warehouses, and railroad lines to supply his great furnaces and mills with raw materials.

Carnegie had a remarkable gift for finding able lieutenants—men like Henry Clay Frick, Charles M. Schwab, Laurence C. Phipps, and Alexander R. Peacock. He pitted these men against one another in jealous competition, rewarding the successful with shares and partnerships. Like other capitalists of his day, he benefited from pools, rebates, patents, and protective tariffs, but in time his power and resources became great enough to make him virtually independent of such devices. At the crest of his power he held the whole steel industry in his grasp except for steel finishing, which he had not entered. His trail to the top was strewn with ruined competitors, crushed partners, and broken labor movements including his bloody victory over labor at Homestead (see p. 439). Carnegie increased his annual production from 322,000 tons in 1890 to 3,000,000 tons in 1900. Over the same decade he and his lieutenants increased the annual profits of the Carnegie Steel Company from $5,400,000 in 1890 to $40,000,000 in 1900. Carnegie's own share of the 1900 profits was approximately $25,000,000.

In the meantime Pierpont Morgan turned his attention from railroads to steel, and the bankers challenged the industrialists for the control of heavy industry. The American Steel and Wire Company, the first big combination in steel, was constructed without his help. Then in the summer of 1898 Morgan swung his support to Judge Elbert H. Gary of Chicago and other Midwesterners who merged several big concerns to form the Federal Steel Company, second in size to Carnegie Steel. Quickly other mergers between hitherto competing steel firms sprang into being, "as if a giant magnet had moved over the surface of the industry," observed one historian. The next obvious move in the drive for mergers was to combine the combinations, that is, consolidate the whole industry into one vast supercorporation, the greatest in the world. Blocking that dream was the mighty Carnegie Steel Company and the known prejudice of its head against banker control. Even Morgan threw up his hands when it was proposed that he buy up Carnegie Steel outright; "I don't believe I could raise the money," he said. The new combinations for making finished steel products then decided in the summer of 1900 to produce their own raw steel, free themselves from dependence on Carnegie, and cancel their contracts with him. Carnegie's response was a cable from Skibo Castle, his summer home in Scotland, declaring open war: "Have no fear as to result. Victory certain." He proposed to go into the production of finished steel, which he had urged on his partners since 1898, and to drive all his competitors to the wall.

Alarmed at the prospect of a war that would place the new steel combinations in deadly peril and demoralize the whole industry, Morgan determined to buy out Carnegie and consolidate the supercorporation. After a night-long conference in the famous Morgan library, Charles M. Schwab agreed to take the matter up with Carnegie. The Scotsman scribbled a few figures on a scrap of paper, and Schwab took it to Morgan. The banker glanced at it and said, "I accept." There was no bargaining. The figure was nearly a half-billion dollars. In a few weeks Morgan pushed and pulled the big steel companies into combination and, on March 3, 1901, announced the organization of the United States Steel Corporation. The new concern brought under a single management three-fifths of the steel business of the country and was capitalized at nearly a billion and a half dollars.

Although U. S. Steel was never without competition within the industry, the uneasy popular sentiment about the gigantic deal was reflected in the words the humorist Finley Peter Dunne put in the mouth of his Irish saloonkeeper, "Mr. Dooley":

> Pierpont Morgan calls in wan iv his office boys, th' presidint iv a national bank, an' says he, "James," he says, "take some change out iv th' damper an' r-run out an' buy Europe f'r me," he says. "I intind to re-organize it an' put it on a paying basis," he says. "Call up the Czar an' th' Pope an' th' Sultan an' th' Impror Willum, an' tell thim we won't need their savices afther nex' week," he says. "Give thim a year's salary in advance."

Rockefeller and the trusts. An industrial giant of power and influence comparable to that wielded by Carnegie was John D. Rockefeller, who did for oil what the Scotsman did for steel. The two contemporaries were strikingly different in temperament and taste: Carnegie was exuberant and communicative, Rockefeller silent and taciturn; Carnegie was a skeptic and an agnostic, Rockefeller a Bible-class teacher and a devout Baptist. In their business methods and their achievements, however, there were many similarities. Both men showed the same astuteness in selecting lieutenants and putting them in the right jobs, the same abhorrence of waste and gambling, the same ability to transform depressions into opportunities for building, buying, and expanding. The Standard Oil Company, founded in 1872 with Rockefeller its head, made ruthless use of railroad-rate discrimination, espionage, bogus companies, price-slashing, and other reprehensible practices. On the other hand, it had positive achievements to its credit, including improved and standardized products, the elimination of waste, and efficiency in distribution.

Rockefeller was the outstanding American exponent of consolidation in industry. Of the trend toward consolidation he wrote:

> This movement was the origin of the whole system of modern economic administration. It has revolutionized the way of doing business all over the world. The time was ripe for it. It had to come, though all we saw at the moment was the need to save ourselves from wasteful conditions. . . . The day of combination is here to stay. Individualism has gone, never to return.

By "wasteful conditions" he meant the glutted markets in crude and refined oil and the disorder, uncertainty, and wild fluctuation of prices and profits that attended free competition among thousands of small producers and hundreds of small refiners. Rockefeller hated free competition and believed that monopoly was the way of the future. His early method of dealing with competitors was to gain unfair advantage over

Industrial empire

them through special rates and secret rebates exacted from railroads.

The most notorious device of the sort was the short-lived South Improvement Company, by means of which Standard joined a few other oil companies in 1872 to demand special rates and secret advantages from the leading railroads in the Pennsylvania oil fields. They received not only large rebates on their own shipments but cash rebates on all shipments made by rivals outside the combination, as well as full and valuable reports on their competitors' business. The South Improvement scheme was soon exposed and had to be abandoned, but Standard continued to receive special advantages from the railroads and to use them to threaten or eliminate competitors. By such methods Standard Oil acquired some seventy-four refining companies and by 1878 was manufacturing a very large percentage of the national product of oil. When pipelines threatened the advantage gained through railroad favors, Standard quickly consolidated most of the pipelines in the Appalachian field into the United Pipe Lines Company, in which Standard had controlling interest. Independent producers and refiners sought to escape the monopoly by building a pipeline across the Appalachian Mountains to the seaboard. Standard waged unrelenting war on the independent Tidewater Pipe Company, which succeeded in completing its line, but in 1883 it signed an agreement that gave Standard 88½ percent of the business.

Rockefeller and his associates dealt competitors crushing blows with their nationwide marketing organization, which could put irresistible pressure on competitors and force surrender. They strengthened their position further by manufacturing all commodities necessary to the trade, from barrels to bungs. Rockefeller was convinced that small-unit enterprise and free competition were things of the past.

Standard Oil speeded up the progress of consolidation and the suppression of competition by forming a trust, first set up in 1879 and then revised in 1882. The trust was an old legal device, but Standard Oil lawyers put it to new use. They created a board of nine trustees and persuaded all stockholders of twenty-seven competing oil companies to turn over their capital stock to the board and receive trust certificates in return. The trustees were now in a position to harmonize and direct the affairs of a huge aggregation of capital, for according to the Standard Oil Trust agreement they were authorized "to hold, control, and manage the said stock and interests for the exclusive use and benefit" of the parties to the agreement. With competition thus brought under control, profits soared.

The Standard Oil Trust became the model for many imitators. Other American industries were plagued by much the same anarchy that had prompted the leaders in railroads, steel, and oil to force consolidation upon warring competitors. They had tried associations, agreements, and pools, but the trust had obvious advantages over the older devices. With the Standard Oil Trust as a pattern, some fifteen new trusts appeared during the 1880s, including the American Cottonseed Oil Trust, the National Linseed Oil Trust, the National Lead Trust, the Whiskey Trust, and the American Sugar Refining Company.

The trust movement encountered active popular suspicion and hostility from the start. The American creed, bred of an agrarian heritage, held that business should be organized in small units, that competition should be unfettered, and that opportunity should be open to all. The trusts were an affront to this traditional faith: they were gigantic, powerful, even awe-inspiring. To the public, the trusts were the product of an evil plot born of greed, and that was the way the cartoonists pictured them in the newspapers and journals and the way popular political leaders described them in their speeches in the eighties. The popular attitude was not without foundation, for the trusts often did use their enormous power to the detriment of both consumers and small businessmen. Businessmen adversely affected were among the most influential antitrust advocates. A demand for government action against the trusts grew as rapidly as the trusts themselves. Even the big-business community, increasingly aware that mergers and trusts were not likely to stabilize and control industry, looked to the federal government for the answer.

As in railroad regulation, the state legislatures took the lead against the trusts. The laws they passed were never very effective, however, and the Wabash decision of 1886 limited the states here as it did in the regulation of railroads and left the problem up to the federal government. The growth of the trusts had stirred uneasiness in the East and the South as well as the West, and by the campaign of 1888 all political parties of significance had inserted antitrust planks into their platforms. In that year John Sherman of Ohio submitted an antitrust bill in the Senate, one of many similar bills introduced that year. Debate in Congress revealed concern for the interests of both the consumer and the small business-proprietor. It illustrated both the "folklore" of the old capitalism and apprehension about the new. The so-called Sherman Antitrust Act became law on July 2, 1890.

On the face of it the new act would seem to have spelled the end of every trust or trustlike combination. In effect it wrote common-law doctrine against monopoly into a federal statute. The opening sentence of the first section declares, "Every contract, combination in the form of trust or otherwise, or conspiracy, in restraint of trade or commerce among

The ordeal of industrialization

the several States, or with foreign nations, is hereby declared to be illegal." And the second section pronounces guilty of a misdemeanor "every person who shall monopolize, or attempt to monopolize, or combine or conspire with any other person or persons, to monopolize any part of the trade or commerce among the several States, or with foreign nations." The word "person" was specifically defined to include corporations, and the act fixed penalties, as the Interstate Commerce Act had not, for violations.

Efforts to enforce the act during the 1890s were not very vigorous, and clever lawyers found loopholes and various ways of evading its provisions. Some trusts merely reorganized as huge corporations, while others pointed the way to the future by finding refuge in holding companies—that is, giant financial structures that held enough stock in member companies to control their policies. In the first five years after the act was passed, twenty-five new combinations came into being. Then in 1895 the first case under the Sherman Act was decided by the Supreme Court. A suit against the E. C. Knight Company of Philadelphia charged that in selling out to the American Sugar Refining Company it was guilty of furthering monopoly. Although the purchase rounded out one of the most complete monopolies in the country, the court decided that it did not violate the antitrust act. The court's reasoning was that manufacturing was not "commerce" within the meaning of the law, and that monopoly of manufacturing without "direct" effect on commerce was not subject to regulation by the federal government. *United States* v. *Knight* was an extreme instance of laissez-faire interpretation of the Constitution. After this signal that the law offered virtually no obstacle, consolidation went forward with a rush, and literally hundreds of new combinations sprang up in the next five years.

The course of Standard Oil from trust to holding company illustrates the trend. The company formally abandoned the trust agreement of 1882 under an Ohio court order in 1892, but in practice the same nine men who had served as trustees continued to conduct the business of the member companies for five years after the trust was formally dissolved. Charged with evading the court order, the trust reorganized in 1899 as a holding company under the laws of New Jersey, which permitted corporations of that state to own and control corporations of other states. The Standard Oil Company of New Jersey simply increased its stock some tenfold and exchanged it for stock of the member companies. These in turn elected directors of the New Jersey company, who carried on in the place of the old trustees. With concentration of control unimpaired and power enhanced instead of diminished, Standard made money as never before. In the eight years following its reorganization as a holding company, annual dividends on its stock varied between 30 and 48 percent.

The merger movement was restricted mainly to a minority of the dominant American industries and lasted only a few years. It reached its peak in 1899, when 1,208 firms disappeared and merger capitalizations rose to $2,263 million. It declined sharply after the formation of U. S. Steel in 1901. Contrary to expectation, most of the mergers brought neither greater profit nor less competition.

The technology of centralization. Concentration of ownership did not always mean centralization of control. But the management of a vast railroad network, a continent-wide industry, or an international market required a new technology of business administration and communication. American inventors outdid themselves to meet these demands. The number of patents issued to inventors jumped from fewer than two thousand a year in the 1850s to more than thirteen thousand a year in the 1870s and better than twenty-one thousand a year in the 1880s and 1890s. In those days the typical inventor was not a trained engineer in an industrial or university laboratory but an individual tinkerer who frequently operated on a shoestring.

Such a man was Christopher L. Sholes, printer and journalist from Pennsylvania and Wisconsin, who invented a typewriter in 1867. He sold his rights to the Remington Arms Company, which put the typewriter on the market in 1875. The year Sholes invented the

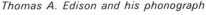

Thomas A. Edison and his phonograph

typewriter, E. A. Callahan of Boston developed a superior stock ticker. In the summer of 1866 Cyrus W. Field employed new techniques to repair and improve his transatlantic cable, broken since 1858, and stock quotations spanned the ocean. Numerous other inventions, including the adding machine (1888), quickened the pace of business transactions.

None of these inventions, however, could rival the importance of the telephone. This was the work of Alexander Graham Bell, a Scotsman who was educated in Edinburgh and London, emigrated to Canada in 1870, when he was twenty-three, and then to Boston two years later. As a teacher of speech to the deaf, he formed the ambition to "make iron talk"—to transmit speech electrically. His experiments over three years resulted in the magnetoelectric telephone. He transmitted the first intelligible sentence on March 10, 1876, and a year later conducted a conversation between Boston and New York. The inventor and his supporters organized the Bell Telephone Company in 1877 and promptly plunged into law suits to defend their patent. The most formidable challenger was the Western Union Telegraph Company, which had originally spurned an opportunity to buy the patent for the "scientific toy" for a mere $100,000. Western Union settled out of court and left the field to Bell and his company, which continued to win hundreds of suits, improve the telephone, buy out competitors, and expand facilities. In 1885 the directors of Bell, led by Theodore N. Vail, organized the American Telephone and Telegraph Company. By 1900 it had become the holding company for the whole system, with some thirty-five subsidiaries and a capitalization of a quarter of a billion dollars.

The use of electricity for light is justly linked with the name of Thomas Alva Edison, who outdid his contemporary Bell as an inventor. The son of a Canadian who settled and prospered in Ohio, Edison grew up without formal schooling. He became a telegraph-operator and while still quite young made some very profitable inventions to improve transmission. He then established himself as a businessman-inventor and built his own "invention factory," forerunner of the modern industrial-research laboratory, at Menlo Park, New Jersey, in 1876. There in 1877 he invented the phonograph, and in later years his laboratories turned out hundreds of inventions or im-

Alexander Graham Bell: he made iron talk

provements, including the storage battery, the motion-picture projector, an electric dynamo, and an electric locomotive. The electric light required a vacuum bulb with a durable filament. Edison made one that burned for forty hours in 1879 and improved it until it was commercially practicable. With the backing of J. Pierpont Morgan he organized the Edison Illuminating Company and moved to New York City to install an electric-light plant. On September 4, 1882, in the presence of Morgan, Edison threw a switch and the House of Morgan, the New York Stock Exchange, the New York *Times*, the New York *Herald*, and smaller buildings in lower Manhattan began to glow with incandescent light.

Edison's plant used direct current, but in order to transmit electricity any distance its voltage had to be stepped up and then stepped down again. For this purpose alternating current and transformers were necessary. George Westinghouse of Pittsburgh, who had invented the railroad air brake in 1869, developed a power plant and a transformer in 1886 that could transmit high-voltage alternating current efficiently, safely, and cheaply over long distances.

For this type of current to be converted into mechanical power, an alternating-current motor had to be developed. In 1888 Nikola Tesla, a Hungarian engineer who immigrated to the United States in 1884, invented such a motor. Westinghouse and his associates bought the patent, improved it with the aid of Tesla, and dramatically demonstrated the practicability of alternating current by illuminating the Columbian Exposition at Chicago in 1893 and by harnessing the might of Niagara Falls and transmitting the power over the countryside. While American industry continued to depend mainly upon steam and water for power until the end of the century, factories no longer had to hover around waterfalls and coal supplies. They were now ready for the electrical revolution that came in the twentieth century.

Laissez-faire conservatism

The Gospel of Wealth. A survey of private fortunes conducted in 1892 revealed that there were 4,047 millionaires in the United States. These were new fortunes; very few of them dated from before the Civil War, when a millionaire was a rarity. Only eighty-four of the millionaires of 1892 were in agriculture, and most of those were cattle barons. The fortunes of the new plutocracy were based on industry, trade, railroads. The new plutocrats were the masters and directors of the economic revolution that was changing the face of American society.

To say that these men were conservative is to put a strain on customary usage of the word, for conservatives are usually opposed to change and devoted to tradition. Yet these men flouted tradition and preached progress. To confuse customary usage further, they adopted the slogan "laissez faire," which was traditionally the doctrine of Jeffersonian and Jacksonian liberals and radicals. In one of the strangest reversals in the history of political thought, the new conservatives took over virtually the whole liberal vocabulary of concepts and slogans, including "democracy," "liberty," "equality," "opportunity,"

433

and "individualism," and turned it against the liberals. In short, they gave an economic and material turn to ethical and idealistic concepts. Man became economic man, democracy was identified with capitalism, liberty with property and the use of it, equality with opportunity for gain, and progress with economic change and the accumulation of capital. God and nature were thus in league with the Gospel of Wealth.

The new doctrine was conservative, however, in the sense that it was bent on defending the status quo, conserving the privileges by which vast accumulations of wealth were gained, and preventing government interference with those privileges. The laissez-faire conservatives naturally found comfort in classical economics, and those who had heard of them found special fascination in the biological theories of Charles Darwin and the sociological theory of Herbert Spencer. The ideas of the great English biologist, which were taken up by American scientists after the Civil War, found early acceptance in the older colleges and were spread abroad by popular writers and lecturers. Herbert Spencer, an English philosopher, found zealous American apostles in John Fiske, a prolific writer and lecturer, and Edward L. Youmans, self-appointed salesman of Spencer's ideas. Spencer applied biological concepts, especially the concept of natural selection, to social principles and justified the unimpeded struggle for existence on the ground that "survival of the fittest" made for human progress. State interference in behalf of the weak would only impede progress. The tooth-and-claw competition of the postwar American economy prepared the perfect market for ideas that glorified laissez faire as the secret of progress. The people could readily see the industrial struggles around them in terms of the Darwinian jungle. It is not surprising that Darwin and

Spencer were more readily acclaimed and more widely admired in America than they were in their native England. "The peculiar condition of American society," wrote the preacher Henry Ward Beecher to Spencer, "has made your writings far more fruitful and quickening here than in Europe." By 1903 more than 368,000 volumes of Spencer's works had been sold in the United States, and many Americans who had never opened one of them or even heard of the author spoke glibly of "the struggle for survival," "natural selection," and "the survival of the fittest." So thoroughly did these concepts become associated with laissez-faire conservatism that the new doctrine has appropriately been called "social Darwinism."

Professors, clergymen, and intellectuals, as well as businessmen, were captivated by the new philosophy. Professor William Graham Sumner of Yale, the most articulate and influential exponent, in an essay called "The Concentration of Wealth: Its Economic Justification," wrote,

> What matters it then that some millionaires are idle, or silly, or vulgar. . . . The millionaires are a product of natural selection, acting on the whole body of men to pick out those who can meet the requirement of certain work to be done. . . . They get high wages and live in luxury, but the bargain is a good one for society.

William Lawrence, the Episcopal Bishop of Massachusetts, announced, "Now we are in a position to affirm that neither history, experience, nor the Bible necessarily sustains the common distrust of the effect of material wealth on morality. . . . Godliness is in league with riches. . . . The race is to the strong." Rockefeller said, "The growth of a large business is merely a survival of the fittest . . . the working out of a law of nature and a law of God." Carnegie admitted

434

Henry George: the nature of property

What constitutes the rightful basis of property? What is it that enables a man justly to say of a thing, "It is mine"? From what springs the sentiment which acknowledges his exclusive right as against all the world? Is it not, primarily, the right of a man to himself, to the use of his own powers, to the enjoyment of the fruits of his own exertions? Is it not this individual right, which springs from and is testified to by the natural facts of individual organization—the fact that each particular pair of hands obey a particular brain and are related to a particular stomach; the fact that each man is a definite, coherent, independent whole—which alone justifies individual ownership? As a man belongs to himself, so his labor when put in concrete form belongs to him....

If production give to the producer the right to exclusive possession and enjoyment, there can rightfully be no exclusive possession and enjoyment of anything not the production of labor, and the recognition of private property in land is a wrong.

From Henry George, *Progress and Poverty*, 1879.

that while this "may sometimes be hard for the individual, it is best for the race, because it insures the survival of the fittest in every department."

By the time it had become fully elaborated, the Gospel of Wealth and its corollaries of social Darwinism included many propositions widely accepted. Among them were the following: (1) that the American economy was controlled for the benefit of all by a natural aristocracy and that these leaders were brought to the top by a competitive struggle that weeded out the weak, the incompetent, and the unfit and selected the strong, the able, and the wise; (2) that politicians were not subject to rigorous natural selection and therefore could not be trusted to the same degree as businessmen; (3) that the state should confine itself to police activities of protecting property and maintaining order and that if it interfered with economic affairs it would upset the beneficent effect of natural selection; (4) that slums and poverty were the unfortunate but inevitable negative results of the competitive struggle and that state intervention to eliminate them was misguided; (5) that the stewardship of wealth obliged the rich to try to ameliorate social injustice.

Through these ideas may be regarded as a rationalization of the rule of a privileged group, they were by no means confined to members of that group. They also became the common assumption of millions, a sort of folk faith. The popular demand for success stories like those in the novels of Horatio Alger, whose 119 books were filled with rags-to-riches heroes for boy readers, suggests that the mass of Americans were as firm in their faith in the Gospel of Work as they were in their faith in the Gospel of Wealth. The business creed absorbed and fostered both faiths for its own purposes.

In the Supreme Court the Gospel of Wealth found institutional support of great prestige and incomparable value. Under the persistent tutelage of Justice Stephen J. Field, the Court had been converted by the late eighties to the view that Herbert Spencer's *Social Statics* coincided remarkably well with the will of the Founding Fathers and the soundest moral precepts of the ages. Interpreting the "due process" clause of the Fourteenth Amendment as a protection intended to cover the substantive interests of corporate enterprise, the Court proceeded to declare state regulatory measures unconstitutional on the ground that they deprived corporations of property without due process of law. By the end of the century, the Court's laissez-faire interpretation of the Constitution had debarred the states in many fields from the exercise of ancient police powers for the protection of the public interest and the welfare of workers.

Social critics and dissenters. The Gospel of Wealth and the Darwinian apology for unrestrained capitalism did not meet with universal acceptance, however, for those doctrines were challenged by social critics, economists, and clergymen. The dissenters themselves were influenced by Darwin, but they interpreted the social implications of his theories in a different way. They rejected the survival-of-the-fittest concept of social progress and found a place for ethical values in economic theory, as well as a need for governmental intervention to restrain the strong and protect the weak. A strong religious impulse often motivated the nonclerical as well as the clerical critics of social Darwinism.

Lester Frank Ward, one of the founders of sociology in America, was an outspoken critic of Spencer's theories. Ward took a job in a Washington bureau in 1865, after service in the Union army, and remained in government work for some forty years. Largely self-educated, he compensated for his impoverished background by astonishing feats of learning. He mastered ten languages and several fields of science in addition to sociology, and, when he finally found acceptance in academic life, he titled a course he gave at Brown University "A Survey of All Knowledge." His first book, *Dynamic Sociology* (1883), was a prodigious work of fourteen hundred pages that was not easily or widely read. He never achieved the acclaim or the influence his conservative rival, Professor Sumner, did. Ward pointed out that there was a difference between animal and human economics. Bears have claws, but men have intelligence. Darwinian laws governed the former, but the human mind transformed the environment of human economics and substituted rational choice for natural selection. This was as it should be, for nature was terribly wasteful in her crude methods of evolution. Unrestrained competition actually prevented the fittest from surviving, and the doctrine of laissez faire killed off whatever benefits competition conferred by encouraging monopoly and by leaving no competitors to compete. For competition to survive, government regulation was necessary. Ward believed in social planning and had great faith in education. "Thus far," he wrote, "social progress has in a certain awkward manner taken care of itself, but in the near future it will have to be cared for." The caring, he said, should be done by social engineers, scientific planners, and managers of society.

A second self-taught social philosopher of the age, and one of the most original economists of the time, was Henry George, author of the famous book *Progress and Poverty* (1879). Born in Philadelphia, George traveled in the Orient and in 1868 settled in California, where he had ample opportunity to observe the land speculation, land monopoly, and social distress that played so important a part in his economics. Addressing himself to the problem of unequal distribution of wealth, he inveighed against the "shocking contrast between monstrous wealth and debasing want." Wealth is produced, he concluded, by applying labor to land, and capital is the surplus above the cost of labor. Labor therefore creates all capital. But capital, by withholding advantageous land sites until their value has been enhanced by labor, improvements in production, and speculation in adjacent areas, reaps a profit out of all proportion to its contribution. This profit George called the "unearned increment." Since land should no more be monopolized than air and sunshine, George's solution was to tax land in such a fashion as to appropriate the unearned increment. This was to be done by a "single tax," which would make other taxes unnecessary. After 1885 he put aside the hope that this would result in common ownership of the land by the people. George's book and his lectures won him a political following at home and abroad and enabled him to make a strong showing as candidate for mayor of New York in 1886.

Another political aspiration born of a book was the Nationalist movement; this time the book was Edward Bellamy's *Looking Backward* (1888). The most successful of several utopian novels published during the eighties, Bellamy's book "looked backward" to the benighted 1880s from the collectivized society of the year 2000 A.D. By that time selfishness has been eliminated by the abolition of corporate property and the nationalization of industry. Competition is seen to have killed nineteenth-century society and its individualism. "Competition," says the protagonist, "which is the instinct of selfishness, is another word for dissipation of energy, while combination is the secret of efficient production." Bellamy's attack on the ethic of "survival of the fittest" appealed to a wide variety of people, who for a time sought to maintain a political organization. Nationalist clubs and periodicals fostered municipal ownership of utilities and public ownership of railroads. As agrarian reform mounted in the nineties, however, the Nationalists tended to join the farmers' parties and abandon their own organization.

From the viewpoint of a later day, the debate over laissez-faire doctrine and social Darwinism appears confused and paradoxical. If free competition was the goal of laissez faire, the industrialists who hated competition and sought to restrain it would seem to have embraced the wrong doctrine. If social Darwinism taught hands off by the government, the businessmen who sought subsidies, protection, and favors from the government again seemed inconsistent. But insofar as these doctrines were useful for the defense of the status quo and the discouragement of efforts to reform or change society by conscious purpose the conservatives were right in embracing them and the radicals in rejecting them.

The house of labor

Man and the machine. In the long run industrialization raises the living standard and increases the opportunities of labor, but around the world labor has discovered that the revolution that establishes industrialization comes at heavy cost and that the worker's adjustment to the machine and the factory way of life is often painful and difficult. In America the labor shortage that had persisted since colonial times had kept the level of wages higher than the level that prevailed abroad; and yet the American worker had his full share of troubles in the grim iron age of industry.

Many of the adjustments the worker had to make were hard to understand and painful to accept, for they meant loss of status and surrender of independence. The skilled craftsman who owned the tools he used was likely to be an individualist who took pride in the quality of his product and enjoyed a strong bargaining position. The new factory discipline offered a humbler role and a lower status. In the factory the worker surrendered his tools, nearly all the creative pride he took in his product, most of his independence, and much of his bargaining power. He became the tender of a machine that set the work pace and the employee of owners whom he probably never met and never saw. The craftsmanship that had been the skilled worker's source of pride and security was no longer of any significance, for his place at the machine could be taken by an unskilled worker. The growing impersonality of his relations to his work and his employer and the ever increasing size of the industrial organization meant a sacrifice in security, identity, and the satisfactions that bestow meaning and value on work.

Adjustment would have been easier had the change been less swift and the worker better prepared. But the mechanization and expansion of the factory system hit a breathtaking pace during the 1880s. Between 1880 and 1890 the total capital invested in the production of machinery increased two and a half times, and the average investment in machinery increased 200 percent for each establishment and 50 percent for each employee. The manufacturer, with all his capital tied up in new machinery, was driven to seek a rapid return on his investment, generally at low prices in a highly competitive market. Real wages actually rose, but the hard-pressed employer often made economies at the expense of the unskilled factory workers, who suffered from working conditions that impaired their safety, their comfort, and their health. While some states had enacted factory laws, the great body of legislation that now protects factory workers had not yet been written in the eighties and nineties. Employers thought nothing of using detectives and armed force to thwart the organization of labor unions, and in "company towns," where all houses, stores, and services were company-owned, employers subjected workers to endless harassments and petty tyranny. There was nothing but the urging of conscience and the weak protest of labor to keep employers from cutting costs at the expense of their workers.

The average weekly wages of common laborers remained less than $9 throughout the nineties, and farm laborers got less than half that amount. After the depression of the seventies, however, there was a fairly steady increase in real wages—for those who had jobs. The rise in real wages helps explain labor's attachment to the system and its relative indifference to socialism. The millions who suffered unemployment during the depressions of the last three decades of the century were not even enumerated, much less assisted, by the government. The most insistent demand of organized labor was for the eight-hour day, but the main result was the adoption of a federal law passed in 1869, and amended in 1892, limiting the work day of federal employees to eight hours. In private industry, however, most workers continued to work a ten-hour day and a six-day week, and in steel and other industries they worked even longer. The accident toll taken by heedless negligence, and the damage done to workers' health by poor ventilation and lighting, dust and fumes—in so far as the facts were known at all—were charged off as the cost of progress.

A special handicap of American labor was its lack of homogeneity. Workers were fragmented by race and color, as well as by geography, philosophy, concepts of organization, style of protest, and national origin. Some formed exclusive groups to protect their own privilege and to keep underprivileged groups at bay. Between 1882 and 1900 there were fifty strikes waged against the employment of black labor. Blacks sometimes served as strikebreakers, thereby increasing the resentment of white workers.

Immigrants formed the largest segment of the American labor force, except in the South, where few of them settled. There had been immigrant workers from the start in the United States, and while the percentage in the labor force remained about the same as it had been since the Civil War, immigrants were coming in greater numbers and from different parts of Europe, mainly the southern and eastern countries. Nineteenth-century immigration reached high tide in the 1880s, when nearly 5¼ million immigrants arrived, 2½ million more than had come in the seventies and 1½ million more than were to come in the nineties. Set apart by language and culture, accustomed to lower wages and living standards, the newcomers often concentrated as ethnic groups in certain industries—Slavs in anthracite, Jews in the garment industry. Native workers often looked down on them with contempt and spoke of work for which they were suited as "foreign jobs." The new immigrants crowded into the coal-mining and steel industries, with each wave pushing the earlier comers a step up the ladder. The bitterest and most implacable labor opposition to immigrants was directed at the Asiatics, particularly the Chinese of California. Supported by labor organizations in the East, the Californians persuaded Congress in 1882 to suspend admission of Chinese immigrants for ten years.

Unions and strikes. For a long time the attitude of American labor toward unions and collective bargaining was typically that of the skilled craftsman or the small shopkeeper. Native workers, and many immigrants as well, were reluctant to abandon the American dream of rising higher and higher in the social scale. Instead of accepting the new industrial order and its conditions, they looked back nostalgically to the past and longed for the good old days. Longings of this sort found expression in such slogans as "every man his own master" or "every man his own employer." Labor unions remained very weak throughout the nineteenth century, embracing not more than 1 or 2 percent of the total labor force and less than 10 percent of the industrial workers.

During and after the Civil War the typical national trade union was designed primarily to protect the status of skilled craftsmen. In 1866 William H. Sylvis, an iron-molder of Pennsylvania, attempted to unite the trade unions into a single organization called the National Labor Union. This organization, of which Sylvis became president in 1868, bore no resemblance to modern labor unions. It was led by visionaries and idealists who did not believe in strikes and who were unconcerned with the immediate needs of working people, apart from the eight-hour day. Sylvis stressed long-range reforms and humanitarian demands, and admitted farmers' societies and advocates of women's rights as members. The organization formed the National Labor Reform party in 1871, and after a feeble showing in the election of 1872 the new party went to pieces.

With many of the same generous impulses and naive assumptions, the Noble and Holy Order of the Knights of Labor was founded in 1869. A secret fraternal order with high-flown titles and elaborate rituals, the Knights sought to unite all labor and welcomed all "toilers" of whatever color, race, nationality, or craft, whether skilled or unskilled. They excluded only gamblers, bankers, lawyers, doctors, liquor-dealers, and a few others—apparently on moralistic grounds. Utopian and nostalgic in many of their views, the Knights frowned on the use of the strike and promoted dreams of restoring the past. Their labor program, however, included demands for a federal bureau of statistics, equal pay for both sexes, the eight-hour day, and the abolition of child and prison labor. In practice they acted like a labor union. The two hundred or more consumer and producer cooperatives the Knights founded elicited great enthusiasm but little profit. Many of their political demands resembled those of contemporary farmers' organiza-

tions, for they included paper money, an income tax, abolition of the national bank, and Prohibition.

The Knights grasped one important fact of the new economy: that the consolidation of industry made necessary the consolidation of labor. They founded their General Assembly in 1878 with a view to centralizing control over labor in order to combat the monopolistic power of corporations. In 1879 they elected Terence V. Powderly as their Grand Master Workman. The dominant figure in the Order during the years of its power and influence, Powderly was described at a labor convention in 1886 as elegantly dressed in "double-breasted, black, broadcloth coat, stand-up collar, plain tie, dark trousers and narrow small shoes," surrounded by "horny-fisted sons of toil" and acting "like Queen Victoria at a national Democratic convention." Powderly constantly preached against strikes, and yet it was as a result of strikes in 1885–86 that the Order made its most sensational gains. These were spontaneous revolts rather than organized strikes, but under their stimulus membership soared from about one hundred thousand to over seven hundred thousand. The strength of the Order quickly ebbed after the upheavals of 1886, and two years later its membership had fallen to two hundred thousand. By 1893 it was virtually defunct.

In the meantime the American Federation of Labor, founded in 1881, was hammering out a labor philosophy somewhat more closely related to the realities of the industrial economy and more in harmony with the future. Rejecting the utopian radicalism of the Knights of Labor, the AFL foreswore political goals for economic objectives. Instead of embracing the brotherhood of all workers, it devoted its attention to gaining concrete benefits for skilled workers organized along craft lines. It was a loose alliance of national trade unions, each of which retained a large amount of autonomy, with jurisdiction over its own affairs and with the power to call its own strikes. By 1900 the AFL did not hesitate to acknowledge the strike and the boycott as legitimate means of collective bargaining. These principles had been formulated by 1881 and reaffirmed when the AFL was reorganized in 1886.

As its first president the AFL elected Samuel Gompers, who retained the office for nearly forty years. An immigrant boy, born in London in 1850, Gompers grew up in the trade-union movement. Under the impact of his experience in America he gradually put aside his earlier leanings to socialism and slowly shaped a more conservative approach to the problems of labor. He felt that labor should accept the economic system and should try to win for itself a respectable place as a "legitimate" group within that system, as legitimate as business or the church. And to do so, he argued, labor would have to struggle day by day for higher wages and lower hours. Gompers

The ordeal of industrialization

Samuel Gompers:
higher wages and lower hours

strove to impose order by resolving jurisdictional disputes between unions and by consolidating local unions in state and national federations. The AFL grew as the Knights declined; in fifteen years its membership topped the million mark.

Labor's struggle to win acceptance and to improve its lot was marked by an extraordinary number of strikes and lockouts, conflicts that sometimes flared into bloodshed, particularly in time of depression. In July 1877 a series of wage cuts and abortive strikes provoked an upheaval of insurrectionary violence along the trunk lines of three big railroads. In the first show of violence, along the B&O, federal troops were called in after a mob intimidated state militia. In Pittsburgh the community joined the strikers against the Pennsylvania Railroad and destroyed $5 million worth of property before being dispersed with heavy loss of life. Other disturbances broke out in Philadelphia, Harrisburg, Reading, Scranton, Buffalo, and Toledo, and farther west in St. Louis, Chicago, and San Francisco. Scores of people lost their lives, and property valued at millions of dollars went up in flames. The courts clamped down, the police became more ruthless, and the public began to withdraw its sympathy from the labor movement. Another upsurge of labor militancy occurred during the mid-eighties. With the Knights of Labor at the peak of their strength the loose rhetoric of labor solidarity ceased to be merely verbal and materialized in general strikes, sympathetic work stoppage, and nationwide boycotts and political demonstrations. During 1886, a climactic year in labor history, 610,000 men were out of work because of strikes, lockouts, or shutdowns due to strikes, more than three times the average of the five preceding years. Then on May 4, during an anarchist demonstration against police brutalities at Haymarket Square in Chicago, a bomb was thrown that killed a policeman and fatally wounded six other persons. A jury found eight anarchists guilty, and four were hanged, though the identity of the bomb-thrower was never established. The incident smeared parts of the labor movement, especially the Knights, with the charge of anarchism and subjected labor to public suspicion and hostility.

Resort to violence was common in the turbulent nineties, but often labor was merely replying to force with force. In the remote Coeur d'Alene district of Idaho, company guards and miners fought it out in 1892 with rifles and dynamite until at last federal troops came in, crushed the strike, and turned the miners' jobs over to strikebreakers. At Carnegie's Homestead steel plant in Pennsylvania the same year, thirty-eight hundred members of the Amalgamated Association of Iron and Steel Workers struck over wage cuts and working conditions. As a preparation for breaking the strike, Henry C. Frick, the manager, imported three hundred Pinkerton detectives. When they arrived at the plant on barges, the strikers resisted and a gun fight ensued that resulted in the death of seven detectives and nine strikers, the wounding of a much larger number, and the surrender of the detectives. The sufferings of the workers stirred great public sympathy, a sympathy that was not entirely alienated by the attempt of an anarchist, who had no connection with the strike, to assassinate Frick. In the end, however, the strike failed miserably, and its failure heralded the end of unionism in the steel industry for many years to come.

The great depression that started in 1893 (see p. 481) brought on a new wave of wage cuts, layoffs, and strikes. More men were thrown out of work by strikes in 1894, a year of exceptional unemployment and labor violence, than in any previous year. The most important strike of that year, and of many years to come, was the big railroad strike centering in Chicago. It originated not among railway workers but among factory workers in George M. Pullman's "model" company town just south of Chicago. The men were driven to desperation by five wage cuts in one year and no reduction in the high rents charged for company houses. The Pullman workers had recently joined the new American Railway Union, headed by Eugene V. Debs and frowned on by the older Railway Brotherhoods of the AFL. Although Debs urged caution, his union voted to refuse to handle Pullman cars if the management would not accept arbitration of the strike. Pullman rejected all arbitration, and the General Managers Association came to his aid by dismissing switchmen who boycotted his cars. The union then struck against the railroads and by the end of June 1894 nearly all railroad men on roads west of Chicago were on strike.

Acting for the railroads, the General Managers Association then appealed directly to the federal government to intervene with armed force and end the strike. There had been no violence so far, and federal intervention with troops was a move that Governor John P. Altgeld strongly opposed. Railroad lawyers had no trouble persuading President Cleveland and Attorney General Richard Olney that intervention could nevertheless be justified on the ground that the strike had obstructed the delivery of United States mail. Actually, the railroads themselves refused, against the union's wishes, to attach mail cars to trains boycotting Pullman cars. Nevertheless, Olney secured an injunction against the union, and on July 4 Cleveland sent some two thousand troops to Chicago to enforce the injunction and protect the mails. After the troops arrived, the union completely lost control of the situation, and mobs of looters destroyed cars and burned and stole property. Twelve people were killed and many arrested at the scene, but none was a striker. The effect of the troop action was to break the strike, a result that Olney, by his own confession, intended to accomplish.

The failure of the Pullman strike had important consequences for the future of American labor. Debs and other union officials were tried and sentenced to jail for contempt of court in disobeying the injunction against the union. The Supreme Court in upholding the sentence gave the use of the injunction in labor disputes a prestige it had never before enjoyed. And the government in suggesting that a strike might be construed as a conspiracy in restraint of trade under the Sherman Antitrust Act placed a powerful weapon in the hands of management for use against unions. Another unforeseen consequence of the Pullman strike and the court's decision was to bring into national prominence for the first time the name of Eugene V. Debs. Within a few years he became the foremost leader of the socialist movement in the country, a position he held during the years when that movement enjoyed its greatest strength.

Any realistic account of the ordeal of industrialization in America will tell of heedless waste and ruthless exploitation, of cutthroat competition and consolidation. Whatever economic progress came out of the grim struggle—and undoubtedly much was gained—was purchased at a high cost in brutalized labor, wasted resources, and deterioration in business and public ethics. Historians who emphasize the necessity for industrialization and the advantages ultimately derived from it remind us that the costs of industrialization have never been low and that when reckoned in human suffering and social turmoil the price has been even more appalling in other countries than in the United States. And in all fairness, the American ordeal should be judged in comparison with that of England, which preceded it, and that of Russia, which came after it. In neither case does the American record, as bad as it was, suffer by comparison.

Suggestions for reading For comparative evaluation see T. C. Cochran, ''The Paradox of American Economic Growth,'' *Journal of American History,* LXI (1975), 925–942. Glenn Porter, *The Rise of Big Business, 1860–1910** (1973), and E. C. Kirkland, *Industry Comes of Age: Business, Labor, and Public Policy, 1860–1897** (1961), are surveys of superior quality. A much briefer sketch of value is S. P. Hays, *The Response to Industrialism: 1885–1914** (1957). J. A. Garraty, *The New Commonwealth, 1877–1890** (1968), R. H. Wiebe, *The Search for Order: 1877–1920** (1968), I. M. Tarbell, *The Nationalizing of Business, 1878–1898* (1936), and T. C. Cochran and William Miller, *The Age of Enterprise** (1942), contain excellent chapters. Two older books still worthwhile are L. C. A. Knowles, *Economic Development in the Nineteenth Century* (1932), and D. A. Wells, *Recent Economic Change* (1890). William Miller, ed., *Men in Business** (1952), has illuminating essays.

The railroad establishment of the period is described in G. R. Taylor and I. D. Neu, *The American Railroad Network, 1861–1890* (1956). The importance of railroads to the economy is questioned by R. W. Fogel, *Railroads and American Economic Growth: Essays in Econometric History** (1964). Railroading in the West is treated in R. E. Riegel, *The Story of the Western Railroads** (1926), and R. C. Overton, *Burlington West* (1941), and *Gulf to Rockies* (1953); in New England by E. C. Kirkland, *Men, Cities and Transportation,* 2 vols. (1948); and in the South by J. F. Stover, *The Railroads of the South, 1865–1900* (1955). On consolidation and management see E. G. Campbell, *The Reorganization of the*

*Available in a paperback edition.

The ordeal of industrialization

American Railroad System, 1893–1900 (1938). Matthew Josephson, *The Robber Barons** (1934), stresses the misdeeds of the capitalists, and T. C. Cochran, *Railroad Leaders, 1845–1890* (1953), emphasizes their attitudes and problems. New light on government regulation comes from Lee Benson, *Merchants, Farmers, and Railroads* (1955), Gabriel Kolko, *Railroads and Regulation, 1877–1916** (1965), and G. H. Miller, *Railroads and the Granger Laws* (1971).

On technological developments, Lewis Mumford, *Technics and Civilization** (1934), is suggestive. H. J. Habakkuk, *American and British Technology in the Nineteenth Century** (1962), is a comparative study. An authoritative work of reference is Charles Singer, *et al.,* eds., *A History of Technology,* Vol. V: *The Late Nineteenth Century, c. 1850 to c. 1900* (1958). Roger Burlingame, *Engines of Democracy* (1940), is a narrative of inventions, and Waldemar Kaempffert, *A Popular History of American Invention,* 2 vols. (1924), is full of interesting detail. Heavy industry and manufacturing generally are treated in V. S. Clark, *History of Manufactures in the United States from 1607–1928,* 3 vols., Vol. II (1929); a briefer account is Malcolm Keir, *Manufacturing Industries in America* (1920). H. C. Passer, *The Electrical Manufacturers, 1875–1900* (1953), reveals much about technical change and economic growth.

On the steel industry, Andrew Carnegie, *Autobiography* (1920), and J. F. Wall, *Andrew Carnegie* (1970), are highly informative. Oil and Rockefeller are the subject of exhaustive studies, including Allan Nevins, *John D. Rockefeller,* 2 vols. (1940); R. W. Hidy and M. E. Hidy, *Pioneering in Big Business, 1882–1911: History of the Standard Oil Company, New Jersey* (1955); and P. H. Giddens, *Early Days of Oil* (1948). For contrasting points of view on Rockefeller, see Earl Latham, *John D. Rockefeller: Robber Baron or Industrial Statesman?** (1949). See also H. F. Williamson and A. R. Daum, *The American Petroleum Industry, 1859–1959,* 2 vols. (1959–63). Jonathan Hughes, *The Vital Few** (1966), is another study of big-business leaders. The trust and early regulatory legislation are most fully treated in H. B. Thorelli, *The Federal Antitrust Policy* (1955); but see also W. Z. Ripley, *Trusts, Pools and Corporations* (1905), John Moody, *The Truth about the Trusts* (1904), and H. D. Lloyd, *Wealth Against Commonwealth** (1894).

The business philosophy of laissez faire is perceptively treated in E. C. Kirkland, *Business in the Gilded Age* (1952) and *Dream and Thought in the Business Community, 1860–1900** (1956), and by R. G. McCloskey, *American Conservatism in the Age of Enterprise, 1865–1910** (1951). Chapters in R. H. Gabriel, *The Course of American Democratic Thought* (1940), are illuminating. Richard Hofstadter, *Social Darwinism in American Thought** (1944, rev. ed., 1959), throws much light on both laissez faire and its critics; and so does Sidney Fine, *Laissez Faire and the General Welfare State: A Study of Conflict in American Thought, 1865–1901** (1956). The authority on Henry George is C. A. Barker, *Henry George* (1955). See Samuel Chugerman, *Lester F. Ward: The American Aristotle* (1939), and A. E. Morgan, *Edward Bellamy* (1944), for the best treatment of these men.

For detailed history, J. R. Commons, *et al., History of Labour in the United States,* 4 vols. (1918–35), is indispensable; Vol. III is on this period. A useful brief survey is Henry Pelling, *American Labor** (1960). On the Knights of Labor, see N. J. Ware, *The Labor Movement in the United States, 1860–1895** (1929), and on its great rival see Philip Taft, *The A. F. of L. in the Time of Gompers* (1957). On trade unionism and reformers see G. N. Grob, *Workers and Utopia* (1961). An important study is Lloyd Ulman, *The Rise of the National Trade Union* (1955). On the South see M. A. McLaurin, *Paternalism and Protest: Southern Cotton Mill Workers and Organized Labor, 1875–1905* (1971). Autobiographies of the two foremost leaders of labor are T. V. Powderly, *Thirty Years of Life and Labor, 1859–1889* (1890), and Samuel Gompers, *Seventy Years of Life and Labour,* 2 vols. (1925).

Industrial life and business struggles have been the subjects of such novels as Henry James, *The American** (1877); John Hay, *The Breadwinners** (1883), an antilabor work; W. D. Howells, *The Rise of Silas Lapham** (1885), the study of a businessman; and Theodore Dreiser, *The Financier** (1912) and *The Titan** (1914), portraits of industrial tycoons. Edward Bellamy, *Looking Backward, 2000–1887** (1888), is a utopian novel that started a reform movement.

*Available in a paperback edition.

CHAPTER 19

The urban society

Elevated railroad, 1885

he United States was born in the country and has moved to the city." A great deal of American history is summed up in this observation by Richard Hofstadter. Old America was rural by birth, by breeding, and in outlook. The Founding Fathers, their children, and their grandchildren were typically country men, and it was inevitable that their problems, their values, and their myths should have been shaped by the setting in which they lived. It was just as inevitable that the problems, values, and myths of modern America should be shaped by the urban environment that eventually replaced the old agrarian setting. The new environment created new problems and strained old institutions. It compelled new adjustments in politics, religion, education, and economic life, and it left a profound imprint upon the whole style of American life, including arts and literature.

America moves to town

The pull of the city. In 1790, the year of the first census, only 3.35 percent of the population lived in towns of eight thousand or more. By the end of the nineteenth century ten times that percentage, a third of the population, was classified "urban" by this definition. The cities grew with the nation, of course, but after about 1820 they grew much faster than the nation. Between 1800 and 1890 the population of the entire country increased twelvefold, but over the same period the urban population multiplied eighty-seven fold. In 1800 there were only 6 cities with more than eight thousand people; by 1890 there were 448, and 26 of them had a population greater than one hundred thousand. More striking still was the rise of the American metropolis, the big city of more than half a million. The ancient world produced only two of that size, Rome and Alexandria, and western Europe had only two by the end of the seventeenth century, London and Paris. By 1900 there were six cities that large in the United States and three of them had a population of over a million. Rapid urbanization was not limited to this country, but the pace was faster in the United States than in Europe. The New World metropolis grew at a pace unprecedented in

history. Chicago more than tripled its size between 1880 and 1900, when it had more than 1½ million, and New York grew from not quite 2 million to nearly 3½ million in those two decades. Buffalo, Detroit, and Milwaukee more than doubled, and St. Paul, Minneapolis, and Denver more than quadrupled their size.

Urban growth was very unequally distributed, and some parts of the country did not really participate in the movement significantly until the twentieth century. In fact, half the entire urban population in 1890 was in the North Atlantic states and only 7.7 percent was in the South Atlantic states. More than half the nation's city-dwellers lived in the five states of New York, Pennsylvania, Massachusetts, Illinois, and Ohio. Four-fifths of them lived north of the Ohio and Missouri rivers. While by 1900 six out of ten people in the North Atlantic states and three out of ten in the Middle West lived in cities, scarcely one out of ten was an urbanite in the South. Urbanization affected all parts of the country, even the most remote, but in large areas toward the end of the century it was less an immediate experience than a distant and powerful lure.

The depopulation of the countryside was especially noticeable in the Middle West and the North Atlantic states. Some of it was due, as in the past, to the lure of the West. But the pull of the city was growing stronger and stronger. Between 1880 and 1890 more than half the townships of Iowa and Illinois declined in population, and yet both states gained substantially in total number of inhabitants. Rural decline was even greater in the North Atlantic states, where the flight to the city had long been in progress. In New England 932 out of the total of 1,502 townships, including two-thirds of those in Maine and New Hampshire and three-fourths of those in Vermont, declined in population during the eighties. Thousands of farms were abandoned, houses were left to decay, and scores of villages were completely deserted. Yet in that decade New England, largely through the growth of its cities, actually gained 20 percent in total population. As early as 1890 the number of industrial wage-earners in the whole country almost equaled the number of farm-owners, tenants, and farm laborers combined.

Rural defenses against the ancient lure of the city reached a new low in the eighties and nineties. The

America moves
to town, 1870

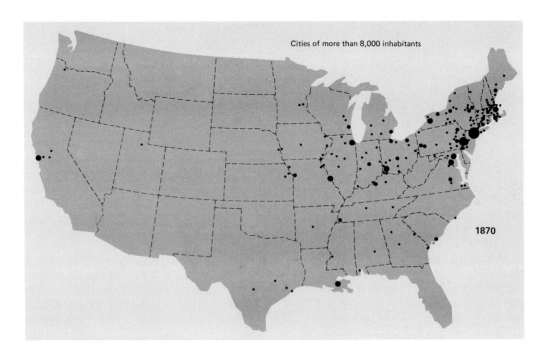

Cities of more than 8,000 inhabitants

1870

seventies and the nineties were the worst decades of agricultural depression (see Chapter 20), when everything seemed to go wrong with the farming economy. Crop prices were lower, debts greater, and mortgages heavier than ever before. At the same time the glamour and attraction of the city were enhanced by the glitter of the new electric lights, as well as by the telephones, the trolley cars, and a thousand other wonders. The city was the only place one could enjoy such amenities, for they did not begin to penetrate the countryside and soften the contrast with urban comforts to any extent until well into the twentieth century. The contrast between rural ills and urban felicity made the farmer regard his harsh lot and isolation as even more intolerable than ever before, as indeed they were. Many farmers resorted to political rebellion for relief. A great many others simply moved to town.

City lights and cesspools. The new technology and the factories probably produced more discomforts and inconveniences than comforts and amenities for the city dweller of the late nineteenth century. But to the outsider the advantages and attractions were more readily apparent. First among these were the bright lights that were replacing the dim gas lamps in the streets and the kerosene lamps and gas jets indoors. Cleveland and San Francisco led the way in 1879 by installing brilliant electric arc lamps in their streets, and their example was quickly followed in cities across the country. The noisy, sputtering arc lamp was impractical for indoor use, but for that purpose the

incandescent light bulb patented by Edison in 1880 (see p. 433) became available in a few years and spread as swiftly as the growth of power plants permitted. In 1882 there were only thirty-eight central power stations in the whole country, but before the end of the century there were three thousand. Improved lighting not only made cities safer at night but enabled factories to run night shifts, proved a boon to theaters and other amusement houses, and extended the hours of libraries, shops, and schools.

Electrical power provided the answer to a city problem that was even more pressing than that of lighting—the problem of moving vast numbers of people rapidly through the streets at rush hours. The old horse cars or mule-drawn coaches, the prevalent means of public transportation into the eighties, were much too slow as well as too small, smelly, and crowded. New York City, later imitated by Brooklyn, Chicago, and Boston, built an overhead railroad with four cars pulled by a tiny steam locomotive. But the heavy elevated roadway was expensive to build and shut out light from the streets, and the locomotives sprinkled pedestrians with soot and hot coals. To master its steep, hill-climbing streets, San Francisco developed cable roads, with the cars pulled by an endless cable sunk under the track level. Midwestern and Eastern cities also used them successfully in their level streets.

In the meantime, inventors had tinkered for years with the idea of an electric street railway, but Lieutenant Frank J. Sprague was the first to install and profitably operate one, a short line built at Richmond,

The urban society

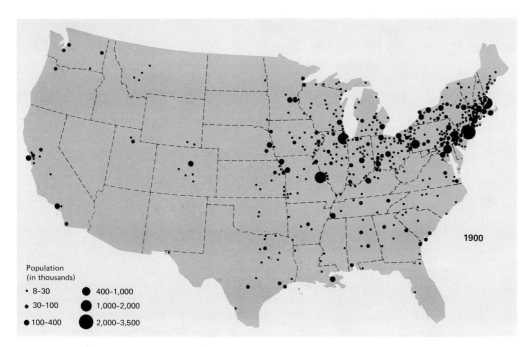

Population
(in thousands)
- 8–30   ● 400–1,000
- 30–100   ● 1,000–2,000
- 100–400 ● 2,000–3,500

1900

Virginia, in 1887. The success of the experiment started a revolution in urban transportation, for the electric trolley cars were faster, cheaper, and more comfortable than any of the older types. By 1895 some eight hundred fifty lines, using ten thousand miles of tracks, were in operation. Boston in 1897 was the first city to put electric cars underground, and New York opened its subway to the public in 1904.

Cities took to the telephone eagerly and naturally, for without it the congestion and concentration of people that was to follow would have been insupportable. Within two years after Bell invented the instrument in 1876 (see p. 432), New Haven had set up the first commercial switchboard, and in two more years eighty-five cities had telephone exchanges. The first telephone connection between cities was effected in 1877 between Boston and New York. Before the end of the century the whole country was laced with interconnecting lines, and eight hundred thousand phones were in use—double the number in all of Europe.

Technology and invention were slower to yield solutions to city problems that were traditionally assigned to the public domain, such as street-paving, water supply, and sewage disposal, and in these matters progress was halting. In the seventies the streets even of the larger cities were poorly paved—usually with cobblestones or granite blocks along the eastern seaboard, with wooden blocks in the Middle West, and with gravel or macadam in the South. Brick became popular as pavement in the mid-eighties, especially in cities where it was manufactured. The na-

tional capital in 1878 set the pace in adapting asphalt to street-paving, the method that eventually proved the favorite, and by 1900 Washington was pronounced the best-paved city in the world.

Water supply and sewage disposal lagged far behind the demands and needs of mushrooming city populations. The typical urbanite of the seventies

Cincinnati trolley, 1890

445

"New" immigrants: the passage

rooting was even more of a shock and a bewilderment.

Many observers have singled out the immigrants as the primary cause of the urban crisis. Actually, the percentage of foreign born in the total population remained about the same; the immigrants came from much the same social class as they always had; and they came for the same old reason—to better their lot. A much larger percentage of the new immigrants than previously returned to their native lands, and there were other significant changes. For one thing they began to come in far greater numbers than ever before. From 1850 to 1880 about 2½ million had arrived per decade, with the rate falling off a bit in the sixties but picking up again in the seventies. Big passenger ships, built for the purpose, altered immigration in many ways. In the eighties the number more than doubled, with nearly 5¼ million arriving during that decade, and with nearly 3¾ million more landing in the next. For another thing immigrants showed a greater tendency than ever to congregate in the large Eastern cities and less disposition to disperse over the countryside. This concentration naturally made them more conspicuous. And finally there came a shift to what was called "new" immigration—from southern and eastern Europe—as contrasted with the "old" immigrants from northern and western Europe. The old immigrants had come typically from Britain, Ireland, Germany, or one of the Scandinavian countries, and they were usually Protestant. The new immigrants were Italians, Austrians, Hungarians, Poles, Serbs, and Russians; they were Catholic or Jewish in religion and had habits and ways that appeared outlandish to older Americans. Immigrants of the new type had made up only 1.4 percent of the total immigration of the sixties and less than 20 percent in the eighties; but in the nineties their proportion suddenly climbed to more than 50 percent and in the next decade to more than 70 percent. This increasing proportion of new immigrants coincided with, and provided stimulation for, two tendencies: (1) an increasing concern over the ills of urban life and (2) an increasing tendency to stress racial differences. Because of this coincidence, the new immigrants were blamed for many serious city problems that had little to do with racial or national origin.

There could be no doubt, however, that the foreigner and the immigrant had become conspicuous in American life. By 1890 one-fourth of the Philadelphians and one-third of the Bostonians and Chicagoans were of foreign birth, and in Greater New York four out of five residents were of foreign birth or foreign parentage. Of the male population of the eighteen largest cities in the country there were two and a half times as many of foreign birth or foreign parentage as there were of the older American stock.

relied on the rural solution of individual well and privy or cesspool: Washington had fifty-six thousand cesspools in the mid-seventies, and Philadelphia even more. Improvement was slow, and large cities of the East and South depended mainly on drainage through open gutters to the end of the century. Pollution of water supplies by sewage as well as by the dumping of industrial waste accounted in large measure for the wretched public-health records and staggering mortality rates of the period. The number of public waterworks multiplied more than fivefold in the eighties, but filtering and purification were slow to be adopted. Throughout the nineties the American city remained poorly prepared to accommodate the hordes that continued to pour in upon it.

The immigrant and the city. The cities grew at the expense of the European as well as the American countryside and village. For the pull of America was felt in Europe more powerfully than ever before, and the great majority of the immigrants crowded into the nation's cities. Like the new native city-dwellers, the immigrants were also country people. In spite of the distance they had come, they were usually no more familiar with city ways and city life than Americans fresh from the farm, and for the immigrants the up-

New York City had half as many Italians as Naples and two and a half times as many Irish as Dublin. The newcomers tended more than the "old" immigrants to huddle together clannishly by nationality. Jacob Riis, a New York journalist and reformer who had emigrated from Denmark in 1870, pictured a map of Manhattan in 1890 colored according to races and nationalities:

> Between the dull gray of the Jew, his favorite color, and the Italian red, would be squeezed in on the map a sharp streak of yellow, marking the narrow boundaries of Chinatown. Dovetailed in with the German population, the poor but thrifty Bohemian might be picked out by the sombre hue of his life. . . . Dots and dashes of color here and there would show where the Finnish sailors worship their *djumala* (God), the Greek pedlars the ancient name of their race, and the Swiss the goddess of thrift.

Less colorfully, Jane Addams described the map of Chicago:

> Between Halsted Street and the river live about ten thousand Italians—Neapolitans, Sicilians, and Calabrians, with an occasional Lombard or Venetian. To the south on Twelfth Street are many Germans, and side streets are given over almost entirely to Polish and Russian Jews. Still farther south, these Jewish colonies merge into a huge Bohemian colony, so vast that Chicago ranks as the third Bohemian city in the world.

Slums and palaces. The city was the way of the future. But there was much about the city of the late nineteenth century to justify the old antiurban prejudice of agrarian America, the prejudice Jefferson voiced when he called the city "a sore on the body politic." To many the city did indeed seem a product of disease rather than a source of social health. The city of that period was the very embodiment of laissez-faire doctrine, for it grew without plan, with a minimum of control, guided mainly by the dictates of industrial enterprise and private greed. Even with an alert and informed citizenry and an honest and efficient municipal government a city would have faced staggering difficulties, and few cities could boast either asset.

The foulest product of the haphazard laissez-faire growth was the city slum, an old evil that took on new life and descended to new depths in 1879 with the invention, in New York City, of the "dumbbell" tenement house, so named for the shape of its floor plan. Designed to get the maximum return for the landlord, the new tenement was no better than a barracks honeycombed with rooms, many of them with no direct

access to light or air. Lacking sanitary facilities, privacy, or health precautions, these tenements rapidly degenerated into human pigsties, vile smelling and vermin infested. According to Jacob Riis, in 1890 there were thirty-seven thousand tenement houses of this type in New York, and more than 1.2 million people lived in them—half the city's population.

William Dean Howells, a realistic novelist, admitted in 1896 that from a distance the tenement might sometimes appear picturesque:

> But to be in it, and not have the distance, is to inhale the stenches of the neglected street, and to catch the yet fouler and dreadfuller poverty-smell which breathes from the open doorways. . . . It is to see the work-worn look of mothers, the squalor of the babes, the haggish ugliness of the old women, the slovenly frowziness of the young girls.

Sources of immigration, 1871–1910

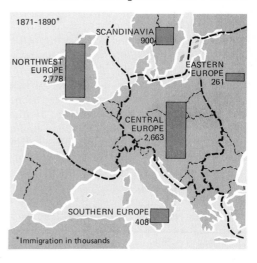

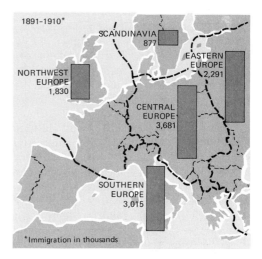

America moves to town

The worst of the tenement slums in New York, which had their counterpart in every urban community in the United States, were known by such names as Bandit's Roost, Misery Row, and Murderer's Alley. Crime and prostitution flourished in these noisome horrors, and organized gangs operated securely within their protection. In years when the homicide rate in England and Germany was less than half that in the United States and when the rate in Europe was declining, the ratio in the United States was increasing, and lawlessness was growing at an alarming pace. Extremes of human misery and degradation had become common sights.

In the eighties and nineties the gulfs between social classes were dramatically emphasized rather than concealed. It was no accident that the economist Thorstein Veblen, in his *Theory of the Leisure Class* (1899), hit on the expression "conspicuous consumption." Displaying habits of consumption that were competitive as well as conspicuous, Chicagoans sported liveried servants and dwelt in lavish palaces built in plain view. The contrast with conspicuous poverty was glaring and unconcealed; squalor and splendor paraded the same streets. The palaces of the wealthy that lined New York's Fifth Avenue were paralleled a few blocks away by the desolation of Shantytown, inhabited by Irish paupers and goats and stretching along the East Side for sixty blocks or more. In the same year in which Jacob Riis published his shocking study of the slums, *How the Other Half Lives* (1890), Ward McAllister published his *Society As I Have Found It* (1890), lovingly recounting the extravagances of New York's Four Hundred, the self-elected social élite. One exploit of this set, a favorite example among protest groups, was the Bradley Martin costume ball, staged in the Waldorf Hotel at a cost of $368,200. It took place on February 10, 1897, when thousands of unemployed roamed the street, and was attended by guests decked in costumes costing as much as $10,000. Scenes of this sort help to explain the violence in the rhetoric of Populism and other protest movements of the nineties.

Howells, in a poem called "Society" (1895), compared the violent social contrasts of his day with "a splendid pageantry of beautiful women and lordly men" playing and dancing upon a magnificent floor that barely covered the crushed and bleeding bodies of the oppressed:

> And now and then from out the dreadful floor
> An arm or brow was lifted from the rest,
> As if to strike in madness, or implore
> For mercy; and anon some suffering breast
> Heaved from the mass and sank; and as before
> The revellers above them thronged and prest.

The awakening of the social conscience

The city was a shock to the American conscience, not merely because of violent contrasts, abuses, and evils, but because the national conscience had taken shape in an agrarian culture and a rural past. So had national values, ideals, morals, folkways, and political

The immigrant in the city

institutions. American country men or European peasants who emigrated were repelled as well as fascinated by the city; they accepted it and rejected it at the same time. Their feelings were torn and their consciences were bruised by the experience.

The challenge of the bosses. Probably the most flagrant offense against public morals in the last quarter of the nineteenth century was the corruption of city government. At least it seemed more conspicuous. The politician bent on corruption could hardly have dreamed of a more promising combination of circumstances. The rapid growth of cities had made necessary the large-scale expansion of public utilities of all sorts—water, gas, transportation, electricity—as well as the construction of public buildings, sewage systems, docks, street and sidewalk pavement. For this work a multitude of valuable contracts, franchises, monopolies, subsidies, and privileges had to be granted. Such prizes were worth the ransom of kings, and there were plenty of predatory operators ready with the price. The corrupt politician was aided in his operations by an antiquated and complex form of municipal government modeled on that of the state. Clumsy city charters saddled the government with inappropriate legislative machinery, weak executive authority, and disorganized courts, making responsibility so difficult to fix that crime went unpunished. State legislatures, by interfering excessively with city affairs, added to the confusion and increased the opportunities for corruption.

Not surprisingly, the cities were excessively burdened with debt. Yet for all their heavy expenditures the cities often received wretched service from the utilities they subsidized and were cynically and repeatedly defrauded by the public servants they elected. "With very few exceptions," wrote Andrew D. White, president of Cornell, "the city governments of the United States are the worst in Christendom—the most expensive, the most inefficient, and the most corrupt." And James Bryce, a generous but well-informed English critic, pronounced city government "the one conspicuous failure of the United States," far more serious, in his opinion, than the shortcomings of state and federal government.

The city machine dominated politics, and the boss dominated the machine. Never has a more colorful set of politicians wielded such power as the great bosses of this period. With a disposition toward large girth, shiny hats, and heavy jewelry, the boss played the role of a freehanded spender, the Robin Hood of the masses. High in the annals of bossdom are the names of "Honest" John Kelley and Richard Croker of New York, Christopher L. Magee and William Finn of Pittsburgh, Ed Butler of St. Louis, "King" James McManes of Philadelphia, and "Czar" Martin Lomasney of Boston. Revenue flowed into their coffers from office-seekers, contractors, public utilities, railroads, prostitutes, gamblers—anybody who happened to need protection or favors. Even pushcart-peddlers and garbage-collectors paid tribute to New York's Tammany. Boss McManes, as head of Philadelphia's gas trust, had 5,630 public jobs at his disposal; he died leaving an estate of more than $2 million.

The city boss and his lieutenants in the wards and precincts found their most reliable supporters among the immigrants. These new voters certainly had no monopoly on ignorance and apathy, and many

The awakening of the social conscience

of them were intelligent and useful citizens. But they were usually unaccustomed to the ballot, unpracticed in the ways of democracy, and bewildered by city life in a strange land. Moreover, the great majority of them were unskilled laborers who lived close to the margin of existence and were often in need of a job and a friend. The boss dealt primarily in jobs and votes. He had sprung from the immigrant community himself, shared its sense of solidarity, knew its members by name, and remained one of them. He was in fact the natural leader of the immigrants, and they responded to him with group loyalty and devotion. They knew him as a man who "got things done," a man to whom they could always take their troubles. The boss made it his business to know their needs and to give them tangible evidence of his interest in them. His favors took the form of getting them jobs, intervening with the law in their behalf, bailing them out of jail, paying burial money, distributing free coal, and handing out Christmas baskets. In short, he performed services for which there was as yet no public agency and which no one else was ready to perform.

Irish politicians were especially adept at these arts, and it was a prevailing conviction that, as one writer put it, "The function of the Irishman is to administer the affairs of the American city." A glance at the names heading the roster of bosses supports this conviction. One of them put his political theory in these words: "I think that there's got to be in every ward a guy that any bloke can go to when he's in trouble and get help—not justice and the law, but help, no matter what he's done." Theodore Roosevelt, who studied the matter, concluded that urban reformers would have to create social agencies to fulfill the role the boss played before they could replace him.

As the reformers found out for themselves, after a little experience, many "good" people supported the bosses and machines—educated, respectable, middle-class people who had been natives for at least three generations. Some of these "good" people were businessmen who were quite willing to cooperate with the machine to secure the favors, privileges, and exemptions they desired. Other respectable citizens voted regularly, if regretfully, for the machine because of their sincere devotion to the national party with which the machine was identified and their desire for a party victory. In short, city machine and city boss were buttressed by some of the strongest as well as by some of the weakest elements of the population. Anyone who undertook to change the system would need to be very powerful indeed.

Humanitarians and reformers. The conscience of the middle class was eventually stirred to indignation and action by the misery and degradation of the city. But first the middle class had to discover what poverty was. Early humanitarians and reformers did not understand the poor—the "depraved classes," as they called them. Attributing their plight to moral shortcomings, they sent agents of the Charity Organizations Society to discover which of the poor were "deserving." But it was the young social workers, nearly all of them women, patiently investigating and visiting the sweatshops and tenement firetraps, who began to establish contact between the middle class and the working class.

Inspired by English social-reform literature and a visit to Toynbee Hall in the slums of London, Jane Addams, the most famous American woman of her time, took up the settlement-house idea and established Hull House on Halsted Street in Chicago in 1889. She wished, she said, "to share the lives of the poor" and to make social service "express the spirit of Christ." One such house had already been established in New York in 1886, and in the next ten years some fifty or more were founded in Northern and Eastern cities. They offered a variety of services, maintained playgrounds, nurseries, club rooms, libraries, and kindergartens, and conducted classes in various subjects. But perhaps of more significance was the education they provided for the young middle-class social workers who came to live in the slums to gain firsthand knowledge of the workers' problems. Within a few years the settlement houses had become the spawning ground of women reformers. Among them were Lillian Wald, founder of the Henry Street Settlement in New York, Florence Kelley, leading spirit in the National Consumers League, and Frances Perkins, with a great future as a Progressive leader.

On the political front the battle for municipal reform began under leaders recruited from the solid and substantial middle class. These included Seth Low and George William Curtis in New York, Edwin U. Curtis and Thomas W. Higginson in Boston, Lyman J. Gage in Chicago, and Joseph W. Folk in St. Louis. Good-government clubs, committees, commissions, and reform organizations for municipal improvement proliferated rapidly in the eighties. Every city of any size had one such organization, and the larger cities had several. One of the most prominent was the National Civil Service Reform League, founded in 1881, which published the magazine *Good Government* to promote its prime object, the merit system for city employees. In the early stages these organizations wasted a good deal of time in mass meetings that drafted wordy resolutions and accomplished nothing except to make the reformers look ineffectual if not ridiculous. Cynics called the good-government people the "goo-goos." They stirred up a good bit of excitement on occasion, but for a long time they seemed to be getting nowhere.

The National Municipal League was launched on a wave of public interest in 1894, and within two years more than two hundred branch leagues were founded. The league put forward as its program a model city charter that embodied such advanced reforms as the short ballot, greater freedom from state interference, limited franchise for utilities, separate city and state elections, the merit system, government by experts, and, above all, more authority for the mayor. In 1880 only one of the nation's twenty-three principal cities was dominated by the mayor, but by 1900 there were twelve. In 1894 the embattled hosts of reform in New York overthrew Boss Richard Croker and elected William L. Strong mayor, though Tammany returned to power after a brief period. Reformers in Chicago, Boston, and St. Louis also scored significant victories over their machines in the next few years.

All these were mere structural reforms, however, and their inadequacy was pointed up by the program of social reforms carried out by Mayor Hazen Pingree of Detroit and Mayor Samuel M. "Golden Rule" Jones of Toledo. Their social reforms provided laws protecting working-class interests and included unemployment relief, the eight-hour day, and a minimum wage. Reforms of this type, overlooked by the good-government reformers, attracted popular support that structural reforms often lacked.

The rights of women. Women reformers responded to the social problems of the city, as we have seen, but another of their preoccupations was the plight of their own sex in a male-dominated society. Their bill of grievances, well documented and long-standing, included political disfranchisement, legal discrimination, economic exploitation, cultural and educational deprivation, and domestic drudgery. If blacks had their "place," women had their "sphere," and to many women its limitations seemed increasingly oppressive. Woman's sphere was The Home, and beyond its walls she ventured, save on religious missions, only at the risk of breaching "the cult of true

Students at Newcomb College, ca. 1900

451

womanhood"—piety, purity, submissiveness, and domesticity. For a growing number of middle-class women technology—gas lighting, domestic plumbing, manufactured ice, and improved furnaces, stoves, washtubs, and sewing machines—provided some escape from the domestic treadmill. For others cheap domestic servants from the immigrant ships furnished release. New women's colleges and older men's colleges turned coeducational were graduating larger numbers of women—2,500 a year by 1890. But they were educated to fill places that, save for underpaid teaching, did not yet exist. Like their sisters who were venturing out of the "sphere," they found themselves in a society that had no use for them.

Turning to organization to battle their frustrations, women established hundreds of clubs, most of them devoted to "self-culture." Founded in 1882, the Association of Collegial Alumnae remained small and exclusive for a long time, limited in 1889 to the graduates of the fourteen colleges that met their rigorous standards. At the opposite extreme of inclusiveness was the sprawling General Federation of Women's Clubs. Organized in 1890, it federated hundreds of clubs, had 150,000 members by 1900, and was soon to top a million. Mainly limited to "self-culture" and entertainment, most members were middle-aged, middle-class, conservative women. The General Federation took pains to avoid antagonizing the cautious rank and file, many of them antisuffragists, and did not endorse woman suffrage until the eve of victory. The leaders of the Federation were usually suffragists, however, and their movement furnished the hard core of feminism. Split into two organizations since the struggle over black suffrage in the 1860s, the rival groups resolved their differences and merged as the National American Woman Suffrage Association in 1890.

A new generation of women leaders had arrived by this time, though veterans like Susan B. Anthony, Elizabeth Cady Stanton, and Lucy Stone were still on the scene. Like them, Anna Howard Shaw met working women as equals, but she was an exception. "The younger women," as historian Eleanor Flexner writes, "were not, for the most part, distinguished by the breadth of their social views." This was true of Carrie Chapman Catt, May Wright Sewall, Rachel Foster Avery, and Harriet Taylor Upton. They reflected the drift of their times toward conservative views on labor and race relations and were more concerned with decorum in pressing their cause. Rejecting their radical origins, the new feminists also turned away from the disturbing and fundamental questions that their contemporary, Charlotte Perkins Gilman, asked in her book *Woman and Economics* (1898). Instead they narrowed their objectives to suffrage, submerged all women's rights in the political struggle, and as a consequence came to exaggerate the value of the ballot as the sovereign remedy for women's ills.

By 1890 seventeen states and territories had given women limited suffrage in school elections, but not until that year did Wyoming enter the Union as the first state with full suffrage for women. Three more underpopulated Western states followed suit, Colorado in 1893 and Utah and Idaho in 1896, but not for fourteen years did another state adopt woman suffrage. Congress gave formal hearings to pleas for a federal woman suffrage amendment, but neither house reported the bill favorably after 1893, and the question disappeared from Congress as an issue for twenty years. Women kept up their campaigns for state action, waging hundreds of them, many heroically under adverse conditions. Among their arguments were some that appealed to nativism and racism. The 1893 convention of the Woman Suffrage Association urged suffrage with literacy instead of sex qualifications, since there were "more white women who can read and write than all negro voters; more American women who can read and write than all foreign voters." For all that they continued to be rewarded with defeat after defeat until the First World War.

The conscience of the church.

The church community was eventually to respond both in faith and in works to the human needs and social problems of city and industry. But in 1876, as Henry May has observed, "Protestantism presented a massive, almost unbroken front in its defense of the status quo." Slums, depressions, and unemployment were but necessary steps to progress, and suffering was the lot of man in good, orthodox theology. Religion was a spiritual and individual, not a social, concern, and salvation came through the striving of the individual with sin and conscience, not through social welfare and betterment. The church, middle class in outlook, was dedicated to the early social creed of individualism and laissez faire, and the mightiest preachers of that era expressed these attitudes forcefully and repeatedly. There was no better exponent of laissez faire and social Darwinism than Henry Ward Beecher in his Brooklyn pulpit.

Revivalism and professional revivalists were usually powerful propagators of the old-time religion—orthodox fundamentalism—and had very little or no social awareness. Throughout the eighties and nineties the annual revival was a regular feature of the program of Methodist, Baptist, Presbyterian, Congregational, and smaller churches. The most famous of the professional revivalists was Dwight L. Moody, an impressive figure of two hundred eighty pounds who got his start with a successful campaign in Britain during the seventies. Returning to America in 1875,

The urban society

Mary Baker Eddy:
prophet of a new faith

he set out with Ira D. Sankey, his equally weighty singer, to "evangelize the world in this generation." Moody brought into play all his great executive and publicity talents to attract huge crowds and with forceful and colloquial sermons converted sinners by the thousands in all parts of the United States. His popularity continued unflagging until his death in 1899. Moody and another famous revivalist, T. DeWitt Talmage, along with numerous imitators, set a new record for professional revivalism in America. Whether as a result of their work or the growth of population, Protestant churches grew rapidly in the last two decades of the century, increasing their membership from somewhat over 10 million to almost 18 million.

In spite of this growth, clergymen complained constantly that the working people were drifting away from the church. Moved either by the pulpit's lack of sympathy for their plight or by the elegance of the clothing they saw in the pews, working people found the churches of the older Protestant denominations less suited to their tastes than they once had been. Investigators reported that large working-class districts in the cities were without church facilities of any kind. Some of the poor and the lowly, as they had in the past, sought solace in new sects founded to restore the lost purity or the original doctrine of the old sects. Many of these "holiness" people were recruited from the Methodists, Baptists, and other Protestant churches. Usually originating in the country and then moving to the city, a dozen or more pentecostal and millennial sects sprang up in the eighties and nineties.

A new sect of a different sort was the Church of Christ, Scientist, usually called Christian Scientist, which was chartered by a small group of the followers of Mary Baker Eddy in 1879. The prophet of the new faith was born in 1821 to a New England family of the pious, humble sort to which Joseph Smith, the Mormon prophet (see p. 238), had been born fifteen years earlier. Inspired by the help she received from a faith healer in her own rather complex health problems, she developed the belief that "disease is caused by mind alone." At the end of her long life in 1910, adherents of her church numbered a hundred thousand, her book *Science and Health* (1875) had sold four hundred thousand copies, and her estate was appraised at more than $2½ million.

Addressing its appeal to the downtrodden, the Salvation Army invaded America in 1879 under the command of George Railton and seven women officers. Founded the year before in London by William Booth, it was born of his desire to reach the city poor. Using revivalist methods and brass bands to attract crowds, the uniformed army and its lassies preached repentance to "rumdom, slumdom and bumdom." Within a decade after the invasion they began to supplement repentance sermons with a social-service program and sent "slum brigades" into the tenement districts to bring relief as well as the gospel to the poor.

It would have been impossible for the Catholic Church to ignore the working class and the social problems of the city. Since the "new" immigration was overwhelmingly Catholic, working class, and urban, the American Catholic Church of the late nineteenth century became more than ever the church of the city, the worker, and the immigrant. The number of Catholics in the country increased from over 6 million to more than 10 million in the last two decades of the century. Responsibility for training and adjusting the new Americans to their country compelled the Church to adjust its social policy to urban needs and persuaded James Gibbons, then in Rome to be installed as cardinal, to defend the cause of American labor before the Holy See in 1887. American Catholics found some support for their social policy in the loyalty of their communicants, which contrasted with the defection and alienation of the masses of which European Catholics complained. The papal encyclical *Rerum novarum*, of May 1891, enunciated social ideals and responsibilities for Catholics

The awakening of the social conscience

that gave additional sanction to the social views of the Americans.

In the meantime a small group of Protestant clergymen, at first responding as individuals to the social crises and labor struggles of the seventies, eighties, and nineties, had begun to shape a reinterpretation of their religion that in later years came to be known as the Social Gospel. Turning away from the traditional emphasis on spiritual and moral concerns, the new gospel stressed the social and pragmatic implications of Christian ethics and called for good works in social reform and betterment. The Reverend Josiah Strong's book *Our Country* (1885), which sold half a million copies in twenty years, has been called the *Uncle Tom's Cabin* of the movement. But Washington Gladden, a Congregational minister who wrote *Applied Christianity* (1886), was probably the most influential leader. Next in importance was R. Heber Newton, a liberal New York Episcopalian and an advocate of more sweeping reform. The Episcopal Church, the most aristocratic denomination and yet the one most influenced by the mildly socialistic doctrines then gaining attention in the parent Church of England, took most readily to the new gospel, while the Methodist Church, traditionally the church of the common man, tended to cling to rural individualism and resisted the Social Gospel at first. With a similar following and the additional restraint of such wealthy benefactors as John D. Rockefeller, the Baptists nevertheless moved earlier toward the Social Gospel under the inspiration of Walter Rauschenbusch. By 1895 the influence of the Social Gospel was being felt through-out American Protestantism and in secular thought as well. Its main impact, however, was not to come until the following century.

The spread of learning

Public schools and mass media. The national determination to educate everybody was best reflected in the growth of public schools, which increased at an unprecedented speed after 1870. Free education for all became a foremost article in the American faith, and the schools were unfairly expected to solve all of democracy's problems, from poorly cooked meals to poorly adjusted races. Growing cities expected the schools to take over many functions that parents, police, and priests had once performed and along the way to Americanize the children of the new immigrants. One measure of the hopes and aspirations thus aroused was the rapid expansion of the school system, especially in the cities. In 1870 only $69 million, or an average of about $15 per pupil, was spent on public education, while in the first school year of the new century $250 million, or nearly $23 per pupil, went into the school budget. By 1900 all but two of the states outside the South had compulsory school-attendance laws of some sort, and both the average school attendance and the length of the average school year had increased markedly. There were only one hundred sixty public high schools in the whole country in 1870, but by the end of the century there were more than six thousand. The cities, with a more concentrated school population and better transportation than rural communities, reaped the greatest benefits from the public-school expansion. More and more of them extended public schools to include kindergartens, normal schools, night classes, and adult and vocational education.

Under the sway of new theories of education the public schools gradually put aside the old authoritarian ways of the drillmaster and disciplinarian in the one-room country school. Just as the preceding generation imported the progressive doctrines of Pestalozzi, the new generation brought from Germany the theories of Johann Friedrich Herbart, who believed that education could be made into a science. The Herbartians encouraged the abandonment of corporal punishment and the teaching of "practical" subjects such as manual training.

Private schools still held on, particularly in the Eastern states, and certain ethnic and religious groups resisted being integrated into a uniform public-school system. Unable to win public support for their own educational efforts, the Catholics in 1884 determined upon an elaborate expansion of their parochial schools. The program was mainly designed to educate the immigrants of that faith in the cities, and most of the schools were located in New England and the Middle Atlantic states.

The federal government had made a gesture of assistance to public schools in 1867, when Congress laid the foundation of a bureau of education, but the Blair Bill for federal aid distributed according to the proportion of illiterates in a state was defeated in the 1880s. Since support of the schools was left to local communities, improvement and growth varied widely with the distribution of wealth. In general, the rural districts lagged behind the urban areas and the West and South behind the East. But the South had a staggering burden of special disadvantages. In the first place it had about twice as many children per adult as the North, and it had considerably less than half the per capita taxable wealth with which to educate them. At the century's end the schools of the South were still miserably supported, poorly taught, and wholly inadequate. Efforts to improve them accomplished little until the next decade.

In spite of the physical growth of the educational plant and the millions of dollars poured into public education, the average American adult by the turn of the century had only about five years of schooling. Illiteracy had been reduced, however, from around 17 percent in 1880 to about 11 percent twenty years later. For all the faddism and quackery, in spite of the low-paid teachers and the attempt to saddle them with all the problems of democracy, the public schools continued to increase in number and grow in popular esteem.

The popular faith in education and the craving for its benefits were reflected in other ways as well. One of these was the highly popular Chautauqua movement, which was started in 1874 at Lake Chautauqua, New York, by Methodist laymen as a camp meeting for training Sunday-school teachers. The idea spread over the country as a sort of informal adult-education movement. It retained its pious, middle-class emphasis on temperance and morality and often made use of Methodist camp-meeting grounds. Small-town audiences sweated earnestly through long lectures on science and religion, thrilled to the illustrated travel lectures of John L. Stoddard, or relaxed with James Whitcomb Riley and Swiss bell-ringers. To supplement the summer meetings a home-study circle was formed in 1878, and ten years later a Chautauqua College began to offer correspondence courses and hand out degrees via the postman.

These years also brought a dramatic expansion of public libraries. Librarians laid claim to professional standing in 1876, when they organized the American Library Association. State and local tax money was tapped, and private donors began to put large amounts into library-building: Andrew Carnegie, the most munificent of them, launched his library benefactions at Pittsburgh in 1881. In the 1890s six library buildings costing more than a million dollars had been either started or completed. The most splendid were the Boston Public Library and the New York Public Library, both opened in 1895, and the Library of Congress, the largest and most costly in the world, opened in 1897. By 1900 there were more than nine thousand public libraries in the country, with a total of more than 45 million volumes.

The repetitive theme of "more and more and more" that drums through all phases of American life in the eighties and nineties (along with *more* unemployment and *more* depression) was nowhere so striking as in journalism, especially in periodicals. In the last fifteen years of the century the number of periodicals published increased by twenty-two hundred, most of them devoted to trades and special interests. More striking was the increase in the number and circulation of periodicals for the general reader. There were only four such monthly magazines in the country in 1885 with circulations of a hundred thousand or more, and they were usually priced at 35 cents a copy. Twenty years later there were twenty such magazines with an aggregate circulation of more than 5½ million, and all but four of them sold at 10 to 15 cents a copy. The 10-cent monthlies created a vast new reading public. More than price was involved in the expansion, however. The older journals, such as

The spread of learning

the *Century*, the *Atlantic*, and the *North American Review*, were sedate, leisurely, rather aloof, and upper class in appeal and sympathy. The new 10-cent competitors, such as *Munsey's*, *McClure's*, and the *Cosmopolitan*, were lighter in tone, with shorter articles and many illustrations. News-mindedness was an innovation of *Public Opinion* (1886), *Current Literature* (1888), and the *Literary Digest* (1890), and reform-mindedness was the theme of the *Forum* (1886) and *Arena* (1889), as well as the older *Nation* (1865) and *Independent* (1848).

Growing cities, increasing literacy, and expanding population combined to create greater and greater markets for newspapers and to heighten the temptation to vulgarize the product in order to exploit the potential market. The number of daily papers, largely confined to the cities, more than doubled, and the number of weekly and semiweekly papers increased more than 50 percent between 1880 and 1900, while subscribers increased even more rapidly. The growth of daily newspapers came as follows:

Year	Number of Dailies	Total Daily Circulation
1860	387	1,478,000
1870	574	2,602,000
1880	971	3,566,000
1890	1,610	8,387,000
1900	2,226	15,102,000

By the end of the century the United States had more than half the newspapers in the world. Two potent influences were at work to change the character of American newspapers: one was advertising, which surpassed sales as a source of revenue in the nineties, and the other was the mass audience. To reach the masses the news columns became more sensational and vulgar. The father of the new school of journalists was Joseph Pulitzer, who bought the New York *World* in 1883 and ran its circulation up from fifteen thousand in 1883 to over a million by 1898. The assault on privacy and taste was continued and intensified by his imitator, William Randolph Hearst of the New York *Journal*.

The higher learning. For all the crassness and materialism that earned for it the name of "Gilded Age," the period could boast of substantial advances in higher education and scholarship. There was obviously much room for improvement. American colleges of 1870, even the better ones, were likely to be strongly sectarian, provincial, and undistinguished. The typical college professor of that year was harshly, but not very unfairly, described as "a nondescript, a

jack of all trades, equally ready to teach surveying and Latin eloquence." The traditional curriculum, designed for the training of ministers, did not permit specialization or allow time for research. Library and laboratory facilities were inadequate, and the natural sciences were neglected. There were no graduate schools and no professional schools to speak of beyond theological seminaries. Collegiate pedagogy, like the Victorian family, was heavily authoritarian, with emphasis upon rules, discipline, rote learning, and recitations.

With Harvard in the vanguard and with Charles W. Eliot at its head, a small group of academicians undertook to reform the old collegiate order. The reforms they made were not universally acknowledged to be improvements in their day, nor are they yet, but they were widely if slowly imitated. One of them was the elective system, which resulted in a proliferation of courses and subjects from which the student chose according to his fancy. Additional reforms, such as an increase in the number of science courses and in the use of the laboratory method of instruction, were taken up rapidly, as were discussion periods as substitutes for rote recitation. Among other changes slowly adopted were the decline of authoritarian norms and traditional curricula and a decrease in the proportion of clergymen on boards of trustees and in presidents' offices.

Accompanying these changes and reflecting the shift to a secular and scientific emphasis was an increase in German influence in academic circles. During the nineteenth century more than nine thousand Americans studied at German universities, all but about two hundred of them after 1850. In the 1880s some two thousand Americans were studying in Germany. The Johns Hopkins University, opened in Baltimore in 1876 with an inaugural address by Thomas Huxley, the Darwinian, was an expression of both English and German influence. Nearly all the faculty of the new university had studied in Germany, and the policies pursued by President Daniel Coit Gilman expressed many of the academic ideals of that country's universities. Among these were a stress on research and graduate study and a shift from the attitude that professors and students were mere conservers of learning to the attitude that they were searchers and advancers of knowledge. The new emphasis implied an increase in the scholar's stature, freedom, and prestige. Inspired more or less by the example of Johns Hopkins, fifteen major graduate schools or departments had been established by the end of the century.

Nearly three thousand students registered in American graduate schools in 1890, as compared with a mere handful two decades before. As quick as their fellow countrymen to organize themselves in national

The urban society

associations, the professional scholars founded scores of learned societies in the seventies and eighties: the Archaeological Institute of America (1879), the Modern Language Association (1883), and in the next ten years the American Historical Association, the American Economic Association, the American Mathematical Society, the American Physical Society, and the American Psychological Association, to mention only a few. Learned journals and books equal to Europe's best began to appear in America, and American-trained scholars began to acquire international reputations.

Medical and legal education was still primitive in the seventies and eighties. None of the schools of medicine or law required a college degree for admission, and the typical medical school turned its graduates loose on a helpless public after only a few months of haphazard lectures. Both medical and legal degrees could easily be bought. Between 1876 and 1900 eighty-six new medical schools were founded, but the Johns Hopkins Medical School, opened in 1894, was the first to require a college degree for admission and the first to have a full-time teaching staff. By the end of the century many states had established boards of medical examiners that tightened license requirements, and the schools themselves began to raise their standards in response. Comparable improvement in law schools was to come only later.

This was an era prolific in the birth of new institutions of higher learning, both public and private. In the last two decades of the nineteenth century the total number of colleges and universities in the country increased by nearly one hundred fifty, though many of them had no valid claim to academic status and were often short lived. Ten new state universities, all of them coeducational from the start, were founded between 1882 and 1895. In the East, where coeducation was slower to win acceptance, Vassar was opened in 1861, Smith in 1871, and Bryn Mawr in 1885, while several of the older men's colleges opened affiliated women's colleges nearby. Numerous land-grant colleges, taking advantage of the Morrill Act of 1862, sprang up to teach both agricultural and mechanical arts. A fraction of the new industrial and commercial fortunes of the age went into the founding of universities bearing the names of Cornell (1868), Vanderbilt (1873), Hopkins (1876), Tulane (1884), Stanford (1885), and Clark (1887). The University of Chicago (1891) was one of the few that did not take the name of its benefactor, in this case John D. Rockefeller.

The history of higher learning of this period was not, however, purely a story of expansion and improvement. A mistaken conception of democracy led to the assumption of equality among all academic pursuits and justified the teaching of courses in al-most any subject, however trivial. Charlatans were often commissioned to teach such courses, and almost anyone could take them. Institutions became over-expanded, overcrowded, and absurdly bureaucratized. A misguided deference to the opinions of alumni, sports enthusiasts, and the unlettered public generally led to an anarchical confusion of values and grotesque distortions of academic purpose. For the first time in recorded history institutions of higher learning assumed the function of providing mass entertainment in spectator sports, and the comparative distinction of a university came to depend on its success in pursuing these commercial enterprises.

The businessmen who replaced the clergymen on the college boards of trustees were slow to acknowledge the status claimed by the new scholar and were sometimes quite unable to distinguish between their relation to faculty members and their relation to "other employees." The trustees of seven well-known universities approved a statement published in the Chicago *Tribune* in 1899 to the effect that college professors "should promptly and gracefully submit to the determination of the trustees" in deciding what should be taught, and that "if the trustees err it is for the patrons and proprietors, not for the employees, to change either the policy or the personnel of the board." During the 1890s nine prominent faculty members were dismissed for presuming to express their opinions on such subjects as labor, railroads, and currency. Though there was no legitimate excuse for the gaucheries that for a time made American colleges a laughingstock of informed world opinion, we must remember that America was trying to spread the benefits of learning far more widely (and as a result more thinly) than had ever been attempted before.

Arts, letters, and critics

Artists and their work. In matters of taste the Gilded Age has acquired and in part deserved a deplorable reputation. Whether it was because the molders of fashion were insecure in the social position or new to their wealth or for some other reason, their taste ran to excesses in all things—in their clothing, their jewelry, and their houses, in interior décor and exterior ornament. They overloaded their rooms with bric-a-brac, their dresses with bustles, and their houses with gingerbread. They had no trouble finding architects, painters, and sculptors of the sort that would cater to their preferences, but the work these people left behind need not detain us.

Beneath the crass surface and behind the clutter of imitative art, however, there were genuinely origi-

457

nal and creative spirits at work in the land. Artists, engineers, architects, sculptors, and painters honestly faced the realities of the new urban, industrial society and contrived original and powerful answers to its problems. It was the new city that gave them both their challenge and their opportunity. The bold spirit with which they met the challenge and seized the opportunity is caught in a statement by a Georgia-bred architect, John Wellborn Root, who did his work in Chicago:

> In America we are free of artistic traditions. Our freedom begets license, it is true. We do shocking things; we produce works of architecture irremediably bad; we try crude experiments that result in disaster. Yet somewhere in this mass of ungoverned energies lies the principle of life. A new spirit of beauty is being developed and perfected, and even now its first achievements are beginning to delight us. This is not the old thing made over; it is new. It springs out of the past, but it is not tied to it; it studies the traditions, but is not enslaved by them.

One achievement of the age that was daring and magnificent enough to meet Root's description was the Brooklyn Bridge, a suspension such as had never before been built, with granite towers 276 feet high and with a central span of 1,600 feet. Sketched by John A. Roebling, who died before construction began, the great bridge was completed by his son Washington A. Roebling in 1883. A product of the new industrialism down to the last of the nineteen strands of steel cable and the last riveted girder, the bridge soared out of the soot and slums of Manhattan, monumental proof that the new society could produce a thing of beauty out of its materials. In the same city a landscape architect named Frederick L. Olmsted demonstrated that it was not necessary for a city to be the seat of an absolute monarch in order to create in its very center spacious, lovely, and exquisitely designed parks, such as Central Park, Olmsted's masterpiece. It was not his only great park, however, for he designed many more and left scarcely a major city in the country untouched by his influence.

The architect whom Root singled out to illustrate the new spirit in American art was Henry Hobson Richardson. Born in New Orleans but educated at Harvard and abroad, Richardson was a man of gargantuan ambitions and appetites, full of zest for any problem and equally ready to design churches, railroad stations, department stores, libraries, office buildings, anything. "The things I want most to design," he said, "are a grain elevator and the interior of a great river steamboat." His massive granite structures created a style and defined an architectural era. Although he died in 1886 at the age of forty-eight, he left his buildings scattered across the country from

Brooklyn Bridge:
symbol of the new industrialism

Amid the immense number and variety of living forms, he [Louis Sullivan] noted that invariably the form expressed the function, as, for instance, the oak tree expressed the function oak, the pine tree the function pine, and so on through the amazing series. And, inquiring more deeply, he discovered that in truth it was not simply a matter of form expressing function, but the vital idea was this: That the function created or organized its form. Discernment of this idea threw a vast light upon all things within the universe, and condensed with astounding impressiveness upon mankind, upon all civilizations, all institutions, every form and aspect of society, every mass-thought and mass-result, every individual thought and individual result.... The application of the idea to the Architectural art was manifest enough, namely, that the function of a building must predetermine and organize its form.

From Louis H. Sullivan, *The Autobiography of an Idea*, 1924.

It became evident that the very tall masonry office building was in its nature economically unfit as ground values steadily rose. Not only did its thick walls entail loss of space and therefore revenue, but its unavoidably small window openings could not furnish the proper and desirable ratio of glass area to rentable floor area.

Thus arose a crisis, a seeming impasse. *What was to do?... The need was there, the capacity to satisfy was there, but contact was not there. Then came the flash of imagination which saw the single thing. The trick was turned; and there swiftly came into being something new under the sun. For the true steel-frame structure stands unique in the flowing of man and his works; a brilliant material example of man's capacity to satisfy his needs through the exercise of his natural powers....*

The social significance of the tall building is in finality its most important phase. In and by itself, considered solus *so to speak, the lofty steel frame makes a powerful appeal to the architectural imagination where there is any. Where imagination is absent and its place usurped by timid pedantry the case is hopeless. The appeal and the inspiration lie, of course, in the element of loftiness, in the suggestion of slenderness and aspiration, the soaring quality as of a thing rising from the earth as a unitary utterance.*

From Louis H. Sullivan, *The Autobiography of an Idea*, 1924.

Trinity Church in Boston to a monument on the Wyoming plains.

The problem of the skyscraper, called into being by the fantastic extravagance of unplanned city growth and overcrowding, could not be solved by masonry. What was required was a steel skeleton for support and walls reduced to mere fireproof curtains instead of supporting buttresses. With contributions from engineers and steelmasters as well as architects, Chicagoans achieved a solution in the Tacoma Building in 1888. With the arrival of the electric elevator and vertical transportation, the age of the skyscraper begins, and with that age the name of Louis Sullivan is intimately associated. Ranking with Richardson as one of the giants of the period, Sullivan was a capri-cious genius who commanded the respect of the ablest critics: Frank Lloyd Wright referred to him as *Der Meister.* Sullivan had been called the "father of the skyscraper," and yet he revealed the inner conflicts of his generation's adjustment to the city when he characterized the structure as "profoundly antisocial."

It is curious that Chicago, which contributed so many new and original architectural techniques, should also have been the host and creator of the White City at the Columbian Exposition of 1893, which represented a return to Renaissance classicism and eclecticism in the extreme. Although Daniel H. Burnham of Chicago supervised the building, the White City was mainly the work of Easterners, partic-

ularly the firm of Charles F. McKim, William R.
Mead, and Stanford White. The architects were assisted by the most famous American sculptor of the
period, Augustus Saint-Gaudens, and by Olmsted,
whose landscaping included the lovely lagoon surrounded by gleaming white-plaster buildings. The
ephemeral dream city was undoubtedly an impressive
spectacle, but Sullivan, who designed the only non-
classical structure in the Exposition, regarded it as "an
appalling calamity" whose influence would "last for
half a century." What he feared was a reversion to the
academic, classical models of architecture; in the
"Federal" style sponsored by McKim, Mead, and
White in the national capital and elsewhere in the
ensuing era, Sullivan's fears were justified. On the
other hand the example of a city intelligently planned
for comfort and beauty stimulated the "city beautiful" movement, and under Burnham's guidance
Washington, Cleveland, San Francisco, and Manila
made impressive achievements in the art of city-plan-
ning.

Some of the fine arts in what Lewis Mumford has
called the "Brown Decades" were creditably served by
American artists. John La Farge, a gifted interior-deco-
rator and art critic, executed thousands of stained-
glass windows and won the admiration of Richardson,
for whom he did the windows of Trinity Church in
Boston. Winslow Homer, a serious illustrator, occasionally struck the note of greatness in his paintings of
the weather-beaten ruggedness of common life. But to
find American painters who deserve to rank with the
best of their European contemporaries one must turn
to Thomas Eakins and Albert Pinkham Ryder. Eakins
worked in relative obscurity outside fashionable currents and left a house full of unsold paintings at his
death. A friend of Walt Whitman, whose portrait he
painted, he had a salty contempt for pretense and

loved to paint boxers, oarsmen, and surgeons at their
work. Ryder was a painter of the sea and the night
and has been compared with Melville in the symbolic
and lyrical qualities of his art. Among his great symbolic paintings are *Death on a Pale Horse, The Flying
Dutchman, Jonah,* and *Macbeth and the Witches*—
all eerie, mystic, and tragic.

Beginnings of realism. In letters as in arts the
post-Civil War decades have had a poor reputation.
Their writers have been tagged with the "genteel" label
and condemned for complacency and blindness to the
glaring faults of their society. Their reputation for
shallowness, complacency, and prudery is not wholly
unjustified, but the age was often as blind to its literary merits as to its social faults. It sometimes overlooked and sometimes misunderstood its best talent.
Contemporaries of Emily Dickinson, the greatest
American poet of the age, and one of the subtlest,
never even heard of her, for she lived the life of a
recluse and published only two poems before her
death in 1886. They mistook Mark Twain, their greatest satirist, for a funny man and a writer for boys.
They were misled by the surface mildness of William
Dean Howells, their major critic and their leading
realist, and they misunderstood (when they did not
neglect) Henry James, their greatest artist. But any age
that could produce Dickinson, Twain, Howells, and
James should command respect and serious attention.

More completely and richly than any other
writer, Mark Twain, who was christened Samuel
Langhorne Clemens, embodied in his life and writings
the sprawling diversity, the epic adventures, the inner
tensions, and the cross-purposes of post-Civil War
America. A Southerner by birth and heritage, he became a Westerner while the West was wildest and
settled in New England to live out his life. He was a

James Bryce: America with a past

child of the frontier and, like his America, a country man who moved to the city, a provincial who was thrust into a strange new world. His literary record of the experience documents a whole epoch. "I am persuaded," the playwright George Bernard Shaw wrote Mark Twain, "that the future historian of America will find your works as indispensable to him as a French historian finds the political tracts of Voltaire."

Mark Twain's American odyssey started in Missouri on the banks of the Mississippi, where the East bordered on the West and the South overlapped the North. He joined the Confederate army when the war broke out, but, after a trivial accident that involved no fighting, he gave up the war and joined his brother in the Far West. He recorded his adventures in the Nevada mining camps in *Roughing It* (1872) and gave the period a name that has stuck in *The Gilded Age* (1873), a broad political and social satire. His boyhood and his later experience as a pilot on the great river found expression in two of his works, *The Adventures of Tom Sawyer* (1876) and *Life on the Mississippi* (1883). But he surpassed all his other work in *The Adventures of Huckleberry Finn* (1884), the finest expression of the age in fiction and a masterpiece of American literature. A composite of satire and nostalgia, it dips deeper into irony than was characteristic of the age, for it aligns the sympathies of every decent reader with Huck, the river rat, against civilization itself and fixes the primitive, superstitious Nigger Jim as one of the noblest figures in American fiction. Mark Twain wrote a great deal more, but like the miners of his Nevada adventure and America itself, he was a spendthrift with his resources and could not always tell the stuff that glittered from real gold.

Howells, the friend of Twain and the generous friend of every creative spirit in letters of his time,

was even more prolific. He wrote thirty full-length novels and five volumes of short stories, not to mention an endless stream of literary criticism. In his time he was rightfully called the dean of American letters and the foremost exponent of American realism. Rejected by a later generation that unfairly associated him with complacency and materialism, Howells deserves better from the present perspective. In mid-life he reached a turning point marked by his reaction to the Haymarket executions in 1886, against which he conducted virtually a one-man protest among the intellectuals. The experience coincided with his reading of Tolstoy and Henry George, and he began calling himself a socialist and demanding a sterner realism that would confront the injustice and suffering of industrial society under plutocratic control. His fiction began at once to reflect his views. *Annie Kilburn* (1889) is an indictment of social injustice and the inadequacies of charity in a New England community, and *A Hazard of New Fortunes* (1890), the best expression of Howells' new phase and the climactic work of American realism, centers around a violent strike. *A Traveler from Altruria* (1894) is a utopian novel that exposes and attacks social injustice.

Henry James continued to develop as a writer after Howells and Twain began to decline. His wonderfully productive life carried over into the twentieth century, though the bulk of his work appeared before 1900. Unlike Howells and Twain, he was not interested in the common man. His typical subjects are Americans and Europeans of cultivated minds, usually in a cosmopolitan setting. *The American* (1877), *The Europeans* (1878), and *Daisy Miller* (1879) are treatments of national attitudes in transatlantic society. This was only the beginning of four decades of writing that included such masterpieces as *The Portrait of a Lady* (1881), *The Ambassadors*

461

Arts, letters, and critics

(1903), and *The Golden Bowl* (1904). Henry James was the most completely dedicated and probably the most wholly fulfilled American writer and artist of his time.

The age affords posterity one unflattering but fascinating portrait of itself drawn by a philosopher-historian who stands in a class by himself: Henry Adams, descendant of the two Presidents whose name he bore. All serious students of the period must make their own acquaintance and their own peace with this querulous and opinionated critic. His main writing dealt with the history of another period, that of Jefferson and Madison. But his novels *Democracy* (1880) and *Esther* (1883) and more particularly his autobiographical *Education of Henry Adams* (1918) and *The Degradation of the Democratic Dogma* (1919) are the keys to his incisive critique. It was characteristic of him that he had the first two books published anonymously and the last two posthumously. Having mastered those, one is then better prepared to find Adams, in *Mont-Saint-Michel and Chartres* (1913), searching the monuments of the Middle Ages for their meaning to modern America, and projecting lines of change from the year 1200 to the year 1900.

After the end of the century and near the end of his life, Henry Adams looked back philosophically over the American experience since the Civil War. He was astonished at how much history had been telescoped into that brief span of years and how frightfully the pace of change had accelerated. At the outset of the period, in his youth, his fellow citizens were still grappling with stone-age men on the Great Plains and debating the issue of African slavery in their midst. America had been a land of villages and farms, a provincial outpost of Western civilization. But now, as he steamed into New York Harbor in 1902, remembering his return from Europe in 1868, he searched in vain for landmarks of the earlier era. "The outline of the city became frantic in its effort to explain something that defied meaning," he observed. Titanic, uncontrollable forces "had exploded, and thrown great masses of stone and steam against the sky. . . . A Traveller in the highways of history looked out of the club window on the turmoil of Fifth Avenue, and felt himself in Rome, under Diocletian. . . . The two-thousand-years failure of Christianity roared upward from Broadway, and no Constantine the Great was in sight." Henry Adams' fellow Americans, less troubled by historical perspective and premonitions of things to come, called the spectacle "progress" and greeted the dawn of the twentieth century with a confidence that was apparently unbounded.

Suggestions for reading

C. M. Green, *The Rise of Urban America** (1965), is a short history, and Blake McKelvey, *The Urbanization of America, 1860–1915* (1963), and C. N. Glaab and A. T. Brown, *A History of Urban America** (1967), are general studies. A. M. Schlesinger, *The Rise of the City, 1878–1898** (1933), furnishes an introduction to the social history of urban America in this period. A. F. Weber, *The Growth of Cities in the Nineteenth Century** (1899), compares statistics of city growth in Europe and America. Lewis Mumford, *The Culture of Cities** (1938), *The City in History** (1961), and several other studies, transcends national history to study the phenomenon theoretically. Several cities are examined as types by C. M. Green, *American Cities in the Building of the Nation** (1956); and the extension of cities in S. B. Warner, *Streetcar Suburbs* (1962).

Contemporary sources on urban slums and poverty include Jacob Riis, *How the Other Half Lives** (1890), *The Children of the Poor* (1892), and *The Battle with the Slum* (1902); see also Josiah Strong, *The Twentieth Century City* (1898), as well as Jane Addams, *Twenty Years at Hull House** (1910). A good history of American attitudes toward poverty is R. H. Bremner, *From the Depths: The Discovery of Poverty in the United States** (1956). A sensitive analysis of immigration is Oscar Handlin, *The Uprooted** (1951). Another is Philip Taylor, *The Distant Magnet: European Emigration to the U.S.A** (1971). On the new immigrants see particularly I. A. Hourwich, *Immigration and Labor* (1922); on their reception in the United States consult Barbara Solomon, *Ancestors and Immigrants** (1956), and John Higham, *Strangers in the Land** (1955) and *Send These to Me: Jews and Other Immigrants in Urban America* (1975). M. A. Jones, *American Immigration** (1960), is an expert synthesis.

On the boss, the machine, and the reformer a contemporary account, James Bryce, *The American Commonwealth,* 2 vols* (1888), is a classic. For reformers of the period, see J. G. Sproat, *The Best Men: Liberal Reformers in the Gilded Age** (1968). A muckraker who deals with this period informatively is Lincoln Steffens, *The Shame of the Cities** (1904). Later studies of value are F. J. Goodnow,

*Available in a paperback edition.

Municipal Problems (1907), C. W. Patton, *The Battle for Municipal Reform: Mobilization and Attack, 1875–1900* (1940), and A. B. Callow, Jr., *The Tweed Ring** (1966).

On women's rights and the suffrage movement see W. L. O'Neill, *Everyone Was Brave: The Rise and Fall of Feminism in America** (1969), Eleanor Flexner, *Century of Struggle: The Woman's Rights Movement in the United States** (1959), and A. S. Kraditor, *The Ideas of the Woman Suffrage Movement, 1890–1920**(1965).

A general history is Sidney Ahlstrom, *A Religious History of the American People** (1972). The reaction of the Protestant churches to social problems is discussed in several books, notably H. F. May, *Protestant Churches and Industrial America** (1949); A. I. Abell, *The Urban Impact on American Protestantism, 1865–1900* (1942); and C. H. Hopkins, *The Rise of the Social Gospel in American Protestantism, 1865–1915** (1940). On evangelists, see B. A. Weisberger, *They Gathered at the River: The Story of the Great Revivalists and Their Impact upon Religion in America** (1958), and J. F. Findlay, Jr., *Dwight L. Moody: American Evangelist, 1837–1899* (1969). On the Catholics there is a fine brief account in J. T. Ellis, *American Catholicism** (1956), and a longer study in Theodore Maynard, *The Story of American Catholicism** (1941). Allan Johnson's long sketch of Mary Baker Eddy in the *Dictionary of American Biography* is helpful on the origins of Christian Science. W. W. Sweet, *Revivalism in America: Its Origins, Growth and Decline** (1944), is a useful survey.

The history of higher learning has been surveyed by Frederick Rudolph, *The American College and University, A History** (1962), elaborated upon by L. R. Veysey, *The Emergence of the American University** (1965), and much illuminated by Richard Hofstadter and Walter Metzger, *The Development of Academic Freedom in the United States* (1955). For a stiff and amusing indictment see Thorstein Veblen, *Higher Learning in America** (1918). Merle Curti, *Social Ideas of American Educators** (1935), is instructive, as is H. K. Beale, *Are American Teachers Free?* (1936). R. H. Shryock, "The Academic Profession in the United States," *Bulletin of the American Association of University Professors* (Spring 1952), is most important.

The history of public education receives vigorous and needed reinterpretation in L. A. Cremin, *The Transformation of the School: Progressivism in American Education, 1876–1957** (1961). A. E. Meyer, *An Educational History of the American People* (1957), is a useful reference work. On the South see C. W. Dabney, *Universal Education in the South,* 2 vols. (1936). R. O. and Victoria Case, *We Called It Culture: The Story of Chautauqua* (1958), is the best account of that movement. F. L. Mott, *A History of American Magazines, 1885–1905* (1957), is an exhaustive and excellent history. The newspapers are treated in W. G. Bleyer, *Main Currents in the History of American Journalism* (1927).

On the graphic arts there are several studies of value, notably Lewis Mumford, *The Brown Decades: A Study of the Arts in America, 1865–1895** (1931); John Kouwenhoven, *Made in America: The Arts in Modern Civilization** (1948); and O. W. Larkin, *Art and Life in America* (1949, rev. ed., 1960). On architecture, see Wayne Andrews, *Architecture, Ambition and Americans** (1955), and on the growth of cities, Christopher Tunnard and H. H. Reed, *American Skyline** (1955).

Literary history in this era is treated by Larzer Ziff, *The American 1890s: Life and Times of a Lost Generation** (1966); Jay Martin, *Harvests of Change: American Literature, 1865–1914** (1967); Everett Carter, *Howells and the Age of Realism* (1954), who discusses Howells' contemporaries as well; and Kermit Vanderbilt, *The Achievement of William Dean Howells: A Reinterpretation* (1968). E. H. Cady, *The Realist at War* (1958); K. S. Lynn, *William Dean Howells* (1971); and V. W. Brooks, *New England: Indian Summer, 1865–1915** (1940) and *The Confident Years, 1885–1915* (1952), are full of biographical incident. Alfred Kazin, *On Native Grounds** (1942), starts his account at 1890 but has two illuminating chapters on that decade. Some good biographies are Justin Kaplan, *Mr. Clemens and Mark Twain** (1966); Ernest Samuels, *Henry Adams: The Middle Years* (1958) and *Henry Adams: The Major Phase* (1964). H. M. Jones, *The Age of Energy: Varieties of American Experience, 1865–1915** (1971), contains essays on the cultural scene.

* Available in a paperback edition.

CHAPTER 20

Political stalemate and agrarian revolt, 1877–1896

National politics had normally been the vital center of American civilization, the arena in which the future was determined and important issues of the present were resolved. Under Presidents Hayes, Garfield, Arthur, Cleveland, and Harrison, Americans still worked up a great deal of excitement over national politics, and voters turned out in great numbers, but it was the excitement more of spectators than of participants. The outcome of the contests meant more to the contestants than to the spectators, for the elections determined which party would enjoy the spoils of victory—and often little else. Great issues were sometimes debated, but most of them were settled around the council tables of industrialists and financiers rather than in the halls of legislatures and in the meetings of cabinets. The doctrine of laissez faire, so popular among businessmen (save when they sought subsidies and protection), was just as popular among politicians, for it spared them a great deal of trouble. Literally applied, it meant permitting men of power to have things their own way so long as they appeared to stay within the law, with little regard for the social consequences. If politicians neglected social purpose, it should be noted that the public they served seemed to share their indifference—and that public was the most completely democratized electorate in the western world. The political game played under these rules attracted men of great skill, but none of true greatness.

The business of politics

The party equilibrium. Politics in the post-Reconstruction period was more a business than a game, a highly competitive business with the two major parties as the evenly matched competitors. The Democrats managed to elect only one of their candidates President (for two terms) in the fifty-two years between 1860 and 1912. And yet this gives a misleading impression of the relative strength of the Democratic and Republican parties. Actually, there was an extraordinarily narrow margin of difference in the popular vote the two parties polled in the two decades following 1876. In none of the presidential elections from 1876 to 1892 did the Republicans carry a majority of the popular votes, and in only one, that of 1880, did they receive a plurality—but even that plurality was less than one-tenth of 1 percent. In three of the five elections, in fact, the difference between the popular votes for the two major-party candidates was less than 1 percent, and in that of 1876, even though the Democrats received a majority of nearly 3 percent, they lost the election. In the Electoral College votes, on the other hand, majorities ranged from 1 in 1876 to 132 in 1892. The narrow margin between victory and defeat encouraged the laissez-faire tendency of politicians, the tendency to avoid vital issues and take few chances.

The Republican party was a loose alliance of regional and interest groups with different and sometimes conflicting interests. The basic regional alliance was between the Northeast and the Middle West—an alliance that had been consolidated in 1860 and had fought and won the Civil War. It hung together afterward partly because of wartime loyalties and memories of the heroic days of Lincoln, when the party had emancipated the slaves and saved the Union. Two other large groups traced their attachment to the party back to the Civil War: the freedmen and the Union army veterans. The blacks remained loyal to the party of emancipation and continued to send one or two congressmen to Washington from the South, but after the Republicans abandoned them in 1877 the political power of the freedmen diminished rapidly. On the other hand the political significance of the war veterans increased as the Grand Army of the Republic grew as a pressure group and as Congress responded with larger and larger pensions for veterans. Economic conflict and political rivalry opened breaches in party unity. Republican policies such as high tariffs, sound money, and favors for railroads pleased Eastern industrialists, but Western grain-growers often resented those policies and threatened revolt. The noisiest quarrel within Republican ranks was the running war between the Half-Breeds, led by James G. Blaine of

465

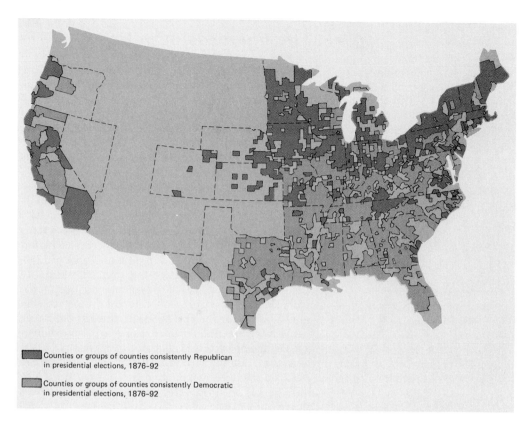

Counties or groups of counties consistently Republican
in presidential elections, 1876–92

Counties or groups of counties consistently Democratic
in presidential elections, 1876–92

Maine, and the Stalwarts, led by Roscoe Conkling of
New York. The long-winded battles between these
factions fascinated the multitude, but the main difference between them was over which of them should
get the spoils of office. Each demanded all the offices.

The post-Reconstruction Democratic party was
even more regional than the Republican. Its most
reliable sources of support were the South and the
machine-dominated cities of the Northeast. And the
disparity of outlook and interest between the provincial, Protestant cotton-farmers of the South and the
underprivileged, Catholic, immigrant, industrial
workers of the big cities was almost as great as that
between the impoverished Negro and the affluent
capitalist supporters of the Republican party. The
Democrats also received support from Northeastern
merchants and bankers who opposed the protective
tariff and favored contraction of the currency—
"sound-money" men, they called themselves. The
leaders of the party in the South, many of them of
Whig background, preferred to be called Conservatives, and were often called Bourbons by their opponents. They had much in common with the dominant Democratic leaders in the Middle West, who
were also business-minded conservatives and were
also known as Bourbons. Rank-and-file Democrats,
farmers, industrial workers, and small businessmen in

the West, the South, and the East, were often restive
and sometimes rebellious under such leaders.

On major issues no important differences, save
those over tariff and monetary policy, existed between the two old parties, which were under equally
conservative leaders. Ethnic, religious, and cultural
issues often took precedence over economic issues.
Not that there was any lack of important economic
and social issues. One has only to recall the recurrent
industrial crises and depressions of the period and the
desperate plight of the victims. Their problems cried
out for vigorous government action. But if they got a
hearing in the political arena, it was through small
third parties. The major parties preferred to avoid
such issues (and so, apparently, did the majority of
the electorate). In the North the Republicans "waved
the bloody shirt," accusing the Democrats of rebellion
and treason, and in the South the Democrats invoked
the menace of "Negro rule" and called for white
supremacy. Yet the rate of voter turnout was unusu-
ally high in these years.

"The American, like the Englishman," observed
James Bryce in 1888, "usually votes with his party,
right or wrong, and the fact that there is little distinction of view between the parties makes it easier to
stick to your old friends." Party allegiance during
these years was in fact remarkably rigid. In Indiana,

for example, thirty-two counties remained unswervingly Republican from 1876 to 1892, and thirty-nine counties stuck as unswervingly with the Democrats, with neither group varying more than 3 percent. In spite of much population mobility, only twenty-one counties shifted parties at all, and with third parties in the picture neither of the major parties could muster a reliable majority in those counties until 1896. The same pattern had prevailed for years: two-thirds of the Democratic counties had been voting Democratic since 1844, and over four-fifths of the Republican counties had gone down the line for the old party since its founding in 1856. These rigid loyalties carried Hoosier voters right through war and peace, through a wide variety of candidates and policies, and through all the economic and social upheavals of the passing years.

Party loyalties seemed less affected by national issues and policies, such as the tariff, than by matters closer to the daily life and experience of voters. And party identifications were more strongly influenced by cultural than by economic interests. Substantive issues such as prohibition versus the "saloon power," Sabbath observance versus "desecration," and public versus parochial schools reflected and symbolized religious and ethnic values. These values and symbols divided "pietists" from "ritualists" and Protestants from Catholics. The Republicans of the period are described as the "Party of Piety," and Democrats as the "Party of Personal Liberty," Men took their party identifications seriously, because they did not take their religious and cultural values lightly.

Neither party was strong enough, however, to rely for victory on the allegiance of certain states or parts of states that could be counted "in the bag." There were always the "doubtful states"—that is, states with enough shifting voters to turn the tide either way. These states were thought to be Connecticut, New York, New Jersey, Ohio, Indiana, and Illinois, but the key states were New York and Indiana. In the 1880s the Republicans had to carry New York and all three of the doubtful Midwestern states to elect their candidate President. Since the whole contest hinged on a few states, it is no wonder that they commanded great bargaining power, absorbed most of the "slush funds" from the campaign treasuries, and gained desirable offices for their politicians. The strategic importance of the few doubtful Midwestern states also helps to explain why five of the six Republican candidates for President from Grant to McKinley came from those states, including three from Ohio and one from Indiana. And as a running mate for their Midwestern candidate, the Republicans almost invariably chose a man from New York. The Democrats, on the other hand, usually reversed the regional order, though they picked their nominees from the same doubtful states. Their presidential nominees, with one exception, all came from New York—three of them had been governors of the state—and their vice-presidential nominees from Ohio, Illinois, or Indiana. In 1876, 1880, and 1884 the second place on the Democratic ticket went to the "strategic" state of Indiana.

The spoilsmen and the reformers. From Grant to McKinley the power and influence of the presidential office were at low ebb. One reason was that no President between 1865 and 1897 enjoyed the advantage of having his own party in control of both houses of Congress throughout his tenure of office, so rapidly did control seesaw back and forth between the evenly matched parties. But more than that, the Presidency was slow in recovering from the blows struck by Congress in its bitter fight with President Johnson and from President Grant's continual acquiescence in the domination of Congress. For a generation congressional supremacy and presidential subordination remained the rule. Senator John Sherman of Ohio, himself a perpetual aspirant to the office, wrote that the President "should be subordinate to the legislative department" and should merely "obey and enforce the laws." Ordinarily the President did not even have a voice in preparing the annual budget, and he was certainly not given the staff or the money to play the role of a real chief executive. To a large degree, Congress itself took care of administration. As Leonard D. White, a leading administrative historian, puts it, "The established course of the public business went on its appointed way, for the most part without requiring or inviting the collaboration of the man who sat in the White House."

Politics was really controlled by oligarchies of party bosses, many of them United States senators, who headed state machines and commanded armies of henchmen whom they paid off with public offices. In addition to Senators Blaine and Conkling were such potentates as Senator Zachariah Chandler, the fat, coarse, and cynical boss of Michigan, and Senator John A. "Black Jack" Logan of Illinois, a power in the Grand Army of the Republic. The patronage system placed at the disposal of the bosses the whole public service, an enormous booty in federal, state, and local offices, the "spoils" of political victory. The spoilsmen sometimes sold offices to the highest bidder, but more regularly they distributed them among faithful workers for service rendered and systematically taxed the holders for "contributions." After the Civil Service Reform Act of 1883 (see p. 471) began to curb patronage as a source of revenue, politicians increasingly turned to big business for money and support. A new type of boss then began to replace the old flamboyant "stump politician," a quieter, more efficient "desk

The business of politics

*Marcus Alonzo Hanna:
industrialist turned politician*

achieving honest and efficient government through civil-service reform. Spoilsmen sneered at "snivel service," and Senator Conkling described the reformers as "the man milliners, the dilettanti and *carpet knights* of politics" and accused them of "canting self-righteousness."

The influence of the Mugwumps was largely confined to the literate upper class, for they were isolated from the mass of voters by their attitudes and their social position. The various reform movements of the period were not on speaking terms with one another, or they spoke different languages. Grangers, Greenbackers, and Alliancemen of the West and the South (see pp. 478–79) demanded reforms in the currency, banking, and credit systems that chilled the blood of Eastern reformers. Agrarian reformers were at the same time divided among themselves: Northerner against Southerner, Republican against Democrat. Both the urban Mugwumps and the rural agrarians had trouble understanding the impulses and strivings of labor reformers. The cause of reform, its forces divided and mutually suspicious, languished and faltered through the eighties.

The conservative ascendancy

Hayes in the White House. We have already seen how the means used to elect Rutherford B. Hayes cast widespread doubt on his title to the Presidency (pp. 382–83). He did not strengthen his position when he announced that he would not run for reelection. Hayes was never an astute politician, but he did not lack courage and determination. From the start of his Administration he set out resolutely to redress the balance between the executive and legislative branches and regain for the Presidency some of the powers that Congress had preempted, particularly the powers of appointment and removal of officeholders.

The nominations for the Cabinet that he sent to the Senate were his first challenge to congressional dominance, for they included names unwelcome to the bosses—notably the name of Carl Schurz for Secretary of the Interior. "Hayes has passed the Republican party to its worst enemies," said Senator Zach Chandler. The Senate balked and refused confirmation on the whole list at first but later yielded to the President. An old device that the House used to coerce the President was the "rider," a piece of legislation the President had to approve in order to secure the needed appropriation to which it was tied. The Democratic majority of the House used the rider repeatedly in an attempt to force Hayes to accept the repeal of Reconstruction laws providing federal pro-

politician," who worked hand in glove with the lobbyists and leaders of public utilities, railroads, heavy industries, and manufactures. Matthew Quay, who kept a card index of the foibles of Pennsylvania politicians; "Easy Boss" Tom Platt, who succeeded Conkling in New York; Arthur P. Gorman, the friend of business in Maryland; Henry G. Davis and his son-in-law Stephen B. Elkins, who ran respectively the Democratic and Republican parties of West Virginia; and Marcus Alonzo Hanna, Ohio industrialist turned politician, were bosses of the new type.

Not all the public men of the age were cynics and spoilsmen. A group of liberal reformers called Mugwumps by their deriders kept up a running crusade against patronage and corruption in office for two decades. Earnest and élitist, the Mugwumps were men of high social position and conservative economic views, usually of Republican background. Foremost among them was George William Curtis, scholarly editor of *Harper's Weekly*, whose cartoonist Thomas Nast made a career of ridiculing and caricaturing the corrupt. Carl Schurz, who called Curtis "the intellectual head, the guiding force" of the movement, was himself a hero of the Mugwumps. Another of the luminaries was E. L. Godkin, editor of the *Nation*. Devoted to laissez-faire principles and unconcerned over the deeper ills of the economy, the reformers of this school confined their economic program to tariff reform and sound money and fixed their hopes on

Political stalemate and agrarian revolt, 1877–1896

tection of elections. Determined to resist the pressure and make the executive "an equal and independent branch of the Government," Hayes vetoed seven such bills, compelled acceptance of his independence, and gained a clear-cut victory over congressional encroachment.

Hayes struck at the spoils system in its most powerful entrenchment, the New York Custom House Ring, the center of Senator Conkling's machine. A commission appointed by the President in 1877 and headed by John Jay of New York investigated the Custom House patronage system and reported that it was "unsound in principle, dangerous in practice, demoralizing in its influence on all connected with the customs service," and ridden with "ignorance, inefficiency, and corruption." Conkling's lieutenants, Collector of the Port Chester A. Arthur and naval officer Alonzo B. Cornell, refused to clean up the corruption and declined to resign. At Conkling's demand the Senate refused to confirm appointment of the successors whom Hayes nominated, but the President stubbornly persisted, dismissed Arthur and Cornell while the Senate was in recess, and eventually filled their places with men of his own choice. He was trying to build his own machine to overcome Conkling's. Hayes had won a battle, but not a war. His orders that officeholders not be assessed for political contributions or required to do political campaigning were ignored. His promise of "thorough, radical and complete" civil-service reform remained unfulfilled, and the spoilsmen continued to rule the roost.

Economic crises and social protest in the worst years of the depression caught the Hayes Administration without a policy and without real comprehension of what was happening. The first great industrial conflict in our history started with a strike on the B&O Railroad in July 1877 (see p. 439). The strike spread spontaneously and rapidly throughout all sections save New England and the South, affecting two-thirds of the railroad mileage in the country. At the request of four state governors, Hayes set the fateful precedent of using federal troops to intervene in a strike and restore order. The President incurred additional ill will from labor, especially on the West Coast, by vetoing a bill passed in 1879 to restrict Chinese "coolie" immigration. He vetoed the bill because it violated the Burlingame Treaty of 1868, but after the veto he began negotiations for a new treaty with China. The Treaty of 1880 acknowledged the right of restriction, and in 1882 Congress passed a bill putting an end to Chinese immigration for the following decade.

Monetary policy in politics. The President also took the unpopular side in a series of debates over national currency policies that divided both parties during his Administration. Hayes held the conservative, laissez-faire doctrine that the sole duty of the government was to maintain the value of currency and that the only way to do this was by the demonstrated ability of the Treasury to redeem currency at face value in gold. His opponents held, on the other hand, that it was the duty of the government to manage the currency so as to prevent or correct injustice and to relieve distress and suffering. While this was not the only explanation for the growing agricultural distress of the time, the farmer was perfectly right that crop prices were falling and that monetary policy was related to this decline.

The first clash between Hayes and the discontented agrarians occurred over a movement to repeal the Specie Resumption Act of 1875, which obliged the Treasury to resume the redemption of legal-tender notes in specie at full face value by January 1, 1879, and to reduce the number of greenbacks in circulation. Though offset by increased issuance of national bank notes, the measure contracted the currency and at the same time appreciated its value, the two things most complained of by farmers and debtors. Advocates of repeal, called Greenbackers, argued that fulfillment of the act would further depress prices and increase the burden of private and public debt. They denounced as outrageous the proposal to redeem war bonds that had been bought with greenbacks worth less than 40 cents to the dollar with currency worth 100 cents to the dollar. A National Greenback party had polled an insignificant vote in the election of 1876, but in the following year the movement gained recruits from labor and additional support from farmers and in February 1878 reorganized as the Greenback Labor party. In the fall elections the new party polled a remarkable total of 1,060,000 votes and elected fourteen representatives to Congress. Resisting all pressure, much of it from his own party, Hayes clung to the policy of resumption and supported Secretary of the Treasury John Sherman in building up a gold reserve to redeem the currency. Two weeks before the deadline of January 1, 1879, however, greenbacks became worth their face value in gold and no run on the gold reserve developed. Resumption was an accomplished fact. The Greenbackers nominated James B. Weaver of Iowa for President in 1880, but their issue was dead, and they attracted little attention.

Inflationist sentiment, by no means dead, found a new outlet in the movement for the free coinage of silver just as the greenback cause was becoming hopeless. Once again Hayes took the unpopular side. The silver question was to become one of the most hotly debated issues in the history of American politics during the next two decades, but before 1875 it attracted no popular interest. The official government ratio of sixteen to one—sixteen times as much silver in a silver dollar as there was gold in a gold dollar—had undervalued silver ever since the gold rush of 1849 had lowered the price of gold. As a consequence, silver-miners sold their product commercially rather than offer it to the Treasury at a loss, and silver dollars virtually disappeared from circulation. Foreseeing a drop in silver prices, a few monetary experts persuaded an ill-informed Congress to abolish the coinage of silver dollars and put the country on the gold standard in 1873. New silver mines in Nevada, Arizona, and Colorado soon flooded the market, and the price of silver began to drop. Miners then discovered that the Treasury rejected their product and that their European market had been reduced by widespread adoption of the gold standard abroad. Denouncing demonetization of silver as the "Crime of 1873," urban publishers of the Midwestern and Middle Atlantic states, not Western miners, started the demand that free coinage at the old ratio be restored. Inflationists eventually took up their cry because they saw in silver a means of halting currency contraction, getting cheaper money, raising crop prices, and securing debtor relief.

So rapidly did the silver movement spread that by the fall of 1877 an overwhelming majority of the lower house of Congress voted for a bill for the "free and unlimited coinage of silver" introduced by Representative Richard "Silver Dick" Bland of Missouri. The Bland bill would have stopped the sale of government bonds for gold and driven that metal out of circulation, since it would have produced silver dollars worth less than 90 cents (and still falling in value) and made them legal tender. Yet the bill commanded so much support in both houses that Hayes knew it would be passed over his veto. Before the Senate acted, however, Senator William B. Allison of Iowa amended and weakened the bill, and in that form it was passed over Hayes' veto in February 1878. The Bland-Allison Act deprived the inflationists of their objective of "unlimited coinage" and substituted the requirement that the Treasury buy not less than $2 million and not more than $4 million worth of silver per month and coin it into dollars. The act did not have the effects that the conservatives feared and the inflationists desired. For one thing the government consistently purchased the minimum amount of silver required by the act and stood ready to redeem the silver coin and notes in gold. And for another, the depression lifted in 1879, gold flowed in from abroad, and crop prices improved temporarily for reasons other than monetary policy. Silverites were to return to the battle in stronger force, but for more than a decade they made no change in the law.

In spite of the unpopularity of his stand on silver and his quarrels with Congress, Hayes ended his Ad-

ministration on an upswing of confidence and respect. Ordinarily such an upturn would have overcome his announced intention to retire, but no such movement developed. His party virtually ignored him, and he became scarcely more than a spectator during the struggle to nominate his successor.

The Garfield tragedy. The Republicans brought their bitter feuds to the Chicago nominating convention under the banners of rival candidates. The Stalwarts were united under Conkling's leadership to name Grant for a third term. The Half-Breeds were determined to nominate Blaine; and Secretary of the Treasury John Sherman maneuvered to make himself available as a compromise candidate. When it became clear that none of the three could marshal a majority, the Blaine and Sherman forces joined on the thirty-sixth ballot and nominated Congressman James A. Garfield of Ohio as a dark horse. Garfield had managed Sherman's campaign and led the anti-Grant forces at the convention. To conciliate the defeated faction, the convention then nominated Conkling's lieutenant, Chester A. Arthur, the deposed spoilsman of the New York Custom House, for Vice President.

Prospects for revenging Governor Tilden by nominating him in 1880 looked promising to the Democrats, but Tilden, like Hayes, declined to run for the Presidency again. The party nominated instead General Winfield Scott Hancock, a Pennsylvanian and a Union hero in the Battle of Gettysburg. Hancock had no political experience, but his nomination was an effective answer to the charge of disloyalty that was so often thrown at his party. His running mate was William H. English, from the "doubtful" state of Indiana. The platforms of the two parties were nearly indistinguishable, and the campaigns they waged demagogic and sometimes unprincipled. The Republican managers did the most decisive work of the campaign in the doubtful states of Ohio, New York, and Indiana, using large amounts of money to carry Indiana by a bare seven thousand votes and New York by twenty thousand. Garfield won by a scant margin of less than forty thousand popular votes in the country at large, though his electoral vote was 214 to 155 for Hancock.

President Garfield's brief tenure in the White House began with embarrassments, continued with unhappiness, and ended in tragedy. A handsome, massive figure of a man, with a reputation for courage under fire in the war and for resourcefulness as party-leader in the House, Garfield was not without a degree of integrity. Under the extraordinary pressures of his new office, however, he wavered in purpose. His first impulse was to conciliate all the warring Republican factions and please as many people as possible. He knew that his major obligation for his office was to Blaine, however, and he acknowledged it by making

the senator Secretary of State. Blaine promptly used his influence over the President to undermine and destroy the power of his sworn enemy Conkling. Garfield's most aggressive move against the Stalwarts was to replace the man whom Hayes had made collector of the port of New York (in the name of civil-service reform) with the leading opponent of the Conkling faction in New York. This precipitated a violent war between the factions of the spoilsmen and a torrent of abuse and charges of bad faith against the President.

At the very height of the furor over spoils and corruption, on July 2, 1881, Charles J. Guiteau, a crazed and disappointed office-seeker, shot the President in the back. Garfield died of the wound on September 19, and the next day Stalwart Chester A. Arthur became President.

The Arthur interlude. The new President was a wealthy, easygoing man with expensive tastes, elegant clothes and carriages, and twenty years of experience as a spoilsman in the Conkling camp of New York politics. His first year as President did little to dispel the fear that Garfield's martyrdom had been in vain and that the spoils system was there to stay. Arthur did not turn over patronage to Conkling, as many expected, but after Blaine resigned the President filled the Cabinet with friends of Grant and Conkling. Arthur did prosecute with vigor the criminals charged with post-office frauds, one of whom claimed to have provided the money for carrying Indiana for Garfield and Arthur. But the guilty men escaped punishment, and the President's efforts not only failed to win over the reformers but alienated his former followers. The fall elections of 1882 drove his party from control of the House of Representatives and gave the Democrats a majority of nearly a hundred seats.

One cause of the Democratic landslide was the nation's shock over Garfield's assassination and revulsion against the system of patronage and spoils associated with the tragedy. Popular indignation put new power behind the demands of the small band of reformers who, having fought the spoilsmen since the 1860s, had in 1881 organized the National Civil Service Reform League, with George William Curtis as president. It was ironic that "Chet" Arthur, long the very symbol of spoils politics, should be cast in the role of civil-service reformer, but he firmly told Congress that "action should no longer be postponed" and promised his full cooperation. In January 1883 large bipartisan majorities in both houses of Congress passed a Democratic bill sponsored by Senator George H. Pendleton of Ohio. The Civil Service Act (often called the Pendleton Act) established a bipartisan Civil Service Commission of three members, appointed by the President with Senate confirmation, who were to administer competitive examinations and select appointees on the basis of merit and an apportionment among the states according to population. Arthur demonstrated his good faith by naming as head of the commission Dorman B. Eaton, an outstanding reformer who drafted the act, and appointing two prominent friends of reform as the other commissioners. At first the act affected only some four-

Chester A. Arthur:
wealthy, easygoing, elegant

The conservative ascendancy

Grover Cleveland:
defender of the right of property

the Civil War to a collection of wooden antiques with cast-iron guns and rotten hulls. It did not boast a steel vessel or a rifled gun afloat. The Arthur Administration awakened Congress out of its indifference and started the construction of new fighting ships. The three cruisers begun in his Administration had numerous defects, but he is properly credited with sweeping away barriers of ignorance and clearing the way for a modern navy. In this as in other ways Arthur proved worthier of the office he held than anyone had reason to believe when he took it.

Changing the conservative guard. The chances of Arthur's succeeding himself as President in 1884, never very strong in any case, were greatly weakened by the Democratic tidal wave of 1882, in which he lost control of his own state. He later won approval from the reform, especially the Mugwump, element, but not their support, and he proved unable to unite his own faction of the party behind his candidacy. Blaine remained the dominant figure in the Republican party, and his nomination seemed more and more likely as the convention approached. Curtis, Schurz, and other Mugwumps spurned Blaine and supported their own candidate, Senator George Edmunds of Vermont, to the end. Ignoring the reformers and overriding the Arthur supporters, the Blaine men nominated their candidate without difficulty and named John A. Logan, favorite son of Illinois, for Vice President. The Yankee Mugwumps promptly decided to bolt the party provided the Democrats nominated the rising hope of the reformers, Grover Cleveland, governor of New York.

Cleveland's rise in New York politics had been recent but rapid. Elected mayor of Buffalo in 1881, he accepted the Democratic nomination for governor in 1882 and won an easy victory because of the split in the Republican party of the state. A burly figure of two hundred forty pounds, determined jaw, and hard eyes, he was known for his rugged honesty and his habits of hard work and thrift—the common man turned reformer. But Cleveland was a thoroughgoing conservative as well, a believer in sound money and a defender of the right of property. As governor he enhanced his reputation for scorn of popularity by vetoing a popular bill reducing the fare on Jay Gould's elevated railroads in New York City to 5 cents. Similarly, he risked the wrath of labor by vetoing a bill limiting the working day of New York streetcar-conductors to twelve hours, and with even greater recklessness he defied "Honest" John Kelley, boss of Tammany Hall. Businessmen, middle-class taxpayers, and reformers of the Mugwump school admired the independence and integrity of Cleveland. The nomination of Blaine and the promise of Mugwump support made Governor Cleveland the logical standard-

teen thousand officials, about one-tenth of the total number of federal employees, but it empowered the President to expand the proportion of "classified" posts—jobs subject to the merit system. By the end of the century 40 percent were classified, and the federal civil service was securely established.

While the Civil Service Commission was the most important achievement of the Arthur Administration, it was not the President's only assertion of independence and conscience, nor his only praiseworthy effort. Two such efforts, both of them futile as it turned out, were in response to the problem of a surplus of over $100 million accumulated in the United States Treasury by excessive tax revenues. The solution favored by Congress was to spend the surplus in lavish appropriations for river and harbor improvements and pork-barrel handouts. In order to win Half-Breed support, Arthur vetoed one such bill, only to have Congress pass it over his veto. The President's solution to the Treasury surplus included the reduction of taxes. His efforts in tariff reduction amounted to little. As an incidental means of reducing the Treasury surplus, Arthur's naval-construction program was more successful. The navy had deteriorated since

Political stalemate and agrarian revolt, 1877–1896

bearer for the Democrats in 1884. He was nominated with the aid of state bosses and financed in his campaign by corporate wealth. His running mate was Thomas A. Hendricks, yet another available candidate from the shifting counties of Indiana.

The presidential campaign of 1884 was one of the most sensational and frenzied in our history, and yet it managed to avoid all vital issues. "The public is angry and abusive," wrote Henry Adams. "Every one takes part. We are all doing our best, and swearing like demons. But the amusing thing is that no one talks about real interests." Cleveland said little at all, and Blaine talked a great deal without saying very much. There was no significant difference between the party platforms. In the absence of public issues, popular attention focused on the private life and personal morals of the candidates. Democrats and Mugwumps took the initiative by reviving the Mulligan Letter charges (see p. 380) that had deprived Blaine of the nomination in 1876 and by publishing additional Mulligan letters to prove that Blaine had been guilty of underhanded deals with railroad-promoters. George William Curtis declared that the issue was "moral rather than political." Thereupon the Republicans retaliated with charges that Cleveland was the father of an illegitimate son. The campaign deteriorated into scandalmongering that became more and more irresponsible.

Cleveland had to carry New York to win the election, and the extreme closeness of the contest in that state concentrated attention on a number of intangible factors, any one of which might conceivably be decisive. Whatever the explanation, the tide turned narrowly in Cleveland's favor. In addition to all the Southern states, he carried the doubtful states of Indiana, New Jersey, Connecticut, and New York—the last by a plurality of a mere 1,149 votes. His share of the votes in the country as a whole was only slightly greater than Blaine's. Mugwumps and reformers rejoiced at the victory, but it is a mistake to conclude that a moral crusade had defeated Blaine. Actually, he polled about the same percentage of the total vote as Garfield had in 1880 and a larger percentage than the Republican candidates were to poll in 1888 and 1892. At any rate, the long Republican rule was at an end, and the Democrats were back in power for the first time in twenty-four years.

Cleveland in command. No one could be sure of the new President's views on any of several leading issues, but everyone could be sure he was a conservative. His inaugural address promising adherence to "business principles" bore this out, and so did his Cabinet appointments, which included representatives of the most conservative and business-minded wing of the party in the East and South. The new Administration signified no break with the past on fundamental issues.

If there was any policy to which Cleveland had a clear commitment, it was civil-service reform, and it was over this issue that he came near to wrecking his Administration. He came to office with two masters to please: the Mugwump reformer and the hungry spoilsman of his own party with an appetite for office whetted by twenty-four years of anticipation. The President's first moves delighted the reformers. Defying the Democratic bosses and spoilsmen, he retained in office some able Republicans and personally examined applications for office far into the night. Party-leaders besieged the President with patronage demands and insisted that he accept their definition of civil-service reform, which, according to one senator, "meant turning out of office of Republicans and putting honest Democrats in their places"—*all* their places. The party press thundered against his "ingratitude." Within a few months he yielded to pressure, and Republican heads began to roll. Carl Schurz wrote, "Your attempt to please both reformers and spoilsmen has failed," and Cleveland broke with the Mugwumps. By the end of four years he had removed about two-thirds of the 120,000 federal officers. He did increase the list of classified jobs to 27,380, nearly double the number when he took office, but he filled the Civil Service Commission with weak and incompetent men.

In the role of Treasury watchdog and thrifty steward of public funds, Cleveland showed more consistency than he did as civil-service reformer. For one thing, he rebuked a pensions racket run by a powerful lobby for Union veterans of the Civil War. Agents of this lobby used private bills to push through Congress thousands of dubious claims, hundreds of them obviously fraudulent. Previous Presidents, who feared the Grand Army of the Republic, had always signed these bills, but Cleveland called a halt and took to investigating individual claims himself, vetoing many of them, often with sarcastic comment. In January 1887, Congress passed a Dependent Pension Bill that provided a pension for all honorably discharged disabled veterans who had seen as much as ninety days of service if they were unable to work, regardless of the cause of their disability. The President defied the wrath of the GAR and its half-million members and vetoed the bill.

Cleveland believed that, except in rare circumstances, the President should confine himself to the execution of the laws and was not obliged to furnish leadership to Congress. In spite of the storms of social protest in the mid-eighties, Congress enacted little legislation of lasting significance, and the President's influence upon that was largely negative. His Secretary of the Interior, L. Q. C. Lamar, showed initiative

473

in compelling railroads and cattle barons of the West to give up 81 million acres of public lands that they illegally withheld from settlement. But Cleveland himself deserves no credit for what was probably the most important act passed during his Administration, the Interstate Commerce Act of 1887 (see p. 425). He regarded the whole idea with suspicion and signed the bill reluctantly and "with reservations."

The tariff in politics. In his fight for tariff reform, however, Cleveland took a more forthright stand that may have contributed to his defeat for reelection. The issue was as old as the republic, but since the Civil War it had taken on a new importance and complexity and was treated with caution and evasiveness by politicians of both parties. The tariff acts of the Civil War had been justified on the grounds that high internal war taxes on American industries put them at a competitive disadvantage that had to be offset with protective tariff duties to enable Americans to compete with foreign manufacturers on equal terms. Beginning with modest rates of 18.8 percent on dutiable goods in 1861, a succession of acts raised the average to 40.3 percent in 1866. No politician at the end of the war would admit publicly that these rates were anything but a temporary expedient. But, while the American producers were soon relieved of the burden of internal war taxes, the protective tariff remained unrepealed. American industry quickly adjusted to the prices, dividends, and profits made possible by freedom from competition from abroad. Producers who enjoyed or desired these advantages organized to press their desires on Congress. Politicians learned the great power of the tariff lobby, and both major parties, the Republicans explicitly and the Democrats tacitly, accepted the principle of protection—though with dissent in each party.

From time to time a President would make a gesture of reform, but Congress would regularly respond with jugglery that left the situation unchanged or made a mockery of reform. The Tariff Act of 1870 reduced the duties on coffee, tea, spices, and other articles not produced in this country but left the protective duties virtually unaltered. Regulars joined reformers in 1872 and actually effected a reduction of 10 percent in the protective duties, but the cut was quietly restored three years later on the ground that the Panic of 1873 had reduced federal revenues. Two Democratic bills for reform in 1876 and 1878 never got out of committee. President Arthur's efforts on Tariff reform came to naught in 1883.

Cleveland hesitated for three years to take an aggressive stand. He knew that a minority of some forty Democratic congressmen had combined with Republicans to defeat tariff-reform bills in 1884 and 1886, and Democratic leaders assured him that an all-out fight on the issue would split the party and lose the next election. Finally deciding, however, the President devoted his entire annual message of December 1887 to the tariff question. He made a slashing attack on the injustice, inequity, and absurdity of existing rates, ridiculed the need to protect century-old "infant industries," and denounced high rates as "the vicious, inequitable and illogical source of unnecessary taxation." The House of Representatives, with a Democratic majority, responded by adopting a bill sponsored by Roger Q. Mills of Texas. Far from radical, it did place such raw materials as lumber, wool, and flax on the free list and made moderate reductions of about 7 percent in rates for finished goods. The Republican-controlled Senate then rejected the Mills bill, as expected, and adopted a highly protective bill that was buried in the House committee by the Democrats. The deadlock of tariff reform produced the first clear-cut economic issue between parties since Reconstruction and provided the leading issue of the 1888 election.

For their presidential candidate the Republicans chose Benjamin Harrison of Indiana, whose chief attractions were that he came from a doubtful state and that he was the grandson of former President William Henry Harrison, "Old Tippecanoe," of log-cabin and hard-cider fame. His running mate was Levi P. Morton, a wealthy New York banker. The Democrats naturally renominated President Cleveland, and for their vice-presidential candidate they chose the elderly and ailing ex-senator Allen G. Thurman of Ohio.

The campaign for Cleveland's reelection was handicapped by halfhearted and ineffective leadership. By contrast, the Republican campaign had a vigorous leader in Senator Matt Quay, boss of a ruthless machine in Pennsylvania. Quay collected and spent a huge campaign fund. Republican strategists made telling use of this fund to purchase votes and rig elections in Indiana and New York.

In spite of much talk about tariff reform, the election did not turn on that issue. Cleveland actually carried the manufacturing states of New Jersey and Connecticut, and the Democrats gained ground in Michigan, Ohio, and California, normally protariff states. Cleveland polled a plurality of almost one hundred thousand popular votes, but Harrison won the electoral vote 233 to 168. It was an extremely narrow victory for the Republicans. As usual, the outcome had hung on a few evenly divided states—Indiana, New York, Rhode Island, and Ohio—and Harrison had carried them all, each by a few thousand votes. Prominent factors in what was probably the most corrupt presidential election of national history up to that time appear to have been trickery in Indiana and New York and division within the Democratic party.

President Harrison paid them off

duced it but to give away the surplus to their friends. With this policy they greeted with open arms the protectionist lobby, the veterans' pension lobby, and the pork-barrel lobby.

The American Iron and Steel Association, the Industrial League, and other protectionists were the first to benefit. Reed appointed William McKinley, a high-tariff representative from Ohio whom he had just defeated in a contest for the speakership, as chairman of the House Ways and Means Committee, and the new chairman assumed the task of fulfilling Republican pledges of higher tariff rates. The McKinley tariff bill, which became law on June 10, 1890, raised an already scandalously high tariff scale even higher, an *ad valorem* increase of about 4 percent. Its purpose was not merely to be protective but to be prohibitive; not merely to discourage foreign competition but to eliminate it; not merely to protect infant industries but to call new industries into being. To aid the Sugar Trust, the bill put raw sugar on the free list but granted American sugar-growers a compensatory subsidy of 2 cents a pound. As a rather hypocritical gesture of help to farmers, duties were raised on farm products that generally needed no protection anyway. Finally, there was a "reciprocity" clause intended not as a means of lowering tariffs but as a threat to raise them in this country if other countries did not lower theirs.

Faced with an indignant reaction in the agricultural sections against the favoritism of the McKinley Tariff, Republican congressmen now hastened to take steps of appeasement. Representatives from the silver-mining states and the Western states in favor of currency expansion had been promised that the party would "do something for silver" in return for their reluctant support of the tariff bill. The measure finally contrived to fulfill this commitment was the Sherman Silver Purchase Act, named for the senator from Ohio. It was designed to replace the Bland-Allison Act of 1878 (see p. 470), which had fixed a minimum amount of silver that the federal Treasury was required to purchase each month in dollars. Under this law the Treasury had put about $378 million in silver into circulation without relieving the scarcity of currency. The Sherman Act fixed the amount of silver to be purchased in ounces rather than dollars: 4½ million ounces per month, approximately the amount of current production of the metal. The silver was to be paid for in Treasury notes of full legal-tender value, which could be redeemed in either gold or silver at the discretion of the government. The bill was passed by a straight party vote, with Democrats opposing on the grounds that it provided no adequate relief. As it turned out, the government subsequently chose to redeem the notes only in gold, and as the price of silver dropped the Treasury was required to spend

Harrison and reaction. President Harrison complained that he could not name his own Cabinet because party-managers "had sold out every place to pay the election expenses." Heavy obligations to Blaine dictated his appointment as Secretary of State, and other appointments paid off regional bosses, high-tariff groups, and donors to the campaign fund. John Wanamaker, a wealthy Philadelphia merchant, became Postmaster General and promptly turned over the Post Office patronage to hungry spoilsmen. In spite of his commitment to civil-service reform, Harrison watched the process in silence.

For the first time since 1875 the Republicans in 1889–91 held the Presidency and a majority in both houses of Congress. Each majority was extremely slight, however, and under existing House rules the Democratic minority could frustrate the majority by simply not answering roll call and thereby depriving the House of a quorum. Speaker Thomas B. Reed of Maine earned the title of "Czar" by sweeping aside the rules over the indignant protest of the minority, strengthening party responsibility, and running House proceedings with an iron will. Under Reed in the House and the protectionist Senator Nelson W. Aldrich of Rhode Island in the Senate, the Republican majority won the name of the "Billion Dollar Congress." Their solution for the growing Treasury surplus was not to lower the tariff revenues that pro-

The conservative ascendancy

fewer and fewer dollars to purchase the stated number of ounces. The act produced no more currency expansion than its predecessor had. The product of weak and shifty statesmanship, it pleased neither side and contributed nothing of importance toward solving the currency problems of the nation.

Another reform act passed about the same time, the Sherman Antitrust Act, bearing the name of the same Ohio senator, became law in July 1890 (see p. 430). Although many congressmen were absent when the vote was taken, the Sherman Antitrust Act was adopted with only one vote against it in the Senate and none in the House. It had little effect during the following decade, for no administration during those years showed much interest in enforcing it.

In order to please Union veterans of the GAR, Harrison appointed Corporal James Tanner, a cynical pensions lobbyist, as commissioner of pensions. The new commissioner publicly declared that he favored "an appropriation for every old comrade who needs it," and as quickly as he could in a brief term of office he added millions to the pension budget. Congress assisted him with the Dependent Pension Act of 1890, similar to the one Cleveland had vetoed in 1887, which declared all Union veterans with at least ninety days' service in the Civil War eligible for a pension if they were unable to provide for themselves for any reason at all. Their widows and children were also made eligible for pensions. The number of pensioners increased by one-third in three years and reached nearly a million, more than the number of Union veterans surviving at the time.

The legislative program of the Billion Dollar Congress did wonders in taking care of the Treasury surplus. The prohibitive tariff rates set by the McKinley Act reduced income, and the combination of excessive pensions and silver purchases increased expenditures. Still in a mood of generosity and still finding some of the surplus left, Congress hastily devised more handouts in the form of subsidies to steamship lines, lavish pork-barrel bills for river and harbor improvements, enormous premiums for government bondholders, and the return of federal taxes paid during the Civil War by Northern states. These handouts and the onset of depression wiped out the surplus in the Treasury by 1894, and the Treasury-surplus problem has never troubled the United States since.

The first Congress of the Harrison Administration promoted the interests of politicians and businessmen—that is, if they belonged to the right party or were engaged in the right business. To other interests, particularly farmers and small businessmen, Congress appeared a wasteful dispenser of favors to the privileged. The congressional elections of 1890 came as a severe rebuke. The Republicans were overwhelmed by a revolt that penetrated traditional strongholds in Ohio, Michigan, Illinois, Wisconsin, and Kansas, even Massachusetts. The shift began in 1889 in Ohio and Massachusetts. Local and cultural issues determined the outcome in several states. Republicans were reduced to 88 seats in the House of Representatives, the smallest number in thirty years, while the Democrats took 235 seats. Republicans hung on to a small majority in the Senate. But the election of 1890 ran up danger signals for conservative leaders of both the old parties, a depression was on the way, a third-party revolt was shaping up, and a new era of reform was in the making.

The agrarian revolt

The decline of agriculture. The spirit of revolt flamed up most fiercely in the agricultural sections of the South and the West, and it was fed by acute economic distress and a deep sense of grievance. American farmers reached the lowest point in their history in the 1890s. The past was not the golden age they sometimes dreamed of, but they had certainly been better off before and were to be much better off in the future. But ever since the 1860s agriculture had been slipping backward, while the cities and factories had been surging forward. Farmers knew they were being left behind, and they suspected the government of indifference, if not hostility, to their interests. They searched everywhere for the causes of their plight and the cure for their troubles. Some of their guesses were shrewd and accurate, but they never grasped the larger causes of their troubles.

What the American farmers did not see was that they were caught up in an international crisis that afflicted agriculture in many parts of the world and provoked rebellion abroad as well as at home. The crisis for producers of export staple crops resulted from a revolution in communication and transportation that created a worldwide market for agricultural products. Ships first steamed through the Suez Canal in 1869, the year locomotives first steamed across the North American continent. The network of railroad and steamship lines was swiftly paralleled by a network of telegraph and telephone lines and transoceanic cables that linked continents and tied the world together. In the meantime vast new tracts of land were brought under cultivation in South America, Australia, and Canada, as well as in the trans-Mississippi West, and simultaneously a new technology of mechanized cultivation increased productivity enormously.

Forced to compete in a world market without protection against their competitors or control over output, American farmers watched the prices of their product decline as productivity mounted. It did not seem fair: the more they grew, the less they earned. Prices of other goods declined too, but farmers said they had to buy expensive farm machinery in a protected market and sell their crops in an unprotected market. As the gap between income and expenses widened, farmers were increasingly forced to mortgage their land or borrow money to cover the gap. They were therefore chronically in debt, and debtors always suffered most keenly from deflationary monetary policies, such as those the government had pursued ever since the resumption of specie payments in 1879 (see p. 469). Contracting the amount of currency in circulation resulted in lowering the price that crops brought and increasing the difficulty of paying off debts. Farmers in debt had reason for opposing contraction and demanding expansion of currency.

It was no wonder that agrarian discontent was most bitter in the South and the West, for the growers of the staple crops of those sections were most dependent on exports. Eastern and Midwestern farmers had different problems and were sometimes at odds with farmers of other sections. The price of cotton and wheat had been falling steadily for two decades. From 1870 to 1873 cotton had averaged about 15.1 cents a pound; from 1894 to 1898 it dropped to an average of 5.8 cents. Over the same period wheat prices dropped from 106.7 to 63.3 cents a bushel, and corn from 43.0 to 29.7. These were market prices, after transportation and warehouse charges had been paid, not the lower prices the farmer received. In 1889 corn was actually selling for 10 cents in Kansas, and farmers were burning it for fuel. Georgia farmers were getting 5 cents a pound for their cotton at a time when economists were estimating that it cost about 7 cents a pound to produce. During several of these years the nation's farmers were running a losing business. Western farmers were kept going sometimes by the appreciation of land values and Southern farmers mainly by sheer habit and the momentum of generations, for in the South land values were declining as well as crop prices.

The ills of agriculture were reflected in the growing number of mortgages (not always an evil) and tenant farmers. Nearly a third of the country's farms were mortgaged by the end of the nineties—45 percent of those in Wisconsin, 48 percent in Michigan, and 53 percent in Iowa. In Kansas, Nebraska, North Dakota, South Dakota, and Minnesota there were by 1890 more mortgages than families. In the Southern states mortgages were far fewer, but only because land was such a drug on the market that it could not be mortgaged. The South's substitute was the lien system, the worst credit system of all (see p. 392). Fewer and fewer farmers owned the land they worked, and more and more labored for a landlord, often an absentee landlord. The number of tenant farms increased from 25.8 percent of all the farms in 1880 to 35.3 percent at the end of the century.

Understandably, the farmer blamed others for his woes. He singled out the railroads as the archenemy, and the offenses he attributed to them were by no means wholly imaginary, though sometimes exaggerated. The complaint that it took one bushel of wheat or corn to pay the freight on another bushel was no exaggeration. The chief complaints of rate discrimination came from the South and the West, where rates were frequently two or three times what they were between Chicago and New York. On the other hand, Eastern farm groups also complained of rate discrimination and charged favoritism for Western competitors. Railroads favored large over small shippers and one locality over another and flagrantly dominated politics and bought up legislatures. The national banks were also a natural target for agrarian abuse, for they were located and run for the convenience of city people, not for countryfolk. They were concentrated in nonagricultural areas, and their rules forbade them to lend money on real estate and farm property. Farmers believed that they manipulated banknote currency against agricultural interests and were indifferent to seasonal needs for money for the movement of crops.

Few could deny the validity of the complaint that the farmer bore the brunt of the tax burden. Stocks and bonds could easily be concealed from the view of the tax-collector, but not livestock and land. Railroads and corporations could pass the taxes on to the consumer, but the farmer could not pass on his taxes. The tax laws, like the bank laws, worked to the farmer's disadvantage. And so did the tariff. The injustice was all the harder to bear for those who believed that the tariff was "the mother of trusts." By fixing prices and defeating competition at home, trusts levied tribute on the consumers of all types of goods. Antitrust and antimonopoly feeling ran high in all farmer organizations. While agrarian theorists were wrong in attributing their plight to a conspiracy, they were right in their contention that they had a number of legitimate grievances against a system that worked so consistently to their disadvantage.

In their more desperate moods the farmers sometimes felt that nature herself was conspiring with their oppressors. In the late eighties and early nineties natural calamities came one on top of another with stunning impact—droughts on the plains that not merely damaged the crops but destroyed them; floods in the lower Mississippi Valley that not merely destroyed the crops but left the land unusable; grim, blizzard-bound winters on the high plains that destroyed not merely domestic animals but wild ones as well and threatened the survival of man himself. Less spectacular,

477

but contrasting sharply with the new urban way of life, was the loneliness, the drudgery, and the isolation of rural life in America in those years. This was the ancient lot of farmers, but the growing glitter of the city made it less tolerable than ever, especially when coupled with the grinding, ceaseless pressure of economic ills and grievances. To Thomas E. Watson of Georgia, who was to whip agrarian wrath into a frenzied crusade, the farmers of his region seemed to move about "like victims of some horrid nightmare . . . powerless—oppressed—shackled." It is not surprising that their protests sometimes sounded a bit irrational.

Agrarian protest. There was nothing irrational, however, about the farmers' impulse to organize and protest against their lot. The Patrons of Husbandry, organized in local "granges" and better known as the Grangers, served as a model for later and more powerful movements. Founded in 1867 by Oliver Hudson Kelley, a government employee in Washington who was moved by the plight of Southern farmers, the Grange grew slowly until the pinch of depression quickened interest in the early seventies. By 1874 the estimated membership was about 1½ million, and growth continued into the next year. In 1875 the Grange was strongest in the Middle West, the South, the Southwest, and the border states of Missouri and Kentucky.

Seeking to eliminate the profits of the middleman, Grangers founded cooperatives for buying and selling, for milling and storing grain, even for banking and manufacturing. These enterprises often suffered from inexperience and lack of capital, but some of them flourished and saved their members money. Membership fell off rapidly after 1875, but the Grangers left their imprint upon law and politics. They actually received more credit than they were due for the so-called Granger laws that were adopted in the early seventies by Midwestern states to regulate grain elevators and railroads. Eight "Granger cases" came before the Supreme Court in 1877, and in *Munn v. Illinois*, the most significant of them, the Court upheld the "police power" of state regulation (see p. 425). Curtailed and hampered by subsequent decisions, the right of the public to control great corporations nevertheless held securely in the future.

The Grange dropped out of political prominence in the late seventies after inspiring a number of similar and smaller agricultural societies. Easily the most important was the Farmers' Alliance, really two organizations of independent origins, a huge one in the South and a much smaller one in the Middle West. Each of them underwent changes of names with reorganizations but were commonly known as the Southern Farmers' Alliance and the Northwestern Farmers'

Grange cartoon: the railroad menace

Alliance. The Southern Alliance had originated in 1875 in a frontier county of Texas, but it amounted to little until it launched a program of rapid expansion in 1886 under the energetic leadership of Dr. C. W. Macune. Farmers joined by the hundreds of thousands—at one time the national organization claimed as many as 3 million members, though it never made a really accurate count. Affiliated with them was a separate Colored Farmers' National Alliance and Cooperative Union that claimed 1¼ million black members.

The Southern Alliance took in tenants and landowners, as well as rural mechanics and other classes of country people. With a highly centralized national organization, it established its own press, which was supported by hundreds of local weekly papers, and a lecture bureau that kept reform ideas circulating among its members. The Alliance went in for cooperatives even more extensively than the old Grange. Hundreds of Alliance stores and warehouses, marketing agencies, gins, tanneries, and mills sprinkled the South, though most of them were short-lived.

The Northwestern Alliance, organized by Milton George of Chicago in 1880, did not agree with the Southern Alliance in its policies of secrecy, centralized control, and separate organization for blacks and resisted pressure to join the larger society for fear of being overwhelmed. But in 1889 the Southern Alliance changed its name to the National Farmers' Alliance and Industrial Union and persuaded the three strongest state alliances of the Northwestern Alliance, those of Kansas and North and South Dakota, to join it. In the same year the Alliance gained the endorsement of the Knights of Labor and formed a political combination with that organization.

The character of the Alliance is reflected in the "demands" drawn up at its annual conventions. The Ocala Demands, for example, voted at the convention in Ocala, Florida, in 1890, called for the government to establish a "Subtreasury System." This would permit farmers to store nonperishable crops in government warehouses or elevators and receive Treasury notes lending them up to 80 percent of the local market value of the grain or cotton deposited. The government loan was secured by the crops and repaid when they were sold, thus enabling the farmer to hold his produce for the best price.* Other demands were for the abolition of national banks, a substantial increase in the amount of money in circulation, the free coinage of silver, a federal income tax, the reduction of tariff rates, the direct election of senators, "rigid" control of railroad and telegraph companies—and, if that did not work, "government ownership" of both.

Though the Alliance, like the Grange, professed to be strictly "nonpolitical," it was clear that its demands could be realized only by political means. Using their demands (similar to the ones adopted later that year at Ocala) as a yardstick, Southern Alliancemen required all Democratic candidates in the 1890 eletions to "stand up and be measured." As a result, the Alliance seemed at the time to have come near taking over the Democratic party in the South, for it elected four governors, secured control of eight legislatures, and elected forty-four congressmen and three senators who were pledged to support Alliance demands. Instead of working within one of the old parties, Alliancemen in the West hastily set up independent third parties, the names of which differed from state to state, and nominated their own candidates. Their most striking successes were in Kansas, where they elected five congressmen and a senator; in Nebraska, where they took control of both houses of the legislature and elected two congressmen; and in South Dakota, where they elected a senator. In other Western states their vote came largely at the expense of the Republicans and accounted in part for the large number of Democratic congressmen elected in 1890. The election served notice on both old parties that the farmers were on the march.

The Populist crusade. Their successes in 1890 inspired Westerners with the ambition to form a na-

tional third party to promote Alliance ideas. Southerners hung back, however, in order to try out their plan of working within the Democratic party. They were quickly disillusioned, for all the Southern Democratic congressmen elected on an Alliance platform, with the exception of Tom Watson, entered the Democratic caucus and voted for a conservative anti-Alliance Georgian for Speaker. Thereupon Watson, redheaded and a rebel by temperament, left his party and became the "People's party" candidate for Speaker with the support of eight congressmen from the West. Thus the new party, often called the Populist party, had a congressional delegation before it had a national organization. The National Alliance, however, under the leadership of President Leonidas L. Polk of North Carolina, was moving rapidly in the Populist direction. On February 22, 1892, a huge Confederation of Industrial Organizations met at St. Louis, attended by delegates from the Knights of Labor, the Nationalists, the Single-Taxers, Greenbackers, Prohibitionists, and other curiously assorted reform groups, but dominated by delegates from the National Alliance. The delegates officially founded the People's party and called for a convention to nominate a ticket for the presidential election of 1892.

Shortly before the convention met in Omaha on July 4, the Populists were deprived of their strongest candidate by the death of Polk. The party nominated the old Greenback campaigner of 1880, General James B. Weaver of Iowa, for President, and, to balance the Union general with a Confederate one, chose General James G. Field of Virginia as his running mate. The platform emphatically reiterated Alliance principles on money, credit, transportation, and land and evoked the wildest enthusiasm for its planks on government ownership of railroads and monetary reform. Populist principles, embodying the agrarian reform ideas of two decades, had become a sacred creed. The fervor and violence of Populist rhetoric is illustrated by the following excerpt from the preamble to the platform, written and delivered by Ignatius Donnelly of Minnesota, foremost Populist writer and orator:

> . . . we meet in the midst of a nation brought to the verge of moral, political, and material ruin. Corruption dominates the ballot-box, the legislatures, the Congress, and touches even the ermine of the bench. The people are demoralized.

Eastern conservatives were frightened by the Populist tone and built up a distorted image of the movement as an insurrection of hayseed anarchists or hick communists. The very nicknames of Populist leaders lent themselves to such propaganda—names such as Lemuel H. "Calamity" Weller of Iowa, Congressman "Sockless" Jerry Simpson of Kansas, Governor Davis H. "Bloody Bridles" Waite of Colorado, and orator

*The idea was embodied in the New Deal measure of 1936 creating the Commodity Credit Corporation.

The agrarian revolt

James H. "Cyclone" Davis of Texas—not to mention
the endlessly quoted advice of Mary E. Lease of Kansas to "raise less corn and more hell." It is quite true
that some of the Populist leaders were fanatical and
narrow-minded, and that the majority of Populist
voters were provincial and ill-informed folk with a
poor understanding of the troubles that beset them.
Populists tended to oversimplify issues, to embrace

Mary E. Lease:
"less corn and more hell"

panaceas, to talk loosely of "conspiracy" against them,
and to use violent and desperate language.

It is only fair to the Populists, however, to recall
that the plight of the people for whom they spoke was
desperate. We must recall also that their conservative
opponents, better educated as a rule, entertained absurd monetary and economic theories of their own
and talked wildly of conspiracies and subversives
themselves (see p. 487). To their credit it should be
remembered that the Populists were the first important movement in this country to insist that laissez-
faire economics was not the final solution to industrial problems and that the federal government had
some responsibility for social well-being. Most of the
Populist demands that seemed so wild at the time
were accepted as respectable within a surprisingly
short time and were eventually written into law. The
Populists' main service was to usher in a long-needed
and long-delayed era of reform and to reveal the
empty pretense of the political game as played by the
old parties.

The first task of the Populists was to bridge the
cleavages between parties, sections, races, and classes
that kept apart the forces of reform that they wished
to unite. First they sought to revive the old agrarian
alliance between South and West that had been effectively broken by the Civil War. Second, they felt that
both the Republicans and the Democrats were bent
on keeping natural allies divided and sought to replace the old parties with a third party. Third, they
tried to unite farmers of the South who were divided
by racial barriers, and some of the whites and blacks
worked hard at the effort. Finally, the Populists sought
to create an alliance between farmers and labor. The
Populists enjoyed some success with all four of these
alliances, but sectional animosities were kept alive by

Kansas House of Representatives, 1895

the bloody-shirt issue, old party loyalties were hard to break, racial antagonism was inflamed by white-supremacy propaganda, and labor did not always see eye to eye with the farmer. In view of all these handicaps the Populists made a surprisingly good showing in their first appearance at the polls. They cast a little more than a million votes for their presidential candidate and also elected ten representatives, five senators, three governors, and some fifteen hundred members of state legislatures.

The depression and the silver issue

Cleveland and the silverites. Somewhat sobered by the Populist threat, the Democrats and the Republicans conducted their 1892 campaigns with more dignity than usual. Cleveland, the choice of conservative Democrats, was nominated by the first ballot of his party's convention, and Harrison was the equally predictable nominee of the Republicans. Adlai E. Ste-

venson* of Illinois became Cleveland's running mate, and Whitelaw Reid, editor of the New York *Tribune,* was the Republican nominee for Vice President. Both platforms were evasive on the monetary issues that stirred the greatest interest among voters. Cleveland improved his poll of 1888, and 1884 as well, winning 5,555,426 votes to 5,182,690 for Harrison, and 277 electoral votes to Harrison's 145. The Democrats carried not only the doubtful states of New York, New Jersey, Connecticut, and Indiana but the normally Republican states of Illinois, Wisconsin, and California. It was not quite a landslide, but it was the most decisive victory either party had won in twenty years.

President Cleveland moved back into the White House and surrounded himself with a thoroughly conservative Cabinet of Easterners and Southerners who were as completely out of touch with the radical discontent of the country as he was himself. Almost immediately the financial panic of 1893 shattered his peace and ushered in the worst depression the nation had experienced up to that time. The panic had actu-

*Grandfather of the Democratic candidate for President in 1952 and 1956.

481

ally started ten days before Harrison left office, when the Philadelphia & Reading Railroad went bankrupt and the New York Stock Exchange was shaken by the greatest selling spree in its history. Two months after Cleveland's inauguration the market collapsed. Banks called in their loans, and credit dried up. Unstable financial conditions abroad, especially the failure of Baring Brothers of London in 1890, had started a drain on the gold reserve that became increasingly severe after 1893. One great railroad after another—the Erie, the Northern Pacific, the Union Pacific, the Santa Fe—went down in failure. "Mills, factories, furnaces, mines nearly everywhere," reported the New York *Commercial and Financial Chronicle* in August, "shut down in large numbers, and commerce and enterprise were arrested in an extraordinary degree." By the end of the year five hundred banks and more than fifteen thousand business firms had fallen into bankruptcy. Populist Donnelly's apocalyptic picture in 1892 of "a nation brought to the verge of ruin" seemed about to be translated into reality.

Learned economists still argue about the causes and remedies of depressions, and there can be no doubt that the causes of the depression that settled over the country in 1893 were highly complex. But President Cleveland had a simple explanation and a simple remedy, and never did a dogmatist cling more tenaciously to his theory. His explanation was that the Sherman Silver Purchase Act (see p. 475) had caused the depression, and his remedy was to repeal the act and maintain the gold standard at all costs— that is, continue to redeem all United States Treasury notes in gold. The economic consequences of Cleveland's remedy do not appear to have been decisive one way or the other, but the political consequences were disastrous. No issue since slavery had divided the people more deeply than silver. It split both old parties, disrupted Populism, and caused a revolution in the Democratic party that overthrew conservative control.

The trouble was that Cleveland's theory clashed head on with a more popular theory held with equal dogmatism by the silverites. According to them, the cause of the economic disaster lay in the "Crime of '73" that demonetized silver, and the remedy lay in the free and unlimited coinage of silver at a ratio of sixteen to one of gold. The arguments and the sources of support for the silver movement acquired new strength and additional recruits. The admission of six new Western states—Montana, North Dakota, South Dakota, and Washington in 1889 and Idaho and Wyoming in 1890—brought reinforcements to the silverites in Congress, especially in the Senate. In the meantime American silver-producers suffered additional reductions in their market from the demonetization of silver in Europe and India and became more desperate for relief through free coinage in the United States. At the same time debtor agrarians saw free coinage of silver as one hope of relief from deflation and currency contraction and increased their cry for "free silver." In place of the inadequate relief provided by the Sherman Silver Purchase Act, they demanded unlimited and free coinage.

Cleveland stubbornly insisted, on the other hand, that the Sherman Act was the whole cause of the trouble and demanded its repeal. The only way to restore confidence and prosperity, he held, was to maintain the gold standard, and that required the maintenance of a gold reserve of $100 million in the Treasury. There was a case to be made in favor of the gold standard in the 1890s, but there were many causes for the drain on the gold reserve, and there were many causes of the depression other than the threat to the gold standard. But under relentless pressure by the President, Congress finally repealed the Sherman Act. Cleveland got his way by relying on Republican support and splitting his own party.

Repeal of the Sherman Act seemed to have no effect, for the drain on the gold reserve continued unabated, and so did the depression. Business confidence was not restored, and the hoarding of gold increased. The Treasury surplus that the Billion Dollar Congress had been so eager to spend was no more, and the McKinley Tariff had sharply reduced tariff revenues. Holders of gold and silver certificates, doubting the ability of the government to maintain the gold standard, started a run on the Treasury; and panic in Europe caused continual withdrawals. The President resorted to a series of highly unpopular bond sales to recoup the gold reserves. The third bond sale, in February 1895, caused the greatest indignation of all. This time the president yielded to the demand of J. Pierpont Morgan that the sale be kept private, and the syndicate of bankers that handled the loan drove a hard bargain for their services and were accused of making large profits, though Morgan refused to reveal how much. The bond issue yielded over $65 million to the government, half of it from Europe, and the bankers scotched some of the drain on the gold reserve. Nevertheless, another issue was necessary in January 1896. The four bond sales did save the gold standard, but they did not stop the decline of the gold reserve or restore prosperity. Each one further intensified the silverites' hatred of the President. These bond sales enhanced Cleveland's reputation for courage but not for wisdom: they failed to cure the depression, and they led to political disaster.

The politics of depression. The blight that had been familiar to farmers for years now began to fall on the factory and the city. Railroad construction fell off drastically, dividends halted, and investment in all

Political stalemate and agrarian revolt, 1877–1896

business declined sharply. Bankers, businessmen, and employers seemed stricken with a failure of nerve. They laid off workers, cut wages, closed factory doors, and swelled the army of the jobless. A hundred thousand of them shuffled through the streets of Chicago, and visitors to the "dream city" at the Exposition in 1893 wondered at the miles of sleeping men who lined the tracks of the elevated railway. "What a spectacle!" exclaimed Ray Stannard Baker, a cub reporter, "What a human downfall after the magnificence and prodigality of the World's Fair."

The year 1894 was the most brutal of the depression. Between 2½ and 3 million, perhaps as many as one out of five workers, were thought to be unemployed, but no one really knew, and the unemployed felt that no one in the government really cared. Some cities provided a little work relief, but this was wholly inadequate, and when hungry men turned to the federal government they were met with cold indifference or angry rejection. Jacob S. Coxey of Massillon, Ohio, a well-to-do businessman who was a Populist and was quite untypical of his class in other ways, proposed a plan of federal work relief on public roads to be financed by an issue of $500 million in legal-tender Treasury notes. The "good roads" bill was designed to end the depression by providing monetary inflation and internal improvements as well as work relief for the unemployed. When Congress refused to pass it, Coxey declared, "We will send a petition to Washington with boots on." "Coxey's Army" marched peacefully from Massillon to the Capitol, picking up sympathizers on the way, including a hundred students from Lehigh University and a few visionaries and eccentrics, and paraded into Washington on May Day, about five hundred strong. They were cheered by crowds, but Coxey and his lieutenants were arrested by the police, and some fifty people were beaten or trampled. No fewer than seventeen "industrial armies" started for Washington in 1894, and some twelve hundred men arrived. They were peaceful and sober as a rule, but it was the obvious sympathy they stirred over the country that frightened the government, even President Cleveland, into the mistaken idea that a spirit of rebellion threatened to bring on mob rule.

Not only the government but private employers resorted to violence in countering labor protest. An extraordinary number of strikes, some fourteen hundred in all, occurred during 1894, many of them provoked by wage cuts. More than 660,000 people were thrown out of work by strikes or lockouts. Management countered by using violence, employing secret police, or securing injunctions from friendly courts. In the Pullman strike of July, as we have seen (p. 440), the federal government used troops of the regular army to crush the workers. Cleveland earned as much

"Coxey's Army" on the march

hostility from labor by his use of troops as he had from agrarians by his sale of bonds.

In the meantime, the only serious piece of reform the second Cleveland Administration undertook, the reform of the tariff, met with complete failure. To fulfill their campaign pledges, the Democrats did put through the House a bill, framed by William L. Wilson of West Virginia, containing modest reductions in the tariff. But in the Senate the protectionists of both parties fell upon it with six hundred amendments that restored the old rates and actually raised some of them. The Wilson-Gorman Act, which Cleveland denounced as "party perfidy and party dishonor" and allowed to become law without his signature, made a mockery of the Administration's pretenses of tariff reform. The only sop to reformers was an amendment, slipped in by the agrarians and deplored by the President, that provided for a small income tax of 2 percent on incomes over $4,000. The Supreme Court, which shared Cleveland's unpopularity as an agency of reaction, promptly declared the income tax unconstitutional by a vote of five to four. For relief of suffering among the unemployed, on the farms, and in the cities, for restoring credit, and for assisting industry afflicted by depression, Cleveland's Administration refused to take any responsibility beyond maintaining the gold standard.

The spirit of despair and resentment abroad in the land was perfectly suited to the appeal of the Populists. In the fall elections of 1894 the third party increased the vote it polled in 1892 by 42 percent. In the West the Populists lost Nevada, which went over to the Silverites, a new party, and Colorado and Idaho

483

went Republican, so that the overall strength of the party declined. But in the South Populists exploited hatred of Cleveland, and with evangelistic campaigns and camp-meeting techniques they piled up gains that frightened the Democrats. In spite of violence and fraud and racist propaganda more blatant than the Democrats had used since the overthrow of Reconstruction, the Populists captured North Carolina, with Republican aid, and mustered more strength in the supposedly conservative states of Georgia and Alabama than they commanded in any Western state save Nebraska. After the defeats of 1894 the Democrats retained only technical control of the Senate and suffered heavy losses in the House. Many prominent Democratic congressmen went down to defeat as the Republicans recouped their losses in the previous election and took control of the House with a majority of one hundred forty seats. No Democrats at all won national office in twenty-four states, and only one each in six others. New York, Illinois, and Wisconsin returned to the Republican fold, and only one Democratic congressman was elected in New England. The elections of 1894 brought about the largest congressional gains and one of the most widespread political realignments in the nation's history. It was this election and not that of 1896 that marked the fall of the Democrats and the beginning of the long Republican ascendancy.

The Democratic party was, in fact, in the midst of revolution almost as profound as that of 1860. Again it was a sectional split, but this time it was the Northeast that was isolated instead of the South. West and South joined hands in the name of the free coinage of silver, but silver merely served as a symbol for dozens of other sectional issues. And Grover Cleveland became the personification of the Northeastern conservatism against which the two agrarian regions were in revolt. Never since Andrew Johnson had a President been so detested and abused by members of his own party as was Cleveland.

Early in 1895 prominent Democrats in the South and West set to work systematically to use the silver issue as a means of taking over control of their party and unseating Cleveland and the conservatives. With financial support from the silver-miners, they held silver conventions all over the South and West to which they invited Populists and urged them to give up their more radical demands and "come down to silver." They distributed great quantities of silver propaganda, such as Ignatius Donnelly's *The American People's Money* (1895) and the famous booklet by William H. "Coin" Harvey, *Coin's Financial School* (1894). In the latter, "Professor Coin" laid bare the "conspiracy of Goldbugs," proponents of the gold standard, and "proved" that the free and unlimited coinage of silver was the panacea for all economic ills. The work of the silver Democrats against Cleveland was so effective that after the state conventions in the summer of 1896 no state Democratic organization south of the Potomac and only three west of the Alleghenies remained in the hands of the President's friends. There was no longer any doubt that the silverites would be able to wrest control of the national Democratic convention from Cleveland.

Joseph H. Choate:

You cannot hereafter exercise any check if you now say that Congress is untrammelled and uncontrollable. My friend says you cannot enforce any limit. He says no matter what Congress does ... this Court will have nothing to say about it. I agree that it will have nothing to say about it if it now lets go its hold upon this law....

I have thought that one of the fundamental objects of all civilized government was the preservation of the rights of private property. I have thought that it was the very keystone of the arch upon which all civilized government rests, and that this once abandoned, everything was in danger.... According to the doctrines that have been propounded here this morning, even that great fundamental principle has been scattered to the winds....

If it be true, as my friend said in closing, that the passions of the people are aroused on this subject, if it be true that a mighty army of sixty million citizens is likely to be incensed by this decision, it is the more vital to the future welfare of this country that this court again resolutely and courageously declare, as Marshall did, that it has the power to set aside an act of Congress violative of the Constitution ... no matter what the threatened consequences of popular or populistic wrath may be.

From Pollock v. Farmers' Loan and Trust Co., 157 U.S. 429, 1895.

Joseph H. Choate

McKinley and gold versus Bryan and silver. Nor was there any doubt that the Republican convention would nominate William McKinley of Ohio when it met at St. Louis in June. McKinley's nomination had been assured by the systematic and patient work of his devoted friend Marcus Alonzo Hanna, who not only rounded up the necessary votes before the convention but financed and managed his friend's preconvention campaign. A blunt and forthright businessman from Cleveland, Hanna had made a fortune in coal, iron, banking, shipping, and street railways before he retired from business in 1895 to devote full time to fulfilling his ambition of putting McKinley in the White House. McKinley's nomination rolled forward as planned on the first ballot, and Garret A. Hobart, a relatively unknown corporation lawyer from New Jersey, was the vice-presidential nominee. A protectionist platform was obviously called for, since McKinley's name had become synonymous with high tariff. The only doubt was how explicit the plank on the gold standard should be. Hanna had already decided upon a forthright endorsement, but he cleverly hung back at the convention and permitted himself to be "persuaded" by Eastern delegates to accept the statement that "the existing gold standard should be preserved." Upon the adoption of the gold plank, Senator Henry M. Teller of Colorado led a small group of Western silver Republicans from the hall, and they withdrew from the party.

Eastern Republicans had reason to doubt McKinley's firmness on gold. In the political lingo of the battle of standards, politicians were classified as "Goldbugs," "Silverbugs," or "Straddlebugs," and the Ohioan was often classed with the third group. He had voted for both the Bland-Allison Act and the Sherman Silver Purchase Act and continued to speak kindly of silver as an American product that deserved "protection" and to favor compromise when compromise had become untenable. In 1896, however, he accepted his party's decision for gold. He was an experienced and skillful politician who had served in Congress from 1876 to 1892, with the exception of one term, and had been governor of Ohio for two terms, completing the second in 1895. A kindly, impressive-looking, rather solemn man, McKinley sincerely shared Hanna's devotion to the interests of American business. The campaign caricature of McKinley as the spineless puppet of the millionaire boss had no foundation in fact, for the evidence is that Hanna constantly deferred to his friend and respected his wishes.

The Democratic convention at Chicago exhibited all the disorder and spontaneity that the Republicans had been spared under Hanna's direction. Cleveland-supporters, still full of fight, arrived from the East to clash with red-hot silver orators from the South and the West amid a din of hisses and catcalls and rebel yells in which only the leather-lunged could make

William Jennings Bryan, 1896: reformers rallied to his cause

had been campaigning for three years to prepare the revolt of the silver forces. Bryan had some naive ideas about money and harbored suspicions of the East, "the enemy's country," as he once called it. He was no radical, and his ties were with the simple agrarian past rather than with the complex future. But conservatives were wrong to dismiss him as a one-idea fanatic. He had an intuitive grasp of the deep mood of protest that stirred the mass of voters, and he expressed that mood in a moral appeal to the conscience of the country. His real service was to awaken an old faith in social justice and to protest against a generation of plutocratic rule.

In their next maneuver, the silver-leaders of the "revolutionized" Democrats persuaded the Populist party, which held its convention in St. Louis after the Democratic convention had met, to make Bryan its candidate as well. The proposal deeply divided the Populists, who neither wanted to split the reform forces with a separate ticket nor give up their own party identity. Western Populists were eager to nominate Bryan, but Southern members, always more radical and less devoted to silver, wanted a separate Populist ticket and no compromise. Bryan's nomination

themselves heard. But the Easterners had neither the strength to control the convention nor a suitable candidate to put before it, and the agrarian rebels rode over them roughshod. They adopted a platform strongly influenced by Governor John P. Altgeld of Illinois, the friend of the Pullman strikers and the pardoner of the Haymarket-riot anarchists. The platform, which denounced virtually everything Cleveland stood for, also struck out fiercely at the protective tariff, the national banks, trusts, and the Supreme Court; it demanded an income tax and, most important of all, free coinage of silver at the ratio of sixteen ounces of silver to one of gold.

Altgeld was disqualified as a candidate by foreign birth, and the convention passed over Congressman Richard P. "Silver Dick" Bland, the most prominent contender. At the strategic moment a handsome young ex-congressman, William Jennings Bryan of Nebraska, captured the attention and the imagination of the silver forces with a speech that mounted to a thrilling peroration: "You shall not press down upon the brow of labor this crown of thorns, you shall not crucify mankind upon a cross of gold." Bryan was nominated on the fifth ballot, and, to balance the ticket, Arthur Sewall of Maine, a banker and businessman who opposed the gold standard, was nominated for Vice President.

While he was only thirty-six and little known in the East, Bryan was already widely known as a peerless orator in the West and the South, where he

William McKinley, 1896: front porch in Canton

Political stalemate and agrarian revolt, 1877-1896

was at last secured when Senator William V. Allen of Nebraska, chairman of the convention, told the Southerners that the Democrats had agreed to withdraw Sewall and accept Thomas E. Watson as their vice-presidential nominee if the Populists would nominate Bryan. Southern radicals bitterly resisted fusion with the Democrats, whom they had been fighting for four years. But when their hero Watson agreed to compromise, they reluctantly consented and nominated Bryan and Watson. Only later did they learn that the Democrats refused to withdraw the banker Sewall.

Two more parties were created out of bolters from the old parties. The National Silver Republicans endorsed the Democratic candidates. Later on, the gold Democrats, with encouragement and financial support from Hanna, organized the National Democratic party and nominated a separate ticket that was intended to contribute to Bryan's defeat.

The contest between McKinley and Bryan in 1896 has taken on the legendary character of the combat between Goliath and David—except that it turned out quite differently. Bryan played the David role admirably—the lone youth armed with nothing but shafts of oratory pitted against the armored Gold Giant and all his hosts. Actually, reformers of many schools rallied to Bryan's cause, including Henry George of the Single-Taxers, Edward Bellamy of the Nationalists, W. D. P. Bliss of the Christian Socialists, Eugene V. Debs of the Railway Union, and Samuel Gompers of the American Federation of Labor, all of whom campaigned for him. Bryan's chief reliance, however, was upon his own voice. In a campaign without precedent at that time, he traveled eighteen thousand miles by train, made more than six hundred speeches, and talked to some 5 million people. He spoke not only of silver but of the price of crops, the cost of mortgages, the need for credit, and the regulation of railroads. The powerful popular response to his campaign aroused great hopes for victory.

It also aroused a hysterical wave of fear among conservatives and facilitated Hanna's collection of campaign funds. He exacted tribute from every great trust, railroad, bank, and tycoon with any stake in the outcome and built up a treasure chest undreamed of before that time. The fund has been estimated everywhere between $3.5 million and $15 million (the latter an exaggeration)—as against a mere $300,000 at Bryan's disposal. Hanna spent the money lavishly but shrewdly, sending out propaganda by the ton and the carload and speakers by the battalion. He also transported trainloads of people from representative groups, all expenses paid, to hear McKinley read well-prepared speeches from his front porch in Canton, Ohio, from which the candidate never stirred. The press assisted Hanna with blasts of ridicule and charges of socialism and anarchism against Bryan. The Philadelphia *Press* described the "Jacobins" of the Chicago convention as "hideous and repulsive vipers." President Cleveland called them "madmen" and "criminals," and the New York *Tribune* referred to Bryan as a "wretched, rattle-pated boy." Employers

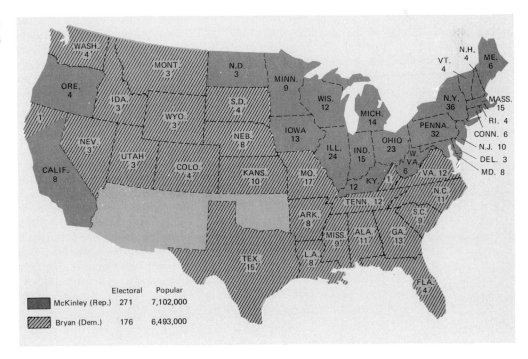

The election of 1896

	Electoral	Popular
McKinley (Rep.)	271	7,102,000
Bryan (Dem.)	176	6,493,000

487

of labor joined in with threats to close up shop or cut wages if Bryan was elected.

The combination of powers was too much for the resources of Bryan. He polled 6,492,559 votes, more votes than any victorious candidate had ever polled before, nearly a million more than Cleveland polled in 1892, but it was still not enough. McKinley won with 7,102,246 votes, a plurality of 609,687, and an electoral vote of 271 to 176. Bryan did not carry a single state north of the Potomac or east of the Mississippi above its juncture with the Ohio. He did not even carry the farming states of Iowa, Minnesota, and North Dakota. What is more significant, he carried no industrialized, no urbanized state. This may well be the main reason for Bryan's defeat. In spite of widespread unrest among labor, Bryan did not win labor's support, which might have given him victory. He really had little to offer either labor or the cities. Like many other American reformers of his day, he had something of significance for the present, but his true ties were with the past. McKinley and Hanna may not have been looking very far into the future, but they clearly had a firmer grip on the present. They were also able to influence labor, and they evidently won the confidence of the urban middle class. Their victory at the polls meant more conservatism and yet another businessman's regime.

The aftermath of '96. The election was followed by a brief revival of the economy and three years later by the end of the long depression. The upturn had little if anything to do with the saving of the gold standard or the victory of McKinley. The price of wheat had started to climb before the election, though hardly enough to have influenced the outcome. But in 1897 the European wheat crop fell off 30 percent, and American farmers doubled their exports of the previous year. Prices continued to rise, and the whole economy began to revive. Discoveries of gold in Aus-

tralia and Alaska revived the flow of gold into the country, and gold production was further increased by discoveries of pay dirt in South Africa and the development of the cyanide process for extracting the metal from ore. The inflation that the agrarians and silverites had demanded came, ironically enough, not through silver but through gold. The influx of gold and capital stimulated industrial expansion, and that in turn touched off a boom in iron and steel.

With a Republican majority in both houses, McKinley called a special session of Congress in the summer of 1897 to further additional protective tariffs. The Wilson-Gorman Tariff of 1894 was already high enough for most protectionists, but Congress passed a bill framed by Nelson Dingley of Maine, which raised duties to an average of 52 percent. McKinley avoided action on the gold standard until gold was flowing in and silver sentiment was waning. But in his annual message of 1899 he called for legislation, and Congress adopted by a party vote the Gold Standard Act, which he signed on March 14, 1900. The act declared that the gold dollar was henceforth the sole standard of currency, thus writing an end to a generation of controversy, but without producing any significant economic effect, either good or bad.

One significant but often overlooked result of the election of 1896 and the return to prosperity was the demoralization of the Populist movement. Fusion with the enemy party and abandonment of principle for the sake of silver had demoralized the Populists and all but destroyed their party. "The sentiment is still there, the votes are still there, but confidence is gone," thought Tom Watson. The following decade was to see a new upsurge of reform and the realization of many of the old Populist demands, but they were achieved under urban, not rural, leadership. Nineteenth-century agrarian radicalism made its last significant bid for leadership of a national reform movement in 1896.

Suggestions for reading

The political history of this period is treated by H. W. Morgan, *From Hayes to McKinley: National Party Politics, 1877–1896* (1969), and by R. O. Marcus, *Grand Old Party: Political Structure in the Gilded Age, 1880–1896* (1971). A revisionary estimate of politicians is D. J. Rothman, *Politics and Power: The United States Senate, 1869–1901** (1966). On the nineties, see H. U. Faulkner, *Politics, Reform and Expansion, 1890–1900** (1959), and L. P. Beth, *The Development of the American Constitution, 1877–1901* (1971). W. E. Binkley, *American Political Parties: Their Natural History* (1943, 4th rev. ed., 1963), is interpretative; E. H. Roseboom, *A History of Presidential Elections* (1957, rev. ed., 1970), is factual; and C. A. M. Ewing, *Presidential Elections from Abraham Lincoln to Franklin D. Roosevelt* (1940), is analytical. Richard Hofstadter, *The Age of Reform: From Bryan to F. D. R.** (1955), is revisionary and challenging. Two sectional studies are Paul Kleppner, *The Cross of Culture: A Social Analysis of Midwestern Politics, 1850–1900* (1970), and R. J. Jensen, *The Winning of the Midwest: Social and Political Conflict, 1888–1896* (1971).

*Available in a paperback edition.

Political stalemate and agrarian revolt, 1877–1896

Key biographies are Harry Barnard, *Rutherford B. Hayes and His America* (1954); R. G. Caldwell, *James A. Garfield: Party Chieftain* (1931); T. C. Reeves, *Gentleman Boss: The Life of Chester Alan Arthur* (1975); D. S. Muzzey, *James G. Blaine: A Political Idol of Other Days* (1934); Allan Nevins, *Grover Cleveland: A Study in Courage* (1933); H. J. Sievers, *Benjamin Harrison: Hoosier Statesman* (1959); and R. E. Welch, Jr., *George Frisbie Hoar and the Half-Breed Republicans* (1971). (On Bryan and McKinley, see below.) See also J. G. Sproat, *The Best Men: Liberal Reformers in the Gilded Age** (1968), and C. E. Rosenberg, *The Trial of the Assassin Guiteau: Psychiatry and Law in the Gilded Age* (1968).

On the politics and issues of reform the literature is rich. On reformist mentality, see Eric Goldman, *Rendezvous with Destiny: A History of Modern American Reform** (1952, abr. & rev. ed., 1956), and the book by Hofstadter cited above. Ray Ginger, *Age of Excess** (1956), is an interpretative study. Civil-service reform is the subject of three excellent works: L. D. White, *The Republican Era: 1896–1901** (1958); P. P. Van Riper, *History of the United States Civil Service* (1958); and Ari Hogenboom, *Fighting the Spoilsmen* (1961). Still valuable on tariff reform are F. W. Taussig, *The Tariff History of the United States** (1894, 8th ed., 1967), and I. M. Tarbell, *The Tariff in Our Times* (1911). Pensions for veterans are treated by J. W. Oliver, *History of the Civil War Military Pensions* (1917), and W. H. Glasson, *History of Military Pension Legislation in the United States* (1900). Monetary controversies of the period are examined in Milton Friedman and A. J. Schwartz, *A Monetary History of the United States, 1867–1960** (1963); Irwin Unger, *The Greenback Era: A Social and Political History of American Finance, 1865–1879** (1964); W. T. K. Nugent, *Money and American Society, 1865–1880* (1968); and Allen Weinstein, *Prelude to Populism: Origins of the Silver Issue, 1867–1878* (1970).

Agricultural conditions and movements are authoritatively examined in F. A. Shannon, *The Farmer's Last Frontier: Agriculture, 1860–1897** (1945). For light on farmers' organizations, see S. J. Buck, *The Granger Movement** (1913); J. D. Hicks, *The Populist Revolt** (1931); Norman Pollack, *The Populist Response to Industrial America** (1962); W. T. K. Nugent, *The Tolerant Populists: Kansas Populism and Nativism* (1963); R. B. Nye, *Midwestern Progressive Politics: A Historical Study of Its Origins and Development, 1870–1958** (1951, rev. ed., 1959); and Theodore Saloutos, *Farmer Movements in the South, 1865–1933** (1960). A suggestive survey is C. C. Taylor, *The Farmers' Movement, 1620–1920* (1953).

The depression of the nineties and its political repercussions are intelligently discussed in S. T. McSereney, *The Politics of Depression* (1972); J. E. Wright, *The Politics of Populism: Dissent in Colorado* (1974); and P. H. Argersinger, *Populism and Politics: William Alfred Peffer and the People's Party* (1974); and economic causes of the trouble in F. B. Webeg, *The Background of the Panic of 1893* (1929). The serious student will be fascinated by source materials in Hamlin Garland, *Main-travelled Roads** (1891), for agrarian ills; W. H. Harvey, *Coin's Financial School** (1894), and Ignatius Donnelly, *The American People's Money* (1895), for silver propaganda; and H. D. Lloyd, *Wealth Against Commonwealth** (1894), for an exposure of monopoly. Scholarly studies of labor protest are D. L. McMurry, *Coxey's Army** (1929), and Almont Lindsey, *The Pullman Strike** (1943). On the latter event, see also Harry Barnard, *"Eagle Forgotten": The Life of John Peter Altgeld** (1938), and Ray Ginger, *Altgeld's America—The Lincoln Ideal Versus Changing Realities** (1958).

On Populism, Bryanism, McKinleyism, and the crisis of 1896, many books already mentioned are relevant. In addition, see Stanley Jones, *The Presidential Election of 1896* (1964); J. R. Hollingsworth, *The Whirligig of Politics: The Democracy of Cleveland and Bryan* (1963); and P. W. Glad, *McKinley, Bryan, and the People** (1964). The best biographies are Margaret Leech, *In the Days of McKinley* (1959); H. W. Morgan, *William McKinley and His America* (1963); and P. E. Coletta, *William Jennings Bryan, Political Evangelist, 1860–1908* (1964). Bryan's own account, *The First Battle* (1897), is worth consulting. Still the best book on McKinley's great friend is Herbert Croly, *Marcus Alonzo Hanna* (1912). Agrarian leaders prominent in 1896 are pictured in C. V. Woodward, *Tom Watson: Agrarian Rebel** (1938), and F. B. Simkins, *Pitchfork Ben Tillman: South Carolinian** (1944).

*Available in a paperback edition.

CHAPTER **21**

Empire beyond the seas

he United States was not born in isolation, nor with any bias against expansionism. On the contrary, the long colonial experience was lived out in the midst of international rivalries. Independence itself was painfully won and precariously defended by taking shrewd advantage of those rivalries. Expansionism was a fundamental policy in the new nation's negotiations with foreign powers. Louisiana, Florida, Texas, New Mexico, California, Oregon, the Gadsden Purchase, and the Alaska Purchase—in fact the acquisition of all the continental area of the country beyond the original colonies—are dramatic evidence of expansionism, vigorously and steadily pursued.

After about a century, ending in 1867 with the purchase of Alaska, the nation lapsed into what might almost be called isolationism, though a better term would probably be withdrawal, or preoccupation. At any rate, the United States called a halt to territorial expansion for a quarter of a century or more. In the 1880s, however, expansionism reawakened in a new form—overseas expansion—and concern over foreign affairs revived. A war with Spain, though not itself prompted by expansionism, actually brought overseas possessions, colonies, millions of colonial subjects, protectorates—a whole empire. A republic became an empire, a country long preoccupied with internal affairs turned its attention outward. One phase of isolationism ended, and with it one phase of American innocence.

Withdrawal and return

The period of withdrawal. The United States' withdrawal from world affairs was not due to any lack of advocates of aggressiveness. William H. Seward,

490

Secretary of State under Lincoln and Johnson, proposed, among other things, intervention in Korea, acquisition of the Hawaiian Islands, and adventures in the Caribbean. He could muster no support for these undertakings, however, and only with difficulty persuaded Congress to accept the Alaska bargain offered by Russia. Moved by scheming friends, President Grant devised a treaty for the annexation of Santo Domingo, though the Senate rejected it in 1870. Other expansionists agitated in vain for the annexation of Canada, for intervention in the Cuban rebellion in 1868–78, for securing a naval station in Samoa in the seventies, and for grabbing naval harbors in Haiti during the eighties. The standard arguments against such schemes were that it was against American principles to govern without the consent of the governed, that we should abstain from foreign entanglements, avoid large naval commitments and expenditures, and refrain from absorbing peoples of alien race and tradition. One name for this policy was "continentalism"—the idea that the nation should acquire no territory outside its continental limits.

American troops
in Peking

491

Uncle Sam:
"I rather like your looks"

Preoccupation with domestic concerns did not blind Americans entirely to opportunities and temptations abroad. The Administrations of Garfield and Arthur sought to advance limited and overlapping goals of prestige, markets, and security, especially in the Caribbean and Central America. Reciprocity trade agreements with countries of these areas were made with a view to exerting economic control over approaches to the proposed isthmian canal region. Arthur's Secretary of State Frederick T. Frelinghuysen pointed out that this would confer "upon us and upon them [Puerto Rico and Cuba] all the benefits which would result from annexation were that possible." Less typical of that period, but suggesting expansionist impulses to come, were the negotiation of a treaty with Korea in 1882 opening up that country to the non-Asian world, and the United States participation in the Berlin Conference of European powers on trade rights in the Congo in 1884–85.

The fact remains, however, that Americans in the seventies and eighties were mainly preoccupied with their built-in empire of the West and their economic colonialism in the South, absorbed in political and economic problems of a domestic character, largely content to stay at home. When Cleveland became President in 1885 the State Department had only sixty employees, including clerks. Secretaries of State were usually political appointees with little knowledge of foreign affairs. Until the 1880s the United States navy was an obsolete and antiquated collection of wooden ships that provoked foreign ridicule. The American merchant marine had virtually disappeared from the seas, and the army was reduced to a handful of Indian-fighters. America still enjoyed—complacently took for granted—nature's mar-velous boon of security, which was not only effective but relatively free. Wide oceans, weak neighbors, and rivalries that kept her potential enemies divided accounted for this blessing of free security. No other great nation enjoyed it, and only the habit of relying upon it can account for the tendency of the United States to engage in heated disputes with foreign powers in which its threats and boasts were out of all proportion to its military strength.

Some of these disputes were with Great Britain, then the mightiest power in the world, and any such dispute was likely to become a game between the major political parties. The game was to see who could "twist the lion's tail" the hardest and who could thereby curry the most favor with the Irish and other anti-British elements. One of the disputes during Cleveland's first Administration was merely a renewal of the perennial bickering over fishing rights along the coasts of British North America. Off the western shores of the continent the United States and Canada were simultaneously embroiled in another dispute—this one over the fur-seal industry in and out of the Bering Sea. The United States advanced an arrogant claim to exclusive jurisdiction over the Bering Sea with the contention that the seals were domestic animals that had wandered out of bounds. The American position was in obvious conflict with the traditional policy of "freedom of the seas." A court of arbitration rejected the American claims and prescribed regulations for the industry that were put into effect by both governments.

The only other embroilment to ruffle the relatively calm waters of foreign affairs during Cleveland's first Administration occurred in the Samoan Islands of the remote South Pacific. The splendid harbor of Pago Pago on Tutuila Island had stirred the interest of naval officers of the United States and other countries. In 1878, after rejecting the proposal of annexation or guardianship made by a Samoan chieftain, the Hayes Administration negotiated a treaty granting the United States the right to establish a naval station at Pago Pago. Germany and Great Britain secured similar treaties the following year, granting them naval-station rights in the same harbor and elsewhere. Competition among the traders of these three nations, and the intrigues of their consuls with rival native chieftains, precipitated a tropical squall of international temper in the mid-eighties. Alarmed by the threat of bloodshed, Cleveland called a conference among the three powers that met in Washington in the summer of 1887 but accomplished nothing. Conditions grew worse when Germany set up a new regime in the islands, and seven warships anchored at Samoa prepared for hostilities. A sudden storm of hurricane force in Apia Harbor brought peace unexpectedly by

Empire beyond the seas

sinking all but one of the warships on March 15, 1889, less than two weeks after Cleveland's term ended. Harrison's Administration worked out a tripartite protectorate of the islands with Germany and Great Britain.

In spite of all these flurries and alarms, little had happened down to 1889 to divert Cleveland from his determination, announced in his first annual message to Congress in 1885, to adhere to "the tenets of a line of precedents from Washington's day, which proscribe entangling alliances," and to oppose "acquisition of new and distant territory or the incorporation of remote interests with our own." Yet the old tradition of isolation, abstention, and withdrawal was near its end, for America was now about to plunge into imperialism and world affairs.

Manifest Destiny revived. The old doctrine of Manifest Destiny (see p. 256) that sped the conquest of California and Oregon in the 1840s had been based on a rather simple faith in the superior vitality of the American people and the beneficence of their political institutions. The new-model manifest destiny that flourished in the late nineteenth century was ornamented by fashionable ideas and scientific notions. Imperialists of the bookish sort found in Darwinism a source of support and rationalization. Practicing imperialists such as Blaine and McKinley found no need for Darwin to justify imperialism. But if industrialists could justify the rise of monopoly in terms of "natural selection," the imperialists could use the same defense for their conquest of "natives" and "backward peoples" in tropical climes. The domination of the "fittest" was thus given the sanction of reputable science. Impulses of aggression and mastery were part of nature's plan for the evolution of man, and to resist them was to go against the law of the universe. Ordinary rules of right and wrong did not apply in this sphere, for responsibility was shifted from conscience to nature. Moreover, the ethics of war and international relations were even more primitive than those of business, for there one was dealing with "the lesser breeds without the law" rather than with "civilized" adversaries.

Nor did the question of who was the "fittest" present the imperialists with any problem: those who were the fittest to rule were those who had the power and craft to do so. The concept of a superior breed of rulers was perfectly attuned to prevailing ideas about race and racial superiority, particularly to the cult of Anglo-Saxon superiority that prevailed among the upper classes of the East and, with a different emphasis, among the whites of the South. Some preferred the term "Teutonic" and others "Aryan" to describe the superior race, but the terms were often used inter-changeably and were sufficiently vague to cover almost all white people with whom one shared friendly feelings.

Religiously inclined exponents of racial superiority believed it had divine sanction. Josiah Strong, an evangelical leader and social reformer, felt this to be a moral obligation. He wrote in his popular book *Our Country* (1885) that the Anglo-Saxon was "divinely commissioned to be, in a peculiar sense, his brother's keeper" and pictured the American branch of the family moving "down upon Mexico, down upon Central and South America, out upon the islands of the sea, over upon Africa and beyond." Professor John W. Burgess of Columbia University assigned the Teutonic nations "the mission of conducting the political civilization of the modern world." A Darwinian lecturer and writer, John Fiske, shared with many historians and philosophers of his time the conviction that it was the "manifest destiny" of the English-speaking people to establish sovereignty of the seas and to bestow the blessings of benevolent rule and superior institutions on less fortunate people around the globe.

But such a grand mission could hardly be accomplished with an antiquated navy. No one was more aware of this fact than Captain Alfred T. Mahan, the foremost exponent of navalism in his time. Mahan was the author of such books as *The Influence of Sea Power upon History* (published in 1890 but delivered as a series of lectures at the new Naval War College in 1886) and *The Interest of America in Sea Power* (1897). "Whether they will or no," wrote Mahan in 1890, "Americans must now begin to look outward." He advanced a program of mercantile imperialism that included the building up of foreign markets, the expansion of the merchant marine, the construction of a navy to protect it, and the acquisition of overseas bases that would enable the fleet to operate in distant seas. Only by these means, he argued, could America keep pace with rival nations. His books were translated into many languages, he was honored in England, and he was studied assiduously in Germany and Japan. His writings were more a reflection than a cause of events, but his influence was strong in shaping naval policy in Washington and in molding opinion and inspiring ambitions among such rising statesmen as Henry Cabot Lodge and Theodore Roosevelt.

Big-navy agitators worked hard and effectively through the eighties. In 1881 Congress established a Naval Advisory Board, which began at once to press for larger naval appropriations, and in 1883 Congress authorized the Secretary of the Navy to construct three cruisers and in 1886 two battleships, the *Maine* and the *Texas*. This construction was still guided by the concept of the navy as a defensive force, but the Naval Act of 1890, which authorized the building of

three more battleships, the *Indiana*, the *Massachusetts*, and the *Oregon*, all heavier and more powerful ships, announced the intention of the government to have a navy that could meet a potential enemy anywhere on the high seas. Before the end of the century the United States had moved up from twelfth to third place among naval powers. Thereafter the big-navy advocates began to reap the cumulative benefits of an expanding fleet: new bases and coaling stations, a stronger argument for a canal to connect the Atlantic and the Pacific, an even larger navy to protect the additional bases, and even more bases to accommodate the larger navy.

Another stimulus that quickened America's response to imperialist propaganda was the example set by the European nations that were carving up Africa and Asia, snatching island kingdoms in the Pacific, and casting eyes on South America. Driven by lust for power and greed for trade, they made protectorates of Morocco, Algeria, Tunis, and Libya in North Africa. The British worked southward from the Sudan and northward from the Cape to realize Cecil Rhodes' dream of an African empire. French, Germans, Belgians, and Italians took all the rest, save Ethiopia. The predatory powers moved in on the crumbling dynasty of China from bases already established in Asia: the French from Indochina, the British along the Yangtze Valley, and the Russians from Siberian possessions. Japan felt cheated when, after her victory over China in 1894, she received only Formosa as booty. Americans began to wonder if they were not falling behind the times, whether they would ever be able to protect their interests if they did not enter even belatedly into the imperialist adventure and "take up the white man's burden" along with the rewards and plunder that went with it.

Domestic affairs furnished further arguments for foreign adventure. The Indians had been subdued and the built-in empire of the West had been "settled" by 1890—at least according to formal census reports. The South had resumed control of the domestic "white man's burden." Some theorists, including young Theodore Roosevelt, believed that foreign adventures might divert farmers and laborers and the nation from preoccupation with economic ills.

All these impulses—the doctrine of racial superiority, the sense of national mission, and the excitement of the Darwinian struggle, along with an expanding navy, an interest in foreign markets, and the example set by old and admired European nations—combined to prepare America for a new era of involvement in foreign affairs.

The new diplomacy

Imperialistic stirrings. The break with the old tradition was finally made by James G. Blaine, Secretary of State under Harrison. Blaine had served briefly in the same office eight years earlier under Garfield and revived the tradition of earlier Republican expansionism under Seward and Grant. Like them he also sought naval bases in Santo Domingo and Haiti, though with no more success. His followers expected him to pursue a "spirited policy" in keeping with his

494

nickname of "Jingo* Jim." Actually Blaine exerted a moderating influence in the settlement of the Samoan incident with Germany and Great Britain held over from the previous Administration. The three-power protectorate over the islands to which he agreed was, however, without precedent and constituted one of the first steps toward overseas imperialism.

Closer to Blaine's interests was Latin America, especially the promotion of United States trade with sister republics, the obtaining of naval bases in the Caribbean, and the construction of an isthmian canal. Eight years earlier he had urged calling an international conference of the American republics, and the idea materialized when he became Secretary of State for the second time. Delegates arrived in the fall of 1889 and were treated to a six-thousand-mile barnstorming tour of the country, but when they settled down to consider Blaine's proposals on trade and arbitration treaties they could not agree. All they would accept was the setting up of an information center, which later became the Pan-American Union. More than a half-century was to pass before Pan-American conferences would finally accept the sort of agreements Blaine tried to effect in 1889.

In the early nineties a new martial spirit in

*The word was originated in England and popularized in America by a jingle printed in the Detroit *News* during the fisheries dispute with Great Britain and Canada:

> We do not want to fight
> But, by jingo, if we do
> We'll scoop in all the fishing grounds
> And the whole Dominion, too.

America found expression in a succession of chauvinistic outbursts, "jingoism" it was called. One such outburst almost brought the United States to the point of war with Chile, a republic with not one-twentieth its population. In October 1891, when a party from the cruiser *Baltimore* went on shore leave in Valparaiso, a mob of Chileans killed two of the American sailors and injured seventeen others. President Harrison inserted a sword-rattling passage in his annual message to Congress and followed this with another message to Congress virtually inviting it to declare war at a time when the apologies he had demanded from Chile were hourly expected. Chile fortunately capitulated with apologies and indemnities, and the war scare passed over.

The bellicose mood of the jingo editors and politicians did not pass over, however. Rather, it continued to mount during the nineties. "The number of men and officials in this country who are now mad to fight somebody is appalling," said the anti-imperialist editor of the *Nation*, E. L. Godkin, in 1894. "Navy officers dream of war and talk and lecture about it incessantly. The Senate debates are filled with predictions of impending war and with talk of preparing for it at once." The irresponsible warmongering of the period was indeed appalling, though it should be remembered that nineteenth-century Americans knew nothing of the total wars to come. They regarded the Civil War as an exception and still thought of war as a heroic affair filled with splendor and glory. It was an illusion slow to die.

Even the antiexpansionist Cleveland was not immune to the new spirit, as he showed in his handling

"That's a live wire, gentlemen!"

of relations with Britain in the dispute over the boundary between British Guiana and Venezuela. It was an old dispute that went back into the colonial history of Venezuela, but the discovery of gold in the disputed territory, combined with a bit of Venezuelan propaganda suggesting that British aggression was a challenge to the Monroe Doctrine, stirred up the Anglophobia and pugnacity of the jingo editors of the United States. In 1895 Cleveland had his Secretary of State, Richard Olney, demand that Great Britain conform to the Monroe Doctrine, as broadly interpreted, by submitting the boundary dispute to arbitration. Olney accompanied this demand with the truculent assertion that the United States today "is practically sovereign on this continent, and its fiat is law upon the subjects to which it confines its interposition." The tone of the note, coupled with his request for a quick reply, gave it the flavor of an ultimatum.

The British foreign minister, Lord Salisbury, took his time in replying, and when he did reply four months later he repudiated Secretary Olney's interpretation of the Monroe Doctrine and flatly refused to submit the dispute to arbitration. After receiving this rebuff, Cleveland sent a special message to Congress deploring "a supine submission to wrong and injustice and the consequent loss of national self-respect." Defusing the situation by delay, he asked that he be authorized to appoint a commission to determine the boundary and that the commission's decision be enforced at whatever cost. Congress promptly complied, and war sentiment mounted. "Let the fight come if it must," wrote Theodore Roosevelt, who hoped to participate personally. "I rather hope that the fight will come soon. The clamor of the peace faction has convinced me that this country needs a war." The risk was altogether disproportionate to the American interest at stake, but it was not at all disproportionate to the chauvinistic mood of the day. Fortunately Britain saw fit to back down. Suddenly finding itself in trou-

ble in South Africa with no ally in Europe on which it could count for support, Great Britain decided to court a friend instead of making an enemy in the New World. It switched to a conciliatory tone and signed a treaty with Venezuela providing for arbitration, which turned out to be mainly in its favor. The upshot of the incident was to enhance American nationalist feeling, but paradoxically it also ushered in an era of Anglo-American understanding.

The Hawaiian question. When it came to expansion overseas, however, Cleveland clung consistently to traditional views and stood firm against the annexation of Hawaii. American interest in these islands dated back to the China trade in the late eighteenth century. Traders were followed by American missionaries, who converted the native Polynesians to Christianity in the second quarter of the nineteenth century, and the missionaries were followed by American sugar-growers. Efforts to annex the islands under President Pierce and again under Secretary Seward failed, but in 1875 a reciprocity treaty was signed opening a free market in the United States to Hawaiian sugar-planters. Sugar production in the islands multiplied tenfold in the next twenty years in response to the free American market. So dependent did the industry become on this market, however, that when the McKinley Tariff of 1890 admitted other foreign sugar on the same terms and subsidized domestic producers, the blow precipitated an economic crisis in the island kingdom and contributed to a political crisis.

King Kalakaua, the next to last of the reigning family, had been forced by the white business community in 1887 to accept a new constitution that curbed his power, made his ministers responsible to the legislature, and brought the legislature under control of the propertied classes. The dissolute old king was succeeded in 1891 by his sister Liliuokalani, who made it apparent that she was determined to overthrow the constitution her brother had accepted, shake off white control, and restore royal prerogatives. In January 1893 a committee of businessmen-revolutionaries demanded that she abdicate. Thereupon United States Minister John L. Stevens, as annexationist whom Blaine had picked for the office, ordered marines ashore from the cruiser *Boston* and raised the American flag. The queen then capitulated, as she said, "to the superior force of the United States of America." A month later, on February 15, Harrison sent to the Senate a treaty annexing the islands. It might have gone through then and there had it not been for the declared preference of Cleveland, who was to begin his second Administration in a few days, that the matter be held over until his inauguration. As soon as he became President again he dispatched a special commissioner to investigate the situation in

Empire beyond the seas

the islands. The commissioner's report convinced Cleveland that the great majority of the natives supported the queen. Cleveland therefore not only withheld the annexation treaty but insisted that it was his duty to restore "Queen Lil." The revolutionary provisional government refused to step down, however, and continued to rule, biding its time until a more imperialist-minded Administration came to power.

Cleveland's firm resistance to annexation, as compared with Harrison's receptive attitude, helped to make the question something of a party issue. The Republican platform of 1896 contained a plank favoring Hawaiian annexation, and though McKinley had previously shown no interest in the matter he was quickly won over after he became President in March 1897. Comparing him with Cleveland, commissioners from Hawaii reported that there was "the difference between daylight and darkness." On June 16, 1897, Secretary of State John Sherman signed a treaty of annexation and McKinley sent it to the Senate. Congress was strongly interested in Hawaii and alarmed by the interest Japan was manifesting in the islands, but the sentiment against overseas expansion was still too strong to be overcome, and the treaty languished for more than a year without action. Only in July 1898, after the war with Spain had opened the floodgates of expansionism, was Hawaii annexed.

War with Spain

The Cuban crisis.   The expansionists and imperialists did not cause the war with Spain. They merely exploited it for their own purposes. The war itself grew out of deplorable conditions in Cuba that seemed intolerable to an aroused popular sentiment in the United States. Spanish misgovernment of the island had given rise to numerous revolts and a Ten Years' War, 1868–78, that brought little relief for Cuban ills. A new civil war broke out in February 1895. As in the case of the Hawaiian revolution, American tariff policy contributed to the uprising, for the tariff law of 1894, by imposing a duty on raw sugar, had added economic suffering to political discontent. Both the Cubans and the Spaniards used savage methods. The Cubans systematically destroyed sugar mills, cane fields, and other property. Early in 1896 the Spanish commander, General Valeriano Weyler, resorted to the brutal policy of "reconcentration." This meant driving the entire population of large areas of Cuba—including women, children, and old people—into cities and towns fortified with barbed wire and under armed guard. Left without food or sanitation, the prisoners fell victim to famine

and disease. Within two years two hundred thousand, or approximately one-eighth of the total population, were estimated to have been wiped out.

The American press exaggerated the Spanish atrocities, but the sufferings of the rebels were horrible enough in any case to arouse deep sympathies among Americans. The sufferings, moreover, were those of a neighbor, and they were incurred in a fight for independence from a manifestly unjust imperial ruler. Little more was required to whip up popular sympathy for the Cuban patriots and animus against Spain, especially in years when the public mind was as susceptible to jingoism as it had recently proved to be in far less serious disputes with Chile and Great Britain. Indications were abundant that influential Americans were "spoiling for a fight," and the Cuban junta that established itself in New York to dispense propaganda, solicit aid, and arouse sympathy was not without support. Those with long memories recalled that the United States had expressed great interest in Cuba since the early years of the century and since 1823 had implicitly regarded European control of the island as unnatural.

One strong ally of the interventionists was the "yellow press" of New York City. Led by William Randolph Hearst's New York *Journal* and Joseph Pulitzer's New York *World*, which were currently engaged in a war for circulation, the press sent a corps of reporters and artists to cover the Cuban conflict and supply the papers with vivid human-interest stories and pictures. The barbarities of the Spaniards were played up and the atrocities of the Cubans glossed over, with the result that the newspaper coverage constituted powerful propaganda for the rebel cause. Waves of sympathy for the insurgents swept the country, and when the struggle continued to drag on with no prospect of Spain's relenting, much of the sympathy began to turn into a demand for American intervention and war with Spain.

American businessmen did not originally share the interventionist sentiment, though important segments of the business community became converts before the intervention. Protestant religious journals and both Republican and Democratic newspapers clamored loudly for intervention and war, though they insisted that they did so on purely humanitarian grounds and disclaimed any desire to annex Cuba or gain territory. Theirs was a moralistic aggression, with imperialism disavowed. Outright imperialists, including Roosevelt, Lodge, and Mahan, were also for war, but for the express purpose of conquest, expansion, and military glory. Two contrasting sets of aggressive impulses, both frustrated in the nineties, sought outlet in an idealistic crusade for Cuban freedom. One set embraced the impulses of protest and humanitarian reform; the other embraced the impulses of national self-expression, aggressiveness, and expansion. The first was embodied in Populism, utopianism, the Social Gospel, and radical labor movements—all of which had suffered frustrations in the nineties, most recently in the downfall of Populism and Bryan and the triumph of conservatism and McKinley. The second group included the big-navy advocates, the patriotic societies, and the statesmen and propagandists of imperialism, whose programs had been blocked by cautious business interests and the antiexpansionist foreign policy that had prevailed since Grant's Administration. The convergence of these two groups in support of intervention in Cuba goes far toward explaining why Americans worked themselves up into a mood for war with Spain.

American intervention.   When Grover Cleveland was President, he had opposed intervention in Cuba on every front. He had resisted pressure from Congress to accord the insurgents belligerent rights, had sought to suppress gun-running into Cuba from the States, and had tendered his good offices to Spain to settle the colonial war. In the summer of 1896, however, Cleveland underwent a change, and in his last annual message to Congress he came near to laying down a rationalization for America's intervention. McKinley tried hard to curb the jingoes and halt the drift to war. Six months after he took office a satisfactory settlement seemed to be in the making. A change of government in Spain brought in a prime minister who recalled General Weyler and offered Cuba a considerable measure of self-government in local affairs. The offer proved unacceptable, however, since the Spaniards in Cuba opposed rule by native Cubans and the insurgents refused to settle for anything short of complete independence. Further hopes for a peaceful solution were disrupted by a series of fateful incidents, or accidents, that brought relations between the United States and Spain to the breaking point.

The first incident was the publication on February 9, 1898, of a stolen private letter from the Spanish minister in Washington, Dupuy de Lôme, who indiscreetly described President McKinley as "weak and a bidder for the admiration of the crowd" and said that the Cuban rebels should be suppressed by force. Dupuy de Lôme resigned before his government had time to respond to Washington's inevitable request for his recall. Then, six days later, the battleship *Maine* blew up in Havana harbor with a loss of two hundred sixty officers and enlisted men. The Spanish government hastened to offer condolence and propose a joint investigation. An investigation by American naval officers reported that the *Maine's* bottom plates had been thrust inward, indicating an external explosion, but the cause of the tragedy was never discovered. It is highly improbable that the Spanish government would have plotted such an act, but the jingo press held Spain guilty and raised the cry "Remember the Maine!" Before the report of the *Maine* explosion was completed, Congress unanimously voted a defense appropriation of $50 million, and on March 19 Senator Redfield Proctor of Vermont delivered a speech painting the shocking conditions he had found in Cuba during a recent unofficial visit. His calm tone, his reputation for moderation, and his matter-of-fact manner convinced many who had heretofore been skeptical of the lurid stories in the yellow press that action was indeed necessary.

On March 27 McKinley proposed to Spain a peaceful settlement in which it would abandon its reconcentration policy at once, grant an armistice until October 1, and enter into peace negotiations with the insurgents through his offices. This was not an ultimatum, though he followed it the next day with a telegram saying that independence would be the only satisfactory outcome of the peace negotiations. Spain was confronted with a cruel dilemma: if it rejected McKinley's demands it faced a disastrous war, and if it complied with them it faced a revolt that might overturn the government and possibly the throne. Spanish appeals for support from European powers won sympathy, but the only tangible response was a visit to President McKinley by the ambassadors of six powers who begged him not to intervene with armed force. Despairing of European aid, Spain replied on March 31 to McKinley's proposals by agreeing to abandon reconcentration and to grant an armistice upon the application of the insurgents. It hedged on the point of independence but volunteered to submit to arbitration the question of who was responsible for sinking the *Maine*. Spain followed up on April 9 by declaring an armistice on its own without waiting for the insurgents to take the initiative. The following day the American minister in Madrid cabled that he believed Cuban independence and a solution satisfactory to all could be worked out during the armistice.

Spain had gone far toward meeting the President's demands, but not so far as conceding independence. The President's insistence on this point made war inevitable. The day after receiving his minister's cable, April 11, McKinley sent a warlike message to Congress. He alluded in passing to Spain's concessions to American demands, but did not stress them. There was, it is true, ground for doubt that the Spanish government could make good its promises. Congress paused only to debate whether it should recognize the insurgent government as well as the independence of Cuba, decided on the latter only, and adopted the resolution on April 19 by a vote of 42 to 35 in the Senate and 311 to 6 in the house. An amendment to the resolution, which was prepared by Senator Henry

Empire beyond the seas

M. Teller of Colorado and adopted at the same time without dissent, renounced any intention of annexing or governing Cuba and promised to "leave the government and control of the Island to its people." The Teller Amendment proclaimed American righteousness and abstention with respect to Cuba but, as the author of the resolution carefully pointed out, left the country a free hand "as to some other islands" that also belonged to Spain. Spain responded by declaring war on April 24, and Congress followed suit the next day. The American declaration of war was made retroactive to April 21, since the President had established a blockade of the Cuban coast on April 22.

The little war. Within ten weeks of the declaration of war the fighting was over and the victory assured. For the country at large—and the readers of headlines in particular—it could not have been a more "splendid little war," as John Hay described it, or one conforming more completely with the romantic imagination of the budding imperialists. The whole war seemed to have been fought to the stirring music of "The Stars and Stripes Forever," the battle song of the war, played by a marine band in dress uniform. Even the participants chose to remember it in the manly prose of Richard Harding Davis or in the heroic sketches of Frederic Remington, two of the numerous writers and artists who "covered" the story of one of the best-publicized wars in history. The Spanish-American War was, in short, the most popular of all

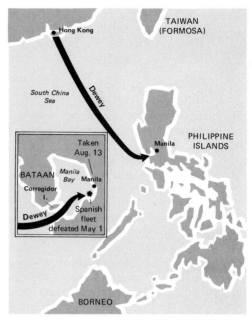

Dewey's campaign in the Pacific, 1898

American wars. Disillusionment takes a bit of time, especially among noncombatants, and this war was over even before weariness could set in—save among combat troops.

The most hardened skeptics were thrown off balance less than a week after the war started by Commodore George Dewey's dazzling naval victory in Manila Bay on the opposite side of the globe. Assistant Secretary of the Navy Theodore Roosevelt, who had secured the commodore's assignment to the command, had directed Dewey two months earlier, in accordance with the navy's previously devised war plan, to be thoroughly prepared for action. McKinley approved this order the next day. On receiving news of the war and his final instructions, Dewey had immediately steamed out of Hong Kong, slipped through the straits of Boca Grande during the night of April 30, and at dawn opened fire on the weak and inferior Spanish squadron at Manila. Before breakfast, and without losing a man, he had sunk the whole fleet to the last of its ten ships. Dewey had crushed Spanish power in the Pacific.

Unfortunately the army was not as well prepared as the navy, but the public did not learn about that until later. The account of the expeditionary force to Cuba that the public read and gloried in was the sort supplied by the debonair reporter Richard Harding Davis:

It was a most happy-go-lucky expedition, run with real American optimism and readiness to take big chances, and with the spirit of a people who recklessly trust that it will come out all right in the end, and that the barely possible may not happen. . . . As one of the generals on board said, "This is God Almighty's war, and we are only His agents."

That was one way of putting it. At least Davis was accurate about the expedition's optimism and recklessness. The army, with only some twenty-six thousand men at the start of the war, had no adequate plans, equipment, or supplies. The War Department was crippled by antiquated methods, utterly incompetent administration, and inefficient and negligent officers. General William R. Shafter, a three-hundred-pound Civil War hero, presided over the chaos at Tampa preceding the embarkation of the expeditionary force. Transportation broke down and confusion reigned. The thousands of volunteers who rushed to the colors eager for glory could not be supplied with guns, tents, or blankets. With hopeless inefficiency they were clad in heavy woolen winter uniforms for a summer campaign in the sweltering tropics. Food was inadequate, repulsive, and sometimes poisonous, sanitation was conspicuously wanting, and medical supplies were almost nonexistent. Over the expeditionary force there spread the stench of dysentery and illness and eventually the horror of plague, the yellow jack. The fact was that blundering inefficiency brought the army to the brink of disaster.

The Spaniards blundered badly, too, but with an unstable government, a tradition-bound leadership, and a backward economy, they had more excuse for inefficiency than the Americans, who had none of those handicaps. Yet for all their pride in industrial progress and their reputation for bustling efficiency and technological know-how, the Americans made a mess of their war effort. The government seemed unable to adopt the vigorous administrative methods that would have made effective use of the country's vaunted industrial superiority. The scandal reflected a quarter-century of federal lassitude and bureaucratic stagnation. As it turned out, the real explanation of the quick American military success lay in the even more incredible inefficiency and blundering of the Spaniards.

The enemy obliged by immobilizing its Cuban naval power, a small force of four cruisers and three destroyers under the command of Admiral Pascual Cervera, in Santiago Harbor, where it was immediately blockaded by a vastly superior fleet commanded by Admiral William T. Sampson. The blockade ended the threat to the landing of the expeditionary force, and after much backing and filling and countermanding of orders a force of some eighteen thousand regulars and volunteers got under way from Tampa, partly equipped, partially trained, and poorly led. The most

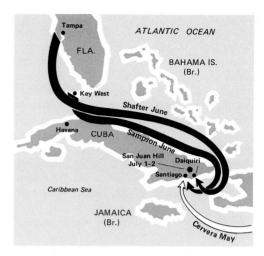

The Cuban campaign, 1898

publicized unit of volunteers was the Rough Riders, commanded by Colonel Leonard Wood, who was loudly supported by Lieutenant Colonel Theodore Roosevelt, second in command. The landing force blundered slowly ashore on June 20 and somehow established a beachhead at Daiquiri, a few miles east of Santiago.

With some two hundred thousand troops in Cuba, the Spaniards could have destroyed the Americans utterly. But they had only about thirteen thou-

T.R.: a "bully fight"

Empire beyond the seas

sand men at Santiago and were so handicapped in transportation that they could not bring their superior forces to bear and so unfortunate in military leadership that they could not employ what power they had at hand to their best advantage. Even so they came near inflicting a disaster upon the invaders. The American objective was to capture the ridges, known as San Juan Hill, that surrounded Santiago and then to take the town in whose harbor Admiral Cervera was blockaded. So poorly was the command organized, however, that the American units were largely without coordinated control in their attack. It was in the capture of Kettle Hill, a flanking outpost of San Juan Hill, that Theodore Roosevelt established his reputation for martial zeal and heroism. Later he was to describe the attack volubly and frequently as a "bully fight" that was "great fun," something of a rollicking skylark. Actually the fight, in which his was by no means the only part, was a pretty desperate and bloody affair marked by a reckless display of courage and a great many needless casualties. The capture of the heights proved decisive in the land fighting, for Santiago was now closely invested. But, under counterattack and without supplies, the American troops were soon in a dangerous plight. On July 3 Roosevelt wrote Lodge, "We are within measurable distance of a terrible military disaster," in desperate need of reinforcements, food, and ammunition.

On that very morning, however, Admiral Cervera hoisted anchor and steamed out of Santiago Harbor to face his doom for the honor of Castile. He knew perfectly well that he was far outclassed and outgunned by the four United States battleships awaiting him just outside the harbor, but he gave battle rather than surrender without a fight. The American battle line opened up with its thirteen-inch guns, and one after another the Spanish ships went down gallantly, guns ablaze. It was all over in a few hours, with four hundred enemy killed or wounded and with only one American killed. The next day was the Fourth of July, and orators had not had such an opportunity since the day after Gettysburg and Vicksburg.

The enemy ashore was now powerless, and the Spanish forces surrendered Cuba on July 16. Puerto Rico was taken within the next two weeks virtually without resistance, and on August 12 a peace protocol was signed. The next day Manila fell to the troops that were sent over after Dewey's victory in May, and the war was over. In actual battle casualties the price of victory was comparatively small. But only after the close of the war did the major losses begin to mount: losses due to disease, mainly typhoid, malaria, and yellow fever. By the end of the year the total deaths in the American army in all theaters of war had risen to 5,462, only 379 of which were the direct result of combat or wounds.

The white man's burden

Mr. McKinley and his duty. The armistice deliberately left open the question of the disposition of the Philippine Islands. They had scarcely figured at all in the war motives of most Americans, who, in Reinhold Niebuhr's phrase, were bent on fighting a "pureminded war." To seize those possessions and to rule them by force without consent of their inhabitants would be to violate both the humanitarian motives that prompted the war and the oldest and profoundest American political traditions. Knowing these things in their hearts, whether they admitted them or not, the imperialist-minded minority scarcely dared hope at the onset of the war that their dreams would materialize. As it turned out they were on the eve of sensational success.

Hawaii was the first sign. In the spring before the war the cause of annexation had looked fairly hopeless. But in the excitement of the Dewey and Sampson victories the traditional arguments were swept aside and the "large policy" of Hay, Lodge, Mahan, and Roosevelt prevailed. The New York *Tribune* maintained that Hawaii was "imperative" as a halfway station to the Philippines, and another expansionist argued later that the Philippines were imperative as an outpost for Hawaii. On June 15 the House of Representatives, and on July 6 the Senate, adopted a joint resolution annexing Hawaii. The large policy was now on the way to further enlargement.

The enlargement was facilitated by the flexible conscience of President McKinley, who once regarded forcible annexation as "criminal aggression" but now saw in it "the hand of Almighty God." He advanced his insights in the form of such epigrams as, "Duty determines destiny," but he did not answer the New York *Evening Post's* query, "Who determines duty?" At any rate the destiny of the Philippines was becoming pretty manifest as McKinley's epigrams and actions multiplied. Even before Dewey's victory was confirmed he sent a force to capture and hold Manila, and before the end of May Lodge was writing Roosevelt, "The Administration is now fully committed to the large policy that we both desire."

The commercial and industrial interests now helped swing the tide toward expansionism. Though they had opposed the war at first for fear of its effect on recovery and the gold standard, once the war started and news of the victories poured in and the potentialities of expansion for the advancement of trade became manifest, the business community swung about in support of the policies it had once opposed. Big business saw the Philippines as a key to the China trade and listened appreciatively to Senator Albert Beveridge's declaration that "the trade of the world must and shall be ours."

501

At the same time the religious press, with the support of the missionary movement, stepped up support for the "imperialism of righteousness." Annexation would further the cause of world evangelization, extend the blessings of civilization and sanitation, and "civilize" more of the heathens. It was this sentiment that McKinley reflected later in recounting how he had reached his decision through prayer "to educate the Filipinos, and uplift and civilize and Christianize them, and, by God's grace, do the very best we could by them, as our fellow men for whom Christ also died."

A more cynical approach to imperialism was that of editor Henry Watterson, who proposed to "escape the menace and peril of socialism and agrarianism" by means of "a policy of colonization and conquest." One popular way of thinking, however, was to attribute imperialism to a determinism of some sort: the hand of God, the instinct of race, the laws of Darwin, the forces of economics and trade—anything but rational and responsible decision. Though many Americans seemed willing to surrender to imperialist policies, few would admit they did so because they wanted to.

McKinley revealed his intentions pretty clearly by the choice of commissioners he sent to negotiate with Spain at the peace conference held in Paris. Three of the five peace commissioners were open and avowed expansionists. Another indication was his seizure of Spain's island of Guam—whose inhabitants mistook the American bombardment for a salute and apologized for having no ammunition with which to return it. In his instructions to the peace commissioners the President took the moral position that "without any desire or design on our part" the United States had assumed duties and responsibilities that it must discharge as became a nation of noble destiny. Impressed by the popular response to speeches he made along this line of "responsibility," he instructed the commissioners in October with regard to the Philippines that "duty requires we should take the archipelago."

John Hay, who had recently become Secretary of State, cabled the delegation in Paris to hold out for the whole of the Philippine Islands. The Spanish commissioners resisted the demand to the point of risking a renewal of hostilities. McKinley stuck to his position that we should "not shirk the moral obligation of our victory" but made one concession, an offer to pay $20 million for the Philippines. The Spaniards capitulated, and the treaty was signed December 10, 1898. By its terms Spain was to give up control over Cuba and surrender Guam, Puerto Rico, and the Philippine Islands to the United States.

In thus abandoning American tradition and his own earlier convictions, President McKinley showed

Uncle Sam's new pupils

little evidence of grasping the implications of his decision for American foreign policy and future involvement in power rivalries and wars in the Far East. There is little reason, however, to doubt the sincerity of the reasons he offered a year later, though some critics question that they came to him in a flood of prayerful illumination. The reasons he offered were that it would be cowardly and dishonorable to give the Philippines back to Spain, "bad business and discreditable" to let France or Germany seize them, impossible to leave them to their own devices since they were unfit for self-rule, and absolutely necessary to follow the humanitarian impulses to "civilize and Christianize" the Filipinos by taking possession of their land. He did not see fit to propose the establishment of a protectorate over the islands with the promise of self-government and later independence.

What McKinley had in mind in his reference to the designs of European powers on the Philippines was a bit of recent history. In November 1897, Germany landed troops at Kiaochow, and a Russian fleet anchored at Port Arthur. The following March the two European powers forced China to sign agreements giving Germany exclusive rights in Shantung province and Russia exclusive rights in Manchuria. Japan had occupied Korea, and France was established in Kwangchau Bay.

The debate on the Philippines. The treaty with Spain committed the United States to open imperialism in the Far East and the Caribbean. But first the treaty had to be ratified by the Senate, and the ques-

Empire beyond the seas

tion of ratification precipitated a debate that spread far beyond the Senate chamber and cast more light on the issues of annexation than had the President's speeches and the expansionists' slogans. After the drums of war were silenced and the people began to think more soberly, it became apparent that there was formidable opposition to the President's policy, perhaps enough to defeat it. Far more opposition came from Democrats than from Republicans, and the sentiment was strong enough to unite even such Democratic extremes as Bryan and Cleveland. But prominent members of McKinley's own party, including Speaker Reed of the House and Senator George F. Hoar of Massachusetts, broke with the Administration over the question, as did Senator Eugene Hale of Maine. To the very last it was doubtful whether the President could muster the two-thirds of the Senate required to ratify his treaty.

Even before the treaty was signed an Anti-Imperialist League was organized that attracted the support of many distinguished men. As president, the league elected George S. Boutwell, formerly Grant's Secretary of the Treasury and later Republican senator from Massachusetts. Among the vice presidents were such contrasting figures as Grover Cleveland and Samuel Gompers, Andrew Carnegie and Carl Schurz, John Sherman and Charles Francis Adams. Intellectuals, novelists, and poets rallied to anti-imperialism in great numbers, among them President Eliot of Harvard and President David Starr Jordan of Stanford, along with William James, William Dean Howells, William Graham Sumner, Hamlin Garland, William Vaughn Moody, and Mark Twain. In a bitter satire Mark Twain assured his countrymen that the "Blessings-of-Civilization Trust" had the purest of motives. "This world-girdling accumulation of trained morals, high principles, and justice cannot do an unright thing, an unfair thing, an ungenerous thing, an unclean thing," he wrote. "It knows what it is about. Give yourself no uneasiness; it is all right."

Some of the anti-imperialist arguments showed remarkable prescience. George Boutwell foresaw a war with Japan as a consequence of American expansion in the western Pacific, and following that the rise of a warlike China in potential alliance with Russia that would turn against American holdings. A favorite argument was based on the doctrine of the Declaration of Independence: no government without the consent of the governed. We had fought the Revolution for that principle and had intervened in Cuba on the same ground; how could we now shamelessly adopt the doctrines we fought to overthrow? Or, as Senator Hoar put it, how could we "strut about in the cast-off clothing of pinchbeck emperors and pewter kings?" Other objections were that the Asiatic people could not be assimilated into our tradition, that im-

perialism would lead to militarism and racist dogma at home, that overseas expansion was unconstitutional and inconsistent with the Monroe Doctrine. Populist opponents of empire in the South and West never fully understood those of the Northeast. Southerners viewed the new imperialism as a revival of carpetbaggery and warned of the difficulties of reconciling races of contrasting color and heritage. Racist arguments were used both for and against imperialism though mainly for it.

The imperialist-minded defenders of the treaty revived with new assurance their old arguments of naval strategy, world power, and commercial interests and incorporated the moralistic line of McKinley on duty, destiny, humanitarianism, and religious mission. In the latter vein Senator Beveridge declared, "It is God's great purpose made manifest in the instincts of our race, whose present phase is our personal profit, but whose far-off end is the redemption of the world and the Christianization of mankind." Senator Lodge dismissed the consent-of-the-governed argument as of no account because that principle had been ignored or violated before, notably in the Louisiana Purchase, in order to advance the national interest. He emphasized and exaggerated the supposed economic advantages of the Philippines: their resources, their trade, and their relationship to the international struggle for China and its trade. He stressed the political expediency of keeping the islands: they were not ready for self-government, would lapse into anarchy, or would be seized by more ruthless powers.

In the meantime the Senate continued its deliberations, the outcome still in doubt. Before the end of the debate the anti-imperialists were confused by a strange maneuver and strategic blunder of William Jennings Bryan. Although he was a strong opponent of the acquisition of the Philippines, he decided that the Senate should approve the treaty to assure peace and should leave the future disposition of the islands to be decided at the polls. He undoubtedly believed that this move would provide him with a winning issue in the presidential election of 1900, but he miscalculated. Approval of the treaty presented the voters with a *fait accompli*. Bryan's advice won some Senate votes over to the side of the Administration, though not enough to assure victory. On February 5, 1899, the very day before the final ballot was set, the drama of the decision was complicated and intensified by the arrival of news that the Filipinos had taken up arms in open revolt against the United States. There could be no more doubt of their desire for freedom or that the United States was now in the same position formerly occupied by discredited Spain. The effect of this news is impossible to estimate. The issue remained in doubt until the roll call the next day recorded fifty-seven in favor of the treaty and twenty-seven

503

against—two more than the necessary two-thirds majority.

In the meantime the American army remained in control of Cuba, and the government refused to withdraw until the Cubans incorporated into their constitution a permanent treaty with the United States, the so-called Platt Amendment, proposed by the United States Senate in 1901. This limited the power of Cuba to make treaties, borrow money, or change certain policies established by the occupation forces and required the sale or lease of lands for a naval base. More important, the United States was granted the right to intervene at will "for the preservation of Cuban independence" and "the protection of life, property, and individual liberty." Having no choice, Cuba submitted.

The motives that prompted America to "take up the white man's burden," as Rudyard Kipling urged it to do, were even more complex than the motives of the war that prepared the way for the decision. Part of the motivation was fear, the fear of appearing silly and playing the fool in the eyes of the world. Part of it was an uglier impulse of aggression. "The taste of empire is in the mouth of the people even as the taste of blood in the jungle," said the Washington *Post*.

Beyond the Philippines. What the other great imperial powers of the world were currently doing to China was a cause more of alarm than of emulation in America. Even before the Cuban war, John Hay had pressed upon President McKinley the common interest of the United States and Great Britain in forestalling exclusion from the China trade. Now the trade opportunities promised in the Far East by the acquisition of Hawaii and the Philippines were threatened by the impending dissolution of China and its partition among imperial powers. A small pressure group of American exporters interested in the China trade added their influence to that of Britain to move the State Department into action.

To meet the problem, Secretary Hay sent his "Open Door" notes to Great Britain, Germany, and Russia in September 1899 and later to Japan, Italy, and France, inviting them to agree to three principles: (1) that no power would interfere with the trading rights of other nations within its sphere of influence, (2) that Chinese tariff duties (which gave America most-favored-nation rights) should be collected on all merchandise by Chinese officials, and (3) that no power should levy discriminatory harbor dues or railroad charges against other powers within its sphere. Great Britain agreed conditionally, Russia equivocated, and Germany, France, Italy, and Japan agreed on condition of full acceptance by the other powers. It was a chilling response, but Hay saved face by blandly announcing that since all powers agreed on the American proposals, their assent was considered "final and definitive." Since Russia had not agreed, and Britain only with conditions, and since the others made acceptance conditional on full acceptance by all powers, Hay's claims were not very impressive. His proposals at this point did not undertake to preserve the territorial integrity or independence of China.

In May 1900, two months after Hay announced his interpretation of the response to the Open Door notes, the Boxers, an organization of fanatical Chinese patriots, incited an uprising that took the lives of 231 foreigners and many Christian Chinese. In June the Boxers began the siege of the legations in Peking and cut the city off from the outside world for a month. The Western powers and Japan then sent in a military force, to which the United States contributed five thousand troops. This expeditionary force relieved the besieged legations on August 4.

American world empire

During the Boxer Rebellion crisis, Secretary Hay labored successfully to prevent the spread of war, limit the extent of intervention, assure the rapid withdrawal of troops, head off the extension of foreign spheres of influence, and keep down punitive demands on China. On July 3, 1900, Hay issued a circular stating it to be the policy of the United States "to seek a solution which may bring about permanent safety and peace to China, preserve Chinese territorial and administrative entity," and protect all trade rights mentioned in the Open Door notes in all parts of the empire. This was an important extension of American policy in the Far East. Although only Great Britain, France, and Germany responded favorably to Hay's circular, its effect was to help soften the punitive terms imposed on China. Unwilling to risk the general war that might be precipitated by a struggle to divide China, the intervening powers were persuaded to accept indemnity in money rather than territory. The United States' share of the reparations was $25 million, more than enough to settle the claims of its nationals. In fact, the United States returned a balance of more than $10 million, and the Chinese government, as a gesture of gratitude, placed the money in trust for the education of Chinese youth in their own country and in the United States.

McKinley's vindication of 1900. It was Bryan's mistake, in planning to make the election of 1900 a popular referendum on imperialism, to believe that the anti-imperialist sentiment of the great debate of 1898–99 could be sustained or even revived, much less strengthened. Nearly two years were to pass between the ratification of the treaty and the presidential election, and by that time much water had passed under the bridge. Empire was no longer a dangerous menace to tradition and a decision that had to be worried out;

it was an accomplished fact to which the people were growing accustomed. They did not like the war that was being waged to suppress Emilio Aguinaldo and his Filipino patriots, even though censorship kept some of its worst aspects from them. That war was to drag on for three years, during which the United States was to use more men to suppress freedom in the Philippines than it had used to bring freedom to Cuba. And the new American rulers were to repeat in grotesque imitation the tortures and brutalities of their Spanish predecessors. But all that was taking place on the other side of the widest of oceans. When pressed, people admitted, "Peace has to be restored."

At home there were plenty of distractions to divert a burdensome conscience. The most important one was the gradual return to prosperity. The war itself served as an additional stimulus. Business regained its nerve, trade quickened, and the economy bustled into activity.

As the farmers and laborers sloughed off the burden of depression, their radicalism declined. "The Spanish War finished us," wrote Tom Watson of the Populist party. "The blare of the bugle drowned the voice of the reformer." The war, coupled with returning prosperity, mounting racism, and the legacy of the Populists' demoralizing fusion with Bryanism in 1896 (see p. 487), did just about finish the party. In the 1900 campaign it split into two feuding factions, neither of which could make a substantial showing. Many of the Populists of the Southwest and Middle West were attracted to the new Social Democratic party, which was founded in 1900 and nominated Eugene V. Debs of Pullman-strike fame as its presidential candidate.

Although McKinley's policies had little to do with the revival of the economy, he was billed as "the advance agent of prosperity," and he prospered politi-

Empire was no longer a menace?

cally with the return of good times. With a Cabinet that was if possible even more conservative than he was himself, McKinley's first Administration had proved as willing and cooperative as Hanna and the business community could have hoped. The Dingly Tariff of 1897 raised the rates to a new high, and the gold standard was now safe.

The presidential nominees of the two major parties in 1900 were pretty much a foregone conclusion. The Republicans had no hesitation about McKinley, but only with some difficulty did they settle upon the military hero and New York governor, Theodore Roosevelt, whom neither McKinley nor Hanna wanted, for Vice President. The Democrats returned to Bryan and picked the Silverite Adlai E. Stevenson, who had been Cleveland's running mate in 1892, for second place. The Democratic platform stressed imperialism as the "paramount issue" and on Bryan's insistence revived the demand for free silver. His strategy of uniting silverites of West and South with gold men of the Northeast in a coalition against imperialism came to grief. Bryan soon discovered that he had two fairly moribund issues on his hands and therefore shifted his emphasis to monopoly and special privilege.

Bryan, in a poorer showing than he had made in 1896, lost his own state of Nebraska, as well as Kansas, South Dakota, Utah and Wyoming—all silver states

Empire beyond the seas

he had carried before. The election neither revived the silver isssue nor provided a mandate on imperialism. Even if the voters opposed imperialism, they could express their disapproval only by voting against prosperity. Republican leaders acknowledged that Americans had lost their appetite for further colonial expansion. To the majority of voters in 1900 McKinley meant prosperity rather than imperialism or gold, and with him conservatism was triumphant once more.

Suggestions for reading

The general histories of American diplomatic relations by Bemis, Pratt, and Bailey see this period from somewhat different points of view. F. R. Dulles, *The Imperial Years** (1956), is an informed and perceptive general study beginning with Cleveland's first Administration. E. R. May, *Imperial Democracy** (1961) and *American Imperialism: A Speculative Essay* (1968), reveal how America emerged as a great power. J. A. S. Grenville and G. B. Young, *Politics, Strategy, and American Diplomacy: Studies in Foreign Policy, 1873–1917* (1966), and Walter LaFeber, *New Empire: An Interpretation of American Expansion, 1860–1898** (1963), contribute insights on this period as does R. L. Beisner, *From the Old Diplomacy to the New* (1974). A neglected period is covered in D. M. Pletcher, *The Awkward Years: American Foreign Relations under Garfield and Arthur* (1962). The world context of imperialism is seen in P. T. Moon, *Imperialism and World Politics* (1926); and the American variant and its rationalization are described and richly illustrated and exposed in A. K. Weinberg, *Manifest Destiny** (1935). On Latin American affairs the most informative studies are S. F. Bemis, *The Latin American Policy of the United States: An Historical Interpretation** (1943), and Dexter Perkins, *The Monroe Doctrine, 1867–1907* (1937); and on the Far East a helpful work is A. W. Griswold, *The Far Eastern Policy of the United States** (1938). W. A. Williams, *The Tragedy of American Diplomacy** (1959), stresses economic expansion.

The revival of the expansionist impulse is traced in David Healy, *U.S. Expansionism: Imperialist Urge in the 1890's* (1970), in Harold and Margaret Sprout, *The Rise of American Naval Power, 1776–1918** (1939), and reflected in many works of the period, particularly Josiah Strong, *Our Country* (1885), and A. T. Mahan, *The Influence of Sea Power upon History, 1660–1783** (1890). Leading expansionists of the 1880s and 1890s are portrayed in W. D. Puleston, *Mahan* (1939); H. K. Beale, *Theodore Roosevelt and the Rise of America to World Power** (1956); and H. F. Pringle, *Theodore Roosevelt: A Biography** (rev. ed., 1956). C. A. Beard and G. H. Smith, *The Idea of National Interest** (1934), takes a skeptical view of expansionism. See also S. K. Stevens, *American Expansion in Hawaii, 1842–1898* (1945). The crisis in Cuba and the war with Spain are treated by J. W. Pratt, *The Expansionists of 1898** (1936), with emphasis on motives; by Walter Millis, *The Martial Spirit** (1931), with coverage of diplomatic and military aspects; and by Frank Freidel, *The Splendid Little War* (1958), with many wonderful photographs and contemporary sketches. R. S. West, Jr., *Admirals of the American Empire* (1948), is useful on naval aspects of the war. The influence of newspapers is examined in C. H. Brown, *Correspondents' War: Journalists in the Spanish-American War* (1967), and J. E. Wisan, *The Cuban Crisis As Reflected in the New York Press, 1895–1898* (1934). Orestes Ferara, *The Last Spanish War* (1937), uses Spanish sources. Penetrating analysis of the theories and motives of American imperialists are found in Richard Hofstadter, *Social Darwinism in American Thought** (rev. ed., 1959). G. F. Kennan, *American Diplomacy: 1900–1950** (1951), has sober reflections on this crusade. Valuable discussions of the peace negotiations and the aftermath of the war are Tyler Dennett, *John Hay* (1933); F. E. Chadwick, *The Relations of the United States and Spain*, 2 vols. (1909–11); and J. W. Pratt, *America's Colonial Experiment* (1950). England's example and approval are pictured in C. S. Campbell, *Anglo-American Understanding, 1898–1903* (1957). Matthew Josephson, *The President Makers, 1896–1919* (1940), throws light on the election of 1900; and Margaret Leech, *In the Days of McKinley* (1959), illuminates not only the same subject but also many aspects of the war with Spain. On opponents of American imperialism, see E. B. Tompkins, *Anti-Imperialism in the United States: The Great Debate, 1890–1920** (1970); and R. L. Beisner, *Twelve Against Empire: The Anti-Imperialists, 1898–1900** (1968); and on China policy, see M. B. Young. *The Rhetoric of Empire: America's China Policy, 1895–1901* (1968), and Thomas McCormick, *The China Market** (1967).

*Available in a paperback edition.

CHAPTER 22

The progressive movement and the Square Deal

hat which strikes the visitor to America today," an English observer wrote soon after the turn of the century, "is its prodigious material development." Industry was growing more swiftly than ever before. Cities spread, wealth increased, and so did "the stress and rush of life." Yet the United States, as another Englishman noted, was still a "land of stark, staring, and stimulating inconsistency." While technology advanced, rural ways of life and habits of mind persisted. Americans had yet to accommodate to the social and cultural changes stimulated by industrial and urban growth. They had yet to adjust their laws and their techniques of government to an age of large and complex private organizations. Americans had yet to recognize the international implications of their national wealth. They had yet to fulfill their national promise of individual dignity, liberty, and decency for all men and women.

The unprecedented productivity of the economy made comfort potentially available to all Americans. That possibility in turn highlighted the striking contrasts between the few and the many, the white-skinned and the dark, the urban and the rural—the striking contrast between national aspiration and national achievement. Out of an awareness of that con-

trast, out of the tensions of material development, out of a consciousness of national mission, there emerged the efforts at adjustment and reform that constituted the progressive movement, a striving by men and women of good will to understand, improve, and manage the society in which they lived.

National wealth and the business élite

During the first two decades of the twentieth century the number of people in the United States, their average age, and their average per capita wealth all increased. In that period total national income almost doubled, and average per capita income rose from $450 to $567 a year. This growth gave confidence to those members of a generation who tended to measure progress in terms of plenty.

There were almost 76 million Americans in 1900, almost 106 million in 1920. Advances in medicine and public health, resulting in a declining death rate, accounted for most of the increase. It was accompanied by a continuing movement of people within the United States. In the West the rate of growth was

Hester Street, New York, ca. 1900

Population 1900

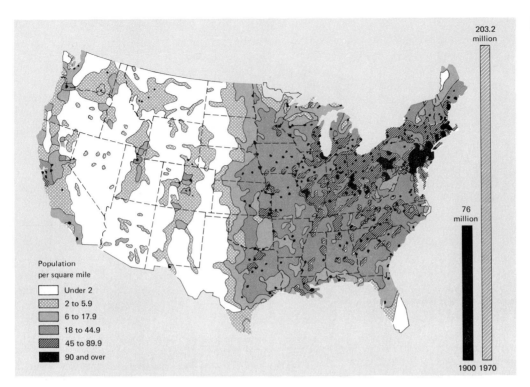

Population
per square mile
- ☐ Under 2
- ▨ 2 to 5.9
- ▤ 6 to 17.9
- ▥ 18 to 44.9
- ▨ 45 to 89.9
- ■ 90 and over

203.2 million

76 million

1900 1970

Population 1920

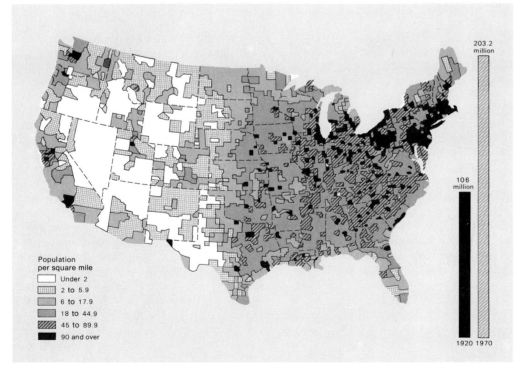

Population
per square mile
- ☐ Under 2
- ▨ 2 to 5.9
- ▤ 6 to 17.9
- ▥ 18 to 44.9
- ▨ 45 to 89.9
- ■ 90 and over

203.2 million

106 million

1920 1970

The progressive movement and the Square Deal

highest—along the Pacific slope, population more than doubled. But growth occurred everywhere, especially in the cities, where it proceeded six and a half times as fast as in rural areas. The cities, in the pattern of the past (see p. 446), absorbed almost all of the 14.5 million immigrants who came largely from central and southern Europe in the years 1900–15. Usually swarthy and unlettered, ordinarily Catholics or Jews, these newcomers differentiated the cities further and further from the patterns of life that rural America remembered and revered. By 1920 more Americans lived in cities and towns of over 2,500 people than in the countryside.

Spurred by the pace of private investment, the nation recovered from the depression of the nineties. During the first two decades of the century, capital investment rose over 250 percent and the total value of the products of industry rose 222. But not all groups shared equally in national wealth. Though unemployment became negligible, the richest 5 percent of American families received about 15 percent of national income in 1913, and 12 percent in 1920.

Those families were at once the agents and the beneficiaries of the process of industrial expansion and consolidation that resumed in the late 1890s. Corporate mergers and reorganizations gave a dominant influence to a few huge combinations in each of many industries—among others, railroading, iron and steel and copper, meatpacking, milling, tobacco, electricals, petroleum, and, by 1920, automobiles. As early as 1909, 1 percent of all the business firms in the nation produced 44 percent of all its manufactured goods. The consolidators had become the richest and in some ways the most powerful men in the United States. They guided the process of investment. They controlled the boards of directors of the great American banks and industries. They interpreted the startling growth of industry as a demonstration of their own wisdom and their optimism about the economic future of the United States. Beyond all that, they were developing, as were the experts whom they hired and consulted, an identification with the entirety of the national economy—the enormous national market, the need for national corporate institutions to reach it, the consequent need for energetic, professional management on a vast scale. Those insights contrasted with the parochialism of smaller institutions and of rural America, and with the traditional (and rewarding) faith of the American folk in their own ability to run their affairs and in their own local institutions. The growth of the great corporations raised questions about scale and control as troublesome as were the questions raised by the related problems of poverty and wealth.

The "leaden-eyed." The magnificence of American wealth contrasted sharply with the sorry lot of the American poor, whom society, as the poet Vachel Lindsey put it, had made "oxlike, limp, and leaden-eyed." In 1910 the nonagricultural laboring force consisted of more than 30 million men and 8 million women, most of whom worked too long, earned too little, and lived meanly. Between one-third and one-half of the industrial population lived in poverty. Their children ordinarily left school to find work—only one-third of the American children enrolled in primary schools completed their courses; less than one-tenth finished high school.

Work for men, women, and children was arduous. Some 8 million laborers were on the job on the average of 52.3 hours a week. Industrial accidents were common and conditions of work unhealthy and sometimes despicable. Usually workers had to suffer their disasters alone. Employer-liability laws, where they existed, were inadequate; there was no social insurance against accident, illness, old age, or unemployment. And the slums, where most workers lived, were as bad as they had been in the 1890s.

Mill worker

ated the 1890s. Still, apart from those fears, the center of American consciousness was slowly acquiring a new conscience. It produced a growing understanding of the efforts of some of the less-privileged to improve their lot, a sympathy for the protests of the best-informed against the inequities of American life, and, though rarely, a tolerance for the outrage of that small minority of Americans who were committed to rapid and radical social improvement.

Organized labor. The craft-union movement, well launched in the nineties, made significant gains during the early years of the twentieth century. Membership in the affiliates of the American Federation of Labor rose from 548,000 in 1900 to 1,676,000 in 1904 and, in the face of strong resistance from employers, to about 2,000,000 by 1914, though even then some 90 percent of industrial workers remained unorganized. The unions and the railroad brotherhoods continued to strive for the bread-and-butter objectives Samuel Gompers and their other leaders had defined earlier. Especially in the building and metals trades, they were able to win from management agreements providing for collective bargaining, higher wages, shorter hours, and safer conditions of work.

The craft unions were effective but in some respects selfish agencies of change. Though they excited opposition from business-managers not yet prepared to grant labor any voice in industrial decisions, they had little quarrel with the concentration of industrial power. The American Federation of Labor did demand the right to organize workers into national trade unions, consolidations that would parallel the consolidations of capital. In order to organize, labor needed to be unshackled from state and federal prohibitions on the strike and the boycott—and needed, too, state and federal protection from antiunion devices. The unions welcomed legislation setting standards of safety and employer liability, but otherwise they preferred to rely on their own power, rather than on the authority of the state, to reach their goals. They continued to distrust the federal government, for it had so often in the past assisted in breaking strikes, and they were eager to enlarge their own power even at the expense of those they had no intention of organizing. So it was that Gompers and his associates persisted in opposing legislation on wages and hours.

Collective bargaining, even when possible, assisted only union members, and the craft unions were generally unconcerned with the unskilled bulk of the labor force. Indeed Gompers, along with other labor-leaders, looked down on the unskilled, particularly on those who were women or immigrants. Craft-leaders feared that management would hire unskilled and unorganized immigrants and blacks to replace skilled

New kinds of mobile slums were developing, the slums of migratory workers—some immigrants, some native Americans, some blacks and Chicanos—who were leaving submarginal small farms to follow the wheat harvest north from Texas or to pick fruits and vegetables along the West Coast. So, too, the mining and lumbering camps of the South and West offered to workers only a life of drudgery, brutality, danger, and poverty.

Complacency and dissent. The inequities in American society evoked a variety of responses ranging from the complacent to the outraged. Most of the well-to-do—the business élite and the professional men who identified with them and served them—believed as they long had that success was a function of virtue and poverty evidence of sin. As the century turned, they were satisfied with existing conditions, and they remained fixed in their belief in minimal government. Other self-respecting men and women of the comfortable middle class harbored some anxieties about their own futures but few doubts about the merit of American institutions.

But there was a minority alike of the rich and of the comfortable who were receptive to the messages of protest and the efforts at particular social remedy that characterized the early years of the new century. That receptivity reflected in part a dread of drastic change and of the kind of radical agitation that had punctu-

The progressive movement and the Square Deal

workers (though in fact skilled workers were competing less with the unskilled than with an advancing technology and mechanization). This fear intensified prejudices against Asians, blacks, and southern and eastern Europeans—prejudices that fed growing sentiments for the restriction of immigration and for racial segregation. Organized labor condoned Jim Crow and sparked the agitation that led in 1902 to the exclusion from the United States of Chinese immigrants and in 1907 to the effective exclusion of Japanese.

American blacks. In short, the unions did no more than management or landlords to help the majority of workers. Within that majority were numbered the 10 million American blacks, of whom almost 90 percent still lived in the South. In 1910 almost a third of all blacks were still illiterate; all were victimized by the inferior facilities for schooling, housing, traveling, and working that segregation had imposed upon them. Worse still, the incidence of lynchings and race riots remained high—a shameful condition dramatized by mass killings in Atlanta in 1906 and by riots in Abraham Lincoln's own Springfield, Illinois, in 1908. As racist concepts spread in the North as well as the South, American blacks experienced their worst season since the Civil War. A few black intellectuals, led by W. E. B. DuBois, a Harvard Ph.D., in 1905 organized the Niagara movement. Abandoning the program of Booker T. Washington, DuBois and his associates demanded immediate action to achieve political and economic equality for blacks. With some support from informed whites, the Niagara movement was transformed in 1909 into the National Association for the Advancement of Colored People. But the NAACP, though a hopeful portent for legal redress of black grievances, was some years from becoming an influential instrument of reform.

American women. With varying success women, too, intensified their struggle for political, economic, and social status equal to that of men. Sarah Platt Decker, president of the General Federation of Women's Clubs, converted the energies of that middle-class organization to agitation for improving the conditions of industrial work for women and children (see p. 452). That was also the objective of the Women's Trade Union League and Florence Kelley's National Consumers' League, which sponsored state legislation for minimum wages and maximum hours. In New York City, the International Ladies' Garment Workers Union, financed in part by wealthy matrons, conducted a prolonged strike in 1909 that won limited gains in spite of opposition from employers and police. The Triangle Shirtwaist Company in New York City did not agree to the union's demand for better wages or for safer conditions of work. The company's stubborn parsimony accounted for the tragedy that occurred in 1911 when fire broke out on its premises and resulted in the death of 146 employees, mostly young women, who could not escape from the building. The episode provoked official investigations that led ultimately to new factory laws and immediately to broader support for the ILGWU, which by 1914 had become the third-largest union in the AFL.

Headquarters, Women's Trade Union League

National wealth and the business élite

Social feminism

The new demand of women for political enfranchisement comes at a time when unsatisfactory and degraded social conditions are held responsible for so much wretchedness and when the fate of all the unfortunate, the suffering, and the criminal, is daily forced upon woman's attention in painful and intimate ways. At the same moment, governments all over the world are insisting that it is their function, and theirs alone, so to regulate social and industrial conditions that a desirable citizenship may be secured....

Governmental commissions everywhere take woman's testimony as to legislation for better housing, for public health and education, for the care of dependents, and many other remedial measures, because it is obviously a perilous business to turn over delicate social experiments to men who have remained quite untouched by social compunctions and who have been elected to their legislative position solely upon the old political issues. Certainly under this new conception of politics it is much easier to legislate for those human beings of whose condition the electorate are "vividly aware."

From Jane Addams, "The Larger Aspects of the Woman's Movement," 1914.

The contributions of women to various movements for social justice demonstrated their creative and organizational abilities, abilities that most Americans—men and women alike—still viewed as inferior to those of men. But women, though exploited by industry, were inferior in no essential sense. To put a stop to the exploitation, social feminists sponsored special factory laws to protect women from hazardous conditions and overlong hours of work. In so doing, they often contended that women needed special care because they were physically frailer than men. But no man worked as hard or accomplished as much for the settlement-house movement in the United States as did Jane Addams at Hull House in Chicago or Lillian Wald at Henry Street in New York. Indeed those extraordinary women trained a younger generation, both men and women, to understand the problems of poverty and to combat the circumstances that caused them.

Women also served among the officers and troops in the war against whiskey. The Women's Christian Temperance Union, strongest in rural America, was an unequaled force in the growing demand for the prohibition of the manufacture and sale of alcoholic beverages. Prohibition, an issue of continuing political importance during the first three decades of the twentieth century, aligned (with exceptions of course) rural, native-born, fundamentalist Americans against their urban, immigrant, Catholic countrymen. Yet in cities as well as small towns, women expressed a special interest in protecting families against the profligacy of alcoholic breadwinners, and the most urbane prohibitionists came to view their objective as a scientifically valid effort to improve human life by controlling part of it. If they were naive about the ability

of the state to govern private behavior, they were more sophisticated than their critics realized in their recognition of the dangers of addiction to any drug, alcohol included.

It was primarily urban women who absorbed the more unconventional messages of Charlotte Perkins Gilman, Emma Goldman, and Margaret Sanger. Gilman, eager to free women from the burdens and constraints of rearing a family and caring for a house, proposed communal arrangements for child care and domestic chores. She influenced fewer women than did Goldman and Sanger, who had begun to advocate free and open instruction in birth control. Birth control, they argued, by gradually reducing the size of the working force, would soon enhance the ability of laborers to bargain with capitalists. Interest in birth control, however, spread largely among women who recognized the physical, social, and psychological advantages of family planning and who were eager to be freed from the constraints of the ordinary American home. Under their auspices, the National Birth Control League in 1915 began its attempt through education and lobbying to effect the repeal of state and federal laws that forbade as obscene the dissemination of information about birth control. But like the NAACP, the NBCL was still many years from becoming an effective political force.

The effectiveness of women as individuals—more and more, for example, were attending college and entering the professions of law and medicine—was matched by the effectiveness of the collective demand for women's suffrage. In the second decade of the new century the suffrage movement gained strength under the quiet leadership of Carrie Chapman Catt, president of the American Women's Suf-

frage Association, and Alice Paul, the more militant head of the new Congressional Union. In 1914 the General Federation of Women's Clubs at last enlisted its significant support for the cause, which was also attracting more and more of those many men who, eager to democratize voting, saw women's suffrage as one part of their program. Indeed suffrage as an issue came to absorb much of the energy of feminism, to stand out as the central goal of American women. Between 1910 and 1914 they won the ballot in six states and were moving close to the national victory they sought.

Protest and reform

American farmers. The new century brought unparalleled prosperity to American farmers. As domestic and world markets revived, the prices of farm products and the value of farm land just about doubled within a decade. The farmer was still suspicious of bankers, of industry and middlemen, of cities and foreigners. But prosperity tempered farmers' hostilities, softened their rhetoric, turned them from outright attack to flanking maneuvers by which they sought to procure for themselves a larger share both of urban culture and comforts and of the business profits of agriculture.

Farm organizations continued to press for political reforms designed to give voters a stronger and more direct voice in government. The reforms, they hoped, would help them obtain public policies that would aid agriculture—better roads and marketing facilities, cheaper credit, technical advice on planting and cultivation, more and cheaper electric power, assistance to cooperatives, lower taxes on land, and

tariff adjustments that would facilitate sales abroad. Those practical goals, some of which entailed special privileges for farmers, challenged the special privileges and the superior power big business had long enjoyed.

In Washington farm spokesmen continued to urge the creation of agencies to monitor the growth and the practices of the great consolidations. Reflecting the agrarian bias against monopoly, they also urged the enforcement of the languishing antitrust laws. Some farm leaders believed that federal programs of assistance should extend to labor. Thus the objectives of farm politics sometimes merged with the objectives of urban reformers.

American radicals. But there remained little of the agrarian radicalism of the 1890s and less of anarchism, which had begun to decline as a cult before the assassination of McKinley revived old, middle-class fears for the safety of the Republic. The radicalism of the early century took other forms.

Socialism consistently gained adherents, especially in the cities, though one strong group flourished for a time in Oklahoma. Most socialists were not proletarians but middle-class, sometimes even quite comfortable, native Americans, though another influential group consisted of New York Jewish immigrants. Intellectuals like Max Eastman and John Reed gave to the Socialist party a brilliant style but recruited few followers. Moderate party leaders like Morris Hillquit in New York and Victor Berger in Milwaukee stood for peaceful, democratic means to effect reform and gradually acquire for the state private means of production, beginning with natural monopolies in such industries as transportation, communications, and other utilities. Their program had only a limited appeal to American workers, who were rarely class-conscious. Most still harbored some faith in the American dream of success, at least for their

Eugene V. Debs:
a stirring rhetoric

children, and skilled workers identified their interests not with socialist doctrines but with the strategy of trade unionism.

Eugene V. Debs, the engaging head of the Socialist party and its continual candidate for President, employed a stirring rhetoric that mixed Jeffersonian and Marxist principles. But even he was no revolutionary. Nor were the almost one million Americans who supported him in 1912, the year of the party's largest vote. Further, Debs stood with the moderates in 1913 in expelling from the party's national executive committee "Big Bill" Haywood, who seemed to consider violence a legitimate tactic of reform.

In 1905 Haywood and others had founded the Industrial Workers of the World, the "Wobblies." Determined to organize the most destitute Americans—itinerant farm workers, Western miners (many of whom were immigrants), the primarily immigrant textile workers of the Northeast, and others whom the AFL ignored—the IWW unhesitatingly employed the strike to obtain recognition of industrial unions (unions of all employees in a plant or mine regardless of skills). The industrial union had earlier support from the Knights of Labor and the American Railway Union, and later was advanced by the Congress of Industrial Workers (CIO) of the 1930s. But the AFL preferred trade unions, objected to any dual unionism—that is, to competition between unions for membership—and feared the IWW would give all

labor a bad name. IWW rhetoric sometimes suggested sympathy for recourse to violence, though the violence of IWW strikes arose largely because of the force with which management resisted. The very appearance of violence disturbed the middle class. Native Americans, moreover, interpreted the combination of the radicalism of the IWW and the union's large immigrant membership as proof of the old stereotype of the immigrant radical. Accordingly, from the time of its founding the IWW knew continued repression from government as well as management, and even occasional victories, as in the Lawrence textile strike of 1913, provided only temporary hopes for the movement's survival.

The growing repression of the Wobblies and the socialists revealed the essential conservatism and ethnocentrism of American culture. The champions of meliorative reform shared those biases with those who opposed any change. But the meliorists, the progressives, in contrast to the stand-patters, advocated reform precisely because they believed that the preservation of American institutions depended upon altering them sufficiently to remove the most disturbing injustices in American life.

Politics had not created those injustices, but politics did reflect and sustain them, so politics might also help gradually to erase them. The early twentieth century witnessed a flowering of ideas that politics might implement, ideas that in one way or another struck against the thoughtless behavior and special privileges of the wealthy and their allies, against the selfishness that was generating the corrosive discontent of moderate and radical dissenters alike.

Bill Haywood and strikers,
Lawrence, Massachusetts, 1913

The progressive movement and the Square Deal

Art and literature of protest. Those ideas took shape as artists, journalists, and social workers exposed the conditions of filth and misery that violated the ideals of middle-class Americans. Realistic literature and art, candid and conscientious journalism, reached the hearts of ladies and gentlemen of good will and helped enlist them in the causes of reform.

Theodore Dreiser, an immigrant's son schooled in poverty, used his powerful novels to describe the barren life of the poor "as simply and effectively as the English language will permit." His *Sister Carrie* (1901), *Jennie Gerhardt* (1911), *The Financier* (1912), and *The Titan* (1914) revealed the human tragedy of inadequate wages, of insecure, hopeless, mechanical existence. Most of Dreiser's characters, driven by greed or sex to bestial violence, tried to fight their way into more splendid circumstances, but Dreiser made it poignantly clear how great were the odds against them, how cruel the cost of success, how sorry the lot of those success left behind. Frank Norris, a lesser talent than Dreiser, made his novel *The Octopus* (1901) a vehicle for condemning the inhumane policies of the Southern Pacific Railroad. In spite of the evils he recounted, he professed a faith that "all things . . . work together for good," but he continued his indictment of wealth in *The Pit* (1903). Jack London, a socialist, was optimistic only about the ultimate triumph of those who had lived, as he had, in "the unending limbo of toil." His fellow socialist and novelist Upton Sinclair, writing *The Jungle* (1906) in a similar vein, showed how those who labored in the poisonous world of the Chicago packinghouses "hated their work . . . the bosses . . . the owners . . . the whole place, the whole neighborhood." The poet Carl Sandburg railed at the stockyards and at "Pittsburgh, Youngstown, Gary—they made their steel with men."

Realistic painters, representatives of the "ash-can school," produced canvases that one of their number, John Sloan, called "unconsciously social conscious." Sloan, Robert Henri, William Glackens, George Luks, and others, experimenting with new brush techniques and new relationships of form, found compelling subject matter in dirty alleys, dank saloons, and squalid tenements—"chapters out of life," which they interpreted with beauty that expressed the sorrow and injustice of an experience previously unrecorded in fashionable galleries.

The art of men like Sloan, Sandburg, and Dreiser, for whom social criticism was often a secondary purpose, supplemented and sharpened the message of outraged authors of a deliberate literature of exposure. Social workers, sociologists, and economists recited the facts of poverty in the magazine *Charities and the Commons*; in reports like *The Tenement House Problem* (1903); in books like Robert Hunter's *Poverty* (1904), Father John A. Ryan's *A Living Wage* (1906),

John Sloan, Sunday, Women Drying Their Hair: *unconsciously social conscious*

John Spargo's *The Bitter Cry of the Children* (1906), Walter Rauschenbusch's *Christianity and the Social Crisis* (1907), and Frances Kellor's *Out of Work* (1915). Those documents demonstrated that between half and two-thirds of all working-class families had incomes too small to buy food, shelter, and clothing—incomes that left nothing for recreation or education, little even for union dues or church contributions. No thoughtful reader of those works could any longer believe that poverty was a function of sloth or moral turpitude; clearly there was something wrong with a society that permitted so much misery while it pretended to a Christian ethic and a generous standard of living.

But humanitarian striving, effective though it was, influenced fewer Americans than did the hortatory, often sensational, journalism of exposure. *McClure's* set the pace for inexpensive, middle-class magazines. It published Ida M. Tarbell's devastating account of the business methods of the Standard Oil Company, Lincoln Steffens' exposés of the role of respectable citizens as well as ward politicians in the corrupt government of a dozen cities and states, Burton J. Hendrick's disclosures of the fraudulent practices of various insurance companies, and Ray Stannard Baker's indictments of railroad mismanagement, labor-baiting in Colorado, and race discrimination in the South. Though other "muckrakers" (the phrase was Theodore Roosevelt's) sometimes enlivened their work with willful exaggerations, they had

But there was the good State of Wisconsin ruled by a handful of men who had destroyed every vestige of democracy in the commonwealth. They settled in private conference practically all nominations for important offices, controlled conventions, dictated legislation, and had even sought to lay corrupt hands on the courts of justice....

The pass abuse had grown to extraordinary proportions in Wisconsin, and the power to give passes, franks on telegraph and telephone lines, free passage on Pullman cars, and free transportation by express companies had become a great asset of the machine politicians....

Clubs were formed in Madison where members of the legislature could be drawn together in a social way and cleverly led into intimate associations with the corporation men who swarmed the capital. In one of the principal hotels a regular poker game was maintained where members who could not be reached in any other way, could win, very easily, quite large sums of money. In that way bribes were disguised.... It was notorious that lewd women were an accessory to the lobby organization. Members who could not be reached in any other way were advised that they could receive good positions with railroad corporations after the legislative session was over.

From Robert M. La Follette, *La Follette's Autobiography, 1913.*

no need to distort. The bare facts stirred the awakening conscience of middle-class Americans.

Protests of the intellectuals.   Meanwhile, American intellectuals were formulating the attitudes and techniques on which reform was to rely. These new attitudes, taken together, suggested the need for skepticism about rigid, formal systems of thought. They suggested also the importance of rigorous, dispassionate inquiry as a foundation for knowledge and of constant testing of hypotheses and modification of them on the basis of experience. These principles, derived from the methods of science, were expected to yield ideas for social action. Indeed for the innovative proponents of the developing philosophy of pragmatism, the value of any idea depended on its utility for the thinker and society.

Among the influential intellectuals of the early century, none better stated the case for enlightened skepticism than did Justice Oliver Wendell Holmes, Jr., who recognized that the prejudices of judges often determined their interpretations of the law. Explaining the divergences between law and ethics, Holmes questioned the propensity of courts to upset the decisions of popularly elected legislatures. Though he understood the fallibility of the majority, he preached judicial restraint, for he understood also the judiciary's fallibility and its tendency to traditionalism and arrogance.

The artificiality and formalism of prevalent theories of social Darwinism invited the attack of William James and John Dewey, the fathers of American pragmatism. A psychologist as well as a philosopher, James emphasized the vagaries and the resilience of the mind, and warned against imprisoning intellectual creativity within arbitrary or mechanistic systems. For him the truth of an idea or an action lay in its consequences, as it did also for Dewey, who conceived of philosophy as an instrument for guiding action, an instrument he himself used in advocating experimentation in education and government. Tolerance and freedom of belief and of expression, Dewey noted, were essential if ideas were to enjoy a competitive chance to prove their merit.

Thorstein Veblen continued to strip away the facade of contemporary institutions as he had in the nineties. His *The Theory of Business Enterprise* (1904) explained the cultural and economic importance of the machine process, and his *The Instinct of Workmanship* (1914) showed that wasteful and destructive monopolistic practices frustrated man's basic drive to create. Veblen's uncompromising analyses contained insights from which reformers, economists, and sociologists—"social engineers"—were then and later to borrow freely and with reward.

Other less angry and less probing students of contemporary economic institutions directed attention to reform. The writings of John R. Commons on labor, Jeremiah W. Jenks on industry, and William Z. Ripley on railroads were characteristic of moderate, but perceptively critical, scholarship. These experts, often counselors to state and federal regulatory or

The progressive movement and the Square Deal

"The System": Pittsburgh

investigatory commissions, understood that business-managers were not ordinarily bad but that they were too often timid or unimaginative. With Ripley, the economists Henry C. Adams, Richard T. Ely, and Simon Patten viewed man not as the creature of deterministic forces but as the maker of beneficent change. They urged that the principles of management be applied to government and that the state be empowered to solve the public problems business could not.

Progressivism in the cities and the states. Democratic government had failed most blatantly in American cities. Now municipal-reform organizations, many of them founded in the nineties, succeeded gradually in winning home-rule charters and permission to regulate franchises or to provide for public ownership of vital services. The experiments of Galveston, Texas, with a commission form of government, and of Staunton, Virginia, with a city-manager, demonstrated how efficient these substitutes for an aldermanic system could be. Over a hundred cities had copied them by 1910. A concern for efficiency in city government contrasted with the purpose of those reformers animated primarily by a desire to root out corruption and to assist the poor. Such men and women drew inspiration from the examples set by mayors like Hazen Pingree of Detroit and Samuel "Golden Rule" Jones of Toledo.

Those developments impinged continually on state government, partly because urban reform could not proceed without improvements in state laws. A wave of reform in the Middle West began in Wisconsin with the election of Robert M. La Follette as gover-nor in 1900. "Battle Bob," who set precedents for the entire region, had tried for years to overcome the regular Republican machine. A loyal party man, he built his own faction of those who shared his worries about the special advantages the state had given many corporations, about high property taxes, and about high prices. He attracted both a rural and an urban following that was essentially middle class in its background and aspiration. Before he became United States senator in 1906, La Follette made his administration a model of honesty and efficiency, established a fruitful liaison between the government and the state university, whose distinguished faculty included many valuable advisers on public policy, and overcame the opposition of the Old Guard in the legislature. At the governor's urging, Wisconsin passed laws providing for a direct primary, civil service, restrictions on lobbying, conservation, state control of railroads and banks, higher taxes on all corporations (previously undertaxed), and the first state income tax. Wisconsin had become, as Theodore Roosevelt later said, "the laboratory of democracy."

Progressive government came also to Iowa, Minnesota, the Dakotas, Oregon, Arkansas, Mississippi, Georgia, and South Carolina. Progressive administrations in those states moved, with variations in each case, to institute programs like La Follette's, though in the South the democratization of politics followed the disfranchisement of blacks and many poor whites.

Progressivism won similar victories in Northern industrial states, where much of the impetus for reform came from the middle class of the suburbs as well as the cities. In New Jersey the "New Idea," a local version of progressivism, arose among prosperous suburbanites who were fighting to prevent valuable rapid-transit and other franchises from falling into exploitative hands, to empower a state commission to regulate commutation fares, to extract taxes from corporations (instead of from real estate alone) to defray the costs of public schooling. Objectives like those, along with the characteristic middle-class hostility toward machine politics, brought the New Idea into alliance with the reform mayor of Jersey City, who had built his strength among the workingmen he befriended. In 1904 the resulting coalition of independent Republicans began to convert New Jersey into a progressive community. In 1910 the state elected a Democratic governor, Woodrow Wilson, and during his administration a bipartisan coalition of progressives completed the program of the New Idea.

New York, Michigan, California, and Ohio, all states with important industrial centers, had political experiences not unlike New Jersey's, though none elected a governor who was so quickly and dramatically successful as Wilson. Reform in these and other industrial states led to major improvements for the working force, which cast some of the crucial votes for progress. Before 1915, twenty-five states passed employer-liability laws; five limited the use of injunctions preventing strikes or boycotts; nine passed minimum-wage laws for women; twenty granted pensions to indigent widows with children; others restricted hours and conditions of work.

The progressive attitudes and motives. The strivings of the progressives revealed a great deal about the progressives themselves—their faith in democratic processes, their hostility to large aggregations of private power, their confidence in public regulatory agencies, their humanitarian temper. And yet they were a diverse group, and their movement was a concatenation of similar but independent movements. In rural areas, it borrowed much from Populism, and it retained an agrarian flavor modified by time, experience, and prosperity. In the cities, where the poor were increasingly conscious of the need to remedy their lot by political action, progressivism was more visible as a political expression of the attitudes of liberal intellectuals of the nineties and the early twentieth century. The middle-class men and women who absorbed those attitudes and swelled the ranks of reform were both goodhearted and worried. They mobilized partly because they had gained a better understanding of the urgency of social reform, partly because they saw that change was needed if they were to preserve the things they valued. Violence, trembling below the surface of society, threatened the comfortable middle-class world. But the middle class had a chance to remove the inequities that bred

disquiet. Further, the state (as middle-class Americans often viewed it) and especially expert agencies created by the state would mediate the tensions between rich and poor, the powerful and the weak.

Professional men, white-collar men, and small businessmen felt their status and their well-being threatened by the advancing power of big business, big city machines, and—more rarely—big labor. They had to organize to protect themselves and their standing and to monitor their giant rivals. Mostly native Americans, they resented the immigrant or second-generation political boss. Mostly men of modest means and often men of old family, they resented the purchased prestige and paraded vulgarity of the newly rich. Though some of them were bureaucrats, successful servants of big business and finance, more of them were the victims of bigness and consequently anxious to regulate it. Where labor unions were strong economically and politically, as in California, they too became targets for the attack on power. But more often the attack was pointed toward corporations that dealt directly with many customers—monopolies or near-monopolies selling transportation, utilities, and food—or that were saddled (sometimes unjustly) with especially bad reputations.

Some managers of large corporations realized that reform sentiment might work to their own advantage. Such men, eager to protect the industrial stability they had achieved, worried about the possibility of renewed competition. They recognized that limited and benign federal regulation—for example, of railroading, of lumbering, of banking, or of the manufacture of pharmaceuticals—could restrict the sharp practices of their smaller but aggressive business rivals. Public policy, in that view, instead of being merely permissive or primarily antimonopoly, had the potentiality of providing positive guidance for industrial behavior, guidance compatible with the interests of big business. Spokesmen of big business who were also reformers—distinctly a minority of their kind—acted in some cases in pursuit of selfish advantage, in some cases out of a sense of social obligation, in some cases out of both motives.

Whatever their motives, they often reasoned from the unstated, paradoxical premises that were characteristic of progressive thought. They had a sense of their own élite status—whether of wealth or social standing or talent—which they felt they deserved. They also believed in representative government, in the agencies it created, and in the electorate to which it was responsible. They reconciled those beliefs with the comforting, private assumption that they and men sympathetic to them would win and hold the confidence of the people. In that assumption, honest businessmen had little to fear from federal

The progressive movement and the Square Deal

regulation of industry, for the regulators would appreciate the problems of those they regulated. Indeed, most progressives believed that the growth and prosperity of industry, properly disciplined, was essential to the national interest.

The progressives, men and women of many stripes, included many middle-class people, but not all—or even most—middle-class people were progressives. Those who were, were the most socially conscious, perhaps the most anxious, but also, by and large, the younger, the better educated, and the more adventurous. They drew much of their inspiration from the most dynamic national exponent of their spirit and purpose, President Theodore Roosevelt. Without Roosevelt, progressivism would doubtless have happened, but it would not have been nearly so exciting.

The Republican Roosevelt

In September 1901 McKinley died, the third President to be assassinated in less than forty years. His successor, Theodore Roosevelt, whom Mark Hanna had called "that damned cowboy," had set his political course for the White House long before McKinley's death. "It is," wrote Roosevelt, "a dreadful thing to come into the Presidency this way; but it would be a far worse thing to be morbid about it." The gift of the gods to Roosevelt—at forty-two the youngest chief executive in American history—was joy in life, and for eight exciting years he brought that joy to his office.

The son of patrician parents, a graduate of Harvard, an accomplished ornithologist and an enthusiastic historian, Roosevelt chose early in life to make politics his career, for he wanted to rule—and he chose to work not as an independent but as a loyal Republican, for he wanted to win. He served successfully, with occasional time out as a rancher in the Dakotas, as an assemblyman in New York, a United States Civil Service commissioner, a New York City police commissioner, Assistant Secretary of the Navy, colonel of the celebrated Rough Riders, and governor of New York. Senator Thomas C. Platt, the long-time boss of the state Republicans, developed serious apprehensions about Roosevelt's successful ventures in reform and managed in 1900 to get him out of New York by arranging his nomination for Vice President, a position Roosevelt accepted with somewhat resigned grace but with characteristic vigor.

Roosevelt and the Presidency. As a campaigner Roosevelt displayed the qualities that were to give

Theodore Roosevelt:
joy in life

him during his Presidency an enormous influence with the people. To the Americans who acclaimed him he was many wonderful things—policeman, cowboy, hero in arms, battler for the everlasting right. He was that toothy grin, that animal energy, that squeaky voice exhorting the worthy to reform. Roosevelt was also a learned man, receptive to the advice of the men of ideas whom he brought to Washington. As one Englishman put it, he was more remarkable than anything in the United States, except perhaps Niagara Falls.

Roosevelt was also a skilled politician who made the Presidency a great office and used it boldly. He conceived of the President as "a steward of the people bound actively and affirmatively to do all he could for the people"; he set out therefore as President to define the great national problems of his time, to propose for each a practicable solution, to win people and Congress to his proposals, and to infuse the executive department with his own dedication to efficient enforcement of the laws.

Roosevelt summoned to federal service a remarkable group of advisers and subordinates. The President's example and support inspired them; his reorganizations of federal agencies gave scope to their

521

talents. They included, among others, Elihu Root, McKinley's Secretary of War whom Roosevelt continued in that office and later made Secretary of State; William Howard Taft, Root's successor in the War Department; Chief Forester Gifford Pinchot and Secretary of the Interior James R. Garfield, both eminent conservationists.

In filling dozens of lesser federal offices, Roosevelt assured his own control of his party. He manipulated patronage so deftly that Mark Hanna had lost control of Republican affairs months before he died in February 1904. By that time Roosevelt, profiting also because he was the incumbent, could count on the support of every important state delegation to the forthcoming national convention. He could rely, too, on the influential party-leaders, for he had satisfied the most urgent demands of the liberal wing without offending or frightening the stand-patters.

Roosevelt and the trusts. Roosevelt, always a gradualist, fashioned a circumspect domestic program, which he dressed in a pungent rhetoric. At the outset of his Administration he indicated that he would accept the advice of the Old Guard in the Senate on tariff and monetary policies, matters about which they were most sensitive. He was himself much more worried about the problems of industrial consolidation. The "absolutely vital question," Roosevelt believed, "was whether the government had power to control" the trusts. The Supreme Court's decision in the E. C. Knight case (1895) suggested that it did not (see p. 431). Seeking a modification of that interpretation, Roosevelt in 1902 ordered his Attorney General, Philander C. Knox, to bring suit for violation of the Sherman Act against the Northern Securities Company.

The President had chosen his target carefully. The Northern Securities Company was a mammoth holding company for the Northern Pacific, the Great Northern, and the Chicago, Burlington, & Quincy railroads. A battle for the stock of the Northern Pacific, key to control of transportation in the Northwest, had led in 1901 to panic on Wall Street. The antagonists made peace by creating the Northern Securities Company for the immediate purpose of quieting the market and for the ultimate purpose of monopolizing the railroads of a rapidly growing region. Those who had fought and then made their profitable peace were titans of finance: J. P. Morgan and Company, the Rockefeller interests, James J. Hill, and E. H. Harriman. The panic they had brought on, a calamity for many brokers, drew attention to their ruthless speculation; the holding company they formed, in which 30 percent of the stock represented only intangible assets, worried the farmers of the

Northwest, who, suspicious as ever of monopolies, expected freight rates to soar.

While several states initiated legal action against the holding company, Roosevelt began his preparations in secret. Announcement of the federal government's suit stunned Wall Street. Morgan, with the arrogance of an independent sovereign, tried in vain to have his lawyer settle things with the Attorney General. His failure, like Roosevelt's attack, symbolized a transfer of power from lower New York to Washington. In 1903 a federal court ordered the dissolution of the Northern Securities Company, a decision the Supreme Court sustained the next year. Roosevelt wrote that it was "impossible to overestimate the importance" of the case.

The government proceeded against forty-four more corporations during Roosevelt's term in office. In 1902 action began against the "beef trust," so unpopular with sellers of livestock and buyers of meat; equally unpopular were four defendants in cases started in 1906 and 1907, the American Tobacco Company, the Du Pont Corporation, the New Haven Railroad, and the Standard Oil Company.

Roosevelt's revival of the Sherman Act won him a reputation as a "trust-buster," but he never believed that the fragmentation of industry could solve the nation's problems. He had, he felt, to establish the authority of the federal executive to use the antitrust law in cases of monopoly or flagrant misbehavior. Trust-busting, however, was in his view an ultimate weapon, inappropriate in the case of most enterprises that had reduced the cost of production and had won for the nation the industrial leadership of the world. The growth of industry was, he argued, natural, unavoidable, and beneficial. Breaking up corporations whose only offense was size would be impossible unless the government also abolished steam, electricity, large cities, indeed all modern conditions. The need was for continuous, informed, and expert regulation, which only the federal government could properly undertake.

The Square Deal. In December 1901 Roosevelt made his first modest recommendations to Congress for creating the efficient system of control on which, he believed, the orderly development of industrial life depended. The President, like many of the consolidators, had a national rather than a local view of economic problems, and a confidence in expert management rather than in popular sentiment. Where some consolidators of that mind looked to the federal government to enhance its authority in order to further their needs, Roosevelt favored that enhancement in order to advance what he considered the public interest. Yet his was not primarily an adversary stance. The public interest, as he saw it, did not call for federal punishment of business but for expert federal regulation to prevent the abuses of predatory business, and thereby to encourage the productive energies of responsible business.

Roosevelt asked first for an act to expedite antitrust prosecutions, which Congress passed in 1903. Without opposition it then also enacted his proposal for forbidding the granting or receiving of rebates, a practice that powerful shippers had forced upon unwilling railroads. The railroads had wanted the protection they received, as did most shippers. More serious opposition developed to Roosevelt's major objective, the creation of a new Department of Commerce and Labor with a Bureau of Corporations empowered to gather and release information about industry. Such a bureau was essential if the government was to learn what businesses to regulate and how. On that account, conservative Republican senators blocked Roosevelt's bill, though many congressmen preferred it to more stringent measures then under consideration. The President saved his bill by announcing that John D. Rockefeller was secretly organizing the opposition to it. The culprit was actually one of Rockefeller's subordinates, but the purport of Roosevelt's charge was accurate, and the consequent public clamor accelerated the passage of the controversial law.

The new act gave to the Bureau of Corporations authority to investigate significant public issues, as that bureau did, for example, in finding the facts on which Roosevelt later based his hydroelectric policy. For its part, the Bureau of Labor, also primarily a fact-finding agency, demonstrated its usefulness to Roosevelt and to workingmen by its fair reporting during the strike of anthracite-coal miners that began in May 1902 and lasted until October. The managers of the Eastern coal-carrying railroads that owned most of the mines would not negotiate with the union, the United Mine Workers, which was demanding recognition, an eight-hour day, and a 10 to 20 percent increase in pay. Labor's orderly conduct and willingness to arbitrate won growing public approval, particularly after the intransigent owners, speaking through George F. Baer, the president of the Reading Railroad, insisted that "God in his Infinite Wisdom has given control of the property interests" to the directors of

Anthracite miners: victims of "arrogant stupidity"

large corporations. This attitude invited public antagonism at a time when fuel was short and the days were growing chilly.

Roosevelt, sympathetic to the workers and worried about the coal shortage, had hesitated to enter the dispute only because his advisers felt that he lacked the legal authority. Early in October he summoned the mine-operators and John Mitchell, the union chief, to the White House. Mitchell again offered to submit to arbitration, but the owners remained obdurate. Indeed, they demanded that the President issue an injunction and, if necessary, use the army to end the strike. Their "arrogant stupidity" provoked Roosevelt instead to let them know indirectly that he was prepared to use troops to dispossess them and produce coal. With this kind of intervention in the offing, Mark Hanna, Elihu Root, and other conservative men who were already working for peace, quickened their efforts, enlisted the help of J. P. Morgan himself, and persuaded the mine-owners to accept a compromise settlement. By its terms the miners resumed work, and a commission appointed by the President arbitrated the questions at issue. In March the commission awarded labor a 10 percent raise, a reduction in working hours to nine and in some cases eight per day, but not recognition of the union. The owners in return received a welcome invitation to raise coal prices 10 percent. Roosevelt was the first President to bring both labor and capital to the White House to settle a dispute, the first to get them both to accept the judgment of a commission appointed by the executive, the first to coerce the owners of a crucial industry by threatening to take it over. All this contrasted vividly with the course of the federal government during the Pullman strike (see pp. 439–40).

In other labor episodes, Roosevelt insisted on the open shop for government-workers and resisted not only all radical unionism but also the principle of the union shop in industry. He believed, as he put it, in "the right of laboring men to join a union . . . without illegal interference." This was less than Gompers advocated, but it was more than most businessmen or conservative politicians were yet willing to concede. It was a position characteristic of Roosevelt—advanced but not radical, cautious but not timorous.

His purpose during the coal strike, Roosevelt explained during the campaign of 1904, had been to give both sides a "square deal." The phrase became a familiar label for his Administration, and for his intention to abolish privilege and enlarge individual opportunity. His "natural allies," he said, were "the farmers, small businessmen and upper-class mechanics," middle-class Americans "fundamentally sound, morally, mentally and physically." Like him, they abhorred extremes; like him, they judged in moral

terms. They warmed to Roosevelt's fusillades against those he later called the "malefactors of great wealth." They accepted and cheered his image of himself as a champion of fairness.

The election of 1904. That was the basis of his campaign for reelection. It was the basis, too, for his appointment to office of qualified men from minority groups, blacks, Catholics, Jews, Americans of Hungarian and German and Irish extraction. His appreciation of the inherent dignity in every man encouraged him to invite to the White House Booker T. Washington, the Negro educator who doubled as an adviser on patronage. There was, to be sure, a happy compatibility between Roosevelt's conscience and the needs of politics, but that did not detract from his conscience, though it manifestly strengthened his campaign. He took no chances. A new pension order, making age alone a sufficient qualification for eligibility, held the GAR to the GOP. The official platform contained standard Republican platitudes about the tariff and prosperity, sops to the Old Guard, as was the lackluster nominee for Vice President, Senator Charles W. Fairbanks of Indiana. Taken together, the platform and the ticket strengthened the basis of the successful Republican coalition of the late 1890s. But the real platform was Roosevelt's record, and the real issue was the man.

That made things difficult for the Democrats. As Bryan complained, Roosevelt had captured his banner. The Republicans now marched as the party of reform. Conservative Democrats returned to the formulas of Grover Cleveland's days, to a platform emphasizing strict construction of the Constitution and a candidate—Judge Alton B. Parker—chosen for his safe views and close ties to New York wealth.

Parker conducted a dull campaign until the vision of impending defeat persuaded him to charge that Roosevelt's campaign-manager, George B. Cortelyou, was blackmailing corporations for contributions. Cortelyou, who had been Secretary of Commerce, had indeed had access to the findings of the Bureau of Corporations, but he neither resorted to blackmail nor needed to. Wealthy Republicans, loyal party men in spite of their reservations about Roosevelt, had responded without stint to the usual appeals for funds. Parker's charges reminded the electorate that Roosevelt's campaign was well endowed but served otherwise only to provoke from the President an indignant denial. Indeed, Roosevelt directed his party treasurer to return any contributions that had come from predatory wealth. The treasurer ignored the order, just as the voters by and large ignored Parker's accusations. Roosevelt could have won without much financial support. In a landslide victory, he received 57.4 per-

The progressive movement and the Square Deal

cent of the popular votes (7,628,461) to Parker's 37.6 percent (5,084,223), and 336 electoral votes to the Democrat's 140.

Roosevelt and reform

The regulation of business. When Congress convened in December 1904, the progress of reform in Washington and in the states was gathering momentum. President now in his own right, Roosevelt took advantage of the mandate he had helped to create. His prime objective was railroad regulation. Decisions of the Supreme Court had stripped the Interstate Commerce Commission of authority over railway rates or rebates, which the roads continued to grant in spite of the government's efforts to enforce the antirebate act of 1903. The only feasible remedy was to give the commission power to set reasonable and nondiscriminatory rates and to prevent inequitable practices. Farmers and small businessmen and their representatives were increasingly demanding that remedy. Some railroad managers saw advantages in dealing with a single federal authority rather than with many state commissions, but even they preferred final decisions to rest with the conservative judiciary rather than with the ICC. Further, most railroads, their privileged customers, and the devotees of conservative economic theory opposed federal rate-making, which would for the first time in American history give the national government authority to determine prices, the sacrosanct prerogative of private enterprise.

For Roosevelt, laissez-faire theory was not sacred, but moral corporate behavior was. In 1904 and 1905 he urged Congress to endow the ICC with the power to adjust rates against which shippers had complained. During the long debate that ensued, Roosevelt advanced his purpose skillfully. Concentrating on the railroad issue, he gave up a tentative plan to press for a downward revision of the tariff, which agrarian Republicans as well as Democrats favored. The President had never considered the tariff a vital matter, for in his opinion it was not a moral question. It was, however, an issue that divided his party. So, rather than risk division, he conceded to the Old Guard on tariff reform. At least partly on that account, the House of Representatives passed the President's railroad bill by an overwhelming margin.

Handling the Senate was more difficult, for the Old Guard delayed a vote while the railroads underwrote a national publicity campaign, which Roosevelt answered in a series of vigorous speeches. In 1906 he outmaneuvered his opponents and, after few modifi-

cations, the Hepburn Act carried. It gave the ICC the authority upon complaint from a shipper to set aside existing rates and to prescribe substitutes, subject to court review. As it worked out during the next several years, the courts did not overrule the commission. The act was less than the most vocal critics of the roads had wanted, for they advocated the physical valuation of railway properties as the proper basis for rate-making. But the act was just what Roosevelt was after. It was a keystone in his intended system of continuous, expert federal regulation of American industry.

Congress in 1906 passed several notable laws. One was an employer-liability act for the District of Columbia and all common carriers. Another was a pure-food-and-drug bill, whose chief exponent was Dr. Harvey W. Wiley of the Department of Agriculture. For several years this measure, twice approved by the House, had faltered. Now a series of articles by Samuel Hopkins Adams exposed the dangers of patent medicine, aroused public opinion, and speeded the enactment of the legislation, though appropriations for its enforcement remained inadequate for two decades.

In a similar way, the publication of Upton Sinclair's *The Jungle*, with its description of the scandalous conditions in meatpacking houses, led Roosevelt to order a special investigation. This confirmed Sinclair's findings and precipitated the passage of a federal meat-inspection law. The act revealed the crosscurrents of purpose that characterized the cautious reform of the Roosevelt era. Sinclair had hoped to obtain remedy for the exploited workers, but the statute ignored them. Progressive senators like Beveridge of Indiana had wanted the packers to pay for federal inspection, but the legislation left the cost with the government, and Congress in later years appropriated stingy sums for enforcement. The large packers, in some cases before the act was passed, in all cases thereafter, preferred unitary federal inspection to irregular and uneven inspections by the many states in which they had plants. The packers also expected that federal inspection would discipline small establishments that could not afford sanitary methods. But those small concerns continued to function in intrastate commerce. Further, though the large packers were eager to retain and enlarge their European markets, Roosevelt threatened that goal by publishing reports about conditions in the meat industry. For his part, the President, who turned to the whole issue rather late, used his influence to keep the House of Representatives, where the packers had influential friends, from subjecting meat inspection to broad judicial review. All in all, then, the legislation, like the Hepburn Act and the Pure Food and Drug

Act, constituted at best a partial victory for each of the various principals involved, and at best, as Roosevelt said, not an ultimate reform but a first step toward a purpose that might require as many as a thousand more. But a first step, he believed, was far better than none at all.

In 1906 Roosevelt also sent Congress a series of recommendations on which it did not act, including proposals for federal control of railway securities and for the abolition of child labor. Labor problems were much on his mind. The National Association of Manufacturers had won a number of victories in its drive to cripple unions by obtaining injunctions against strikes and boycotts, the unions' most effective weapons. The NAM was also exhorting legislators to oppose all labor legislation. Fighting back, Gompers and his associates submitted to Roosevelt and the Congress a Bill of Grievances voicing their traditional demands, especially for relief from injunctions granted under the Sherman Act. The American Federation of Labor struck politically as well, campaigning in 1906 against congressmen unfriendly to labor, most of whom were Republicans. Caught between his growing sympathy for labor's goals and his partisan loyalties, Roosevelt endorsed all Republican candidates but exhorted them to mend their ways.

New ideas and the Old Guard. The gulf between the President and the Old Guard widened in 1907 and 1908. They especially differed over conservation. In 1902 Roosevelt, an ardent conservationist, had spurred the passage of the Newlands Act, which set aside a portion of receipts from the sale of public lands for expenditures on dams and reclamation. Pushing on, largely on the advice of Gifford Pinchot, he had withdrawn from private entry valuable coal and mineral lands, oil reserves, and waterpower sites. He had proceeded vigorously against cattlemen and lumbermen who were poaching on public preserves. These policies offended the Western barons who had become rich by exploiting the nation's natural resources (see p. 411). In 1907 their representatives attached a rider to an appropriation bill for the Department of Agriculture that prevented the creation of new forest reserves in six Western states without the consent of Congress. Roosevelt had to sign the bill, for the department had to have funds, but before signing he added 17 million acres to the national reserves. He later vetoed bills that granted waterpower sites to private interests but that did not provide for federal supervision of waterpower development.

In 1908 Roosevelt called a National Conservation Congress, which forty-four governors and hundreds of experts attended. It led to annual meetings of governors and to the creation of state conservation commissions. Congress, more and more hostile, ignored recommendations for river and flood control made by the Inland Waterways Commission, which Roosevelt appointed, and refused to provide funds to publish the report of another of his boards, the Country Life Commission, which advocated federal assistance for rural schools and roads and for farmers' cooperatives. Yet Roosevelt had succeeded in making the conservation of human and natural resources an issue of the first importance to thousands of Americans. He believed in the preservation of threatened species and of areas of great natural beauty. He believed just as strongly in conservation for use, that is, in protecting natural resources from ruthless private exploitation and for the needs of generations yet to be born. Further, he shared the spirit of progressive reform that stressed the ability of the mind and will of man to alter and improve his environment. Conservation provided an obvious laboratory for testing that belief.

Roosevelt's general policies jarred many businessmen who blamed him for the financial panic that occurred in the autumn of 1907 and for the brief depression that preceded and followed it. The basic causes of the slump were beyond his control. Productive facilities had expanded beyond the country's immediate capacity to consume, but the differential would probably have led to no serious trouble if the nation's banking and monetary systems had been stronger and if financiers had not been guilty of speculative excesses. Panic began only after depositors learned that several New York trust companies had failed in an expensive attempt to corner the copper market. As runs began on these and other (sound) banks, some had to close and all had to call in loans from creditors in New York and throughout the country. J. P. Morgan, at his most magnificent in this crisis, supervised a pooling of the funds of the leading Manhattan banks to support the threatened institutions. Undoubtedly this action prevented general disaster.

Morgan and his fellows could not have succeeded without assistance from the Treasury Department, which moved government deposits into threatened New York banks. The complex maneuvers depended in part on the purchase by the United States Steel Corporation of controlling shares of stock in the Tennessee Coal and Iron Company. That transaction, however, was unthinkable if there was any danger that it might lead immediately to an antitrust suit. So informed, Roosevelt, without making "any binding promise," urged Morgan's associates to proceed.

Though the panic quickly subsided, it had demonstrated the urgency of financial reform. It was ridiculous for a great nation in a time of crisis to have to fall back on Morgan or any other private banker. And it was vital to relax the general monetary stringency that intensified the crisis. Both the President

The progressive movement and the Square Deal

T. R. on the rights of labor

and his detractors endorsed the action of Congress authorizing a commission, with Senator Nelson Aldrich as chairman, to study and report on monetary and banking policy.

Roosevelt meanwhile had condemned the "speculation, corruption and fraud" that contributed to the panic. His messages to Congress of December 1907 and January 1908 disclosed his zeal for further reform. Indeed he now favored measures that he would have considered radical a few years earlier—measures that seemed far too sweeping to the conservatives who dominated Congress. After repeating many of his earlier recommendations, the President called for federal incorporation and regulation of all interstate business, federal regulation of the stock market, limitation of injunctions against labor, compulsory investigation of labor disputes, extension of the eight-hour law for federal employees, and personal income and inheritance taxes. He went on to castigate the courts for declaring unconstitutional a workmen's-compensation law and to condemn "predatory wealth" for its follies and its unscrupulous opposition to "every measure for honesty in business." Roosevelt in private warned that a revolution would break out if rich men and blind judges made the lot of the worker intolerable. Without reform, capitalism could not survive.

The goals Roosevelt defined and the principles he enunciated were the chart and compass of progressives in 1908 and for many years thereafter. He did not invent them, but he gave them effective expression, put the dignity of his high office at their service, and converted to them the thousands who felt the vitality of his person. All this he did with a faith in the progress that conserves, a belief that power prop-erly inheres in the federal government rather than in any private group, a conviction that the holder of power has an obligation to promote justice and enforce orderly and moral behavior, and a confidence in his own ability to handle power to those ends. Those beliefs and that confidence also guided his foreign policy.

Roosevelt and world power

National power and responsibility. During the first decade of the twentieth century, more and more Americans, including those who considered themselves progressives, subscribed to a new doctrine of manifest destiny (see p. 493). Along with that concept there grew up other ideas about the international role of the United States. The writings of Alfred T. Mahan, the experience of the Spanish War, and awareness of the swelling ambitions and power of Germany and Japan persuaded an influential minority of Americans of the importance of naval preparedness and national defense. Some, like Roosevelt, Root, and Senator Henry Cabot Lodge, also believed that every powerful nation had a stake in world order and an obligation to preserve it, that a great country like the United States could not escape involvement in international affairs.

Roosevelt as President continually reminded Americans of the oneness of the world. Nineteenth-century progress in transportation, communication, and production, he warned, had created situations of

527

It is idle to assume, and from the standpoint of national interest and honor it is mischievous folly for any statesman to assume, that this world has yet reached the stage, or has come within measurable distance of the stage, when a proud nation, jealous of its honor and conscious of its great mission in the world, can be content to rely for peace upon the forbearance of other powers.... Events still fresh in the mind of every thinking man show that neither arbitration nor any other device can as yet be invoked to prevent the gravest and most terrible wrongdoing to peoples who are either few in numbers, or who, if numerous, have lost the first and most important of national virtues—the capacity for self-defense....

I can not recommend to your notice measures for the fulfillment of our duties to the rest of the world without pressing upon you the necessity of placing ourselves in a condition of complete defense.... There is a rank due to the United States among nations which will be withheld, if not absolutely lost, by the reputation of weakness. If we desire to avoid insult, we must be able to repel it; if we desire to secure peace, one of the most powerful instruments of our rising prosperity, it must be known that we are at all times ready for war.

From Theodore Roosevelt, Special Message to Congress, 1908.

potential chaos in which only the availability of power and, when necessary, the application of force could establish a tolerable equilibrium.

He therefore preached preparedness to the frequently reluctant public. For Roosevelt, preparedness was not simply militarism. It entailed, too, the preservation and development of natural and human resources. Sharing the Anglo-Saxon bias of his time, Roosevelt urged Americans of old stock to increase their birth rate. But all Americans, regardless of national origin, could contribute, he maintained, to national well-being if they saw to their physical fitness and cultivated clear minds, clean souls, and brave hearts.

High character and the strenuous life were not in themselves enough, for preparedness ultimately involved the size, equipment, and leadership of the military services. The President heartily supported the reform of the outmoded army organization that Secretary of War Root had begun to plan under McKin-

ley. Root set up an Army War College, demanded rigorous tests for the promotion of officers, and in 1902 asked Congress to authorize the creation of a general staff and the incorporation of the state militia into the regular army. Congress hesitated, partly because the national guard and its aggressive lobby, as well as some senior regular officers, opposed incorporation of the guard, partly because of the belief, especially among rural Americans, that the militia was a democratic institution and a general staff a "Prussian" agency. Roosevelt and Root had to give up their plan for the militia, but Congress approved a modification of the general-staff plan that permitted the proposed modernization of the army to get under way.

Roosevelt also demanded the construction of a modern navy strong enough to protect American interests and to further his "large view" of national obligations. The United States, he realized, could no longer depend on the British fleet for protection. It had to keep pace with the building programs of Japan and Germany and with rapid changes in naval technology. Before he left office, Congress acceded to his constant prodding. The navy and army profited, too, from the enthusiastic recognition the President gave to military service and to dedicated and imaginative commanders like General Leonard Wood and Commander William S. Sims.

His zeal for discipline and morale, however, led him to discharge without honor the black troops who refused to reveal the names of the few soldiers who had allegedly shot up the anti-Negro town of Brownsville, Texas, in 1906. That hasty, unjust decision reflected the racism of both the President and the army. American blacks properly resented it, but it was not reversed until 1972.

A strong nation, in the view of Roosevelt and others who subscribed to the new manifest destiny, had the duty of imposing civilization and justice in the backward territories it ruled. In the Insular cases of 1900 and 1901, the Supreme Court held that inhabitants of the recently acquired American empire were not American citizens and did not have a right to the liberties guaranteed by the Constitution unless Congress expressly conferred them. Except for Hawaii and Alaska, which were destined for statehood, the Court's rulings left the determination of colonial policy to the Roosevelt Administration. It adopted a variety of expedients. The navy administered Guam and Tutuila, where it had coaling stations. Puerto Rico elected its own house of delegates, though its decisions had to be confirmed by a council and executed by a governor appointed in Washington. The American protectorate in Cuba ended in May 1902 with the inauguration of the first government under Cuba's new constitution. The next year, however, a formal treaty between Cuba and the United States provided for American intervention in the event of a foreign threat or domestic disturbance. Insurrection in Cuba in 1906 persuaded Roosevelt to exercise the right of intervention. After three years the Americans withdrew their troops but retained a major naval base at Guantanamo and continued to exercise a monitory influence over Cuban policy. Earlier, the President had insisted that in return for the rights accorded by the Cuban treaty, the United States had a moral duty to aid the Cuban economy by granting special tariff rates to Cuban sugar, a concession he wrung from protectionist congressmen after a stiff legislative struggle in 1903.

He was unable, in spite of repeated attempts, to obtain tariff concessions for the Philippines. Those islands presented a number of difficult problems. Occasional episodes of cruelty by the American army during the suppression of the independence movement (see p. 503) had whetted native resentment. That resentment began to abate (though for a brief time the revolt continued) when Congress in 1902 passed an organic act for the Philippines, when Roosevelt abolished the office of military governor, and when William Howard Taft, the first civilian governor, proclaimed a general amnesty. A patient proconsul, Taft got along well with the elected assembly and furthered municipal home rule, improvements in public health, civil affairs, education, and transportation. He was successful, too, in delicate negotiations with the Vatican and with Catholic friars in the islands for the purchase of lands that the Church claimed but the Filipinos held and deserved to keep. Like Roosevelt and Root, Taft did not believe the Philippines would be ready for independence for many years. Though native patriots and American anti-imperialists remained impatiently committed to that goal, Taft's benign administration gradually won the confidence of the islanders, assisted the development of their economy, and helped them prepare for ultimate self-government. Still, the inability of Roosevelt and his associates to understand the urgency of sentiment for self-government among subject peoples made American policy as it developed, indistinguishable from the imperialism of European powers.

Policing the hemisphere. Roosevelt's foreign policies, like his colonial policies, were derived from his assumption that it was "incumbent on all civilized and orderly powers to insist on the proper policing of the world." This was, of course, a highhanded assumption, which Roosevelt defended when he had to

International interests in the Caribbean

by arguing that only with stability could there be justice. An imperious manner characterized his methods as well as his objectives. As President, he believed, he had to conduct foreign policy himself, for in that field the Congress and "the average American" did not "take the trouble to think carefully or deeply."

Stretching his constitutional authority to its limits, Roosevelt intervened to preserve stability and American hegemony in the Caribbean, where, with Mahan, he felt the United States could not afford a rival. Like the other small states in that area, Venezuela had borrowed money in Europe, which Cipriano Castro, her prodigal dictator—Roosevelt considered him a "villainous little monkey"—lacked either the means or the will to repay. In December 1902 England, Germany, and Italy, demanding payment for their citizens, blockaded Venezuela and fired on one of its ports. Venezuela asked the United States to arrange arbitration, to which England and Germany agreed. But a German ship again bombarded a port, infuriating the President and many other Americans, and later Germany briefly opposed referring the dispute to arbitration. During the controversy Roosevelt implied to the German ambassador that the United States would insist on that solution. He recalled years later that he threatened, if necessary, to dispatch a naval squadron under Admiral George Dewey. His memory probably exaggerated his role, but whatever he actually did he certainly was indignant over Germany's conduct, and he was determined to make the Caribbean an American area of influence.

The best way to keep Europe at home, the President believed, was to keep order in the Caribbean. Yet a selfish conception of order gave Roosevelt a flimsy basis for incontinent behavior in Panama. In December 1901 the Senate ratified the second Hay-Pauncefote Treaty by which England acknowledged the right of the United States alone to build and fortify an isthmian canal, so long an American dream. Such a canal would facilitate intercoastal shipping and would make it easier for the navy to move from ocean to ocean. The preferred route had at one time been through Nicaragua, where a sea-level canal could be built, but the commission of experts that Congress had authorized had come to prefer a lock canal through Panama, which would provide the cheapest and shortest route between the coasts of the United States. Accordingly, in June 1902 Congress directed the President to negotiate with Colombia for the acquisition of a strip of land in Panama, provided that the old French canal company, which had begun work decades earlier, agreed within a reasonable time

The progressive movement and the Square Deal

and on reasonable terms to sell the United States its titles and equities in the area. Members of the American commission had valued the French holdings at not more than $40 million. This was only half of the company's own official estimate, but the company gratefully accepted the revised figure.

With that matter settled, Roosevelt pressed Colombia to surrender control of the land in return for $10 million and an annual rental of $250,000. A treaty to that effect was rejected by the Colombian government, which wanted more money and greater rights of sovereignty in the zone. Roosevelt, outraged at what he considered "blackmail," though the Colombian request was scarcely that, let it be known privately that he would smile upon insurrection in Panama. Predictably, in November 1903 insurrection occurred (if it had not, the President was prepared to ask Congress for authority to take the zone from Colombia). The United States aided the revolutionists, used a warship to prevent Colombian forces from landing, and immediately recognized the new, inde-

pendent Republic of Panama, which promptly accepted Roosevelt's terms for a canal zone.

Roosevelt boasted that he "took Panama," and most Americans at the time condoned his behavior. But the episode was a national disgrace. There was even suspicion of scandal. Agents of the French company, eager to unload their otherwise worthless assets, had influenced the State Department and members of Congress to favor the Panama route and had helped to foment the insurrection. Roosevelt's ruthless pursuit of his own interpretation of national advantage was no more ethical than was their pursuit of profit. Yet he persuaded himself that his conduct was impeccable, for, he argued, he had stamped out lawlessness in Colombia and disorder in Panama. Thus he perverted his insistence on stability in the Caribbean into a rationalization for imperialism.

That perversion took much of the gloss off his message to Congress of December 1904, in which he announced that the United States would not interfere with Latin American nations that conducted their

Building the Panama Canal

Roosevelt and world power

affairs with decency, but that "brutal wrongdoing" might require intervention by some civilized power, and that the United States could not "ignore this duty." The Monroe Doctrine told Europe to stay out of the Americas; the Roosevelt Corollary asserted that the United States had a right to move in. In 1905 Roosevelt interceded in Santo Domingo to end the cycle there of debt, revolution, and default. He imposed American supervision of customs collections and finance and established a trust fund to repay the European-held debt. The convention containing those terms was blocked in the United States Senate, which was growing restive under the President's single-handed conduct of foreign affairs, but Roosevelt substituted an executive agreement that protected his policy until the Senate accepted a modified treaty in 1907.

The balance of power.   The international police power that Roosevelt arrogated to the United States he expected other civilized nations to exercise elsewhere—Japan in Korea, England in Egypt and India. Stable and prosperous nations, however, had in his view no right to proceed against one another. World order depended on their restraint and on the shifting balances of their power. British restraint preserved the growing Anglo-American entente during a dispute about the Alaskan boundary. Canada in 1902 claimed Alaskan lands that cut off newly discovered Canadian gold fields from the sea. Roosevelt rightly judged the claim weak, but he wounded Canadian sensibilities by his blustering refusal to arbitrate (for, he said, arbitration usually resulted "in splitting the difference"). To help Canadian officials save face, in 1903 he submitted the issue to negotiation but instructed the commissioners he appointed to concede nothing. He also took pains to inform London of his order. The single English commissioner voted with the three Americans against the two Canadians, thereby straining temporarily the bonds of empire but serving both the merits of the issue and the cause of transatlantic friendship.

As he contemplated the balance of power in Europe, Roosevelt was grateful for England's friendship, dubious about Russia's immediate strength (though he recognized its great potential), and more and more anxious about Germany. Had the Kaiser had the "instinct for the jugular," Roosevelt thought, he would have kept a sharp eye on Russia. As it was, Germany was more jealous of France and England, and the Kaiser entertained "red dreams of glory" that might disrupt Europe and thus the whole world.

Aware of the network of European alliances that would engage every major continental power in a contest between any two, the President worried about the tensions that flared in 1905 over French and German rivalry in Morocco. The Kaiser secretly asked Roosevelt to persuade England not to support France. Roosevelt at first hesitated to intervene, for, as he put it, the United States had "no real interest in Morocco." It did have a major stake in preserving peace, however, and Roosevelt overcame his disinclination to appear "a Meddlesome Mattie" and carried on the difficult negotiations that brought all parties, including the United States, to a conference at Algeciras, Spain, in January 1906.

Roosevelt's instructions to the American delegates revealed his anti-German bias and his conviction that the entente cordiale between France and England preserved the essential balance of power in Europe. Though American participation had little effect on the outcome of the conference, at which France won a diplomatic victory, Roosevelt's role was nevertheless significant. He had served peace. Furthermore, he had demonstrated to Europe and to the American people, many of whom criticized his departure from the course of isolation, that the President of the United States recognized the nation's unavoidable concern in any European crisis.

In Asia, Roosevelt judged, slumbering China was of no account, but to prevent dislocations of power he accepted the prevailing fiction of her territorial integrity, and he gave lip service to the principle of the Open Door. He was little interested in Chinese markets, but to stabilize the Orient politically he counted on a balance between Russia and Japan. He welcomed an Anglo-Japanese defensive alliance of 1902, which committed both signatories to preserve the status quo in Asia, but in 1904, when the Russo-Japanese War began, he brooded about its "immense possibilities . . . for the future." A Russian triumph, he concluded, would be "a blow to civilization"; on the other hand, the elimination of Russia's "moderative influence" on Japan would be equally unfortunate. That possibility seemed imminent after Japan's initial naval and land victories and the outbreak of revolution in Russia. Though Roosevelt was partial to the Japanese, he intensified his effort through mediation to arrange a peace that would preserve an equilibrium. Proceeding without the knowledge of Congress, he worked secretly and deftly through personal friends in the diplomatic corps of Japan, Germany, and Great Britain. By the summer of 1905 Russian distress and Japanese financial infirmity brought both belligerents to accept a peace conference at Portsmouth, New Hampshire.

The President's brilliant diplomacy continued at the conference, which produced a settlement that suited his purpose and earned him a Nobel Prize for Peace. Japan took over the southern half of the island of Sakhalin, Port Arthur, and the South Manchuria

The progressive movement and the Square Deal

Railroad, but Manchuria remained legally a part of China, where the Open Door still presumably permitted all nations to trade and invest. Russia retained effective control over northern Manchuria and all of Siberia, the source of her basic weight in Asian politics. The Japanese failed to get the huge indemnity they had wanted, which made the treaty and Roosevelt the object of considerable public criticism in Japan. But the Japanese government was satisfied, particularly because the United States, like Russia, had recognized Japan's primacy in Korea.

Also in 1905 Taft and Japanese Foreign Minister Taro Katsura reached an agreement by which the United States permitted Japan to occupy Korea and Japan disavowed any ambitions in the Philippines. This, too, was a victory for the President's realistic and essentially cautious diplomacy. Though he sometimes sounded fierce, he never undertook ventures beyond his means to execute them. The United States, he knew, lacked the means to interfere in Korea, and Japan had to be kept friendly or it could easily conquer those islands, which Congress would not arm.

Japanese-American relations might have remained excellent had it not been for the problem of immigration. In 1900 Tokyo agreed to deny passports to emigrant laborers bound for the United States. But Japanese workers continued to make their way to the West Coast through Hawaii, Mexico, and Canada. Especially in California, where deep-rooted prejudice against all Asians had resulted in the national exclusion of Chinese immigrants, anti-Japanese feeling rose, revealing itself in the press, in the debates of the legislature, and in race riots. In 1906 San Francisco segregated Asian school children. The proud Japanese protested officially to Washington. Roosevelt assured them that he had no sympathy with the "outrageous agitation" of the Californians. He could not, however, silence the yellow press or control the "idiots" in the California legislature, nor could he prevent racial discrimination by barring the immigration of all laborers, for Congress opposed so stringent a law. Yet he was wholly unwilling to ask the Japanese to concede any racial inferiority. The State Department resolved the crisis by negotiating the "Gentlemen's Agreement" of 1907, an official but informal understanding that bound both countries to stop direct immigration between them.

This crisis focused attention on the whole immigration question. Roosevelt understood why organized labor objected to unrestricted immigration, Asian or European, and to a degree he shared the middle-class prejudice against the unrestricted entry of southern and eastern Europeans. Still, he feared that a general debate about immigration in 1906 would complicate relations with Japan and possibly divide the Republicans, some of whom were urging enactment of a literacy test for immigrants. He recommended the appointment of a fact-finding commission, a solution that would delay debate, appease the restrictionists, and, he believed, throw light on a complex subject. Modifying his proposal, Congress in 1907 authorized a commission of nine members, of whom three were to be selected by the President, three by the Speaker of the House, and three by the President of the Senate. Those who were appointed to the commission, of which Senator Dillingham became chairman, approached the task with a formidable bias for the restriction of immigration.

Besides provoking a debate on immigration policy, the Japanese-American crisis stirred up loose talk of war. There was less hostility in Japan than in the United States, where racists spoke of irreconcilable conflict and where the President was apparently worried in 1907 that Japan intended to provoke war. His anxiety may have been contrived to stir Congress into pushing ahead with the naval building program. In any case, there was no need for alarm, although years later Roosevelt said that he had detected "a very, very slight undertone of veiled truculence" in Japan's communications. "It was essential," he then decided, "that we should have it clearly understood by our own people especially, but also by other peoples, that the Pacific was as much our home waters as the Atlantic." He sailed the battle fleet around the world to make his point clear.

Had Japan been belligerent, it could have demolished the American ships that entered Tokyo Bay. Instead it welcomed them heartily. Yet Roosevelt believed their presence curbed any Japanese urge toward aggression and was therefore "the most important service" he ever rendered to peace. It was certainly a fine example of one of his favorite adages: "Speak softly but carry a big stick." Good will rather than fear led the Japanese ambassador to propose a declaration of friendship. In the Root-Takahira Agreement of 1908, both nations promised to uphold the status quo in the Pacific and to respect the Open Door and China's territorial integrity.

Prospects for American commerce and investment in China, the objectives of the Open Door, remained important to the Department of State, but the President, according to his own accounts, was concerned primarily with the balance of power in the Pacific. "A council of war never fights," Roosevelt wrote in his *Autobiography*, "and in a crisis the duty of a leader is to lead." As President he personally conducted the nation's foreign policies, acting sometimes with skill, sometimes with daring, sometimes with scant regard for the opinion of public or Congress or for the rights or sensitivities of other nations. His magisterial manner and imperialistic ventures set potentially dangerous precedents that his critics deplored. Still, as he knew, and as he instructed, the United States had become part of an interdependent world; the use of force could keep isolated trouble spots from erupting into general war; power was a pervasive element in world affairs; and, as Roosevelt saw it, the United States, a powerful nation, had an obligation to keep its power in a state of readiness and, when necessary, to use it intelligently but with restraint.

The election of 1908. No harm came from the concentration of power in one man's hands, Roosevelt observed, "provided the holder does not keep it for more than a certain, definite time, and then returns it to the people from whom he sprang." An American President, he believed, should serve only two terms. So he had announced in 1904 that he would not run again, and, though he gloried in his office, he resisted the strong sentiment for his renomination in 1908 and used his power in the party to ensure the nomination of William Howard Taft, whom he had selected as the man most able to continue his policies.

Some progressive Republicans would have preferred New York's governor, Charles Evans Hughes, but the President's endorsement and Taft's own excellent reputation kept the party united. With the tide of progressivism rising, the Democrats turned again to Bryan, who ran with more prudence but less vigor than before. He had the support of the leaders of organized labor, who applauded the Democratic plank urging the restriction of injunctions, and he made what he could of an attack on the Republican tariff. But Taft polled 52.0 percent of the popular vote and carried the Electoral College 321 to 162. Taft's identification with Roosevelt elected him. In 1901 Roosevelt had inherited a conservative administration. Increasingly he had enlisted with reform. When he bowed out in 1909, off to hunt in the African jungles, a majority of Americans had come to adulate him and to accept his policies. It remained to be seen what Taft would do with his inheritance.

Suggestions for reading

GENERAL

G. E. Mowry, *The Era of Theodore Roosevelt** (1958), provides a comprehensive account of the developments during the first twelve years of this century. There is a stimulating interpretation of progressivism in Richard Hofstadter, *The Age of Reform** (1955). Another spirited account appears in the relevant chapters of Eric Goldman, *Rendezvous with Destiny** (1952), which should be compared to C. Lasch, *New Radicalism in America, 1889–1963** (1965); Arthur Ekrich, *Progressivism in Practice* (1974); and J. D. Buenker, *Urban Liberalism and Progressive Reform* (1973). S. P. Hays, *The Response to Industrialism** (1957), and R. H. Wiebe, *The Search for Order: 1877–1920** (1966), offer interpretations suggested by their titles. G. Kolko, *The Triumph of Conservatism** (1963) and *Railroads and Regulation, 1877–1916** (1965), attributes the reforms of the progressive era largely to conspiratorial and selfish influences of big-business leaders; R. H. Wiebe, *Businessmen and Reform** (1962), emphasizes divisions of opinion about reform issues within the business community; and Albro Martin, *Enterprise Denied: Origins of the Decline of American Railroads, 1897–1917* (1971), reveals business resistance to reform.

PROGRESSIVISM

Among the best places to begin reading about progressivism are the lucid studies of the underprivileged and their champions in R. H. Bremner, *From the Depths** (1956), and Roy Lubove's *The Progressives and the Slums* (1962) and *The Professional Altruist: The Emergence of Social Work as a Career, 1880–1930* (1965). See, too, Allen Davis, *Spearheads of Reform: The Social Settlements and the Progressive Movement, 1890–1919* (1967). Two of the champions revealed their concerns in J. A. Riis, *How the Other Half Lives** (1890), and Jane Addams, *Forty Years at Hull House** (1935). The contributions of the churches receive analysis in H. F. May, *Protestant Churches and Industrial America** (1949). Philip Taft, *The A. F. of L. in the Time of Gompers* (1957), provides an account of the trade unions as does Bernard Mandel, *Samuel Gompers, A Biography* (1963). Contrasting accounts of the struggle for women's rights are in W. L. O'Neill, *Everyone Was Brave: The Rise and Fall of Feminism in America** (1969), and D. M. Kennedy, *Birth Control in America: The Career of Margaret Sanger** (1970); also important on the subject of women are Aileen Kraditor, *The Ideas of the Women's*

*Available in a paperback edition.

The progressive movement and the Square Deal

Suffrage Movement, 1890–1920 (1965), and Lois Banner, *Women in America** (1974). On American blacks, see Elliott Rudwick, *W. E. B. DuBois* (1969); B. J. Ross, *J. E. Spingarn and the Rise of the NAACP** (1972); and Nancy Weiss, *The National Urban League, 1910–1940* (1974), as well as the indispensable contemporary classic, W. E. B. DuBois, *Souls of Black Folks** (1963). There are good accounts of dissident radicals in Patrick Renshaw, *The Wobblies* (1967); Melvyn Dubofsky, *We Shall Be All: A History of the Industrial Workers of the World** (1969); David Shannon, *Socialist Party in America* (1967 ed.); and J. P. Diggins, *The American Left in the Twentieth Century** (1973). Among the important interpretations of progressive intellectuals, besides the volumes listed in the preceding paragraph, are Daniel Aaron, *Men of Good Hope** (1951); Morton White, *Social Thought in America: The Revolt Against Formalism** (1949); D. W. Noble, *The Paradox of Progressive Thought* (1958); Sidney Fine, *Laissez Faire and the General-Welfare State** (1956); James Weinstein, *The Corporate Ideal in the Liberal State, 1900–1918** (1969); Samuel Haber, *Efficiency and Uplift: Scientific Management in the Progressive Era, 1890–1920* (1964); and H. F. May, *The End of American Innocence** (1959). These should be read in conjunction with the contemporary works mentioned in the text and with such revealing autobiographies as those of Lincoln Steffens and William Allen White. Progressive ferment and achievement in various regions, states, and cities have had excellent treatment in C. V. Woodward, *Origins of the New Sowth, 1877–1913** (1951); David Thelen, *The New Citizenship, 1885–1900* (1972), on the rise of La Follette; R. B. Nye, *Midwestern Progressive Politics, 1870–1958** (1951, rev. ed., 1959); G. E. Mowry, *The California Progressives** (1951); R. E. Noble, *New Jersey Progressivism Before Wilson* (1947); R. M. Abrams, *Conservatism in a Progressive Era: Massachusetts Politics, 1900–1912* (1964); H. L. Warner, *Progressivism in Ohio, 1897–1917* (1964); and Arthur Mann, *Yankee Reformers in the Urban Age: Social Reform in Boston, 1880–1900** (1954).

ROOSEVELT AND HIS ADMINISTRATION

The best introduction to Theodore Roosevelt remains his autobiography, which can be profitably supplemented by reading in his voluminous collected works (the National Edition [1926] is handiest) and published letters, E. E. Morison, ed., *Letters of Theodore Roosevelt,* 8 vols. (1951–1954). Carleton Putnam provides a glowing account of Roosevelt in *Theodore Roosevelt: The Formative Years* (1958). Two good biographies are G. W. Chessman, *Theodore Roosevelt and the Politics of Power** (1968), and W. H. Harbaugh, *Power and Responsibility** (1961). J. M. Blum, *The Republican Roosevelt** (1954), focuses on Roosevelt as politician and President, and H. K. Beale, *Theodore Roosevelt and the Rise of America to World Power** (1956), offers an analysis of Roosevelt's foreign policy. Among other special studies of important public policies in Roosevelt's time, some of the most rewarding are E. L. Peffer, *The Closing of the Public Domain* (1951), which should be supplemented by Gifford Pinchot's autobiography; O. E. Anderson, Jr., *The Health of a Nation* (1958); B. H. Meyer, *History of the Northern Securities Case* (1906); and Raymond Esthus, *Theodore Roosevelt and the International Rivalries* (1970). There is a wealth of good autobiography by and biography of the men around Roosevelt. Besides those autobiographies noted earlier, Robert La Follette's is important, and among the most readable and instructive biographies those that most successfully introduce the period are John Braeman, *Albert J. Beveridge* (1971); N. W. Stephenson, *Nelson W. Aldrich* (1920), a sympathetic treatment of a great conservative; P. C. Jessup, *Elihu Root,* 2 vols. (1938); D. E. Anderson, *William Howard Taft* (1973); E. E. Morison, *Admiral Sims and the Modern American Navy* (1942); and D. P. Thelen, *Robert M. La Follette and the Insurgent Spirit* (1976).*

*Available in a paperback edition.

CHAPTER **23**

Progressivism: retreat and resurgence

Republicans celebrating the inauguration of William Howard Taft in March 1909 had no cause for complacency. Their party had won four successive presidential elections, and its national leaders had preserved the alliances on which its majority rested. But the partners in those alliances—the Old Guard, urban progressives, and Western agrarians—were growing uneasy with one another. The Democrats, secure in the South and in many Northern cities, were gaining strength among labor unions and farmers. In 1906 and 1908 the Republicans had lost seats in the House of Representatives, and in 1908 they had also lost several governorships. If they hoped to remain in power, they would have to satisfy their restive factions and close ranks against their opposition.

Insurgency

President Taft. Taft, the new President and head of the party, had excellent intentions. A kindly, learned man, he saw the need for social-welfare legislation, understood the purposes of the Roosevelt reforms, for which he had worked with skill, and meant to keep his promise to preserve and further his predecessor's program. He was also a loyal Republican who hoped to strengthen his party, which in his opinion was the only fit instrument of government. In a placid time he might have done well.

He was, however, seriously handicapped for the job he had to do. Taft was almost a caricature of the fat man—genial, usually easygoing. He was also both indecisive and untrained in politics. His career had been on the bench and in appointive administrative offices. He had no instinct for manipulation, no nerve for controversy. His reluctance to use the full powers of the Presidency grew out of his interpretation of the Constitution, which led him to believe that he should not interfere in the course of legislation. He was uncomfortable in the company of men who did not share his background of old family, personal means, and Eastern education. He preferred talking with Nelson Aldrich to conversing with La Follette, whom he considered one of the party's troublemakers.

The President was by nature and conviction a conservative whose highest confidence was in the law as he and other judges had shaped it. The bench, he believed, was the appropriate arbiter of social issues. He was suspicious of direct democracy, because he did not trust the majority to make laws. He was also cautious about enlarging the power of the executive for fear that it might encroach upon the traditional authorities of the other branches of government.

Taft was not unresilient. He accepted the need for change. But he did not particularly like it, and he did not at all like to be rushed. Yet he came to his office when the progressives were in a hurry. And they expected him, on the basis of his commitment to Roosevelt's programs, to keep pace with them. He preferred an easier pace, an advance in which each forward step was measured carefully against the footprints trailing through the past.

The tariff. Taft began boldly by calling a special session of Congress to revise the tariff. He and Roosevelt had insisted upon a plank in the Republican platform promising modification of the tariff, and his speeches had suggested that he preferred a moderate downward revision. Republican representatives of manufacturing interests were still wedded to high protectionism, but the Midwestern farmers and their party spokesmen were convinced that the Dingley duties (see p. 488), by protecting the trusts from foreign competition, were sustaining artificial prices for manufactured goods. Furthermore, as proponents of the "Iowa Idea" argued, Europeans had to sell in the American market in order to earn dollars to buy American agricultural surpluses.

The Western progressives counted on the President's support in getting the tariff lowered, but even before the special session got under way they experienced their first disappointment. Taft appointed a Cabinet of conservatives, five of them corporation lawyers. He also turned down young George Norris of Nebraska and other insurgents in the House of Representatives who appealed for his support in their effort to restrict the power of the Speaker, "Uncle Joe" Cannon of Illinois, an arch-Tory and protectionist. And when debate on the tariff began, Taft made no gesture in behalf of the revision he had advocated.

The House of Representatives passed a tariff bill that made modest concessions to reform. It reduced some duties and imposed an inheritance tax graduated from 1 to 5 percent.

In the Senate, however, the Old Guard carried the day. The Finance Committee struck out the inheritance tax, made over eight hundred amendments to the House bill, and even slightly increased the average rates of the Dingley Tariff. On the floor of the Senate, progressives attacked the swollen tariff schedules one by one and joined the Democrats in urging

Speaker Cannon and his hogs

an income tax. Taft's intercession fostered a compromise that set a 2 percent tax on corporate income and assured passage of a constitutional amendment authorizing a personal income tax. But the compromise little affected the tariff itself. A conference committee of the two houses made modest changes in a number of schedules, but most of those revisions benefited manufacturers rather than farmers or consumers.

The Payne-Aldrich Act as it finally passed was a triumph for the protectionists. During the struggle Taft had alienated the insurgent Midwesterners and their constituents. Stubbornly, the President in September widened the breach. In a series of implausible speeches he scolded the progressives who had voted against the tariff, which he declared the best the party had ever enacted.

A divided party. When Congress met again in 1910, the insurgents no longer expected help from the White House. Attacking at once, Norris and his associates made common cause with the Democrats and passed a resolution transferring much of Speaker Cannon's authority to the House Rules Committee. The insurgents then joined the Democrats to amend Taft's railway bill, though the President made support of that bill a test of party loyalty. Taft's measure empowered the Interstate Commerce Commission to fix rates on its own initiative. But it established a Court of Commerce with broad powers of review over the commission's decisions, thereby giving the traditionally conservative judiciary a determining veto. The bill also permitted railroads to acquire competing lines. The Democratic-progressive coalition supported the first of those three provisions, attacked the others,

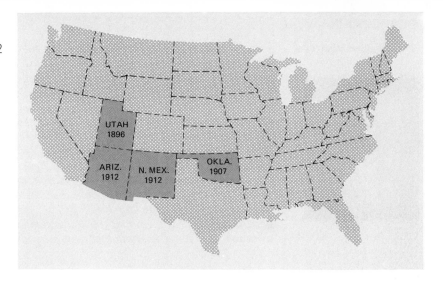

New states, 1896–1912

and succeeded in eliminating the third. It further amended the bill to bring telephone and telegraph companies under the commission's jurisdiction and to provide for the physical valuation of railway properties as a basis for determining fair rates.

In the Senate Aldrich eliminated the provision calling for physical valuation and preserved the Commerce Court by making a trade with the Democrats. In return for their help on the railway bill, he agreed to the admission of Arizona and New Mexico, which were sure to elect four Democratic senators in 1912. This was a Pyrrhic victory: it saved the Administration's face, but it did not long prevent a physical-valuation law (which Congress passed early in 1913), and it precipitated open warfare within the Republican party. The insurgents had defied the President, who had unwisely raised the question of party regularity. Now he retaliated by denying them patronage and starting a campaign to defeat them in the fall elections of 1910.

Meanwhile Taft had got caught up in a damaging controversy. With his approval, his Secretary of the Interior, Richard A. Ballinger, had reopened to private sale millions of acres of public land and many valuable waterpower sites that Gifford Pinchot, Roosevelt's trusted friend, had previously arranged to have closed. Pinchot, still chief forester of the United States, became suspicious of Ballinger's motives when he learned from Louis R. Glavis, an investigator in the General Land Office, that Ballinger had been instrumental in selling certain government coal lands in Alaska to a wealthy syndicate controlled by J. P. Morgan and David Guggenheim. Pinchot took the case to Taft, who ruled for Ballinger on every count and discharged Glavis. Though he considered Pinchot a "crank," Taft politely urged him to drop the issue and stay in office.

The indignant Pinchot had other plans. He supplied material for two magazine articles attacking Ballinger. He also wrote a letter praising Glavis that was read to the Senate. Taft had no choice but to dismiss Pinchot, though he knew that in so doing he would seem to oppose Roosevelt's conservation policies and possibly antagonize the Colonel. His worst fears materialized. A joint congressional committee in 1910 exonerated Ballinger, but Louis D. Brandeis, counsel for the opposition, revealed that Taft and his Attorney General had tampered with evidence they sent to Congress. Though Taft was an effective conservationist, Brandeis' argument hurt his reputation. The political damage was compounded when Pinchot greeted Roosevelt after the Colonel emerged from the African jungles. In the future Roosevelt always saw the matter Pinchot's way.

The election of 1910. Taft felt that Roosevelt's friends had plotted to cause a rupture between him and their hero. After Roosevelt's triumphant return to New York, the insurgents set out for his home at Oyster Bay to enlist his help. Roosevelt, who was temperamentally incapable of remaining out of politics and who was sensitive to a coolness on Taft's part, now decided that his principles needed defending. He embarked on a speaking tour during which he endorsed the Administration but gave stronger praise to the insurgents. He also reemphasized the points he had made in his last messages to Congress. At Osawatomie, Kansas, invoking the spirit of John Brown, Roosevelt announced his New Nationalism, a program of social welfare, federal regulation of business and industry, and direct democracy. In that address he frightened conservatives by attacking the courts for having invalidated progressive labor legislation.

The friction within the Republican party contributed to its losses in the elections of 1910. The Democrats in many states managed to identify themselves with progressivism and to identify the Republi-

can tariff with the rising cost of living, a particularly sensitive issue among city-dwellers. The Democrats won several governorships, including those of New York and New Jersey, which had been safely Republican for many years. For the first time since 1892, the Democrats elected a majority to the House of Representatives. The Republicans' loss of New York and the defeat of Senator Beveridge in Indiana saddened Roosevelt. The Democratic victories over Old Guard candidates in the East and the victories of progressive Republicans in the West repudiated Taft. Overall, the returns suggested that only an insurgent could save the Republicans in the presidential election of 1912, but the Old Guard, tense and defensive, prepared to resist the temper of the time.

Taft's closest political associates began in 1911, by the adroit use of patronage, to strengthen their factions in the North and to wrap up the Republican organizations in the South. At the same time, La Follette began to recruit support for his own candidacy, which was endorsed by many progressives. Some of them, however, privately hoped to draft Roosevelt, whose personal appeal remained strong even after his announcement that he had retired from politics.

A divisive foreign policy. During the year Taft succeeded in intensifying party discord and stirring the Colonel to action. In January 1911 the President submitted to Congress a reciprocity agreement with Canada. It put on the free list many agricultural products, including important raw materials for industrial use, and some manufactured goods. Western progressives, fearing the competition of Canadian farmers, opposed the measure. So did most high-tariff advo-

cates, who objected to any breach in the wall of protection. Together they rejected the agreement. But Taft called a special session in April during which the Democrats, delighting in the discomfort of the Republicans, helped Administration forces to put the measure through. The Canadians, however, disturbed by the prospect of economic competition and Americanization, in September repudiated the agreement. Another tariff debate had produced only more wounds. The Democrats kept them open, with help from Republican insurgents, by passing a series of bills reducing specific schedules—"pop-gun" tariffs that the President systematically vetoed.

Taft's foreign policy also aroused opposition. His Secretary of State, Philander C. Knox, negotiated treaties with Nicaragua and Honduras providing for the assumption of their European-held debt by American investors and for the appointment of Americans to direct their finances and thus assure the collection of those debts. Though the Senate rejected the treaties, Knox pursued his policy throughout the Caribbean with considerable success.

Taft and Knox also emphasized the possibilities for American investments in China. At the instigation of the State Department, American bankers agreed to join in various commercial projects there, including an international railway consortium. Roosevelt disapproved of that "dollar diplomacy." He had urged Taft to abandon commercial competition with the Japanese in China. It was more important, the Colonel argued, to cultivate Japanese friendship and to arrange a clearer understanding about Japanese immigration.

Roosevelt also opposed arbitration treaties that Taft negotiated with France and England. Taft was confident that international problems could be solved

A case against bigness

by courts of law. In the summer of 1911 he submitted to the Senate treaties with France and Great Britain that bound the signatories to arbitrate all differences "susceptible of decision by the application of the principles of law or equity." Those treaties excited the hopes of the thousands of Americans who considered them an important step toward avoiding wars. But Roosevelt wrote angry articles denouncing the arbitration of questions involving "territory" or "national honor," and he cooperated with like-minded senators who succeeded in amending the treaties so drastically that the President scrapped them. Taft was dismayed by the outcome and offended by Roosevelt's scathing language.

Roosevelt revolts. Roosevelt in turn was offended by Taft's antitrust policies. The Supreme Court in 1911 in the Standard Oil and American Tobacco cases, both of which had been initiated during Roosevelt's Administration, found that the corporations were monopolies guilty of violating the Sherman Act. Yet the decisions also pronounced the "rule of reason," which held that only unreasonable restraints of trade were unlawful. That was a necessary corollary to antitrust law, for an undiscriminating application of the Sherman Act would destroy the structure and impede the functioning of American business. But whereas Taft was content to have the Court take upon itself the authority to define reasonableness, Roosevelt believed that an administrative agency should make that judgment and should base it on considerations of economic efficiency and business behavior.

This difference of opinion was exemplified in the case of the United States Steel Corporation, then the largest of all holding companies, which Taft chose to

prosecute. Roosevelt, who considered the company guiltless, concluded that Taft had acted largely to embarrass him, for the prosecution, which resulted ultimately in an acquittal, and the congressional hearings that it provoked, publicized Roosevelt's negotiations of 1907 with J. P. Morgan (see p. 526).

Taft's antitrust and foreign policies gave Roosevelt a chance to rationalize what he would undoubtedly have done anyway. In February 1912 he announced that his hat was in the ring. A furious battle for the Republican presidential nomination was under way.

The struggle was really between Roosevelt and Taft, who denounced each other with unrestrained personal vehemence. Though La Follette remained in the race, most of his supporters of 1911 deserted him for Roosevelt. Now just as progressive and vastly more sophisticated and popular than La Follette, Roosevelt had in his New Nationalism formulated a program that promised to distribute the abundance of industrialism, while controlling and preserving the institutions which had made that abundance possible. Roosevelt stood an excellent chance of winning the election. Taft had no such chance, but his dander was up, and the Old Guard cared more about nominating him, defeating Roosevelt, and dominating the party than about beating the Democrats.

The Taft forces, moreover, had in their hands the party apparatus through which they could control the convention. In some states Roosevelt's supporters managed to pass legislation establishing preferential primaries for the nomination, but in the end only thirteen states held such elections. They gave 36 delegates to La Follette, 48 to Taft, and 278 to Roosevelt—an overwhelming mandate for the Colonel. Taft, how-

"Strong as a Bull Moose"

ever, controlled the South, New York, and the crucial national committee, which with its affiliates disposed of 254 contested seats at the convention. With a cynical disregard for the merits of the contestants, it allotted 235 of the contested seats to Taft delegates. The rigged convention then renominated the President on the first ballot.

The Bull Moose. Before the balloting took place, most of the Roosevelt men bolted, crying fraud. In August they reconvened as delegates of the new Progressive party. To that convention there came social workers, feminists, intellectuals, and industrialists attracted by Roosevelt's personality and program, and Republican politicians disenchanted with their factional rivals—all imbued with a revivalist spirit that led them to choose "Onward, Christian Soldiers" as their marching song. Roosevelt, "strong as a Bull Moose," told them they were standing at Armageddon battling for the Lord and accepted the nomination they tendered with thundering unanimity.

The Progressive party was a politician's Gothic horror, hastily and inadequately organized but with a powerful leader. Roosevelt probably knew in his heart that by splitting the Republican party he was assuring the election of a Democrat. He and Taft, however, had by June gone too far to turn back toward compromise, which the events of four years had in any case made difficult. The split was much more than just a personal falling out. Taft's adherents by and large stood for the status quo. Some, to be sure, were of a progressive mind but were unwilling to break with their party. Many were genuinely frightened by Roosevelt's advocacy of the recall of state judicial deci-

sions by referendum, a proposal that in their view would substitute the fickle and untutored will of the majority for the presumed majesty of the courts. For the most part they stayed with Taft because they considered him and his sponsors safe, whereas they considered Roosevelt, along with his friends and his platform, downright alarming.

The Bull Moose platform was incontestably adventurous, a charter of progressive reform for its own time and for years to come. It advocated the familiar devices of popular democracy—presidential primaries, women's suffrage, the initiative and referendum, and popular election of United States senators. It advocated, too, a comprehensive social-welfare program—conservation of natural and human resources, minimum wages for women, the restriction of child labor, workmen's compensation, social insurance, a federal income tax,* and the limitation of injunctions in labor disputes. Finally, in keeping with Roosevelt's ideas about the proper role of government, it called for expert federal commissions to adjust the tariff and to regulate interstate business and industry. Party and candidate alike stood for social justice and popular rule, and stood, too, for the application of efficiency to the management of public problems, an objective attractive at once to many progressives and to many men of affairs. As it developed, however, they faced formidable competition as champions of reform from a united and inspired Democratic party.

Progressivism at zenith

Woodrow Wilson. The Democratic candidate in 1912 had found his way into politics by an unusual route. Woodrow Wilson, the son of a Southern Presbyterian minister, had abandoned a brief and unrewarding career in law for one in education. After earning his doctorate at The Johns Hopkins University, Wilson taught history and political science at Bryn Mawr, Wesleyan of Connecticut, and Princeton, his own alma mater, of which he became president in 1902. He first won national attention for his writings, especially his earliest book, *Congressional Government* (1885), which criticized the weakness of the executive and the inefficiencies of Congress and praised the British parliamentary system. As president of Princeton Wilson initiated a number of celebrated educational reforms, but he lost his battle with faculty

---

*The Sixteenth Amendment, which provided for an income tax, was already before the states, as was the Seventeenth, providing for popular election of senators. Both were ratified in 1913.

members and wealthy alumni over plans for a graduate school. That struggle brought on his resignation but also gave him a reputation as a champion of democracy in education.

Wilson resigned in 1910 to accept the Democratic nomination for governor of New Jersey. He had always had political ambitions; now he owed his nomination to Democratic machine leaders who were impressed, as were his wealthy New York friends, by his stature and his presumably conservative economic views. But during the campaign Wilson adopted the program of New Jersey progressives. As governor he made a brilliant record that put New Jersey in the van of progressive states (see p. 520) and put Wilson in the lead for the Democratic presidential nomination.

But in 1912 the Democrats, like the Republicans, were caught in a momentous struggle over selecting a candidate. Wilson had offended his conservative sponsors, who now helped organize a movement to defeat him. In spite of his appeal to many Southern progressives, his opponents were particularly successful in the South, where they captured most of the state delegations. In the East, the city machines, alarmed by Wilson's treatment of their counterparts in New Jersey, embarrassed him by publicizing sections of his *History of the American People* (1902), which disparaged the new immigrants. In the farming West, moreover, the favorite candidate was Champ Clark, the folksy "Ol' Hound Dawg" of Missouri. Bryan Democrats there rightly judged that Wilson was not one of them.

During the national convention at Baltimore Bryan, probably more to further his own ambitions than Wilson's, took the floor to castigate any candidate supported by Tammany. Tammany had just moved New York into the Clark column, thus contributing to his majority. But it took a two-thirds vote to nominate, and Wilson's floor-leaders gradually made the deals that turned the convention their way. One of those deals assured the vice-presidential nomination to Thomas R. Marshall of Indiana, a politician best remembered for his fetching assertion that what the country needed was "a good five-cent cigar." On the forty-third ballot Wilson won a majority of the votes; on the forty-sixth, the nomination.

The election of 1912. The basic contest in 1912 was between the Democrats and the Progressives. Certain of the South, assisted elsewhere by the Republican schism, the Democratic leadership took pains to preserve party unity by placating the factions that had opposed Wilson and by appealing to the urban ethnic groups that had long sustained the party's political machines. But Wilson, though the odds were with him, could not take Roosevelt for granted. He had to meet the challenge for progressive votes.

In many respects the Bull Moose and Democratic platforms were similar, but there were several significant differences between them. Where the Progressives endorsed a protective tariff, the Democrats called for sharp downward revision. Where the Progressives demanded powerful federal regulatory agencies, the Democrats emphasized state rights. The Democrats did not spell out a broad social-welfare program, but they did advocate limiting the use of injunctions against labor unions. The party's continuing insistence on that issue held the allegiance of Gompers and most of his associates in the American Federation of Labor. Moreover, farmers responded enthusiastically to Democratic promises to make loans for agriculture cheaper and more readily available.

More than the platforms, the attitudes of the candidates marked the differences between the parties. Roosevelt's New Nationalism assumed that the consolidation of the economy was inevitable and healthful. He welcomed big business but demanded big government to supervise it and to promote the welfare of nonbusiness groups. The political theorist Herbert Croly expressed these ideas forcefully in *The Promise of American Life* (1909), an influential book that helped Roosevelt and like-minded men articulate their principles. It demanded positive, comprehensive federal planning for the national interest and for social reform.

Wilson had reached dissimilar conclusions. There lingered in his mind a complex of ideas he had cherished since youth. He was a devout Presbyterian who held men individually responsible to God for their actions. Guilt in business affairs, he believed, was also personal guilt. Where a corporation misbehaved, his instinct was to punish its officers as the Lord punished sinners. He was more the stern prophet than the stern promoter. He was also convinced that laissez-faire principles of economics would work if only the state would protect and encourage competition. It should, he felt, act as a handicapper resolved to make the race equitable at the start and as a policeman determined to keep the runners in their lanes. An enemy of political and business corruption, a believer in popular democracy, a proponent of regulation to prevent industrial abuses, Wilson was a progressive, but of a type uncomfortable with Croly's formulations.

Another able intellectual, Louis D. Brandeis of Massachusetts, one of the splendid legal thinkers of his time, helped Wilson organize his developing ideas. The great corporations, Brandeis argued, controlled credit, raw materials, and markets. They prevented competition and guarded their own inefficient methods, excessive profits, and overcapitalized values. They had corrupted government, Brandeis went on,

and had to be prosecuted and broken up. He also urged that the rules of competition be defined by law and that federal programs be launched to provide credit for small and new businesses. His ideas and the data with which he supported them confirmed Wilson's own theories, which the candidate set forth in the program he called the New Freedom.

Roosevelt's plans, as Wilson said, would result in "partnership between the government and the trusts." The Democratic alternative would ensure a free economy and preserve free government. "Free men," he asserted, "need no guardians." Indeed they could not submit to guardians and remain free, for submission would produce "a corruption of the will."

Wilson called for "regulated competition" in preference to "regulated monopoly." He feared that individuals were being "swallowed up" by great organizations, and he condemned what he considered "an extraordinary and very sinister concentration in . . . business." He demanded "a body of laws which will look after the men . . . who are sweating blood to get their foothold in the world of endeavor." Roosevelt called Wilson's program "rural Toryism." In a sense it was. But Wilson affirmed the hopes of the farm, of the

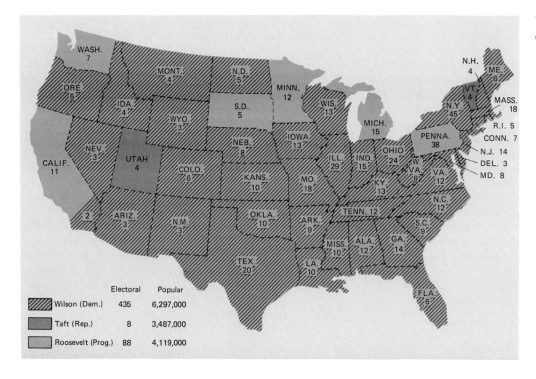

The election of 1912

		Electoral	Popular
	Wilson (Dem.)	435	6,297,000
	Taft (Rep.)	8	3,487,000
	Roosevelt (Prog.)	88	4,119,000

small town, of middle-class America. His party, furthermore, retained the allegiance of the South and of urban ethnic groups that had long voted Democratic.

Wilson won a telling victory, though he got only 41.9 percent of the popular vote and a smaller total vote than Bryan had in 1908. Roosevelt received only 27.4 percent and Taft only 23.2. In the electoral count Wilson led his rivals 435 to 88 and 8, and the Democrats carried both houses of Congress. The Democrats, who ran best in the areas of their traditional strength, had needed the Republican division to win. The returns were just as clearly a triumph for reform. Taft's miserable showing revealed the voters' disdain for standpat government, while the dissatisfaction with existing conditions was evidenced by the nearly 1 million votes for Socialist candidate Eugene V. Debs and by the remarkable support won by the Bull Moose party in its initial test.

It was also remarkable that so lively a contest produced a turnout of voters that, as in other presidential elections of the first decades of the century, fell short of the percentage of eligibles who had voted in the 1880s and 1890s. Apart from those voters who had been disfranchised in the South, many other Americans were obviously either preoccupied with questions that politics did not address or persuaded that the choices politics offered made little difference. Yet the degree of voter participation never alone measured the significance of elections, for politics had never been wholly rational. In 1912 there was a choice. At the least, the election signaled a temporary end of the Taft Administration's retreat from reform and a beginning of the progressive resurgence that marked Wilson's first term in office.

Wilson and the tariff. Wilson realized that he could work most efficiently through his own party. Indeed he considered himself a party-leader in the English style, with the right to hold party members in Congress to his programs and, if necessary, to appeal over their heads to the electorate. From the first he set out to unite the Democratic factions—the Southerners, the Northern city machines, the progressives; to use his united party to legislate; and to endow it with a record and reputation that would make a majority of Americans prefer it to any rival.

Wilson, however, had neither the temperament nor the experience to get along with professional politicians. A tense and angular man, he was incapable of displaying good fellowship he did not feel. But he knew his limitations and compensated for them by selecting a group of skilled advisers. Among others they included Bryan, the new Secretary of State, influential as always with the agrarian liberals; Albert S. Burleson, Postmaster General, a veteran Southern congressman popular among the party regulars on the

Hill; Secretary of the Treasury William G. McAdoo, a progressive businessman who had the confidence of those who had made Wilson's nomination possible; Joseph P. Tumulty, the President's private secretary, a young Irishman wise in the ways of machine politicians and professional journalists; and Colonel Edward M. House, an urbane Texan who attached himself to Wilson and became his "second personality." Though House had neither title nor office, he quickly acquired important responsibilities as a liaison man between the President and leaders of the party and the Congress, as well as between the President and foreign heads of state.

Informed and assisted by his subordinates, Wilson made his own major decisions and gave a personal stamp to his executive leadership. Right after his inauguration he called a special session of Congress to fulfill the Democratic pledge of tariff revision. He dramatized the session and his intended role by appearing personally, as had no President since Jefferson's time, to address the Congress. He had already begun a fruitful cooperation with the committees responsible for tariff recommendations. In May 1913, only a month after the President's address, the House passed a bill reducing average *ad valorem* rates about 11 percent; adding a number of consumer goods to the free list; and eliminating the protection of iron, steel, and various other products of the trusts. To make up for the attending loss in revenue, the bill

Edward M. House:
urbane Texan

levied a modest graduated income tax, which ratification of the Sixteenth Amendment had legalized two months earlier.

The test of Wilson's leadership came in the Senate, where the Democrats had a majority of only three votes. Democratic senators from sugar- and wool-producing states were reluctant to leave those products on the free list where the House had placed them. Wilson urged them to vote with their party, but they wavered, and lobbyists for protection tried to exploit the chance for logrolling. The President then called on public opinion to "check and destroy" the "intolerable burden" of "insidious" lobbyists. His statement helped to initiate an investigation of the private interests of all senators, some of whom, it developed, stood to profit personally from the protection of wool and sugar. With a refreshed sensitivity to public opinion, all but two Democrats voted for the party's bill. It kept sugar and wool on the free list and reduced the general level of rates another 4 percent. It also, thanks to the efforts of progressives in all the parties, doubled the maximum surtax on personal incomes.

The tariff of 1913, the Underwood-Simmons Act, removed an accumulation of privileges and, without abandoning protection, reduced previously swollen schedules. It also made a significant modification in the federal tax structure by shifting some of the burden to those best able to bear it. It was a convincing demonstration that the Democrats could achieve the goals of the New Freedom, and it was an acknowledged triumph for Wilson's leadership.

Banking reform. Pressing his gains, the President had urged the special session of Congress to correct the nation's anachronistic money and banking system. The Panic of 1907 (see p. 526) had underscored the inflexibility of currency and the inelasticity of credit. The events of the panic also suggested that financial power was concentrated in the hands of a small group of Eastern private bankers. That situation had been the subject of investigation by a House committee chaired by Congressman Arsène P. Pujo. Its findings, later popularized in Louis Brandeis' *Other People's Money* (1914), persuaded many progressives that there existed a "money trust."

Southern and Western farmers had long assumed that there was a bankers' conspiracy against their interests and had long agitated for monetary reform. By 1913 the bankers themselves were in favor of reform, but of their own kind. The experience of the panic and the report of Aldrich's Monetary Commission (see p. 527) led most of them to advocate central control of the banking system and the creation of a currency responsive to, and partly based on, the expansion and contraction of commercial paper—that is, loans that banks made to business.

The bankers, taking as their models the Bank of England and the controversial Second United States Bank, wanted a central bank to be authorized by the government but privately controlled. They also wanted it to issue currency on its own liability. The conservative Democrats modified those proposals by replacing a single central bank with a number of regional banks supervised by a federal board. This modification, the plan Wilson at first favored, failed to satisfy the party's progressive and agrarian factions. To meet their minimum demands, the President agreed that the government should appoint the supervising board and that the bank notes issued by the new system should be obligations of the United States.

Those concessions fell short of the program advanced by Southern farmers. They called for a prohibition of interlocking directorates, for public control of the regional banks, for permitting reserve banks to discount agricultural paper, and for preventing the use of commercial paper as a basis for currency. Bryan mediated their differences with Wilson, who met them part way. The President conceded the discounting of agricultural notes and promised later to take care of interlocking directorates. In return, the militants supported the rest of the bill, which the House passed in September 1913.

There was resistance again from conservatives in the Senate. Wilson overcame some of it by another appeal for party responsibility and by a timely use of patronage. Again he took his case to the people, asserting that bankers were trying to defeat the measure by creating artificial fears of impending panic. Although Senate conservatives managed to increase the percentage of gold reserves required for the issue of bank notes and to reduce the authority of the Federal Reserve Board, the Democrats were sufficiently united to pass the bill without further changes in December 1913.

The Federal Reserve Act was the most significant statute of Wilson's Administration. The Federal Reserve Board and the regional Reserve Banks gave the United States its first efficient banking system since the time of Andrew Jackson. Their power over currency and credit put into responsible hands the means to provide the flexibility of short-term credit that was so badly needed. Though private banking interests dominated the regional banks with their large powers, the regulatory authority of the board assured a greater degree of public control over banking than ever before. Indeed the act remedied almost all the deficiencies in American banking and currency that informed observers then recognized. Without the new system the country could not have adjusted to the financial strains of the First World War. There was still need to ease long-term agricultural credit and (though it was not yet understood) to endow public authorities with effective instruments to modulate the business cycle. But the new law was nonetheless impressive. Americans of all points of view and parties applauded it and the President's "great exhibition of leadership" in guiding it through Congress.

The New Freedom completed. When Congress met in regular session in 1914, Wilson presented his program for regulating industry. The tariff had furthered the New Freedom by reducing protection for the products of the trusts. The Federal Reserve Act had made credit more readily available to small and new enterprises. The obvious drift of public opinion and public policy had helped to persuade the Morgan partners to resign from many of their directorates. Now the President asked Congress to make it impossible for interrelated groups to control holding companies, to create a commission to help dissolve corporations found in restraint of trade, and to define unfair business practices.

Those recommendations, too strong for conservatives, did not satisfy either labor-leaders, who urged that unions be exempted from the Sherman Antitrust Act, or Bull Moosers, who advocated a strong regulatory agency. Louis Brandeis had moved closer to the Bull Moose point of view, and he now drafted a bill that Wilson supported. It created a Federal Trade Commission to prevent the unlawful suppression of competition. The measure passed, but only after Southern conservatives had helped the Republicans amend it to provide for broad court review of the commission's order, a review that soon proved to be debilitating.

A companion measure, the Clayton Bill, was also amended before enactment. As the House passed it, it followed the prescriptions of Wilson's message, defined unfair practices, and forbade interlocking directorates. Senate conservatives modified that prohibition by exempting instances that did not tend to decrease competition. That standard failed to assure prosecution of the largest holding companies. It was also in the Senate that friends of labor added to the bill a statement declaring that labor was not to be considered a commodity, a mere article of commerce. The House had earlier included a clause exempting labor unions and farm organizations from antitrust prosecutions, but only when those groups were lawfully pursuing legitimate aims. As the courts were to interpret the Clayton Act, the reservation about legitimate aims just about canceled the exemption.

The antitrust laws of 1914 failed to prescribe business conduct to the extent Wilson had sought, and they failed to give unions the freedom of activity Gompers had urged. The Federal Trade Commission, moreover, had less power than many progressives had recommended. But the weaknesses of the legislation were not immediately apparent, and the laws seemed to constitute another, though limited, victory for the Administration. In less than two years Wilson had reached the major statutory goals of his new freedom.

The voters responded favorably in the elections of 1914. Superficially the Democrats suffered that year, for the Republicans made sizable gains. But the Democrats retained control of both houses of Congress. The collapse of the Progressive party helped the Republicans in the Northeast, where they made their best showing. Elsewhere the Democrats picked up progressive support, and in the new Congress that sat in 1915 and 1916 Southern and Western farmers had a larger voice than they had had before. The returns convinced perceptive Democratic strategists that they could carry the nation in 1916 only by winning the progressives of the West. Once more, reform had won a mandate.

In behalf of social justice. That mandate made an impression on Wilson, who had given signs of turning toward the right. Before the election he had blocked bills that outlawed child labor and that established federal banks to make long-term loans to farmers. His appointments to the Federal Reserve Board and the Federal Trade Commission had on the whole been conservative. After the election he adjusted to the demands of congressional and national politics. He encouraged the progressive Democrats, who in 1916 succeeded in passing the Federal Farm Loan Act and the Child Labor Act. Though he also endorsed legislation permitting firms engaged in export trade to combine to meet foreign competition, he did so primarily in order to strengthen American competition against foreign cartels. On matters of international trade the President had come to respect the arguments of the Progressive party, and he supported an act in 1916 creating a nonpartisan, expert tariff commission designed, among other things, to prevent the dumping of unprotected goods on the American market.

In 1916 Wilson also practically ordered Congress to establish the eight-hour day at ten-hour pay for railway labor. Congress responded with the Adamson Act. In this case the President acted largely to prevent a threatening strike that would have tied up shipments of war materials for France and England, but his intercession won plaudits from organized labor. Labor-leaders and reformers had earlier found convincing evidence of Wilson's progressive intentions in his nomination of Louis D. Brandeis as Associate Justice of the Supreme Court.

Wilson's effective use of influence to overcome the opposition to the Brandeis appointment symbolized the President's commitment to progressivism, and the President's adherence to new objectives dem-

onstrated his own flexibility. He had moved a long way from his position of 1912 toward that of Roosevelt and the Bull Moose. Indeed he had a right to boast that the Democrats had opened their hearts to "the demands of social justice" and had "come very near to carrying out the platform of the Progressive Party" as well as their own.

Wilson and moral diplomacy

The force of moral principle. In making foreign policy Wilson and Secretary of State Bryan were guided by attitudes they shared with most progressive Americans, particularly rural reformers, social workers, and Protestant Social Gospelers. "The force of America," the President said during one crisis, "is the force of moral principle." Moral principle, as he interpreted it, involved a duty to work for peace both by example and through diplomacy. It also involved obedience to the law. Wilson and Bryan felt that they had a mission to teach semideveloped countries to live according to the kind of legal and constitutional system that existed in the United States. They believed that that system was not only especially efficient but especially ethical. They believed, too, that there was a definable body of international law that moral nations should obey in their relations with one another. And they placed their hope for peace, as well as for American commercial interests, in that law rather than in systems of alliances or in defensive or deterrent military buildups.

Those attitudes led Wilson and Bryan to distrust the career men in the navy, the army, and the State Department, whom they considered conventional and even cynical. The President and the Secretary of State were willing to risk offending the experts in order to strike out along new diplomatic paths. Bryan launched his program in 1913 and 1914 by negotiating treaties with Great Britain, France, Italy, and twenty-seven lesser powers. Those treaties provided for submitting all disputes among the signatories to permanent commissions of investigation. For one year, while investigation proceeded, the parties to the treaties promised that they would neither go to war nor increase their armaments. At the end of that year they could either accept or reject the findings of the investigation, but Bryan expected the "cooling-off" period to remove the chance of war. Though Roosevelt ridiculed the plan, humanitarians throughout the Western world applauded the treaties and the spirit that produced them.

That spirit impelled Wilson in 1913 to withdraw American support from the Chinese railway consortium that Taft had helped to arrange (see p. 540). The United States, Wilson said, could not be a partner to foreign interference in Chinese affairs. He also recognized the new Republic of China, the first major recognition that government received.

The most imminent threat to China's national integrity was Japan, whose relations with the United States had deteriorated because of the troublesome race issue. Wilson had characteristic Southern prejudices about race. During his Administration there was increasing segregation of Negroes within the federal service. Never an enemy of Jim Crow, Wilson made no effort to dissuade California politicians who were in any case determined in 1913 to prohibit Japanese from owning land in their state. On the President's advice, they passed a statute that achieved that end indirectly, and without violating American treaty obligations. But the Japanese were nonetheless humiliated. Their ambassador protested to the State Department; there were anti-American disturbances in Japan; and the Joint Board of the Army and Navy, deeming war probable, advised Wilson to move warships into Chinese and Philippine waters. The President resorted instead to conciliatory diplomacy. The ensuing exchange of notes eased the crisis and ended talk of war, but the issue remained unresolved, and the Japanese remained understandably resentful.

That resentment contributed to a new controversy in 1915. The preoccupation of European powers with the war then raging on their own continent gave Japan a chance to make twenty-one extraordinary demands of China. Had China agreed to the treaty containing the demands, she would have become a political and economic dependency. American protests, supplemented by pressure from England, persuaded the Japanese temporarily to moderate their terms. The episode revealed how tenuous the balance of power in Asia had become. It also disclosed Bryan's commitment to long-standing national policies and to American commercial interests. The United States, Bryan warned Japan in a portentous note, could not recognize any agreement impairing the Open Door policy, the treaty rights of Americans, or the political or territorial integrity of China.

Confusion in Latin America. As in Asia, so in Latin America, Wilson intended to abandon "dollar diplomacy" with its attendant intrusions on the sovereignty of weak nations. He hoped also, while preserving the strategic lifeline to the Panama Canal, to cultivate the friendship of Latin American peoples and to help them achieve a higher standard of living and a more democratic government. He began convincingly by negotiating a treaty with Colombia providing both apology and indemnity for Roosevelt's Panamanian adventure. But Roosevelt's friends in the Senate prevented approval of that treaty, and the Administration's benign purposes soon produced policies that seemed imperialistic to those countries they were designed to assist.

A combination of circumstances made moral diplomacy difficult. The small nations in and around the Caribbean were, as they had long been, impoverished and turbulent. Unwilling to have the United States government assume and service their debts, Wilson relied on private bankers, whose motives he suspected. He could not permit turmoil in the area to breed revolutions or European intercessions that might endanger the approaches to the isthmus. Consequently he turned to American troops and American dollars to keep order. Since the local forces of order were often also the forces of reaction, Wilson at times resisted reform. Further, he let Bryan send to the Caribbean area "deserving Democrats" lacking any qualifications except faithful party service.

Yet the President tended to attribute qualities of justice and legality to the reactionary government Bryan supported in Nicaragua and to the protectorates the Administration established in Santo Domingo and Haiti. Wilson never fully appreciated how closely his policies resembled "dollar diplomacy" or the intensity of the anti-American feeling those policies provoked.

The President also plunged into Mexican affairs. During the late nineteenth century, large landholders, the army, the hierarchy of the Church, and foreign investors had sustained a dictatorial government in Mexico that had suppressed the landless, uneducated, impoverished peasants and workers. In 1911 a revolution overthrew the government, but in 1913 General Victoriano Huerta engineered a *coup d'état* that restored a reactionary regime under his domination. The revolutionists, who called themselves Constitutionalists, continued to resist under Venustiano Carranza, their able and implacable leader. Though his forces controlled much of the country, the major European powers recognized the Huerta government. President Taft had delayed recognizing the Huerta regime only because he hoped first to settle various outstanding American claims.

Americans with financial interests in Mexico urged Wilson to recognize Huerta, but the President would have no formal dealings with a government of assassins. He therefore refused to appoint an ambassador to Mexico. He did, however, send a series of special agents, whose reports intensified his dislike for the regime but also led him erroneously to believe that the United States could decree a solution to her neighbor's problems.

Wilson followed a policy of "watchful waiting" until October 1913, when Huerta, supported by British oil interests, proclaimed himself military dictator. The President then demanded that Huerta retire. The United States, he assured the Mexicans, sought no territory but only the advancement of "constitutional liberty."

To cut off the dictator's support, Wilson promised to protect British property if a Constitutionalist victory endangered it. He also, in 1914, drove through Congress a law repealing the exemption from tolls for American coastal shipping using the Panama Canal. That exemption, as the British had argued, violated an Anglo-American treaty that pledged the United States not to discriminate against British shipping using the canal. In full agreement, Wilson timed his action to serve his Mexican policy as well as international good faith. The danger of war in Europe made the British

Wilson and moral diplomacy

Occupying Vera Cruz

particularly solicitous of American friendship, and in March 1914 they withdrew their recognition of Huerta.

Meanwhile Wilson had told Carranza that the United States would join him in war against Huerta if he would keep the revolution orderly. Opposed to any American interference, Carranza rejected the indiscreet offer. But, since he needed the arms that an American embargo denied all Mexicans, his representatives assured Wilson that he would respect property rights. Somewhat skeptically, the President lifted the embargo in February 1914.

Armed conflict in Mexico. Soon thereafter Wilson seized an excuse for intervention. On April 10, 1914, an Huertista colonel arrested some American sailors who had gone ashore at Tampico. Though the Mexicans immediately apologized, they refused to make a formal salute to the American flag. Wilson therefore prepared to occupy Vera Cruz, Mexico's most important port. On April 20 he asked Congress for authority to use military force "to obtain from General Huerta . . . the fullest recognition of the rights and dignity of the United States."

The next day, before Congress could act, Wilson ordered the navy to seize Vera Cruz in order to prevent a German merchant ship from landing arms for Huerta. Both Americans and Mexicans were killed in the action that followed. While American newspapers predicted war and Wilson ordered war plans drawn up, the Constitutionalists as well as the Huertistas denounced the violation of their national sovereignty.

Fortunately both countries accepted an offer of mediation from Argentina, Brazil, and Chile. The resulting proposals were never signed by the Constitutionalists, who had become the dominant faction in Mexico. Huerta abdicated in July, and Carranza marched into Mexico City in August 1914, angry with the United States and disdainful of Wilson.

During 1915 the revolution in Mexico reached high pitch. Violence sometimes accompanied reform. The destruction of private property and attacks on priests and nuns excited American demands for intervention, especially among Catholics, Republicans eager to embarrass Wilson, and jingoes spoiling for a war. The President had no affection for Carranza, but he resisted the pressure of the jingoes, partly because he respected Carranza's objectives, partly because he dared not let embroilments in Mexico tie his hands in the crisis then developing with Germany. In October 1915 he recognized the Constitutionalists as the *de facto* government.

Within a few months the bandit leader Pancho Villa created a new crisis. An opponent of Carranza, Villa had earlier won some support from Wilson. In January 1916, however, Villa murdered a group of Americans whom he had removed from a train in Mexico. In March he killed nineteen more during a raid on Columbus, New Mexico. Again there were

Pancho Villa:
brazen bandit and friends

Progressivism: retreat and resurgence

demands in the United States for war, but Wilson tried to contain the situation. He ordered an expedition to cross the border and punish Villa but to avoid engaging the Constitutionalists.

The futile pursuit of Villa aroused Mexican tempers. In April Carranza insisted the Americans leave his country. Wilson refused. When Villa brazenly raided Texas, the President called up the national guard for service on the border and commissioned plans for a full-scale invasion. Twice there were serious skirmishes between American and Constitutionalist soldiers. Carranza, however, needed to devote his full energies to his domestic affairs, and Wilson had growing problems in Europe. Both men, moreover, genuinely desired peace. In July 1916 they agreed to appoint a joint commission to resolve their differences. Although Carranza later rejected its decision, the danger of war had passed. In January 1917 Wilson called the troops home, and two months later he granted the Constitutionalists *de jure* recognition.

In the balance Wilson's restraint outweighed his moralism. In attempting to impose American standards upon the Mexicans, the President offended those he wanted to help. But he also succeeded in withstanding the demands for war that he had inadvertently fanned. He succeeded most of all in grasping the need for reform in Mexico. The American people in varying degree shared his confusions and his distaste for the excesses of revolution. Most of them, however, also shared his sympathy for Mexico's troubles and his reluctance to permit disagreement and discord to grow into war.

Problems of neutrality

War in Europe. In August 1914 a crisis within the empire of Austria-Hungary brought on the war in Europe that had been brewing for more than a decade. Ambitious Germany dominated the alliance of the Central Powers, including Austria-Hungary and Turkey. On the other side were the western powers, France and England, their ally, Russia, and soon also Italy, a partner bought by promises of more lands.

Though most Americans had known that war was threatening, they were shocked by the outbreak of hostilities and unprepared to face the problems war imposed on them. Relieved that war seemed so far away, they had yet to learn that distance alone could not insulate the United States. Most progressives tended to believe that selfish commercial rivalries had moved the European nations toward disaster. They

The European powers at war

Central Powers
Allied Powers
Neutral nations

believed, too, that the United States could serve the world best by concentrating on further reform at home, by setting a noble example of peace and democracy. Even those who were not progressives were slow to recognize the intensity of nationalistic emotions that war bred, slower still in seeing how those emotions blocked a return to peace. Americans, like other Western peoples, had no experience with the shocks of total war, calculated brutality, and mass hatred.

The Administration's initial statements of policy gave official sanction to attitudes that prevailed throughout the nation. Wilson expressed his faith that the United States could play "a part of impartial mediation," and he urged Americans to be "neutral in fact as well as in name." But impartiality of sentiment was impossible. Many Americans of various national origins identified themselves with the loyalties of their forebears. The German- and Irish-Americans particularly supported the Central Powers. British-Americans favored the western Allies. The similarities between British and American speech and institutions, furthermore, fostered widespread sympathy for

England. Wilson himself had long been an admirer of England's culture.

Belligerents in both camps tried to enlist American emotions. The Germans circulated stories alleging that the British blockade was causing mass starvation; the British published accounts of atrocities allegedly committed by German soldiers. Both sides exaggerated, but propaganda won few converts. The course of the war itself, however, made a deeper impression. Germany's invasion of Belgium in August 1914, which violated a treaty pledging Germany to respect Belgian neutrality, offended many Americans. Propaganda could not erase that evidence of German ruthlessness, and evidence was to come of German intrigue within the United States. The Allied cause gradually gained adherents, though very few even among them favored American participation in a war across the Atlantic.

Neutral rights. While Wilson remained firm in his purpose to be neutral in fact, he upheld neutral rights to trade and to the use of the ocean. Those traditional objectives of American diplomacy had, the President believed, a clear basis in law and morality. His stand-

Neutral in fact

552

Progressivism: retreat and resurgence

ards for defining neutral rights were "the existing rules of international law and the treaties of the United States." But those rules were uncertain, especially under the unprecedented conditions created by the tactics of the submarine, the novel weapon on which Germany counted heavily. Particularly with Germany, but also with England, troubles arose over Wilson's interpretations of American neutral rights.

The British, who controlled the seas, were determined that the Allies alone should receive munitions and other essential war materials from the United States. They therefore established a tight blockade of Germany and narrowly limited the kinds of goods that American ships could carry to neutral ports from which they could be sent on to Germany. The British also diverted suspect shipping to their own ports, confiscated many cargoes, interfered with American mail in order to intercept military and economic information, and ultimately forbade British subjects to do any business with American firms "blacklisted" for violating British rules.

Wilson protested often and vigorously against these and other British practices that infringed upon traditional neutral rights. The British, engaged in total war, considered him peevishly legalistic. But, since they had to have American supplies, they made the basic objective of their diplomacy "the maximum blockade that could be enforced without a rupture with the United States."

The success of that policy owed much to the increasing good will Americans felt for England. It owed something, too, to the growing importance of war production for the American economy. Allied demands for war materials stimulated American heavy industry and provided a market for American agriculture. Indeed, with a wise solicitude the British even provided funds to help stabilize the price of cotton at a level satisfactory to the Democratic South.

There were no international rules against selling war materials to the Allies. And if Wilson had refused to permit such sales, he would have indirectly aided the Central Powers. Nor were there any rules to prevent American bankers from making loans to finance Allied purchases. Bryan at first maintained that such loans violated "the true spirit of neutrality," but early in 1915, when the Allies were desperate for funds, he partially reversed himself. Before the end of that year the State Department had approved enormous loans, arranged by American financiers, without which England and France could not have continued to buy the materials they had to have. Thereafter almost every segment of the national economy would have suffered from a diplomatic rupture with the Allies or from a German triumph.

The Germans, who were unable to transport supplies through the British blockade, protested against

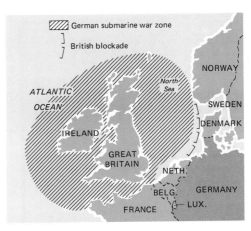

The war at sea

American sales of war materials to the Allies and against British interpretations of maritime law. They also sent out submarines to destroy Allied shipping. These U-boats created the issue on which German-American relations ultimately foundered.

The submarine problem. Submarines could not operate according to the traditional rules governing the conduct of ships bent on destroying commerce. Their effectiveness depended upon surprise. They could not warn their prospective targets before attacking them or remove crews or passengers from stricken ships. They were too small to rescue survivors of their sinkings. Yet Wilson insisted that the Germans observe traditional international law.

The submarine issue arose in February 1915, when Germany proclaimed a war zone around the British Isles. Enemy ships, Germany warned, would be sunk on sight, and neutral ships would be in danger of misidentification. In a sharp reply Wilson called the sinking of merchant ships without visit and search "a wanton act." The destruction of an American ship, he declared, or the loss of American lives on belligerent ships, would be regarded as "a flagrant violation of neutral rights." It would be an offensive act for which he would hold Germany to "strict accountability." His note expressed the horror most Americans felt toward the barbarity of modern weapons. It left the Germans with a choice between abandoning their strategic plan or risking American antagonism.

They chose to take the risk. In April 1915 an American went down aboard a British ship. On May 1 an American ship was torpedoed. Six days later the Germans sank the British passenger liner *Lusitania* and with it died more than 1,200 men, women, and children, 128 of them Americans whom the Germans had warned not to embark. That sinking shocked the nation. A minority wanted to break off relations with

Problems of neutrality

NOTICE!

TRAVELLERS intending to embark on the Atlantic voyage are reminded that a state of war exists between Germany and her allies and Great Britain and her allies; that the zone of war includes the waters adjacent to the British Isles; that, in accordance with formal notice given by the Imperial German Government, vessels flying the flag of Great Britain, or of any of her allies, are liable to destruction in those waters and that travellers sailing in the war zone on ships of Great Britain or her allies do so at their own risk.

IMPERIAL GERMAN EMBASSY
WASHINGTON, D. C., APRIL 22, 1915.

Germany, which in their view was guilty of "murder" and "piracy," as Theodore Roosevelt put it. Most Americans of that mind hoped soon to see the United States at war. At the other extreme, those who sympathized with Germany and those who considered war the worst possible calamity were eager to arbitrate the issue, if necessary to prohibit travel on the ships of belligerents. The majority of Americans were angry but anxious to avoid hostility. Like Wilson, they hoped the problem could be negotiated away.

"There is such a thing," the President told one audience, "as a man being too proud to fight. There is such a thing as a nation being so right that it does not need to convince others by force." In that spirit he began his negotiations. It did not matter, he told Berlin, that the *Lusitania* carried munitions as well as passengers. That was a secondary consideration. The United States was concerned with the "sacred . . . rights of humanity," particularly "the right to life itself." The sinking was an "illegal and inhuman" act, and Wilson demanded an apology and reparations. Since submarines could not be used without violating "principles of justice and humanity," he also by implication demanded that they should not be used at all.

The extremists were dissatisfied. Roosevelt called the President "yellow." Bryan, who had urged Wilson

to adopt the principles of the "cooling-off" treaties, considered the notes to Germany too harsh. Sadly he resigned from the Cabinet, to be replaced by Robert Lansing, a New York lawyer with a talent for diplomatic phraseology. As he and the President continued to negotiate, the Germans met them part way. They would not admit the illegality of the sinking, but in February 1916 Germany offered an apology and an indemnity. By and large the American people were relieved. As Lansing put it, they desired only honorable friendship.

Peace with honor. So long as the war continued, however, the submarine issue might involve the United States. The national interest as well as the interests of the besieged people of Europe impelled Wilson to attempt to arrange a peace. He had sent Colonel House to Europe in January 1915 to investigate the possibility of mediation, but House had found the Germans adamant in their decision to hold Belgium and to destroy England's naval power. In October, however, the Colonel concocted a plan for peace, which Wilson approved. They intended to force Germany to negotiate by warning that otherwise the United States might enter the war on the Allied side. If the Germans were agreeable to negotiations, House hoped to bring them to reasonable terms at the conference table. Again, failure, according to the plan, would invite American participation in the war. In London in January and February 1916 House made progress toward his goal. Indeed it looked as if the British would accept an offer from Wilson for a peace conference in the autumn. But the enterprise collapsed when Lansing tried to revise American policy toward the submarines.

Wilson and Lansing had decided to ease the submarine issue by attempting to persuade the Allies not to arm their merchantmen. In that event the U-boats could issue warnings before attacking. The Germans naturally welcomed the idea, for their purpose was not to kill sailors but to destroy cargoes and bottoms. To their delight, just as House was completing his negotiations in England, Lansing suggested that Allied merchantmen be disarmed. The British of course refused. Lansing had earlier suggested to the Germans that if the Allies declined, Germany might declare unrestricted submarine warfare against all armed ships. In February 1916 the Germans made precisely that declaration. But Lansing then doubled back, reasserted Wilson's original submarine policy, and announced that the United States would not warn Americans against travel on armed ships. "Strict accountability" still applied.

The Roosevelt Republicans prepared to make a major campaign issue during 1916 of the embarrass-

Progressivism: retreat and resurgence

ment the President had caused the Allies. At the opposite pole of opinion, Bryan, La Follette, and other agrarian progressives saw a "sort of moral treason" in letting American citizens create crises by sailing on endangered ships. Resolutions forbidding such travel failed in Congress only because Wilson exerted all his influence to defeat them.

One month later, in March 1916, a German submarine without warning torpedoed an unarmed French steamer, the *Sussex*, which was carrying some American passengers. The President's policy seemed to have failed completely. But he did not retreat from his principles. After much reflection, in April he sent Germany an ultimatum. Unless it immediately abandoned "its present method of submarine warfare," the United States would "sever diplomatic relations." The Kaiser's advisers decided that since they lacked the submarines to conduct a useful blockade of England, it was more important to keep the United States neutral. In May Germany acceded to Wilson's demand. Submarines would observe the rules of visit and search, the Germans said, but they might remove that limitation unless the United States compelled England to obey international law.

In spite of the threat that Germany might revert to its earlier tactics, most Americans were again relieved. Unaware of the reasons for the German decision, they felt that the President had avoided war, maintained justice, and conquered the submarines with his pen. The *Sussex* pledge seemed to promise peace with honor—a happy formula, especially in a campaign year.

Americanism and preparedness.

As the war went on, it revealed to Americans as well as to Europeans the terrors of organized brutality and the dangers of organized passions. Intelligence and decency and orderliness gave way before the strains of continual fear. Though the United States was far from the fields of battle, even here timid men sought some symbol that would protect them from the disturbances around them. Other men seized the chance to create nationalistic symbols they could use for their own selfish ends. The most avid foes of labor unions underwrote a campaign to equate the open shop with "Americanism." Those who distrusted blacks or Catholics or Jews now did so in the name of Americanism. It was a word that the opponents of women's suffrage used, a word used also by the advocates of a literacy test for immigrants. The Senate blocked an amendment to enfranchise women, and Congress in 1915 passed a bill establishing a literacy test. Wilson vetoed it, pointing out that it abridged the traditional right of asylum and tested education rather than talent.

Preparedness parade

The President resisted the spirit of frightened conformity that Roosevelt exalted in the name of Americanism. The name, however, had a political magic no politician could safely ignore, and Wilson himself used it to describe his foreign policy. In 1915, condemning the sabotage of munitions production for the Allies, he attributed it to extremists among the German- and Irish-Americans. Calling on all others to dedicate themselves to the national honor, the President planned to make his version of Americanism the keynote of his campaign for reelection.

The position Wilson and his party took on preparedness also accorded with the middle-of-the-road attitudes of most Americans. Even after the war began, they tended, like the President, to consider arms and munitions the unnecessary tools of evil men. Again like the President, they had an instinctive dislike for widespread military training and a large standing army, neither of which had any place in the American tradition. That tradition persisted, in spite of the nature of modern war, in defining the militia and a citizen-soldiery as proper safeguards for national security. Four months after the sinking of the *Lusitania*, Wilson expressed a popular sentiment when he said he saw no need "to stir the nation up in favor of national defense."

Moved by the possibility of war in Europe and Mexico, a vocal minority began to preach the need to prepare, pointing out that it took time to produce weapons and to train armies and navies for twentieth-century warfare. Theodore Roosevelt led these advocates of preparedness. He was sometimes too strident to be convincing, but more moderate men gradually put their ideas across. During 1915 Secretary of War Lindley M. Garrison and his three Republican predecessors all urged preparedness. It had become a political issue, and Wilson's Democratic advisers warned him that he had better do something about it.

In July 1915 the President instructed the armed services to make plans for expansion. In November, asking for much less than they had recommended, he proposed a volunteer army of four hundred thousand men who were to serve only a few months in each of several successive years. Even this modest proposal met opposition from rural liberals in Congress, most of them Democrats, some of them with great influence. Preparedness also incurred the hostility of a passionate peace party, its membership recruited not least from among women who saw all war as a needless exercise of raw masculinity. To win more moderate support for his program, Wilson went on a speaking trip that took him halfway across the continent. During that tour he came out for a "navy second to none."

Yet in 1916 the President had to make concessions to his opponents. Still close to the middle of the road, he first rejected the War Department's plan for creating a large reserve force under the regular army, and he appointed a new Secretary of War,* Newton D. Baker, a progressive with a reputation for antimilitarism. Wilson and Baker then worked out a compromise that satisfied the Congress. The resulting law of May 1916 doubled the regular army but left the national guard still largely independent of the authority of the War Department. The President's influence helped, too, to carry a measure accelerating the building of a strong navy.

The agrarians scored one success: in the face of Administration opposition, they fashioned the revenue legislation to pay for the defense program. It increased surtaxes on personal income and put new taxes on inheritances. Those best able to pay would have to foot the bill for preparedness.

The Democrats had given the preparedness issue a progressive stamp and had identified their party with national defense. The measures fell short of the demands of the armed services, but they met the most

urgent requirements of a nation that still hoped and expected to remain at peace.

The election of 1916. For the Republicans one major problem in 1916 was how to reassimilate the Progressive party. Roosevelt had kept it alive largely to further his own ambitions, but the Old Guard would not countenance his nomination on the Republican ticket, and the Colonel cared more about defeating Wilson than about nursing old grudges. In order to regain Bull Moose votes, the Republicans selected a candidate with a progressive record, Charles Evans Hughes. He had been a successful reform governor of New York and in 1912, as an Associate Justice of the Supreme Court, had stayed neutral in the party split. He was an able man and a strong candidate whose cause may have been hurt rather than helped by Roosevelt's obsessive attacks on Democratic foreign policy.

Although Wilson had planned to run on the issues of Americanism and progressivism, foreign policy became a central factor in the campaign. At the Democratic convention, as the keynote speaker described the recurrent crises in foreign policy, he explained how Wilson had resolved each one and concluded each time with the phrase: "We did not go to war." Each time the delegates responded jubilantly. The party-managers sense that their most effective slogan would be: "He kept us out of war." Its effectiveness probably grew as Roosevelt sounded more and more bellicose and as Hughes explained that he would have been tougher on Mexico and Germany than Wilson had been. The President himself told the voters that he was "not expecting this country to get into war," and Democratic propagandists advertised: "Wilson and Peace with Honor? or Hughes with Roosevelt and War?"

There were, of course, other issues. The Irish-American and German-American extremists embarrassed Hughes by supporting him openly; but he failed to repudiate them publicly, while Wilson deliberately attacked them. The Democrats had made a progressive record that was especially persuasive with those from the defunct Bull Moose who could not yet tolerate the idea of voting Republican again.

By and large, rural America voted for Wilson, as did labor, the liberals, and most intellectuals. That coalition was still tenuous, but it foreshadowed the profile of Democratic hegemony years later. In 1916 the contest was so close that it hinged on the ballots in California and Minnesota, which were counted only after early Eastern returns had put Hughes ahead. Hughes went to bed election night thinking that he had won. But the South and the West reversed the verdict. Wilson received 49.4 percent of the popu-

---

*Garrison had resigned partly because of his view on national defense, partly because he opposed Wilson's policy for increasing home rule in the Philippines.

Progressivism: retreat and resurgence

Charles Evans Hughes: candidate with a progressive record

lar vote to Hughes' 46.2 percent and carried the Electoral College 277 to 254. Peace and progressivism had helped to put Wilson across again, but his victory had also depended upon traditional Democratic loyalties and the continuing Republican division.

The road to war

Wilson knew very well how uncertain was the nation's hold on peace. Before election day the British had tightened their regulations on neutral trade, and the Germans had intensified their submarine campaign against the Allies. The war could not be contained much longer. Either Wilson had to find ways to end it or else he would have to sacrifice peace or honor—or both.

The President planned to send a dramatic note to the belligerents. He was ready, his draft said, to pledge the "whole force" of the United States to end the "war of exhaustion and attrition" and to keep the future peace. The draft asked each side for "a concrete definition" of the objectives for which it was fighting. It also demanded that a peace conference be called immediately. Furthermore, Wilson intended to employ every pressure short of war to assist the more reasonable side. While he was still reworking his draft, in December 1916, the German chancellor announced his government's readiness to negotiate. For a brief time Wilson was encouraged.

The offer, however, hid a calculating spirit. The Germans made the gesture out of confidence of impending victory. Masters of the eastern front, where the Russians were collapsing, the Germans expected to smash France and England if their terms were re-

jected. They had also secretly decided that, if negotiations failed, they would resume unrestricted submarine warfare. And their secret terms were harsh—they would insist on territory along the Baltic, in the Congo, and in Belgium, France, and Luxembourg.

Slowly Wilson discovered the truth. He dispatched the note he had been drafting, but the Germans replied that they wanted no neutral at the peace table. The Allies publicly rejected the President's proposal but privately let him know they would negotiate if the German conditions were reasonable. Then in January 1917 the Germans at last revealed their greedy terms and announced that their submarines would sink at sight all ships, belligerent or neutral.

For several weeks Wilson would not admit that he had either to surrender his principles or go to war. He broke off relations with Germany, but he told Congress he wanted no conflict. He remained outwardly temperate even after learning on February 25 that Germany was plotting against the United States. That day the British communicated to Washington secret orders of the German foreign minister, Arthur Zimmermann, which they had intercepted. Those orders told the German minister to Mexico that, in the event of war with the United States, he should invite Mexico and Japan to join the Central Powers.

Wilson, while still hoping to avoid war, had meanwhile pressed his interpretation of neutral rights. He had asked Congress for authority to arm American merchant vessels and to employ any other means that might be necessary to protect American ships and citizens at sea. To win votes for his proposal, he made the Zimmermann note public on March 1, 1917. A wave of anti-German sentiment swept the country, but the Democratic House of Representatives withheld the broad authority the President wanted, and in the Senate a dozen antiwar progressives talked a stronger bill to death.

That "little group of willful men," as Wilson called them, struggled in vain. The Zimmermann note had dissolved the myth that the war was strictly European. The President on his own ordered the merchantmen armed, and on March 18, two weeks after his second inauguration, U-boats sank three American ships. Moreover, the first Russian revolution established a limited monarchy and a responsible parliament, temporarily destroying the despotism that had made Americans reluctant to associate with the Allied cause. And the Allies could no longer fight without American men, money, and material. The combination of events convinced even the most ardent peace advocates in the Cabinet of the necessity for war.

Wilson was agonized by a conclusion he could not escape. War, he allegedly told one confidant,

The world must be made safe for democracy. Its peace must be planted upon the tested foundations of political liberty. We have no selfish ends to serve. We desire no conquest, no dominion. We seek no indemnities for ourselves, no material compensation for the sacrifices we shall freely make. We are but one of the champions of the rights of mankind. We shall be satisfied when those rights have been made as secure as the faith and the freedom of nations can make them....

It is a fearful thing to lead this great peaceful people into war, into the most terrible and disastrous of all wars, civilization itself seeming to be in the balance. But the right is more precious than peace, and we shall fight for the things which we have always carried nearest our hearts,—for democracy, for the right of those who submit to authority to have a voice in their own governments, for the rights and liberties of small nations, for a universal dominion of right by such a concert of free peoples as shall bring peace and safety to all nations and make the world itself at last free.

From Woodrow Wilson, War Message to Congress, 1917.

"would overturn the world we had known," lead to "a dictated peace," require "illiberalism at home." Sadly he predicted that "the spirit of ruthless brutality" would enter the very "fibre of our national life." His pain was shared by every progressive, for progressivism had based its faith on the peaceful, reasonable improvement of the lot of man in a world of quiet and intelligence. It was also, however, a moral faith, and in the view of Wilson and other progressive intellectuals, Germany had violated moral principles. It had forced war on France and Belgium. It was bent on conquest. Whatever the definitions of neutral rights, so Wilson had concluded, no one was immune from German aggression, and there could be no real peace while it went unpunished.

With those thoughts in mind, Wilson on April 2 addressed the special session of Congress he had summoned. On April 4 the Senate by a vote of 82 to 6, and on April 6 the House of Representatives by a vote of 373 to 50, passed a resolution recognizing the existence of a state of war with Germany.

The decision of the German General Staff to resume unrestricted submarine warfare had rested on the calculation that American belligerency would cost Germany less than continuing shipments of American supplies to the Allies. That decision, as the Germans expected it would, led to the American declaration of war, for Wilson and his supporters had staked the grandeur of the nation on his policies. If Americans had not been allowed to travel upon the ships of belligerents, if American bankers had been forbidden to make loans to England and France, if the United States had surrendered its historic commitment to neutral rights, the crisis of war would not have developed as it did. But American business interests would not have abandoned their markets without protest. More important, the sense of national greatness that had been growing since the 1880s precluded an easy acceptance of limitations on the country imposed by any foreign power. Wilson gave a special cast to American pride and sensitivity, but those sentiments were not his alone. Most important, though no one of

Progressivism: retreat and resurgence

the great powers of Europe was uninvolved in the contest for supremacy that brought on the war, the Germans did precipitate the war and pursue it without the delicate and deliberate care for American sensibilities that the British cultivated. Further, had the Germans prevailed, they intended to impose upon Europe and much of the rest of the world a Carthaginian settlement. German intentions, as well as the special conditions of war-making that guided German maritime strategy, created the problems that American policy-makers found no way to resolve, in the end, short of war itself.

Suggestions for reading

GENERAL

The best general account of the Taft years and of the breakup of the Republican party is in G. E. Mowry, *The Era of Theodore Roosevelt** (1958). A. S. Link, *Woodrow Wilson and the Progressive Era** (1954), covers the succeeding years to the American entry into the war. Both books are challenged by Gabriel Kolko, *The Triumph of Conservatism** (1963). Also useful are relevant parts of Eric Goldman, *Rendezvous with Destiny** (1952), and Richard Hofstadter, *The Age of Reform: From Bryan to F. D. R.** (1955). An older book of G. E. Mowry, *Theodore Roosevelt and the Progressive Movement** (1946), contains a more detailed account—and less friendly to T.R.—than that in the same author's later work.

PROGRESSIVES AND REGULARS

A case for Taft is set forth in D. E. Anderson, *William Howard Taft* (1973), which should be compared with the Roosevelt biographies listed in connection with the preceding chapter and with A. T. Mason, *Bureaucracy Convicts Itself* (1941). For an understanding of progressive social ideas, see the books suggested in the previous chapter. It is also essential to read Herbert Croly, *The Promise of American Life** (1909); Walter Weyl, *The New Democracy** (1912); and Walter Lippmann, *Drift and Mastery** (1914). See also Otis Graham, Jr., *Encore for Reform: The Old Progressives and the New Deal** (1967). Two significant studies of progressive thought, besides those referred to in the previous chapter, are Walter Johnson, *William Allen White's America* (1947), and C. B. Forcey, *The Crossroads of Liberalism** (1961). There are no comparable studies of conservative thought, but that subject gets useful treatment in Richard Leopold, *Elihu Root and the Conservative Tradition** (1954), and in the introduction by E. E. Morison to Vol. V of *The Letters of Theodore Roosevelt* (1952). Useful in the context of its title is Walter and Marie Scholes, *The Foreign Policies of the Taft Administration* (1970).

WILSON

The outstanding work on Wilson is A. S. Link's multivolume biography. Two brief studies of Wilson are J. M. Blum, *Woodrow Wilson and the Politics of Morality** (1956), and J. A. Garraty, *Woodrow Wilson** (1956). Of the special studies of Wilson's diplomacy, the best are A. S. Link, *Wilson the Diplomatist** (1957), and N. G. Levin, Jr., *Woodrow Wilson and World Politics** (1968). There are keen analyses of the issues of American foreign policy in R. E. Osgood, *Ideals and Self-Interest in America's Foreign Relations** (1953), and E. R. May, *The World War and American Isolation 1914–1917** (1959). W. A. Williams, *The Tragedy of American Foreign Policy* (1962), presents the most influential interpretation of the dominance of economic considerations. Other important monographs include D. G. Munro, *Intervention and Dollar Diplomacy in the Caribbean, 1900–1921* (1964); R. E. Quirk, *An Affair of Honor: Woodrow Wilson and the Occupation of Vera Cruz** (1962); P. E. Haley, *Revolution and Intervention: The Diplomacy of Taft and Wilson with Mexico, 1910–1917* (1970); R. W. Curry, *Woodrow Wilson and Far Eastern Policy, 1913–1921* (1968); Ross Gregory, *The Origins of American Intervention in the First World War** (1971); D. M. Smith, *The Great Departure: The United States in World War I, 1914–1920* (1965); and J. M. Cooper, Jr., *The Vanity of Power: American Isolationism and the First World War, 1914–1917* (1969). Of the various studies of the Wilsonians, one is indispensable: Charles Seymour, ed., *The Intimate Papers of Colonel House*, 4 vols. (1921–28). Also useful, particularly on domestic issues, is A. T. Mason, *Brandeis: A Free Man's Life* (1946). J. A. Garraty, *Henry Cabot Lodge* (1953), presents an understanding account of one of Wilson's foremost antagonists. The literature on Wilson and his time has been richly expanded with the continuing publication of his letters and papers under the editorship of A. S. Link.

*Available in a paperback edition.

CHAPTER **24** **_War and its sequel_**

"Over There"

The American nation was unprepared for the First World War. To begin with, the country had no clear sense of purpose. Many German- and Irish-Americans were unreconciled to fighting on the side of the Allies. Smaller groups of pacifists saw no excuse for any fighting, and some progressives believed that the United States had no business involving itself in what they considered to be a struggle between European imperialists. The majority of Americans were in full accord with the decision to go to war, but they were confused about its origins and objectives. Like the President, they had hoped to remain neutral. Like the President, they regarded the submarine issue as a matter of morality. They had little if any understanding of world politics.

Indeed the moral temper of the times led Americans to seek utopian rather than realistic reasons for the actions to which they were committed. To accommodate that temper, and to convert the dissenters, Wilson defined American war aims in idealistic terms. The spirit of his war message and later addresses was noble as well as persuasive. It helped transmute the fervor of progressivism into the selfless bravery of the "great crusade." But it also turned some fervor into frenzy, and it led Americans to expect a paradise that no war could give them. The failure to achieve that expectation tinged the persisting frenzy of the immediate postwar years with bitterness and vindictiveness.

The United States was also unprepared for the total mobilization demanded by modern war and for the special strengths required to fight a war overseas. The nation lacked the necessary army, the plans and facilities to raise it, the guns and tanks and airplanes to equip it, the ships to transport it, and even the tools and the organization to produce the materials of war. In every respect—emotional, economic, military—mobilization was urgent but erratic.

The armed forces on land and sea

Selective service. The President and his military advisers agreed that conscription was the only efficient and democratic way to recruit a large army. Yet the Speaker of the House and the Chairman of the Military Affairs Committee, both Democrats, led the opposition to the Administration's selective-service bill. Many of the bill's opponents considered conscription a threat to democracy. Others had a romantic attachment to the tradition of voluntary military service. But if war had ever been romantic it was no longer so, and selective service, as Wilson argued, spread the obligation to serve among all qualified men without regard to their social position. The House passed the bill in May, but only after mollifying American mothers by raising the minimum draft age from nineteen, which the army recommended, to twenty-one.*

In the Senate the Republicans wasted three weeks in a futile effort to force the Administration to accept the volunteer division Theodore Roosevelt was organizing. Roosevelt and his admirers believed that even though his troops were half-trained they would make up the deficiency in dash. Wilson prudently preferred professional to political generals. The Selective Service Act finally passed by the Senate left Wilson free to dispose of volunteer units as he saw fit, and he saw fit to reject Roosevelt's.

Early in June 1917 over 9 million men registered quietly with the local officials whom the War Department authorized to supervise the draft. Before the war ended, over 24 million had registered and almost 3 million had been inducted into the army. There was no significant opposition to conscription, and the drafted troops fought as heroically as the 2 million volunteers who enlisted in the various armed services.

The army's top command was strictly professional. Bypassing General Leonard Wood, an intimate of Roosevelt, Wilson made General John J. Pershing head of the American Expeditionary Force and gave his decisions consistent support. "Black Jack" Pershing, a laconic, stern West Pointer, pursued two controversial policies. He refused to send troops into battle until they had completed their training, and he insisted on preserving a separate identity for the American Expeditionary Force, though the French and British were impatient for reinforcements and eager to merge American units with their own.

The war in the west. In the fall of 1917 German offensives routed the Italians and destroyed the Russian army. The Bolshevik Revolution of November removed Russia from the war and left the western front, manned by war-weary French and British troops, exposed to the full attack Germany was certain to mount the following spring. The alarmed Allies created the Supreme War Council to direct their resistance and urged Pershing to supply men, trained or untrained. But Pershing still declined. In the spring,

*It was necessary in 1918 to lower the minimum age to eighteen.

War and its sequel

An obligation to serve

however, as the Allied lines crumbled before a furious German offensive, Wilson agreed to the appointment of French Marshal Ferdinand Foch as supreme commander, and Pershing put his four available divisions at Foch's disposal.

During May 1918 the Germans pushed the French back to the Marne River, only fifty miles from Paris. Foch then called up one American division and a few regiments of marines who met the Germans at

Foch and Pershing

Gas? What do you know of it, you people who have never heard earth and heaven rock with the frantic turmoil of the ceaseless bombardment? A crawling yellow cloud that pours in upon you, that gets you by the throat and shakes you as a huge mastiff might shake a kitten, leaves you burning in every nerve and vein of your body with pain unthinkable; your eyes starting from their sockets; your face turned yellow-green.

Rats? What did you ever read of the rats in the trenches? Next to gas, they still slide on their fat bellies through my dreams.... Tens of thousands of rats, crunching between battle lines while the rapid-firing guns mow the trench edge—crunching their hellish feasts....

Stench? Did you ever breathe air foul with the gases arising from a thousand rotting corpses? Dirt? Have you ever fought half madly thru days and nights and weeks unwashed, with feverish rests between long hours of agony, while the guns boom their awful symphony of death, and the bullets zip-zip-zip ceaselessly along the trench edge that is your sky-line—and your death line, too, if you stretch and stand up?

Quoted in the *Independent*, June 19, 1916.

Chateau Thierry, carried the intensive battle there, and in June drove the enemy out of Belleau Wood.

Gambling for a quick victory before more American forces could reach France, the Germans in July struck at the sector of the Marne between Rheims and Soissons. Here some eighty-five thousand Americans helped to turn the attack, and eight divisions of Yanks participated in the French counteroffensive that cleaned out the sector early in August. The American First Army under Pershing then took over the southern front near St. Mihiel and routed the Germans there in an independent offensive in September. Late that month Pershing attacked the German lines between Verdun and Sedan. This Meuse-Argonne engagement produced a costly but crucial American victory. Along with the success of French and British forces on the northern and central fronts, it crushed the German army and set the stage for an armistice (see p. 569).

The triumph exacted extraordinary expenditures of nerve and flesh, for in some respects the First World War was the most ghastly in history. Casualties ran

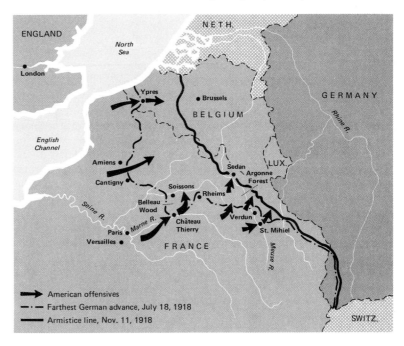

American operations on the western front, 1918

Legend:
→ American offensives
–·– Farthest German advance, July 18, 1918
━━ Armistice line, Nov. 11, 1918

The Meuse-Argonne: extraordinary expenditures of nerve and flesh

high, particularly during offensives, and American troops, along with their allies and foes, suffered a high incidence of shell shock, a form of battle fatigue, and of tuberculosis, a companion of the poison gas and the mud, cold, wet, and filth of the trenches. For most soldiers the war was an awful combination of fear, drudgery, and exhaustion.

The signal exceptions were the aviators. Their craft were simple and slow, their tactics rudimentary. Yet the new knights of the air wrote a chapter of military history in their man-to-man combat in the skies, and American aces dramatized for their countrymen the potentialities of aerial warfare.

The Yanks had reached France just in time. The Allies needed the new manpower to stop the Germans' gamble for victory—a gamble that would probably have succeeded had reinforcements failed to appear. Yet the Americans, indispensable during the last months of war, and gallant and effective then, arrived only after the Allies had held the Germans for almost four terrible years. Over 50,000 Americans died in France, but the war took the lives of 3 million English, French, and Russian soldiers. The role of the American army was both relatively small and absolutely vital.

The war at sea. So too was the role of the American navy. In all but one respect the war at sea had been won by the success of the British navy in bottling up the German fleet. As the British Admiralty admitted, however, the German submarines also had to be brought under control. During 1917 U-boats sank more than twice the tonnage of shipping that the Allies and Americans built that year. Hard pressed to supply themselves, the British could not guard the American lines of supply to Europe, and the Americans could not afford to risk transporting an army aboard ships unprotected from enemy submarines.

The United States navy had the ships and the men to take over the patrol of the Western Hemisphere and to assist the English in patrolling the waters around the British Isles. But the Allies lacked the antisubmarine vessels to root the U-boats out of the ocean. An American plan proved to be at least as important as the ships themselves. Admiral William S. Sims, the ranking American naval officer in Europe, was the primary exponent of the idea of using destroyers and other men-of-war to escort convoys of merchantmen across the Atlantic. Though British skippers preferred to sail alone rather than to proceed in formation under naval command, Sims in the summer of 1917 overcame their objections and the resistance of the British Admiralty. By the end of 1917 the use of convoys had cut shipping losses in half.

The escorted convoys and the patrolling American destroyers were so effective that not one American soldier was lost in transit to Europe. The bridge of ships to France carried the troops and supplies that the Germans had expected to destroy, and the miracle of transportation turned the tide of war. That great

American achievement was possible only because the British also provided bottoms for men and equipment, and only because the Yanks at the front could use Allied cannon, tanks, and airplanes.

The home front

Problems of production. By themselves the eventual prodigies of American war production would have been too little and too late for victory. Since there were no precedents for economic mobilization, the Administration had to feel its way along in creating agencies to supervise production and distribution and to allocate vital goods and services. When war came, the army did not even have information about the uniforms and shoes it would need. There was no inventory of national resources, no adequate plan for priorities or for stockpiling critical materials. Most of the first nine months of the war were spent in learning about mobilization, and in tooling up for production.

The lost time was especially serious for the aviation program. American planners were so slow in designing and manufacturing aircraft that American aviators had to fly in British and French machines all through the war. The situation was almost as desperate in the production of artillery and tanks. The building program for transports and cargo vessels collapsed completely, and the government had to rely on ships seized from neutrals or purchased from private industry.

These and other difficulties spurred the Senate Military Affairs Committee to investigate the conduct of the war. As 1918 began, the Democratic chairman of that committee asserted publicly that the military effort had been impeded by waste and inefficiency. Republican senators, joined by several Democrats, urged that a war cabinet of three distinguished citizens be set up to exercise the powers the Congress had conferred upon the President. If that measure had passed, Wilson would have become a figurehead. Even as it was, the Senate committee was close to assuming the role of its predecessor that had harassed Lincoln during the Civil War.

The President, however, had already begun to solve the problems of mobilization. Neither during 1917 nor later, moreover, did any scandal taint the administration of the war. Aware of the threat from the Senate, Wilson prepared a bill giving him sweeping authority to reorganize and manage all executive agencies. This measure, which Senator Lee S. Overman sponsored, passed Congress in April 1918 and enabled the President to complete his own plans.

Economic mobilization. As those plans matured, the Administration put the nation's economy on a satisfactory war footing. In the spring of 1917 England, France, and Italy urgently needed food. Stretching the mandate of the Council of National Defense, which Congress had authorized the year before, the President established a food-control program in May under Herbert C. Hoover, who had acquired an international reputation as director of the Belgian Relief Commission. Wilson also asked Congress for emergency authority over agricultural production and distribution. The Lever Act of August 1917 granted him that authority, together with limited power to control the prices of certain scarce commodities. Wilson at once created the Food Administration. With Hoover at its head, that agency controlled prices to stimulate the production of wheat and pork, managed the distribution of those and other foodstuffs, and persuaded the public to observe meatless and breadless days. To that last objective, as to the selling of war bonds, American women contributed impressive energy. The success of Hoover's policies made possible the victualing of the nations fighting Germany.

To mobilize American industry proved more difficult. The General Munitions Board, another offshoot of the Council of National Defense, showed itself incapable of coordinating the conflicting demands of the American armed services and the Allied purchasing commissions. Consequently, in July 1917 Wilson appointed a War Industries Board with authority to pass on all American and Allied purchasing, to allocate raw materials, to control production, and to supervise labor relations. The WIB, however, failed to elicit the full cooperation either of industry or of the armed services. In March 1918 the President rewrote its charter and named a new chairman, the wealthy and influential Democrat, Bernard M. Baruch, who enlisted the help of some hundred outstanding business-leaders. Now concerned largely with establishing industrial priorities, the WIB eliminated bottlenecks and speeded the conversion of plants to war production. The agency was helped in its task by a reorganization of the general staff of the army into functional divisions, each under an experienced officer selected without regard to seniority. With the army and the WIB cooperating, the abundance of the country could now be funneled into the war effort, though both government and business remained hesitant and ambiguous about the proper role of the modern state in wartime.

As in agriculture and industry, so in fuel, transportation, and labor, peacetime practices faltered under the stress of war. To relieve the critical coal shortage, the Lever Act empowered the President to fix the price of coal high enough to encourage operators to work marginal mines. In August 1917 he estab-

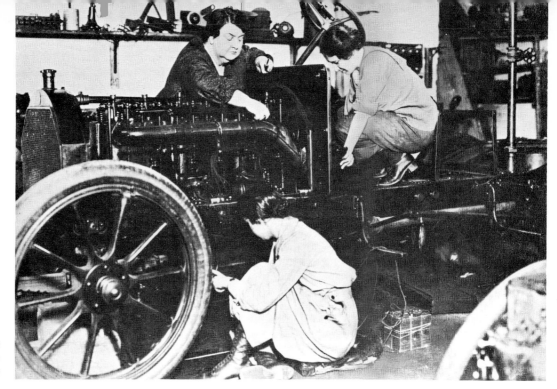

Wartime
assembly
plant

lished the Fuel Administration under Harry A. Garfield, president of Williams College. The agency set an attractive price for coal, and the resulting production was ample for the nation's needs. Snarls in railway transportation, however, impeded coal deliveries, and for four days in January 1918 Garfield closed all East Coast plants that used coal for any but vital purposes.

That emergency order underlined the crisis in railroading. The roads had tried to handle the extraordinary wartime traffic on the basis of voluntary cooperation, but in the absence of unified authority delays became worse and worse, and the snow and freezing weather of December 1917 precipitated a collapse of internal transportation. With congressional approval, Wilson therefore established the United States Railway Administration under William G. McAdoo. Exercising an even greater authority than Baruch had over industry, McAdoo improved the railways' equipment, strengthened their finances, and successfully adjusted their operations to the demands of war.

Labor in wartime. In April 1918 the President created the National War Labor Board, which unified the various agencies that had been established to prevent labor disturbances and the attending losses in production. Under the joint chairmanship of former President Taft and Frank P. Walsh, a labor lawyer, the WLB heard more than twelve hundred cases and forestalled many strikes, but it lacked the information it needed to set labor policies for the entire country. To remedy

that deficiency, Wilson in May 1918 appointed the War Labor Policies Board under Felix Frankfurter, a young law professor who had been the War Department's labor adviser. The WLPB surveyed national labor needs and practices and standardized wages and hours. At its recommendation, the President created the United States Employment Service, an agency that placed almost 4 million workers in essential war jobs.

While keeping the country free from serious strikes, the government's labor agencies and policies also advanced some peacetime objectives of social reformers and union-leaders. Industry hired more women, though by no means enough to satisfy the reasonable expectations of American feminists. Membership in the American Federation of Labor grew more than 50 percent, reaching over 3,200,000 by 1920. The government demanded an eight-hour day for war industry wherever it could and insisted on decent working conditions and living wages. Even though the cost of living rose 50 percent, booming wages and full employment permitted a gratifying increase of 20 percent in average *real* income. Though management groups hostile to labor were impatient with wartime controls, their profits were high. The overall experience demonstrated dramatically that enlightened federal labor policies could bring to the laboring force unprecedented comfort and personal dignity without damping business enterprise.

Indeed the wartime experience confirmed the insights of men like Herbert Croly (see p. 543). Working together in the emergency agencies, businessmen and public servants refined the techniques of organization and administration and applied them vigorously in the national interest. The organization of agriculture and labor proved to be as rewarding as the organization of industry, which had proceeded so much further during the days of peace. The wartime experience provided a pattern of some voluntary, some federal, organization of an economy beset by crisis.

Propaganda, public opinion, and civil liberties. This very increase in efficiency, however, gave some of the wartime agencies a dangerous authority over the minds of citizens. A week after war was declared, Wilson created the Committee on Public Information to mobilize public opinion. George Creel, chairman of the CPI, worked out with newspapermen a voluntary censorship that kept the public reasonably well informed while safeguarding sensitive information. He also hired hundreds of artists and writers to mount a propaganda campaign without precedent in American history.

The CPI stressed two major points. One argued, as Wilson did, that the United States was fighting only for freedom and democracy. The other maintained that the Germans were all Huns, diabolic creatures perpetrating atrocities in an effort to conquer the world for their lust and greed. The releases of the Creel committee intensified the unreasoning attitudes of a nation at war. They hinted that German spies had an ear to every wall. Often they carried antiunion overtones, labeling as treason all work stoppages, whatever their real cause. More often they implied that all dissent was unpatriotic and that pacifists and socialists had hidden sympathies for the enemy.

This propaganda helped to sell war bonds, combat absenteeism in the factories, and reconcile some doubters to the war. But the price was high. The attitudes the CPI encouraged were the same as those fostered by private vigilante groups like the National Protective Association, which cultivated a kind of war-madness. There were continual spy scares, witch hunts, even kangaroo courts that imposed harsh sentences of tar and feathers. The innocent victims were usually German-Americans or antiwar radicals. The orgy of hatred had its ridiculous as well as its outrageous side. Americans stopped playing German music and stopped teaching or speaking the German language; they called sauerkraut "liberty cabbage"; and in Cincinnati they even removed pretzels from the free-lunch counters of saloons.

It was essential, of course, to protect the country from espionage and sabotage, but wartime legislation and its administration exceeded reasonable bounds. The Espionage Act of 1917, which Wilson requested, provided penalties of up to twenty years in prison and a $10,000 fine for those who helped the enemy, obstructed recruiting, or incited rebellion within the armed services. One section gave the Postmaster General authority to deny the use of the mails to any publication that in his opinion advocated treason or forcible resistance to the laws. The Trading-with-the-Enemy Act, which Congress passed in October 1917, added sweeping authority to censor the foreign-language press.

In 1918 Congress went still further. The rising hysteria was stimulated by the demands of the Attorney General and by the antipathy toward the Industrial Workers of the World. Copying state statutes, Congress passed the Sabotage Act and the Sedition Act, which empowered the federal government to punish any expression of opinion that, regardless of whether or not it led to action, was "disloyal, profane, scurrilous or abusive" of the American form of government, flag, or uniform. Subsequent systematic persecution effectively destroyed the Wobblies, and in one characteristic case, Eugene V. Debs was imprisoned for a decade for expressing his revulsion against the war.

The recklessness of Congress in stocking such an arsenal had its source in the frenzy of the people. Timid in the face of public opinion, state and federal officials and judges made a mockery of the right of freedom of speech and belief. Just as those administering the draft subjected conscientious objectors to needless humiliations, often imprisonment, so those administering the espionage, sedition, and other wartime laws made conformity a measure of loyalty. The mails were closed to publications whose only offense was a statement of socialism, a plea for feminism, or anti-British bias. People were haled into court who had done no more than criticize the Red Cross or the financing of the war or who had merely declared that war was contrary to the teachings of Jesus Christ. Of over fifteen hundred arrests for sedition, only ten were alleged to be for actual sabotage. The government's own immoderation and its failure to control private vigilantes shocked men and women of good will and good sense, blemished the Administration's war record, and exaggerated passions that long outlived the crisis itself.

Politics in wartime. Those exaggerated passions sometimes found expression in partisan, sectional, and factional politics. Though Wilson expressed the wish that politics might be adjourned for the duration, wartime problems raised conflicts of interest and irresistible opportunities to pursue partisan advantages. The Republicans, determined to prevent the Democrats from getting all the credit for American successes, criticized the conduct of the war. But that criticism, much of it valid, hurt the Democrats less

than did the behavior of a few Southerners in key congressional posts who consistently voted against war legislation.

Southern agrarians and Western progressives demanded heavy income, inheritance, and excess-profits taxes to prevent war profiteering. Conservatives, in contrast, preferred federal borrowing and excise or sales taxes of various kinds. They argued that future generations should share the cost of a war fought in the national interest and that taxes on consumption would help check wartime inflation. The Administration took a sensible middle position. In all, the war cost about $33.5 billion, of which $10.5 billion was raised by taxes, the balance by Treasury borrowing. Secretary of the Treasury McAdoo had intended taxes to carry a larger share, but the soaring cost of the war upset his calculations. As it was, wartime taxes were heavier than they had ever been in the United States. The Revenue Act of October 1917 imposed new and larger excise and luxury taxes, a graduated excess-profits tax on business, and increased estate and personal income taxes. It raised the maximum surtax on income to 63 percent, and the Revenue Act of 1918 lifted it and the excess-profits tax still higher.

The revenue measures passed during the war established a truly progressive tax structure, which placed a heavy but equitable burden on those best able to carry it. They paid, but they also complained. And, especially in the Northeast, Republican politicians won middle-class support by contending that the agrarian Democrats were deliberately punishing the nation's industrial regions. By 1918 the tax issue was being hotly debated by moneyed men who had once supported less expensive progressive policies.

The Republicans also made gains among Midwestern farmers who had defected to the Democrats in 1916. The Lever Act empowered the Administration to control the price of wheat but not the price of cotton, and the Western farmers resented the larger profits of their Southern brethren and blamed the Democratic policies that had created the inequity.

The Democratic coalition of 1916 was hurt by other issues as well. Southern votes were crucial in overriding Wilson's veto of an act of 1917 establishing a literacy test for immigrants. The urban laboring force found the Southerners' support of Prohibition even more exasperating. Advocates of the prohibition of the manufacture and consumption of alcoholic beverages achieved their goal during the war. First, a section of the Lever Act limited the production of whiskey, and a section of the Selective Service Act limited its sale near army camps. Later, in December 1917, Congress adopted the Eighteenth Amendment—the Prohibition Amendment—and submitted it to the states for ratification (completed in January 1919).

Prohibition offended many Irish-, German-, and Scandinavian-Americans who were also dubious about Wilson's foreign policies. While most of them did not openly oppose the war, they questioned the virtue of the Allied nations and they resented the domestic pressures for conformity that sometimes seemed to denigrate their native lands.

For their part, Northern liberals, disturbed by the Administration's threats to civil liberties, were also irritated by Southern resistance to the woman-suffrage amendment, which senators from Dixie blocked to Wilson's disappointment. As he had learned from the suffragists, democratic principles included the right of women to vote. But only in January 1919 did Congress remove the injustice of limiting suffrage on the basis of sex. (Ratification followed in August 1920.)

As the coalition of interests that had elected Wilson in 1916 fell apart, the Republicans effected a powerful reorganization of their party under the direction of their aggressive national chairman, Will Hays. They approached the elections of 1918 (see p. 569) with more confidence than they had had in a decade, and their campaign threatened not only Democratic control of Congress but the program for a liberal peace on which Wilson pinned his most fervent hopes.

Constructing the peace

A liberal program. During the war, sentiment for a liberal peace developed on both sides of the Atlantic, especially in England and the United States. The plans of various humanitarian groups differed in detail, but they usually advocated four common principles: the substitution of an international comity for the alliance system, the substitution of arbitration for armaments, the institution of self-government among all peoples, and the avoidance of seizures of territories and of demands for reparations.

Wilson embraced these objectives. In 1916 he publicly advocated the idea of a league of nations. In 1917 he began to meditate seriously on the components of a generous peace—a peace without victory. Soon after the United States declared war, he assigned the task of preparing detailed peace plans to Colonel House and a staff of experts. While they were at work, the President in a series of addresses spelled out his own goals, which reflected the principles that had previously characterized his New Freedom and his neutrality policies.

It was necessary, Wilson believed, to remove the military party, including the Kaiser, from authority in Germany, to divest Germany of power over other peoples, to establish democratic self-government in Germany and among each of the national groups rescued from its domination or the domination of its allies. It was necessary then to bring all nations into a world parliament whose collective democratic judgment would guard the peace. "Peace," he said, "should rest upon the rights of peoples, not the rights of governments—the rights of peoples great or small . . . to freedom and security and self-government and to . . . economic opportunities."

This grand vision underestimated the role of power in world affairs and the selfishness of nations torn by war. Even so, Wilson might have won commitments from the Allies to a liberal peace if he had tried. He did not. By his own choice the United States had fought not as one of the Allies but as an "associated" belligerent, with the others but not of them. This was the Administration's way of paying tribute to the questionable tradition of avoiding "entangling alliances." Wilson chose, too, to avoid facing squarely the punitive intentions of the Allies, intentions that they had recorded in secret treaties. He simply ignored the existence of those treaties, with their clauses providing for the division of German, Austrian, and Turkish territories and for the exaction of huge indemnities. In so doing he surrendered the opportunity to insist that America would help the Allies only if they agreed to give up those plans.

The course of revolution in Russia focused the attention of the world on the problems of peace. After taking over the government in November 1917, the Bolsheviks began to arrange a separate and humiliating surrender to Germany. They also set out, in the midst of ruthless civil war, to solidify their hold at home and to advance the communist revolution elsewhere. In order to embarrass the Allies, they disclosed the terms of the secret treaties they found in the czar's archives. Both David Lloyd George, the British prime minister, and Wilson countered by reasserting their dedication to a just peace.

In January 1918, while the war was still raging, Wilson announced his celebrated Fourteen Points. They expressed his belief in the inextricable interconnections among free trade, democratic institutions, and human liberty. Five were broad: open diplomacy, by which he meant an end to secret agreements; free use of the seas in peace and war; the reduction of armaments; the removal of barriers to free trade; and an impartial adjustment of colonial claims. Eight points pertained to the principle of national self-determination: German evacuation of Russian territory; the restoration of Belgian independence; the return to France of Alsace-Lorraine (which Germany had conquered in 1870); the establishment of an independent Poland; and the autonomous development of each of the peoples of Austria-Hungary and European Turkey. The fourteenth and crowning point called for forming "a general assembly of nations" to afford "mutual guarantees of political independence and territorial integrity."

Those objectives conflicted not only with the ambitions of the Allies but with the attitudes of many Americans. Though there was much enthusiasm for the President's ideals, there was also opposition from those who wanted protective tariffs, from those who resisted internationalism of any kind, and particularly from those whose war-born hatreds demanded revenge, a march on Berlin, and gallows for the Kaiser.

The armistice and the election of 1918. The President was by no means soft. In October 1918, as the Allies drove through the German lines, the German high command urged the chancellor to propose an armistice to Wilson on the basis of the Fourteen Points. During the ensuing exchange of notes, Wilson took a position charitable enough to lead the Germans on, but firm enough to make them admit defeat. This satisfied all the Allied chiefs of state and military commanders except Pershing, who urged unconditional surrender. The British and French, exhausted by four years of war and frightened by the westward surge of Bolshevism, were eager for an armistice so long as it gave them security.

569

Aware of those views, Wilson demanded withdrawal of German forces from all invaded territory and immediate cessation of aerial and submarine warfare. When the Germans acceded to these conditions, which were designed to make renewed hostilities impossible, Wilson on October 23 opened negotiations with the Allies and suggested to the Germans that reasonable terms would depend on their establishing a democratic government. This suggestion precipitated the overthrow of the Kaiser, who abdicated on November 9.

The Allied leaders chafed at the Fourteen Points; the British explicitly rejected the point on the freedom of the seas, and the French demanded reparations for civilian damages. They would have insisted on further changes had Colonel House not threatened to make a separate peace if they did not assent to the rest of the Fourteen Points, which were to be the basis for an armistice. The Americans for their part ultimately agreed to add terms forcing the Germans to withdraw well beyond the east bank of the Rhine and to surrender vast quantities of war materials, including their submarines.

Those were tough conditions. But even so the Republicans attacked the President's foreign policy, insisting, as Roosevelt put it, on dictating peace to the hammer of guns instead of to the clicking of typewriters. This demagoguery frightened many Democratic leaders who, with a congressional election coming on, were tempted to seek votes by flag-waving. But Wilson refused to let politics interfere with his carefully devised program. He yielded, however, to his advisers' demand for a blanket endorsement of all Democratic candidates. Angry himself at the onslaughts of men like Roosevelt, Wilson on October 25 urged the people to vote Democratic if they approved of his policies at home and abroad. The return of a Republican majority, he said, would be a repudiation of his leadership.

This appeal made Wilson's foreign policy more than ever a partisan issue. It infuriated the Republicans, and though it helped some Democratic candidates it did not prevent the Republicans from gaining control of both houses of Congress. Republican leaders later claimed that it was foreign policy that had determined the outcome. On November 11, 1918, only a few days after the election, men of all parties rejoiced at the news that an armistice had been arranged. Now, as Wilson turned to negotiating the terms for peace, he had to reckon with a Republican majority in the Senate, where partisanship could delay or even prevent approval of any treaty he submitted.

Negotiating peace

The background of the Paris conference. Wilson failed to appoint any influential Republican to the American delegation preparing to leave for the peace conference at Paris. To advance his liberal program he chose to head the delegation himself, thus becoming the first President to go overseas on a diplomatic mission. Though his critics complained that he would slight his duties at home, his able performance at Paris justified his decision. Wilson named to the delegation Secretary of State Lansing and Colonel House, in his view obvious choices, and two others: General Tasker H. Bliss, a military expert, and Henry White, a career diplomat, ostensibly a Republican but in no sense a politician or a representative of the Senate. The delegation was to be Wilson's instrument, under his dom-

Dover, England: crowds greeted Wilson as a savior

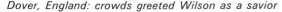

ination, but any advantage this control gave him during negotiations was overshadowed by the disadvantages inherent in slighting the Republicans.

Wilson also slighted public opinion. He had little talent for dealing with journalists, many of whom distrusted his official press representative, George Creel. Moreover, at the peace conference he had to yield to the other negotiators' insistence on secret sessions. The American press interpreted this decision as a violation of the principle of open diplomacy, even though there was no secret about the decisions reached at the conference. If Wilson's press relations had been better, American newspapers could have helped explain the President's difficulties to a public that did not fully understand the necessity for give-and-take.

Wilson had to bargain endlessly with the Allies, for their objectives often conflicted with his. He felt strongly that the Fourteen Points should be accepted as guides for the peace settlement. He did not expect a perfect peace, but he thought that a league of nations could continually improve the terms of a peace treaty, and he counted on enlisting the moral force of the world behind the league. His optimism grew during his tour of Europe before the conference opened. Crowds greeted him as a savior, and he mistook their gratitude for victory as an endorsement of his goals.

Actually, the peoples of Europe and Asia, with unimportant exceptions, supported the demands of their own spokesmen. Four of these men were, with Wilson, the major architects of the peace. There was the self-controlled and resourceful Count Nobuaki Makino of Japan, ambitious for territory, as was the cultured and adroit Vittorio Orlando of Italy; there was the perspicacious but shifty British prime minister, David Lloyd George, who had promised his electorate vast reparations; there was the French premier, Georges Clemenceau, cynical, tenacious, weary, aloof, determined to crush Germany forever. These men were bound by treaties to support one another's claims. Their armies, moreover, actually held most of the lands they planned to annex or assign.

Over large parts of the world neither they nor Wilson could exercise much influence. The Bolshevik Revolution had made Russia unwelcome at the conference, and she stood apart brooding, dissatisfied, potentially a mighty and ominous force. There was, furthermore, continuing war within her borders while the peace conference sat. British troops in the northern part of European Russia were trying to assist anti-Bolsheviks there, and in Siberia a Japanese army was pushing west with an eye to conquest. In order to keep watch on them the United States also sent troops to Siberia. The Bolsheviks, resenting the presence of foreigners, believed the Japanese and the Americans were agents of counterrevolution, as some authorities

in Washington, London, and Tokyo intended them to be.

Revolution and counterrevolution infected all of Russia's European neighbors. The empire of Austria-Hungary had simply ceased to exist. In the territories it once had ruled, the quarrels of self-conscious ethnic groups, complicated by the conniving of communists, were forging the new states that were to mark the map of central and eastern Europe whether the men at Paris willed it or not. Within Germany the new republican government faced revolution at the borders, Red plots within, and a populace exasperated by a food shortage imposed by the continuing Allied blockade. With the world in turmoil and Europe exhausted by war, the Paris conference had an unpropitious setting. With the Allies opposed to a liberal peace, moreover, the odds against Wilson's program were enormous.

The League of Nations. Wilson's plans for a charter for a league of nations included the disposition of former German colonies. In order to bring about an impartial and equitable settlement of colonial claims, as the Fourteen Points promised, Wilson hoped to put the German colonies under the guardianship of small neutrals like Switzerland and Sweden. These neutrals were to be trustees for the league and were to help the backward colonial peoples to move toward independence.

The British and Japanese, however, would not surrender the territory in Africa and the Pacific that they had seized during hostilities. According to a secret treaty between them, German islands in the Pacific north of the equator were to go to Japan and islands south of the equator were to go to Australia and New Zealand. Wilson prevented the outright transfer of colonies by persuading the Allies to accept instead a system of "mandates," which obliged their holders to render annual accountings and theoretically to help subject peoples to stand alone. The compromise gave the Allies a pocketful of territory, but it also subjected them to some surveillance in their administration of that territory. Though the mandate system was imperfect, Wilson felt that the league would gradually better it (though the League never did so).

The concepts of a league met opposition from the French, who wanted a military alliance of the victors against Germany. Japan further complicated Wilson's negotiations by demanding a statement of racial equality pledging member nations of a league not to discriminate against the nationals of other members. But the President had help from the Italians, who were pleased by his endorsement of the northern boundary they wanted, and from the British, who shared his hopes for the league. The racial pride of the

Never forget that this league is primarily—I might say overwhelmingly—a political organization, and I object strongly to having the politics of the United States turn upon disputes where deep feeling is aroused but in which we have no direct interest. It will tend to delay the Americanization of our great population, and it is more important not only to the United States but to the peace of the world to make all these people good Americans than it is to determine that some piece of territory should belong to one European country rather than to another. For this reason I wish to limit strictly our interference in the affairs of Europe and of Africa. We have interests of our own in Asia and in the Pacific which we must guard upon our own account, but the less we undertake to play the part of umpire and thrust ourselves into European conflicts the better for the United States and for the world.

Henry Cabot Lodge, Speech in the Senate, August 1919.

Japanese was assuaged by their new mandates, and the French accepted the idea of a league after they realized that they could obtain their objectives elsewhere in the treaty. Wilson in return let the French and British dodge the question of self-disarmament. In the end his draft served as the basis for the Covenant of the League of Nations, which the responsible committee approved and reported to the peace conference in February 1919.

It was a simple document. Each signer of the treaty was to have one vote in a Body of Delegates of the League. Larger authority rested with the Executive Council, which was to consist of representatives from the United States, the British Empire, France, Italy, Japan, and four states selected by the Body of Delegates. Decisions of the council required a unanimous vote except when a council member was itself a party to a dispute. The covenant also established a permanent secretariat, an international Bureau of Labor, and the mandate system. It provided for the admission of new members by a two-thirds vote of the delegates and for amendment by a three-fourths vote.

The main purpose of the League was to keep the peace. To that end the covenant obliged signatories, before they resorted to war, to submit disputes either to inquiry by the council or to arbitration by the Permanent Court of International Justice which the council was to create. Member nations were to punish any breach of this article by severing economic relations with the offending state. The council, moreover, might recommend that members of the League contribute military and naval units to protect its principles. And the council was to advise on means of ensuring that member nations lived up to Article 10, which Wilson considered the heart of the covenant. This article bound signatories "to respect and preserve against external aggression the territorial integrity and

. . . political independence of all members of the League."

The League was not a superstate. It could only recommend, but not compel, the recruitment and use of military force. Its deliberations would not bind Germany or Russia until the victorious powers invited them to join. Those powers had sufficient authority, moreover, to use the League to try to perpetuate the status quo. But the covenant did create the first promising international organization in modern history. It also fulfilled Wilson's purpose of recognizing war and the threat of war as everybody's business and of providing a forum for the nations of the world to discuss problems that might lead to conflict. In his view, the covenant organized the moral force of the world.

Consequently the President was distressed by the opposition to the League that he confronted during a brief trip home. The essence of that opposition was Republican partisanship, but it fed on other attitudes as well. Many German-Americans still resented the war and its outcome. Many Irish-Americans believed Wilson should have insisted on Irish independence. The President pointed out that that was a question for England to resolve, but he was pointedly cool toward his Irish critics. He was even less patient with those Americans who hesitated to depart from what to them was a national tradition of isolation from Europe. They thought of the past as having been sterilized from the Old World, and they viewed the covenant as an "entangling alliance." These and other sentiments bred susceptibility to the propaganda of Wilson's opponents.

On March 4, 1919, the day before the President returned to Paris, Senator Henry Cabot Lodge produced a round robin signed by thirty-seven Republican senators, four more than were needed to defeat

Need for the League

the treaty. It stated that the covenant was unacceptable and insisted that consideration of the League be deferred until after a treaty had been completed. In a speech that night, Wilson condemned the "careful selfishness" of his critics and their "ignorance of the state of the world." The covenant would be intimately tied to the treaty itself, he said. That interrelationship was essential for working out the problems of the conference, and the President was understandably annoyed. But his strong language intensified the partisanship that provoked it.

The Treaty of Versailles. Though Wilson would not separate the League from the treaty, he realized that the covenant would have to be modified to meet the suggestions of American moderates. The revisions the President sponsored on his return to Paris would certainly have been demanded by the Senate in any event. They defined procedures for withdrawal from the League, stated that the acceptance of mandates was optional, and excluded from the purview of the League domestic issues such as immigration and regional agreements such as the Monroe Doctrine. By reopening the question of the covenant, however, Wilson exposed himself to the bargaining of his associates, who once more pressed their demands for Europe and Asia. The President secured his revisions, but only at an inflated price.

Clemenceau, still determined to assure French security, insisted that Germany be dismembered. He urged that two new states, Poland and Czechoslovakia, be set up on Germany's eastern border. Both states would absorb some German land and population. He also asked for the creation of a Rhenish buffer state, to be splintered off from Germany's west, and for the cession to France of the Saar Basin, a

bountiful source of coal and iron, as well as of Alsace-Lorraine. Wilson balked at these extreme demands and argued that the League itself would protect France from German aggression. Clemenceau scoffed and called the President pro-German. For ten days the conference stalled, but when Wilson threatened to leave, Clemenceau bowed to the proponents of compromise.

The treaty drew generous boundaries for Poland and Czechoslovakia, but it also arranged for the League to conduct a plebiscite to determine the disposition of a part of Silesia coveted by both Germans and Poles. The treaty gave Poland access to the sea through a narrow corridor that put some Germans under Polish rule. France received Alsace-Lorraine and temporary economic concessions in the Saar, but the League was to administer the Saar and after fifteen years was to conduct a plebiscite there. France could also occupy the Rhineland for fifteen years; after that time the area was to be demilitarized but left a part of Germany. The German army was limited to a token force.

Furthermore, Wilson and Lloyd George agreed to a special security treaty pledging their nations to assist France if it were attacked. Clemenceau realized, even if Wilson did not, that the United States Senate would reject the special treaty, but in that case the Rhineland could be occupied indefinitely. All in all, Clemenceau obtained as much safety for France as any treaty cowld reasonably provide.

The French and the English also pushed Wilson into accepting their demands for reparations far in excess of what Germany could pay and in violation of the prearmistice agreement to limit payments to the cost of civilian damages. The President let the Allies include the cost of pensions, which later permitted

- - -	1914 boundaries
▨	New nations
▦	Plebiscite areas
▓	Occupied area

FINLAND

NORWAY

SWEDEN

ESTONIA

LATVIA

DENMARK

LITHUANIA

RUSSIA

IRELAND

Danzig

GER.

GREAT
BRITAIN

Berlin •

POLAND

London •

NETH.

GERMANY

Silesia

BELG.

Rhineland

CZECHOSLOVAKIA

LUX.

Saar

Vienna •

Paris •

Alsace-
Lorraine

AUSTRIA

HUNGARY

RUMANIA

SWITZ.

FRANCE

• Fiume

YUGOSLAVIA

BULGARIA

ITALY

ALBANIA

TURKEY

PORTUGAL

SPAIN

GREECE

Europe in 1920

the reparations commission to calculate that the Germans owed some $120 billion, the fantastic figure that had been the British objective. The reparations clause of the treaty, moreover, specifically attributed the cause of war to "the aggression of Germany," a phrase that rankled in German minds for years to come, however accurate it may have been. Along with the economic dislocations that grew out of the exorbitant reparations imposed on Germany, the war-guilt clause proved to be an emotional threat to future peace.

At the time, however, the President's troubles with Italy seemed more ominous. Before the conference Wilson had agreed to a northern frontier for Italy at the line of the Brenner Pass, which put two hundred thousand Austrians under Italian rule. This left him with nothing else to trade when the Italians also insisted on taking Fiume, an Adriatic port surrounded by Yugoslav land. When the Italians discovered that all the powers were antagonistic to their claim to Fiume, they boldly marched into the city. Wilson appealed to the Italian people in the name of justice, but they, with their leaders, resented the President's miscalculated intrusion. The Italians left Paris in a rage, and, though they returned to sign a treaty that did not give them Fiume, the incident alienated Italian-Americans from Wilson's treaty and almost disrupted the conference.

The Japanese seized on the confusion to advance their own claims. They were seeking endorsement for their economic ambitions in China and for their assumption of the German leasehold at Kiaochow and of German economic privileges in the Shantung Peninsula. The Chinese, of course, opposed the whole program, which Japan's secret treaties with France and England condoned. Furthermore, late in 1917 Secretary of State Lansing had reached an understanding with Viscount Kikujiro Ishii by which Japan affirmed its support of the Open Door and of China's territorial integrity; but in return the United States recognized Japan's special interest in Chinese provinces adjoining Japanese possessions. Since Shantung was just such a province, Wilson found it hard to oppose the Japanese demands, especially after the whole conference seemed about to disintegrate. He accepted a compromise that by and large restricted the Japanese to former German holdings, less Kiaochow, which Japan promised to surrender. Though many Americans, including two of the delegates, thought the President conceded too much, he felt he had obtained a solution "as satisfactory as could be got out of the tangle."

The same could be said of the whole treaty that the victors and the vanquished signed at Versailles in 1919. It was punitive, but Germany had lost the war it had expected to win, and the Allies were much less severe than the Germans would have been. The treaty followed the Fourteen Points as closely as world conditions permitted. Europe had a new map that approximated ethnic groupings as closely as possible.

The major architects of the peace:
Clemenceau, Wilson, Lloyd George, Orlando

This, to be sure, involved some compromises of the principle of self-determination and created some boundaries that conflicted with the military defense and the economic needs of the new states. But these difficulties and others could be negotiated later in the forum of the League. As Wilson had predicted, the League was inextricably part of the treaty, a "convenient, indeed indispensable" instrument. He had yet, however, to bring two-thirds of the Senate over to his way of thinking.

The struggle over ratification

The Senate and the treaty. Wilson brought the treaty home to a people initially predisposed in its favor. Though few Americans were familiar with the whole long document, most had learned something about the League, and millions were enthusiastic about it. But the people could not vote on the treaty. The question of its approval, and therefore the portentous question of what direction American foreign policy would take, were for the Senate to decide.

Of the ninety-six senators forty-nine were Republican, but only fourteen were irreconcilably against the League and the treaty. Those irreconcilables, many of them progressives, believed that the mission of the United States was to create a model society for other nations to emulate, not to get involved in international affairs. Indeed they shared the distrust of foreigners so common among the American people. The other thirty-five Republicans intended not to reject the treaty but to make its adoption contingent on a number of reservations, of which the most significant had to do with Wilson's League of Nations. Twenty-three Republicans favored a list of

strong reservations drafted and sponsored by Senator Lodge; twelve were willing to settle for milder reservations. Since only four of the forty-seven Democrats opposed the treaty, a coalition of Democrats and moderate Republicans would have commanded a majority vote. And a majority was all that was needed to settle the kind of reservations that would be demanded. Such a coalition, moreover, could probably have attracted the necessary two-thirds vote for approval. But the crucial coalition was never formed.

The Democratic leaders knew they had to make concessions to their opponents, but they felt that they also had to wait for instructions from the President. They never received those instructions, for Wilson refused to compromise an issue he considered both personal and moral.

It was Lodge who had made the issue personal. Lodge had endorsed the round robin and the strategy of insisting on reservations; Lodge had packed the important Foreign Relations Committee with irreconcilables and strong reservationists. Lodge, the majority leader of the Senate, was determined to hold his party together and to win in 1920. Further, he honestly believed that the League as Wilson had planned it was a threat to national sovereignty. Lodge was not an isolationist, but he put his faith in armies and navies and the balance of power, the "large view" of his old friend Theodore Roosevelt, who had just died. A ruthless, often exasperating man, Lodge was also moved by mean considerations, including the prejudices of his many Italian- and Irish-American constituents. He was a formidable antagonist who hated Wilson as Wilson hated him.

Lodge's reservations struck the President as unnecessary and immoral. Wilson objected to the very idea of making the approval of the treaty subject to reservations. He also held that reservations would mean that the treaty would have to be renegotiated, though the British, the French, and the State Department did not think so. Two of the reservations would have made Congress the sole judge of whether the United States should accept a mandate and whether it should withdraw from the League. Two others reserved to the United States exclusive authority over tariff policy, immigration, and the Monroe Doctrine. As Wilson argued, the revised covenant already covered those issues. Another reservation exempted the United States from any decision of the League on which any member and its self-governing dominions had cast in the aggregate more than one vote. The American veto in the council, Wilson noted, made superfluous such an ungracious protest against the seats of the British dominions in the Body of Delegates. The President especially opposed the reservation on Article 10, which stated that the United States would assume no obligation to preserve the territorial integrity or political independence of any other country without the approval of Congress. To Wilson this would be a violation of the essential spirit of the League—the moral obligation to protect the peace of the world.

In the abstract Wilson may have been right, but the politics of the Senate made compromise necessary. Even if Lodge's reservations did make the United States seem timid and selfish, they would have damaged the League far less than would outright rejection of treaty and League alike. Senator Gilbert Hitchcock, the Democratic minority leader, advised Wilson to work out some sort of compromise with Lodge, as did Colonel House, Robert Lansing, Bernard Baruch, and many other friends of the President.

But Wilson would not listen, and his personal efforts to persuade individual Republicans to adopt his point of view were futile. Moreover, as the days passed, the public tended to become bored with the whole question and amenable to Lodge's purpose. Wilson had advocated a degree of national involvement in foreign affairs greater, in all probability, than most Americans, after reflection, were willing to accept. The idealism of wartime was fading into the problems of the postwar period. Inflation, unemployment, and fears of Bolshevism reduced public enthusiasm for a generous peace and for a genuine internationalism.

The President's collapse. In order to arouse new enthusiasm for the League, Wilson set out in September 1919 on a speaking tour across the country. He hoped to stir up a passion for his program that the Republican senators would not be able to withstand. His train moved through the strongholds of isolationism, over eight thousand miles, stopping thirty-seven times for him to address the voters. As he proceeded through the Middle West to the Pacific Coast, then south, and then east, he was greeted by larger and larger crowds. But their applause did not change one vote in the Senate. Indeed Wilson's attacks on his opponents stiffened their resolution to resist, and his absence from Washington impeded Democratic efforts to find a basis for compromise. The President was superbly eloquent, but his strenuous efforts taxed his limited strength without achieving his political purpose.

On September 25 Wilson spoke at Pueblo, Colorado. That night his head hurt mercilessly. Frightened by the President's exhaustion, his physician canceled the remainder of the trip. Back in Washington Wilson was too tired to work, too tense to rest. On October 2 he fell to the floor unconscious, the victim of a cerebral thrombosis, a blood clot in his brain.

The stroke did not kill the President, but it paralyzed his left side, thickened his speech, totally disabled him for almost two months, and prevented him thereafter from working more than an hour or two at a time. For six months he did not meet with the Cabinet. For six weeks he could not execute the minimum duties of his office. Though his mind was not injured he became petulant, suspicious, and easily moved to tears. He was unable to assess men or situations with accuracy. His collapse was a tragedy not only for himself but for a nation facing a momentous crisis in foreign plicy.

On November 6, while Wilson was still bedridden, Lodge presented his reservations to the Senate. It was obvious that the Republicans had the votes to adopt them but not the two-thirds needed to approve the treaty after the reservations had been attached. The Democratic leaders hesitated to move without the President's consent, and he gave stringent orders on November 18 that they were to reject the treaty so long as it was shackled by the Lodge reservations. They were then to move that the treaty be accepted either as it stood or with mild interpretive reservations of which Wilson approved. This order conceded nothing to the Republican moderates, who stood behind Lodge. Though nonpartisan friends of the League preferred accepting Lodge's reservations to rejecting the whole treaty, the Democrats on November 19 voted to reject the treaty with those reservations. Consequently the resolution to adopt the treaty as Lodge had modified it failed by thirty-nine to fifty-five. Lodge blocked debate of the interpretive reservations that the Democrats then proposed, and minutes later a resolution to approve the unamended treaty also failed, thirty-eight to fifty-three.

The final rejection. But the treaty was still not dead. The moderate Republicans and the Democrats were stunned by what they had done and felt they had to try again. Furthermore, organizations representing some 20 million Americans petitioned for compromise and ratification. The same hope was voiced by the British and French press and by the British government. Influential Democrats without exception tried to persuade the President to relieve his party of the hopeless battle to defeat the Lodge reservations.

But Wilson, the victim of fantasies produced by ill health, would still not hear of concessions. Instead, on January 8, 1920, he wrote a blistering letter to his fellow Democrats. The majority of the people wanted ratification, he said. Let the Senate accept the treaty without tampering with it or else reject it. If there was any doubt about public opinion, Wilson warned, the issue could be resolved at the next election, which would be "a great and solemn referendum."

This was the counsel of a deluded man, for presidential elections turn on many issues, not just one.

The Democratic party had been losing strength for three years, and the treaty, if the Senate rejected it again, would be impossible to resuscitate. Recognizing the folly of Wilson's position, Senator Hitchcock and other Democrats tried to work out a satisfactory compromise on the reservations. They failed, partly because the Republican irreconcilables warned Lodge against compromise, partly because Lodge himself probably did not want to rescue the treaty. The President, increasingly peevish, on March 8 again instructed the Democrats to hold the line.

His adherents prevailed. The Lodge reservations, only slightly modified, were adopted, this time with some Democratic help. On March 19, the day of the final test, half the Democrats voted to approve the treaty with the reservations. But twenty-three Democrats, twenty of them Southerners, did the President's bidding. Together with twelve irreconcilables, they voted against approval and thus prevented by a margin of seven the two-thirds majority needed for adoption.

There was to be no "solemn referendum." The Democratic presidential nominee in 1920, James M. Cox, supported the League, but sometimes with hesitation. The Republican plank on the treaty was deliberately vague, as was the Republican candidate, Warren G. Harding. Though Harding enjoyed the full support of both Republican isolationists and Republican internationalists, he chose to consider his smashing victory a repudiation of the treaty.

The Senate had made the telling decision. In rejecting both treaty and League, the Senate had for the while turned America's back to Europe. The rejection destroyed the best available chance for developing world peace. Perhaps the irreconcilables, the forceful spokesmen of isolation, could have defeated the treaty in any event, but it was not they who did so, though they helped. Wilson's stubbornness and Lodge's partisanship helped even more. Indeed partisanship was the real culprit, and the outcome of the fight revealed how severely domestic politics could damage foreign policy.

The damage, in the end, affected the whole world, for without the United States the League became an instrument for preserving the status quo. Even if the United States had been a member, the League would probably have acted just about the way it did. But as it was, the League never had a chance to fulfill Wilson's vision. That vision, which rested on the moral intent of the President's peace program, was the most compelling image democracy then offered to the world. With the defeat of the treaty, the United States seemed to have renounced its claims to the imagination of people everywhere. The renunciation came just at the time when Bolshevism was advancing its revolutionary claims more effectively than ever

before. The American retreat eased the way for both the advocates of reaction and the advocates of communism. It cost the United States the only available fruits of a gallant victory. It made a travesty of the noble effort to create a world safe for the ideals Wilson cherished.

Transition from war

Demobilization. When the war ended, the government had no plans for demobilization. It simply lifted the controls it had imposed on the economy during the war. In accord with public sentiment, it hastened the discharge of the soldiers, many of whom were unable to find jobs when they returned to civilian life. Though unemployment declined after February 1919, it persisted in troubled areas for another half-year, and it soured thousands of veterans who had expected a hero's welcome to include a job.

Immediately after the armistice the War Industries Board began to close up shop, confident that private industry would be able to switch back to a peacetime economy with no help or direction from the federal government. That was a miscalculation. While industry bid for new plants and machinery, consumers dug out their wartime savings to make the purchases they had long postponed. Inflation struck the country. During 1919 the cost of living climbed to 77 percent above prewar levels; during 1920, another 28 percent.

The government developed only piecemeal and inadequate remedies for unemployment and inflation. There was as yet no body of economic ideas to explain the need for overall federal policies that would ease the process of reconversion. Wilson, moreover, was preoccupied with peacemaking and hampered by an opposition Congress. Yet the Revenue Act of 1919 carried on the policy of progressive taxation, ensured the government the income it needed, and helped check inflation.

Both Congress and the public were anxious to settle the question of what should be done with the railroads, which the government was still running. Private management wanted them back, but labor had found that public administration was more generous and more efficient. An attorney for the railway brotherhoods, Glenn E. Plumb, proposed a plan for nationalizing the roads. The AFL supported the Plumb plan, but elsewhere it evoked little enthusiasm. Congress, in the Transportation Act of 1920, extended the tradition of mixed capitalism by turning the railroads back to their private owners while subjecting them to increased but deliberately benign supervision. In a similar spirit, the Water Power Act of 1920 set up a Federal Power Commission, consisting of the Secretaries of War, Agriculture, and the Interior, to license the building and operation of dams and hydroelectric plants. This clumsy arrangement by its very failure drew attention to the need for genuine public control.

Labor strife. In the years right after the war, the once-progressive fervor of Americans seemed to have spent itself. The nation's policy-makers, like the American people, turned more and more to the past. The Administration, which had sympathized with organized labor, now began to favor management. That reversal was prompted by several forces: Wilson's advisers were growing impatient with the strikes that continued to cripple the nation's industries, and management had launched a successful campaign to associate all unions with radicalism, about which the country at large was harboring hysterical fears.

The enforced wartime truce between labor and management ended in 1919. The unions then set out to consolidate their gains and to bring wages into line with the rising cost of living. And the National Association of Manufacturers and other management groups set out to reestablish the open shop, which they liked to call "the American way." Management propaganda extolled the beneficence of business and warned that unions and union demands were inspired by foreign and radical influences. Nevertheless, many of the first strikes after the war were successful, notably those of clothing, textile, telegraph, and telephone workers.

The most celebrated postwar strikes occurred in Seattle and Boston. In February 1919 the Seattle Central Labor Council called a general strike to support shipyard workers who had walked out in quest of higher pay and shorter hours. Those workers and others in Seattle, something of a wartime boom town, were also worried about postwar unemployment. Some of the local labor leaders were unquestionably radical, and a general strike was itself a radical technique, perhaps especially in the view of the residents of a city where the IWW had been active. But Mayor Ole Hanson grossly exaggerated the Red menace and used troops to stamp out the strike.

In Boston the police found that they could not stretch their prewar wages to cover postwar living costs. Denied a raise and restive because of other grievances, they secured a charter from the AFL and threatened a strike in August 1919. The mayor appointed a citizens' committee, which suggested that most of the policemen's demands, except recognition of their union, be granted. The police commissioner, however, a declared enemy of organized labor, rejected the suggestion and fired nineteen of the union's leaders. On September 9 the policemen went out on strike. Volunteer vigilantes were unable to control the gangs of looters who brought Boston to the point of anarchy. The American middle class was shocked and scared. But just then the governor of Massachusetts, Calvin Coolidge, called out the national guard to restore order. The strike failed, and many of the police were dismissed.

The whole episode was as unnecessary as it was lamentable. Coolidge could have supported the mayor and overruled the police commissioner before the strike began. Instead, he won a national reputation by putting down the strike. The American people knew little about the facts of the case, but they long remembered the governor's characteristic response to Gompers' request that the policemen be reinstated: "There is no right to strike against the public safety by anybody, anywhere, any time."

The AFL faced its crucial test in the steel industry. The secretary of its organizing committee, William Z. Foster, had been radical enough in his beliefs for management to persuade the public that he was a Red. He was also less than an effective organizer. Still, the steelworkers had grave grievances. Most of them put in a twelve-hour workday in return for subsistence wages. After attracting a substantial minority of workers, the union called a strike in September 1919, after management had rejected its demands for recognition, an eight-hour day, and decent pay. Episodes of violence punctuated the strike. Public opinion, misled by the steel companies' propaganda, condoned the widespread use of state and federal troops to prevent picketing. United States Steel alone used thousands of strikebreakers. In January 1920 the union gave up, thoroughly beaten.

Meanwhile, in November 1919, the bituminous-coal miners had walked out under the leadership of their new and colorful president, John L. Lewis, who was radical only in his pugnacious manner. A wartime agreement had governed wages in the mines, but the union claimed that the armistice had made that agreement inapplicable. As Lewis observed, there was no ceiling on the rising price of coal. The miners demanded a 60 percent wage increase, a six-hour day, and a five-day week. When the operators refused to negotiate, the miners prepared to strike. With Wilson's approval, Attorney General A. Mitchell Palmer ruled that the wage agreement was still in effect and obtained an injunction against the union. Lewis then called off the strike because, as he put it, "we cannot fight the government." Still the miners refused to go back to work until the government ordered an immediate 14 percent increase in pay and set up an arbitral commission, which ultimately awarded another 27 percent. The miners' other demands were denied.

Race hatred. Old prejudices, whetted by new fears, had also provoked a wave of persecution and violence that engulfed American blacks. In response to wartime labor shortages, several hundred thousand blacks had moved from the South to Northern industrial centers. Segregated there in urban slums, they were the continuing objects of the race hatred of their white neighbors, especially of unskilled workers who viewed blacks as competitors for their jobs. More and more blacks, for their part, educated by the experience of military service, by the war's avowedly democratic aims, and by the inequities they met in the North, began to demand rights long denied them, particularly higher wages, equal protection under the law, and the chance to vote and hold political office. Those were key goals of the increasingly militant National Association for the Advancement of Colored People and of its foremost leader, W. E. B. DuBois. Yet white supremacists were determined "to keep the Negro in his place," by force if necessary, and many of them applauded irresponsible statements of men like Congressman James F. Byrnes of South Carolina, who warned that the Reds were inciting a black uprising in the South.

Turning to terrorism, lynch mobs in the South made victims of more than seventy blacks in 1919, ten of them veterans in uniform. The new Ku Klux Klan (see p. 596), committed to the intimidation of blacks, gained some one hundred thousand members. In 1919 South and North alike saw the worst spate of race riots in American history to that time. Two of the most tragic occurred in Washington, D.C., where a majority of the offenders were white veterans, and in Chicago, where for thirteen days a mob of whites fought blacks in the black slums. Before the year ended, twenty-five race riots had resulted in hundreds of deaths and injuries and millions of dollars of property damage.

Most blacks resisted their attackers, as the NAACP advised them to, and liberal whites organized to fight intolerance and to lobby for antilynching

Race riot, Chicago, 1919

Marcus Garvey: black nationalist

laws, but by and large blacks were neither hopeful of remedy nor yet ready to campaign in their own behalf. Instead, by 1923 about half a million blacks had joined the Universal Negro Improvement Association of Marcus Garvey, a Jamaican black nationalist who proposed to create a new empire in Africa with himself on the throne. That scheme collapsed, but its transient appeal to American blacks rested on the need they felt for self-identity, racial pride, and an escape from a society that denied them dignity, opportunity, and even personal safety.

The Red scare. American radicals also felt the sting of old prejudices and new fears. There was, to be sure, genuine cause for concern over the spread of Bolshevism in Europe. In March 1919 Soviet leaders organized the Third International as an agency for world revolution, and during the rest of that year the communists made striking gains in Germany, Hungary, and along Russia's frontiers. The International fed on the postwar disintegration of eastern Europe—a disintegration the United States did little to check.

Within the United States, however, communism was feeble. In 1919 the Socialist party, its ranks depleted and its morale low, broke into three factions. Some forty thousand moderates retained the old name. One left-wing faction of about twenty thousand, almost all of them immigrants, formed the Communist Labor party. Another militant group of between thirty thousand and sixty thousand, also largely immigrant, joined the Communist party of America under native-born leaders. But the three groups together constituted less than half of 1 percent of the population.

During the war public and private propaganda had generated hatred and fear of the Germans, and Americans had already begun to fight the shadows of

Transition from war

their anxieties. In the postwar months they transferred much of this hate to the nation's immigrants, whom the suspicious middle class had long stereotyped as radical. Hysteria reached pathological proportions under the influence of business propaganda that branded all labor as radical, under the spur of politicians who exploited the mood of the nation for their own advantage, and under the stimulus of sporadic episodes of violence.

Scare headlines and legislative investigations of alleged Red activity kept the public edgy. In April the handiwork of a few lunatic radicals created near-panic when bombs were mailed to thirty-eight eminent citizens, including John D. Rockefeller, Justice Holmes, the Postmaster General, and the Attorney General. The Post Office intercepted all the bombs but one. In June there were several direct bombings. One weapon exploded in front of the Washington home of Attorney General A. Mitchell Palmer, damaging the building and dismembering his would-be assassin, an Italian anarchist.

The bombings of April and June had been plotted by dangerous criminals. They were not, however, a part of communist strategy, for the leaders of international communism recognized that simple terror would be an ineffective weapon for overturning a strong capitalist state. But most Americans did not differentiate among radicalisms. They grew more frightened every day, and they saw Red in everything they feared or disliked.

The mood of the nation endorsed the witch hunts conducted by Attorney General Palmer. A Quaker, a progressive Democrat who had worked effectively for women's suffrage and labor reforms, an enthusiast for the League of Nations, Palmer had enjoyed a deserved reputation as a liberal until he took office in March 1919. Then he threw his department, especially the newly created Federal Bureau of Investigation, into a strenuous campaign against aliens and radicals. He may have been hoping to advance his candidacy for the Democratic presidential nomination in 1920. If so, he overreached himself. But he did succeed in violating the Anglo-American heritage of civil liberties.

Congress refused to pass a sedition bill that Palmer had drafted, but the Attorney General on his own authority ordered a series of raids, many against the remnants of the IWW, beginning in November 1919. During the first raid his agents arrested 250 members of the Union of Russian Workers and beat many of them up, but the Justice Department could find cause to recommend that only 39 of them be deported. In December Palmer cooperated with the Labor Department in deporting 249 aliens to Russia, most of whom had committed no offense and were not communists. A nationwide raid on January 1, 1920, led to the arrest of some 6,000 people, many of whom were American citizens and noncommunists. They were herded into prisons and bull pens; some were seized on suspicion only, taken without warrants from their homes, and held incommunicado. The raids revealed no evidence of a grand plot. Nevertheless, outside of the small membership of the incipient Civil Liberties Union, few Americans spoke out against the highhanded tactics of the Attorney General, the chief legal officer of the United States.

Still worried about preventing a revolution that was not brewing, Palmer continued to warn the nation about Red plots. But the outbreak he predicted for May 1, 1920, failed to materialize, and gradually

the public began to tire of his unfounded alarms. The tide of Bolshevism had started to recede in Europe, and Palmer and his imitators had made themselves ridiculous. They could, of course, also be ruthless, as was the New York legislature, which expelled five innocuous Socialists, all properly elected members of the Assembly. This travesty on the American elective system evoked sharp denunciations, the most influential from Charles Evans Hughes. By the summer of 1920 the Red scare was largely over, the hysteria spent. In September Americans were horrified by a bomb explosion at the corner of Broad and Wall streets in New York; but they accepted the episode for what it was, the work of a crazed individual, not the product of a Bolshevik conspiracy as Palmer maintained.

The Red scare left ugly scars. The constitutional rights of thousands of Americans had been violated. Hundreds of innocent people had been deported. Many states had enacted sedition laws even more extreme than those passed during the war. And there lingered a less strident but still pervasive nativism that in the years ahead was to condone the new Ku Klux Klan, an organization dedicated to the hatred of blacks, Catholics, Jews, and foreigners. Nativism set the stage for a major reversal of immigration policy, which had for so many decades kept the gates of America open to newcomers. In February 1921, over Wilson's veto, Congress passed a law limiting the number of immigrants in any year to 3 percent of the foreign-born of each national group who had been living in the United States in 1910. Even this restrictive quota, which just about choked off immigration from Asia and central and southern Europe, was later to be reduced (see p. 596).

Hatred of aliens and radicals made a mockery of justice in the celebrated case of two Italians, confessed anarchists, Nicola Sacco and Bartolomeo Vanzetti. They were arrested, tried, and convicted for murder-ing two employees of a shoe company in South Braintree, Massachusetts, during a payroll robbery in 1920. Yet there was no conclusive evidence against them, and they were condemned essentially for their language and their beliefs. The judge who conducted the trial referred to them privately as "those anarchist bastards." Many Boston patricians felt the same way, and most of them, including the presidents of Harvard and M.I.T., approved the decision to deny a retrial. Felix Frankfurter, the novelist John Dos Passos, the poet Edna St. Vincent Millay, and other defenders of justice tried for six years to save Sacco and Vanzetti, but they failed. The cause attracted attention throughout the world and engaged the hearts of men and women who were to provide liberal leadership in the years to come. But in 1927, when Sacco and Vanzetti were electrocuted, the wounds of the Red scare festered again. The forces of respectability and conformity and repression seemed to be united against justice and decency and democracy.

The election of 1920. The Red scare drained away the vestiges of progressive zeal. Americans, weary of public matters great and small, withdrew to a private world of pleasure, entertainment, and sensationalism. The political parties reflected the nation's fatigue and selfishness. The confident Republicans met in Chicago, where the professionals who controlled the party intended to name a candidate they could manage. After six ballots, the bosses met in the Blackstone Hotel suite of George Harvey, a New York editor, once a friend but now a bitter foe of Wilson. In this, the most celebrated of smoke-filled rooms, they arranged for the nomination to go to Senator Warren G. Harding of Ohio. The convention selected Harding on the tenth ballot, and then the delegates, ignoring the orders of the bosses, named Calvin Coolidge for Vice President.

Harding was a handsome, semieducated political hack with a modest talent for golf; a larger taste for women, liquor, and poker; a complaisant disposition; an utterly empty mind; and an enduring loyalty to the Republican creed of 1890. He was probably the least-qualified candidate ever nominated by a major party. His platform fitted his creed exactly. It promised lower taxes, a higher tariff, restriction of immigration, and—with opportunistic generosity—aid to farmers. It damned the League of Nations but called vaguely for an "agreement among nations to preserve the peace"—a phrase that made the isolationists happy and that Harding's wordy speeches did nothing to clarify.

The Democrats were at odds with themselves. The failure of President Wilson, in spite of his illness, to disclaim ambition for the nomination impeded the candidacy of his son-in-law, William G. McAdoo, probably the ablest of the hopefuls. Attorney General Palmer had begun to lose support before the convention met. And in any event the Democratic bosses, almost as powerful as their Republican counterparts, wanted no candidate who was identified with the Wilson Administration. They preferred Governor James M. Cox of Ohio, a good vote-getter and an opponent of Prohibition.

On the forty-fourth ballot the convention selected Cox. As his running mate, the delegates chose a young Wilsonian with a magic political name, Assistant Secretary of the Navy Franklin D. Roosevelt. The platform was pro-League (though it allowed for amendments to the covenant), in favor of tax reduction and Philippine independence, noncommittal about Prohibition, and otherwise undistinguished. So, except in contrast to Harding, was the Democratic candidate. Cox had about him a pleasant way, a certain prim yet persuasive manner, and a satisfactory record; but he had little of the stature of most of the national candidates of the preceding decade.

The movement toward the Republicans, still the normal majority party, had begun in 1918 (see p. 568), and it accelerated in 1920. Midwestern farmers, alienated by wartime controls, were now troubled by falling prices. Much of the once-progressive middle class had come to resent high taxes, inflation, and labor strife. Urban Democrats of the North were suspicious of Southern "drys," and Irish-Americans were hostile toward Wilson's foreign policy. Many independents could not forgive Palmer his behavior or Wilson his sometimes open endorsement of it.

All these factors combined to produce a Republican "earthquake," as one Democrat put it. Harding received 61 percent of the popular vote, which now included women, carried every state outside the South and also Tennessee, and led Cox by 404 to 127 in the Electoral College. The Republicans also swept

New voters

the congressional elections, obtaining a majority of 22 in the Senate and 167 in the House of Representatives. Not only had the voters repudiated Wilson and internationalism; they had repudiated progressivism. They restored to power the Republicans who had stuck with the party when Roosevelt bolted in 1912. Harding, for all his limitations, had caught the purpose of his constituency when he called for a return to "not nostrums, but normalcy."

Normalcy

All the advantages. Harding, his Secretary of State, Charles Evans Hughes, and the Republican majority in the Senate quickly buried the issue of the Treaty of Versailles. In his first message to Congress the President stated that the United States would have nothing to do with the League of Nations, not even with its health program. Since the rejection of the treaty left the United States still technically at war with the Central Powers, the Senate passed again a resolution establishing a separate peace with Germany—a resolution that Wilson had vetoed. Harding signed it in July 1921, and Hughes then negotiated peace treaties with Germany, Austria, and Hungary. Like the resolution, these treaties claimed for the United States all the rights and advantages, but none of the responsibilities, of the Paris settlement.

The pursuit of advantages without responsibility—in Wilson's words "an ineffaceable stain upon . . . the honor of the United States"—also engaged the Harding Administration as a diplomatic partner to American oil companies. Their pressure persuaded the President to champion a treaty with Colombia, ostensibly designed only to indemnify that republic with $25 million for its loss of land and honor when

Roosevelt assisted the Panamanian revolt. The treaty had been under consideration for several years, but Roosevelt's friends had blocked it while he still lived. In 1921, two years after his death, Colombia was preparing to withdraw all private rights to subsurface oil deposits. That possibility helped to move even Lodge to seek the good will that would permit Standard Oil to obtain concessions from the Colombian government. In April 1921 the Senate approved the treaty; Colombia ratified it in 1922; and American investments there, largely in oil, grew from about $2 million to $124 million by 1929. The State Department opened even richer prospects for profit by persuading the British to share with American companies the enormous oil fields of the Middle East.

The outstanding diplomatic venture of Harding's term was a 1921 conference on naval disarmament, which the President was rather reluctant to summon. At the time of his inauguration, the Navy Department was urging the completion of the vast building program that had been launched five years earlier (see p. 556). But businessmen were impatient to cut federal expenses so that taxes could be reduced, and they grumbled about the cost of the program. Continued naval expansion, moreover, was provoking an armament race with two recent associates, Great Britain and Japan, sea powers who were unwilling to stand idly by while the American navy grew. Senator William E. Borah of Idaho suggested a three-power meeting on naval limitation, and large majorities in both houses of Congress endorsed that scheme in a resolution attached to the naval-appropriations bill of 1921.

This move was welcomed by the British, who were eager to terminate the defensive alliance made with Japan in 1902, an alliance that the dominions, especially Canada, disliked. The British also felt that the arms race was intimately associated with stability in the Far East, particularly because the United States and Japan had been at odds over such questions as China's future, the Siberian intervention, and the disposition of former German islands in the western Pacific. Harding proposed a conference on naval limitations on the same day the British called for a conference on the Far East. They agreed to discuss both matters at a single meeting in Washington.

The double agenda made it necessary to invite all the major naval powers—the United States, Great Britain, Japan, France, and Italy—as well as smaller powers with interests in the Far East—China, Portugal, Belgium, and the Netherlands. Everyone agreed that Bolshevik Russia, though a Pacific power, should be excluded, and her protests were ignored.

The delegates assembled on November 11, 1921, to commemorate the third anniversary of the armistice. The next day Harding greeted them with an emotional speech. Then they heard an address by Secretary of State Charles Evans Hughes, who had been named presiding officer. Instead of dealing in the usual platitudes of such occasions, Hughes presented the conference with a detailed plan for naval disarmament. The United States was to scrap thirty capital ships, half old and half being built; the British were to give up twenty-three; Japan, seventeen. This destruction of more than 1,878,000 aggregate tons afloat, on the ways, or planned, would establish a capital-ship tonnage ratio among the three nations of 5:5:3. The ratio was to persist for ten years, during which the powers would observe a moratorium on the construction of capital ships. France and Italy were each to have one-third the tonnage allotted the United States and Great Britain.

Hughes' speech, one of the most dramatic in diplomatic annals, stirred the amazed delegates to cheers. The Japanese, however, disliked being on the short end of the ratio, which wounded their pride and might threaten their national security. They bargained successfully to keep their newest battleship, which Hughes had destined for the junk heap. They accepted the Five Power Naval Treaty only after the United States and England had agreed not to fortify their possessions in the western Pacific.

Another agreement, the Four Power Treaty, bound the United States, Great Britain, Japan, and France to respect each other's rights affecting insular possessions in the Pacific, to refer disputes in that area to a joint conference, and to consult each other in the event of a threat from another power. Moreover, the treaty specifically supplanted the Anglo-Japanese alliance.

Now Hughes pressed on to conclude a Nine Power Treaty that committed all the nations at the conference to observe traditional American policies in the Far East. They agreed to respect the territorial and administrative integrity and the independence of China and to uphold the Open Door.

The Washington treaties were a considerable achievement. As the British had intended, and as the United States later maintained, they were integrally related to each other, and together they reduced tension in the Far East. Japan restored Shantung to China's sovereignty, withdrew from Siberia, and granted the United States cable rights on the former German island of Yap. The naval treaty, moreover, marked the first time in history that major powers had consented to disarm. Hughes had made a virtue of necessity, for he had really given up nothing he had any reasonable chance of getting. The economy-minded Congress, as Lodge reported, would not have continued to expand the navy and would have looked askance at the cost of fortifying Guam or the Philippines.

Yet the Washington settlement also had shortcomings. It left the powers free to construct auxiliary naval vessels, such as destroyers, cruisers, and submarines, which were to prove vital weapons in the future. It provided no mechanism for the consultations the four major powers had agreed to. All in all, it perpetuated the postwar status quo, for the western Pacific was still a Japanese lake. Japan when she chose could build up her fleet, fortify her mandate islands, and encroach upon China, unless the United States and the other powers were prepared to defend their stated policies. The test of the settlement lay not in its terms but in whether or not the powers chose to honor them. As Wilson had asserted, peace was a matter of continuous negotiation and accommodation. And, as Roosevelt had preached, power was ever a factor in the affairs of nations.

Hughes had done remarkably well, but the spirit with which Americans greeted his accomplishment was ominous. In ratifying the Four Power Treaty, the Senate added a reservation asserting that the United States recognized "no commitment to armed force, no alliance, no obligation to join in any defense." Congress in 1922 and for years thereafter was unwilling to maintain the navy even at treaty strength. In short, the American people accepted words as realities, and the Washington settlement proved to be another case of seeking all the advantages and none of the responsibilities.

The best minds. Advantages rather than responsibilities were also the goal of the representatives of business and finance who shaped the domestic policies of the Harding Administration. The President had promised to recruit for government the "best minds" of the country. Hughes met that standard, as did Secretary of Commerce Herbert C. Hoover and Secretary of Agriculture Henry C. Wallace, who had long devoted himself to the cause of agricultural reform. But Wallace's influence was outweighed by that of Hoover who used his department to promote the interests and enlarge the markets of American business. Hoover, in Harding's view, had proved his worth by acquiring a magnificent fortune. That was the President's surest criterion for finding the "best minds."

Foremost among Harding's advisers was Secretary of the Treasury Andrew Mellon, a reticent multimillionaire from Pittsburgh whose intricate banking and investment holdings gave him, his family, and his associates control, among many other things, of the aluminum monopoly. A man of slight build, with a cold and weary face, Mellon exuded sober luxury and contemptuous worldliness. "The Government is just a business," he believed, "and can and should be run on business principles."

Great businesses, as Mellon knew, thrive on innovation and expansion. Yet the only business principle he considered relevant to government was economy. With small regard for the services that only government could furnish the nation, Mellon worked unceasingly to reduce federal expenditures. Expenses had to be cut if he was to achieve his corollary purpose: the reduction of taxes, especially taxes on men of means. It was better, he argued, to place the burden of taxes on lower-income groups, for taxing the rich inhibited their investments and thus retarded economic growth. A share of the tax-free profits of the rich, Mellon reassured the country, would ultimately trickle down to the middle- and lower-income groups in the form of salaries and wages. Robert La Follette paraphrased that theory succinctly: "Wealth will not and cannot be made to bear its full share of taxation."

The quest for economy in government had some beneficial results. In 1921 Harding signed the Budget and Accounting Act, which improved the budgeting procedures of the federal government. It also served Mellon's purpose, for Harding's first Director of the Budget, Charles G. Dawes, a Chicago banker, made economy the touchstone of the budget that was presented to Congress in 1922.

Primarily to hold expenditures down, Harding opposed a veterans'-bonus bill that Congress debated in 1921, and he vetoed it when it passed the next year. The American Legion, an organization of World War veterans, led the lobby that demanded "adjusted compensation" for all servicemen. The Legion argued that soldiers had fought for a pittance while civilians were drawing high wartime wages. The bonus was to set matters right. Perhaps veterans did indeed deserve something more than gratitude from their country, but this bonus was little more than a raid on public funds supported by the American Legion, an energetic and increasingly influential pressure group. The newly created Veterans Administration was already taking care of the disabled. Veterans were not necessarily the neediest candidates for public assistance. Yet the veterans were simply acting in the spirit of the time when they continued to seek special advantages. Congress overrode a second veto in 1924 and granted a bonus in the form of paid-up twenty-year insurance policies, against which the veterans could immediately borrow limited funds.

Meanwhile, Mellon had advanced the tax program of the business community. In 1921 he urged Congress to repeal the excess-profits tax and to reduce the surtax on personal income from a maximum of 65 percent to 32 percent for 1921 and 25 percent thereafter. These proposals would have prevailed had it not been for the opposition of a group of Western Republican senators who joined with the Democrats to preserve the progressive principles of wartime revenue legislation. The Revenue Act of 1921 fell short of Mellon's goals. It held the maximum surtax on per-

sonal income at 50 percent, and it granted some tax relief to lower- and middle-income groups.

The Administration had better luck with its tariff policy. Following the tradition of their party, Republican leaders set out to restore the protective rates that had prevailed before 1913. Two developments eased their way. The spread of industry in the South had dispelled much of the traditional Democratic resistance to tariff protection. More important, farm representatives had concluded that they would profit from protective rates on farm products. This was a delusion, for the farmer really needed larger markets abroad, but during the discussion of the tariff the leaders of the farm bloc, except for Senators William E. Borah, George Norris, and Robert La Follette, rivaled the spokesmen of industry in their zeal for protection. Consequently there was no spirited debate on the tariff, as there had been in 1909.

With no significant dissent, Congress in 1922 passed the Fordney-McCumber Act, which reestablished prohibitive tariff rates. The act did instruct the Tariff Commission to help the President determine differences in production costs between the United States and other nations. And it did empower the President to raise or lower any rate by 50 percent, on the commissions' recommendation. In practice, however, the commission was strongly protectionist, and of the thirty-seven rates that were altered during the life of the act, thirty-two were actually increased.

The Tariff of 1922 and its administration damaged foreign trade. By preventing Europeans from selling their goods in the United States, it made it impossible for them to buy American products, including agricultural surpluses, except by borrowing dollars and thus increasing the large debts they had incurred during the war. This was an unhealthy situation both for the United States and for Europe.

Nullification by administration. The restoration of tariff protection was only one part of a concerted effort by the Administration to restore the conditions of the nineteenth century. Wherever they could, Harding and his associates rolled back the accomplishments of the progressive movement.

The President could not tear down the apparatus that had been constructed for regulating business and industry, but he succeeded in rendering that apparatus useless by turning it over to the very interests it had been designed to regulate. His appointments to federal commissions, as Senator Norris said, "set the country back more than twenty-five years." They achieved "the nullification of federal law by a process of boring from within."

The Administration also stood aside while management continued its attack on labor unions and labor legislation. In 1922 Harding interceded to stop the violence that attended a nationwide coal strike. The report of the commission of inquiry he appointed revealed the pitiful, even desperate, state of life in the coal towns. The commission supported neither compulsory arbitration, which the operators wanted, nor complete unionization, which the miners had advocated. Instead, it recommended various federal controls over the mining industry, but Congress and the Administration ignored the report. In the same year, the national Railway Labor Board approved a 12 percent reduction in the wages of railway shopmen, a decision that precipitated a strike that lasted two

A virtuous poor? *The standard furnished by the statute ... is so vague as to be impossible of practical application with any reasonable degree of accuracy. What is sufficient to supply the necessary cost of living for a woman worker and maintain her in good health and protect her morals is obviously not a precise or unvarying sum—not even approximately so.... Morality rests upon other considerations than wages; and there is, certainly, no such prevalent connection between the two as to justify a broad attempt to adjust the latter with reference to the former.... Nor is there ground for distinction between women and men, for, certainly, if women require a minimum wage to preserve their morals, men require it to preserve their honesty. For these reasons, and others which might be stated, the inquiry in respect of the necessary cost of living and of the income necessary to preserve health and morals, presents an individual and not a composite question, and must be answered for each individual considered by herself and not by a general formula prescribed by a statutory bureau.*

From Adkins v. Children's Hospital, 261 U.S. 525, 1923.

months. It ended only when the Attorney General got an injunction that forbade the union to picket or in any way to encourage workers to leave their jobs.

In this and other rulings the federal courts, acting in the spirit of the executive establishment, took advantage of the permissiveness of the Clayton Act (see p. 547). Contrary to Gompers' hopes, the injunction was still a handy instrument for breaking strikes. In the same spirit, the courts sustained "yellow-dog" contracts that bound employees not to join unions. The courts' hostility toward labor not only helped management's campaign for the open shop but destroyed social legislation designed to protect the poorest and weakest workers. The Supreme Court in 1922, in the case of *Bailey* v. *Drexel Furniture Company*, declared unconstitutional a federal statute levying a prohibitive tax on products manufactured by children. The Court had ruled earlier, in *Hammer* v. *Dagenhart* (1918), that federal laws to control child labor were an unconstitutional invasion of the police powers of the states. In the Bailey case, it said that Congress could not use its tax power to accomplish this unconstitutional purpose. The decision perpetuated child labor, especially in the Southern textile mills.

The Supreme Court was just as opposed to regulation of wages, hours, and working conditions. In 1923, in *Adkins* v. *Children's Hospital*, it held unconstitutional a District of Columbia statute establishing minimum wages for women. Ignoring the social and economic arguments for the act, the majority of the Court found it a violation of the freedom of women to contract to sell their labor as they pleased. The Adkins decision contravened the spirit of the Clayton Act, which asserted that labor was not a mere com-

modity. The decision also left labor defenseless, for neither federal nor state governments could insist on minimum standards of health and decency, and the attitudes of the courts denied the unions much of their opportunity to recruit membership or to strike for fair treatment.

The farmers fared better politically, but not economically, under the Harding Administration. In 1922 agricultural prices began to recover from their postwar slump, but the farmers were harassed by high interest charges on mortgages and by heavy taxes on land. Agricultural technology raised production and expanded surpluses even though the number of farms and of agricultural workers was steadily declining. And advancing industrialism continuously reduced the farmers' share of the national income. Agriculture during the early 1920s was not generally impoverished, though segments of it were. But even the more privileged farmers were anxious about their future and resentful of their diminishing influence on American life. They were jealous, too, of the conveniences, especially electricity, automobiles, and entertainment, that were becoming more and more common in the cities.

In 1921 and 1922 the discontent of farmers generated considerable political force in the South and the Middle West, and the farm bloc in Congress won a series of victories. With few exceptions, however, the leaders of the farm bloc failed to understand the basic difficulties. They made their mark instead where the objectives of the fading progressive movement helped them to define their goals. Legislation in 1921 authorized the Secretary of Agriculture to compel commission merchants, grain merchants, and stockyard owners to charge reasonable rates. An act of

War and its sequel

1922 exempted farm cooperatives from the antitrust laws, and Congress added a representative of agriculture to the Federal Reserve Board. In 1923 the Agricultural Credits Act established twelve Intermediate Credit Banks to make loans to cooperatives and other farm groups for six months to three years. The loans were to help cooperatives to withhold crops from the market when prices were temporarily low. These statutes strengthened the farmer's ability to conduct his business, and they created instruments for controlling the middlemen to whom he sold his produce. But they did not ease his mortgage burden, and they helped the small farmer, sharecropper, and farm laborer not at all.

In the off-year elections of 1922, agrarian dissent carried anti-Administration candidates to victory in Republican primaries in most of the West. In November the resurgent Democrats reduced Republican majorities to eight in the Senate and eighteen in the House. And, of the Republicans who were elected, so many were disenchanted that the Administration no longer controlled Congress. The elections assured key committee assignments to strong men in both parties who were dubious about the Administration's program and methods. Those men, using Congress' power of investigation, soon exposed the Harding regime to publicity it could not afford.

The Harding scandals.

The President of the United States sets the tone of his Administration. The first two decades of the twentieth century had been marked by McKinley's kindness, Theodore Roosevelt's strenuosity, Taft's decent ineffectuality, and Wilson's soaring idealism. Warren Harding brought to government the qualities of his own weak person. To his credit, he stopped the repression of dissent that marked the late Wilson years, and he pardoned Debs. But he was an ignorant, naive, confused man whose loose standards made him particularly vulnerable to his intellectual deficiencies and to the corrupt character of the hail-fellows with whom he instinctively surrounded himself.

Harding was ruefully aware of some of his limitations. As he once admitted, he did not know whom to trust. Uncomfortable with the "best minds," he preferred the kind of tawdry companionship he had known in his native Marion, Ohio. The "Ohio gang" and their friends met continually with Harding at a house on K Street. There councils of state had an incidental but insinuating part in the rounds of poker, whiskey, and women that made the President feel at home.

For two years the Ohio gang flourished. Early in 1923, however, Harding learned that the head of the Veterans Bureau had pocketed an impressive fraction of the $250 million his agency spent lavishly for hos-

"My God-damned friends"

pitals and hospital supplies. Though Harding permitted the culprit to go abroad and resign, he was later exposed, tried, convicted, and sentenced to prison.

It also developed that Harding's Attorney General, Harry M. Daugherty of Ohio, had peddled his power for cash, but two divided juries in 1926 saved Daugherty from prison.

Secretary of the Interior Albert Fall was less fortunate. In 1921 he persuaded Harding to transfer to the Interior Department control over naval oil reserves at Elk Hill, California, and Teapot Dome, Wyoming. The next year Fall secretly leased Elk Hill to the oil company of Edward L. Doheny and Teapot Dome to the company of Harry F. Sinclair. But the leases could not be kept secret very long. In October 1923 a Senate committee under the chairmanship of Thomas J. Walsh, a Montana Democrat, began an investigation, which a special commission completed in 1924. The inquiries disclosed that Doheny had "lent" Fall $100,000 and that Sinclair had given the Secretary of the Interior a herd of cattle for his ranch, $85,000 in cash, and $223,000 in bonds. In 1927 the government won a suit for cancellation of the leases. Though another remarkable verdict acquitted Doheny, Sinclair, and Fall of conspiracy to defraud the government, Sinclair was convicted of tampering with a jury, and in 1929 Fall was convicted of bribery, fined $100,000, and sentenced to a year in jail. He was the first Cabinet officer ever to go to prison.

Harding knew of only the earliest scandals. In June 1923, before setting out on a speaking tour through the West, the President unburdened himself to William Allen White: "My God, this is a hell of a job. I have no trouble with my enemies. . . . But my damned friends, my God-damned friends . . . they're the ones that keep me walking the floor nights!" Depressed and tired, Harding grew "nervous and dis-

traught" as he traveled. Late in July, while in Seattle on the way home from Alaska, the President suffered acute pain. His doctor diagnosed it as indigestion, but other physicians in the party believed that Harding had had a heart attack, a diagnosis that was confirmed by a San Francisco specialist. On August 2, in a room at the Palace Hotel, Harding died, the victim of a coronary or cerebral thrombosis.

Vulgarity and scandal were the sordid fruits of normalcy, of a government that sought all the advantages of power but none of the responsibilities, of organized self-interest that sought special favors in bonuses, bounties, lower taxes, and higher tariffs. Pressure groups had gained advantages for big business even during the progressive years. After the war those interests dominated the federal government as they had not since the 1890s. The scandals passed, but the equation of national interests with privileged interests did not. That equation satisfied the "best minds" during the decade that followed the great war. It contradicted the best hopes cultivated before that war began.

Suggestions for reading

THE WAR

Historians have given the experience of the United States during the First World War less attention than it merits. The biographies of Wilson and the Wilsonians, noted in connection with the preceding chapter, provide some useful data and insights. More complete is F. L. Paxson, *American Democracy and the World War,* 3 vols. (1936–48). There are adequate discussions of economic mobilization in B. M. Baruch, *American Industry in War* (1941) and *The Public Years** (1960), but more important is R. D. Cuff, *The War Industries Board* (1973). The relevant chapter of Sidney Ratner, *American Taxation* (1942), is useful on its subject. On congressional developments, see S. W. Livermore, *Politics Is Adjourned** (1966). On the administration of the War Department, Frederick Palmer, *Newton D. Baker,* 2 vols. (1931), offers considerable information; the Navy Department receives perceptive treatment in Frank Freidel, *Franklin D. Roosevelt: The Apprenticeship* (1952). The most rewarding of the war memoirs is J. J. Pershing, *My Experiences in the World War,* 2 vols. (1931), but there are more useful accounts of military developments in J. G. Harbord, *The American Army in France* (1936), E. E. Morison, *Admiral Sims and the Modern American Navy* (1942), and Russell Weigley, *The American Way of War* (1973). There are a number of admirable studies of propaganda, censorship, and civil liberties in wartime, including J. R. Mock and Cedric Larson, *Words That Won the War: The Story of the Committee on Public Information, 1917–1919* (1939); H. C. Peterson, *Propaganda for War* (1939); H. C. Peterson and G. C. Fite, *Opponents of War, 1917–1918** (1957); J. M. Jensen, *The Price of Vigilance* (1968); William Preston, *Aliens and Dissenters: Federal Suppression of Radicals, 1903–1933* (1963); and the classic Zechariah Chaffee, *Free Speech in the United States** (rev. ed., 1941).

THE PEACE

Students of peacemaking and of the American rejection of the peace treaty have at their disposal a voluminous literature that is continually growing. One excellent place to begin reading is in the penetrating analysis of H. R. Rudin, *Armistice, 1918* (1944). On the significance of the Bolsheviks in the fashioning of peace terms, see J. M. Thompson, *Russia, Bolshevism, and the Versailles Peace*

*Available in a paperback edition.

(1966), and A. J. Mayer, *Political Origins of the New Diplomacy, 1917–1918** (1959) and *Politics and Diplomacy of Peacemaking** (1968). Two detailed accounts of the negotiations at Paris, which applaud Wilson's efforts, are D. F. Fleming, *The United States and the League of Nations, 1918–1920* (1932), and Paul Birdsall, *Versailles Twenty Years After* (1941). On the United States and the Soviet Union, there are two superb volumes by G. F. Kennan, *Russia Leaves the War: The Americans in Petrograd and the Bolshevik Revolution** (1956) and *The Decision to Intervene: The Prelude to Allied Intervention in the Bolshevik Revolution** (1958). Also scholarly, and essential on its topic, is R. J. Bartlett, *League to Enforce Peace* (1944). There is a critical but persuasive analysis in T. A. Bailey, *Woodrow Wilson and the Lost Peace** (1944). The same author, in *Woodrow Wilson and the Great Betrayal** (1945), provides a trenchant study of the rejection of the treaty. Also significant on that subject are: R. A. Stone, *The Irreconcilables: The Fight Against the League of Nations** (1970); N. G. Levin, Jr., *Woodrow Wilson and World Politics** (1968); J. A. Garraty, *Henry Cabot Lodge* (1953); R. W. Leopold, *Elihu Root and the Conservative Tradition** (1954); and M. C. McKenna, *Borah* (1961). There are conflicting views about the conduct of government during Wilson's illness in E. B. Wilson, *My Memoirs* (1938), and J. M. Blum, *Joe Tumulty and the Wilson Era* (1951). Among the accounts of contemporaries friendly to Wilson, two of the most valuable are D. F. Houston, *Eight Years with Wilson's Cabinet, 1913–1920,* 2 vols. (1926), and Herbert Hoover, *The Ordeal of Woodrow Wilson** (1958). Two important unfriendly statements appear in H. C. Lodge, *The Senate and the League of Nations* (1928), and J. M. Keynes, *Economic Consequences of the Peace** (1919). Several of the books here listed cover the question of the League in the election of 1920, a subject further explored in J. M. Cox, *Journey Through My Years* (1946), and Frank Freidel, *Franklin D. Roosevelt: The Ordeal* (1954).

THE RED SCARE
R. K. Murray, *The Red Scare** (1955), contains the most comprehensive narrative about the subject. It has to be supplemented, however, by the studies of civil liberties listed above and the perceptive biography by Stanley Coben, *A. Mitchell Palmer: Politician* (1963); the masterful analysis of G. L. Joughin and E. M. Morgan, *The Legacy of Sacco and Vanzetti** (1948); Kenneth Jackson, *The Ku Klux Klan in the City, 1915–1930** (1967); the excellent studies of labor in Irving Bernstein, *The Lean Years** (1960), and D. Brody, *Labor in Crisis: The Steel Strike of 1919** (1965); the analysis of blacks in A. I. Waskow, *From Race Riot to Sit-In, 1919 and the 1960s** (1966), E. D. Cronin, *Black Moses** (1955), A. S. Spear, *Black Chicago** (1967), and N. I. Huggins, *et al., Key Issues in Afro-American Experience,* 2 vols.* (1971); and the penetrating treatments of nativism in John Higham, *Strangers in the Land** (1955), and Oscar Handlin, *Race and Nationality in American Life** (1957) and *The American People in the Twentieth Century** (1954, 2nd rev. ed., 1966).

HARDING AND NORMALCY
W. E. Leuchtenburg, *The Perils of Prosperity, 1914–32** (1958), provides a crisp and thoughtful account of the Harding period. Also lively, but less judicious, is F. L. Allen, *Only Yesterday** (1931). There is a short but incisive evaluation of the Harding years in A. M. Schlesinger, Jr., *The Crisis of the Old Order** (1957), and a fuller narrative in J. D. Hicks, *Republican Ascendancy, 1921–1933** (1960). The economy and its problems receive able handling in George Soule, *Prosperity Decade: From War to Depression, 1917–1929** (1947); but for a richer discussion of taxation and agriculture, respectively, the relevant chapters of R. E. Paul, *Taxation in the United States* (1954), and Theodore Saloutos and J. D. Hicks, *Twentieth Century Populism: Agricultural Discontent in the Middle West, 1900–1939** (1951), are particularly valuable. The Harding scandals get the treatment they merit in S. H. Adams, *Incredible Era** (1939), and Karl Schriftgiesser, *This Was Normalcy* (1948). Andrew Sinclair, *The Available Man** (1965), tries to redeem Harding's reputation, as does R. K. Murray, *The Harding Era* (1969). Two stimulating accounts of the Washington Conference are H. H. and M. T. Sprout, *Toward a New Order of Sea Power* (1946), and J. C. Vinson, *The Parchment Peace: The United States Senate and the Washington Conference, 1921–1922* (1950). Also important are the pertinent parts of A. W. Griswold, *The Far Eastern Policy of the United States** (1938), and F. R. Dulles, *Forty Years of American-Japanese Relations* (1937). Two biographies have given first-rate attention to the diplomacy of Harding's Secretary of State: M. J. Pusey, *Charles Evans Hughes,* 2 vols. (1951), and Dexter Perkins, *Charles Evans Hughes and American Democratic Statesmanship* (1953).

*Available in a paperback edition.

CHAPTER **25**

A new age
of business

*American city,
1923*

alvin Coolidge believed in the kind of luck that Horatio Alger had immortalized. If a man worked hard, saved his pennies, respected the authorities, and kept his mouth shut, an invisible hand would contrive an occasion to make his reputation. Coolidge took no chances while he waited for his breaks. The son of a Vermont storekeeper, he worked his way through Amherst College, studied law in Northampton, Mas-sachusetts, and entered politics there, winning successively those minor state offices on which undistinguished politicians build their careers. His patient course endeared him to the Massachusetts Republicans, who valued his unquestioning acceptance of things as they were, his unwavering preference for inaction, and his obvious personal honesty.

In 1919, twenty years after he first won public office, Coolidge achieved national prominence for his role in stopping the Boston police strike. His delay in dealing with that episode invited anarchy, but his friends used his new reputation to generate the boom that made him the Republican choice for Vice President. In that post Coolidge dispatched his ceremonial duties with quiet pleasure, warned Americans against the "Reds in Our Women's Colleges," and awaited his next break. When Harding died, Coolidge's luck had him at home, where his father, a notary public, administered the oath of office. The event was a blessing for the most privileged Republicans, for the accession of Calvin Coolidge gave them a new President who cloaked normalcy with respectability.

A new cult of enterprise

Coolidge and the business creed. Personally neat, even prim, deliberately laconic and undemonstrative in public (though given in private to temper and garrulity), Coolidge scrubbed the White House clean of the filth that Harding had left. Grace Coolidge, the new first lady, erased scandal with her natural dignity, charm, and warmth. The President chose two lawyers of impeccable integrity to prosecute the rascals in government. When the mounting evidence against the Attorney General forced his retirement in March 1924, Coolidge named to his place an eminent former dean of the Columbia Law School, Harlan Fiske Stone, whose appointment completed the shift from rascality to virtue.

In other respects Coolidge left the national government unaltered. As much as Harding, Coolidge subscribed to the creed of American business. "The business of America is business," Coolidge believed. "The man who builds a factory," he once said, "builds a temple. . . . The man who works there worships there." The President himself worshiped wealth and those who had it. Worldly possessions were for him evidence of divine election. He stood in awe of

Calvin Coolidge: he worshiped wealth

Andrew Mellon. He took a smug delight in his own eminence, but he was absolutely euphoric when his office commanded for him the deference of the rich. Coolidge, as William Allen White put it, was "sincerely, genuinely, terribly crazy" about wealth.

This passion coincided exactly with the theories of business spokesmen. There were, they preached, a superior few and an inferior many. And they were easy to distinguish, for "a man is worth the wages he can earn." Material success marked the élite, and to them the others should leave the important decisions about society. The 1920s witnessed a renaissance of the conservative dogmas of the 1880s, now clothed in new metaphors. Bruce Barton, a magnificently successful advertising man, gave the gospel its most popular phrasing in his best-seller of 1925, *The Man Nobody Knows*. To his infinite satisfaction, Barton, the son of a minister, discovered that Christ was a businessman. "Jesus," he wrote, ". . . picked up twelve men from the bottom ranks of business and forged them into an organization that conquered the world." The parables made incomparable advertisements; the gospel, an incomparable business school.

Coolidge was devoted to the dominant values of his time, to business, materialism, élitism, and their corollaries. If only the rich were worthy, it followed that government should beware the counsels of the majority. Since poverty was the wage of sin, government should not tax the virtuous rich in order to assist the unworthy poor. And since the rich best understood their own interests, government should not interfere with the businesses they ran, though it should help promote them.

No devotee of laissez faire ever abhorred government more than Coolidge did. "If the Federal Government should go out of existence," he said, "the common run of people would not detect the difference . . . for a considerable length of time." Government's grandest service was to minimize itself, its activities, and its expenditures. So persuaded, Coolidge slept more than any other President in this century. He also said and did less when he was awake. "Four-fifths of all our troubles in this life," he told one agitated senator, "would disappear if we would only sit down and keep still." Silence, inactivity, gentility, complacency—those were the sum and the substance of the Coolidge calculus.

Productivity and plenty. The extraordinary prosperity of the 1920s cast a mantle of credibility over the doctrines of business and its representative President. It was easy for him and others of like mind to interpret prosperity as majestic proof of their beliefs. As the country came out of the short slump of 1921, unemployment became negligible except in sick industries like textiles and coal. By 1923 the average money wages of industrial workers were twice what they had been in 1914, and they continued to advance through 1928. Real wages rose, too, steadily though less dramatically. By 1928 they were about one-third higher than they had been fourteen years earlier. Several factors accounted for those increases. Many employers had begun to realize that higher wages removed one of the incentives that prompted workers to join unions and also provided purchasing power that swelled the market for industrial products. Wages stretched further as prices fell, especially the price of food and of goods manufactured in industries where mechanization pushed productivity to new peaks.

The profits that came with mechanization invited investment in new plants and new tools. Investment was encouraged also by the growing national market, by the permissive climate of inactive government, and by Mellon's gradual success in persuading Congress to reduce taxes on large incomes. While investment provided the means for building more and more productivity into American industry, management was mastering new ways to use machinery and to organize production more effectively.

The American system of manufacturing that flowered during the 1920s had deep roots. It depended on the concept of continuous fabrication, by which raw materials entered a plant to emerge after multiple operations as finished products. That concept was at

A new age of business

least as old as the first Lowell textile mills. It depended also on machine tools capable of producing standard, complex artifacts with interchangeable parts—the kinds of tool and the kind of standardization that Eli Whitney had developed for guns a century before Coolidge's inauguration. More immediately, the American system of manufacturing depended on two recent and interrelated developments. One was the emerging profession of industrial engineering, with its concern for continuous process, improved machinery, specialization of jobs, and time-motion studies of performance. The other was an emerging cult of productivity, a rationalization of the glories of making and distributing and consuming ever more bountifully. Americans had long honored that objective, but never more avidly than in the 1920s.

The founding father of "scientific management" was Frederick W. Taylor. Born into a comfortable family in Germantown, Pennsylvania, in 1856, Taylor had to interrupt his gentleman's education at Harvard because of poor eyesight. Moving into an entirely different environment, he learned the trades of patternmaker and machinist and in 1878 went as a common laborer to the Midvale Steel Company. By 1885 he had earned his Master of Engineering degree at Stevens Institute; a year later he became chief engineer at Midvale. His driving concern was with making machines and the men who attended them produce more and faster. Those interests led him to establish his own consulting practice on production, on "systematizing shop management."

Taylor's system started with a close study of every step in manufacturing. By applying the resulting data, by breaking the process of manufacturing into separate parts, and by specializing the function of the man and machine involved in each part, he could substantially increase the rate of production. His classifications of jobs and of capacity, he believed, would lead also to higher wages as workers first met and then exceeded their calculated goals. The aim of every establishment, Taylor wrote in *Shop Management* (1911), should be to give each workman the highest grade of work of which he was capable, to call on each to turn out his maximum, and to pay each in accordance with his product. "This means," he argued, "*high wages* and *low labor cost.*" It also meant time-motion studies, discipline, pressure, and incentives for speedup. For Taylor efficiency was a fetish, but he got results. Before he died in 1915 (with a watch in his hand, John Dos Passos surmised), he had caught the attention of management and had aroused the fears of labor-leaders, who suspected that piecework and the speedup would grind profits out of workers' fatigue. In spite of those fears, Taylorism spread. It was praised by Louis Brandeis and other progressives, and institutionalized by a Taylor Society.

Taylor was the philosopher of the machine process; Henry Ford was its commanding general. In 1911

Ford opened his plant at Highland Park, Michigan. There he and his fellow executives arrived at Taylor's principles along their own routes and began to turn out automobiles at prodigious rates. The Ford Motor Company outsped all industry in specializing the tasks of men and machines. After 1913 it also applied the idea of continuous motion, using conveyor belts, gravity slides, and overhead monorails to feed the machinery by which workers stood. The modern assembly line turned out the Model T's that put America on wheels. As his production and market grew, Ford cut prices and increased wages. To be sure, the wages he claimed to pay did not reach all his workers, the speedup at the Ford company was notorious, and the company tolerated no unions. But the $5 day that Ford announced in 1914 seemed to mark the dawn of a new era, and so did Ford's staggering profits. In the mid-1920s Ford had become, in the phrase of Upton Sinclair, the Flivver King.

By that time Ford's production techniques had become standard in the automobile and other industries. The Model T was a very stark car, but America's machines were also producing more comfortable, more sumptuous, and more complex mechanisms. During Coolidge's tenure in office, for the first time in the history of any nation, a mass market developed for cars, for radios, for refrigerators and vacuum cleaners. There was, in a sense, no longer any problem of production. The available stocks of American raw materials, workers, machines, and techniques could saturate the nation, and much of the world, with the necessities and conveniences of modern civilization.

Businessmen, however, were interested in more than just the science of production. Their restrictive labor policies during the 1920s kept the rise in real wages well below the rise in profits. And they guarded their market jealously, trying to produce only as much as the market could absorb without a break in prices. Large firms in heavy industries had long since learned the importance of administered, noncompetitive pricing and had long since contrived the consolidations that made for industrial stability. During the 1920s the tendency toward consolidation proceeded at an accelerating tempo, in old industries as well as new. And, as consolidation advanced, managers became more and more skillful in governing costs, price, and output. They also learned to husband enough of their profits to permit their companies to invest for further growth without recourse to traditional financial markets.

These developments disturbed Americans for whom the production and distribution of wealth were

A market developed for radios

A new age of business

more precious objectives than amassing profits. The Nobel Prize-winning novelist Sinclair Lewis, in *Dodsworth* (1929), told of an automobile-manufacturer who was forced to sell out to a giant holding company, a fictional General Motors. Dodsworth, deprived of the satisfaction of producing cars himself, and unwilling to serve as a subordinate in a great corporation, sought vainly to find new satisfactions in the culture of Europe. But in the end he came back to the United States to embark on the manufacture of mobile homes. He was the kind of business engineer who adhered to a commitment to production that Lewis felt ordinary business-managers were destroying.

Thorstein Veblen made the most devastating comparisons between those who made goods and those who made money. In *The Engineers and the Price System* (1921) and *Business Enterprise* (1923) he condemned businessmen for artificially curtailing output for the sake of profit—a practice he labeled "sabotage." He called for a revolution of technicians, of men committed to production, who would free industry of pecuniary restraints and use the machine process to provide plenty for all mankind. There was a naiveté in Veblen's attitude toward competition, and a strong dose of Marxism. But his simplifications had both merit and influence. Whereas business-managers often planned only for profit, Veblen urged public planning for the general welfare. His message helped to bridge the space between the progressive era and the next era of reform.

Republican symbols: 1924.
In the Coolidge era, however, the impulse for reform flagged. The spirit of that time saw no conflict between profits and productivity. It found a symbol in the person of Herbert Hoover, who seemed to have walked right out of American mythology. Son of an Iowa farmer, descended of pioneer stock, orphaned at ten, Hoover went west, worked his way through Stanford University, married a banker's daughter, and as an engineer in Asia earned his first million before he was forty. He was the hero of Belgian relief, the successful Food Administrator of Wilson's war Cabinet, and, in the opinion of one London newspaper, "the biggest man . . . on the Allied side" at Paris. By 1920 Hoover's name stood for personal success, for food for the hungry, and for rigor in administration. His reputation reached its height while he was serving under Harding and Coolidge as Secretary of Commerce.

To that office Hoover applied, as it were, the principles of scientific shop management. His department studied business trends, fought economic waste through its Office of Simplified Practice, and promoted American commerce and investment abroad. Concurrently it encouraged trade associations to sus-

Thorstein Veblen: perceptive critic

tain prices and profits by adjusting production to demand. Hoover personally organized the relief of victims of the Mississippi flood of 1927, avoided associating with politicians, and harbored an ambition as broad and inconspicuous as his conservative blue suits. He stood at once for laissez-faire doctrines, humanitarian endeavor, and quiet and humorless efficiency. Coolidge, increasingly jealous of Hoover's reputation, could barely tolerate "the wonder boy."

The President did not suffer any rival kindly. A shrewd political manipulator, he rapidly brought the machinery of the Republican party under his control. As the nominating convention of 1924 approached, he had only one possible opponent—not Hoover, who was biding his time, but Henry Ford. The Flivver King had run as a Democrat, and lost, in the race for senator from Michigan in 1918. His publicity men, who wrote much of what he signed, had begun in 1922 to suggest that he might be available as a Republican candidate for the White House. The prospect was both preposterous and alarming. Away from his machines, Ford was a ludicrous, semiliterate figure, the captive of folk prejudices. He was opposed to tobacco, liquor, and ballroom dancing. He had published and circulated anti-Semitic propaganda. He detested labor unions and Wall Street, both of which he felt were the tools of an international Jewish conspiracy. But this nonsense had an unfortunate appeal to the uneducated, and a third of those who were polled by *Collier's* in a straw ballot of 1923 named Ford as their first choice for President.

Ford's candidacy may not have been serious, though many people thought it was. He was, however, deadly serious in his proposal to take over the government dam, nitrate plant, and other facilities constructed during the war at Muscle Shoals on the Tennessee River. He proposed to purchase the nitrate works for less than 5 percent of what they had cost the government, to lease the waterpower facilities for a hundred years for less than 10 percent of what it would cost the government to complete them, and to have the government pay him simply by issuing new paper money. In return, he hinted that he would be able to produce fertilizer for American farms at half its current price. As Senator Norris said, this was the "most wonderful real estate speculation since Adam and Eve lost title to the Garden of Eden."

Norris exposed and defeated the scheme, which would have destroyed his cherished plans for the public development of the Tennessee. Yet before the chimera vanished, Coolidge, after talking with Ford, recommended that Congress sell Muscle Shoals to private interests. Ford himself soon put an end to his presidential boomlet by announcing that the nation was "perfectly safe with Coolidge." There may have been no bargain, but the coincidence of events suggested that both men were trading in character.

It was a striking commentary on the times that Ford's nitrate project was even proposed. It was no less striking that Ford's candidacy seemed to be the only barrier to Coolidge's renomination. Robert La Follette and Hiram Johnson, dedicated, doughty old progressives, could muster between them only forty-four votes at the Republican convention that gave Coolidge over a thousand votes on its first and decisive ballot. Only a dozen years earlier almost half the Republicans had cast their lot with Theodore Roosevelt.

One nation divisible

For white Protestants only. The temper of the twenties was marked by narrowness and provincialism as well as by prosperity and complacency. The attitudes on which the Red scare had fed survived the passing of the scare itself. Among many Americans there lingered an intolerance of all "isms," a distrust of foreign nations, and a dislike, often bordering on hatred, of people of foreign origin. Much of the farm community had long been susceptible to those feelings, and organized labor had endorsed the racial as well as the economic arguments of those who advocated that immigration be restricted.

In 1924 Congress adopted the recommendations of the Dillingham commission (p. 533) and passed the National Origins Act. This based annual immigration quotas temporarily on the proportion of descendants of each nationality resident in the United States in 1890 and limited immigration after 1927 to 150,000 a year, selected on the proportion established by the census of 1920. Those quotas ended all but a trickle of immigration from southern and eastern Europe. The act, furthermore, included a provision that West Coast racists had been urging for years. It forbade the immigration of Asians, thus terminating the Gentlemen's Agreement (see p. 533) and insulting the race-sensitive Japanese. "It has undone the work of the Washington Conference," Charles Evans Hughes wrote, "and implanted seeds of . . . antagonism."

Asians, blacks, Catholics, and Jews were all victims of the prejudice based on the ethnic self-consciousness of white, Protestant Americans of older stock. Even many educated and comfortable people, who should have known better, attributed to race, religion, or national origin varying qualities of character and intelligence, always with the assumption that Americans of old stock were a superior breed. That kind of bigotry thrived even among college professors and more virulently among Southern whites, and it also appealed to the poorer and semieducated who lived or had grown up in rural or small-town America. That America, as the census of 1920 indicated, now contained a minority of the American people. Rural folk felt threatened. More and more they tended, as they had for at least half a century, to blame their personal disappointments on the growth of cities and industry and to express their anxieties in hostility toward those who peopled the cities.

Those prejudices were the stock in trade of the Ku Klux Klan, an organization founded in Georgia in 1915 on the model of its Reconstruction predecessor. It recruited only "native born, white, gentile Americans," and it gave them a sense of importance by admitting them to membership in a group dedicated to persecuting an alleged enemy within the country. It also gave them a uniform, a hierarchy, and a ritual.

In 1920 two professional fund-raisers organized a membership drive and arranged to share with local officers the profits from increased initiation fees and from the sale of uniforms and insignia. By 1925 membership approached 5 million. The Klan used floggings, kidnapings, cross-burnings, arson, even murder to terrorize whole communities. It was especially vicious in its treatment of Catholics. An Alabama jury acquitted a Klansman who had murdered a priest; a Klan mob burned a Roman Catholic church in Illinois; the Klan and its sympathizers attempted to crush parochial schools in Oregon; and in Oklahoma they inspired the impeachment of a governor who had declared martial law in a brave effort to rout the organization. Increasingly powerful in politics, the

Klan held the balance of power in several states.

At its zenith in 1923 and 1924, the Klan by its very excesses attracted increasing opposition. In 1924 William Allen White, its implacable enemy, lost the Kansas governorship to one of the Klan's friends, but White's campaign set a sensible example. In some states the Klan began to fade, especially after "Dragon" David Stephenson of Indiana kidnaped and assaulted his secretary and connived to keep her from medical attention after she took poison. Convicted in 1925 of second-degree murder and sentenced to life imprisonment, Stephenson demanded a pardon from his fellow Klansman, Governor Ed Jackson. When Jackson refused, the vindictive "Dragon" opened a "little black box" whose contents provided evidence that sent one congressman, the mayor of Indianapolis, and various lesser officers to jail. Most important, the Klan, which had pretended to guard civic purity and feminine virtue, now stood exposed for what it was—corrupt, sordid, and licentious.

Prohibition. The Prohibitionists, who were always strongest in rural areas and particularly among fundamentalist sects, considered liquor an instrument of the devil. Unaware of the complex personal and social problems that provoke excessive drinking, they insisted that alcoholism was created by alcohol itself and by the saloon keepers who sold it. Whiskey and beer seemed to them, moreover, the potions of immigrants and political bosses, the poison of the corrupt city.

The Prohibition Amendment of 1919 also drew strength from the delusion of many Americans that legislation could somehow control personal behavior of all kinds. Yet before long only the most rabid or stubborn "drys" failed to recognize the difficulties of enforcement. The Prohibition commissioner, in his quest to prevent the manufacture, transportation, and sale of alcoholic beverages (defined by the Volstead Act of 1919 as one-half of 1 percent by volume), had to depend on a small force of agents who were often third-rate political appointees with neither the background nor the intelligence to resist bribes or needless violence. They simply could not police the millions of Americans who wanted to drink and who either made their brews at home or, more often, bought their beer or whiskey from the hundreds of "bootleggers" who earned an illegal, sometimes dangerous, but remunerative living supplying it.

Speakeasy

597

Smugglers brought whiskey in across the Canadian border, or on fast boats from the Caribbean. To supplement the supplies of these "rum-runners," there were countless domestic distillers of illicit whiskey, much of it bad and some of it poisonous. It was easy to buy whiskey by the case, the bottle, or the drink. Indeed "speakeasies," illegal saloons, did business in every major city, and obliging policemen and cab-drivers were glad to tell strangers where they were.

The traffic in bootlegging provided a new and rich source of income and influence for organized crime. In 1920 the most notorious gangland chief, "Scarface" Al Capone, moved to Chicago, where within seven years he had established a $60-million enterprise in whiskey, drugs, gambling, and prostitution. His private army of about a thousand gangsters, who were charged with protecting his domain, accounted for most of the one hundred and thirty murders in the Chicago area in 1926–27. Such was Capone's influence that not a single murderer was convicted. In New York, Philadelphia, Kansas City, and elsewhere, gangsters put high public officers on their payroll and transformed machine politics into agencies for crime.

Prohibition, manifestly unenforceable, had not created organized crime, but it had given gangland a vast privilege to exploit—a privilege that repeal of Prohibition would at least remove. Urban "wets," who had opposed Prohibition from the first, led the movement for repeal, supported by more and more former "drys." The most adamant foes of repeal were the moralists of the countryside who had failed to distinguish between liquor and crime and who identified both with immigration and the city.

Last-ditch fundamentalism.
Rural hostility to urban culture also showed itself in matters of the mind. The unsophisticated have always fallen prey to antiscientism, partly because they do not understand the methods of science, partly because they resent many of the changes that science and technology bring about. Though most Americans admired the technological advances of the 1920s and recognized them as the products of earlier scientific strivings, some were distressed by the complexities and uncertainties of a machine civilization, by its speed, its capacity for destructive as well as constructive power, its overwhelming challenge to the ways of the "good old days." To those Americans science seemed threatening and mysterious. In the rural areas that modern culture had just begun to reach, Protestant fundamentalism seized on science as an archenemy.

The fundamentalists insisted that the Bible must be accepted as literal truth. More than sixty years after the publication of Darwin's *Origin of Species*, they still rejected the concept of biological evolution and attacked those who taught it. In the postwar years William Jennings Bryan, a "dry," a fundamentalist, a folk hero of a kind, and now an old and frustrated man, enlisted in the antievolutionist crusade. Strengthened by his leadership, the antievolutionists scored partial victories in several Southern states. Bryan himself in 1925 assisted the lobby that pressured the Tennessee legislature into passing a statute making it illegal to teach any theory that denied the account of creation recorded in Genesis.

The American Civil Liberties Union, responding to this challenge to the freedom of inquiry, offered counsel to any Tennessee teacher who would test the

Darrow and Bryan
at Dayton:
creation took centuries

law. More in amusement than in anger, John T. Scopes of the mountain town of Dayton lectured from a Darwinian text and was arrested. Among the lawyers who defended him were Clarence Darrow, the most famous pleader of the time, and Arthur Garfield Hays, a celebrated advocate of civil liberties. Assisting the prosecution was Bryan, who had been retained by the World's Christian Fundamental Association. The all-star cast in the Dayton "monkey trial" engaged the interest of the entire nation.

The prosecution contended that the only issue was Scopes' violation of the law, but the defense raised the question of the validity of the law itself. The case reached its climax when Bryan took the stand as an expert on the Bible. Joshua had made the sun stand still, the Commoner said; the whale had swallowed Jonah; if it was in the Bible, it was so. As Darrow pressed the cross-examination, Bryan revealed an invincible ignorance of modern learning. Exhausted by the strain of testifying and by the laughter of the spectators, he died, heartbroken, soon after the trial.

Scopes was convicted for violating the law, but the state supreme court reversed the decision on a technicality, and the constitutionality of the statute could not be tested. There was no longer any reason to test it. Bryan had admitted in his testimony that creation took centuries; a "day" in Genesis might be an eon. That admission cost the fundamentalists their argument, and the ridicule of Bryan's performance had lost them their cause.

But by 1925 the blind innocence of fundamentalism, together with the pernicious zeal of the Klan, had estranged the ordinary citizen from the intellectual and had divided the underprivileged of the farms from the underprivileged of the cities. Protestant laborers had been set against Jewish and Catholic laborers, whites against blacks. Americans whom prosperity either did not reach or did not beguile had been sealed off into separate and often hostile groups.

The election of 1924. This estrangement made it difficult for the Democratic party to select a national candidate to oppose Coolidge in 1924. One of the two leading contenders was William G. McAdoo, who had won the acclaim of liberals for his administration of the railroads during the war (p. 566), but who had lost their favor by taking a job as counsel to Edward L. Doheny, one of the scoundrels of Teapot Dome. Yet McAdoo, ardently "dry" and equivocal about the Klan, held the support of the South and the West. His major rival, Alfred E. Smith, the governor of New York, was a "wet," a Catholic, and a Tammany man. The darling of the Eastern cities, Smith was anathema to the rural delegates in spite of his progressive record.

The convention met in New York's Madison Square Garden during a July heat wave. To the party's shame a motion not to include a plank in the platform condemning the Klan by name passed by $543\frac{3}{20}$ to $542\frac{3}{20}$. There followed a nine-day deadlock over the nomination. Through ninety-five ballots the hoarse voice of the aged Bryan vied with the raucous noise of the Tammany gallery, and the contest was relayed by radio to millions of American homes. The split in the party had become irremediable; the sweltering delegates had become exhausted. At last Smith and McAdoo withdrew by mutual agreement. On the 103rd ballot the convention nominated John W. Davis for President and Charles Bryan as his running mate. They were an unlikely brace. Davis, who had served as Solicitor General and briefly as ambassador to Great Britain during the Wilson Administration, was a cultivated gentleman and an eminent corporation lawyer identified with the House of Morgan. The liberals who disdained him could find small solace in Bryan's younger brother Charley, at best a cockboat in the wake of the Commoner's leaky man-of-war. Wall Street and Nebraska could not be squeezed onto a single ticket, but the prolonged bitterness of the convention had made a saner choice impossible.

A third nomination stirred wider interest. The resurgence of reform candidates in the congressional election of 1922 had owed much to the Conference for Progressive Political Action, an organization of farm leaders, social workers, former Bull Moosers, and Socialists. Now the leaders of the Conference began to talk about running a separate ticket in 1924. The communists forced their hand by taking over the Farmer-Labor party and offering its nomination to "Battle Bob" La Follette. Then almost seventy, iron-gray, still the indomitable Daniel in the lion's den of "the interests," La Follette scorned the offer. That response prompted his supporters to form a new Progressive party, which named La Follette and the liberal Montana Democrat Burton K. Wheeler as its national candidates.

La Follette's candidacy attracted a host of tireless battlers for reform, among them Felix Frankfurter, John R. Commons, and Jane Addams. It was endorsed by the American Federation of Labor and, curiously, by the Socialists. La Follette stood for conservation, public ownership of waterpower, increased taxes on wealth, curbing the authority of the Supreme Court, limiting the use of injunctions in labor disputes, the popular election of judges, the direct election of Presidents, the end of child labor, and a national referendum on declarations of war. But he emphasized the evil of monopoly, ringing again the changes of his early campaigns in Wisconsin. The *Wall Street Journal* called his platform "Wisconsin Bolshevism"; the head of the Communist party in the United States called it "the most reactionary document of the year." Both statements were nonsense. The platform and the campaign were simply refurbished Grangerism, still appealing to many farmers, and the only haven for those who could stomach neither Coolidge nor Davis.

The Republicans ignored Davis and harped on La Follette's radicalism. They need not have worked so hard as they did nor have spent the millions they poured into the campaign, for the nation voted overwhelmingly to "keep cool with Coolidge." The President carried thirty-five states to Davis' twelve and La Follette's one, Wisconsin. Coolidge won 382 electoral votes to his opponents' 149. And his popular vote, over 15,000,000, exceeded the combined total of Davis, who polled fewer than 8,500,000, and La Follette, who had slightly more than 4,800,000. Prosperity and "Silent Cal" had enjoyed a major triumph.

Yet the new Progressive party had made a point, though it died in 1925 with La Follette. The point was simply that there was room in politics for dissent from the business creed. The lesson was not lost on the Democrats, who realized that they had to close ranks and reconstruct a coalition that welcomed men of all colors, all parentages, all sections. If the Democrats were to win in the future they would have to be "unequivocally the party of progress and liberal thought." That phrase was Franklin Roosevelt's, who saw small chance for a victory before 1932. When it came, at its core would be the combination of Davis and La Follette voters.

Grandiose illusions

The good life. Americans were optimistic during Coolidge's second term. The middle class in particular, more comfortable than ever before, experienced a sense of well-being. They admitted no limit to a personal success symbolized by material possessions. They neither liked nor trusted the "knockers," but preferred the "boosters," the men with their eyes and hearts set on the rosy future.

Some of the boosters channeled their optimism into the expanding advertising profession. National advertising flourished in the twenties. It offered an attractive substitute for more painful forms of competition, like price-cutting, which, in any event, were being curtailed by trade agreements and informal arrangements among manufacturers. Advertising also helped identify brands for consumers, who were buying more and more of their goods in stores and producing fewer and fewer at home. Advertising men believed they were "inspiring citizens to live a more abundant life." They were creating new wants and encouraging discontent with possessions outmoded but not necessarily outworn. Advertisers sold the ingredients of the good life—health in orange juice, cleanliness in soap, popularity in deodorants, romantic love in voguish clothes.

As one General Motors executive put it, advertising had to make people "healthily dissatisfied with what they have. . . . The old factors of wear and tear . . . are too slow." Built-in obsolescence paved the road to business success. Manufacturing prettier, more comfortable cars than Ford did, changing models annually (while also meeting competitive standards in engineering), General Motors won primacy in the automobile industry largely by catering to luxury and fashion.

Advertising also created and sold reputations, both corporate and personal. Public-relations experts, taking over the new game of ballyhoo as their own, fabricated heroes on demand. Some of the celebrated athletes of the 1920s, for example, owed part of their fame to sheer ballyhoo. To be sure, Bobby Jones in golf, Bill Tilden in tennis, Jack Dempsey in boxing, and Babe Ruth in baseball were athletes of genuinely

Babe Ruth: heroic proportions

A new age of business

The mission of advertising

heroic proportions. But their proportions were overdrawn, and cynical public-relations men learned to conceal the boorish behavior of Ruth, among others, by planting stories of fictitious noble deeds.

The prospering tabloid newspapers catered to a mass audience that delighted in sensationalism and hero worship. The art of sham was especially effective when it could concentrate on sex. It publicized the new heroes and heroines of the booming motion-picture industry—Rudolph Valentino, the Casanova of the silent films, whose untimely death broke thousands of adolescent hearts; Clara Bow, the ''It'' girl, whose curves and curls entranced a male multitude; Mary Pickford, the sweet charmer whom a plucky lad could more properly admire; and Charlie Chaplin, the incomparable clown.

Outside Hollywood, standard success stories followed classic forms—farm boys conquered the city while remaining pure, poor boys struggled and saved their way to wealth, nice boys met and married beautiful rich girls. The protagonist's gleaming teeth, curly hair, lithe muscles, humility, and hard work assured a happy ending. And ordinary Americans could do just as well through diligent use of the right toothpaste, hair lotion, and correspondence course. But the plot was used too often to boost sales and circulation, and it was beginning to wear thin. Just then a real hero revived the faith.

In the spring of 1927 there was startling news of a young man flying solo, eastward across the Atlantic, in a small monoplane. No one before had made that flight alone. The prayers of the nation followed Charles A. Lindbergh, Jr., to France. His safe landing set off a jubilee; Coolidge sent a cruiser to bring him home; New York extended ecstatic greetings. Briefly,

sham and commercialism hid from authentic daring and clean-cut youth. Lindbergh took it calmly. After writing another stanza to his saga by marrying Anne Morrow, the daughter of a Morgan partner, he tried to escape the tabloids and the confetti. Myths need a foundation in truth, and the Lindbergh story had been as genuine as it was refreshing. When it faded from the headlines, myth fed once again on the exploits of hired muscle men who drew crowds to mammoth stadiums.

Advertising and public relations and ballyhoo, like the newspapers and magazines and radio that

The ''It'' girl: Clara Bow

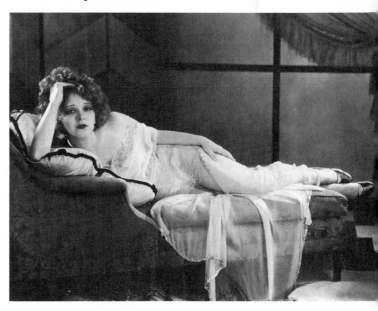

Urban ways

carried them, exported urban ways to rural people. They disseminated a common set of symbols to diverse groups. They told farmers and laborers and suburbanites to admire the same success stories and buy the same cars and cosmetics. They told them all to spend their money to increase their comfort, to prove their mettle, to live "the good life." They encouraged installment buying to ensure the sale of an expanding national product. They helped Americans with rising wages to forget about the frustrations of their dull and routine jobs. The spurious self-esteem that sprang from possession and fashion would endure only so long as Americans could count on steady income and easy credit; but so long as prosperity lasted, advertisers gilded the promises of a commercial culture, the only brand of Americanism they really understood. This crass and transient boom was rooted in illusion, in calling things by the wrong names and then accepting the names as true. The illusions of public life were similarly deceiving.

The image of America abroad. The Coolidge Administration was continually involved in Latin American affairs. But often it succeeded only in obscuring national purpose and generating ill will among Latin Americans. Secretary of State Hughes, moved by a concern for peace and order, had helped bring about

the peaceful settlement of several Latin American boundary disputes. During his tenure, the United States also sponsored a conference of Central American powers, which agreed to withhold recognition from any government established by a *coup d'état*. But this genuflection to stability ignored the realities of Central American politics, for where the government in power had complete control over elections, a *coup d'état* or revolution was the only means of ousting it.

In Nicaragua Coolidge acted unilaterally. First, in 1925, he withdrew a token force of marines from that nation, which then seemed capable of servicing its foreign debt and preserving its internal stability. But the appearance was deceptive. Almost at once revolution broke out, and Coolidge again landed the marines, in time some five thousand. Regrettably, in its quest for order and for commercial opportunity the United States chose to support the reactionary faction, whose identification with large landowners and American investors had helped provoke the revolution in the first place.

The marines contained the fighting, but they could not bring it to an end. American bankers were lending money to the conservative faction for the purchase of munitions in the United States, and the rebels were receiving some arms from sympathetic Mexico. Increasingly uncomfortable, Coolidge in 1927 named Henry L. Stimson as his personal emissary to negotiate a peace. Stimson succeeded in arranging an effective truce and an honest election, in which the rebel general triumphed. The marines, however, remained until 1933. They also remained in Haiti but in 1924 left the Dominican Republic, where President Wilson had sent them.

Though the United States had no territorial ambitions, Yankee investors were seeking bonanzas in Latin America, and Latin Americans resented the Yankee habit of intervening in their local affairs. At the Pan-American Conference of 1928 the Argentine delegation sponsored a proposal that "no American country have the right to intervene in any other American country." The United States succeeded in defeating the proposal but in doing so heightened the resentment. Late in 1928 the State Department concluded that intervention was not justified by the Monroe Doctrine or by the interests of American investors. But it was still not ready to announce that conclusion or to surrender its claim to unilateral intervention. This offense to the sensitivities of Latin Americans continued to cloud hemispheric friendship.

Latin American liberals, moreover, identified the United States with the forces of reaction. Even more than the Nicaraguan episode, developments in Mexico contributed to that view. In 1925 Plutarco Elias

Calles, the new president of Mexico, revived the spirit of the revolution of 1910, which had for several years been in eclipse. He sponsored laws that permitted foreigners to acquire land only if they renounced the protection of their own government, and laws that defined all subsoil deposits as the inalienable property of the Mexican nation. Oil companies, American and other, were required to apply for a renewal of their concessions before 1927. Four large American companies refused. Their spokesmen in the United States, asserting that Mexico was on the road to Bolshevism, called for military intervention, but in January 1927 the United States Senate by unanimous vote passed a resolution demanding the peaceful settlement of all contested issues—by arbitration, if necessary.

Several months later Coolidge appointed a new ambassador, Dwight W. Morrow, with the overriding commission "to keep us out of war with Mexico." Morrow's patient negotiations led to a temporary relaxation of the Mexican land laws and restored friendly relations. Yet Morrow's admirable performance could not erase the hostility created by earlier American diplomacy. To reformers south of the border American amity was colored by oil.

Europeans resented a different kind of diplomacy of the dollar. During the First World War the United States had lent the Allies $7 billion and after the war another $3.3 billion. The recipients had spent their loans almost entirely on American military products and relief supplies. With the return of peace, they regarded the loans merely as one part of the total Allied resistance to Germany, an American contribution toward a victory to which Europeans had given a larger share of flesh and blood. So they were reluctant to repay either the loans or the interest on them. And even those who wanted to square accounts found it difficult to pay. The European nations had depleted their own reserves before borrowing from the United States, and now they found it impossible to replenish those reserves in an American market sealed off by the tariff.

The only way they could meet their obligations to the United States was to draw on the huge reparations that had been imposed on Germany at Versailles. But Germany lacked both the means to pay and the will to scrimp in order to exonerate a war guilt it did not really accept. In 1923 it defaulted, and French and Belgian troops occupied the Ruhr Valley. The Germans there cut down coal production, while the German government inflated its currency recklessly, and the resulting economic distress in both France and Germany seemed to forebode economic collapse and possibly even armed conflict.

The crisis commanded American as well as European attention. Earlier, Charles Evans Hughes had suggested that an international commission of experts, including Americans, be appointed to examine the whole reparations problem. The deadlock in the Ruhr now persuaded the French to agree. The committees that then met recommended what was called the Dawes Plan, in recognition of the participation of Charles Gates Dawes, who was soon to become Coolidge's running mate. That plan, which went into effect in 1924, arranged for an international loan to stabilize German currency and for a flexible, graduated scale of reparations payments. Five years later another American, Owen D. Young, headed a second committee, which substantially reduced the payments. The Allies, satisfied by these terms and concurrent European political agreements, withdrew their forces from the Ruhr and the Rhineland.

American money, however, played a more significant role in the European crisis than did either Dawes or Young. Between 1924 and 1931 Germany managed to meet its payments only because its government, its municipalities, and its businessmen were able to borrow $2.6 billion in the United States. In turn, only the reparations collected by the Allies enabled them to keep up their payments on their American war debts. The interdependence of debts and reparations payments was obvious, but the United States refused to acknowledge it. Most Americans, moreover, most of their congressmen, and certainly their President rejected the notion that the debts had in any sense been offset by the Allied losses in battle. For Coolidge, as for most of his constituents, the debts were business obligations pure and simple. When the French proposed that the burden of debt be eased, the President unhesitatingly turned them down. "They hired the money," he said. The spirit behind that phrase overshadowed all the efforts of Dawes and Young. So long as it prevailed, Europe regarded Uncle Sam as Uncle Shylock.

Deluded diplomacy. The Administration resisted the facts of international politics as strongly as it resisted the facts of international economics. Like most Americans, Coolidge believed in disarmament, not only because he knew that it would reduce federal expense, but because he presumed that it would assure peace. But he did not understand, or at least would not admit, the continuing importance of power in international affairs.

Further, the conventional men in control of the army and the navy husbanded their meager appropriations and resisted spending anything on airplanes and submarines, even though those weapons had clearly made traditional military tactics and strategy obsolete. The failure to develop aircraft infuriated General William ("Billy") Mitchell of the Army Air Service, whose bombers had sunk a battleship in 1921. In an oracular report two years later, he warned the

Grandiose illusions

authorities of the vulnerability of battleships. In 1925, after the navy's sheer incompetence had resulted in the destruction of a dirigible, Mitchell attacked his superiors in public and urged the creation of a separate air command. A court-martial suspended him from duty for five years. The flurry over the episode persuaded Coolidge to appoint a civilian board of inquiry under Dwight Morrow, but it shrugged off Mitchell's arguments. The Administration denied public funds to promote commercial aviation as well. By 1929 the productive capacity of the American aircraft industry had fallen to seventy-five hundred planes a year, little more than a third of the capacity available at the war's end. In the absence of responsible public policy, the United States alone of the major powers slept smugly through the morning of the air age.

Coolidge was less complacent about international naval competition. The Five Power Treaty had applied only to battleships and aircraft-carriers, and the signatories had continued to build auxiliaries. Late in 1924 Congress authorized the construction of eight cruisers. Hoping to avoid the expense of further construction and to end the naval rivalry, the President invited the powers to a conference in 1927. Italy, already infected by Mussolini's fantasies of military glory, refused to attend. So did France, unhappy with the small ratio it had already received at Washington and reluctant, in the face of Italian resurgence, to commit itself to further self-restraint. Coolidge, dedicated to a policy of isolation from European affairs, had failed to assess these obstacles to disarmament. He failed also to negotiate a preliminary understanding essential to any agreement with the British. As a consequence, the English-speaking delegates at the 1927 conference wrangled to no purpose, while the Japanese stood contentedly aside.

Coolidge had already retreated from an earlier, cautious gesture toward internationalism. The Permanent Court of International Justice called for by the League of Nations Covenant had been established in 1921. The purpose of this World Court was to adjudicate certain types of case, to render advice whenever the League requested it, and to arbitrate cases brought before it. Americans had long hoped for the development of a body of law that could be applied to international affairs and in 1923 Harding, influenced by Hughes, recommended conditional American adherence to the court. Coolidge made the same recommendation in his first annual message. But, even though Hughes had drafted four reservations to the court's protocol to protect the United States from contact with the League itself, the isolationists in the Senate balked. After a long delay the Senate adopted a fifth reservation that would limit the court's right even to render advisory opinions to the League. Fur-

ther, the court could give no opinion, without American consent, on any question in which the United States claimed an interest. In 1926 the Senate finally voted adherence to the court on those conditions. When the members of the court then tried to clarify the meaning of the reservations, Coolidge declared that clarification constituted rejection and that there was no prospect of American adherence to the court.* That denouement, followed by the failure of the naval-armaments conference, left the Administration's diplomatic record singularly barren.

During his last months in office, however, Coolidge's diplomacy won wide acclaim. Salmon O. Levinson, a Chicago lawyer, had been recommending that the great powers sign an agreement condemning war. Professor James T. Shotwell, who had been advancing the same suggestion independently, also proposed sanctions to enforce such an agreement. The idea of outlawing war caught the attention of many Americans, including William E. Borah, chairman of the Senate Committee on Foreign Relations. Shotwell urged it upon Aristide Briand, the French foreign minister, who promptly used it for his own purposes. In April 1927, in a gesture of good will to compensate for Franco-American friction over disarmament and war debts, Briand wrote an address to the American people in which he proposed a pact outlawing war. Coolidge was irritated by Briand's resorting to irregular channels to announce his scheme, but the popular enthusiasm for the proposal forced the President's hand. The State Department asked Briand to submit his plan formally.

Secretary of State Frank B. Kellogg now outflanked Briand. Intent on avoiding a bilateral agreement that would imply some sort of alliance between the United States and France, Kellogg recommended instead "an effort to obtain the adherence of all the principal powers of the world to a declaration renouncing war as an instrument of national policy." While Briand stalled, the Secretary of State circulated the draft of a declaration he had drawn up on his own. He also let it be known that the United States would consent to sign the pact in Paris. Briand then accepted the American scheme, and in August 1928 fifteen nations meeting in Paris endorsed a treaty by which they renounced war and promised to settle all disputes, whatever their nature, by "pacific means."

Americans were jubilant over the banishment of war—so jubilant that they tended to ignore qualifications made in diplomatic notes exchanged by the signatories. These set down reservations safeguarding

---

*Both Hoover and Franklin Roosevelt later recommended adherence to the court on terms like those contemplated by Hughes. But the Senate declined.

A new age of business

France's interpretations of its own self-defense and Great Britain's obligations to its empire. In recommending ratification of the pact, the Senate Foreign Relations Committee reported that ratification would not, in its view, curtail the right of the United States to self-defense and to its own interpretations of the Monroe Doctrine, nor would ratification oblige the United States to take any action against a violator of the Kellogg-Briand pact. So interpreted, the pact won approval by a vote of eighty-five to one. But so interpreted, it was, in the words of Senator Carter Glass of Virginia, "worthless, but perfectly harmless."

For most Americans the Paris pact constituted a triumph. To declare perpetual peace without assuming the responsibility for preserving it suited the nation's mood. Now the nation could cut its expenditures, disarm, collect its debts, and trust to reassuring words for sunny safety. Yet the hocus-pocus that sold peace in multilingual print was not unlike the hocus-pocus that sold beauty in a bottle.

Get rich quick. Of all the grandiose illusions of the 1920s none was more beguiling than the prospect of easy riches. It rested on the simple faith that the value of property would constantly increase, and that the man who bought today could sell tomorrow at a handsome profit. Those who had property to sell nourished this faith, and they were helped by the ready credit that enabled speculators to borrow what they needed. The hucksters and the boomers, more-

over, made the allure of speculation a favorite fantasy of the time.

For a while in the mid-twenties the quest for a bonanza drew thousands of Americans to ventures in Florida real estate. The population of Miami more than doubled between 1920 and 1925, and other Florida cities and resorts along the Atlantic and Gulf coasts also mushroomed. Florida's boomers pointed to the warm winter climate, the ready accessibility of their region to vacationers from the North, the prospect of an American Riviera. Imagination covered swamps and barren sands with towns and building lots. As the greedy rushed to buy the dream, a few who invested early and sold at the peak of the boom made fortunes. Their success lured others. Most of the transactions took the form of binders—agreements to buy property, which could be had for a fraction of the value of the property itself. The binders could be sold and sold again, each time for more money.

For every sale, of course, there had to be a buyer. The trade in binders was profitable only so long as someone came along to bid them up, and once people began to compare the dream with the reality the buyers were bound to disappear. The balloon began to deflate in the spring and summer of 1926. That fall it burst when a hurricane swept through the Miami area, destroying developments that had emerged from the dream stage, and wrecking the railroad to Key West. The grand plans of the boomers were laid away;

Miami
after the hurricane

Grandiose illusions

the millions of dollars in speculative profits were wiped out; and the Florida craze was over.

But a much larger boom was already under way. During the prosperous twenties most of the gains from increased productivity and from the growing market for manufactured goods were funneled into corporate profits. And as profits rose, enhanced by Mellon's tax favors to business, so did the value of corporate shares. Initially that rise reflected a genuine increase in the worth of corporate properties and in the earning potential of the corporations themselves. In the mid-twenties, however, the price of stocks began to soar at a dizzying pace. Investors who were looking for securities that would give them a reasonably safe return now had to compete with speculators who were after overnight fortunes. To meet the demand for stocks, promoters organized investment trusts and multitiered holding companies whose only assets were hope and good will. They offered their new issues to eager buyers deluded by greed and by a naive confidence in the surging market. In 1923 new capital issues totaled $3.2 billion; in 1927, $10 billion, much of it purely speculative. The volume of sales on the New York Stock Exchange leaped from 236 million shares in 1923 to 577 million in 1927 and to 1,125 million a year later.

Corporations themselves speculated. As the market rose, corporations found that they earned less by investing their reserves in new facilities than by putting them into brokers' loans—that is, loans that brokers made to their customers to enable them to gamble far beyond their cash resources. In "buying on margin," as this practice was called, customers relied on brokers' loans to cover most of the cost of their stock purchases. Brokers and customers alike expected that the growing value of the stocks would

make it easy enough to repay the loans. Meeting the pressing demand for brokers' loans, or "call money," corporations emptied their surpluses into the money market, where they received staggering returns.

Instead of tempering the boom, public officials encouraged it. The Federal Reserve System had means to tighten credit—that is, to make loans more expensive. But it chose to use its power to keep interest rates low. It did so in order to discourage the import of gold from Europe, and thus to protect the value of European currency and also to facilitate American loans to Europe, then still in need of investment funds for economic rehabilitation and development. (If interest rates had gone way up, Europeans and Americans would both have tended to invest more of their money within the United States.) Even if the Federal Reserve had tightened credit, however, it could not have controlled the call-money market that the corporations were feeding, for speculators were willing to borrow at usurious rates to finance their march to riches.

In the absence of federal authority over either credit or the chicanery of promoters, the best weapon available to the government was simple candor. There was, however, none of that. Secretary of the Treasury Mellon knew exactly what was going on; indeed he was himself deep in speculation. Yet whenever sober businessmen questioned the state of the market, he or his colleagues in the Administration invariably responded with soothing reassurances. And Coolidge went along. Early in 1927 William Z. Ripley, a Harvard economist, lectured the President on the prevalent "double-shuffling, honey-fuggling, hornswoggling and skulduggery." Coolidge, feet on desk and cigar in teeth, asked gloomily: "Is there anything we can do down here?" Ripley answered that the regulation of securities was the responsibility of the states, not of the federal government. Relieved, the President relaxed and put the incident out of his mind.

By the end of the year brokers' loans had reached nearly $4 billion. In January 1928 Coolidge reassured the dubious few by announcing that this volume of loans was perfectly natural. Shortly thereafter Roy Young of the Federal Reserve Board, a close friend of Herbert Hoover, told a congressional committee that the loans were "safely and conservatively made." Those sanctions hastened the tempo of the boom and gave a Midas touch to 1928, an election year.

To Coolidge the ascending figures on the ticker tape were evidence of the nation's prosperity and of his own sagacity. He was as much honey-fuggled as hornswoggling. Like the brokers and speculators, he was at once the prisoner and the propagator of the grandiose myths that bemused the nation.

Nonconformity and dissent

The Jazz Age. Some Americans, however, were repelled by materialism and its delusions. Disappointed by a progressive faith that seemed to have failed, they were alienated by the emptiness of business civilization. Some few thousands sought a solution in communism, but all kinds of radicalism recovered only slowly from the postwar repression, and the American communists during the 1920s spent their zeal in factionalism and debate. Most of the disenchanted were equally cynical about serving mankind and about striving for worldly success. Finding only futility in the past and the future, they chose to seek out the pleasures of the present, to live for their private selves and for immediate self-expression.

Those men and women, many of them young, were no more immoral or promiscuous than men and women had been before. But they dropped pretense. They revealed their impatience with traditional standards of conduct openly and often. One symbol of their protest was jazz, with its sensuality, its spontaneity, its atavistic rhythms, and with the sinuous and intimate dancing it inspired. Jazz was ungenteel, even un-Caucasian, above all uninhibited. It expressed not only protest and art of a kind but a controversial change in sexual mores.

That change sprang largely from the ways in which city living altered family life. The nuclear

The Jazz Age: above all, uninhibited

family of the city and suburb (man, wife, children) existed in a private world quite different from that of the kinship family of the country, where grandparents, aunts, uncles, and cousins provided support and where community was more common than aloneness. The very impersonality of the city obliged its inhabitants to meet and resolve the problems of their lives with neither help nor impediment. Not every marriage was equal to the challenge.

Increasingly, women demanded easier and more equitable divorces, and they struggled for equal rights to jobs, to income, to their own apartments, to cigarettes, to whiskey, and to sexual satisfaction in matrimony or sometimes outside it. Much of the energy of feminism concentrated on the birth control movement. That movement, so Margaret Sanger claimed, freed the mind from "sexual prejudice and taboo." Not the least of its functions was to increase the quantity and quality of sexual relationships. Probably the incidence of premarital and extramarital sexual experience also rose. To some extent, especially for young people, adventures in sex released part of a rebellion against the reigning culture and its neopuritanical code.

During the twenties, moreover, even the unrebellious were learning to understand the significance of sex in human nature. The most important contributions to that understanding were made by Sigmund Freud, whose doctrines had first reached America in the years before the war. After the war Freudian psychology rapidly became a national fad, ordinarily in vastly simplified and distorted forms. Freud himself, while demonstrating that neurotic symptoms and behavior could usually be attributed to sexual origins, did not advocate promiscuity. His first concern was with creating a system of analysis that would enable a doctor to help a patient find the emotional sources of his disorders, behavioral or somatic. On the basis of that discovery sick people could then reconstruct their lives. His popularizers, however, interpreted his works as a rationale for sexual freedom. The average American met Freudian ideas only in that sense.

A literature of alienation. "Society was something alien," Malcolm Cowley wrote about himself and his literary contemporaries of the 1920s. "It was a sort of parlor car in which we rode, over smooth tracks, toward a destination we should never have chosen for ourselves." Gertrude Stein called the young writers of the time "a lost generation." It was lost, Cowley later concluded,

> because its training had prepared it for another world than existed after the war . . . because it accepted no older guides to conduct and because it had formed a false picture of society. . . . The

generation belonged to a period of transition from values already fixed to values that had to be erected. . . . They were seceding from the old and yet could adhere to nothing new.

This generation of artists turned its back on progress, on economics, on Main Street, and on Wall Street. "It was characteristic of the Jazz Age," said novelist F. Scott Fitzgerald, one of its high priests, "that it had no interest in politics at all." And the editor of *The Smart Set*, H. L. Mencken, wrote: "If I am convinced of anything, it is that Doing Good is in bad taste."

These men and their fellows detested the business culture. Many of them fled, some to Paris, others to Greenwich Village, still others to an impenetrable privacy of creativity. And they attacked the civilization they had left. Sinclair Lewis peopled the Middle West with confused men and women, trapped by their own futile materialism and unthinking gentility, narrow, unhappy, stifled. Lewis' *Main Street* (1920) and *Babbit* (1922) created satirical symbols of American life that persisted for a quarter of a century, not in the United States alone, but in Europe as well.

Sherwood Anderson exercised a large influence on his literary compatriots. A compassionate critic of small-town America, Anderson abandoned a business career, after a nervous breakdown in 1912, to devote himself to writing. His *Winesburg, Ohio* (1919) was a moving, autobiographical novel of alienation. Perhaps more important, he exemplified the religion of art, for he had escaped Babylon and had succeeded in his career of the spirit.

Seeking in art a distillation of experience, the young masters experimenting with literary form gave a new beauty and vitality to American letters. Encouraged particularly by Ezra Pound and Gertrude Stein and inspired by their prewar poetry, the novelists Ernest Hemingway and William Faulkner and the poet T. S. Eliot raised the national literary reputation to its all-time zenith. Hemingway's *The Sun Also Rises* (1926) and *A Farewell to Arms* (1929) expressed a deep revulsion against nineteenth-century standards of conduct and idealizations of war. In *The Sound and the Fury* (1929) Faulkner used Freudian insights and adventurous prose to expose the awful tensions between self and society and the exacerbation of those tensions in the culture of the Deep South. Eliot's "The Love Song of J. Alfred Prufrock" (written in 1911, published six years later) made impotence the weary symbol of modern man. His *The Waste Land* (1922), probably the most emulated poem of the decade, provided a text in fragmentation and despair.

All these works revealed alienation and spoke of protest, but their authors were first, and most self-consciously, artists. So, too, were the other Americans

Jazz and the black artist

who shared in the extraordinary literary renaissance of the period. They included an impressive number of talented black artists and authors, among them James Weldon Johnson, Countee Cullen, and Langston Hughes. Though some of the prose and poetry of the "Harlem Renaissance" repudiated black themes, much of it borrowed self-consciously from black culture, and the best of it, like the poetry of Hughes, ranked with the best work of white Americans.

The great outburst of artistic creativity had begun before 1920; it continued beyond 1929; but it came to a crescendo during the Coolidge era. But the religion of art, then so prevalent, could be as futile as materialism itself. Alienation ordinarily denied social responsibility. The artists who rejected their national culture also accepted most of its claims. They turned away from the Coolidge era not because of its inequities but because of its superficial accomplishments. In contrast to the progressive intellectuals who had preceded them, they sought private escapes and private satisfactions, and they surrendered society to its shortsighted masters. This escapism deprived the nation of the assistance of many of its most imaginative minds.

Worse still, some Americans cast off democracy along with materialism. They agreed with the Mellons and the Fords and the Coolidges who believed that the business cult was the democratic ideal. They concluded that democracy necessarily generated a vulgar, selfish, pecuniary civilization. The critic Van Wyck Brooks, in his *The Ordeal of Mark Twain* (1920), wrote about the Gilded Age, with the twenties much in mind, as "a horde-life, a herd-life, an epoch without sun and stars," which condemned the artist, and the soul, to frustration. Eliot also scorned democracy and remained rootless until he found salvation in the church, as Brooks did in sentimentality. H. L.

Mencken was more acid. He ridiculed not only Prohibition, the Ku Klux Klan, and censorship, but the whole American people, whom he considered a sodden, brutish, ignorant mob. Democracy, for him, was government by orgy. As for democracy as a theory, "all the known facts lie flatly against it." Irving Babbitt, who formulated an aristocratic doctrine of the "inner check," had no patience with the "sickly sentimentalizing of the lot of the underdog," no confidence in social reform, no hope except in pseudo-Platonic comforts, and thus no real hope. The price of complacent materialism was alienation; and the bill of despair that went with alienation was ominously high.

Progressive hopes and failures. Yet disenchantment did not lead all critics to alienation. Some drew on the legacy of progressivism and on their own undaunted spirit to point out anew the paths toward a good society. John Dewey (see p. 518) continued to examine the practical consequences of social policies in *Human Nature and Conduct* (1922) and *Individualism Old and New* (1929). These books urged experimentation in education for selfless citizenship, and public rather than private planning for social rather than pecuniary goals. Charles Beard in his *The Rise of American Civilization* (1927) stressed optimistically the historical significance of economic change. A year later he called for social engineering, national planning, to organize advancing science and technology for the general good. John R. Commons (see p. 518) worked out theories and techniques for social insurance, and among his fellow economists Irving Fisher showed that the government had to manage the nation's money supply if it was to achieve desirable social and economic ends. William T. Foster and Waddill Catchings advanced even more novel ideas.

They attacked the beliefs that savings flowed automatically into investment and that business cycles righted themselves. If the nation was to avoid depressions, they insisted, government would have to resort to public spending when private investment faltered.

In public life, too, the progressive faith persevered, though it suffered major setbacks. Militant feminists, by no means satisfied with suffrage, now worked through the Women's party for the goal of total equality with men, a goal to be achieved through the proposed equal rights amendment to which Congress had yet to give serious consideration. Indeed the militants lost influence during the decade after 1919. The League of Women Voters, however, a growing organization almost wholly of middle-class membership, reached a broader constituency in its efforts to educate the electorate about reform issues familiar to prewar progressives, including the protection of working women. But the League won no important legislative victories, partly because women, who did not vote in a bloc, shared the indifference to politics or the conservative bias of most men of the time.

So it was that in 1926, when Mellon again advocated tax relief for the rich, his dwindling opponents could find no telling argument against cutting taxes. Federal revenues were then more than ample for the costs of government, and no one had yet developed a cogent program for spending to improve the nation's housing, roads, and natural resources. Without difficulty, the Administration put through Congress a revenue act that cut in half the estate tax and the maximum surtax on individual incomes. Two years later Congress eased the tax on corporations. Mellon had carried the field.

Private utility companies were almost as successful. Sales of electric power doubled during the twenties, and ingenious promoters with very little cash managed to monopolize the industry by setting up complex holding companies. By the end of the decade ten utility systems controlled approximately three-fourths of the nation's light and power business. The promoters kept the cost of electricity unreasonably high and through financial sleight of hand manipulated securities at the expense of bewildered stockholders. They also carried on a massive propaganda campaign and financed a powerful lobby to beat back demands for public supervision and for public distribution of electrical power.

The reformers, led by George Norris, included Governor Smith of New York and his successor, Franklin Roosevelt, who advocated state ownership and operation of public power. Gifford Pinchot, governor of Pennsylvania, organized a survey in 1923 that paved the way to public rural electrification. Many municipalities built or acquired their own power plants, and Nebraska, Norris' home state, established a public power system.

Farm politics particularly exercised Washington during Coolidge's second term, when farmers stepped up their demands for a government marketing plan. Such a plan had first been suggested in the lean years right after the war. Now it became the basis for legislation sponsored by Senator Charles L. McNary of Oregon and Representative Gilbert N. Haugen of Iowa. At the heart of the proposal was a two-price scheme—a high domestic price and a low foreign price for staple crops. By purchasing farm surpluses, the government was to sustain a balance of supply and demand that would keep commodity prices at "parity" (see p. 636). In that manner the government would be underwriting the prosperity of the American farmers. The government would sell farm surpluses abroad for whatever price it could get, and any loss would be offset by an equilization tax levied on farmers or on those who processed and transported farm products.

Congress rejected the McNary-Haugen bill in 1924. But it passed a revised measure in 1927 and another one in 1928. Coolidge vetoed both versions. The bill, he said, would create a vast and clumsy bureaucracy, would improperly delegate taxing power from Congress to the administrators of the program, and would involve the government in trying to fix prices. Such prices, he argued, would be artificial and would encourage farmers to overproduce. Moreover, if the American government began to dump farm surpluses abroad, foreign governments would be bound to retaliate. The last two objections were undoubtedly sound, but Coolidge's concern for minimized government and a laissez-faire economy was unconvincing. After all, the government used the tariff, which was simply one kind of taxation, to aid industry. And the tariff, combined with the marketing practices of big business, led to artificial prices for manufactured goods. Those very prices kept farmers' costs high while their incomes lagged. Coolidge's vetoes, as the economist Rexford G. Tugwell put it, revealed "a stubborn determination to do nothing."

The debate over farm policy, like the debate over public power and taxation, highlighted the policy issue that dominated the late twenties: Was the federal government to be the handmaiden of business, the servant of the wealthy? Or was the government to build an equitable society in which all could obtain a fair share of the nation's wealth? Intellectuals like Dewey and Commons and politicians like Norris and Smith insisted on the second alternative. They were insisting that Americans, both in their private lives and in their conduct of public affairs, accept a responsibility that the spirit of the times rejected.

A new age of business

A Catholic for President

The election of 1928. Calvin Coolidge announced that he "did not choose to run" in 1928. He might have been persuaded to accept a draft, but the Republican convention nominated Herbert Hoover on its first ballot. Professional politicians had little liking for Hoover, who was never one of them, and Midwestern farmers had little enthusiasm for a man who had opposed the McNary-Haugen bill precisely as Coolidge had. But businessmen trusted Hoover; his reputation for efficiency and humaneness was at its peak; and his personal success more than compensated for his lack of public glamour.

Hoover stood stolidly on a platform that attributed good times to Republican rule, praised the protective tariff, endorsed Prohibition, offered only platitudes to labor, and warned farmers of the evil of "putting the government into business." In his campaign speeches Hoover emphasized the virtues of individualism and "the American system" of free enterprise. There lay the source of prosperity. "We in America," Hoover said, "are nearer to the final triumph over poverty than ever before in the history of any land. . . . Given a chance to go forward with the policies of the last eight years, we shall soon with the help of God be in the sight of the day when poverty will be banished from this nation."

The Democrats nominated Al Smith. Those who had kept the nomination from him in 1924 could no longer deny his claims. As governor of New York he had made a record for efficiency as compelling as Hoover's. He had reordered the state's finances and reorganized its administration. He had promoted public health and public recreation, workmen's compensation, and civil liberties. As a national candidate, Smith stood for public ownership of the principal power sites and generating plants, and he endorsed the McNary-Haugen Plan.

"Socialism," Hoover retorted. But Smith was no radical. Indeed, he, too, deferred to the temper of the time. He accepted the need for protective tariffs. He chose as his campaign-manager John J. Raskob, a Republican industrialist, identified with Du Pont and General Motors. The Democratic campaign may have reassured the conservatives, but it converted almost none of them, and it disappointed the liberals.

Raskob's appointment, furthermore, reopened the party wounds of 1924, for, like Smith, Raskob was a Catholic and a "wet." Rural America dug out its old suspicions of the city, booze, Tammany, and the pope. Particularly in the South, fundamentalist preachers associated Smith with all the old fears and hates. Smith explained that his religion had not and would not affect his policies, and his record confirmed his words. But the suspicious took their cue instead from his East Side accent, his brown derby, his open advocacy of repeal, his unabashed cityness. Hoover, for his part, made no convincing effort to dispel the religious issue.

More than bigotry, prosperity defeated Smith, for probably no Democrat could have outraced Santa Claus. Smith received only 87 electoral votes to Hoover's 444; some 41 percent of the popular vote to Hoover's 58. Five Southern states and all the border states went Republican. The Grand Old Party had won another landslide.

The returns, however, were not that unambiguous. Smith carried the dozen largest cities, which the Republicans had won handily four years before. The Democrats also cut into the traditionally Republican agricultural vote in the West. The farmers had doubts about Santa Claus, and in the cities the ethnic issue cut both ways, helping the Democrats in the urban North as much as it hurt them in the rural South. In 1928, as in 1924, the vote dramatized the need for Democratic unity and for a positive commitment to social reconstruction. But the prospects seemed poor, for the Coolidge era ended much as it had begun.

Prejudice had divided the underprivileged, and prosperity had obscured public irresponsibility. Most Americans, as they had shown at the polls, were remarkably content. And confident, as well. The stock market boomed as it eagerly awaited Hoover's inauguration and the nation's final triumph over poverty.

Suggestions for reading

GENERAL

The outstanding general accounts of the Coolidge years and their implications are in A. M. Schlesinger, Jr., *The Crisis of the Old Order** (1957); W. E. Leuchtenburg, *The Perils of Prosperity, 1914–32** (1958); and John Braeman, ed., *Change and Continuity in 20th Century America: The 1920's* (1968). F. L. Allen, *Only Yesterday** (1931), has charm and flair; and J. D. Hicks, *Republican Ascendancy: 1921–1933** (1960), is sober. The most entertaining biography of Coolidge is W. A. White, *A Puritan in Babylon** (1938); but see also Donald McCoy, *Calvin Coolidge* (1967). Coolidge speaks often but rarely well in H. H. Quint and R. H. Ferrell, eds., *The Talkative President: The Off-the-Record Press Conferences of Calvin Coolidge* (1964).

BUSINESS ENTERPRISE

The economics of prosperity are described in George Soule, *Prosperity Decade: From War to Depression, 1917–1929** (1947); the institutions of business, in A. D. Chandler, Jr., *Strategy and Structure** (1962), and T. C. Cochran, *The American Business System: A Historical Perspective, 1900–1955** (2nd ed., 1957); the business creed, in J. W. Prothro, *The Dollar Decade: Business Ideas in the 1920's* (1954); and the techniques of advertising, in Otis Pease, *The Responsibilities of American Advertising* (1958). On the Ford Motor Company, its master, and the automobile industry in general, the preeminent works are Allan Nevins and F. E. Hill, *Ford: The Times, the Man and the Company* (1954) and *Ford: Expansion and Challenge* (1957). There is also an acid analysis in Keith Sward, *The Legend of Henry Ford** (1948). See, too, John Rae, *The Road and Car in American Life* (1971). The best introduction to F. W. Taylor is his own *The Principles of Scientific Management** (1907). Siegfried Giedion, *Mechanization Takes Command: A Contribution to Anonymous History** (1948), offers brilliant observations about technology, which is handled on a more elementary level in Stuart Chase, *Men and Machines* (1929). By far the fullest and best account of labor during the 1920s is in Irving Bernstein, *The Lean Years** (1960). See also Robert Zieger, *Republicans and Labor, 1915–1929* (1969). Two studies of the first rank on corporate concentration and on the business cycle, respectively, are A. A. Berle, Jr., and G. F. Means, *The Modern Corporation and Private Property** (1932, rev. ed., 1969), and Thomas Wilson, *Fluctuations in Income and Employment* (1948). E. A. Goldenweiser, *American Monetary Policy* (1951), deals expertly with its subject.

IDEALS AND IDEOLOGIES

The works mentioned in the text, and other works of the authors noted there, provide a good point of departure for studying the artists and intellectuals of the 1920s. For that purpose, Malcolm Cowley, *Exile's Return** (1934), is rewarding; and so are Alfred Kazin, *On Native Grounds** (1942), and Edmund Wilson, *The Shores of Light** (1952) and *The American Earthquake** (1958). The outstanding anthology of the social and cultural expressions of the time is Loren Baritz, *The Culture of the Twenties** (1969). On black artists, see Nathan Huggins, *Harlem Renaissance** (1971), and Eugene Levy, *James Weldon Johnson* (1973). Among the helpful literary studies are Mark Schorer, *Sinclair Lewis** (1961); Grover

*Available in a paperback edition.

612

A new age of business

Smith, Jr., *T. S. Eliot's Poetry and Plays: A Study in Sources and Meaning** (1956); Cleanth Brooks, *William Faulkner: The Yoknapatawpha Country** (1963); F. J. Hoffman and O. W. Vickery, eds., *William Faulkner: Three Decades of Criticism** (1960); and H. D. Piper, *F. Scott Fitzgerald: A Critical Portrait* (1965). See also C. A. Fenton, *The Apprenticeship of Ernest Hemingway** (1954), and C. H. Baker, *Hemingway: The Writer As Artist** (1956). American anti-intellectuals and bigots receive their just rewards in N. F. Furniss, *The Fundamentalist Controversy, 1918–1931* (1954); and Don Kirschner, *City and Country: Rural Responses to Urbanization in the 1920's* (1970); Ray Ginger, *Six Days or Forever?** (1958), on the Scopes trial; and J. M. Mecklin, *The Ku Klux Klan* (1924). More sympathetic is W. B. Gatewood, Jr., ed., *Controversy in the Twenties* (1969). Among the engaging works on the ideology and politics of Prohibition, and on the crime it helped to spawn, are Andrew Sinclair, *Prohibition: The Era of Excess** (1962); Herbert Asbury, *The Great Illusion* (1950); Charles Merz, *Dry Decade** (1932); Virginius Dabney, *Dry Messiah: The Life of Bishop Cannon* (1949); F. D. Pasley, *Al Capone* (1930); and Raymond Moley, *Tribunes of People* (1932).

On women during the 1920s, see William Chafe, *The American Woman: Her Changing Social, Economic, and Political Roles, 1920–1960* (1972); J. S. Lemons, *The Woman Citizen: Social Feminism in the 1920's* (1973); and Lois Banner, *Women in Modern America** (1974).

PUBLIC ISSUES AND PUBLIC MEN

Two important accounts of major federal public policies in the period 1923–29 are in the pertinent parts of R. E. Paul, *Taxation in the United States* (1954), and Theodore Saloutos and J. D. Hicks, *Twentieth Century Populism: Agricultural Discontent in the Middle West, 1900–1939** (1951). Agricultural matters also receive useful treatment in J. D. Black, *Agricultural Reform in the United States* (1930), and M. R. Benedict, *Farm Policies of the United States, 1790–1950* (1953). On the campaign of 1924, there is a brief review in R. B. Nye, *Midwestern Progressive Politics, 1850–1958** (1951, rev. ed., 1959), and a longer analysis in K. C. MacKay, *The Progressive Movement of 1924* (1947). The fullest study of the election of 1928 is E. A. Moore, *A Catholic Runs for President* (1956). Oscar Handlin, *Al Smith and His America** (1958), is short and thoughtful, while Matthew and Hannah Josephson, *Al Smith: Hero of the Cities* (1969), is laudatory. For electoral trends, see David Burner, *The Politics of Provincialism** (1968). Among the autobiographies and biographies of other public men of the time, some of the more rewarding are B. C. and Fola La Follette, *Robert M. La Follette*, 2 vols. (1953); Frank Freidel, *Franklin D. Roosevelt: The Ordeal* (1954); Arthur Mann, *La Guardia: A Fighter Against His Times, 1882–1933** (1959); G. W. Norris, *Fighting Liberal** (1945); Richard Lowitt, *George W. Norris: The Persistence of a Progressive* (1971); William Harbaugh, *Lawyer's Lawyer: The Life of John W. Davis* (1973); Herbert Hoover, *Memoirs*, 3 vols. (1951–52); E. E. Morison, *Turmoil and Tradition: A Study of the Life and Times of Henry L. Stimson** (1960); and H. L. Stimson and McGeorge Bundy, *On Active Service in Peace and War* (1948). The last two shed significant light on the foreign policy of the Coolidge years, on which R. H. Ferrell, *Peace in Their Time** (1952), J. H. Wilson, *American Business and Foreign Policy, 1920–1933** (1971), and Hicks, cited above, are also useful; for an influential point of view, see W. A. Williams, *The Tragedy of American Diplomacy** (1959).

*Available in a paperback edition.

CHAPTER **26**

The end of an era

The United States met the new year of 1929 with a smile and a swagger. The national habit of confidence had grown during three decades in which both the reformers of the early century and the merchants of the new age of business believed they were fashioning a national Eden. A college graduate of the class of 1901, fifty years old in 1929, could believe with them that they had succeeded. As evidence of success, he might point to the statutes left over from progressivism, the great war won, the apparent unlikelihood of future war, the excitement of new inventions, and the largess of good times. Not since the mid-nineties, not for a generation, had the nation suffered a serious depression.

President Hoover

Business plans. "I have no fears for the future of our country," the new President announced at his inauguration. "It is bright with hope." There was no nonsense about Hoover, none of T. R.'s boyishness or Wilson's dreaminess, none of Harding's incontinence or Coolidge's folksiness. The President was a serious man who kept in shape by playing medicine ball in the early morning. He would, most people thought, keep the nation in shape and lead it to ever higher plateaus of prosperity.

Hoover approached his office like a businessman with a business plan. He reorganized the inefficient presidential staff by creating a secretariat in which each member was assigned a specific place and duty. Government was to be neat. It was also to be respectable. Hoover appointed a Cabinet of men who stood for what the business community admired. Mellon continued as Secretary of the Treasury. The others, with one exception, were undistinguished. The exception was Secretary of State Henry L. Stimson, a conservative whose superior perceptions soon made him as uncomfortable as he was valuable.

From the first active in pursuit of his own beliefs, Hoover, according to the solicitor of the Federal Power Commission, interceded to prevent private companies from being regulated rigorously. The President also proposed that the federal government withdraw its control from all public lands and from all new reclamation and irrigation projects. The states, he said, were "more competent to manage . . . these affairs." This was a debatable assertion, but it suited Hoover's purpose. In conservation, as in most other matters, he was determined to keep federal government small in both size and power.

Hoover's farm program reflected that determination. Still, he recognized the need for some aid to agriculture, and he summoned a special session of Congress to provide it. The President suggested that the best way to help the American farmer would be to raise the tariff and to give him federal assistance in marketing his produce—policies that would not, he said, undermine the farmer's initiative. In the Agricultural Marketing Act of 1929, Congress acted on Hoover's suggestions. It created a Federal Farm Board that was to be advised by committees representing the cooperative associations that marketed each of the major commodities. It also provided a revolving fund of $500 million from which the board could make loans to cooperatives to help them market their crops more effectively. Another provision, inserted by the farm bloc, permitted loans to be made to stabilization corporations "for the purpose of controlling any surplus." In other words, these corporations could influence prices so long as the Farm Board lent them enough money. But the Farm Board had no control over production. Consequently, not even generous loans for stabilization could long sustain prices if they should begin a major decline in the face either of gross overproduction or of adverse general economic circumstances. From the first, farmers were dissatisfied with the legislation of 1929.

They gained nothing at all from Hoover's proposal to give them more tariff protection. The President lacked the political skill to guide a tariff bill through Congress. In 1929 Congress put the matter aside. In 1930 industrial lobbyists and their friends in the Republican majority carried protection to its all-time high. The Hawley-Smoot Tariff of that year raised average *ad valorem* rates from about 32 percent to about 40 percent. It increased rates on some seventy farm products and over nine hundred manufactured goods. More than a thousand economists urged Hoover to veto the bill. It would, they pointed out, raise the cost of living, encourage inefficient production, hamper American export trade, including trade in agricultural surpluses, and provoke foreign bitterness and retaliation. Though those arguments were entirely correct, Hoover signed the measure. It reflected the continuing influence of business interests in Washington and their continuing shortsightedness.

The crash. Dramatic evidence of that shortsightedness had already appeared in the stock market, the barometer of prosperity. It soared during the early months of 1929, but unbridled speculation began to worry conservative financiers and the President too. He privately urged the New York Stock Exchange to curb the manipulation of securities, but with no success. Hoover would not ask Congress to interfere, for he "had no desire to stretch the powers of the Federal Government" that far. Instead he supported the Federal Reserve Board when it warned banks against making loans for speculative purposes, and he approved the board's 1 percent increase in the interest rate first in June and again in August 1929. But the higher cost of funds for speculation did not check the speculative fever.

Gamblers in stocks paid no heed to other warnings. The first signs of danger began to appear during the summer of 1929. Residential construction, important for the many industries that supplied its needs throughout the nation, fell off more than a billion dollars; business inventories trebled; the rate of advance in consumer spending dropped some 400 percent. From June onward, industrial production, employment, and commodity prices declined steadily. Indeed the August increase in the interest rate came at a time when legitimate enterprise could ill afford it.

Yet the stock market boomed on. Ignoring the evidence of industrial decline, undeterred by the advancing costs of brokers' loans, speculators bid shares to new peaks. The morning after Labor Day the New York *Times* average of selected industrial stocks stood at 452, up more than 200 points since early 1928. The market seemed strong, but it was sustained only by deluded confidence. In one week brokers' loans had risen $137 million and New York banks had borrowed $64 million to carry the weight of speculation.

During September and most of October the market wavered, moving gently downward. Some days were worrisome, but none of the captains of finance in New York or their lieutenants in Washington voiced alarm. Then on October 23 security prices crumbled in a wave of frenzied selling. Panic was temporarily averted when a group of New York bankers met next morning at J. P. Morgan and Company and agreed to pool their resources to hold the market up. The senior Morgan partner assured reporters that the heavy selling had been "due to a technical condition," not to any basic cause. The following day President Hoover announced that "the fundamental business of the country . . . is on a sound and prosperous basis."

They were wrong. During the next fortnight the market shuddered to collapse. As values fell, all the bets made on a rising market paid off in panic. An uncontrollable decline swept past the support the bankers had organized. By mid-November the New York *Times* average had fallen to a shattering 224. In less than a month the securities listed on the New York Stock Exchange lost $26 billion—more than 40 percent—of their face value. Nor was the descent over. In July 1932 the *Times* average hit bottom at a mere 58.

Contrary to Hoover's assertion, the fundamental business of the country was unsound. Excessive industrial profits, along with skimpy industrial wages, were distributing one-third of all personal income to 5 percent of the population. Some two years before the crash, the annual rate of increase of national investment (as contrasted to speculation) had started downward, not the least because corporations and their executives had diminished expectations for profits from an economy in which purchasing power could no longer keep pace with productivity. That rate of increase of investment, as economists came to understand a decade later, had to continue to rise if

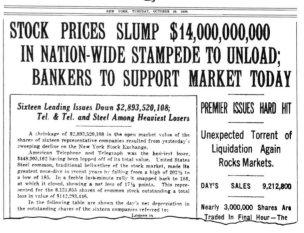

Tuesday, October 29, 1929

economic growth was to be sustained. Since 1927 the shortage of purchasing power among consumers had had a particularly bad effect on the vital construction and automobile industries. The falling market for homes and cars, expensive items, reflected the uneven distribution of American income and wealth that left even the middle class without sufficient cash or credit to continue the buying splurge of the earlier years of the decade. But in the 1920s the level of economic intelligence, like the level of both private and public economic policy, was still relatively low. The surfeit of disposable income among the rich, together with the swollen profits of corporations, had encouraged speculation. When trouble came, the jerry-built corporate structures of many businesses, especially the utilities, toppled. Nor could the American banking system meet the strain, for bankers, though they had been aware of the loose practices of their profession, had long refused to discipline themselves.

Business had failed to keep its house in order. Even worse, it had persuaded the government to follow the unwise economic policies of the decade preceding the crash. The crash itself brought the sagging economy down. It wiped out savings and confidence alike. The mood of despair that settled over the nation stifled any renewal of private investment that might have encouraged recovery. It also dispelled the confidence of Americans in the business élite. The dominance of businessmen and industrialists, in government and out, had brought, not a new Eden, but a panic that marked the onset of the most baleful depression in all history.

The onset of depression

The Hoover policies: first phase. Few of the leaders of American business and politics, either Republican or Democrat, had expected the crash. And when it came, very few of them understood what had

caused it or foresaw the severity of the depression it was to bring. Most of them agreed with the head of Bethlehem Steel, who announced in December 1929 that "never before has American business been as firmly entrenched for prosperity as it is today." Most of them agreed also with Andrew Mellon, who recommended letting the economy run down to the depths, from which it would presumably recover automatically, as it had in the 1870s and 1890s. That policy would entail great suffering, but those who believed that the economy operated according to mechanical laws believed too in the inexorability of business cycles and in the wisdom of leaving them alone, suffering or no. "Liquidate labor," Mellon advised, "liquidate stock, liquidate the farmers."

Hoover knew better. Though he remained convinced that the economy was basically sound and that

THERE IS A SANTA CLAUS!

617

government should not interfere with business, he took steps to prevent the spread of depression. In a series of conferences he tried to persuade business-leaders to keep wages and prices up voluntarily. He called on the Federal Reserve to make it easy for business to borrow. He encouraged the Farm Board to provide funds to help the stabilization corporations in their efforts to sustain commodity prices. Above all, he hoped, by offering private advice and by making public pronouncements, to restore the nation's confidence in business.

Hoover welcomed the Tariff Act of 1930 (see p. 616), for he was convinced that business would be encouraged by a continuation of protection. To hearten businessmen further, he recommended, and Congress in 1930 provided, cuts in personal and corporate income taxes. The reductions gave the wealthy more disposable income to use for investment, but they gave lower-income groups, who paid little taxes anyway, no additional money to spend on consumption. In the absence of confidence in business, the investments were not forthcoming. Following Hoover's advice, Congress did make modest appropriations for public works. These gave some boost to the sick construction industry and to the heavy industries that supplied it, and indirectly to the men who were employed in those industries.

But those efforts were too meager to check the contraction in private spending, investment, and employment that followed the crash. Both Hoover and the Federal Reserve Board opposed a rapid, deliberately inflationary expansion of currency and bank deposits, which the board might have attempted with some possible healthy effect. The President would not countenance any more spending, because he was determined to keep the federal budget balanced, or as close to balanced as possible. This, he believed, as did most Americans, was sound finance, and it was also an unshakable article of business faith. Large federal deficits, like inflation, would have frightened the business community, which the President wanted to soothe. To that purpose, during 1930 the President continually applied the balm of official optimism. True, official gloom would have caused further alarm; but Hoover, while privately dubious, acted as if his conferences with business-leaders had succeeded, whereas wages and prices actually continued to decline.

The blight of depression. "We have now passed the worst," Hoover announced wishfully in May 1930, "and . . . shall rapidly recover." The statistics told a different story. In 1929 new capital issues in the United States, a rough yardstick of investment, had totaled $10 billion; in 1930 they dropped to $7 billion. As the depression deepened, the figure reached $3

"If you die, you're dead, that's all."

billion in 1931 and $1 billion in 1932. Investment was discouraged by the decline in corporate profits, which fell off steadily from $8.4 billion in 1929 to $3.4 billion in 1932. At the same time, the rate of business failures rose—over 100,000 businesses went under in the period 1929–32. And banks were failing too. In 1929, 659 banks with total deposits of about $200 million closed their doors; in 1930, 1,352 banks with deposits of $853 million; in 1931, 2,294 banks with deposits of almost $1,700 million, at the rate of almost 200 a month. Each collapse buried the cash and savings of depositors, most of whom had no other resources.

By the last quarter of 1930, industrial production had fallen 26 percent below the 1929 level. By mid-1932 it was off 51 percent from that level. Unemployment mounted: 4 million in October 1930; nearly 7 million a year later; almost 11 million by the fall of 1932. Even those who kept their jobs were earning less and less. Between 1929 and 1933 the total annual income of labor dropped from $53 to $31.5 billion. Average manufacturing wages came down 60 percent, average salaries 40 percent. Farmers fared even worse: their income declined from $11.9 to $5.3 billion. In 1929 national income touched $81 billion; by 1932 it had shrunk to $49 billion.

Liquidation carried a frightful burden of human suffering. Thousands of middle-class families, their incomes dwindling, sometimes entirely gone, lost

The end of an era

For years it has been an article of faith with the normal American ... that America, somehow, was different from the rest of the world.... The smash of 1929 did not, of itself, shake this serene conviction.... It looked, at the time, just because it was so spectacular and catastrophic, like a shooting star ... disconnected with the fundamental facts.... So the plain citizen, no matter how hard hit, believed. His dreams were shattered; but after all they had been only dreams; he could settle back to hard work and win out....

Then he found his daily facts reeling and swimming about him, in a nightmare of continuous disappointment. The bottom had fallen out of the market, for good. And that market ... had a horrid connection with his bread and butter, his automobile, and his installment purchases.... Worst of all, unemployment became a hideous fact, and one that lacerated and tore at self-respect....

That is the trouble that lies ... at the back of the American mind.... If America really is not "different," then its troubles, the same ... as those of Old Europe, will not be cured automatically. Something will have to be done—but what?

From M. A. Hamilton, *In America Today*, 1932.

Impact of depression

next their savings, then their insurance, then, unable to pay their mortgages, their very homes. The optimism of the twenties gave way to gloom and fear. The times were even harder on laboring men and their families. The lost job, the fruitless search for work, the shoes worn through and the clothes worn thin, the furniture and trinkets pawned, the menu stripped of meat and then of adequate nutrition, no rent, no joy, no hope; and finally the despair of bread lines—these visited every city, leaving in their path sullen men, weeping women, and hungry children. So, too, on the farm—vanished incomes, foreclosures, tenancy, migrancy, and with them, as in the cities, the death of self-respect.

Hoover had predicted the abolition of poverty in America. Instead, within two years there mushroomed around America's cities settlements of shacks built of empty packing boxes, where homeless men squatted, reduced to desultory begging. A new Eden? "Brother, can you spare a dime?"

The Hoover policies: second phase. In the congressional elections of 1930 the Democrats conducted a rousing campaign against Hoover, though they offered no clear alternatives to his policies. The intensification of depression hurt the Republicans, as depression had always hurt the party in power. Though Hoover had been by no means unenlightened, he was, by virtue of his office, the most exposed target for abuse. The Democrats made his name a synonym for hardship. A "Hoover blanket" was yesterday's newspaper; a "Hoover flag" was an empty pocket turned inside out. Rough tactics and national discontent produced a slim Democratic victory, the first since 1916. The Republican majority in the Senate was reduced to a single vote, leaving that body dominated by a coalition of Democrats and Western agrarians. The Democrats won a bare majority in the House.

The new Congress was not to meet for a year (see Twentieth Amendment, Section 5), but in December 1930 the Democratic minority of the old Congress (which had been elected in 1928) used the rump session to develop a program for unemployment relief. Hoover, irritated by the Democratic campaign and appalled by its success, reasserted his own policies.

The President felt that relief was strictly a local problem. The cities, he insisted, with help from private charity, should and could take care of the needy. This was a fallacious assumption, for nowhere in the nation was there an adequate system of relief. Local public funds in 1929 paid three-fourths of the cost of relief (by 1932, four-fifths), but the localities had neither the means to raise revenue nor the capacity to borrow to defray their mounting obligations. Their relief agencies and programs, moreover, had concentrated on helping unemployables, people unable to work. Local administrators had neither the experience nor the facilities to cope with mass unemployment, and private charity was incapable of meeting the nation's massive need for immediate relief.

As the winter of 1930–31 came on, cold and hunger moved into the homes of the unemployed. Relief payments were only $2.39 a week for a family in New York and even less in most other cities. Two Texas cities barred relief for blacks. Detroit, unable to tax or borrow, dropped a third of the needy families from its relief rolls; St. Louis cut off half, and children there combed the dumps for rotting food.

In October 1930 the President appointed an Emergency Committee for Employment under Colonel Arthur Woods. Though Hoover told the committee that relief was a local responsibility, Woods recommended a federal public-works program. The President rejected it, and in April 1931 Woods resigned.

Meanwhile Senator Robert Wagner, a New York Democrat, had introduced bills providing for federal public works and a federal employment service. Along with Wagner, Senator Robert M. La Follette, Jr., "Battle Bob's" son and successor, and Republican Senator Bronson Cutting of New Mexico urged federal spending for public works and relief. All this Hoover opposed on the ground that federal action was unnecessary.

Instead, in February 1931 Hoover expressed his continuing dedication to individualism, local responsibility, and mutual self-help. But in the face of depression, the virtues of economic individualism and private charity were outweighed by the needs of the helpless. The sheer shock of the depression and the pervasive ignorance about the causes of the business cycle impeded the search for remedies. Like others in government, the President was a captive of those circumstances as well as an honest man whose convictions had glued him to inaction.

Hoover's interpretation of the economic ups and downs of 1931 strengthened his convictions. Between February and June of that year the economic indexes rallied slightly, partly because of a normal seasonal upturn. The gains, though tiny, persuaded the President, and others bent on optimism, that recovery was under way. Then in the spring and summer of 1931 financial panic swept over Europe. The American crash had precipitated the collapse abroad by drying up the loan funds on which the European economy and the interrelated reparations and war-debt payments had come to depend. And the European collapse in turn drove foreigners to dump American securities in their scramble for dollars, thereby driving American stock prices down even further. Moreover, shortages in exchange forced one European nation after another to devalue its currency. This action disrupted international trade, and the prices of American agricultural commodities plummeted. Before the end of the summer, the indexes had resumed their decline. Again the depression deepened.

No rent, no joy, no hope

"Brother, can you spare a dime?"

The fault, Hoover concluded, lay in Europe. All the calamities since 1929, he came to believe, had originated in the Old World. The war had taxed the world economy beyond repair; the United States had regrettably become involved not only in war but in a morass of bad loans as well. European bankers had collaborated with their New York associates to create the easy-money conditions on which speculation had fed (see p. 606), and from that collusion was born the Panic of 1929. Then, just as recovery beckoned, European disaster in 1931 had reversed the gains so arduously won. This view of the causes of the depression reasserted the persistent myth of American innocence—even wounded innocence—for as Hoover saw the situation American business shared little of the blame; he himself shared none. Hoover's theory, moreover, excused him from embracing the domestic policies he had rejected, for if the basic cause of depression lay outside the United States the most appropriate action would be to ease the strains abroad and to protect the American economy from them.

Diplomacy in depression

A set of good intentions. The foreign policies on which the Hoover Administration embarked in 1929 were marked by good will and peaceful purpose. The President and his able Secretary of State, Stimson, believed, as had their immediate predecessors, that the world had fought its last major war a decade earlier. Europe, they expected, could take care of itself, as could Asia and Latin America, with occasional advice from the United States. The aroused morality embodied in the Kellogg-Briand pact would prevent aggression and discourage militarism. Indeed Hoover expected the powers to put an end to their arms race in the very near future.

Initially Hoover and Stimson made some progress toward their benign goals. While still President-elect, Hoover had carried friendship to Latin America during a ten-week tour that publicized the "good neighbor" policy.* In Argentina he promised to abstain from intervention in the internal affairs of the nations south of the border. He kept his word. In 1930 Stimson announced that the United States henceforth would grant diplomatic recognition to *de facto* governments. Moreover, Hoover set about withdrawing the marines from Nicaragua, a task that was completed in 1933, and he arranged to remove them from Haiti.

In 1930 the President formally repudiated the Roosevelt Corollary to the Monroe Doctrine (see p. 532). A memorandum written by former Assistant Secretary of State J. Reuben Clark, which Hoover ordered published, denied that the doctrine justified American intervention in Latin America. Nor did Hoover regard the doctrine as a mandate for collecting the private debts of Americans. Some fifty revolutions or attempts at revolution shook the "good neighbors" of the hemisphere during his Administration. But he kept hands off, even though those disturbances often resulted in the repudiation of debts owed to American citizens and in the nationalization of their properties. Although the State Department fell into argumentative negotiations that ran on for many years, the United States did not resort to force. By abandoning dollar diplomacy and protective imperialism, Hoover created an improved atmosphere in hemispheric relations.

This success contrasted with the Administration's diplomatic disappointments in Europe and its agonies in Asia. Intent on naval disarmament, Hoover welcomed the cooperation of Ramsay MacDonald, the head of the new Labor Cabinet in England. Their preliminary negotiations prepared the way for the multipower conference that met in London in 1930. There the Americans, the British, and the Japanese extended the "holiday" on the construction of capital ships, and American and British representatives evolved a formula for limiting the construction of cruisers, destroyers, and submarines. Naval experts of the English-speaking nations, however, deplored a compromise that increased Japan's ratio for cruisers and destroyers and gave it equality in submarines. In

---

*A phrase later used by and ordinarily associated with Franklin Roosevelt.

effect, this arrangement recognized Japan's primacy in the western Pacific. It would have accepted nothing less, and neither the Hoover nor the MacDonald government wanted to engage in an expensive naval race. Neither, moreover, considered Japan unfriendly. They confirmed, therefore, only what they had already conceded.

Even so, they failed to close the door on a naval race. The French, frightened by the militarism of fascist Italy, refused to limit their naval program unless the United States promised to help France in the event of aggression. Such a pledge was unthinkable to Hoover, the Senate, or the American people. When France and Italy would not subscribe to significant parts of the London treaty, the British insisted on adding a clause permitting England, the United States, or Japan to expand their fleets if their national security was threatened by the building program of some other power. This "escalator" clause made naval limitation conditional upon the self-restraint of a resurgent Italy and an alarmed France. Yet the Hoover Administration and the American people accepted disarmament as a fact.

Monetary diplomacy. When the panic struck European banks and security markets in 1931 (see p. 621), the focus of Hoover's diplomacy shifted to money. American investors, hard hit by the depression, cut off the loans to Germany that had so far enabled it to pay reparations for its part in the First World War. Without this source of income, the former Allies were unable to keep up payments on their debts to the United States. Even before the distressed German president appealed for help in the spring of 1930, Hoover had begun to think about a one-year moratorium on all intergovernmental debts and reparations payments. The idea was admirable, but Hoover said nothing about it until he had made sure of congressional support, and he failed to consult the French. When he announced his proposal late in June, England and Germany endorsed it, but France held back, still hopeful of collecting reparations. The French also suspected that the American proposal was partly designed to enable Germany to pay back private debts it owed in the United States. During the two weeks before France endorsed the moratorium, the accelerated flight of funds from Germany forced widespread bank failures.

To his shock, the President discovered that Europe's distress directly embarrassed American banks. They had lent some $1.7 billion, on a short-term basis, without collateral, to central European banks, especially in Germany. Bank runs in Europe made those loans impossible to collect, and the solvency of the American banks that had made them was threatened. The loans were part of a complex network of obliga-

tions among banks in many countries. In order to stop demands for payments back and forth among them, Secretary Stimson and other American representatives in July 1930 negotiated an emergency "standstill" agreement. It was later extended to September 1931, and again to March 1933. The standstill agreements froze private debts just as the moratorium had frozen public debts. This gave financiers time to try to protect the banks of the Western world from bankruptcy, and time to delay putting pressure on borrowers for loans due.

But the freezing came too late to stop panic. Depositors, their confidence in banks shaken, demanded their money, which they intended to hoard. A run on the Bank of England, for decades the world's foremost symbol of financial stability, drained its gold and forced Great Britain off the gold standard in September 1931. That nation made gold the property of the government, refused to convert paper currency into gold except under conditions the government set, and devalued the pound—that is, increased the cost of gold in terms of British currency. England also established a special government fund to manage the value of the pound in terms of other currencies. By the end of 1931 every major power except Italy, France, and the United States was also forced off the gold standard, and each depreciated its currency and attempted to control its value in international exchange. These efforts at control were often designed to produce selfish advantages in trade, as were the prohibitive tariffs that invariably accompanied devaluation. Exchange controls and high tariffs actually impeded world trade and, worse still, gave rise to international suspicion and distrust.

Hoover had shown commendable initiative in arranging the moratorium and the standstills, but he never saw to the bottom of the problem. He failed to recognize that America's high protective tariffs impeded international commerce and invited foreign retaliation. And he would not support the cancellation of war debts. At the Lausanne Conference of 1932, England and France finally admitted Germany's bankruptcy and agreed to scale reparations down to an insignificant sum provided that the United States would scale war debts down equivalently. Most American bankers favored that plan, as did Stimson, who urged cancellation of "these damn debts." But Congress, reflecting public opinion, would not even consider a new debt commission, and Hoover, equivocal himself, demanded that the European nations resume payments on their debts after the moratorium expired. The debtor nations—except for Finland, whose obligation was tiny—had no choice but to default.

The defaults, like the demand that forced them and the long stalemate over debts and reparations that

preceded them, engendered ill feeling on both sides of the Atlantic. The resulting distrust weakened the will of the democracies to cooperate in order to resist the black forces gathering around them.

Fire bells in the Orient. Japan broke the peace of the world. Since its victory over Russia in 1905, it had dominated the economy of southern Manchuria, the northeastern section of China. Tokyo was willing to acknowledge China's political claim to the area so long as that claim did not collide with Japanese military interests and economic privileges. During the late twenties such a collision grew increasingly likely. In China, Chiang Kai-shek took over the central government and broke with the communists who had been his allies. Chinese nationalists hoped soon to have the whole country under their control. But the Russians still managed the Chinese Eastern Railway and were developing its Pacific terminus, the Siberian city of Vladivostok. Alarmed by the construction there, Japan resolved to reinforce southern Manchuria. Here it confronted Chiang Kai-shek, who was determined to yield nothing further to any foreign power.

In the fall of 1931 the Japanese army in effect took over the Tokyo government. In September Japanese troops occupied Mukden and other Manchurian cities and moved rapidly to establish political control over the province. This violation of the Nine Power Treaty and the Kellogg-Briand pact was perfectly timed. China turned to the League of Nations for help, but the West was paralyzed by depression.

Even in good times Japan would probably have had little to fear. The British were opposed to any strong action in Manchuria. American public opinion, though it condemned Japan's behavior, was vehemently against any measures that might precipitate war. Hoover, anxious to avoid war at any cost, rejected Stimson's suggestion that the United States might have to cooperate with the League in imposing economic sanctions on Japan.

At Hoover's insistence, Stimson proceeded cautiously. He hoped at first to strengthen the civilian moderates in the Japanese cabinet and to persuade them to end the occupation of Manchuria. But in January 1932 the Japanese army drove on. Now Stimson resorted to moral condemnation, the only weapon Hoover would countenance. In identical warnings to China and Japan, he revived the doctrine Bryan had enunciated in 1915. The United States, Stimson warned, would not recognize any change brought about by force that impaired American treaty rights or Chinese territorial integrity. Japan scoffed politely.

Before the end of January the Japanese invaded Shanghai, bombarded the city, and killed thousands of civilians—all on the pretext that they were retaliating against a Chinese boycott. America's warning had

Japanese in Shanghai

proved no deterrent. Yet once again Hoover refused to consider economic sanctions. Stimson could turn only to sterner words.

In February he published a long letter to Senator Borah, in which he reiterated his nonrecognition doctrine and lamented the failure of other nations to endorse it. He also recalled the interdependence of the various Washington treaties of 1922. Stimson wrote:

No one of these treaties can be disregarded without disturbing the general understanding and equilibrium. . . . The willingness of the American government to surrender its commanding lead in battleship construction and to leave its positions at Guam and in the Philippines without further fortification, was predicated upon, among other things, the self-denying covenants contained in the Nine Power Treaty.

Stimson had hoped that his letter would encourage China, inform the American public, exhort the League and Great Britain, and warn Japan. But sentiment did China no good. Americans, like the League and its members, shared Hoover's determination to confine deterrence to words, and Japan was confident that neither the President nor his constituents were prepared to heed Stimson's counsel.

The Assembly of the League, with Japan abstaining, unanimously adopted a resolution incorporating the nonrecognition doctrine. A year later a League commission of inquiry named Japan the aggressor in Manchuria and called on the Japanese to return the province to China. They simply withdrew from the League, though they left Shanghai temporarily.

Stimson, a disciple of Theodore Roosevelt, believed that power and the will to use it were essential to world peace. The vast majority of Americans, including Congress, disagreed. Indeed, as Hoover understood, there neither would nor should have been any support for a war against Japan, or a policy that invited war. For its part, Congress early in 1933 passed a bill granting independence to the Philippine Islands, largely in response to pressure from American interests eager to raise the tariff barrier between themselves and their Filipino competitors. The measure, enacted over Hoover's veto, demonstrated that Congress was willing to throw the islands to the mercy of Japan, and it canceled the veiled warning in Stimson's letter to Borah.

The story was very much the same in Europe, where the German Nazis were marching to power. At a World Disarmament Conference in Geneva in 1932, the French proposed that an international army be established and that all powers submit to the compulsory arbitration of disputes. Hoover countered with a plan for the immediate abolition of all offensive weapons and the reduction by one-third of existing armies and navies. But with the United States still unwilling to guarantee their security, the French were unimpressed by the arithmetic of arms reduction, and the conference adjourned in July with nothing accomplished. In 1933 Germany was Hitler's.

Good will and high moral purpose had no meaning in the Germany of the Nazis or the Japan of the Imperial Army. For men who hoped for disarmament and peace and the rule of law, the hour of peril was close. Neither the American people nor their leaders had brought mankind to the edge of disaster, nor could they alone have prevented the collapse of world order. But the foreign policies of the United States lacked the force to check depression or aggression.

The depths of depression

The Hoover policies: third phase. Hoover, William Allen White once said, was "constitutionally gloomy, a congenital pessimist who always saw the doleful side of any situation." The President took no joy in his office or in its potentialities for leadership. As he put it himself, "I can't be a Theodore Roosevelt." Grim and aloof, Hoover was nonetheless resolute. Just as he tried to halt the panic in Europe in 1931, so did he try to buttress the United States against the effects of that panic. By the fall of that year he had reached certain conclusions that were to shape his policies during the coming months. He intended to do everything he could to keep the nation on the gold standard, in his view an indispensable condition of economic health. The business and financial community shared that belief passionately, as it had for almost a century. The President also intended, again with ardor and with the blessing of men of means, to strive for economy and a balanced budget. He was prepared, however, to use federal funds and federal authority on an unprecedented scale to rescue the banks and industry from their troubles. The effects of their recovery, he thought, would reach down to the farmers and laborers, who were to receive little direct aid from the federal government.

The new Congress convened in December 1931. At Hoover's suggestion it appropriated $125 million to expand the lending powers of the Federal Land Banks. Also at his urging, but not until July 1932, it established a system of home-loan banks with a capital of $125 million for discounting home mortgages. The purpose of this scheme was to enable savings banks, insurance companies, and building-and-loan associations to obtain cash for the mortgages they held instead of having to foreclose them. The act not only helped to keep the assets of the lending institutions liquid but also, as Hoover said, spared hundreds of Americans the "heartbreaking . . . loss of their homes." And it set a significant precedent for more extensive legislation later on.

In February 1932 Congress amended the Federal Reserve Act of 1914 as requested by the President and Secretary of the Treasury Ogden Mills. (Hoover had rid himself of the increasingly unpopular Mellon by appointing him ambassador to Great Britain.) The act of 1914 had required that Federal Reserve currency be backed by gold or certain safe kinds of commercial paper—bank loans to business. By 1932 there was so little commercial activity that gold had come to form almost 70 percent of the reserve stock. Yet foreigners were withdrawing gold at an increasing rate, and domestic hoarding had reached alarming proportions. Hoover and Mills therefore recommended making government bonds and larger classes of safe commercial paper acceptable as collateral for Federal Reserve notes.

The new law, the Glass-Steagall Act, freed about a billion dollars' worth of gold to meet the demands of Europeans who were converting their dollars to gold. This enabled the United States for the time being to retain enough gold to remain on the gold standard without putting controls on gold movements or on transactions in foreign exchange. Yet the continuing outflow of gold even further reduced bank reserves and thus the availability of bank loans to business. That situation further depressed prices and added to the burden of debts contracted when prices were high. To hold to the gold standard was in keeping with the theories of classical economics, with their emphasis on the automatic workings of domestic and international trade and of the business cycle. Yet now that mechanism spun the business cycle downward and helped depression feed upon itself.

In spite of the Glass-Steagall Act, moreover, many banks remained weak. To supplement their resources, Hoover in the fall of 1931 persuaded New York bankers to create a National Credit Association with a $500-million pool. But the halfhearted use of this fund doomed the effort to failure. The President then gave in to the urgings of Eugene Meyer, governor of the Federal Reserve Board and formerly head of the War Finance Corporation established in 1918. Meyer proposed reviving that agency in order to rescue American finance. Hoover, hoping that the psychological lift provided by this scheme would justify the cost of financing it, made it the keystone of his recovery policy in 1932.

In January Congress created the Reconstruction Finance Corporation with a capital stock of $500 million and the power to borrow three times that sum in guaranteed, tax-free bonds. It was authorized, as Meyer and Hoover had recommended, to lend money to banks and insurance companies and, with the approval of the Interstate Commerce Commission, to railroads. Most of the $1.5 billion the RFC disbursed before March 1933 went to banks and trust companies. The RFC, however, could lend funds only against adequate collateral, and it could not buy bank stock. Its loans increased bank indebtedness, but it could not satisfy the banks' basic need for new capital.

The RFC kept its transactions secret for five months, largely because Hoover feared that publicity would incite runs on the weak banks that were receiving the loans. More than half of the $126 million that the RFC dispersed during those months went to three large banks. One of them was the bank of Charles G. Dawes, who resigned as president of the RFC only a month before the loan went through. In July 1932 the Democrats in Congress, to Hoover's dismay, put through an amendment compelling the RFC to report its transactions. Thereafter the number of loans made to large institutions fell off.

The muddle of relief. Late in 1931 Hoover appointed a new committee on unemployment with Walter S. Gifford as its head. Gifford, the president of the American Telephone and Telegraph Company, agreed with Hoover that relief was the responsibility of local government and private charity. Yet Gifford could not convincingly defend this view. In January 1932 he confessed to a Senate committee that he did not know how many people were out of work; he did not know how many needed help, how much help they needed, or how much money localities were raising or could raise. But of one thing he seemed certain: the "grave danger" of taking "the determination of these things into the Federal Government."

The gravest danger, in the view of the President and most congressmen of both parties, was that the budget might be thrown further out of balance. Yet throughout 1932 the need for federal spending increased. In the words of Senator Edward P. Costigan, Colorado's progressive Democrat, "nothing short of federal assistance . . . can possibly satisfy the conscience and heart and safeguard the good name of America." With La Follette, Costigan introduced a bill granting a modest $375 million for relief, but the Administration blocked it. Sensing the political importance of the issue, the Democratic leadership now began to press for direct federal aid to the unemployed and for deficit spending for public works.

Hoover insisted on limiting any relief program to RFC loans to localities and on limiting public works to self-liquidating projects, like bridges and housing, which could return enough income from tolls or rent-

I want to tell you about an experience we had in Philadelphia when our private funds were exhausted and before public funds became available....

One woman said she borrowed 50 cents from a friend and bought stale bread for 3½ cents per loaf, and that is all they had for eleven days except for one or two meals.

With the last food order another woman received she bought dried vegetables and canned goods. With this she made a soup and whenever the members of the family felt hungry they just ate some of the soup....

One woman went along the docks and picked up vegetables that fell from the wagons. Sometimes the fish vendors gave her fish at the end of the day. On two different occasions this family was without food for a day and a half....

Another family did not have food for two days. Then the husband went out and gathered dandelions and the family lived on them.

From Hearings Before a Subcommittee of the Senate Committee on Manufactures, 1932.

als to pay back the initial cost of construction. But many states had nearly exhausted their legal authority to borrow from any source, and few projects had emerged from the drawing board. Consequently the President's restrictions put a low ceiling on spending.

Even so, Hoover endorsed a federal program without precedent in American history. After a partisan wrangle, on July 21, 1932, he signed a bill that authorized the RFC to lend $1.5 billion for local self-liquidating public works and $300 million at 3 percent interest to supplement local relief funds.

The relief loans, the President said, were to be based on "absolute need and evidence of financial exhaustion." That limitation kept them small. The governor of Pennsylvania asked for a loan of $45 million (three-fourths of the sum, he noted, that would allow the jobless in the state a mere 13 cents apiece a day for food for a year). The RFC let him have only $11 million (enough for little more than 3 cents a person a day). By the end of 1932 the RFC had allotted only $30 million for relief loans and even less for public works.

The outlook of the nation's farmers seemed as hopeless as that of the unemployed workers in the cities. Even before the depression destroyed the European market for farm commodities, the Federal Farm Board had recognized that it could never stabilize farm prices without some control over farm production. When in 1932 American prices followed world prices down to bewildering lows, the stabilization corporations made a brief but futile effort to brake the decline. They lost $354 million in market operations, accumulated huge stocks of unsalable commodities, and finally in the summer simply gave up. Wheat, which had brought $2.16 a bushel in 1919 and $1.03 in 1929, sank to 38 cents. Cotton, corn, and other prices suffered comparably. Farmers found themselves without enough income to meet their mortgage payments or even to buy food for their families. And certainly they lacked the money to buy manufactured goods, which still sold at prices sustained by industry.

The members of the Federal Farm Board urged Congress to do something about regulating acreage and production as a first step in setting up some sort of program for boosting farm prices. The only alternative was agricultural bankruptcy. Yet Hoover and Secretary of Agriculture Hyde rejected the idea of imposing federal controls on agriculture. Before the year ended, farmers were burning corn in Nebraska to keep warm, forming angry posses in Minnesota to prevent foreclosures, and joining Milo Reno's militant Farmers' Holiday Association in Iowa to block the shipment of produce until prices rose.

Moods of despair. Father John Ryan, the Catholic social reformer, despaired for the state of the nation. "I wish," he said, "we might double the number of Communists in this country, to put the fear, if not of God, then . . . of something else, into the hearts of our leaders." Communism had a particular appeal for the intellectuals who had been alienated by the culture of the Coolidge era, men like Malcolm Cowley and Sherwood Anderson. But the theories of Karl Marx had little appeal for the general public. The communists organized "hunger marches" in Washington and Detroit and preached revolution elsewhere, but Communist party membership was little more than one hundred thousand.

Though desperate Americans spurned communism, they gave way to hatred and violence. Farmers, brandishing shotguns to prevent foreclosures, defied the law to defend their homes. The president of the

Rural violence

Farmers' Union damned the rich as "cannibals . . . who live on the labor of the workers." Some of the prosperous took out "riot and civil commotion insurance" and began to suggest that the United States needed a fascist dictator like Mussolini.

In the spring of 1932 some fifteen thousand unemployed veterans converged on Washington from every region of the country. They announced that they planned to stay in the capital until Congress voted full and immediate payment of the bonus. The year before, over Hoover's veto, Congress had authorized loans up to 50 percent of the value of each adjusted service certificate (see p. 584). But those funds had been spent, and the unemployed veterans, like all other unemployed Americans, were in dire need of help. When the Senate voted down the bonus bill, half the veterans went home. But the rest had no place to go and no way of getting there, so they camped in a muddy shantytown on Anacostia Flats and in vacant government buildings.

Their plight evoked the sympathy of the chief of the District of Columbia police, who treated them generously and intelligently. But their presence worried the Administration. Hoover, anxious to get rid of

Anacostia Flats: the bonus army fighting back

Hoover on federal relief

The proposals of our opponents will endanger or destroy our system.... I especially emphasize that promise to promote "employment for all surplus labor at all times." At first I could not believe that anyone would be so cruel as to hold out a hope so absolutely impossible of realization to these 10,000,000 who are unemployed. And I protest against such frivolous promises being held out to a suffering people. It is easily demonstrable that no such employment can be found. But the point I wish to make here and now is the mental attitude and spirit of the Democratic Party to attempt it. It is another mark of the character of the new deal and the destructive changes which mean the total abandonment of every principle upon which this government and the American system is founded. If it were possible to give this employment to 10,000,000 people by the Government, it would cost upwards of $9,000,000,000 a year.... It would pull down the employment of those who are still at work by the high taxes and the demoralization of credit upon which their employment is dependent.... It would mean the growth of a fearful bureaucracy which, once established, could never be dislodged.

From Herbert Hoover, Campaign Address in New York, October 1932.

them, had Congress pass a bill that permitted them to borrow against their bonus certificates in order to get funds for transportation home. Still most veterans waited around after Congress adjourned. They hoped at least for a conference with the President.

Late in July the Administration ordered the eviction of all squatters from government buildings. In the ensuing melee, brought about largely by the small corps of communists among the veterans, two men were killed and several policemen wounded. Secretary of War Patrick Hurley had been looking for just such an incident. At his request, the White House now called in the army—four troops of cavalry and four infantry companies, with six tanks, tear gas, and machine guns. Under the personal command of General Douglas MacArthur (whose junior officers included Dwight D. Eisenhower and George Patton), the troops rode into Anacostia Flats, drove out the veterans and their families, and burned their shacks. Crowing over his triumph, MacArthur called the veterans "a mob . . . animated by the essence of revolution." The Administration published reports claiming that most of them had been communists and criminals.

Neither a grand jury nor the Veterans Administration could find evidence to support those charges. The bonus marchers were destitute men. Whether or not they merited special treatment, they deserved, as did unemployed Americans everywhere, compassion and assistance. They received first indifference and veiled hostility, then vicious armed attack. That treatment appalled the nation.

With government callous and blundering, with the business élite defensive about the disrepute it had brought on itself, with depression still spreading,

Americans began to fear that the whole political and economic system might collapse. Yet they waited patiently, as they had so often before in times of trouble, to see whether the presidential campaign would give them a vote for a brighter future.

The changing of the guard. In the summer of 1932 the Republicans renominated Hoover and his Vice President, Charles Curtis. A minority of the delegates to the convention were dissatisfied with the Administration's policies but were unwilling to repudiate the President. The convention was listless, for the delegates realized that the electorate, rightly or wrongly, blamed the party for the depression and regarded Hoover as the symbol of the party.

The Democrats, in contrast, sensed victory ahead. A majority of the delegates came to Chicago pledged to Franklin D. Roosevelt, who had been the front runner for the nomination since his easy reelection as governor of New York in 1930. He had the nerve for politics, the sense of fun, and the zest with people that had once made his distant cousin, Theodore Roosevelt, the most popular man in America. Franklin Roosevelt, moreover, had worked effectively with Tammany Hall, had made friends with the masters of other Northern machines, and yet had always preserved close relations with the Southern wing of the party. He closed the gap that had divided the party in 1924. Further, though conservative in his economic thinking, Roosevelt believed in positive, active, humane government.

Roosevelt stood to the left of his serious opponents. Their one hope was to organize a coalition to keep him from getting the two-thirds vote necessary

for nomination. Al Smith, still a favorite of the machines, hoped to be nominated once again. Ambition had soured Smith's best instincts. When Roosevelt before the convention called for help for "the forgotten man at the bottom of the economic pyramid," Smith remarked testily, "This is no time for demagogues." But Smith lacked allies. The McAdoo faction still opposed him and now backed Speaker of the House John N. Garner. After Roosevelt had failed to win the necessary vote in three ballots, McAdoo, evening up the old scores of 1924 (see p. 599), switched California's delegation to the New York governor. This put Roosevelt across and in return his lieutenants arranged second place on the ticket for Garner.

In a characteristically dramatic gesture, Roosevelt

Putting Roosevelt across, Chicago, 1932

F.D.R. in Indianapolis, 1932: a real choice

broke precedent by flying to Chicago to accept the nomination before the convention adjourned. "Let it . . . be symbolic that . . . I broke traditions," he told the cheering delegates. "Republican leaders not only have failed in material things, they have failed in national vision, because in disaster they have held out no hope. . . . I pledge you, I pledge myself to a new deal for the American people."

Roosevelt began to define that New Deal during his campaign. He was often deliberately vague and took pains to avoid offending any large bloc of voters. He hedged on the tariff. He made much of his party's demand for the repeal of the Eighteenth Amendment: Prohibition was still an important political issue in 1932, but it had no immediate bearing on the depression, which was the overriding concern of Americans. But he also set forth strong lines of attack on the nation's economic ills. At the Commonwealth Club in San Francisco, Roosevelt said that "government . . . owes to everyone an avenue to possess himself of a portion of that plenty sufficient for his needs, through his own work." In its dealings with business, government was to "assist the development of . . . an economic constitutional order." And such an order, he pointed out, demanded national planning.

Roosevelt's plans drew on the ideas reformers had nurtured throughout the twenties and promised assistance to the victims of depression. He called for strict public regulation of the utilities and federal development of public power. He advocated federal controls on agricultural production as a part of a program to support commodity prices and federal loans to refinance farm mortgages. He expressed interest in the schemes for currency inflation that agriculture-leaders were urging as a means to raise prices and reduce the weight of debt. He appealed to the business community by demanding cuts in government spending in order to balance the budget, but in the same speech he also promised to incur a deficit whenever human suffering made it necessary.

Roosevelt's oratorical flair and personal ebullience contrasted with Hoover's heavy speech and grim manner. The President emphasized his dedication to budget-balancing and the gold standard, defended his record, and charged his opponent with recklessness. The policies Roosevelt advocated, Hoover said, "would destroy the very foundations of our American system." If they were adopted, "grass will grow in the streets of a hundred cities, a thousand towns."

That rhetoric reflected Hoover's gloom. It obscured his own expansion of federal control, and it exaggerated Roosevelt's intentions. Actually the Democrat's campaign disappointed many intellectuals who felt, as Walter Lippmann earlier had, that Franklin Roosevelt was "a highly impressionable person . . . without strong convictions. . . . a pleasant man, who, without any important qualifications for the office, would very much like to be President."

But there were significant differences between the two candidates and their ideas, between Hoover's pessimism and Roosevelt's effervescence, between Hoover's belief that the origins of the depression lay

The end of an era

outside the United States and Roosevelt's belief that they were internal, between Hoover's impulse toward caution and Roosevelt's impulse toward experiment, between Hoover's identification with industry and finance and Roosevelt's identification with the forgotten and with the intellectuals and social workers who championed them. Hoover in his last campaign speech was right in associating Roosevelt with Norris and La Follette, right in asserting that the contest was between two philosophies of government. Both philosophies were fundamentally American, but Hoover's looked backward, while Roosevelt's looked cautiously ahead.

The people had a real choice when they went to the polls in November. Dismissing radicalism (the Socialists—rent by factionalism—polled 881,951 votes, the Communists, only 102,785), they swept the Democrats into office. Roosevelt won over 57 percent of the popular vote and carried the Electoral College 472 to 59. The Democrats also gained a large majority in both houses of Congress. The vote, a protest against the Administration, gave Roosevelt a clear mandate for change, though the nature of that change was clear neither to the voters nor the victor. Roosevelt lost only six states—Maine, New Hampshire, Vermont, Connecticut, Delaware, and Pennsylvania. He carried the agricultural West as well as the South; he carried the great cities by majorities larger than Smith's in 1928.

Depression had stripped the American people of most of their illusions. After twelve years the farmers and the workers once again had the determining voice in Washington. They had repudiated business and its policies and servants, had thrown out the Old Guard, and had taken the direction of government back into their own hands.

Suggestions for reading

HOOVER AND HIS POLICIES

A. M. Schlesinger, Jr., *The Crisis of the Old Order** (1957), provides a critical and detailed analysis of the Hoover Administration and its problems. Also critical, though the authors intend to be sympathetic, are H. G. Warren, *Herbert Hoover and the Great Depression** (1956), and J. A. Schwarz, *The Interregnum of Despair* (1970); the relevant chapters in J. D. Hicks, *Republican Ascendancy: 1921–1933** (1960), and J. H. Wilson, *Herbert Hoover* (1975), are unsympathetic and those in W. E. Leuchtenburg, *The Perils of Prosperity: 1914–32** (1958), lucid but brief. An incisive work is Albert Romesco's *The Poverty of Abundance: Hoover, the Nation, the Depression** (1965). The most ardent defense of the Administration appears in Herbert Hoover, *Memoirs: The Great Depression, 1929–1941* (1952), which may be supplemented by another book of similar spirit, R. L. Wilbur and A. M. Hyde, *The Hoover Policies* (1937). On Hoover's foreign policies, there is significant material in both W. A. Williams and the biographies of Stimson mentioned in connection with the preceding chapter, and in R. H. Ferrell, *American Diplomacy in the Great Depression: Hoover-Stimson Foreign Policy, 1929–1933** (1957).

DEPRESSION

All the volumes noted above of course deal with the depression. Its impact is also poignantly revealed in the pertinent parts of Irving Bernstein, *The Lean Years** (1960); Caroline Bird, *The Invisible Scar** (1965); Bernard Sternsher, ed., *Hitting Home** (1970); and D. A. Shannon, ed., *The Great Depression** (1960). There are excellent descriptions of the stock-market crash in F. L. Allen, *Only Yesterday** (1931), and J. K. Galbraith, *The Great Crash, 1929** (1955). The skillful analysis of the latter should be compared with the also able view in Thomas Wilson, *Fluctuations in Income and Employment* (1948), with the important chapters on Hoover in Herbert Stein, *The Fiscal Revolution in America** (1969), and in C. P. Kindelberger, *The World in Depression, 1929–1939** (1973); and with the special view of central banking policy in Milton Friedman and A. J. Schwartz, *The Great Contraction, 1929–1933** (1965). Within his excellent general study of American radical intellectuals, *Writers on the Left** (1961), Daniel Aaron discusses the influence of the depression on the spread of radicalism.

F.D.R. AND 1932

Franklin D. Roosevelt's governorship and first presidential campaign receive important treatment in A. M. Schlesinger's work, mentioned above, which is brilliant and panoramic on those subjects, and in Frank Freidel, *Franklin D. Roosevelt: The Triumph* (1956), a work of outstanding scholarship. Less comprehensive but still useful are parts of J. M. Burns, *Roosevelt: The Lion and the Fox** (1956), and R. G. Tugwell, *The Democratic Roosevelt** (1957).

*Available in a paperback edition.

CHAPTER **27** *The New Deal*

During the winter of 1932–33, the despair born of depression gripped the United States ever more tightly. The four-month interval between the November election and the inauguration of March 1933 found Hoover without influence and Roosevelt without power. Hoover frustrated any chance of collaboration with his successor by insisting on policies Roosevelt had condemned. In February, when the President called on Roosevelt to make a series of conservative declarations, he privately wrote a Republican senator, "I realize that if these declarations be made by the President-Elect, he will have ratified the whole major program of the Republican Administration." The incoming President, recognizing Hoover's invitation as a request for capitulation rather than cooperation, naturally rejected it, as he was, in any event, inclined to.

Without making public commitments to any program, Roosevelt awaited his day to take charge. Americans, worried and gloomy, also awaited the change of command, their anxieties deepened by an attempt upon Roosevelt's life by a madman in Miami, Florida, in February. The electorate had no sure sense of what a new deal might bring them, but they had clinching evidence that the old deal was ending in disaster.

The spreading panic was beginning to concentrate on one of the weakest links in the economy—the banking system. As the economy continued downward, more and more people played it safe by converting their savings to cash. The mounting pressure on financial institutions, the lines of depositors waiting to draw out their savings, the threat of further runs on the banks, led the governor of Michigan in mid-February to proclaim a bank holiday—that is, to order the temporary closing of the banks in his state. That act set off a chain reaction in other states. On the last day of Hoover's Administration, with banks shutting their doors across the land, the retiring President said, "We are at the end of our rope. There is nothing more we can do."

Franklin D. Roosevelt

His background. The new President was fifty-one years old. Like his distant cousin Theodore, he had come from a patrician background that gave him both a high sense of civic responsibility and a certain disdain for those whose chief achievement was making money. Like Theodore, Franklin Roosevelt was a man of charm, vivacity, and energy. He had been much influenced by Theodore, and their careers offered

633

TVA: Fontana Dam

curious parallels. Both had made their political debuts in the New York legislature; both had served as Assistant Secretary of the Navy in Washington; both had been governor of New York; both had been candidates for the Vice Presidency.

Unlike Theodore, Franklin was a member of the Democratic branch of the Roosevelt family. He was less of an intellectual than Theodore, but he was also less moralistic and evangelical. His urbane and conciliatory manner, indeed, led some observers to suppose him too compliant for hard responsibilities and decisions. But as second in command in the Navy Department during the First World War, he had been a resourceful executive. As candidate for Vice President in 1920, he had been a vigorous campaigner. In 1921 he had been stricken by poliomyelitis. That illness deprived him of the use of his legs; many thought it would end his public career. The determination of his comeback revealed an inner spirit that was not only gallant but tough. He had been an imaginative governor of New York; no state had taken so many positive measures to meliorate the effects of depression. His capture of the Democratic nomination in 1932 was the work of a seasoned politician.

The superficial affability of Roosevelt's manner concealed a complex personality—at once lighthearted and somber, candid and disingenuous, open and impenetrable, bold and cautious, decisive and evasive. Throughout his life he pursued certain public ends—especially the improvement of welfare and opportunity for the great masses of people—with steadiness of purpose; but the means he employed to achieve those ends were often inconsistent and occasionally unworthy. Yet his capacity to project the grand moral issues of his day—and his readiness to use the resources of presidential leadership to prepare the country for necessary action—enabled him to command the confidence of a great majority of Americans during his terms in office, despite the persistent opposition of a powerful minority.

His ideas. Roosevelt was a child of the progressive era. Theodore Roosevelt and Woodrow Wilson had been his early inspirations. Government seemed to him a necessary instrument of the general welfare, and he had no inhibitions about calling on the state to redress matters when "rugged individualism" left parts of the population or sections of the country without adequate protection. But the problems of 1933 were novel. Progressivism had been a gospel of social improvement rather than a program for economic growth, and progressives were no less baffled than conservatives by economic collapse. But, where faith in laissez faire constrained conservatives from taking positive government action, progressives like Roosevelt, with activist temperaments and an adventurous attitude toward social policy, were ready to invoke affirmative government to bring about economic recovery.

In economics, Roosevelt had leanings rather than theories. In his campaign for the Presidency, he had identified himself with two main ideas—action and planning. As to what should be tried, his views were sometimes incompatible.

Certain of his advisers had more clear-cut ideas. A group of college professors, mostly recruited from Columbia University, had served as his campaign brain trust. A book of 1932, *The Modern Corporation and Private Property*, by Adolf A. Berle, Jr., and Gardiner C. Means, provided one foundation for their analysis. The trend toward economic concentration, they contended, was irreversible. Already it had transformed great parts of the old free market of classical economics into "administered" markets, in which basic economic decisions were made, not by equations of supply and demand, but by the policies of those who ran the great corporations. In Berle and Means' opinion this change in the structure of the market rendered classical laissez-faire theory obsolete.

So persuaded, another Columbia economist, Rexford G. Tugwell, urged the President-elect to bold conclusions. If concentration was inevitable, Tugwell argued, then control over the nation's economic life could not be safely left in private hands. Such private control had brought about the depression. In the twenties the gains of economic productivity had gone into profits, savings, and speculation when they should have gone into a buildup of purchasing power through the payment of higher wages to workers and higher prices to farmers. The only way to operate the modern integrated economy at capacity, in Tugwell's view, was organized public planning.

Men like Berle, Tugwell, Means, and Raymond Moley, who acted as nominal head of the brain trust, were in a sense heirs of Theodore Roosevelt's New Nationalism. Their predisposition toward new institutions for central planning was reinforced by the views of those who, recalling America's last national emergency, the First World War, reverted to wartime economic agencies in the battle against depression. The Reconstruction Finance Corporation of the Hoover Administration was itself a revival of Wilson's War Finance Corporation (see p. 625). Now men who had once been associated with the War Industries Board, men like Bernard Baruch, Hugh S. Johnson, and George N. Peek, began to sponsor schemes of industrial and agricultural planning, though with little of Tugwell's zeal for accompanying social reform.

Not all those around Roosevelt accepted the virtues of national planning. Others close to him—especially Associate Justice Louis D. Brandeis of the Supreme Court and Professor Felix Frankfurter of

Harvard—rejected the thesis of inevitable economic concentration. They distrusted the idea of central planning and advocated policies designed to encourage more competition. Still others, though these were more powerful in the Democratic party in Congress than in the President's immediate circle, were inflationists in the tradition of William Jennings Bryan. And others, like Lewis W. Douglas, whom Roosevelt was about to appoint Director of the Budget, were sound-money, laissez-faire Democrats deeply committed, like the Republicans, to the gold standard and the annually balanced budget. As now one, now another, of these groups exerted a telling influence, the resulting policies on occasion clashed.

Roosevelt, concerned more with action than consistency, presided benignly over the clash of debate and policy alike. Disagreement stimulated him, enabled him to compare the merits of competing arguments and personalities, and reassured him that crucial questions would come to him for decision. His choice of Cabinet members reflected his desire for a variety of views and his confidence that he could control men of divergent opinion. To the State Department he named Cordell Hull, a Tennessee Democrat who had sponsored the Income-tax Amendment during the Wilson Administration but who was now cautious in his views except as a passionate foe of international trade barriers. Two vigorous progressive Republicans—Henry A. Wallace of Iowa and Harold L. Ickes of Illinois—were appointed to Agriculture and Interior; the first woman in history to go into the Cabinet, Frances Perkins of New York, a veteran social worker, became Secretary of Labor; and the other posts were filled by Democratic politicians or, in the case of the Treasury, by William Woodin of New York, a flexible-minded businessman.

The Hundred Days

The inauguration. On March 4, 1933, millions of Americans clustered around their radios to hear the new President deliver his inaugural address. "Let me assert my firm belief," Roosevelt began, "that the only thing we have to fear is fear itself." Then he assailed the business-leaders whose incompetence and misconduct, he said, had been largely responsible for the economic disaster. "This Nation asks for action, and action now," he concluded, adding that he would seek from Congress "broad Executive powers to wage a war against the emergency, as great as the power that would be given to me if we were in fact invaded by a foreign foe."

Action itself was quick to follow. Immediately after the inauguration, Roosevelt declared a national bank holiday and called Congress into special session. When Congress convened on March 8, it received at once a special message on the banking crisis and a draft of emergency banking legislation, on which Roosevelt's advisers had collaborated with some of Hoover's outgoing Treasury staff. In less than eight hours the House and Senate shouted through the bill and returned it to the President for signature. The unprecedented combination of decision and speed in the passage of the act electrified the country.

Quick to seize advantage of the national mood, the President put forward a bill calling for the reduction of government expenses, including veterans' pensions. He followed his economy message with a call for the amendment of the Volstead Act to legalize light wines and beers. The prompt enactment of both the economy and the beer bills involved the defeat of the two most powerful lobbies in the nation's capital—the veterans and the Prohibitionists. All this ac-

*Inauguration Day, 1933:
action was quick to follow*

*Troy, Wisconsin:
to raise the price
of milk*

tivity increased the national sense of exhilaration. "In one week," wrote Walter Lippmann, "the nation, which had lost confidence in everything and everybody, has regained confidence in the government and in itself."

Planning for agriculture. So far the Roosevelt program had been dashing in style but orthodox in content. Now, focusing on the problem of recovery, the President followed the path of the planners who advocated using the power of the federal government to "rationalize" and to help to manage agriculture and industry. On March 16, Roosevelt sent to Capitol Hill a message calling for a bold national policy in agriculture. "I tell you frankly that it's a new and untrod path," he said, "but I tell you with equal frankness that an unprecedented condition calls for the trial of new means."

The condition was indeed unprecedented. The per capita cash net income of the American farmer had declined from $162 to $48 between 1929 and 1932. Because farm prices had fallen faster than industrial prices, the farmer's purchasing power was only about 60 percent of what it had been in 1929. The farmer's fixed charges—especially the burden of mortgage debt assumed at higher price levels—weighed more heavily than ever on him. Since the individual farmer saw no way to fight falling prices except to increase his production, he put more pro-

duce on the market and drove prices down faster and further. Some farmers, instead, burned their crops or threw them away.

The central idea in the Administration proposal was "agricultural adjustment." This plan aimed to increase farm income by controlling production; and it aimed to control production by offering benefit payments to farmers who agreed to regulate their plantings according to a national plan. The adjustment programs were to be financed by processing taxes collected at the flour mill or textile mill or packinghouse. No program would go into effect until a majority of farmers indicated they wanted it by voting in a referendum. The local administration of the plan was to be as much as possible in the hands of the farmers themselves. The ultimate object was to restore to the farmer substantially the purchasing power he had had in 1909–14. That concept was known as "parity."

The agricultural-adjustment bill that emerged from conferences between the Department of Agriculture and leading farm organizations incorporated, in addition to benefit payments, a number of other approaches to the farm problem. It gave the government authority, for example, to maintain prices through loans on or purchase of nonperishable crops, which would then go into government storage; it also conferred authority to withdraw land from cultivation through leasing and to regulate the release of commodities for sale through marketing agreements and quotas. Through the use of those powers the government could not only prevent gluts on the market but could build up reserves against lean years, and, in the phrase of Henry Wallace, maintain an "ever normal granary." The inflationists in Congress added an important amendment giving the President power to issue greenbacks, to remonetize silver, and to alter the gold content of the dollar. In the meantime, the newly created Farm Credit Administration provided quick and effective mortgage relief.

While Washington laid its plans, trouble was mounting on the countryside. In late April a mob marched on a judge in Le Mars, Iowa, who had refused to suspend foreclosure proceedings, and nearly lynched him. The Farmer's Holiday Association, the most radical of the farmers' groups, renewed its threat of a farm strike. Alarmed by the rising agrarian wrath, the governor of Iowa called out the national guard and placed half a dozen counties under martial law.

Those developments speeded passage of the Agricultural Adjustment Act on May 12. It established the Agricultural Adjustment Administration and opened the New Deal's campaign to raise farm income. The first task was to cut down production in areas already overwhelmed by surpluses. Thus a carry-over from previous years of 8 million bales of cotton had driven cotton prices down to 5 cents a pound. Yet, by the time the act had passed, some 40 million acres had already been planted in new cotton. The only way to save the cotton-grower was to persuade him to plow under the planted crop in return for benefit payments. This the AAA proceeded to do in a whirlwind plow-up campaign of some 10 million acres in the spring and summer. Acting on the recommendation of the Farm Bureau and the Grange, the AAA dealt with the market glut in corn and hogs by buying and slaughtering some 5 million little pigs.

No one perceived more sharply the irony of destroying plenty in the midst of want than the men who ordered the job to be done. "To destroy a standing crop goes against the soundest instincts of human nature," said Henry Wallace. Yet industry, the Secretary of Agriculture pointed out, had in effect plowed under much of its potential output after 1929 by cutting down on production; how, in all logic, could agriculture be denied the same right of self-protection?

The terrible logic of scarcity worked. As production declined—aided, in the cases of wheat and corn, by the searing droughts of 1933–34—prices rose. Between 1932 and 1936 gross farm income increased by 50 percent, and cash receipts from marketing (including government benefit payments) nearly doubled. The parity ratio rose from 55 in 1932 to 90 in 1936. The chief beneficiaries were commercial farmers, owners of large holdings and recipients of a disproportionate share of benefit payments. To reduce acreage, they often forced their tenants or sharecroppers off the land and into migrancy, usually as itinerant farm-laborers or unemployed newcomers to the cities. But many owners of family-sized farms also benefited, and though the AAA was occasionally disturbed by top-level policy conflicts, it conducted its complex administrative operations with smoothness and effect.

Planning for industry. Agricultural planning covered only the lesser part of the American economy. By 1933 American industry was employing some 5 million fewer workers than in 1929 and producing less than half the value of goods. Businessmen, striving to maintain a margin of profits, saw no choice but to cut costs—that is, to lower wages and lay off employees. But the more wages and employment were reduced, the more mass purchasing power declined.

There was increasing agreement that the only way to stop the industrial decline was through joint planning by government and business. This view was backed not just by Tugwell, with his belief in public management of the economy, and by Johnson, with his memory of the War Industries Board. Powerful voices in business, especially the United States Chamber of Commerce, now urged that private trade associations be given authority to fix prices, divide markets, and "stabilize" industrial production. Recovery, they argued, depended on limiting the play of what Johnson called "the murderous doctrine of savage and wolfish individualism."

In the spring the Administration worked out a so-called national-industrial-recovery bill, divided into two parts. The first part was designed "to promote the organization of industry for the purpose of cooperative action among trade groups" through codes of fair competition that granted exemption from the antitrust laws. An important provision—the celebrated Section 7a—sought to win labor support by offering federal guarantees of the right of trade unions to organize and bargain collectively. The second part of the bill provided for the establishment of a Public Works Administration with an appropriation of $3.3 billion. Roosevelt signed the bill on June 16, calling it "a challenge to industry, which has long insisted that, given the right to act in unison, it could do much for the general good which has hitherto been unlawful. From today it has that right."

Two agencies were set up under the National Industrial Recovery Act—the National Recovery Administration, with General Johnson as head, and the Public Works Administration under Harold L. Ickes. Johnson saw the NRA as a national crusade designed to restore employment and regenerate industry in an excitement of torchlight processions and giant rallies. Finding the negotiation of codes with specific industries disappointingly slow, Johnson came up in July

637

The Blue Eagle:
symbol of compliance

labor, an improvement of working conditions, an encouragement of labor organization, an extension of fair-trade practices.

Soon the NRA began to overextend its efforts. Instead of concentrating on codification in the major industries, it allowed itself to be tempted into setting up codes for local and service trades. There was good humanitarian reason for this effort, for these were the trades where the sweatshop was most deeply entrenched. But it involved the NRA in a host of petty enforcement problems, which at once distracted its energies and dissipated its credit. Johnson was reluctant to use the NRA's coercive powers, since he wanted to avoid a court test of the NRA's constitutionality. Consequently his chief reliance against those whom he denounced as "chiselers" was the compulsion of public opinion. So long as the nation felt itself in acute crisis, this compulsion worked. But as soon as economic conditions began to grow better, more and more employers tried to beat the codes.

Within the NRA, moreover, there was constant pressure from trade associations to use the code mechanism as a means of raising prices. Many businessmen felt that price-fixing would be an appropriate *quid pro quo* for their concessions on wages, hours, and collective bargaining. On the other hand, many inside the NRA and out argued that excessive price increases would defeat the whole policy of expanding purchasing power. They feared that price-fixing would turn the codes into a vehicle for the sort of monopoly Congress had tried to outlaw in the Sherman Act. An investigation by a special committee in 1934 under the chairmanship of Clarence Darrow, the criminal lawyer, seemed to substantiate the charge that the NRA had become the instrument of monopoly.

In the meantime the labor provisions in Section 7a had given a great stimulus to trade-union organization, and this embittered many employers. Hugh Johnson's unstable personality and his increasingly erratic course further complicated the NRA's existence. Roosevelt forced him out in the fall of 1934 and replaced him by a five-man board. By now the NRA had lost its allure. In 1933 nearly everyone had been for giving it a chance. By 1935 most people—except for the trade associations and the trade unions—were against it. When the Supreme Court finally declared the National Industrial Recovery Act unconstitutional in 1935, the Administration accepted the verdict with relief. From the outset it had been seeking other roads to recovery and reform.

The end of the Hundred Days. The AAA and the NRA set the pattern of national planning and were, in this sense, crucial measures of the early New Deal. But they by no means exhausted the achievement of the special session of 1933. During the Hundred Days

with the idea of a "blanket code" in which cooperating employers would pledge themselves to observe NRA standards on minimum wages and maximum hours. The Blue Eagle, modeled on the Indian thunderbird, became the symbol of compliance. Briefly, in the revivalist atmosphere conjured up by Johnson, the Blue Eagle soared. Two million employers accepted the blanket code, and the great industries of the country began to accept special codes.

Protected from competition by those codes, managers were able to stop cutting prices and with them wages. But the codes also protected marginal firms that might best have been allowed to fail, as well as strong firms that could have produced at a profit at prices lower than those that tended to obtain. Further the codes decreased the probability of investment in new, improved facilities. Yet new capital investment would have helped to stimulate the overall economy.

Those liabilities were balanced in part by the attempts of the NRA to pursue some of the long-term objectives of American reformers. In the economic field, it hoped to bring about permanent reemployment by raising wages and shortening working hours. In the social field, it sought the abolition of child after March 4, 1933, Roosevelt sent fifteen messages to Congress and saw fifteen major bills through to enactment.

Advocates of inflation, strongest in Congress but vocal also within the executive branch, were eager to relieve the burden of debt contracted when the price level was much higher. Since the closing of the banks and the Economy Act had a deflationary impact, the Administration looked, too, for means to induce a general price increase. Conservative officials, especially Budget Director Douglas, opposed anything that savored of inflation. On the other hand, many Southern and Western congressmen demanded either a massive printing of greenbacks or an extensive monetization of silver. Those prospects had broad support among farmers and even some members of the business community. Roosevelt himself had no desire for currency inflation, but he was determined to bring about a rise of prices—not so fast as to absorb the increases in wages and farm income but fast enough to reduce the drag of debt on the economy. It seemed increasingly evident to him that the United States had to choose between the old gold standard and the price-raising policy, and he had no hesitation about the choice. On April 18, 1933, the President determined to abandon the gold standard officially by executive orders authorizing the control of the flow of gold from the United States. In a few weeks Congress confirmed the departure from gold by passing a resolution providing for the abrogation of the gold clause in public and private contracts.

In the meantime, the inflationist amendment to the Agricultural Adjustment Act (see p. 637) had bestowed a variety of monetary powers on the President. He protected the independence of American monetary policy by refusing at the London Economic Conference in July to peg the dollar at a fixed value in international exchange, and, when farm prices sagged in November, Roosevelt, always eager for action, embarked on a gold-purchase program designed to raise the level of prices, especially commodity prices, by Treasury purchases of gold. The program was of doubtful economic validity. But the exercise permitted Roosevelt to retain control of monetary policy at a time when both inflationists and bankers were demanding that he take action that he deemed positively harmful. By January 1934 the experiment had obviously failed to raise prices, but the pressure for inflation had abated. The Administration then stabilized the dollar at $35 for an ounce of gold, 59.06 percent of the pre-1933 gold value. Roosevelt also guided through Congress the Gold Act of 1934, which gave the Treasury large new authority in managing the value of the dollar abroad and the conditions of credit at home.

The gold policy, along with the banking and securities legislation of 1933–34, shifted the financial capital of the nation from Wall Street to Washington. The adventure in inflation and the Treasury's use of its new powers established a continuing policy of "cheap money"—that is, low interest rates. Those low rates made private borrowing more attractive and the financing of government borrowing less expensive. But the inducement to private or public investment proved inadequate, for the private sector still envisaged small opportunities for profit and the Administration still hesitated deliberately to incur heavy deficits. Like planning for industry, inflation and cheap money did not produce recovery. They did establish public authority over an area of economic activity that private power had previously dominated. That authority was expanded by a landmark act of 1935 that amended the Federal Reserve Act of 1913. The earlier statute had left most of the authority over the banking system with the regional Federal Reserve Banks, which were dominated by private bankers. The new law concentrated authority in the Board of Governors of the Federal Reserve System, the public agency in Washington, which now had direct control over the significant instruments affecting the volume of money and credit.

The Securities Act of 1933, a first step toward disciplining the practices of Wall Street, required full disclosure of relevant information in the issuance of new securities, and the Glass-Steagall Act, also of the Hundred Days, provided for the separation of commercial and investment banking in order to limit speculation by banks. Legislation in 1934 strengthened the Securities Act, and a further measure of 1935 established the Securities and Exchange Commission to prevent and punish misrepresentation and fraud in the securities business.

Other actions of the Hundred Days were designed at once to help the banks and to reduce the human cost of depression. The House Owners' Loan Act saved countless homes by providing means for the refinancing of mortgages. That refinancing, along with the similar operations of the Farm Credit Administration for agricultural mortgages, protected homes and farms from foreclosure and assisted banks and insurance companies as well. In return for mortgages that were not being paid, those lending institutions received government bonds that they could always convert to cash and on which regular interest payments were assured. Still another New Deal measure, the Federal Deposit Insurance Corporation, set up a system for the insurance of savings and demand deposits and thereby helped restore confidence in the banks. That restoration revealed the New Deal's commitment to saving capitalism while reforming it.

More precedent-breaking was the Federal Emergency Relief Act, which established for the first time a

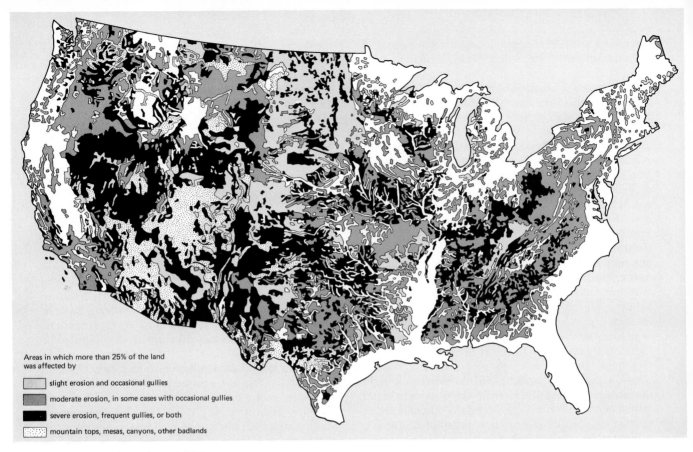

Areas in which more than 25% of the land was affected by

- slight erosion and occasional gullies
- moderate erosion, in some cases with occasional gullies
- severe erosion, frequent gullies, or both
- mountain tops, mesas, canyons, other badlands

The extent of erosion, 1935

system of federal relief. Under the resourceful direction of Harry L. Hopkins, a New York social worker, the new relief agency rapidly supplied the states with cash for immediate assistance to the indigent unemployed. Hopkins the next winter began to experiment with "work relief"—jobs rather than handouts—a program that pointed toward the policies Congress endorsed in 1935.

Another measure of the Hundred Days linked work relief to the conservation of natural resources. This was the Civilian Conservation Corps, an organization that recruited young men between the ages of eighteen and twenty-five to work in the countryside. CCC camps were set up in all parts of the country, and CCC boys played a useful role in protecting and developing reservoirs, watersheds, forests, and parks. The dust storms of the early thirties, whirling up from the parched and eroded land of the Great Plains, emphasized the need for a revitalized national conservation policy. A "shelterbelt" of trees was planted along the one-hundredth meridian from Canada to Texas; other measures were undertaken to promote reforestation, to control overgrazing, and to encourage farmers to plant soil-improving crops and adopt other soil-conservation practices.

In some respects the most striking innovation of the Hundred Days was an effort to rescue an entire region. The Tennessee Valley was a conspicuous example of what later generations would know as an

The CCC: protecting the forests

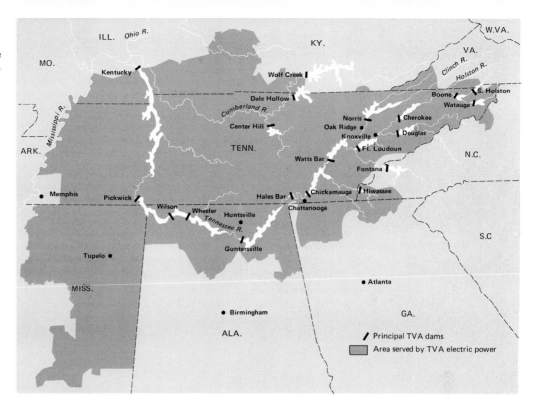

The Tennessee Valley Authority

Principal TVA dams

Area served by TVA electric power

"underdeveloped" territory. Recurrent floods washed away the topsoil; the forests were thin and overcut; income was less than half the national average; and in the highland counties, over half the families were on relief. Only two out of every hundred farms had electricity. Yet the Valley also contained one of the most valuable power sites in the country, at Muscle Shoals, Alabama; and some people, especially Senator George W. Norris of Nebraska, saw in cheap electric power the means of transforming life in the valley. But Norris' bills providing for government operation of hydroelectric plants had fallen under the vetoes of Republican Presidents.

Many factors—some opportunities, some problems—converged in the Valley: not only electric power and conservation but fertilizer production, flood control, inland waterways, and, above all, the hopeless cycle of human poverty. In a bold change of perspective, Roosevelt now saw all these elements as parts of a single problem. The answer, he believed, was not a collection of separate and unrelated reforms but multipurpose development under the direction of a single authority. In April 1933 he called on Congress to establish "a corporation clothed with the power of Government but possessed of the flexibility and initiative of a private enterprise" charged with "national planning for a complete river watershed."

Despite the opposition of the power companies of the area, whose executives claimed that the Valley already had all the power capacity it could absorb for

years to come, Congress passed the bill establishing the Tennessee Valley Authority in May 1933. The TVA proved to be one of the most dramatically successful of all New Deal undertakings. Seeking at every opportunity to win local collaboration under TVA director David E. Lilienthal's slogan of "grassroots democracy," the TVA built dams and powerhouses, cleared the rivers, replenished the soil, rebuilt the forests, and brought the magic of electricity into the farthest corners of the Valley. Grassroots democracy in the Valley proved to be for whites only. Without protest from Washington local agencies working with TVA systematically excluded blacks from participation and benefits. Yet for whites at least the region vibrated with a new life. Soon visitors came from all over the world to inspect the result. No other New Deal agency had such an international impact.

The struggle for recovery

The conquest of fear. The Hundred Days induced a tremendous revival of confidence. In this revival the personality of the President himself played a basic role. As late as the 1932 campaign, Franklin Roosevelt had still been a hazy figure. Now his speeches, his radio "fireside chats," his twice-a-week press conferences made him seen almost a constant presence in the homes of Americans. He radiated energy, deci-

Share the wealth

What I have proposed is....

1. A capital levy tax on the property owned by any one person of 1% of all over $1,000,000; 2% of all over $2,000,000 etc., until, when it reaches fortunes of over $100,000,000, the government takes all above that figure; which means a limit on the size of any one man's fortune to something like $50,000,000—the balance to go to the government to spread out in its work among all the people.

2. An inheritance tax which does not allow any one person to receive more than $5,000,000 in a lifetime without working for it....

3. An income tax which does not allow any one man to make more than $1,000,000 in one year, exclusive of taxes....

The foregoing program means all taxes paid by fortune holders at the top and none by the people at the bottom; the spreading of wealth among all the people and the breaking up of a system of Lords and Slaves in our economic life....

Then ... the food of the land will feed, the raiment clothe, and the houses shelter all the people....

Then ... EVERY MAN A KING.

From Huey P. Long, *Every Man a King*, 1933.

---

sion, and good cheer. His superb personal faith, along with the explosion of administrative inventiveness and political audacity in Washington, convinced the people that they had a chance to recover control of their economic destiny.

During 1933 Roosevelt enjoyed almost universal support. As the crisis receded, however, opposition began to emerge—first from the business community on Roosevelt's right, then in a clamor of discordant voices on his left. At the start his critics made little dent in his popularity. The congressional election of 1934 provided an almost unprecedented national endorsement of the President's program. The Administration actually increased its strength in both the House and the Senate, and the Republicans were left with the governorship of only seven states. Many of the new Democrats came to Congress from urban districts and were especially responsive to labor and welfare concerns.

Critics, right and left. Roosevelt confronted the congressional session of 1935 with top-heavy majorities in both houses, but the policy momentum of 1933 had begun to slacken. Full economic recovery still seemed distant, and the voices of criticism were now speaking out with new confidence. The American Liberty League, an organization formed in 1934 by a group of conservative businessmen and politicians, offered the most active opposition on the right. On the left the most powerful of the new leaders was Huey Long of Louisiana.

As governor of Louisiana, Long had brought new roads and schools and textbooks to the state; but the price of his impressive program of social improvement was spreading corruption and repression. By 1935 he ruled his native state almost as a dictator. In national politics, Long's role was more purely that of a demagogue. His "Share Our Wealth" movement, which stressed heavy taxation of the rich and large handouts to the poor, reminded Americans of the need for social justice. But Long used his program primarily as a means of stirring existing resentments in the hope that the Kingfish, as Long fondly called himself, could be propelled into the Presidency.

Another rising leader was a California physician, Dr. Francis E. Townsend, who proposed a two-hundred-dollar monthly pension for all over sixty-five. The aged had suffered deeply from the depression, and the Townsend Plan seemed for a while in 1935 to be developing genuine mass support. Both Long and Townsend were openly hostile to the New Deal. A third leader, Father Charles E. Coughlin, the famous "radio priest" of Royal Oak, Michigan, had originally endorsed Roosevelt but by 1935 was drifting into opposition. He established in that year the National Union for Social Justice, an organization that appealed especially to the Populist and inflationist traditions of the Middle West and to Irish-Catholics of the great cities. Coughlin's particular nostrum was the nationalization of the banks.

Long, Townsend, and Coughlin were hawking competing patent medicines for the nation's economic ills. But they drew their following from much the same audience—baffled and disoriented members of the lower-middle class who were seeking attention and protection. The emergence of these new movements signified a discontent that the President could not ignore.

Stalemate in 1935. Though the policies of the Hundred Days had ended despair, they had not produced recovery. The gross national product, though nearly $20 billion larger than in 1933, was still $30 billion less than in 1929. Four million more workers were employed in 1935 than in 1933, but 9 million were still unemployed. Roosevelt was still in economic trouble and, as the clamor of the demagogues and the fractiousness of the new Congress made clear, might well be in increasing political trouble. He needed a new forward thrust of policy if he was to maintain his control.

The Supreme Court further increased the pressure against the policies of 1933. For two years the Administration had delayed tests of the constitutionality of New Deal legislation, but now the dam was breaking. Early in 1935 the Court invalidated a provision of the National Industrial Recovery Act prohibiting interstate shipment of "hot" oil—that is, oil produced in violation of production quotas fixed by state laws. A few weeks later, the gold resolution of 1933, one of the foundations of the nation's monetary policy, barely escaped judicial veto in a bitter and somewhat ambiguous five to four decision. Then the Court, in another five to four decision, declared against the whole idea of a federal pension act for railroad employees. And on May 27, 1935, the celebrated "Black Monday" of New Deal annals, the Court in three sweeping decisions killed a farm-mortgage-relief act, rebuked the President for what it declared to be an illegal exercise of his removal power, and condemned the entire National Industrial Recovery Act as unconstitutional.

The NRA case, irreverently known as the "sick chicken" case, involved some Brooklyn poultry-dealers, the Schechter brothers, who had been charged with violations of the Live Poultry Code. The Court pronounced unanimously against the Recovery Act on two grounds: that it delegated excessive powers to the executive and that it ascribed to Congress powers of economic regulation that could not be justified under the commerce clause. This second objection was particularly devastating. The language used in the decision seemed to say that the Court regarded mining, manufacturing, agriculture, and construction as "essentially local" activities. In a press conference a few days later Roosevelt concluded, "We have been relegated to the horse-and-buggy definition of interstate commerce."

New directions in policy. In invalidating the NRA, the Supreme Court knocked out the keystone of the early New Deal experiment in national planning. The Court's action came at a time when Roosevelt himself was perhaps losing faith in the efficacy of national planning and when the New Dealers most identified with the planning idea were beginning to lose their political usefulness. Roosevelt, always the activist, turned to those best prepared to offer him a convincing program of action. He found this program in the Brandeis-Frankfurter group (see p. 634).

During the Hundred Days, that group had played a subordinate role except in their influence on banking and securities legislation. They disapproved of the NRA, both of the philosophy of irreversible economic concentration on which it was based and the program of national planning to which it led. In 1935 the group moved to the forefront. It influenced both the President and his program for that year. In a message to Congress on June 19, 1935, the President committed himself to the view that "without . . . small enterprises our competitive economic society would cease. Size begets monopoly." Roosevelt moved equivocally along the new lines, but the mounting hostility of business and the Court's condemnation of the NRA pushed him on.

With the revival of Roosevelt's leadership, the 1935 session broke the log jam that had blocked action for months. The result was a stunning program of legislative achievement. A $4.8 billion relief bill had already passed in April. It gave Harry Hopkins the

The WPA: schools, roads, flood relief

The struggle for recovery

authority and some of the appropriations he had been seeking to establish the Works Progress Administration and thus to pursue his belief that the solution for aid to the unemployed lay in work relief. Though his new program led to a small amount of made work, known invidiously as "boondoggling," it also built roads, airports, and schools, improved parks and waterways, produced plays and concerts, maps and guidebooks, and sustained the morale and preserved the skills of millions of Americans unable through no fault of their own to find private employment. Where Hopkins' WPA specialized in light public works, Ickes' Public Works Administration, which shared the $4.8 billion, concentrated on heavy and durable projects, ranging from dams and bridges to irrigation projects and aircraft-carriers. The activities of the PWA not only gave some stimulation, albeit inadequate, to the national economy but permanently improved the national estate in many ways.

Meanwhile the elimination of the NRA had created an urgent need for new laws continuing elements of the NRA program. Thus the Wagner Labor Relations Act, to which the President now gave his support, replaced Section 7a of the National Industrial Recovery Act. The act outlawed unfair labor practices, including the firing or blacklisting of employees for union activities. It also established the National Labor Relations Board to enforce its provisions, which provided more reliable guarantees for collective bargaining. The Public Contracts Act applied NRA wage and hour standards to firms doing business with the federal government. The Guffey Coal Act tried to put the NRA Coal Code into constitutional form. No one could be sure whether these laws would survive the Supreme Court, though they had been drawn up to avoid the more obvious defects of the National Industrial Recovery Act.

The defects of the Agricultural Adjustment Act also needed remedy. The crop limitation and support programs of the AAA operated to the disadvantage of tenant farmers and sharecroppers, especially in the South. Owners of the land they tilled took much of that land out of cultivation in order to qualify for federal subsidies. The displaced tenants and croppers either drifted to the cities, where they had difficulty finding employment, or became migrant agricultural workers who followed the harvest from place to place. The dust storms of the Great Plains were forcing small farmers there to join the migration, primarily toward California. The poverty both of the migrants, and of the croppers who remained near starvation on the land where they had grown up, contrasted with the growing prosperity of the large landowners, the chief beneficiaries of the AAA. In 1935 Roosevelt first addressed the problem by establishing the Resettlement Administration, financed by part of the $4.8 billion

The statute goes no further than to safeguard the right of employees to self-orga-nization and to select representatives of their own choosing for collective bargain-ing....

Respondent says that whatever may be said of employees engaged in inter-state commerce, the industrial relations and activities in the manufacturing department of respondent's enterprise are not subject to federal regulation....

The congressional authority to protect interstate commerce from burdens and obstructions is not limited to transactions which can be deemed to be an essen-tial part of a ''flow'' of interstate or foreign commerce. Burdens and obstructions may be due to injurious action springing from other sources. The fundamental princi-ple is that the power to regulate commerce is the power to enact ''all appropriate legislation'' for its ''protection and advancement.'' ... That power is plenary and may be exerted to protect interstate commerce ''no matter what the source of the dangers which threaten it.'' ... Although activities may be intrastate in character when separately considered, if they have such a close and substantial relation to interstate commerce that their control is essential or appropriate to protect that commerce from burdens and obstructions, Congress cannot be denied the power to exercise that control....

The close and intimate effect which brings the subject within the reach of federal power may be due to activities in relation to productive industry although the industry when separately viewed is local.

The scope of congressional power: a broader view

From the Majority Opinion of the United States Supreme Court by Mr. Chief Justice Charles E. Hughes, National Labor Relations Board v. Jones and Laughlin Steel Corporation, 301 U.S. 1, 1937.

---

relief appropriation. The RA was to rehabilitate ten-ants and small farmers, establish cooperative farm communities, and resettle farm families existing on submarginal land. The program, bold in its intentions, never received adequate funds from Congress, as the President's Committee on Farm Tenancy reported in 1937. That report, an encyclopedia of agricultural distress, provoked Congress to reorganize the RA as the Farm Security Administration to provide financial help for tenants hoping to become landowners, to refinance small farmers, and to assist migratory work-ers. The new program assured many of the neediest farmers of federal aid, though never on the scale that the largest landowners enjoyed.

Most important for the future, the Congress passed in August 1935 the Social Security Act, setting up the Social Security Board to operate both a na-tional plan of contributory old-age and survivors in-surance and a federal-state plan of unemployment compensation. Both programs, though at first limited in their coverage, provided the men and women they affected with a measure of protection against hazards and vicissitudes beyond their control. They started the government toward a permanent and inclusive system of social welfare. In addition, the Social Secu-rity Act, along with other measures of the session,

helped further to consolidate a political alliance be-tween the New Deal and organized labor.

Other acts of the 1935 session were designed to restore competition to the economy. The Public Utili-ties Holding Company Act limited each holding com-pany after 1938 to a single integrated public-utility system unless it could make a convincing economic case for holding more than one system. The tax law of 1935, with its increased surtaxes and estate taxes and its substitution of a graduated for a uniform corpora-tion income tax, sought to discriminate in favor of small business and the small taxpayer. The tax act of 1936, deeply resented by business, made an attempt to force management to distribute most corporate profits to shareholders. Once distributed, those profits would be subject to the high personal surtax rates. Most important, the forced distribution of profits would reduce the power of management and enhance the options of shareholders who might spend their larger incomes or seek alternative investments. Still another tax act in 1937 aimed to close the loopholes through which Andrew Mellon, Alfred Sloan, the du Ponts, and other rich men had been escaping taxes.

The philosophy of the New Deal. Alike in its earlier and later emphases, the New Deal strove con-

Dust storm, Oklahoma, 1936

tinuously for both economic recovery and social reform. The focus of policy shifted partly as a consequence of the change in national mood between 1933 and 1935. The desperation of 1933 seemed to demand sweeping economic measures; at the same time, it produced a large measure of political unity. The partial recovery of 1935 increased political disunity and decreased the desire for centralized economic control. By 1935 the New Deal had abandoned its early adventures in inflation. More important, while the New Deal had at first accepted the logic of the administered market and tried to devise new institutions to do what competition had once done to keep the economy in balance, the New Deal by 1935 was stressing a more competitive market and a more egalitarian distribution of income, wealth, and private power. It was politically more radical. Earlier the New Deal had sought government-business cooperation to achieve national objectives. Now the New Deal, persuaded that equitable competition could be restored only through rigorous government enforcement of the rules of the competitive game, was zestfully antibusiness in rhetoric. If "a concentration of private power without equal in history" was the great menace to the American economy, as Roosevelt told Congress in 1938, then the way out was a program "to stop the progress of collectivism in business and turn business back to the democratic competitive order." His basic thesis, Roosevelt said, was "not that the system of free enterprise for profit has failed in this generation, but that it has not yet been tried." In 1938 the antimonopoly drive picked up new speed with the appointment of Thurman Arnold as head of the Antitrust Division of the Department of Justice and with the establishment of the Temporary National Economic Committee to survey the concentration of economic power.

The fight against economic concentration, however, constituted only part of the second phase of the New Deal. A new philosophy of recovery through the use of the federal budget was beginning to emerge within the Administration. The chief spokesman for this new view was Marriner Eccles of the Federal Reserve Board, who contended that, when the decline of private spending brought about a depression, it was the obligation of government to offset the decline by increasing public spending. Eccles felt that the deliberate creation of compensatory government deficits would stimulate capital formation and purchasing power until the consequent rise in national income produced enough revenue to bring the budget once again into balance. In 1935 these ideas were still tentative and unorthodox, even among New Dealers. The New Deal was spending large sums and was running budgetary deficits (the largest in the prewar years was $4.5 billion, in 1936); but it was doing these things in response to conditions, not to theories. Further, the deficits were too small effectively to spur recovery. In 1936 the English economist John Maynard (later Lord) Keynes gave Eccles' approach its first extended theoretical justification in his influential book *General Theory of Employment*. Many of the younger New Dealers found Keynesian ideas increasingly congenial, and their alliance with the compensatory spenders was decisive in the final evolution of New Deal policies.

F.D.R. looks at his record

The 1936 election

The estrangement of business. The emergence of big government and big labor in the early thirties meant that the business community no longer enjoyed unchallenged primacy in American society. Resentment over loss of status, resentment over government regulation and taxation, resentment over uncertainty and strain—all these emotions, joined in many cases to a sincere conviction that the New Deal was a first step toward a totalitarian state, gradually produced among many businessmen a state of bitter opposition to Roosevelt's Administration. In alienating those businessmen, the New Deal also discouraged them from new investment, but they had not invested while Hoover cultivated their interests and solicited their confidence. Further, had the New Deal ignored social problems, and had it used taxation not to redistribute income and reform business but instead to provide favors for business, the Administration would have surrendered the social interests of the whole people to the possibility, by no means certain, of a recovery beneficial primarily to the wealthy. Even if recovery had occurred under those conditions, it would have left unaltered the many injustices of American society in the twenties. New Deal social reforms may have involved some short-run economic and political liabilities, but, for the long run, Roosevelt's emphasis was indispensable for preserving democratic possibilities in the United States.

Still the attitude of the Supreme Court seemed to validate the notion of businessmen that the New Deal was using unconstitutional means to achieve unconstitutional objectives. When the Court returned in 1936 to its assault on the New Deal—vetoing the Agricultural Adjustment Act in January, the Guffey Coal Act and the Municipal Bankruptcy Act in May, and a New York minimum-wage law in June—its actions deepened convictions on both sides that an impassable gulf existed between the America of individualism and the America of reform. Hoover denounced the New Deal as an attack on "the whole philosophy of individual liberty." Some conservatives began to trace the New Deal to subversive foreign ideas—to fascism or, more generally and fashionably, to communism. At the height of the holding-company fight, and on occasion thereafter, rumors were even put into circulation that Roosevelt was a madman given to wild bursts of maniacal laughter.

The 1936 campaign. The "hate-Roosevelt" feeling, the conviction that the New Deal represented the end of the American way of life, permeated the conservative wing of the Republican party. Other Republicans, however, recognizing the hard fact of Roosevelt's popularity and, in many cases, agreeing with his policies, opposed Hoover's notion of making the 1936 campaign an all-out fight against the New Deal. This view prevailed in the Republican convention of 1936. The Republicans nominated Governor Alfred M. Landon of Kansas, a former Bull Moose Progressive, who, while conservative on matters of public finance, had shown himself tolerant of many aspects of the New Deal. Frank Knox, a newspaper-publisher from Chicago, was chosen as Landon's running mate. The Democrats meanwhile renominated Roosevelt and Garner. The forces of Coughlin, Townsend, and Long (Long himself had been assassinated in September 1935) coalesced in the Union party and nominated Congressman William Lemke of North Dakota for the Presidency.

At the start Landon took a moderate line, accepting New Deal objectives but arguing that only the Republican party could achieve them thriftily and constitutionally. In the later stages of the campaign, however, he found himself making more and more extreme accusations, until in the end his line was almost indistinguishable from Hoover's. In a moment of last-minute desperation the Republican high command even decided to make an issue of the social-security program, which was due to go into effect on January 1, 1937. The Social Security Act, declared Frank Knox, "puts half the working people of America under federal control." The Republican national chairman said that every worker would have to wear metal dog-tags carrying his social-security number.

Such efforts were unavailing. Roosevelt conducted his campaign in a mood of buoyant confidence. He was aware, however, of the bitterness of feeling against him; and, in indignation over the social-security panic, he gave vent to bitterness of his own before the campaign was over. "Never before in all our history have these forces [of selfishness and greed] been so united against one candidate as they stand today," he said. "They are unanimous in their hate for me—and I welcome their hatred." The election revealed that the attacks on Roosevelt had made little impression on the voters. In a victory without previous precedent in American politics, Roosevelt carried every state except Maine and Vermont. The Republicans were routed, and the Union party sank without a trace. In 1936, the celebrated Roosevelt coalition had emerged in its full strength. The coalition of 1936 included the farmers, West and South, who had supported the party in 1916. It included also the city machines and workingmen of all ethnic origins, most of whom had rallied to Al Smith in 1928. In 1936 increasing numbers of blacks in Northern cities were also voting Democratic, as they had never before. So were reform-minded intellectuals, as they had not consistently since 1916, and so was much of the middle class, its confidence revived since 1932, its debt to the New Deal considerable, and its previous Republicanism in eclipse. Though with continuing shifts of influence and support within it, that coalition was to dominate national elections, especially presidential elections, for a generation.

The Supreme Court fight

The Court versus the New Deal. Roosevelt opened his second Administration by issuing a vigorous call for an extension of the New Deal. "I see one-third of a nation ill-housed, ill-clad, ill-nourished," he said in his inaugural address. But he faced a formidable roadblock in his determination to push ahead his reform program. That roadblock was the Supreme Court. By the end of its 1936 term the Court had heard nine cases involving New Deal legislation. In seven of those cases a majority of the Court had found the legislation unconstitutional, though three verdicts of unconstitutionality were by the narrow margin of five to four and two more by six to three. In addition, the Court, having in 1923 (*Adkins* v. *Children's Hospital*) denied the federal government power to set minimum wages, had now denied that power to the state of New York, thereby apparently saying that no power existed in the United States to outlaw the sweatshop.

So sustained and devastating a use of the judicial veto to kill social and economic legislation had never before occurred. Moreover, the minority, which in several cases had affirmed its belief in the constitutionality of the disputed laws, comprised by far the more distinguished members of the Court—Louis D. Brandeis, Benjamin N. Cardozo, Harlan F. Stone, and, on occasion, Chief Justice Charles Evans Hughes. "Courts are not the only agency of government that must be assumed to have a capacity to govern," Stone had warned his conservative brethren.

The whole future of the New Deal appeared uncertain. Such laws as the Social Security Act, the Wagner Act, and the Holding Company Act seemed the next candidates for execution by the Court. And, so long as the majority's narrow reading of the Constitution prevailed, there was little chance that the New Deal could take further steps to meet the problems of the forgotten third of a nation. During 1936 Roosevelt and his Attorney General, Homer Cummings of Connecticut, came to feel that, before anything else could be done, something had to be done about the Court. They considered and then dismissed the idea of a constitutional amendment, partly because of the difficulties of the ratification process, partly because the amendment itself would be at the mercy of judicial interpretation. In any case, the trouble seemed to lie, not with the Constitution, which they regarded as a spacious charter of government, but with the Court majority. They concluded that the best solution would be to do something directly about the personnel of the Court.

"Packing" the Supreme Court. In February 1937 Roosevelt sent a message to Congress calling for the reorganization of the federal judiciary. He contended that the Supreme Court could not keep up with its work burden, and that the interests of efficient administration required the appointment of an additional justice for each justice aged seventy or over. The argument about overcrowded dockets was disingenuous and gave the Court plan an air of over-

John L. Lewis:
United Mine Worker

slickness from which it never recovered. Chief Justice Hughes was soon able to demonstrate that the Court had, in fact, been keeping abreast of its responsibilities. In two speeches in March, Roosevelt tried to wrench the debate back to the real issue. The Court, he said, had "cast doubts on the ability of the elected Congress to protect us against catastrophe by meeting squarely our modern social and economic conditions." His object was "to save the Constitution from the Court and the Court from itself." But it was too late. The protest against the measure was now too great to be diverted.

Those who had disliked the New Deal from the start found in the Court plan verification of their claim that Roosevelt was trying to destroy the American system. And many who had supported the New Deal were genuinely shocked both by the idea of "packing" the Court and by Roosevelt's circuitous approach to his objective. The proposal set in motion a bitter national debate. In Congress the Republicans held back and allowed dissident Democrats to lead the fight against the President. The measure might have carried with some modifications had not the Court itself suddenly changed its attitude toward New Deal legislation. On March 29, 1937, the Court in effect reversed its decision of 1936 and affirmed the constitutionality of a Washington minimum-wage law. Two weeks later it sustained the Wagner Act. Plainly the Court majority had abandoned the narrow ground of 1935–36; in Robert H. Jackson's phrase, it had retreated to the Constitution. The way had ap-

parently been cleared for the New Deal without the appointment of a single new justice. And the resignation of one of the conservative justices in June, giving the President his first Supreme Court appointment, made his plan of enlarging the Court seem less necessary than ever. The bill was defeated, though Roosevelt could later claim with some justice that if he had lost the battle he had won the war. But the New Deal had lost momentum in Congress, where the Court fight both revealed and widened the rift between reform Democrats and the conservatives in the party.

Social and economic crises

The rise of the CIO.   The Court battle had struck a blow at Roosevelt's prestige as well as at the unity of the Democratic party. And the surging militance of organized labor was creating new problems. The NRA had given the trade-union movement its first impetus to mass organization since the First World War. Under the leadership of John L. Lewis and the United Mine Workers, a great campaign had begun in 1933 to organize the unorganized in the mass-production industries. This campaign soon led to a major conflict within the labor movement itself. The American Federation of Labor was dominated by craft unions; under the craft theory, the automobile industry, for example, was to be organized, not by a single union, but by as many different unions as there were different crafts involved in making a car. But Lewis, as head of one of the few industrial unions in the AFL, thought instinctively in terms of organization, not by craft, but by industry. Moreover, craft unionism had failed to organize the basic industries, to which industrial unionism seemed peculiarly adapted. The consequence was a fight within the AFL between craft unionism and industrial unionism, culminating in the expulsion of Lewis and his associates in 1936 and their formation of a rival labor federation, the Congress of Industrial Organizations.

The CIO came into existence at a time when workers throughout the country, especially in the mass-production industries, were hungering for organization in unions of their own choosing. The spontaneous character of the labor uprising was shown in 1936 and 1937 by the development of a new strike technique, frowned upon by national labor leadership—the "sit-down strike," in which workers sat down by their machines in factories and refused to work until employers would concede them the right of collective bargaining. To many employers, the sit-down strike threatened property rights and smacked of revolution; its vogue led them to fight all the more savagely against any recognition of industrial unions as bargaining agents.

But the CIO pushed its organizing campaigns ahead vigorously, especially in automobiles and steel. There were shocking moments of violence. In May police shot and killed ten pickets outside the Republic Steel plant in Chicago. In Detroit, Walter Reuther and other leaders of the United Automobile Workers were brutally beaten by company guards at Henry Ford's River Rouge plant. But the decision of General Motors to negotiate with the UAW in February 1937 and of United States Steel to negotiate with the Steel Workers Organizing Committee in March dated the beginning of the end. The battle for collective bargaining was not yet wholly won. But union membership, which had been less than 3 million in 1933 and barely over 4 million at the start of 1937, grew to 7.2 million by the end of the year and to 9 million by 1939.

The recession of 1937–38. The years 1935 and 1936 had been years of slow but steady economic improvement. So marked was the trend that leading bankers began to worry about inflation, though resources and labor were still widely underemployed. Under pressure from the bankers, the Federal Reserve Board tried to put on the brakes by raising reserve requirements and thus interest rates in 1936 and 1937. This action had some effect. But it was less significant in arresting the upward swing than the decline between 1936 and 1937 in the federal government's net contribution to the economy. In 1936 the payment of the veterans' bonus of $1.7 billion on top of relief and public-works expenditures and the normal costs of government resulted in a net federal government contribution of $4.1 billion. In 1937 several factors—the collection of taxes under the Social Security Act as well as the attempt to reduce public spending and to move toward a balanced budget—resulted in a decrease of the net government contribution to $800 million, a drop of $3.3 billion in a single year. Private business spending, contained by the apprehensions of investors, did not fill the gap created by the contraction of public spending.

The collapse in the months after September 1937 was actually more severe than it had been in the first nine months of the depression. National income fell 13 percent, payrolls 35 percent, durable-goods production 50 percent, profits 78 percent. The increase in unemployment reproduced scenes of the early depression and imposed new burdens on the relief agencies.

The recession brought to a head a policy debate within the Administration. One group, led by Henry Morgenthau, Jr., the Secretary of the Treasury, had supported the policy of government retrenchment and favored balancing the budget as soon as practicable. Those steps, they believed, though historical evidence contradicted them, would restore business confidence and lift private investment. Another group, led by Hopkins of the WPA and Eccles of the Federal Reserve Board, urged the immediate resumption of public spending. Economists advising them and like-minded New Dealers could now buttress their case by reference to the theories of J. M. Keynes, which were gradually winning converts in Washington (see p. 646). Roosevelt himself favored for a while the first group; but, as the downward slide speeded up, he reluctantly accepted the necessity for spending. In March 1938 he announced a new spending program. Again too small to achieve its intended results, this program, which included as much as Congress would tolerate, did begin to reverse the decline. It sopped up some unemployment and by 1939 effected a gross national product larger than in 1937. The recession, however, killed Roosevelt's hope of attaining full economic recovery before the end of his second term.

1938 and the purge. The Court fight, the new aggressiveness of organized labor, and the resumption of the spending policy all tended to widen the gap between the liberal and the conservative wings of the Democratic party. The liberals were mostly Northerners, the conservatives mostly Southerners, and other events of 1938 hastened the alienation of the Bourbon Democrats from the New Deal. Southern employers were bitterly opposed to the Administra-

Steel strike:
shocking moments of violence

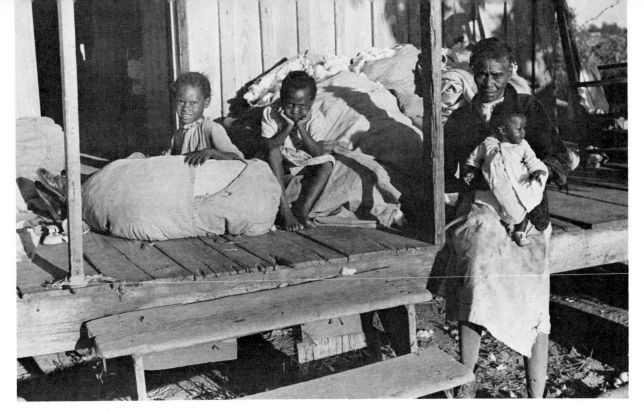

The South: "the nation's No. 1 economic problem"

tion's Fair Labor Standards (or Wages and Hours) Act, which was passed in June 1938. They objected that its policy of setting minimum wages and maximum hours and outlawing child labor would increase labor costs. Southern planters were equally bitter against the Farm Security Administration and its activities on behalf of tenant farmers and sharecroppers. The release in August 1938 of a government report on economic conditions in the South and Roosevelt's description of the South as "the nation's No. 1 economic problem" seemed to express a determination to extend the New Deal into the South. Conservative Democrats in Congress prepared to resist; and the alliance between Southern Democrats and Northern Republicans, tentatively initiated in 1937 during the Supreme Court fight, began to harden in 1938 into a major obstacle to further New Deal legislation. The House Committee on Un-American Activities, dedicated under the chairmanship of Martin Dies of Texas to the harrying of radicals in and out of government, became an instrument of conservative retaliation against the New Deal.

The defection of the Southern conservatives raised difficult problems for the Administration. Roosevelt felt that many conservative Democrats had taken a free ride on the popularity of the New Deal; their refusal to support liberal policies, in his judgment, served to blur essential distinctions in Ameri-

can politics. "An election cannot give a country a firm sense of direction," he said in June 1938, "if it has two or more national parties which merely have different names but are as alike in their principles and aims as peas in the same pod." Accordingly he decided to make the New Deal itself an issue in the Democratic primary elections. In August he began to intervene personally in state primaries in the hope of replacing anti-New Deal Democratic senators and congressmen with liberals. Such intervention was a striking departure from precedent, and his opponents were quick to denounce it as a "purge." The almost complete failure of Roosevelt's efforts was a prelude to Administration setbacks in the general election: the Republicans gained seven seats in the Senate and eighty in the House.

The year 1938 marked the end of the forward thrust of the New Deal. The public demand for reform seemed to be slackening, Congress, now controlled by a conservative coalition, rejected the Administration's Lending Bill of 1939, a measure based on Keynesian principles. By that time the drift toward war in Europe was leading both the President and the people to shift their attention to foreign policy. In his state-of-the-union message in January 1939 Roosevelt had spoken significantly of the need "to invigorate the processes of recovery in order to *preserve* our reforms."

651

The American people in the depression

The trauma of depression. The depression had been a severe shock to the American people—to their expectations, their values, and their confidence in themselves and their future. Mute evidence of a declining faith in their prospects was the sudden slowdown of the marriage and birth rates. Population grew at a rate of less than a million a year; the total population increase (to 131.7 million in 1940) was hardly more than half that of the preceding decade. In 1938 there were 1.6 million fewer children under ten than there had been five years before. With the increase in life expectancy (from fifty-six in 1920 to sixty-four in 1940), the proportion of people over sixty-five increased from 5.4 percent in 1930 to 6.9 percent in 1940. In the perspective of depression America began to look like an aging country, its future limited. The demographic trend led economic theorists to argue that the nation had reached "economic maturity" and could not hope to resume growth without aggressive government intervention.

Americans brought up in the tradition of the bright future and the happy ending found it hard to adjust to bread lines, government relief, and mass unemployment. Some fell into listlessness and apathy. Others, unwilling to concede that the old story had come to an end, flocked behind one or another of the social demagogues with their promises of miraculous deliverance. A few believed that depression was an inherent and ineradicable evil of the capitalist system and concluded that the only way out was to abolish capitalism.

Some of these, excited by the success of fascism in Italy and Germany, formed fascist groups, bearing such names as the Silver Shirts. In a vivid novel, *It Can't Happen Here* (1935), Sinclair Lewis showed how a 100 percent American fascist movement might take over the United States. But, though the American fascists diligently imitated many of the Nazi techniques and appeals (including anti-Semitism), they had little impact on American life.

More of those who despaired of capitalism turned toward Marxism. In 1932 just under a million Americans voted against the capitalist system. Most of the votes went to the Socialist party, a reformist group under the appealing leadership of Norman Thomas; but over one hundred thousand voted for the Communist party ticket. The communist movement, the more serious of the two, was controlled by a hard core of disciplined devotees, faithfully conforming to the turns and twists of the party line laid down in Moscow. Not all those who joined the party, however, were aware of its whole nature. At one time or another during the decade, a large number of people passed rather quickly through the movement, attracted primarily by the apparent idealism of communist promises but soon bored by the sectarian inflexibility of communist analysis or repelled by the ruthless dishonesty of communist performance, especially in Europe. Secret communists had some success in penetrating certain labor unions and even a few government offices, though without significantly influencing American policy.

The shake-up of the people. If depression induced despair, it also compelled change. In particular, it discredited and disrupted the structure of status and prestige that had ruled the United States in the twenties. The businessman had been the culture hero of the prosperity decade. In 1929 his New Era had exploded in his face. In the thirties his pretensions to wisdom were derided, his leadership rejected, and he himself often dismissed as a fool if not a crook. A midget perched impudently on the knee of the mighty J. P. Morgan at a congressional investigation became the symbol of the new skepticism about men of wealth.

People from outside the business community—especially politicians and intellectuals—were now in power. Still smarting from their own sense of inferior status in the twenties, they often took undue pleasure in rubbing the nose of the once-arrogant businessman in the mess he had helped create. And in their wake came a rush for status of the "forgotten men" of America—men who had been denied opportunities in the past because of their class or ethnic origin. The New Deal, by revising the structure of status, brought about profound social changes, including visible gains for previously disadvantaged ethnic groups, that diminished the attractiveness to Americans of radical ideologies.

The social revolution. Organized labor's rise to respectability typified the tendencies of the decade. In 1933 the presidents of the six great steel companies blanched and fled when Secretary of Labor Frances Perkins proposed to introduce them to William Green of the American Federation of Labor for a discussion of the NRA steel code. Four years later, when United States Steel signed up with the CIO, labor had achieved substantial recognition. The business community had reluctantly accepted the right of other groups to participate in national economic decisions. Even though the depression continued to restrict economic opportunity, members of once-marginal groups—not only wage-earners but tenant farmers, sharecroppers, old folks, and even intellectuals and women—now had larger chances for fulfilled lives.

The social revolution also enhanced the quality

of life, particularly in the countryside. Though the Supreme Court knocked out the original AAA in 1936, the principle of national responsibility for the agricultural economy was established and reaffirmed in legislation of 1938. No other federal agency had such an impact on the quality of country life as did the Rural Electrification Administration. When it was founded in 1935, only about one farm in ten had power-line electric service, and these were mostly in the neighborhood of towns or cities. Through low-interest loans to cooperatives, the REA enabled farmers to build their own power lines and generate their own electricity. The spread of electricity transformed the countryside. Had distribution been kept in the hands of privately owned utilities, this expansion would not have taken place so quickly.

The ethnic revolution. Immigration substantially stopped in the thirties (except for refugees from fascism toward the end of the decade). The last wave of immigrants, mostly from southern and eastern Europe, in the earlier part of the century had not yet achieved full acceptance in American society; the upheaval of depression gave many Italians, Poles, South Slavs, and Jews their first opportunities. Where craft unions, for example, had often discriminated against the "wops" and the "hunkies," as against the blacks, the industrial unions of the CIO opened their doors to them. Similarly the New Deal gave them their first chance in politics and public service.

Roosevelt himself had no patience with the old American attitude of superiority toward more recent immigrants. "Remember, remember always," he once told the Daughters of the American Revolution, "that all of us, and you and I especially, are descended from immigrants and revolutionists." Of the 214 federal judges appointed by Harding, Coolidge, and Hoover, only 8 were Catholics; of the 196 appointed by Roosevelt, 51 were Catholics. Political figures in the great cities, like Mayor Fiorello La Guardia of New York, acted as brokers in gaining recognition for ethnic minorities previously shut out from political preferment. Concurrently there was a notable decline in the foreign-language press and a more effective acculturation of ethnic minorities into American life.

Most striking of all, perhaps, was the rise in expectations of American blacks, for many years the victims of economic and political neglect. During the depression, the Negro was, in the phrase of the day, "the first man fired and the last man hired." And, though blacks had voted Republican since the Civil War, the Republican administrations had shown little concern for their welfare; black leaders had denounced Hoover as "the man in the lily-White House." Roosevelt brought to Washington an unprecedented sympathy for black problems. New Deal

agencies generally conformed to local folkways that perpetuated segregation and discrimination within the CCC and in the distribution of work relief in the South, for two of many examples. But the New Dealers appointed many able blacks to senior administrative positions from which they were able not only to symbolize new opportunities for their race but to mount programs to assist their fellows. Roosevelt himself repeatedly denounced lynching, though he would not provide direct support to the Northern Democrats in the Senate who took the initiative in sponsoring bills to make lynching a federal crime. The New Deal did far less for American blacks than their circumstances warranted, but it did far more than had any administration since Reconstruction. By 1936 black voters had begun to shift to the Democratic party.

New Deal policies also mitigated, though they did not eliminate, discrimination against women. As they had during the 1920s, so during the 1930s educated women confronted formidable obstacles to entering the professions. A much larger number of women than ever before needed industrial or clerical employment in order to support themselves or to help support their families. Yet with the onset of depression, employers tended to discharge women before they discharged men, and during the 1930s women found it harder than did men to secure new jobs. Consequently many women dropped out of the working force. Those who remained ordinarily earned less than did men in similar positions and normally received no consideration for promotion to supervisory posts. New Deal policies provided partial remedies for those conditions. First the NRA codes and later the Fair Labor Standards Act at least set minimum wages for women as well as men. The WPA created some jobs for women clerical workers, teachers, and lawyers. And the CIO, flourishing under the New Deal, set out, as the AFL had not, vigorously to recruit women into industrial unions and thus to assure them of the gains obtained through collective bargaining.

The New Deal also succeeded in recruiting women voters. The President and particularly his wife encouraged women to work for the Democratic party, as did their friend Molly Dewson, a leader of the National Consumers League. Dewson enlisted thousands of women in the precincts and helped to persuade the Democratic national committee to appoint eight women as vice-chairmen. In 1936 the Democratic convention required each delegate to the platform committee to have an alternate of the opposite sex, a reversal of earlier policy. Dewson also solicited federal patronage for women, who received more postmasterships than ever before and more recognition in major offices—in the Cabinet, where Frances Perkins was Secretary of Labor, on the bench, in executive positions with the WPA. Eleanor Roosevelt, the most visible and influential woman New Dealer, be-came a national symbol for advocates of social justice. Though feminism as a social movement remained subdued, her spirit heartened all women, workers and intellectuals alike.

The release of energy brought about by the New Deal, the invigorating sense that the "forgotten" man and woman could still make a place for themselves in American life—all this gradually began to heal the trauma of depression. The sense of America as an exhausted nation gave way to the image of a purpose-

Eleanor Roosevelt: symbol of social justice

ful society capable of meeting its problems with en-ergy and conviction.

In the twenties, the intellectuals who scorned the American present had turned to "debunking" the American past. In the thirties, when the American present was acquiring purpose and dignity, they began to read this purpose and dignity back into American history. The title of John Dos Passos' book *The Ground We Stand On* (1941) summed up the new attitude. "In times of change and danger," Dos Passos wrote, "when there is a quicksand of fear under men's reasoning, a sense of continuity with generations gone before can stretch like a lifeline across the scary pres-ent." Other skeptics of the twenties joined Dos Passos in taking a more affirmative view of American tradi-tions. Van Wyck Brooks, who had once seen Ameri-can culture as pinched and sterile, now portrayed it, in *The Flowering of New England* (1936) and suc-ceeding volumes, as rich and abundant. Even H. L. Mencken, though he took small comfort in the Amer-ica of the thirties, dedicated his main energies to bring up to date his loving study of *The American Language* and to writing his own nostalgic recollec-tions of an earlier America. The publication of a number of important biographies helped meet the new national desire to repossess the past in all its solidity. This impulse came into happy conjunction with the New Deal in the valuable series of state guidebooks produced by the WPA.

The new pattern of American society. The re-covery of American faith in the thirties both derived from and contributed to the capacity of the American people to reassert a measure of control over their social and economic destiny. In so doing, American society was countering the prevailing ideologies of the day. Both laissez faire and Marxism were philosophies of economic determinism with narrow views of social possibility. The New Deal, with all its improvisations, contradictions, sentimentalisms, and errors, did have the signal advantage of rejecting economic fatalism and of affirming a faith in intelligent experiment.

By Roosevelt's second term the essential pattern of the new society was complete for his generation. The American nation had renounced laissez faire without embracing socialism. Government had acquired the obligation to underwrite the economic and social health of the nation. The budget provided the means by which the government through the use of fiscal policy could compensate for a decline in private economic activity. The state had abandoned efforts aimed at the direct control of industrial production, but industry had to accept ground rules covering minimum standards of life and labor; and the state continued to intervene to maintain, in modified form, the free play of competition. Special areas of economic activity required more comprehensive government control—banking, transportation, public utilities, agriculture, oil. Human welfare was to be protected through various forms of public insurance. A collection of "built-in stabilizers"—minimum wages, unemployment compensation, farm-price supports, social-security payments—were to help secure the economy against future crashes like that of 1929.

Was the Roosevelt way possible? These measures involved more government intervention in the economy than some had thought the economy could stand and still remain free. This was the critical question raised by the New Deal—whether a policy of limited and piecemeal government intervention in economic life was feasible; whether a mixed system was possible that gave the state power enough to assure economic and social security but still not so much as to create an all-powerful dictatorship or so little independence as to remain uncorrupted by the large influence of powerful industrial, labor, and agricultural groups.

The New Deal especially assisted the American middle class. It protected their savings, homes, and farms. It opened the way to middle-class comforts and status for previously stigmatized ethnic groups and many clerical and blue-collar workers. But the New Deal also knew many failures. It did not achieve recovery. It did not sufficiently redistribute income and wealth, though it proposed more effectual policies than Congress would accept. It did not bring American blacks or women an equitable share in the country's social and economic life. It could not overcome the conservative social and regressive economic policies of most American states. It could not permanently insulate its new regulatory agencies from the tendency of regulators to develop excessive sympathy for those they were supposed to control.

Those failures, clearer in retrospect than at the time, suggested that the particular middle way of the Roosevelt years would later need modifications. But to the question of the viability of any middle way, doctrinaires returned a categorical *no* through the decade. Ogden Mills stated the issue with precision for the conservatives: "We can have a free country or a socialistic one. We cannot have both. Our economic system cannot be half free and half socialistic. . . .

There is no middle ground . . . between tyranny and freedom."

In such sentiments, at least, the critics of capitalism agreed enthusiastically with the conservatives. "Either the nation must put up with the confusions and miseries of an essentially unregulated capitalism," said a radical weekly in 1935, "or it must prepare to supersede capitalism with socialism. There is no longer a feasible middle course." The proponents of individualism and the proponents of collectivism agreed on this if on nothing else: no regulated capitalism was possible, no mixed economy, no middle way between laissez faire and socialism.

But the New Dealers cheerfully rejected the conclusion. They believed that there was more on heaven and earth than could be found in any ideology. Roosevelt himself was blithe and humane in his undeviating rejection of any all-encompassing doctrine. He might have undertaken social experiments either more or less bold than those he chose. But his aim was consistent—to steer "slightly to the left of center," avoiding alike "the revolution of radicalism and the revolution of conservatism." The New Deal faith in intelligence, compassion, and experiment postulated that a managed capitalist order could combine personal freedom and economic growth. For the generation that lived through it, the decade of the New Deal, with all its confusion and recrimination, rekindled confidence in free society, not in America alone, but throughout the Western world.

Suggestions for reading

GENERAL
The most comprehensive account of domestic developments, 1933–36, is in A. M. Schlesinger, Jr., *The Coming of the New Deal** (1959) and *The Politics of Upheaval** (1960). W. E. Leuchtenburg, *Franklin D. Roosevelt and the New Deal, 1932–40** (1963), provides the best short account. There are valuable insights in J. M. Burns, *Roosevelt: The Lion and the Fox** (1956). Paul Conkin, *The New Deal** (1967), criticizes Roosevelt and his policies from the point of view of the disenchanted revisionists of the 1960s and 1970s. Caroline Bird, *The Invisible Scar** (1965), provides a lively account of the social impact of continuing depression. For a trenchant analysis of that point of view and of various others, see O. L. Graham, Jr., ed., *The New Deal: The Critical Issues** (1971).

MEMOIRS AND BIOGRAPHIES
Memoirs of the New Dealers and biographies based on their papers throw important light on Roosevelt and his problems. R. E. Sherwood, *Roosevelt and Hopkins: An Intimate History** (1948, rev. ed., 1950), provides a view of an important friendship and a favorable account of relief policies. Frances Perkins, *The Roosevelt I Knew** (1946), is significant for its compassion but must be compared to George Martin, *Madam Secretary: Frances Perkins* (1976); see R. G. Tugwell, *The Democratic Roosevelt** (1957), for its retrospective reflections; *The Secret Diary of Harold L. Ickes,* 3 vols. (1953–54), for its gossip and atmosphere. On politics, two illuminating memoirs are J. A. Farley, *Behind the Ballots* (1938), and Edward Flynn, *You're the Boss** (1947). J. M. Blum, *Roosevelt and Morgenthau** (1970), recounts in detail the activities of the Secretary of the Treasury, one of the President's influential advisers. H. S. Johnson, *The Blue Eagle* (1935), presents a contemporary view of the National Recovery Administration. There is a valuable contemporary critique of the early New Deal in Raymond Moley, *After Seven Years** (1939); this may be supplemented by his retrospective *The First New Deal* (1966). In *Beckoning Frontiers* (1935), M. S. Eccles provides an important account of the evolution of economic policy. Samuel Rosenman writes as a close counselor to the President in his *Working with Roosevelt* (1952). R. G. Tugwell's work, cited above, is an important memoir-history, as is his *The Brain Trust** (1968). J. J. Hutchmacher, *Senator Robert Wagner and the Rise of American Liberalism* (1968), is a telling study of a leading liberal senator. There is indispensable personal material in Eleanor Roosevelt, *This I Remember** (1949), and in J. P. Lash, *Eleanor and Franklin** (1971). Frank Freidel has completed four volumes of his long biography of Roosevelt. Though there is no useful edition of Roosevelt's private papers, one vital source for study of the man and his times is Samuel Rosenman, ed., *The Public Papers and Addresses of Franklin D. Roosevelt,* 13 vols. (1938–50).

NEW DEAL POLITICAL THOUGHT
Students wishing to study New Deal political thought in the important works of the time should consult, as the text suggests, at least the following influential sources: A. A. Berle, Jr. and G. C. Means, *The*

*Available in a paperback edition.

*Modern Corporation and Private Property** (1932, rev. ed., 1969), significant on economic concentration; M. S. Eccles, *Economic Balance and a Balanced Budget* (1940), significant on countercyclical spending; R. G. Tugwell, *The Battle for Democracy* (1935), and H. L. Ickes, *The New Democracy* (1934), both important on social goals and public planning, as is H. A. Wallace, *New Frontiers* (1934); and D. E. Lilienthal, *TVA** (rev. ed., 1953), on regional development. Two incisive books by Thurman Arnold—*The Symbols of Government** (1935) and *The Folklore of Capitalism** (1937)—well express the iconoclastic and deflationary side of the New Deal. For a revisionistic view, see Howard Zinn, ed., *New Deal Thought** (1966).

SPECIAL STUDIES

Outstanding studies of economic problems in the 1930s include the analytical T. Wilson, *Fluctuations in Income and Employment* (1948); K. D. Roose, *Economics of Recession and Revival: An Interpretation of 1937–38* (1954); and R. E. Paul, *Taxation in the United States* (1954). Some of the most useful of more recent works are Irving Bernstein, *Turbulent Years** (1970), which describes the labor movement; Robert Lekachman, *The Age of Keynes** (1966), which discusses the rate and range of acceptance of the ideas of the new economics, as does Herbert Stein, *The Fiscal Revolution in America** (1969); and E. W. Hawley, *The New Deal and the Problem of Monopoly** (1966), which analyzes pressure-group influences on federal policies. Significant, too, are Richard Kirkendall, *Social Scientists and Farm Politics in the Age of Roosevelt* (1966); J. T. Patterson, *The New Deal and the States: Federalism in Transition* (1969); Roy Lubove, *The Struggle for Social Security, 1900–1935* (1968); Thomas McCraw, *TVA and the Power Fight, 1933–1939* (1970); and Michael Parrish, *Securities Regulation and the New Deal* (1970). O. L. Graham's work, cited above, includes an excellent bibliography of still other good studies.

Among the stimulating works about social and intellectual currents are R. A. Lawson, *The Failure of Independent Liberalism, 1930–1941** (1971); Richard Pells, *Radical Visions and American Dreams: Culture and Social Thought in the Depression Years** (1973); Charles Alexander, *Nationalism in American Thought, 1930–1945** (1969); Edward Purcell, Jr., *The Crisis of Democratic Theory** (1972); and Donald Meyer, *The Protestant Search for Social Realism, 1919–1941** (1960). For a thoughtful account of the appeal of communism and other radical ideas, see Daniel Aaron, *Writers on the Left** (1961); Richard Crossman, ed., *The God That Failed* (1949); F. A. Warren, *Liberals and Communism: the "Red" Decade Revisited** (1966); Irving Howe and Lewis Coser, *The American Communist Party** (1957); and Bernard Johnpoll, *Pacifist's Progress** (1970), on Norman Thomas. R. G. Swing, *Forerunners of American Fascism* (1935), offers a contemporary account of the lunatic right, which is modified in A. P. Sindler, *Huey Long's Louisiana** (1956), and D. H. Bennett, *Demagogues in the Depression* (1969), and challenged by T. H. Williams, *Huey Long** (1969). On the problems of blacks during the 1930s, see Bernard Sternsher, ed., *The Negro in Depression and War: Prelude to Revolution** (1969); Raymond Wolters, *Negroes and the Great Depression* (1970); and D. T. Carter, *Scottsboro: A Tragedy of the Modern South* (1969). On women, see William Chafe, cited after Chapter 26.

Samuel Lubell, *The Future of American Politics** (1952), identifies important political changes in the period; also revealing about politics are Theodore Loewi, *The End of Liberalism** (1969); Grant McConnell, *Private Power and American Democracy** (1969); and Bruce Stave, *The New Deal and the Last Hurrah* (1970). George Wolfskill, *The Revolt of the Conservatives* (1962), displays the reaction on the right, as does his volume with J. Hudson, *All But the People* (1969). The career of the ablest Republican senator of the era receives admirable treatment in J. T. Patterson, *Mr. Republican, A Biography of Robert A. Taft* (1972). On the Supreme Court fight, four especially rewarding studies are R. H. Jackson, *The Struggle for Judiciary Supremacy** (1941); A. T. Mason, *Harlan Fiske Stone* (1956); Joseph Alsop and Turner Catledge, *168 Days* (1938); and M. J. Pusey, *Charles Evans Hughes*, 2 vols. (1951). The same subject is treated by one of the masters of constitutional history, E. S. Corwin, in his *Twilight of the Supreme Court* (1934), *Court over Constitution* (1938), and *Constitutional Revolution, Ltd.* (rev. ed., 1946). New and important studies on the Court are soon to be published by W. E. Leuchtenburg and P. A. Freund.

*Available in a paperback edition.

CHAPTER **28**

The decay of the peace

When Franklin D. Roosevelt became President, the American people were absorbed in gloomy domestic problems. The crusading internationalism of 1917 was a distant, and for most a distasteful, memory. The rejection of the League of Nations had been followed by growing disenchantment about the motives and results of the First World War; and the renewed American determination to go it alone in world affairs was only slightly tempered during the twenties by such symbolic gestures as the Kellogg-Briand pact and the Stimson Doctrine. If the Republican Administrations sought to enlarge world markets for American products, they simultaneously undercut the policy of commercial expansion by raising tariffs and thereby denying foreign nations the opportunity to earn dollars for the purchase of American goods. After 1929 depression intensified tariff warfare and economic nationalism in both the United States and Europe. By 1933 isolationism, both political and economic, was the dominant American mood.

There were more and more signs, however, that the uneasy peace established after the First World War was in jeopardy. Japanese expansionism in East Asia was accompanied by German militancy in Europe. On January 30, 1933, Adolf Hitler became the new chancellor of Germany. In March, nineteen days after Roosevelt's inauguration, the Reichstag gave the Nazi leader dictatorial powers to carry forward his program of rearmament, anti-Semitism, and messianic nationalism. The German *Führer*'s fanatical resolve to overthrow the system established at Versailles in 1919 offered an ominous challenge to international order.

Roosevelt and world affairs

Preparation for statesmanship. Few American politicians could rival Roosevelt in the breadth of his world experience. Between 1885 and 1931 he had made thirteen trips to Europe, and, though he had never visited the Far East, family tradition—his maternal grandfather had been active in the China trade—gave him a lively interest in Asia and especially in China. He had come of age, moreover, when the United States, under Theodore Roosevelt, was first beginning to exercise the responsibilities of world power. As a young man, he was also greatly influenced by the strategic ideas of Admiral Alfred T. Mahan.

659

Storm Troopers, Nuremberg, 1938

His service under Woodrow Wilson as Assistant Secretary of the Navy provided him varied experience in international affairs. Almost alone among the members of the Administration, he instantly perceived the catastrophic implications of the events of the summer of 1914. The young Roosevelt then made no secret of his desire to build up American naval power or of his passionate belief in the Allied cause. When America entered the war, he dealt effectively both with problems of economic mobilization at home and with problems of coalition strategy and diplomacy abroad.

But the war also placed his principles of strategy in a new setting. To Mahan's realism, Roosevelt now added Wilson's idealism: the combination defined his own future approach to foreign affairs. He became an ardent supporter of Wilson in his fight for the League, and he made the League a key issue in his campaign for the Vice Presidency in 1920. He retained his sharp concern with the actualities of national power but now saw power in the context of international order.

During the twenties Roosevelt opposed the drift toward isolationism, condemned the Republican tariff policy, derided the pretensions of the Kellogg pact, and pleaded the case for international collaboration. "If the World War showed anything more than another," he said, "it showed the American people the futility of imagining that they could live in smug content their own lives in their own way while the rest of the world burned in the conflagration of war." But, as depression accentuated the isolationist mood, he announced in 1932 that in existing circumstances he no longer favored American participation in the League.

The Roosevelt style in foreign policy. Nevertheless Roosevelt named as Secretary of State Cordell Hull, an unregenerate Wilsonian and low-tariff man. "In pure theory," he once wrote Hull, "you and I think alike but every once in a while we have to modify principle to meet a hard and disagreeable fact!"

Roosevelt was far more ready than Hull to modify principle. Toward the State Department itself, the President's attitude was one of disdain. He instinctively understood the problems of military as of political leaders, but he was often impatient with the professional diplomat. Foreign-service officers, he tended to believe, represented a narrow social group and knew little of American life.

This attitude molded his own style in foreign affairs. His conduct of foreign policy was marked by imagination and also a certain dilettantism. He remained the brilliant amateur, better in the main than the professionals, bolder, more creative, more compelling, but often deficient in steadiness and follow-

Cordell Hull:
Wilsonian Secretary of State

through. He tended toward personal diplomacy and used his own agents and emissaries to bypass the professionals. His basic preference, not always realizable in practice in these early years, was for direct negotiation among heads of state.

Uniting the Western Hemisphere

The good neighbor. "In the field of world policy," Roosevelt said in one of the scant references to foreign affairs in his inaugural address, "I would dedicate this Nation to the policy of the good neighbor—the neighbor who resolutely respects himself and, because he does so, respects the rights of others—the neighbor who respects his obligations and respects the sanctity of his agreements in and with a world of neighbors." Though this thought was evidently intended to be general in its import, its immediate sphere of application was Latin America. Soon the Good Neighbor policy came to refer specifically to United States policy in the Western hemisphere.

During the twenties Roosevelt and others of his generation, among them his old friend Sumner Welles, a former diplomat, had become critical of the policy of intervention. Yet, Roosevelt's Latin American policy got off to an ambiguous start. Welles went to Cuba as ambassador to get rid of the brutal Machado dictatorship. The dislodgment of Machado, however, eventually brought into power a revolutionary government that the United States declined to recognize. In response to the American attitude, a conservative regime received recognition. Though Roosevelt at the same time speeded up plans for withdrawing the marines from Haiti, Latin Americans in the fall of 1933 were suspicious of Washington.

From Montevideo to Buenos Aires. The Seventh International Conference of American States met at Montevideo in December 1933 in an atmosphere of hostility toward the United States. The American delegation soon induced a change in that attitude. The United States, reversing its policy of five years before in Havana, now accepted (with minor qualifications) a proposal declaring that "no state has the right to intervene in the internal or external affairs of another." The Montevideo Conference, by establishing inter-American relations on the principle of nonintervention, brought into being a new epoch in hemispheric relations.

The United States proceeded to show that it meant to live up to its Montevideo pledge. In May 1934 it abrogated the unpopular Platt Amendment, thereby abandoning its treaty right to intervene in the affairs of Cuba. In 1934 in El Salvador, it abandoned the policy of nonrecognition of revolutionary governments in Central America. The establishment of the Export-Import Bank the same year provided a means of extending credit to Latin American states. The Panama Treaties of 1936 renounced the right to intervene in Panama and recognized Panama's responsibility in the operation and protection of the canal. A treaty of 1940 terminated United States financial controls in the Dominican Republic.

Relations with Mexico provided a test of the new policy. The hostility of the radical Mexican government toward the Roman Catholic Church in the early thirties had produced demands in the United States that Washington intervene in Mexico. The expropriation of foreign-owned petroleum companies renewed this pressure in 1938. Washington declined to intervene, however, confining its activities to urging the Mexican government to provide American owners their due compensation. A State Department memorandum of 1939 summed up the new attitude: "Our national interests as a whole far outweigh those of the petroleum companies."

Those national interests, in the State Department's interpretation, included increased trade with and investment in Latin America. Both the reciprocal trade treaties with Latin American states and the activities of the Export-Import Bank furthered those objectives. For Roosevelt, however, political considerations outweighed economic.

His policies by 1940 had inspired confidence throughout the hemisphere in the reality of the Good Neighbor policy. By December 1936, when Roosevelt himself attended the Inter-American Conference at Buenos Aires, the warmth of his reception attested to a transformation in Latin American attitudes toward the colossus of the north.

Early relations with Europe

The London Economic Conference. American relations with European nations had been bedeviled since 1919 by the question of war debts. Beset by depression, most European nations, except for Finland, began to suspend payment in 1933. War debts thereafter became a dead issue—except to the United States Congress, which retaliated in 1934 by passing the Johnson Act prohibiting loans to defaulting governments.

From the European viewpoint, war debts were only a part of the larger problem of world economic relations. Governments everywhere were building walls of protection in the hope of defending their national economies against the worldwide decline. Economic nationalism took more than one form. The Hoover version was nationalist in trade, internationalist in finance: Hoover thus advocated raising the protective tariff to new levels and at the same time argued that recovery depended on the restoration of a world gold standard. In this belief, he agreed to United States participation in an international economic conference favored by the gold-bloc nations and scheduled for London in the spring of 1933.

Roosevelt and the early New Dealers, on the other hand, believed that recovery was to be achieved primarily through domestic planning. "I shall spare no effort to restore world trade by international economic readjustments," the new President said in his inaugural address, "but the emergency at home cannot wait on that accomplishment." The New Dealers consequently mistrusted the international gold standard as a threat to national programs for recovery. Yet, unlike Hoover, they rejected the steeply protective tariff, favoring instead the system of reciprocal trade agreements, which Hoover assailed in 1932 as "a violation of American principles." The Roosevelt version of economic nationalism was thus internationalist in trade, nationalist in finance.

When the London Economic Conference opened in June 1933, it became evident that the gold bloc, led

661

by France and Italy, was determined to force through an agreement stabilizing foreign exchanges. By now the American government was fully committed to its program of raising commodity prices through reducing the value of the dollar in terms of gold—a policy obviously incompatible with immediate stabilization of the dollar in terms of an international gold standard. Roosevelt declined to subordinate his domestic policy to international stabilization. This view emerged only gradually in the course of the conference. Meanwhile the antics of an odd American delegation had dissipated American influence in London. As the gold bloc continued to press for stabilization, Roosevelt, in what he conceived as an effort to recall the conference to more fruitful topics, sent a testy message scolding the conference for succumbing to the "old fetishes of the so-called international bankers." Though some Englishmen, among them J. M. Keynes, defended Roosevelt, the "bombshell" message precipitated the unsuccessful end of the conference.

During the next several years, the financial policies of the great powers reflected the mutual suspicions that the London Conference had intensified. But in 1936, with the American economy much improved and the dollar again fixed, in practice, in terms of gold, Roosevelt permitted the negotiation of a stabilization agreement with Great Britain and France. The President was moved to that decision also by his hope for closer political relationships with those democratic countries. The new agreement, to which other European democracies soon adhered, called for consultation and cooperation among the treasuries of the three nations to manage the value of their currencies in their common interest.

Liberalizing American trade. Roosevelt made it clear that his opposition to the international gold standard did not mean that he believed in economic self-containment. In March 1934 he asked Congress for authority to enter into commercial agreements with foreign nations and to revise tariff rates in accordance with such agreements up to 50 percent either way. This proposal for the executive negotiation of reciprocal trade agreements raised a storm of opposition, partly because some congressmen—and the protectionist lobbies—objected to the weakening of the congressional role in tariff-making, partly because businessmen feared the new system would result in lower rates. Only two Republicans supported the bill in the House, only three in the Senate. But with Hull's devoted backing, the bill became law in June 1934.

By the end of 1935, reciprocal trade agreements were in effect with fourteen countries; by 1945, with twenty-nine countries. While the program did little in the thirties to relieve the balance-of-payments problem between the United States and foreign countries (indeed debts owed to the United States grew steadily during the thirties), it did display Hull's hope of bringing about a large measure of economic internationalism with attending gains for American trade.

Disarmament. In an effort to compose matters after the breakup of the London Economic Conference, Roosevelt wrote to Ramsay MacDonald, the British prime minister, "I am concerned by events in Germany, for I feel that an insane rush to further armaments in Continental Europe is infinitely more dangerous than any number of squabbles over gold or stabilization or tariffs." From an early point—earlier, indeed, than any European statesman of comparable rank—Roosevelt was convinced that Hitler meant war. Yet, while he saw the approaching horror with clarity, he also saw it with aloofness. This was partly the result of geography, which conferred on the United States the luxury of detachment; partly the result of politics, for Roosevelt had little choice but to defer to the isolationist preferences of the vast majority of the people; partly the result of the depression, which gave the American domestic scene first claim on his attention.

The combination of concern and aloofness produced a basic contradiction in the heart of his foreign policy. Roosevelt addressed himself to two problems: first, how to stop the world drift toward war; and, second, if that drift proved irresistible, how to make sure that the United States would not be involved. Plainly the goals of international peace and national isolation—of world disarmament and American neutrality—were in latent conflict. World disarmament implied American cooperation in a world system. Rigid neutrality implied a systematic reduction of America's international commitments. In 1933 and 1934 the tension between these two ideas complicated the conduct of America's foreign policy.

Disarmament had been a major theme of foreign affairs in the twenties, though efforts to work out formulas for land armaments had proved unsuccessful. A new disarmament conference, beginning in Geneva in 1932, had bogged down because of Germany's demand for equality in armed strength, which was impossible to reconcile with the insistence of other nations, especially France, on having reliable protection against a possible recurrence of German aggression.

The replacement of the Weimer Republic by the Nazi regime gave the German demand for equality an ominous cast. In May 1933 Roosevelt authorized the American representative at Geneva to say that, if a substantial reduction of armaments was effected by international agreement, the United States was prepared to consult with the other states in case of a threat to peace. If the other states identified an aggres-

The decay of the peace

Hitler meant war

The Administration tried in vain to defeat the amendment. Failing, it dropped the resolution itself, thereby canceling the effect of the American initiative at Geneva. What the President had proposed the Congress had now disowned. The episode confirmed the skepticism in European chancelleries over the seriousness of American diplomacy.

Even congressional approval of the arms embargo would probably not have saved the Geneva conference. Hitler, hell-bent on rearmament, was committed to a revolt against the entire Versailles system. When Germany walked out of the League in October 1933, land disarmament was dead. And the withdrawal of Japan from the League in 1933 and the Japanese decision in 1934 to terminate the Washington Naval Treaty signaled the end of naval disarmament. By 1934 the hope of averting war through disarmament had gone.

The American government had been prepared to cooperate in the supervision of a disarmed world. It was not prepared to cooperate in keeping the peace at the risk of war in a world intent on rearmament. Since disarmament had failed, the alternative, in the American view, was neutrality.

Relations with Great Britain and the Soviet Union. The collapse of disarmament was accompanied by a deterioration in American relations with the leading anti-Hitler powers. Roosevelt's bombshell message had exasperated London, and the policies of the British government exasperated Washington. An important faction in the British Cabinet, led by Neville Chamberlain, the chancellor of the exchequer, so deeply distrusted the United States that in 1934 it seriously considered whether Britain should base its strategy on cooperation with Japan instead of with the United States. At this point Roosevelt instructed his roving emissary, Norman Davis, to impress British Foreign Secretary Sir John Simon "and a few other Tories" with the fact that

> If Great Britain is even suspected of preferring to play with Japan to playing with us, I shall be compelled, in the interest of American security, to approach public sentiment in Canada, Australia, New Zealand and South Africa in a definite effort to make these Dominions clearly understand that their future security is linked with us in the United States.

The Japanese themselves soon took care of the problem by presenting the British with rearmament demands so extreme that even the pro-Tokyo Cabinet members had to abandon their policy.

Roosevelt's efforts to establish friendly relations with the Soviet Union were hardly more successful. Support for the recognition of the communist regime

sor and took measures against aggression, the United States, if it concurred in their judgment, would "refrain from any action tending to defeat such collective effort which these states may thus make to restore peace." In other words, the United States would forgo its traditional insistence on neutral rights, including the freedom of the seas, in the interest of supporting measures of collective security. But, when the Administration asked Congress to pass a resolution authorizing the executive at his discretion to embargo arms shipments to aggressor nations, the Senate Foreign Relations Committee amended the resolution to compel the President to embargo arms shipments to *all* nations involved in a war. This amendment destroyed the original purpose of the resolution, which was to discriminate against aggressors. Its effect would now be to strengthen those who had arms already and to abandon those who had none.

663

had been growing for some time before 1933. Businessmen saw in Russia a market for American surplus production. The renewal of Japanese aggression argued for a normalization of Soviet-American relations as a means of restraining the Japanese. "The world," Cordell Hull told Roosevelt, "is moving into a dangerous period both in Europe and in Asia. Russia could be a great help in stabilizing this situation."

In October 1933 Maxim Litvinov, the Soviet commissar for foreign affairs, came to Washington to work out a set of agreements. In one document Litvinov gave a remarkably detailed pledge to refrain from any intervention in American internal affairs—a pledge that covered not only the Soviet government itself but any organizations "under its direct or indirect control." Another memorandum provided what seemed to be a formula for the settlement of Russian debts to the United States. The discussions concluded in the establishment of formal relations between the two governments.

Despite this beginning, relations soon returned to a state of mistrust. The attempt to make the Soviet government live up to its promises on propaganda and debts led to interminable negotiation, recrimination, and frustration. American representatives in Moscow encountered harassment and hostility. Finally, when American communists came to Moscow in July 1935 for the seventh congress of the Comintern, their presence seemed, in the view of the American ambassador, to constitute "a flagrant violation of Litvinov's pledge" and a justification for the severance of diplomatic ties. Though the government did not go that far, relations with Soviet Russia reached a new low less than two years after recognition.

Isolationism at flood tide

The rout of the internationalists. The breakdown of attempts to strengthen relations with Britain and the Soviet Union coincided with a crystallization of isolationist sentiment in the United States. By the early 1930s, few Americans were prepared to make an all-out defense of Wilson's decision of 1917. "Revisionist" historians had launched a reconsideration of such problems as German "war guilt" and American entry into the war. Their scholarship seemed to reveal the war, not as a struggle of democracy against autocracy, but as a sordid scramble among imperialist powers. If this was so, then the United States had been drawn into the war under false pretenses.

The next question was: Who had drawn the United States in and why? The new disillusion was clinched in 1934 and 1935 by the work of a Senate committee set up under the chairmanship of Gerald P. Nye of North Dakota to investigate the munitions industry. The Nye Committee unearthed a wealth of documentation purporting to show that the United States had been shoved into war when international bankers, especially the House of Morgan, saw no other way to guarantee repayment of the vast credits they had granted to the western Allies. To demonstrate that no President could be trusted with discretionary power in matters of war and peace, Nye charged Wilson with duplicity in pretending to be ignorant of the secret treaties.

The Nye Committee consolidated the isolationist argument. The isolationists could conceive of no world war that would present a moral issue between the antagonists or a strategic threat to American security. They were also convinced that American freedom could not survive participation in another holocaust. America's best contribution to peace and democracy, in their judgment, lay in absolute rejection of the power struggles of Europe and Asia.

Roosevelt was quickly to learn the new power of organized isolationism. In January 1935, a short time after the stunning Democratic victory in the 1934 elections, he sent the Senate a recommendation that the United States join the World Court. "At this period in international relationships," he said, "when every act is of moment to the future of world peace, the United States has an opportunity once more to throw its weight into the scale in favor of peace." Joining the World Court could hardly have been a more innocuous act, but the isolationist bloc staged an extraordinary appeal to public opinion, and an outpouring of protest defeated the resolution. Roosevelt wrote to Elihu Root, who had proposed a world court at The Hague a generation before, "Today, quite frankly, the wind everywhere blows against us."

The design of neutrality. The next problem, as Nye, Arthur Vandenberg, and their Nye Committee colleagues saw it, was to make sure the forces that had brought about American participation in the First World War would never have their way again.

If the United States had been drawn into that war to ensure the repayment of debts owed to American bankers and munitions-makers, then to keep out of war it would be necessary to forbid loans and the export of arms to belligerents. If the United States had been drawn into that war because American ships carried supplies to belligerent nations or because Americans citizens insisted on traveling on belligerent ships, then to keep out of war such actions should be prohibited. If the United States had been drawn into war by the unneutral decisions of a President with too much discretion in the conduct of foreign policy, then the President should be denied the opportunity

The decay of the peace

to tamper with neutrality. The Nye group demanded a new neutrality policy—one that might even involve the surrender of certain classical neutral rights, such as the freedom of the seas.

The Administration, yielding to isolationist pressure, agreed that the President should have authority to prohibit American ships from carrying arms and munitions, to withdraw the protection of the government from Americans traveling on belligerent vessels, and to impose an embargo on arms and loans. But the Administration wanted the President to be able to use these powers at his discretion. The senators, with the image of the perfidious Wilson in their mind, wanted to make it mandatory that he use them against *all* belligerents—which would, of course, nullify American influence in the case of conflict. In the end the Senate passed a mandatory bill, the House a discretionary bill. The resulting compromise of August 31, 1935, contained a mandatory arms embargo but made it good only until March 1, 1936. In other respects—such as American travel on belligerent vessels—the bill gave the President discretion. The Administration decided to accept the measure rather than risk further exacerbation of isolationist sentiment through a veto. On signing the act, Roosevelt warned that "the inflexible provisions . . . might have exactly the opposite effect from that which was intended."

Neutrality on test

Italy invades Ethiopia. Early in October 1935 Italian troops invaded Ethiopia from Eritrea and Italian Somaliland. In his message to Congress in January 1936, Roosevelt indicted nations that had the "fantastic conception that they, and they alone, are chosen to fulfill a mission and that all the others among the billion and a half of human beings in the world must and shall learn from them and be subject to them." At the same time, he issued a proclamation of neutrality and invoked the mandatory arms embargo.

The supposition in Washington was that the embargo would hurt Italy more than Ethiopa, since Ethiopa lacked dollars to buy arms in the United States and ships to carry them away. Actually the arms embargo did Italy little initial harm, since it had its own munitions industry. Where the restriction of American exports really could hurt the Italian warmaking capacity was in raw materials, especially in oil. But the Neutrality Act covered only implements of war. Roosevelt accordingly followed up the arms embargo with a call for a voluntary restriction of other exports. This action initiated the experiment in what became known as the "moral embargo."

The moral embargo aroused the protests of the Italian government as well as of American oil companies, and moral suasion did not turn out to be effective. Oil shipments to Italy were 600 percent larger in August and September 1935 than they had been for the same two months in 1934. Nevertheless, the American policy preceded by many weeks any comparable action by the League, and it strengthened the hands of those in Geneva contending for economic sanctions against Italy. The League decision was finally taken in a limited way (not including oil, for example) on November 18, 1935.

When Congress convened in 1936, one of its first tasks was to replace the neutrality resolution of 1935. The Administration tried to increase the presidential role in the management of neutrality; but the legislative situation grew hopelessly confused, and in the end it seemed simpler to extend the existing act until May 1, 1937, with an amendment banning credits to belligerents. One apparently minor change did increase executive discretion: it was now up to the President to decide that a state of war existed before the act could be invoked.

The outbreak of civil war in Spain on July 17, 1936, deepened Roosevelt's sense of a general European disintegration. In a speech four weeks later, he set forth with earnestness his hatred of war, his commitment to neutrality, and his determination to resist the forces that might draw the United States into another world conflict. His private correspondence reflected a belief that somehow a conference among heads of state might avert the drift to Armageddon; but he found no formula that offered any promise of success and thus took no action.

The attempt of Spanish fascists under General Francisco Franco to overthrow the democratic government of Spain created new problems. The mandatory embargo applied to wars between nations, not to civil wars. Early in January 1937, Congress, with Roosevelt's full support and with but one negative vote in both houses, enacted a resolution aligning the United States with Britain and France in a program of nonintervention and in banning shipments of implements of war to either side in Spain. Neutral in intention, the resolution in fact helped Franco, for he received far more military assistance from Italy and Germany than his opponents received from the Soviet Union.

Then Congress faced once again the question of renewing or rewriting the existing neutrality legislation. The main innovation in the 1937 debate was the so-called cash-and-carry proposal, which provided that, once the President had proclaimed the existence of a state of war, no nonmilitary goods could be shipped to a belligerent until the purchaser acquired full title and took them away himself. The Administration supported this idea in order to head off a drive

The emphasis on trade expansion, and upon the Open Door Policy, served to define the nature and the causes of danger and conflict in international affairs.... For the New Deal administration as for its predecessors, therefore, American recovery and prosperity were made dependent upon the acceptance of American policies by the rest of the world. By externalizing good, so also was evil externalized: domestic problems and difficulties became issues of foreign policy. In the immediate context of the mid-1930's and as Roosevelt, Hull, Sayre, and others explicitly noted as early as 1935, that meant that Germany, Italy, and Japan were defined as dangers to the well-being of the United States. This happened before those countries launched military attacks into or against areas that the United States considered important to its economic system. It occurred instead as those nations began to compete vigorously with American entrepreneurs in Latin America and Asia....

Men who began by defining the United States and the world in economic terms, and explaining its operation by the principles of capitalism and a frontier thesis of historical development, came finally to define the United States in military terms as an embattled outpost in a hostile world. When a majority of the leaders of America's corporate society reached that conclusion, the nation went to war—at first covertly, then overtly.

From William Appleman Williams, The Tragedy of American Diplomacy, 1959.

for an automatic embargo on all goods. Ironically, the amendment would clearly have the unneutral effect of favoring the maritime powers, notably Britain and Japan, and of closing American markets to nations like Germany and China. Nevertheless, Congress adopted the provision by sweeping majorities.

Aggression in the Far East

The problem of China. For many Americans the problems of Europe had come to seem more remote, or at least less America's business, than the problems of the Far East. As far back as the announcement of the Open Door doctrine, the United States had conceived of itself as playing a direct role in the affairs of East Asia. By the First World War Washington had concluded that the great threat to the Open Door would come from Japan. Both the Washington Naval Conference and the Stimson Doctrine were designed to restrain Tokyo's imperial aspirations.

In addition, years of missionary endeavor had given many Americans warm sympathy with China in its struggle for nationhood. Roosevelt, who shared this sympathy, himself endorsed the Stimson Doctrine. Then the Tangku truce of May 1933 suspended hostilities between China and Japan. But in April 1934, Eiji Amau, spokesman for the Japanese foreign office,

demanded for Japan a free hand in China and warned the West against coming to China's assistance. Soon Japan denounced the Five-Power Treaty.

Those developments confronted the United States with perplexing problems. Some historians have argued that the American motive was to secure markets and investment outlets in China for American capitalism. But American trade with China was negligible, and American investment there far below British. Similarly, American economic interests in the Philippines yielded to domestic economic interests when Congress in 1934 again enacted legislation providing for the independence of the islands after a period of transition. Japan was the most profitable American market in Asia. Nor was the tendency of the Roosevelt Administration to carry out the desires of the business community ever marked. What concerned Roosevelt was the Japanese challenge to international order—the fear that, if aggression ran on with impunity, the peace system would collapse and war might engulf the United States. The preservation of that system therefore seemed a vital American interest. In addition, an expanding Japan could deny the United States strategic materials, like natural rubber, that were essential to national security.

But what could America do? To the State Department, the cornerstone in a containment policy had to be the buildup of the United States navy. So long as America remained weak in Asian waters, Cordell Hull reasoned, any attempt to oppose the Japanese or to help the Chinese would be pinpricks that would serve only to provoke Tokyo unnecessarily. Naval superiority became not only the indispensable condition for a future American policy in East Asia but a powerful argument against present action. Thus the State Department generally opposed proposals to condemn Japan or aid China.

The renewal of Japanese aggression. In the meantime, the Chinese, under the leadership of Chiang Kai-shek, were making progress toward the unification of their nation. Perhaps wishing to halt the process before it went too far, the Japanese used troop clashes at the Marco Polo Bridge in July 1937 as an excuse for an invasion of China. By the end of the month, Japanese soldiers had seized Peking and Tientsin. The subsequent bombing of Shanghai by Japanese planes and the sack of Nanking in December horrified Americans. The Chinese retreated to the interior, established their capital at Chungking, and prepared to keep up their resistance.

Popular sympathy in the United States was wholly with the Chinese, but official reaction was cautious. Britain and America warded off Chinese pressure for invocation of the Nine-Power Treaty (see p. 583) and instead allowed the matter to go to the League for perfunctory condemnation. The President, however, displayed his solicitude for the Chinese

cause by refusing to proclaim the existence of a state of war between China and Japan. Without such a proclamation, the arms embargo and the cash-and-carry provision for nonmilitary commodities would not go into effect. Most observers felt that these provisions would hurt China, which had to import implements of war, more than they would Japan, which had ample stockpiles and a productive capacity of its own. Between July and November 1937 the value of licensed munitions shipments to China was $86 million; to Japan, $1.5 million. But an arms embargo could not cut off what Japan needed most—oil and scrap metal. And cash-and-carry would favor Japan as a solvent customer and naval power.

Awakening the nation

The quarantine speech. The disintegration of the peace system promised to loose war upon the world—a war contemporaries believed would be vastly more destructive than the war of 1914–18. Moreover, as the peace system collapsed, Nazi Germany might well seize control of the power and resources of Europe. Roosevelt regarded that prospect as a mortal threat to the security of the United States.

Japanese attack Tientsin

F. D. R.: the contagion of war

It seems to be unfortunately true that the epidemic of world lawlessness is spreading.

When an epidemic of physical disease starts to spread, the community approves and joins in a quarantine of the patients in order to protect the health of the community against the spread of the disease....

War is a contagion, whether it be declared or undeclared. It can engulf states and peoples remote from the original scene of hostilities. We are determined to keep out of war, yet we cannot insure ourselves against the disastrous effects of war and the dangers of involvement. We are adopting such measures as will minimize our risk of involvement, but we cannot have complete protection in a world of disorder in which confidence and security have broken down....

Most important of all, the will for peace on the part of peace-loving nations must express itself to the end that nations that may be tempted to violate their agreements and the rights of others will desist from such a course. There must be positive endeavors to preserve peace.

From Franklin D. Roosevelt, Speech at Chicago, October 1937.

Fearing the strategic consequences of Nazi expansion, detesting the cruel and tyrannical Nazi ideology, American leaders watched Hitler with increasing anxiety. Roosevelt even proposed a personal meeting with Neville Chamberlain, now British prime minister. But Chamberlain had no confidence in the United States—"it is always best and safest," he said in 1937, "to count on nothing from the Americans but words"—and he dedicated himself instead to the hope of making Hitler reasonable through a program of appeasement.

The renewal of warfare in China heightened the sense of international urgency. It also turned Roosevelt's attention to an idea that had been in the back of his mind for many years—the deterrence of aggression by holding over potential aggressors the threat (as he had put it in a "Plan to Preserve World Peace," written for a prize competition in 1923) of "the severance of all trade or financial relations, and the prohibition of all intercourse." Carrying his campaign to alert the nation to the heart of American isolationism, Roosevelt, in a speech at Chicago in October 1937, declared that "the present reign of terror and international lawlessness" had reached a stage "where the very foundations of civilization are seriously threatened." If aggression continued, he said, "let no one imagine America will escape." In a cryptic passage, he compared "the epidemic of world lawlessness" to an epidemic of physical disease and advocated a "quarantine" to protect the community against the contagion.

Aftermath of the quarantine speech. Roosevelt's main purpose was undoubtedly educational: he wanted to awaken the nation to the dangers of world war. A secondary purpose was very likely to explore the readiness of the American people to support some form of boycott of aggressors—moral, diplomatic, perhaps economic.

In the international sphere, the quarantine speech encouraged the British to call the signatories of the Nine-Power Treaty to a conference at Brussels to deal with the new Sino-Japanese conflict. But first the British sent word to Washington that they could do nothing about imposing sanctions against Japan unless they received "assurance of military support" in the event of Japanese retaliation. Roosevelt declined to give such guarantees; the British declined to act without them; and the Brussels Conference came to nothing.

In the meantime, Under Secretary of State Sumner Welles suggested that Roosevelt follow up his quarantine speech by convening a conference of neutral nations to set forth a peace program based on certain standards of international behavior. But Chamberlain, absorbed in the appeasement policy, rejected the American initiative on the ground that it ran the danger of "cutting across our efforts here." Winston Churchill later wrote that Chamberlain's decision was "the loss of the last frail chance to save the world from tyranny otherwise than by war."

Within the United States the reaction to the quarantine speech was so unfavorable that the President at a press conference seemed to retreat from what he had said. Further, most Americans, while sharing Roosevelt's detestation of dictators, detested war even more. When Japanese planes sank the American gunboat *Panay* in the Yangtze River in December 1937, the nation accepted Japanese apologies and indemnification with relief. Interest was ris-

ing in a constitutional amendment offered by Congressman Louis Ludlow of Indiana proposing that declarations of war be subject to popular plebiscite except in case of invasion. The country, moreover, was sinking into an economic recession, and the Administration needed congressional support for its new recovery program. The quarantine idea, vague enough at best, now perished between American reluctance and British indifference.

The road to war

The end of appeasement. In 1936 Germany moved into the Rhineland. In March 1938 it invaded and annexed Austria. In the following months Hitler began to use the plight of the German minority in the Sudetenland as a pretext for demands on the government of Czechoslovakia.

As the Czech crisis deepened in September, Chamberlain requested a personal conference with Hitler. There followed a series of meetings attended by Hitler, Chamberlain, Prime Minister Daladier of France, and eventually Mussolini. No representatives of Czechoslovakia were present. In the interval between the talks at Godesberg (September 23) and those at Munich (September 29), when it seemed as if Chamberlain was standing firm against Hitler, Roosevelt sent him an encouraging cable ("GOOD MAN") and brought pressure on Hitler to resume negotiations. But at the Munich meeting the democratic powers swallowed Hitler's terms. Czechoslovakia had no choice other than to acquiesce bitterly in the German annexation of the Sudetenland.

The first reaction in the United States was one of heartfelt relief: the appeasement policy seemed to have averted war. But soon people began to compute the price of appeasement: not just the establishment of German hegemony in Central Europe, but the incentive offered everywhere to intimidation and aggression.

Rearmament. During the 1920s the regular army had fallen well below the size authorized by the National Defense Act of 1920 and the navy below the levels permitted by the various international agreements. When Roosevelt came into office in 1933, the army ranked seventeenth in the world in active strength. From the start of his Administration, he had tried to rebuild American military and naval power. Thus the Public Works Administration constructed cruisers and aircraft-carriers; and in 1935 Congress authorized the army to increase its enlisted strength. In a message to Congress in January 1938 Roosevelt called for larger defense appropriations. In May Congress passed the Naval Expansion Act. In the months after Munich, he requested further increases in the defense budget and encouraged British and French purchasing missions to place defense orders in the United States.

In other respects Roosevelt began to tighten his ship in preparation for storms ahead. Following the failure of his "purge" in 1938 (see p. 650), he moved toward a tacit political truce, moderating his liberal objectives in the hope of gaining support for his foreign and defense policies. He also gathered support in the American hemisphere. In December 1938 in the Declaration of Lima the American republics announced their collective determination to resist fascist threats to peace.

Aggressions leading to the Second World War in Europe

The Neutrality Act remained the greatest obstacle to a positive policy. In 1939, as the Munich settlement seemed to be growing increasingly unstable, Roosevelt considered how he might modify the neutrality system in order to make American aid available to democratic nations. Hitler's invasion of Czechoslovakia on March 15, 1939, persuaded even Neville Chamberlain of the bankruptcy of appeasement. The State Department denounced Germany's "wanton lawlessness," and the Administration stepped up its campaign for the modification of the arms embargo. As Cordell Hull put it, the law "plays into the hands of those nations which have taken the lead in building up their fighting power. It works directly against the interests of the peace-loving nations." But isolationist senators, confident there would be no war in 1939, insisted that the matter be laid over to the next session of Congress.

In Europe events rushed toward climax. The invasion of Czechoslovakia was followed by the German occupation of Memel (March 23), the collapse of the Spanish Republic (March 28), and the Italian invasion of Albania (April 7). Through the summer Hitler carried on a war of nerves against Poland, using a German minority in Danzig as his tool. In the meantime his emissaries were secretly negotiating a nonaggression pact with the Soviet Union. On August 23 the German-Russian pact was signed in Moscow. The next day Britain and Poland signed a pact of mutual assistance. On September 1 Germany attacked Poland. Two days later Britain and France declared war on Germany. The Second World War was under way.

America and the war

First reactions. "When peace has been broken anywhere," Roosevelt said in a fireside chat on the evening of September 3, 1939, "the peace of all countries everywhere is in danger." He reaffirmed his determination "to use every effort" to keep war out of America. But, in marked contrast to Wilson's appeal in 1914 that his countrymen be "neutral in fact as well as in name," he added that he could not ask that "every American remain neutral in thought. . . . Even a neutral cannot be asked to close his mind or his

conscience." When he issued the proclamation of neutrality, he also indicated that he would call Congress into special session in order to repeal the arms embargo.

The isolationist leaders in the Senate, backed by former President Hoover and by such national figures as Colonel Charles A. Lindbergh, as well as by the American Communist party (following the Soviet-Nazi pact), declared that Roosevelt's course was leading straight to war. The opposition was strong enough to compel the Administration to accept restrictive compromises in exchange for the elimination of the embargo. The neutrality-revision bill then passed Congress, and the President signed it on November 4, 1939. The law placed the arms trade on a cash-and-carry basis. Where the previous legislation had favored Germany, with its well-established war industries, the new law enabled Britain and France to buy war materials in the United States so long as they were willing to pay cash and to carry their purchases away in their own ships.

Meanwhile the Nazi air force and Panzer divisions had subdued Poland in a three-week campaign. The French and British had been able to do little to create a diversion on the western front, and the war settled into an aspect of apparent quiescence that won it the derisive name of "the phony war." While opinion polls showed an overwhelming public preference in America for the western Allies against Germany (in October 1939, 62 percent of the population favored all possible aid to the Allies short of war), less than 30 percent favored American entry into the war even if Britain and France were in danger of defeat.

American emotions were perhaps more engaged when the Soviet Union, having advanced into eastern Poland in September, moved into the small Baltic republics of Latvia, Estonia, and Lithuania in October and invaded Finland in late November. The American people, remembering Finnish punctiliousness in the payment of war debts, grew indignant over the onslaught on the "gallant little Finns." Roosevelt sharply condemned "this dreadful rape." Isolationists, however, were alert not to let emotion over Finland drag the nation closer toward war. The Administration's cautious program of aid to Finland encountered strong opposition in Congress and had hardly gone into effect when the Winter War came to an end in March 1940.

Blitzkrieg. Hitler was already preparing the blow that he hoped would break the will of his western antagonists. On April 9, 1940, Germany attacked Denmark and Norway. An Anglo-French attempt to land forces in Norway miscarried, and by the end of the month Norwegian resistance was broken. Popular discontent in Britain over the Chamberlain government now forced Chamberlain to resign, and Winston Churchill, who had long criticized the appeasement policy and, after the outbreak of war, had served as first lord of the admiralty, became prime minister.

Chamberlain was in the course of resigning on May 10 when Nazi mechanized divisions invaded the Netherlands, Belgium, and Luxembourg. In a week they were thrusting deep into northern France. The British and French were unable to cope with the speed of the German attack. The main part of the British forces retreated to Dunkirk, where they were evacuated across the English Channel by a heroic flotilla of small boats conjured up from British ports. In a few days Italy, joining the war, invaded France from the south. "The hand that held the dagger," Roosevelt said grimly, "has struck it into the back of its neigh-

Evacuation at Dunkirk, 1940

bor." Soon Paris fell, Marshal Pétain became head of the French government, and on June 22 France and Germany signed an armistice at Compiègne. The next day, from London, General Charles de Gaulle, then an obscure and lonely figure, pledged continued French resistance.

The success of the Nazi blitzkrieg had a stunning effect on American opinion. Citing "the almost incredible events of the past two weeks," Roosevelt asked Congress for more than a billion dollars in additional defense appropriations. He called in particular for the annual production of fifty thousand warplanes. He also set up a National Defense Advisory Commission to plan defense production. And he began to consider how he could aid Britain, now standing alone against the Berlin-Rome Axis. Churchill's rise to power ended the glumness that had marked Anglo-American relations during the Chamberlain period. Roosevelt, who had for some months exchanged letters with the new prime minister, recognized him as a man of congenial temperament and stature. When Churchill offered his own people nothing but "blood, toil, tears and sweat," when he promised to "wage war by sea, land and air, with all our might and with all the strength that God can give us," he made a profound appeal to the American imagination.

But Britain needed more than sympathy. On May 15 Churchill sent Roosevelt a long list of specific requirements, including old destroyers, new aircraft, and materials of war. For the moment Washington could do little, partly because of America's own defense needs, partly (as in the case of the destroyers) because Roosevelt feared that congressional assent would not be forthcoming. After Dunkirk the American government did scrape together small arms and ammunition for the British to use in the desperate eventuality of a German invasion. But the problems of American policy were now further complicated by the approach of the 1940 presidential campaign.

The election of 1940

The third term. The struggle between isolationists and interventionists cut across party lines. Roosevelt found some of the most effective supporters of his foreign policy in the ranks of internationalist Republicans—a fact he acknowledged in June 1940, when he appointed Henry L. Stimson of New York as Secretary of War and Frank Knox of Illinois as Secretary of the Navy. However, the basic sentiment of the Republican party, especially in Congress, was isolationist. When the Republicans gathered in Philadelphia to select a presidential candidate, they read Stimson and Knox out of the party and prepared to choose between two candidates, Senator Robert A. Taft of Ohio and Thomas E. Dewey of New York, both identified with isolationism though neither held the rigid views of Senator Nye.

The Republican regulars did not allow for the enthusiasm with which a group of internationalists

The decay of the peace

rallied support for a dark-horse candidate, Wendell L. Willkie of Indiana. Willkie, an affable and articulate businessman, had magnetic qualities of personality that justified the title of "the rich man's Roosevelt." As president of Commonwealth & Southern, a leading public-utilities holding company, Willkie had won attention as an antagonist of the New Deal during the fight over the Tennessee Valley Authority. Actually he had been a Democrat himself most of his life; his personal views and values were on the liberal side; and, most critically of all in 1940, he sympathized with the Roosevelt policy of aid to Great Britain. To general astonishment, the Willkie forces staged a blitzkrieg of their own at Philadelphia, and the former Democrat emerged as the Republican candidate.

As for the Democrats, Roosevelt had failed, whether through design or negligence, to develop an heir apparent. For many months ardent New Dealers had demanded that he stand himself for a third term. Conservative Democrats, led by Vice President Garner and Postmaster General Farley, sought to organize opposition on the ground that a third term would violate a sacred American tradition. But the international urgencies made Roosevelt seem to most Democrats the indispensable candidate. The Democratic convention accordingly renominated him at Chicago in July, though it swallowed hard at his insistence on Henry A. Wallace, the Secretary of Agriculture, for Vice President.

Foreign policy and the campaign. While Americans concerned themselves with presidential politics, the German Luftwaffe launched a savage air war against England. The Royal Air Force put up a magnificent defense in what became known as the Battle

Wendell Willkie: he had magnetic qualities

of Britain. But if Britain hoped to repulse an anticipated German invasion—as well as maintain its own lines of supply—it needed immediate reinforcement of its battered destroyer fleet. Churchill, renewing his request for American destroyers, cabled Roosevelt on July 31, "I must tell you that in the long history of the world this is a thing to do *now*."

Though the United States had over-age destroyers to spare, the Naval Appropriations Act required prior

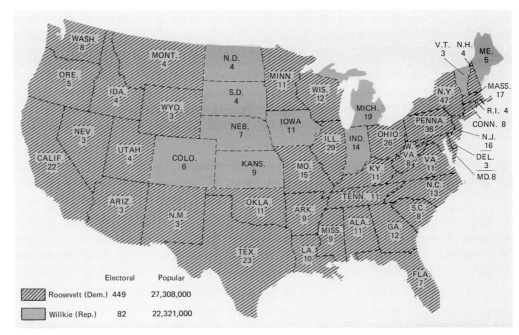

The election of 1940

	Electoral	Popular
Roosevelt (Dem.)	449	27,308,000
Willkie (Rep.)	82	22,321,000

approval of the Chief of Naval Operations before they could be released. Moreover, Roosevelt feared the political repercussions in a campaign in which he was already under attack for unneutral acts. But he was persuaded that he could legally release the destroyers without amending the law; he consulted his cabinet and congressional leaders; and he received assurances that Willkie, the Republican candidate, would not oppose the transaction. Accordingly, on September 2 the United States by executive agreement transferred fifty destroyers to Britain in exchange for ninety-nine-year leases of bases in Newfoundland and the Caribbean.

Willkie's support of conscription also enabled the Administration to obtain a Selective Service Act in August. Still, though Willkie's internationalism minimized the role of foreign policy in the campaign, it did not altogether eliminate peace and war as an issue. Indeed, as the campaign wore on, the Republican candidate, rattled both by his own inexperience and by discordant counsel among his advisers, assailed Roosevelt's foreign policy more and more extravagantly in terms which he would later dismiss as "campaign oratory." Soon he predicted that Roosevelt, if elected, would have the nation in war by April 1941. By the end of the campaign Roosevelt was himself assuring American parents: "I have said this before, but I shall say it again and again and again: Your boys are not going to be sent into any foreign wars."

The election showed that Roosevelt still retained the national confidence. He received 27 million popular votes against 22 million for Willkie; the Electoral College margin was 449 to 82. But he received only 54.8 percent of the vote as against 60.8 percent in 1936, and more than ever before he needed his pluralities in the cities. Because of the equivocal way in which both candidates had presented the foreign issues—had, indeed, somewhat misrepresented their own convictions—the election did not serve either to clarify public thinking or to produce a setting for future action.

Aid short of war

The Lend-Lease Act. Through 1940 Britain had been able to get the goods it needed under the system of cash-and-carry. But, as Churchill urged on Roosevelt in December, both features of the system were in peril—"cash" because Britain's supply of American dollars was nearing exhaustion, "carry" because of the effectiveness of the German submarine campaign against British shipping.

"The thing to do," Roosevelt now told Secretary of the Treasury Morgenthau, "is to get away from a dollar sign. I don't want to put the thing in terms of dollars or loans." As he explained to his press conference, if a neighbor's house was on fire, you would not waste time arguing about the cost of the hose; you would put the fire out and get the hose back afterward. Why not say to England, "We will give you the guns and the ships you need, provided that when the war is over you will return to us in kind the guns and ships we have loaned to you"?

In January 1941 the Administration introduced the so-called lend-lease bill to carry out Roosevelt's intention. The measure authorized the President to sell, transfer, exchange, lend, lease, or otherwise dispose of war equipment and other commodities to the "government of any country whose defense the President deems vital to the defense of the United States." So sweeping a proposal aroused bitter isolationist opposition. "The lend-lease-give program," said Senator Burton K. Wheeler, "is the New Deal's triple A foreign policy; it will plow under every fourth American boy." Senators Taft and Vandenberg feared that Congress, if it passed the bill, would surrender much of its constitutional authority over foreign policy. Among those who testified against the bill were Charles A. Lindbergh, Charles A. Beard, the historian, and Joseph P. Kennedy, the former ambassador to England; Wendell Willkie led a parade of witnesses in its favor. But public sentiment strongly supported the proposal. Assured of biannual review of lend-lease appropriations, Congress passed the bill. It became law on March 11, 1941. "Through this legislation," Roosevelt said, "our country has determined to do its full part in creating an adequate arsenal of democracy."

The Battle of the Atlantic. The Lend-Lease Act decisively committed the economic power of the United States to the support of Britain. It also implied, as its opponents had predicted, at least a partial commitment of American naval power; for, if the United States deemed aid to Britain vital to American security, then clearly the United States had better make sure that goods intended for Britain actually arrived there. Shortly after the passage of lend-lease, the Germans joined the challenge by extending the North Atlantic war zone westward to the coast of Greenland. As German submarines and destroyers sank increasing numbers of British ships, Roosevelt sought means for protecting the Atlantic lifeline and strengthening the defenses of the Western Hemisphere. In April 1941 he concluded an executive agreement with the Danish minister to send American troops to Greenland, a part of the Western Hemisphere, and he extended to that area American naval and air patrols. Those moves lessened but did not resolve the problem of the Atlantic lifeline.

Unlimited national emergency. Roosevelt's policy of aid to Great Britain was not limited only by the fear of an adverse public reaction. The President him-

The U.S.-British destroyer-bases agreement, 1940

Bases acquired by U.S. from British

self apparently cherished the hope, which many around him had abandoned by the spring of 1941, that Hitler might be defeated without direct American military involvement.

Yet Britain's situation seemed to be growing steadily worse. In the United States itself the attitude of business as usual impeded full mobilization of the economy for defense production. The Office of Production Management had succeeded the National Defense Advisory Commission in January 1941, but the new agency lacked adequate authority over allocations and priorities. Many businessmen were disinclined to convert their facilities to defense needs. Strikes in defense industries, some of them instigated by communists, further kept the country from living up to its full responsibility as the "arsenal of democracy." Some positive step seemed necessary to galvanize America and to reassure Britain. On May 27, 1941, the President in a speech to the nation proclaimed "that an unlimited national emergency exists and requires the strengthening of our defense to the extreme limit of our national power."

Roosevelt's proclamation called for preparing American defenses to repel any attack on the Western Hemisphere. To that end, in July by executive agreement he dispatched American troops to Iceland, outside the hemisphere. Had the Nazis reached Iceland first, he argued, they would have threatened the flow of munitions to England, a matter of policy Congress had approved in the Lend-Lease Act. Senator Robert Taft disagreed. The President, he said, had no constitutional right to send troops to Iceland without congressional approval, for there had been no attack upon the United States, nor was there a threat of an attack. Though only one senator supported Taft's protest, the President was stretching his authority at least to its limits and in so doing moving American forces to the very edge of the war.

Isolationism's last stand

The great debate. The slow unfolding of American policy had been accompanied by an intensification of public debate. In 1940 the Committee to Defend America by Aiding the Allies was established under the chairmanship of the Kansas editor William Allen White to argue the moderate interventionist position. In 1941 the Fight for Freedom Committee contended for American entry into the war. On the other side, the America First Committee argued that Hitler's victory would not menace American security. Each side took its case to the public through newspaper advertisements, radio broadcasts, and mass meetings.

The resulting debate became more bitter even than the arguments of the thirties over the New Deal. It was, in addition, unpredictable, cutting across political, economic, and geographical lines. Isolationists were to be found in all parts of the country, in all social classes, and in all political parties. Still, to a considerable degree, isolationism as a political force represented the conservative Republican wing of the business community, with special strength in the Middle West. Progressives like Burton K. Wheeler, Socialists like Norman Thomas, and the communists also criticized Roosevelt's policies. The German-American Bund and the fringe of pro-Nazi groups in America endorsed the isolationist position.

The isolationist dilemma. Most Americans remained uncertainly in the middle of the violent debate. "I am 100 percent plus against our participation in this criminal war," wrote Josephus Daniels, the old Wilsonian, once Roosevelt's chief as Secretary of the Navy in the First World War, now ambassador to Mexico, "but, of course, I trust that Europe will be delivered from totalitarian governments and the scourge of force." This was the isolationist dilemma: at some point, the two sentiments were bound to collide.

An analysis of votes in Congress during these years shows, not a rigid isolationist-interventionist division, but a large middle bloc trying to steer a course between the two extremes. Most members of Congress, like most Americans, wished that all-out support of Britain short of war would somehow bring British victory without American participation. In providing Britain such support, they edged steadily toward involvement. Yet involvement was not their purpose; it was rather the last resort they earnestly hoped to avoid. Men like Henry L. Stimson, Harold L. Ickes, and the members of the Fight for Freedom Committee felt that Roosevelt himself, by refusing to call for an American declaration of war, was engaged in self-delusion. Still, the President's policy of hoping for the best while preparing for the worst expressed the predominant sense of the American people in 1941. Had he been more forthright about the risks he took, he might have appeared less duplicitous to his opponents. He might also in so doing have heightened the fears of his countrymen, lost their support, and thus constrained his ability to combat the terror that was threatening the world.

Hitler widens the war. After the Soviet Union attacked Finland, Roosevelt had condemned Stalin's regime as "a dictatorship as absolute as any other dictatorship in the world." Nonetheless, American diplomats, noting growing evidence of tension between Germany and Russia, told a skeptical Kremlin

The decay of the peace

The first summit:
Argentia, 1941

Most Americans supported this decision. The American communists, of course, rapidly called off their antiwar agitation and became passionate proponents of national defense. From an isolationist viewpoint, however, Hitler's new embroilment strengthened the case against American participation.

The Atlantic Charter. In August, Roosevelt and Churchill met on a warship off Argentia on the coast of Newfoundland. While Roosevelt avoided military commitments, he did agree with Churchill on "certain common principles in the national policies of their respective countries on which they base their hopes for a better future for the world." In the Atlantic Charter, Britain and the United States disclaimed territorial aggrandizement, affirmed the right of all peoples to choose their own form of government and to express freely their wishes concerning territorial changes (though Churchill excepted the peoples within the British empire), assured all states equal access to trade and raw materials ("with due respect to their existing obligations"), proposed collaboration among all nations in the economic field, and promised "after the final destruction of the Nazi tyranny" the disarmament of all aggressor nations "pending the establishment of a wider and permanent system of general security."

By the time of the conference American destroyers were escorting convoys as far as Iceland, leaving the British navy to conduct them the rest of the way. The question of what American ships should do if they encountered a German raider was left unanswered until a U-boat fired on the destroyer *Greer* early in September. Though the President did not so inform the American people, the *Greer* had provoked the attack. Saying the time had come for "active defense," Roosevelt instructed the navy to "shoot on sight" any Axis ships in the American neutrality zone. In October the Germans badly damaged one American destroyer and sank another, the *Reuben James*, with considerable loss of life. In November Congress revised the Neutrality Act to allow merchantmen to carry arms and to proceed to British ports. Roosevelt had consulted Congress about that measure, but he had not told the whole truth. To have done so, he feared, would have risked too much, for the House of Representatives had renewed the Selective Service Act by a margin of only one vote. Accordingly the President had been disingenuous, as he knew, but in what he believed was a commanding cause.

Both the Argentia meeting and the new Atlantic policy goaded the isolationists into ever more impassioned attacks on the Administration. In an angry speech at Des Moines, Iowa, in September, Charles A. Lindbergh declared that "the three most important groups who have been pressing this country toward

in the winter of 1940–41 that a German attack might be in the making. Stalin remained impervious to warnings. When Hitler, despairing of an early defeat of Britain, decided to eliminate the potential threat of Russia by a sudden blow, the Soviet regime was taken by surprise. The Nazi invasion of the U.S.S.R. on June 22, 1941, brought the European war into a new phase.

Winston Churchill had long since decided that, in such an eventuality, he would offer Russia full British support. "I have only one purpose," he said, "the destruction of Hitler. . . . If Hitler invaded Hell, I would make at least a favorable reference to the Devil in the House of Commons." Roosevelt was ready to accept this policy. Despite warnings that Russia could not be expected to hold out against the Nazi onslaughts, he sent Harry Hopkins to Moscow in July. Hopkins' relatively optimistic report confirmed Churchill and Roosevelt in their decision to do what they could to stiffen Soviet resistance.

Isolationism's last stand

Charles A. Lindbergh:
impassioned isolationist

war are the British, the Jewish and the Roosevelt administration." Most isolationists disowned Lindbergh's anti-Semitism, but the course of the war and of the American role in it was rapidly diminishing the range of maneuver between the Nazis and their enemies.

Thunder in the East

The Japanese dilemma. Despite the Japanese occupation of coastal China in 1937 and the failure of the Brussels Conference (see p. 668), the Chiang Kai-shek government and the Chinese communists under Mao Tse-tung had kept up stalwart resistance. The Chinese plight increasingly enlisted the sympathy of the United States and Britain. Though both governments were reluctant to provoke Japanese retaliation, they began in 1938 to seek ways to get financial assistance to China.

The Japanese response was less explosive than the State Department had predicted. One reason for this restraint was the extent to which the Japanese war effort had itself become dependent on the United States. In 1938, for example, the United States supplied Japan with 90 percent of its metal scrap, 91 percent of its copper, and 66 percent of its oil. This trade confronted Washington with embarrassing problems. It was sanctioned by the Japanese-American commercial treaty of 1911, and the commodities involved were beyond the reach of existing neutrality

legislation. To call for a "moral" embargo of the sort used in the Italo-Ethiopian conflict would penalize China as well as Japan. Its hands thus tied, the United States was left in the position of fueling a war machine of which it profoundly disapproved. In an effort to regain freedom of action, Washington informed Tokyo in July 1939 of its intention to terminate the commercial treaty, though, it added in January 1940, it would not for the time being disturb the existing trade.

Then the Nazi successes in Europe transformed the situation. The expansionists in Tokyo felt their long-awaited opportunity had come to seize the colonial empires of France and the Netherlands, even perhaps of Britain. The relatively moderate government was overthrown. In its place came a tough government, dominated by the military and dedicated to the achievement of a "new order in Greater East Asia." In September Japan joined Germany and Italy in the Tripartite Pact. The Axis now extended to Asia.

The American response. The American response was an embargo on essential materials, especially aviation gasoline and scrap metal. Since this action could be justified in terms of America's own defense needs, it did not have the flavor of an open affront to Japan. Behind the scenes, American representatives took part in staff discussions with British and Dutch officials to consider plans for the defense of the western Pacific in case a Japanese attack forced the United States into war.

Roosevelt, however, was primarily concerned with the crisis in Europe. He therefore wished to stave off a showdown with Japan. Accordingly 1941 was marked by long, intricate, and repetitious discussions between the two countries. In June the German invasion of the Soviet Union relieved Japan of its anxieties about a possible attack from Siberia. In mid-July 1941 Japanese troops invaded southern Indochina and occupied Saigon. Roosevelt told the Japanese ambassador that if Japan withdrew from Indochina he would secure its neutralization and assure Japan access to its raw materials. If Japan persisted in its course, and especially if it moved into the Dutch East Indies, the United States would help the Dutch and probably cut off oil exports to Japan. When Japan did not reply, Roosevelt on July 26 froze Japanese assets in the United States and a few days later embargoed oil shipments.

These actions brought about a reappraisal in Tokyo. Prime Minister Fumimaro Konoye, a moderate, in August proposed a meeting with Roosevelt. Japan, Konoye's foreign minister promised, would withdraw its troops from Indochina as soon as the "China incident" was settled, would not expand southward or make war on the Soviet Union unless attacked, and would not feel bound by the Tripartite Pact to go to war if the United States became engaged in a defensive war with Germany. Though Roosevelt considered those terms favorable as a basis for peace in the Pacific, Hull insisted on an agreement about China, which he viewed as the major issue, before any conference took place between the President and the prime minister. The Secretary of State and his advisers made the territorial integrity of China the crux of their diplomacy partly out of long habit and conviction, and partly in the false belief that Japan would in no event attack the United States. Persuaded by their belief, Roosevelt in his reply to Konoye on September 3 made China the key to negotiations. That was unacceptable to the Japanese war party. Late in September Konoye tried again, only to be rebuffed as before by Hull's demand for a prior agreement on China. Had Hull done otherwise, he would have agreed to giving Japan a free hand in China.

There was to be no turning back from that breakdown of diplomacy. As Roosevelt had long recognized, the first interest of the United States lay in preventing Nazi domination of Europe and Great Britain. Pursuit of that interest entailed avoiding, or at the least postponing, war with Japan. On that account the question of China might have been left until after the end of the European war. There was, however, no assurance that Konoye could have continued to restrain the Japanese army, which any concessions might have emboldened, as Roosevelt and Churchill agreed. Japan, moreover, had no right to dominion in China, and the Chinese resistance did evoke a natural American sympathy. But the timing of Hull's advice

to Roosevelt, and the adamancy of both the American and Japanese positions on China, eliminated the last chance for a Pacific armistice, however transitory.

The Rising Sun over the Pacific. In mid-October the militants in the Japanese cabinet forced Konoye's resignation. Though his successor, General Hideki Tojo, was a leader of the war party, debate continued until November 5. The army then agreed to a last effort at accommodation with the United States provided that the emperor approve plans for an immediate attack if negotiations failed. Earlier the Japanese leaders had defined their minimum demands to include the abandonment of China by the United States and the restoration of normal commercial relations, with renewed delivery of oil and scrap metal. Now Tojo told Admiral Kichisabura Nomura, Japanese ambassador, that other matters would be negotiable but that Japan could never yield on the question of China.

By decoding secret Japanese messages, the Americans had been able to follow some of the Japanese moves. Officials in Washington realized that the end was drawing near. Late in November American forces in the Pacific, including those in Hawaii, were sent the first of a number of alerts ordering them onto a war footing. Everyone expected attack, but the conviction was absolute that the Japanese would move toward the south. In Washington, Cordell Hull continued to meet with Japanese representatives. On December 6 Roosevelt sent a final appeal to the emperor.

In the meantime, a striking force of Japanese aircraft carriers had left the Kuriles on November 26 and was making its way toward Pearl Harbor. On

Pearl Harbor, December 7, 1941

December 7, 1941, while discussions continued in Washington, the Japanese launched a devastating attack on the fleet and air force in Hawaii. An epoch in American history had come to an end.

"In the past few years—and, most violently, in the past few days—we have learned a terrible lesson," said Franklin Roosevelt two days later. "We must begin the great task that is before us by abandoning once and for all the illusion that we can ever again isolate ourselves from the rest of humanity." He added, "We are going to win the war, and we are going to win the peace that follows."

Suggestions for reading

THE MAKING OF AMERICAN FOREIGN POLICY

Selig Adler, *The Uncertain Giant: American Foreign Policy Between the Wars** (1966), and R. A. Divine, *The Reluctant Belligerent: American Entry into World War II** (1965), cover the main events of the period. For a cogent transatlantic view, see Jean-Baptiste Duroselle, *From Wilson to Roosevelt: Foreign Policy of the United States, 1913–1945* (1963). J. E. Wiltz, *From Isolation to War, 1931–1941** (1968), provides an incisive discussion of leading issues. R. E. Osgood, *Ideals and Self-Interest in America's Foreign Relations** (1953), offers a stimulating analytical framework from which to view American foreign policy. See also G. F. Kennan, *American Diplomacy, 1900–1950)* (1951), and Walter Lippmann, *U.S. Foreign Policy: Shield of the Republic* (1943).

For Roosevelt's first term, the raw material of foreign affairs can be conveniently found in E. B. Nixon, ed., *Franklin D. Roosevelt and Foreign Affairs,* 3 vols. (1969). Merze Tate, *The United States and Armaments* (1948), describes the frustrations of disarmament in the years between the wars. The story from 1937 to Pearl Harbor is splendidly recorded in two magisterial volumes by W. L. Langer and S. E. Gleason, *The Challenge to Isolation** (1952) and *The Undeclared War** (1953). 1941 is well covered in J. M. Burns, *Roosevelt: The Soldier of Freedom** (1970). For military aspects, see M. S. Watson, *Chief of Staff: Prewar Plans and Preparations* (1950). On intelligence problems, the outstanding work is Roberta Wohlstetter, *Pearl Harbor* (1962).

Cordell Hull, *Memoirs,* 2 vols. (1948) supplies the view from the office of the Secretary of State. It may be supplemented by J. W. Pratt, *Cordell Hull,* 2 vols. (1964). Sumner Wells, *A Time for Decision* (1964), and Herbert Feis, *Seen From E. A.: Three International Episodes** (1947), amplify the State Department view. For H. L. Stimson, there are three works: his own book with McGeorge Bundy, *On Active Service in Peace and War* (1948); a perceptive biography E. E. Morison, *Turmoil and Tradition** (1960); and a prosecutor's brief by R. N. Current, *Secretary Stimson* (1954). R. E. Sherwood, *Roosevelt and Hopkins** (1948, rev. ed., 1950), is vivid and penetrating; and the second volume of J. M. Blum, *From the Morgenthau Diaries: Years of Urgency* (1965), is valuable for the years before Pearl Harbor.

Two waves of revisionism have washed over these years. The old isolationist school can be consulted in two books by C. A. Beard—*American Foreign Policy in the Making, 1932–1940* (1946) and *President Roosevelt and the Coming of War, 1941* (1948). C. C. Tansill sums up the isolationist case in *Back Door to War* (1952). A recent restatement of isolationist ideas is in Bruce Russett, *No Clear and Present Danger* (1972). In *Roosevelt: From Munich to Pearl Harbor* (1950), Basil Rauch provides a careful rebuttal. The contemporary school of revisionism, committed to the thesis that American foreign policy has always been the expression of the imperialist necessities of American capitalism, is represented in L. C. Gardner, *Economic Aspects of New Deal Diplomacy** (1964), and in the relevant chapters of W. A. Williams, *The Tragedy of American Diplomacy** (1959; rev. ed., 1962).

THE POLITICS OF FOREIGN POLICY

Selig Adler, *The Isolationist Impulse** (1957), Manfred Jonas, *Isolationism in America, 1935–1941** (1966), and Samuel Lubell, *The Future of American Politics** (1952), consider the sources of isolationism. Frank Waldrop, *McCormick of Chicago* (1966), is an illuminating essay on the isolationist mood. J. K. Nelson, *The Peace Prophets: American Pacifist Thought, 1919–1941** (1967), discusses the

*Available in a paperback edition.

peace movement. Congressional reactions to foreign affairs can be traced in F. L. Israel, *Nevada's Key Pittman* (1963), M. C. McKenna, *Borah* (1961), B. K. Wheeler, *Yankee from the West* (1962), and W. S. Cole, *Senator Gerald P. Nye and American Foreign Relations* (1962). See also J. E. Wiltz, *In Search of Peace: the Senate Munitions Inquiry, 1934–1936* (1963); for the neutrality debate, R. A. Divine, *The Illusion of Neutrality** (1962); and for Willkie, D. B. Johnson, *The Republican Party and Wendell Willkie** (1960).

The angry controversy of 1939–41 is well covered in Walter Johnson, *The Battle Against Isolationism* (1944), M. L. Chadwin, *The Hawks of World War II* (1968; in paperback as *The Warhawks: American Interventionists before Pearl Harbor*); and W. S. Cole, *America First: The Battle Against Intervention* (1953). The musings of a leading isolationist can be followed in C. A. Lindbergh, *Wartime Journals* (1970).

EUROPE
J. W. Gantenbein, *Documentary Background of World War II* (1948), lives up to its title. For interpretations, Keith Eubank, *The Origins of World War II** (1969), sums up the accepted view; and A. J. P. Taylor, *The Origins of the Second World War** (1962), is a stimulating essay in heterodoxy. W. S. Churchill's classic volumes, *The Gathering Storm** (1948) and *Their Finest Hour** (1949), are majestic and indispensable.

Alan Bullock, *Hitler: A Study in Tyranny** (1952), is the best biography. Five useful works discuss Nazi Germany and America; H. L. Trefousse, *Germany and American Neutrality* (1951); J. V. Compton, *The Swastika and the Eagle* (1967); Alton Frye, *Nazi Germany and the Western Hemisphere, 1933–1941* (1967); A. A. Offner, *American Appeasement: United States Foreign Policy and Germany, 1933–1938** (1969); and Robert Dallek, *Democrat and Diplomat: The Life of William E. Dodd* (1968). For American relations with the Soviet Union, see R. P. Browder, *The Origins of Soviet-American Diplomacy** (1953); Beatrice Farnsworth, *William C. Bullitt and the Soviet Union* (1967); and E. M. Bennett, *Recognition of Russia: An American Foreign Policy Dilemma* (1970). Brice Harris, *The United States and the Italo-Ethiopian Crisis* (1964), displays the American response to the events of 1935; and F. J. Taylor, *The United States and the Spanish Civil War* (1956), and Allen Guttmann, *The Wound in the Heart: America and the Spanish Civil War* (1962), consider the problems of 1937–38. Four books throw light on Anglo-American relations at various points: Herbert Feis, *1933: Characters in Crisis* (1966); W. F. Kimball, *'The Most Unsordid Act': Lend-Lease, 1939–1941* (1969); T. A. Wilson, *The First Summit: Roosevelt and Churchill at Placentia Bay, 1941* (1969); and H. D. Hall, *North American Supply* (1955).

FAR EAST
Dorothy Borg, *The United States and the Far Eastern Crisis of 1933–1938* (1964), is a basic work. The Japanese problem is assessed from various angles in Herbert Feis, *The Road to Pearl Harbor** (1950); D. J. Lu, *From the Marco Polo Bridge to Pearl Harbor: Japan's Entry into World War II* (1961); P. W. Schroeder, *The Axis Alliance and Japanese-American Relations* (1958); C. E. Neu, *The Troubled Encounter: The U.S. and Japan* (1975); and Robert Butow, *Tojo and the Coming of the War** (1961). For American diplomatic reactions, see Walter Johnson's rendering of the papers of J. C. Grew, *Turbulent Era: A Diplomatic Record of Forty Years*, 2 vols. (1952), and W. H. Heinrichs, *American Ambassador: Joseph C. Grew and the Development of the United States Diplomatic Tradition* (1967).

LATIN AMERICA
Bryce Wood, *The Making of the Good Neighbor Policy** (1961), is the best historical account; Laurence Duggan, *The Americas: Search for Hemispheric Security* (1949), is the testimony of a participant. David Green, *The Containment of Latin America* (1971), is a revisionist critique of the Good Neighbor policy.

*Available in a paperback edition.

CHAPTER 29

The world in flames

The bitter wreckage of ships and planes at Pearl Harbor ended the illusion that the United States could be a world power and remain safe from world conflict. In the shocking strike from the placid Hawaiian skies, the Japanese crippled the Pacific fleet, destroyed nearly 200 planes, and killed nearly 2,500 men. The navy lost three times as many men in this single attack as it had lost in the Spanish-American and First World wars combined. Four days after Pearl Harbor, on December 11, 1941, Germany and Italy declared war on the United States. America was now committed to global war.

America organizes for war

Arms for global war. War brought profound changes to American society. The first problem was to produce the machines and weapons for global warfare. In 1941 military spending had reached a monthly rate of about $2 billion; but only 15 percent of industrial output had gone for military purposes, and businessmen had resisted pressure to shift to war production. Roosevelt now laid down unprecedented objectives for 1942—60,000 planes, 45,000 tanks, 20,000 antiaircraft guns, 8 million tons of shipping—and set up the War Production Board under Donald Nelson to convert the economy to a war basis.

In the first six months of 1942, the government placed over $100 billion in war contracts—more goods on order than the economy had ever produced in a single year. The structure of central control buckled under the strain. An effective priority system was essential, but sometimes more priorities were issued than there were goods to satisfy them. In the confusion the military, who had already gained authority over procurement, demanded control over production. Nelson, backed by the President and Congress, fended off this proposal. In 1943 the WPB's Controlled Materials Plan introduced order into the allocation of critical materials, about which the military continued to have considerable voice.

Roosevelt, in his characteristic style, assigned important areas of authority to other civilian agencies. In December 1942 the War Food Administration assumed direction of the nation's food program. Shortages in oil and rubber brought about the appointment, also outside the WPB, of "czars" with exceptional powers to expedite production. The War Manpower Commission supervised the mobilization of men and women for both civilian and military purposes. And the Office of Scientific Research and Development, under the direction of Dr. Vannevar Bush, conducted scientific and technical mobilization; its scientists and engineers were responsible for short-range rockets (especially the "bazooka"), the proximity fuse, and other remarkable gains in military technology.

In 1942 the proportion of the economy committed to war production grew from 15 to 33 percent. By the end of 1943 federal expenditures for goods and services constituted a sum larger than the total output of the economy when Roosevelt took office a decade earlier. The gross national product grew from $99.7 billion in 1940 to $211.9 billion in 1945 (in 1975 dollars, from about $319 billion to about $678 billion). The WPB continued to be shaken by feuds, both internal and external. In the interest of efficiency in procurement, the army and navy relied increasingly on big business in the awarding of war contracts. Nelson tried without success to divert a substantial proportion of those contracts to smaller concerns, for which he also attempted to get reconversion privileges in 1944. Convinced that any move toward reconversion was premature, the army and navy persuaded Roosevelt to force Nelson to resign. Still, in one way or another, the WPB had succeeded in guiding the productive energies of the economy to enable America in a surprisingly short time to outproduce all other nations in the world.

The fight for stabilization. This extraordinary feat was a result of the stimulus provided by government spending to the productive talents of American managers and workers. Federal purchases of goods and

Guadalcanal

services rose from $6 billion in 1940 to $89 billion in 1944. Total federal spending during the war years came to over $320 billion—an amount twice as great as the total of all previous federal spending in the history of the republic.

How was this prodigious expenditure to be paid for? The first resort was to a broadening and deepening of the tax structure. By 1944 surtaxes were taking away 94 percent of net income in the highest brackets; and people at every level were paying taxes that would have seemed inconceivable a short time before. Total tax revenues in the war years came to about $130 billion. This was far less than Roosevelt had requested, however, and, as a result, the government was able to meet only about 41 percent of the cost of the war on a pay-as-you-go basis–not enough, though a much larger proportion than during the First World War.

The rest of the defense bill was made up by borrowing. In 1944 alone the excess of expenditures over receipts amounted to more than $50 billion—a figure over twice the total size of the accumulated debt in 1941. By the end of the war the national debt had grown to about $280 billion, nearly six times as large as it had been when bombs fell on Pearl Harbor. The budgetary deficits so loudly bewailed in New Deal days now seemed negligible compared to the deficit spending of war. An incidental effect was to prove the Keynesian argument that public spending would end the depression: unemployment rapidly vanished in 1941 and 1942, and Congress abolished old New Deal agencies like the Works Progress Administration. The problem became, not to find jobs for people, but to find people for jobs.

The tremendous increase in public spending released strong inflationary pressures. The shift from civilian to war production reduced the quantity of goods available for purchase just as the quantity of money jingling in people's pockets was increasing. By 1944, for example, the production of civilian automobiles, of washing machines and other consumer durables, of nondefense housing and the like had virtually come to an end. Unless prices were to soar out of sight, means had to be found to hold the volume of spendable money down to the volume of available goods.

One recourse was to fiscal and monetary policies. Taxation was an obvious means of reducing the supply of spendable money in people's hands. The war-bond drive was another way by which the government sought to persuade people to put their money away instead of using it to bid up prices; nearly $100 billion worth of the various series of war bonds were sold in these years. But it was evident from an early point that indirect measures would not be enough to eliminate the "inflationary gap"—the gap, that is,

Assembly line

between too few goods and too much money. As early as August 1941 Roosevelt had accordingly established the Office of Price Administration under the direction of Leon Henderson, a hard-driving New Deal economist.

Price control presented one of the toughest problems of war administration. Every economic interest wanted rigid policing of the other fellow's prices but tended to regard attempts to police its own prices as subversive of the free-enterprise system. In April 1942 the OPA imposed a general price freeze, joining to this a system by which necessities of life in short supply—meat, gasoline, tires—were rationed to the consumers through an allotment of coupons. The farm bloc, however, succeeded in gaining exceptions for agricultural prices; and the increase in the cost of food brought about demands for wage increases. The War Labor Board, set up in January 1942, sought to meet this problem by the Little Steel formula of July, permitting wage increases to keep pace with the 15 percent rise in the cost of living since January 1941. In September Roosevelt requested new authority to stabilize the cost of living, including farm prices and wages. The Stabilization Act of 1942 established the Office of Economic Stabilization under the direction of former Supreme Court Justice James F. Byrnes.

Special interests nevertheless continued unabashed guerrilla warfare against price control in their own sectors. The farm bloc was unrelenting in its demand that exceptions be made for itself. John L. Lewis led the United Mine Workers in a fight against the Little Steel formula; for a time in 1943 the government was forced to seize and operate the coal mines. Henderson, who had affronted Congress by the unquenchable zeal of his war against inflation, had been forced to resign in December 1942. But a "hold-the-line" order in April 1943, followed by a campaign in May to "roll back" food prices, helped bring the price level to a plateau by mid-1943. For the rest of the war the OPA, under the able direction of Chester Bowles, was able to maintain substantial price stability. From October 1942 to the end of the Pacific war, consumers' prices rose only 8.7 percent. For all its unpopularity, especially among businessmen, politicians, and farm leaders, the OPA was one of the war's brilliant successes.

The problem remained of concerting the efforts of various agencies dealing with production and stabilization. In May 1943 Roosevelt set up the Office of War Mobilization and put Byrnes in charge. Employing his judicial and political skill to intervene when operating agencies disagreed, Byrnes did an effective job in pulling together the infinitely ramified strands of America's domestic war effort.

The people behind the lines. The attack on Pearl Harbor ended the isolationist-interventionist debate and caused a surge of national unity. Throughout the war popular confidence in the government remained high. Nevertheless, like any period of war, this was a time of upheaval and anxiety.

To combat the threat of enemy activity within the United States, Roosevelt gave new authority to the Federal Bureau of Investigation, including the power to tap wires in national security cases. Under the astute direction and relentless self-advertisement of J. Edgar Hoover, the FBI had already established itself in congressional and public opinion. Its new mandate

Nisei evacuees: victims of American brutality

encouraged it to widen its investigations into the beliefs as well as the deeds of Americans. But the years 1941–45 were not marred by the widespread assaults on civil freedom that had characterized the years 1917–20 (see pp. 567, 579). Perhaps because they were not perceived to constitute a real threat to the nation, German-Americans and Italian-Americans were not subjected to jingoistic harassment. In contrast, the tragic exception to this general tolerance was the fate of the over one hundred thousand Japanese-Americans—the Nisei—who were brutally removed from their homes along the Pacific Coast and relocated in internment camps in the interior—an act of national hysteria wholly unjustified.

Of native Americans suspected of sympathy for fascism, some had their publications—for example, Father Coughlin's *Social Justice*—denied the mails. Toward the end of the war, an effort to convict a number of American fascists in a mass sedition trial miscarried. In the meantime, the Department of Justice had taken effective steps against Nazi agents and organizations. So far as is known, no acts of enemy sabotage were committed in the United States during the war. In the main, Attorney General Francis Biddle strove with success to maintain an atmosphere of moderation.

If war meant anxiety, it also meant opportunity. It uprooted people from familiar settings, exposed them to new experience, changed the direction of their lives. The rise in output and employment was accompanied by a tremendous increase in real income, partly from the prevalence of overtime pay for workers. Wartime tax policies strengthened the tendency toward income redistribution that had begun under the New Deal. The wealthiest 5 percent of Americans had received 30 percent in 1929 and 24 percent in 1941; by 1944 their share was down to 20.7 percent.

After the long years of depression, both workers and the middle class savored the prosperity of the war years. They spent freely for available consumer goods and saved with the expectation of buying refrigerators and radios, and especially automobiles and houses, after the war. Facilities for housing, transportation, schooling, and recreation were critically short in communities impacted by war industries, particularly in the rapidly growing cities of the South, the Southwest, and the West Coast. Those shortages intensified yearnings for a comfortable tomorrow. For the duration, most civilians, though irritated by rationing, lived better lives than they had for more than a decade.

Between 1941 and 1945 shortages of labor brought some 6.5 million women, most of them middle-aged and married, into the working force. Except for the rare feminists, they did not yet question conventional

America organizes for war

Black power: 1942

We know that our fate is tied up with the fate of the democratic way of life. And so, out of the depths of our hearts, a cry goes up for the triumph of the United Nations. But we would not be honest with ourselves were we to stop with a call for a victory of arms alone.... Unless this war sounds the death knell to the old Anglo-American empire systems, the hapless story of which is one of exploitation for the profit and power of a monopoly capitalist economy, it will have been fought in vain. Our aim then must not only be to defeat nazism, fascism, and militarism on the battlefield but to win the peace, for democracy, for freedom and the Brotherhood of Man without regard to his pigmentation, land of his birth or the God of his fathers....

While the March on Washington Movement may find it advisable to form a citizens committee of friendly white citizens to give moral support ... it does not imply that these white citizens ... should be taken into the March on Washington Movement as members. The essential value of an all-Negro movement such as the March on Washington is that it helps to create faith by Negroes in Negroes. It develops a sense of self-reliance with Negroes depending on Negroes in vital matters. It helps to break down the slave psychology and inferiority-complex in Negroes which comes and is nourished with Negroes relying on white people for direction and support. This inevitably happens in mixed organizations that are supposed to be in the interest of the Negro.

From A. Philip Randolph, Keynote Address to the Policy Conference of the March on Washington Movement, September 1942.

---

attitudes toward women's roles or protest against the disparity between men's and women's wages or the lack of day-care centers for the children of working mothers. Women war-workers for the most part did not intend to remain on the job after the war (though many of them either did not leave or soon returned). Rather, they took satisfaction in their contributions to wartime tasks, a point the federal government stressed. They were also beguiled by their new income. Supplementing their husbands' earnings, that income gave their families, often for the first time, access to the necessities and some of the comforts of a middle-class standard of living.

Ultimately the demand for labor also provided new opportunities for blacks, though throughout the war they received much less than equal treatment Their resulting resentments fostered an unprecedented and often effective militancy. During the defense boom before Pearl Harbor, blacks were, as ever, the last hired. Many remained unemployed. Those who found jobs ordinarily received low wages, small chance for promotion, and often no chance to join self-consciously segregated labor unions. Worse, the army and navy persisted in the segregation of the armed forces, consigned most blacks to menial tasks, and with few exceptions denied blacks training for commissions or for élite service like that of the air corps. "A jim crow army," as one critic said, "cannot

fight for a free world." So persuaded, the head of the Brotherhood of Sleeping Car Porters, A. Philip Randolph, one of the great black leaders of the century, organized the Negro March on Washington Committee, which planned to recruit thousands of blacks for a rally at the Lincoln Memorial in the spring of 1941 to demand equal rights to work and the desegregation of the armed forces. Roosevelt persuaded Randolph to call off the march in return for Executive Order 8802 of June 1941, which made it national policy to forbid discrimination in employment in defense industries. Roosevelt also appointed the Fair Employment Practices Committee to enforce that policy by investigating complaints and taking steps to redress grievances.

The FEPC, detested though it was in the South, lacked the authority to fulfill its mission. Though war industries did hire blacks and other minorities, discrimination in wages and seniority remained the rule in spite of efforts of the FEPC to combat it. The War and Navy Departments, moreover, took only token steps toward desegregation in the services. Consequently Randolph kept alive his March on Washington Movement with its black membership and its commitment to mass, nonviolent protest. Ghandian nonviolent techniques became the tactics of newer organizations, most notably the Congress on Racial Equality (CORE), which included whites among its members and successfully employed sit-ins during the war to desegregate various Northern restaurants, theaters, and skating rinks. By 1945 CORE was planning freedom rides to desegregate public transportation in the South.

The movement of thousands of black workers to industrial centers, south and north, provoked the hostility of many prejudiced whites who objected to black neighbors and even more to their competition for jobs, housing, and schooling. Episodes of racial violence visited a dozen cities and culminated in 1943 in riots in Los Angeles, New York, and most grimly in Detroit. There in June over thirty people, white and black, died during two days of guerrilla fighting that ceased only with the intervention of the National Guard. Continuing evidence of white racism, official and private, discouraged blacks and damped but did not dispel the new militancy. The achievements of the FEPC, inadequate though they were, raised hopes for the future, as still more did the occasional victories of nonviolent protest. Even the head of the moderate NAACP foresaw that only continuing protest—"a rising wind," as he put it—would fasten public policy to the cause of civil rights.

Early politics of the war. Political developments after Pearl Harbor quickly refuted the isolationist prediction that war must doom democracy and free discussion. In Congress the dominating conservative coalition of Republicans and Southern Democrats seized the opportunity to liquidate New Deal agencies that appeared to have lost their function. On the other hand, Congress also provided responsible counsel on many aspects of the war effort—most notably in the

Senate War Investigating Committee, which, under the able chairmanship of Harry S Truman of Missouri, exposed waste and confusion in the defense effort and made many valuable recommendations to the executive.

Relations with Congress presented Roosevelt with difficult problems. The 1942 congressional election took place in a time when military defeats had yet to be offset by any striking victories, and in an atmosphere suffused with wartime irritations, especially over the OPA's efforts to hold prices and rents down. It resulted in striking Republican gains—ten seats in the Senate, forty-seven in the House. This outcome confirmed the conservative complexion of the Congress, increased Roosevelt's difficulties in dealing with that body, and filled the Republicans with high hopes for the presidential election of 1944.

The war in Europe

Beat Hitler first. The manifold activities at home, however, provided only the backdrop for the essential problem of war—victory over the enemy. For the United States there were two enemies—the Japanese, advancing rapidly into Southeast Asia in the weeks after Pearl Harbor; and the European Axis, now engaged in savage warfare on the Russian front and presumably preparing an eventual invasion of England. The immediate problem for the United States was whether to throw its military might against Germany or against Japan.

American military planners had already concluded by March 1941 that, if the United States entered the war, American strategy must be to beat Hitler first. There were several reasons for this decision. For one thing, Germany, with its command of most of the western coast of Europe and its access to the Atlantic, presented a direct threat to the Western Hemisphere; there was particular concern over Axis penetration of Latin America. For another, Germany seemed far more likely than Japan to achieve some revolutionary breakthrough in military technology. In addition, Great Britain was fully engaged in fighting the Axis, while in the Far East, China was both less active in its resistance to Japan and less accessible to outside support.

The Nazi attack on the Soviet Union in June 1941, far from reversing the Europe-first argument, was considered to reinforce it; for the Russo-German war increased both the chance of defeating Germany and the urgency of doing so before Germany conquered Russia. Nor did the Japanese attack on Pearl Harbor shake the American decision. When Winston

Detroit, 1943: two days of guerrilla fighting

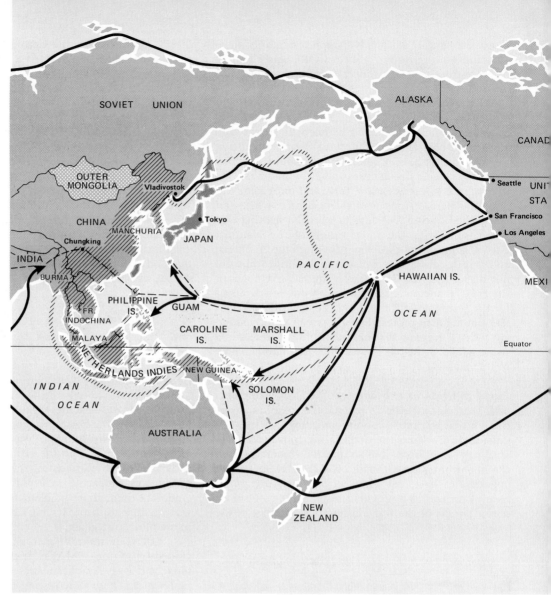

Churchill came to Washington in December 1941, he found complete agreement on his proposition that "the defeat of Germany, entailing a collapse, will leave Japan exposed to overwhelming force, whereas the defeat of Japan would not by any means bring the World War to an end."

Diverging strategies in Europe. The agreement between the United States and Britain on beating Germany first was not matched, however, by agreement on the best way of doing it. The British strategy was to postpone direct assault on Germany until a combination of naval blockade, aerial bombing, psychological warfare, and military attack on the Axis periphery had sufficiently weakened Germany's capacity to resist. In Churchill this strategy had an

exceptionally eloquent and resourceful champion. The British prime minister had long been identified with the circuitous approach to the German foe. "No plan could be more unpromising than the plan of frontal attack," he had written in his history of the First World War. "It is a tale of the torture, mutilation, or extinction of millions of men, and of the sacrifice of all that was best and noblest in an entire generation."

Where the British strategy was to attack the enemy where he was weakest, the American was to attack the enemy where he was strongest. From the American viewpoint, the Churchill plan of "pecking at the periphery" would waste resources without winning victory. As Roosevelt used to observe when Churchill advocated a landing at one or another Euro-

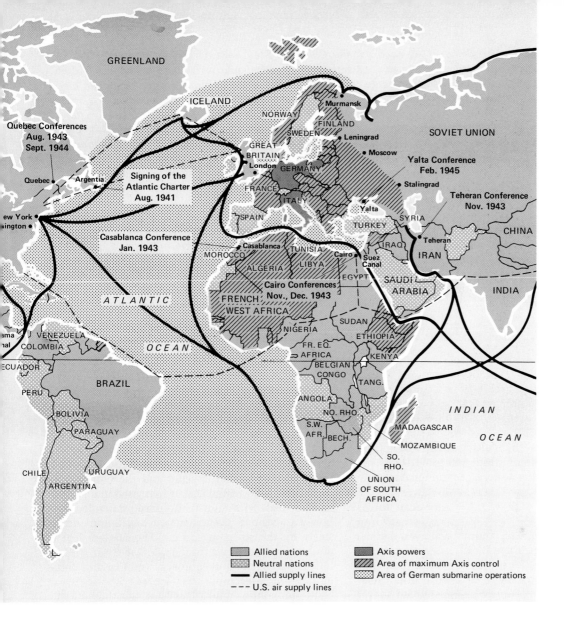

Allied nations	Axis powers
Neutral nations	Area of maximum Axis control
— Allied supply lines	Area of German submarine operations
--- U.S. air supply lines	

pean point remote from Germany, "All right, but where do we go from there?" The American Joint Chiefs of Staff, ably led by General George C. Marshall, felt that only a massive thrust across the English Channel and France into the heart of Germany would achieve victory. In their view—a view generally shared by Roosevelt—all Anglo-American efforts should be concentrated on establishing a second front in France.

Detour to North Africa. The Soviet Union, in desperate need of relief from the hammer blows of the German army and air force, brought strong pressure for a second front in 1942. But, though the British accepted a cross-Channel invasion in principle, they continued to object in practice. They felt that the

Americans underestimated the difficulties of amphibious landings on fortified coasts; they regarded American troops as untried; and they doubted whether the American economy could quickly achieve the production levels necessary to sustain a great invasion. There were particularly ominous shortages in landing craft and in modern tanks. Accordingly, when the American Joint Chiefs submitted in the spring of 1942 a plan for the invasion of France later that year, the British turned it down.

Still, something had to be done in 1942, if only to reassure the hard-pressed and bitterly disappointed Russians. Churchill consequently proposed an invasion of North Africa. The American Joint Chiefs felt that a North African diversion, by committing Anglo-American forces to a Mediterranean campaign

Across the Channel in '42: an advocate

My advice is: As soon as your Chiefs of Staff have completed the plans for the northern offensive to your satisfaction, you should send them by a most trusted messenger and advocate to Churchill and his War Council as the American plan which you propose and intend to go ahead with if accepted by Britain....

And then having done that, you should lean with all your strength on the ruthless rearrangement of shipping allotments and the preparation of landing gear for the ultimate invasion.... It should be pushed with the fever of war action, aimed at a definite date of completion not later than September. The rate of construction of a number of landing barges should not be allowed to lose the crisis of the World War. And yet that is the only objection to the offensive that, after talks with British critics here, I have heard made.

If such decisive action is once taken by you, further successful dispersion of our strength will automatically be terminated. We shall have an affirmative answer against which to measure all such demands; while, on the other hand, so long as we remain without our own plan of offensive, our forces will inevitably be dispersed and wasted.

From Henry L. Stimson, Letter to President Roosevelt, March 1942.

---

as well as by preempting necessary men and materiel, would delay the invasion of France, perhaps until 1944. But Roosevelt accepted Churchill's argument that an invasion of North Africa in 1942 could be a preliminary to a cross-Channel attack in 1943. In July the decision was made to invade North Africa in the autumn. The operation was placed under the command of General Dwight D. Eisenhower.

On November 8, 1942, Anglo-American forces disembarked at Casablanca in Morocco and at Oran and Algiers in Algeria. The landings achieved tactical surprise. Within short order, local resistance came to an end. But military success raised political problems. The collaborationist regime of Marshal Pétain, established at Vichy and in control of unoccupied southern France, exercised nominal authority in North Africa. The United States, which had maintained diplomatic relations with the Vichy government, had some hope of winning the support of pro-Vichy officials and military leaders in Algeria and Morocco. Roosevelt and Churchill supposed that General Charles de Gaulle, commander of the Free French in London, would be unacceptable to the North African French, who had sworn oaths of loyalty to Pétain. But the Americans believed that General Henri Giraud, who had recently escaped from a German prison camp, would be exempt from de Gaulle's unpopularity.

But Giraud, as a condition for cooperation, at first demanded supreme command of the invasion for himself. The situation was further complicated by the presence in Algiers of Admiral Jean François Darlan, a prominent French collaborationist and Pétain's suc-

cessor-designate. Darlan proved as ready to collaborate with the Americans in 1942 as he had been with the Germans in 1940. On November 11 he signed an armistice agreement. As part of the arrangement, Eisenhower recognized Darlan as *de facto* political chief in North Africa—an action that provoked a storm of criticism in England and the United States from those who feared that it inaugurated a policy of making deals with fascists. Roosevelt defended Eisenhower's action as "a temporary expedient, justified solely by the stress of battle." The Darlan deal undoubtedly accelerated the Anglo-American military success in Algeria and Morocco, and Darlan's assassination on December 24 spared Roosevelt and Churchill political embarrassment. But they offended de Gaulle again by giving much of Darlan's authority to Giraud, whose prestige in North Africa turned out to be overrated.

In the meantime, Hitler, after ordering the occupation of Vichy France, rushed German troops by sea and air to Tunisia. Eisenhower promptly advanced into Tunisia from the west, while the British Eighth Army, under the command of General Bernard Montgomery, entered from Tripoli to the east. The Anglo-American forces encountered the brilliant generalship of Field Marshal Rommel, who came to be known as the Desert Fox. Nonetheless, the Anglo-American vise closed inexorably. On May 12, 1943, the Axis troops surrendered. The British and Americans had captured or destroyed fifteen Axis divisions, had regained the Mediterranean for their shipping, and had thereby laid open to attack what Churchill called the "soft underbelly" of the Axis.

Across the Channel in '42: the opposition

The Mediterranean or France? "All right, but where do we go from there?" Roosevelt had asked. As the Joint Chiefs of Staff had feared, the British advocated moving on into Sicily and Italy in order to maintain the initiative in the Mediterranean. The Americans reluctantly accepted this logic. The result was the invasion of Sicily in July and of Italy in September. When Mussolini fell from his dictatorial seat, Eisenhower, with the approval of Roosevelt and Churchill, reorganized a new Italian government under Field Marshal Pietro Badoglio and the reigning king, both fascists. As part of that deal, Badoglio made haste to surrender, and it seemed as if the campaign would produce quick results. But, despite the Italian collapse, the German forces in Italy put up dogged resistance. The Italian front soon was marked by the most bitter and bloody fighting of the European war. When Allied progress up the spine of Italy was stopped at Monte Cassino early in 1944, an attempt was made to circumvent the enemy by amphibious landings at Anzio near Rome late in January. But for many weeks Allied troops could not break out of the Anzio beachhead, and Rome itself did not fall for another four months. In the end, the Italian campaign—especially beyond Rome—cost more and achieved less than its proponents had expected.

In the meantime, argument continued over the invasion of France. The British service chiefs still wanted to delay Overlord (the code name for the cross-Channel operation) for the sake of new adventures in the Mediterranean. But the American Joint Chiefs, with Soviet backing, insisted on a firm commitment to a second front in France. Postponement had already soured the Soviet temper, for the Russians were bearing the brunt of the fighting against the Nazis. At the end of November 1943, Churchill finally consented to May 1944 as a target date.

The actual invasion, scheduled, as Churchill said, "mainly by the moon and the weather," did not take place until June 6. The Germans, deceived by

Normandy beachhead, June 6, 1944

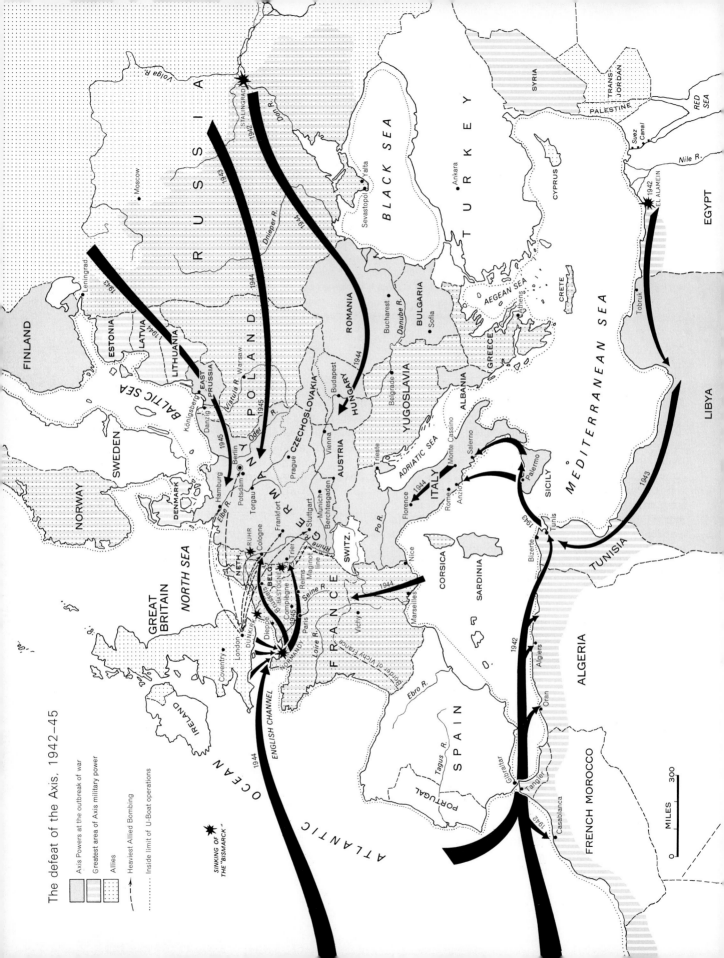

The defeat of the Axis, 1942–45

Axis Powers at the outbreak of war

Greatest area of Axis military power

Allies

Heaviest Allied Bombing

Inside limit of U-Boat operations

SINKING OF THE "BISMARCK"

GREAT BRITAIN

IRELAND

NORTH SEA

ATLANTIC OCEAN

ENGLISH CHANNEL

NORWAY

SWEDEN

FINLAND

BALTIC SEA

DENMARK

Leningrad

Moscow

R U S S I A

Volga R.

Don R.

Dnieper R.

STALINGRAD 1942

Yalta

BLACK SEA

Sevastopol

T U R K E Y

Ankara

CYPRUS

SYRIA

TRANS-JORDAN

PALESTINE

RED SEA

Nile R.

Suez Canal

EGYPT

EL ALAMEIN 1942

LIBYA

Tobruk

MEDITERRANEAN SEA

CRETE

AEGEAN SEA

Athens

GREECE

ALBANIA

ADRIATIC SEA

YUGOSLAVIA

Belgrade

Trieste

BULGARIA

Sofia

Danube R.

Bucharest

ROMANIA

HUNGARY

Budapest

Vienna

AUSTRIA

Prague

CZECHOLOVAKIA

P O L A N D

Warsaw

Vistula R.

Odel R.

Danzig

EAST PRUSSIA

Königsberg

LITHUANIA

LATVIA

ESTONIA

Berlin

Potsdam

Torgau

Hamburg

Elbe R.

RUHR

Cologne

Frankfort

Trier

NETH.

BELG.

BASTOGNE

Brussels

Dunkirk

London

Coventry

Dieppe

Paris

Compiègne

Reims

Seine R.

Maginot line

Rhine R.

Stuttgart

Munich

Berchtesgaden

SWITZ.

Po R.

Florence

Rome

Anzio

Monte Cassino

Salerno

I T A L Y

SICILY

Palermo

SARDINIA

CORSICA

Nice

Marseilles

F R A N C E

Loire R.

Vichy

Border of Vichy France

Ebro R.

Tagus R.

S P A I N

PORTUGAL

Gibraltar

Tanger

FRENCH MOROCCO

Casablanca

Oran

Algiers

ALGERIA

TUNISIA

Tunis

Bizerte

G E R M A N Y

MILES

0   300

THE DEFEAT OF GERMANY

WESTERN FRONT			EASTERN FRONT
		January 20, 1942	Russian counteroffensive begins, reaches Kharkov May 12
		June 28, 1942	German summer offensive begins. Reaches Stalingrad Aug. 22
British stop German African drive at El Alamein	June 29, 1942		
British offensive begins with victory at El Alamein; Tobruk falls Nov. 13, Bengasi Nov. 20	November 4, 1942		
U.S. and British landings in North Africa. French sign armistice Nov. 11	November 8, 1942		
		November 19, 1942	Russian counteroffensive begins at Stalingrad
		January 18, 1943	Russians raise siege at Leningrad
British take Tripoli	January 24, 1943		
		February 2, 1943	Germans surrender at Stalingrad
		February 14, 1943	Russians take Rostov, followed by Kharkov Feb. 16, Rzhev Mar. 9
U.S. and British lines meet in North Africa	April 7, 1943		
British take Tunis, Americans take Bizerte	May 7, 1943		
Surrender of Axis in North Africa	May 13, 1943		
Invasion of Sicily, completed August 17	July 10, 1943		
Resignation of Mussolini	July 25, 1943		
		August 4, 1943	Russians reverse German offensive and take Orel and Belgurod
British troops invade Italy	September 3, 1943		
Unconditional surrender of Italy	September 8, 1943		
Americans invade Salerno. Allied advance begins, crosses Volturno River Oct. 14, reaches Sangro River Dec. 25	September 9, 1943		
		September 25, 1943	Russian advance takes Smolensk, moves on to Kiev Nov. 7, enters Poland Jan. 3, 1944
Landing at Anzio	January 22, 1944		
		January 29, 1944	Moscow-Leningrad area clear of German forces
		April 10, 1944	Russians take Odessa
		May 9, 1944	Russians take Sevastopol
Cassino falls after two month battle	May 18, 1944		
Allied invasion of Normandy	June 6, 1944		
		June 23, 1944	Russians begin summer offensive south of Leningrad
Cherbourg captured	June 27, 1944		
Caen falls	July 9, 1944		
American "Break Out" at St. Lo	July 25, 1944		
British take Florence, Italy	August 12, 1944		
Americans invade southern France	August 15, 1944		
Liberation of Paris	August 25, 1944		
Liberation of Brussels and Antwerp	September 4, 1944		
		September 8, 1944	Surrender of Bulgaria
Liberation of Luxembourg	September 11, 1944		
American forces enter Germany	September 12, 1944		
		September 22, 1944	Russians take Tallinn
		October 20, 1944	Russians enter East Prussia; seize Belgrade, Yugoslavia
Americans take Aachen, followed by Metz, Nov. 22, Strasbourg, Nov. 23	October 21, 1944		
German counteroffensive and Battle of the Bulge until Dec. 26	December 16, 1944		
		December 29, 1944	Russians take Budapest, Hungary
		January 12, 1945	Russians advance in Poland, Warsaw falls Jan. 17, Lodz Jan. 19. Russians at Oder River Jan. 23
British offensive in Holland	February 8, 1945		
Americans cross Saar River	February 22, 1945		
Fall of Cologne and Düsseldorf. Americans capture Remagen Bridge across Rhine	March 7, 1945		
Americans reach Elbe River	April 11, 1945		
		April 13, 1945	Russians begin drive to Berlin, enter Apr. 24
Americans take Nuremberg	April 21, 1945		
Americans meet Russians at Torgau	April 25, 1945	April 25, 1945	Russians meet Americans at Torgau
		May 2, 1945	Berlin falls
Unconditional surrender of Germany. May 8 end of war in Europe	May 7, 1945		

elaborate stratagems, did not expect an attack in Normandy. The Allied forces were thus able to consolidate their position and fan out for movement along a larger front. On July 25 General George Patton's Third Army broke through into Brittany. The war in France now developed extraordinary mobility. American and British divisions raced toward Paris, which was liberated on August 25; and by September 13 Allied forces had penetrated deep into Belgium and crossed the German frontier at Aachen.

These developments, on top of the long-sustained Anglo-American air offensive against Germany, made Hitler's situation more desperate every day. From 1942, when the British and American air forces took substantial command of the air, Germany had been subjected to a series of devastating air raids. Though they were less effective than their advocates claimed at the time, by the autumn of 1944, Allied air attacks—which by the end of the war amounted to 1.5 million bomber sorties and 2.7 million tons of bombs dropped—were exerting a heavy toll on German production (most essentially, of fighter aircraft), and rail and road transportation. The raids also destroyed German cities with inevitable cruelty and ultimately damaged German civilian morale.

In addition, a Soviet offensive, timed to coincide with the Anglo-American landings in France, was driving the Germans back in the east. Indeed, on D-day there were 165 German divisions on the eastern front as against 131 in the west and south. The Russians, who suffered enormous losses throughout the war, seemed to most Germans to be their most fearful enemies. As morale dropped even among high-ranking German officers, an attempt on Hitler's life on July 20, 1944, provided heartening evidence of resistance within the *Reich*.

General Montgomery, the top British commander in the west, now urged Eisenhower to concentrate all Allied resources on ending the war by a single decisive thrust into Germany. Eisenhower, looking at Allied port and trucking facilities, concluded that logistic support was lacking for the Montgomery plan. Accordingly, in a controversial decision, he settled instead for a "broad-front" strategy of building up strength along the entire western front in preparation for a general advance into Germany.

Southern France or the Ljublana Gap? A final argument over strategy remained. The Americans had long wished to follow up the invasion of Normandy with troop landings in southern France; Eisenhower regarded this as essential to the invasion of Germany. The British wanted to switch the whole operation to the east and mount instead an invasion through Trieste and the Ljublana Gap of Yugoslavia toward Vienna.

This debate gave rise to the subsequent myth that Churchill, wishing to forestall the Soviet advance into Eastern Europe, favored a Balkan invasion rather than a second front in France. Actually Churchill's Mediterranean strategy of 1942–43 was based on military considerations. Churchill never advocated an invasion of the Balkans, as an alternative to the second front or otherwise. The proposed attack through the Ljublana Gap in 1944—the "stab in the Adriatic armpit," as Churchill called it—would have left most of the Balkans untouched.

By 1944, it is true, Churchill was becoming increasingly concerned over the spread of Soviet power, and a definite object of the Ljublana plan was to beat the Russians to Vienna. The Americans rejected the proposal, partly because of the logistic difficulties presented by an Istrian campaign, partly because Roosevelt expected to be able to resolve any postwar political difficulties with the Soviet Union. And so the invasion of southern France took place according to schedule on August 15, 1944. With the fresh Allied advance up the Rhone Valley, the iron ring around Germany was drawing tight.

The war in the Pacific

Holding the line. Though the European theater of war had priority, the United States and Great Britain did not neglect the Far East. Pearl Harbor had marked only the beginning of a period of exultant Japanese aggression. "For three months after the Pearl Harbor attack," Admiral Samuel Eliot Morison has written, "the Pacific was practically a Japanese lake." One after another the bastions of western empire fell to the Japanese: Guam, Wake Island, and Hong Kong in December 1941; Singapore in February 1942; Java in March; and, after the terrible holding action on Bataan, the Philippines in May. Japanese forces were moving into Burma and threatening advances as far to the west as India and to the south as Australia. Japanese politicians were looking forward to the formation of the Greater East Asia Co-Prosperity Sphere, where Japan would mobilize the power of East Asia behind a wall of air and naval defense.

The Allied forces in the Pacific felt themselves the stepchildren of the war. Still, even when they believed themselves starved for supplies, their situation was by no means hopeless. The Japanese had failed to destroy a single aircraft-carrier at Pearl Harbor; and the American carrier striking force was not only able to secure the South Pacific supply line between Hawaii and Australia but could conduct sporadic harassments of the enemy (including an air raid on Tokyo in April 1942).

Moreover, the Japanese themselves, instead of pausing for consolidation, struck out on ambitious new programs of conquest in the spring of 1942. Japanese political leaders hoped to extend the sway of the emperor by isolating and perhaps invading Australia; and Admiral Yamamoto, the chief Japanese sea lord, wished to force the American Pacific Fleet into a final engagement before it had a chance to recoup the losses of Pearl Harbor. In May 1942, therefore, the Japanese occupied Tulagi in the Solomon Islands and launched a naval expedition across the Coral Sea toward Port Moresby in Papua, New Guinea. But an American carrier task force intercepted the Japanese ships, and, in an extraordinary battle of carrier-based aircraft, the Americans turned back the enemy. This was the first sea battle in history in which the ships involved exchanged no shots—indeed, did not even come within sight of one another.

The Battle of the Coral Sea marked the high point of Japanese initiative in the south. Yamamoto now shifted his operations to the north-central Pacific. A month later, the bulk of the Japanese navy—some two hundred ships—headed toward Midway Island and the western Aleutians. But the Americans, having broken the Japanese code, were able to anticipate enemy intentions. There followed the decisive naval battle of the war, in which the American fleets, brilliantly led by Admirals Raymond A. Spruance and Frank J. Fletcher, destroyed four Japanese aircraft-carriers and many other ships and forced the enemy into

Tarawa

General Douglas MacArthur:
emotional arguments and a solemn promise

disorderly retreat. The Japanese never again had sufficient naval air strength to take the long-range offensive.

The road to Tokyo. The threat to communications from Hawaii to Australia remained, however, so long as the Japanese held bases in the Solomons and the Bismarcks. Moreover, the Bismarck Barrier, a chain of small islands, gave the Japanese a powerful defense block athwart the road to Tokyo. Intelligence reports that the Japanese were building an airstrip on the island of Guadalcanal in the Solomons precipitated American action in August 1942. There followed six months of grueling combat in the steaming, fetid jungles of Guadalcanal and in the serene waters around the island. By February 1943 the Japanese abandoned Guadalcanal.

In January 1943 the Joint Chiefs, noting that only 15 percent of Allied resources was applied to the Pacific, argued for enough additional strength to permit the launching of an offensive. The British acquiesced, stipulating only that Pacific operations should be kept within such limits as would not handicap the war against Germany. The American planners—for the Pacific war was accepted as essentially an American responsibility—now considered the question of the best route to Tokyo.

If European strategy was a compromise between diverging American and British views, Pacific strategy was a compromise between the diverging views of the American army and navy. General Douglas MacArthur, who had been American commander in the Philippines and had been evacuated to Australia early in 1942 to take command of the army in the South Pacific, argued forcefully for an advance from the South Pacific through New Guinea to the Philippines and then to Japan. Admiral Chester Nimitz, on

THE DEFEAT OF JAPAN

ISLAND WARFARE The South Pacific: MacArthur			ISLAND WARFARE The Central Pacific: Nimitz
Marines land on Guadalcanal, campaign to control Solomon Islands begins. Feb. 9, 1943, Japanese abandon Guadalcanal	August 7, 1942		
Counteroffensive at Papua begins reconquest of New Guinea, completed Sept. 16, 1943	January 23, 1943		
Landings at Rendova, New Georgia	June 30, 1943		
Landings at Bougainville, Northern Solomons. Solomons secure by end of year	November 1, 1943		
		November 21, 1943	Landings at Tarawa and Makin Islands begin battle for the Gilbert Islands and campaign for the Central Pacific. Tarawa secure November 24
		January 31, 1944	Invasion of Marshall Islands. Roi and Namur fall Feb. 3, Kwajalein Feb. 6, Eniwetok Feb. 22
Invasion of Admiralty Islands. Secure Mar. 25	March 1, 1944		
Conquests of air base, Hollandia, Dutch New Guinea	April 22, 1944		
		June 15, 1944	Invasion of Saipan, Marianas Islands. Secure July 9. Air raids of super-fortresses against Japan from Saipan begin November 24
		July 21, 1944	Invasion of Guam, Marianas Islands. Secure Aug. 9
Invasion of Morotai	September 15, 1944	September 15, 1944	Invasion of Peleliu, Palaus Islands. Islands secure Nov. 25
Invasion of Leyte, Philippine Islands	October 29, 1944		
Invasion of Mindoro, Philippine Islands	December 15, 1944		
Invasion of Luzon, Philippine Islands. Fall of Manila Feb. 25	January 9, 1945		
		February 17, 1945	Invasion of Iwo Jima. Secure March 17
		April 1, 1945	Invasion of Okinawa. Secure June 21
		August 6, 1945	Hiroshima. Soviet Union enters war Aug. 8. Nagasaki Aug. 9
		August 10, 1945	Japanese offer of surrender

behalf of the navy, contended for an advance through the central Pacific to Formosa, the Chinese coast, and thence to Japan. MacArthur protested that this would be a gravely mistaken diversion of limited resources. But the navy responded persuasively that a single axis of advance would allow the Japanese to concentrate their defensive action. In the end the Joint Chiefs in Washington decided on parallel offensives along both routes.

The invention of new tactical techniques facilitated the American offensive. In March 1943, in the Battle of the Bismarck Sea, General George Kenney's bombers destroyed a Japanese troop convoy headed for New Guinea—an action that dissuaded the Japanese thereafter from attempting to move large bodies of troops within range of Allied air power. Knowing that the Japanese would not risk large-scale reinforcement, American forces could simply bypass the stronger Japanese bases. This "leapfrogging" technique became the basic pattern of the American counteroffensive.

By March 1944 Nimitz' forces had leapfrogged at Tarawa and Kwajalein, and MacArthur's forces had broken the Bismarck Barrier. Nimitz was now moving into the Marianas; in June the Pacific Fleet under Admiral Spruance smashed the Japanese navy again in the Battle of the Philippine Sea; MacArthur continued to press along the northwest coast of New Guinea toward the Philippines (see map, p. 697). The time was approaching for a final decision about the road to Tokyo.

Luzon or Formosa? MacArthur insisted on the recapture of the Philippines, and especially of Luzon, as the indispensable preliminary. He invoked not only strategic arguments—that Luzon would be a safer staging area for invasion than Formosa (Taiwan)—but political and emotional arguments. Was the President willing, the general asked, "to accept responsibility for breaking a solemn promise to eighteen million Christian Filipinos that the Americans would return?" (The promise had been MacArthur's.) Admirals King and Nimitz advocated leapfrogging part or all of the Philippines in the interest of an immediate attack on

The world in flames

The Second World War in the Pacific

Formosa. In a conference at Pearl Harbor in July 1944, Roosevelt leaned toward the MacArthur view but did not settle the question in MacArthur's favor until early October.

Once given the signal, MacArthur lost no time. On October 20 he disembarked on the beach at Leyte, saying, "People of the Philippines: I have returned." A few days later, in the Battle of Leyte Gulf, the American navy in the Philippines completed the destruction of Japanese naval striking power; in number of ships engaged, this was the greatest naval battle of all history. MacArthur's troops meanwhile pressed on toward Manila, while Nimitz' forces were making their way toward Japan from the central Pacific. Japan itself was now under a stern naval blockade and ever more devastating air attacks.

The riddle of China. Washington had hoped that China could play a leading role in the war against Japan. Indeed, through the war, Roosevelt, despite Churchill's skepticism, persisted in treating China as if it were a major power. However, the Nationalist regime of Chiang Kai-shek—driven into the interior, cut off from sources of supply, exhausted by four years of war, and demoralized by inflation, intrigue, and graft—was increasingly incapable of serious action.

Keeping China in the war nevertheless remained a major American objective. In 1941 and 1942 the Chinese government, now established in Chungking, received a trickle of supplies flown over the "hump" of the Himalayas from India. Then in 1943 an assortment of Chinese, Indian, and American troops, under the command of General Joseph W. Stilwell, began to construct a road and pipeline across northern Burma to Kunming. Soon Stilwell was sent to Chungking as commander of the American forces in China, with orders to maximize the Chinese contribution to the war against Japan. But, where Stilwell saw only one enemy, he discovered that Chiang Kai-shek saw a second—the increasingly powerful Chinese communists, spreading out from their base in Yenan.

Seeking particularly to mobilize the poverty-stricken and land-hungry peasants, the communists won respect, even among Westerners, as an embodiment of reform, austerity, and discipline. War sharpened the contrast between the self-indulgence of Chungking and the dedication of Yenan. Chiang himself seemed to be paying less and less attention to Japan in his preoccupation with the threat of Mao

Tse-tung and his Eighth Route Army. By 1944 four hundred thousand Nationalist troops had been diverted to check the spread of communist influence. Stilwell, eager to get as many Chinese divisions as possible—whatever their politics—into action against the Japanese, soon came to consider Chiang a main obstacle to the fulfillment of his mission.

In June 1944 the Fourteenth Air Force began to attack Japan from Chinese airstrips. This action provoked the Japanese into counterattacking the bomber bases and renewing their offensive against Chungking. Now the difficulties between Stilwell and Chiang came to a head. A brave, narrow, intense man, Stilwell was devoid of diplomatic skill and baffled by the unfathomable depths of Chinese politics. When the Joint Chiefs recommended that the Chinese army be placed under Stilwell's command, Chiang instead demanded his dismissal. Roosevelt complied. The military potential of China was disappearing in the swirl of Chinese civil discord.

The fourth term

Politics as usual. The congressional elections of 1942 brought into office the most conservative Congress Washington had known for a decade. Congressional refusal in the spring of 1943 to continue the National Resources Planning Board was a symbolic rejection of the whole idea of New Deal planning. Passage in June of the Smith-Connally Act over Roosevelt's veto bestowed on a reluctant government new powers to crack down on trade unions in labor disputes. Congress liquidated the National Youth Administration, harassed the Farm Security Administration, and sought in a variety of ways to curtail social functions and expenditures.

Roosevelt himself gave ground before the conservative attack. In a press conference in December 1943 he explained that the New Deal had come into existence because the United States was suffering from a grave internal disorder. But in December 1941 the patient had been in a bad external smashup. "Old Dr. New Deal didn't know 'nothing' about legs and arms. He knew a great deal about internal medicine, but nothing about surgery. So he got his partner, who was an orthopedic surgeon, Dr. Win-the-War, to take care of this fellow who had been in this bad accident." Roosevelt went on to praise the ministrations of Dr. New Deal but added, "At the present time, obviously, the principal emphasis, the overwhelming first emphasis should be on winning the war."

The occupation of the White House by Dr. Win-the-War had already engendered a certain disenchantment in the American liberal community. Though Roosevelt retained the essential confidence of liberals, he was no longer articulating their day-to-day hopes. Many of them had been upset by his wartime suspension of antitrust proceedings, by his relationships with Darlan and Badoglio, and by his tepid policies toward civil rights. In their frustration, they listened to other voices. They found consolation in particular in Vice President Henry Wallace, with his celebration of "the century of the common man," and, more surprisingly, in Wendell Willkie, the Republican presidential candidate of 1940 (see p. 673). In the years after his defeat, Willkie had shown himself a political leader generous in disposition and courageous in utterance. Increasingly he was a champion of civil rights and a critic of big business. His book *One World*, published in 1943 after his trip as a presidential emissary to Britain, the Soviet Union, the Middle East, and China seemed to sum up the best aspirations of American liberal internationalism.

The campaign of 1944. As the titular leader of the Republican party, Willkie retained hopes of a second presidential nomination in 1944. But his liberal tendencies, on top of a chronic political maladroitness, had estranged most of the leaders of his party. After suffering a bad defeat in the Wisconsin presidential primary in April, he withdrew from the race. Thomas E. Dewey, who had been elected governor of New York in 1942, was now emerging as the favored Republican contender. A young man—he had just passed his forty-second birthday—he had already gained a reputation for executive efficiency and vigor. The Republican convention, meeting in Chicago at the end of June, promptly nominated Dewey on the first ballot. To balance Dewey's growing inclinations toward liberalism and internationalism, Governor John W. Bricker of Ohio, a conservative isolationist, was named for second place.

The Democrats renominated Roosevelt without suffering the trauma of 1940. "For myself, I do not want to run," he wrote the chairman of the Democratic National Committee in July. "All that is within me cries to go back to my home on the Hudson. . . . But as a good soldier . . . I will accept and serve." The struggle was over the vice-presidential nomination. Wallace, with the ardent support of the labor-liberal wing of the party, sought renomination. But the Democratic bosses opposed him, and, though Roosevelt said he "personally" would vote for Wallace if a delegate, he did not insist on Wallace's renomination. For a time Roosevelt leaned toward James F. Byrnes. When Ed Flynn of New York and Sidney Hillman of the Amalgamated Clothing Workers vetoed Byrnes, Roosevelt said he would be "very glad to run" with either Senator Harry S Truman of Missouri or Justice

William O. Douglas of the Supreme Court. The contest narrowed down to Truman and Wallace, and Truman, with Roosevelt's private support, won on the third ballot.

The campaign was overshadowed by the war. The initial restraint of Dewey's speeches failed to stir the electorate. He stepped up the harshness of his attack, but his main achievement was to force Roosevelt himself into the arena. An uproariously successful speech by Roosevelt before the Teamsters Union in Washington on September 23 showed that the old campaigner had lost none of his magic. In October he sought to meet doubts about his health by riding around New York City all day in an open car through pouring rain. In the meantime, he spoke with eloquence about the need for internationalism in the postwar world and for a postwar economic bill of rights with federal guarantees to education, employment, and expanded social security. On November 7 Roosevelt received 25.6 million popular and 432 electoral votes as against 22 million and 99 for Dewey. The Democrats lost one seat in the Senate, gained twenty in the House, and captured five governorships. The election, though the closest of his triumphs, was a categorical confirmation of Roosevelt as America's chosen leader for the peace.

The diplomacy of coalition

The question of war aims. Even before Pearl Harbor Roosevelt had outlined his broad ideas on the postwar settlement. In his message to Congress on January 6, 1941, he said that the United States looked forward to a world founded upon "four essential human freedoms—freedom of speech and expression, freedom of worship, freedom from want, freedom from fear." In August of the same year, the Atlantic Charter (see p. 677) further particularized the American conception of the postwar world, laying stress on national self-determination, equal access to trade and raw materials, and a lasting peace to be achieved through a permanent system of general security. On January 1, 1942, twenty-six nations (led by the United States, Britain, the Soviet Union, and China) signed a joint declaration subscribing to the Atlantic Charter, pledging their full resources to victory, promising not to make a separate peace, and dedicating themselves to "defend life, liberty, independence, and religious freedom, and to preserve human rights and justice in their own lands as well as in other lands." Roosevelt called this a "declaration by United Nations," and his phrase was employed thereafter to describe the grand alliance.

In practice, three of the United Nations—the United States, Britain, and the Soviet Union—were more important than the rest. The United States and Britain, with common traditions and interests, had little difficulty in establishing partnership. Roosevelt and Churchill regarded each other with mutual respect and delight and were almost immediately on intimate terms. The formation of the Anglo-American Combined Chiefs of Staff in December 1941 guaranteed close military coordination; combined boards were subsequently set up in other fields. Friction, of course, was not entirely eliminated. There were persistent differences over European strategy, and Churchill quickly made it clear that he had no intention of applying the Atlantic Charter to British possessions. "We mean to hold our own," he said. "I have not become the King's First Minister in order to preside over the liquidation of the British Empire." Nonetheless, disagreements were held within a framework of reciprocal confidence.

With regard to the postwar world, Churchill, though by instinct a balance-of-power man, was prepared to go a considerable distance with Roosevelt's version of the United Nations as the keystone of a peace system. In Wilsonian rhetoric, Roosevelt declared that peace must "spell the end of the system of unilateral action, the exclusive alliances, the spheres of influence, the balances of power, and all the other expedients that have been tried for centuries—and have always failed." A reversion to those principles, he believed, would create the conditions for future wars; it would also mean the repudiation of the Atlantic Charter, the Four Freedoms, and the values for which the war had presumably been fought. Roosevelt expected the four great powers—the United States, the United Kingdom, the Soviet Union, and China—to work in concert to keep the peace. He also viewed the United States as the dominant influence in the Americas. Still, he recognized that all nations had an interest in all the affairs of the globe, and all would therefore deserve representation in a postwar international organization. As he saw it, moreover, international prosperity was to be assured by the reduction of barriers to an expanding world trade.

The Russians viewed the world primarily in terms of spheres of influence and balances of power. They placed little confidence in the United Nations. Their physical safety, as they read their bitter historical experience, demanded the absolute guarantee that all states along the Russian border in eastern Europe should have "friendly governments," by which they meant governments reliably subservient to Moscow. They had no intention of allowing other states a role in eastern Europe. In 1939 the Soviet-Nazi pact had enabled Russia to begin to fulfill part of what it considered its security requirements through the acquisition of the Baltic states, Karelian Finland, and eastern Poland. In November 1940 Moscow had pressed further demands on Hitler—a free hand in Finland, predominance in Romania and Bulgaria, bases in the Dardanelles. After the German attack, Stalin hoped to gain from the West what Hitler had not dared yield him.

These were traditional Russian objectives not dependent on ideology. But ideology intensified the possibilities of discord. The Soviet view, grounded in the Marxist-Leninist analysis of history, excluded the idea of long-term peace between communist and capitalist states. The very existence of the United States as the citadel of capitalism was, by definition, a deadly threat to the security of the Soviet Union. Even the existence of independent communist states, like Yugoslavia, turned out to be objectionable to Stalin. While short-term accommodations with capitalism might be undertaken for tactical reasons, such arrangements would at best be an armed truce. But Stalin was not necessarily the helpless prisoner of this ideology. He saw himself less as the disciple of Marx and Lenin than as their fellow prophet. Sensing that Stalin was the only force capable of overcoming Stalinism, Roosevelt placed great emphasis on his personal relations with the Soviet leader.

So long, however, as Russian survival depended on the establishment of a second front, Moscow's purposes, whether strategic or ideological, were muted. Thus the Soviet government adhered to the Atlantic Charter (though with a reservation about adapting its principles to "the circumstances, needs, and historic peculiarities of particular countries") and acquiesced in the British refusal, under American pressure, to recognize the Soviet conquest of the Baltic republics. But Stalin's basic hope, as expressed in a proposal to Britain at the end of 1941, was for a straight sphere-of-influence deal.

The early wartime conferences. It soon became evident that the diplomacy of coalition required not only constant communication among the nations but periodic face-to-face meetings among their leaders. Thus Churchill followed his Washington visit in December 1941–January 1942 with a visit to Moscow in August, where he explained to an angry Stalin the reasons for the postponement of the second front ("Now they know the worst," he wrote Roosevelt, "and having made their protest are entirely friendly; this in spite of the fact that this is their most anxious and agonizing time").

The successes in North Africa at the end of 1942 opened a new phase of the war and emphasized the need for a conference among all three leaders. Stalin, however, felt that he could not leave the Soviet Union; so Roosevelt and Churchill met with their staffs at Casablanca on the Atlantic coast of Morocco in January 1943. The Casablanca Conference laid plans for future military action in the Mediterranean. Roosevelt and Churchill also sought, with little success, to unite the anti-Vichy French by bringing about a reconciliation between General de Gaulle and General Giraud. The main contribution of Casablanca, however, was the doctrine of "unconditional surrender."

By unconditional surrender Roosevelt meant no more than the surrender by Axis governments without conditions—that is, without assurance of the survival of the political leadership that had brought on the war. "It does not mean," he explained at Casablanca, "the destruction of the population of Germany, Italy, or Japan, but it does mean the destruction of the philosophies in those countries which are based on conquest and the subjugation of other people." Unconditional surrender was not a last-minute improvisation. It had been discussed in the State Department since the preceding spring and had been raised with Churchill (who, in turn, raised it with the British War Cabinet) before the press conference at which it was announced. The doctrine was designed partly to overcome misgivings generated by the Anglo-American willingness to deal with Darlan but even more to prevent Hitler from breaking up the Allied coalition by playing off one side against the other. The fear that the Soviet Union might seek a separate peace with Germany haunted British and American policy-makers in 1942–43, and unconditional surrender seemed the best insurance against such an eventuality.

Critics have subsequently claimed that unconditional surrender stiffened Axis resistance and prolonged the war. This argument is not easy to substantiate with regard to the European war. Unconditional surrender had no effect at all in delaying the Italian surrender. In the case of Germany, no one seems to have been deterred from surrendering who would have surrendered otherwise, and up to the last moment such Nazi leaders as Goering and Himmler were sure they could work out their own deals with the Allies. An associated argument that unconditional surrender played into the hands of the communists by creating a power vacuum in central Europe seems odd in view of the fact that Stalin tried hard in 1944 to persuade Roosevelt and Churchill to modify the doctrine.

From Big Two to Big Three. Roosevelt and Churchill met again in Washington in May 1943, and in Quebec in August. Both meetings dealt mainly with Anglo-American military questions. The Soviet Union still remained outside the conference circuit until October, when Cordell Hull and Anthony Eden journeyed to Moscow to pave the way for a meeting of the Big Three.

Relations between the Soviet Union and its western allies were now somewhat ambivalent. On the one hand, a temporary recession of ideology was evident when Stalin, in order to rally his people against the invader, replaced the appeal of Marxism with that of nationalism. "We are under no illusions that they are fighting for us," he once observed to Averell Harriman, the American ambassador. "They are fighting for Mother Russia." In May 1943 the Comintern, the instrumentality of communist revolution, was dissolved.

On the other hand, shadows of future problems were casting themselves ahead, especially in the liberated nations. The Soviet Union protested its exclusion from the Allied Control Commission for Italy. It had made clear its disinclination to relinquish the part of Poland it had seized in 1939, and in April 1943 it broke off relations with the Polish government-in-exile in London because the Poles asked the International Red Cross to investigate German charges, probably accurate, that the Russians had massacred several thousand Polish officers at Katyn. In Yugoslavia, the communist partisans, led by Marshal Tito, were already in conflict with a monarchist resistance movement of Chetniks led by General Mihailovich. A similar feud between communist and noncommunist guerrillas divided the resistance movement in Greece. Further, Roosevelt, at Churchill's instigation, had decided to keep secret Anglo-American development of certain weapons, of which the most important was the atomic bomb, then still far from completion. That secrecy reflected an uncertainty about Soviet intentions, a reservation about postwar cooperation, of which Stalin was aware. He harbored similar reservations himself.

But such events remained in the background when the foreign secretaries met in October. Molotov, the Soviet foreign secretary, went agreeably along with a statement of pieties advocated by Hull and soon issued as the Declaration of Moscow. This included affirmation of "the necessity of establishing at the earliest practicable date a general international organization . . . for the maintenance of international peace." The Moscow Conference also established the European Advisory Commission to plan for German collapse.

The next step was the long-delayed meeting of the three leaders, arranged for Teheran in late November. This was preceded by a separate conference in Cairo where Roosevelt and Churchill met with Chiang Kai-shek; Stalin did not take part because Russia was not in the Far Eastern war. The Cairo Declaration promised to strip Japan of its conquests, to free Korea, and to return Manchuria and Taiwan to China. The Teheran meeting concentrated on military problems, including an Anglo-American commitment to a cross-Channel invasion within six months. The meeting also considered the future of Germany, problems in Eastern Europe and the Far East, and the shape of the postwar peace system. "We came here with hope and determination," the three leaders wrote in the Declaration of Teheran. "We leave here, friends in fact, in spirit and in purpose."

Postwar planning. More progress was made in defining the structure of the future international organization when the Allies met at Dumbarton Oaks in Washington in August–September 1944. But the creation of broad frameworks for postwar collaboration did not solve the concrete problems of the postwar settlement. The fate of Germany posed especially perplexing questions. All members of the Big Three had played at one time or another with notions of German dismemberment; this approach seemed to prevail as late as Teheran. But when the European Advisory Commission took over, dismemberment receded into the background. The EAC concentrated instead on determining the zones of Allied occupation. In the end, Britain took the northwestern zone, America the southwestern, and Russia the eastern. Berlin, though situated in the Soviet zone, was to be jointly held; the question of access to Berlin was left, on military advice, to the commanders in the field.

As for the German economy, the most drastic proposals came from the United States Treasury Department in August 1944. Secretary Morgenthau urged both territorial transfers and partition; in addition, he recommended the dismantling of German heavy industry and the transformation of Germany into an agricultural state. For a moment Roosevelt fell in with the Morgenthau plan. Even Churchill accepted it briefly during the second Quebec Conference in September, partly in the hope of securing postwar economic aid in exchange. But in a few weeks this scheme dropped by the wayside, though its emphasis on a Spartan treatment of occupied Germany remained American doctrine.

Growing doubts about Soviet policy compounded the uncertainty over the future. The Polish question was more acute than ever. Churchill, in an effort to restore the position of the Polish government-in-exile in London, had been urging that government to accept Soviet territorial demands, including the Curzon line to the east and (in compensation) the Oder-Neisse line to the west (see map, p. 714); in November 1944 the British government pledged support for the Oder-Neisse line even if the United States refused to go along. But Stalin, who saw Poland as "the corridor for attack on Russia," considered the Polish question as "one of life and death" and refused to accept the

London regime. In August the Polish Home Army, whose affiliations were with London, set off a revolt against the Germans in Warsaw. The Red Army, a few miles outside the city, declined to aid the uprising; the Soviet Union would not even permit planes carrying supplies to Warsaw from the west to land on Russian soil. This seemed a calculated attempt to destroy noncommunist Poles. In addition, the Soviet Union was setting up a group of procommunists in Lublin as the nucleus of a postwar Polish government. And, citing the Anglo-American example in Italy, the Russians, after the surrender of Bulgaria, denied the western Allies any role in the Bulgarian Control Commission.

In October Churchill paid another visit to Moscow. His effort to bring about a reconciliation between the London and Lublin Poles failed; but he and Stalin agreed on a scheme for southeastern Europe, according to which in the period after liberation Britain would recognize Russia's predominant interest in Romania, Bulgaria, and Hungary, and Russia would recognize Britain's predominant interest in Greece, with Yugoslavia split fifty-fifty. Roosevelt went along with this only as a temporary wartime arrangement, but Stalin and perhaps Churchill too probably expected it to register postwar realities.

Triumph and tragedy

The Big Three at Yalta. Roosevelt's reelection in November 1944 found the Allied forces pressing hard down the last mile to victory. But bloodshed was far from over. With Eisenhower's forces deployed along the length of the Siegfried line, the Germans saw an opportunity in December 1944 to launch an attack in the Ardennes Forest. The desperate German offensive resulted in some early breakthroughs, but the Americans held at Bastogne, and, after weeks of severe fighting, the Battle of the Bulge came to an end in January. On the other side of the world, the Japanese continued their resistance. Manila was not liberated until February 1945; and the forces of Admiral Nimitz coming in from the central Pacific had to fight every step of the way before they could gain such islands to the south of Japan as Iwo Jima (in February) and Okinawa (in April).

The approach of victory did not simplify the political problems of the triumphant coalition. In December communist resistance groups revolted against the British-backed provisional government of newly liberated Greece. Though Stalin, respecting the October agreement, made no objection to Churchill's military intervention in Greece, the fact that local

Yalta, 1945: hopeful assumptions were soon to be falsified

The Big Three on Eastern Europe

communists had taken such initiative seemed a poor omen. The Polish tangle showed no signs of unraveling. The fate of Germany remained undecided. The future of eastern Europe and the Far East was still swathed in obscurity. The persistence of these problems argued for another meeting of the Big Three. They met in a conference at Yalta in the Crimea in February 1945.

Some of the decisions taken at Yalta pertained to Europe. The most critical of these had to do with the liberated nations of eastern Europe. Roosevelt and Churchill rejected Stalin's proposal that they accept the Lublin government in Poland. Instead, the three leaders agreed on a reorganization of the Polish government to include leaders from abroad—this provisional government to be "pledged to the holding of free and unfettered elections as soon as possible." For liberated Europe in general, the conference promised "interim governmental authorities broadly representative of all democratic elements in the population and pledged to the earliest possible establishment through free elections of governments responsive to the will of the people." With regard to Germany, the conference postponed decisions on dismemberment and on future frontiers, endorsed the EAC provisions for zonal occupation (adding a zone for France) and for an Allied Control Council, and evaded a Soviet demand

of $20 billion for German reparations while conceding the figure as a "basis for discussion."

The Yalta discussions also dealt with the Far East, where the American Joint Chiefs were eager to secure from Stalin a precise commitment about entering the war. While Stalin had said vaguely in 1943 that the Soviet Union would declare war on Japan after the defeat of Germany, some feared that Russia would let the United States undertake a costly invasion of Japan and then move into Manchuria and China at the last minute to reap the benefits of victory. Moreover, the military estimated that the invasion of Japan, scheduled for the spring of 1946, might cost over a million casualties to American forces alone—another reason for desiring early Soviet participation. In secret discussions with Roosevelt, Stalin agreed to declare war on Japan within two or three months after the surrender of Germany on condition that the Kurile Islands and southern Sakhalin be restored to Russia and that the commercial interest of the Soviet Union in Dairen and its rail communications be recognized. When Roosevelt obtained the assent of Chiang Kai-shek to these measures, the Soviet Union would agree "that China shall retain full sovereignty in Manchuria" and would conclude a treaty of friendship and alliance with the Chiang Kai-shek government.

A third topic at Yalta was the organization of the

United Nations. Here the Soviet Union accepted American proposals on voting procedure that it had opposed at Dumbarton Oaks and agreed that a United Nations conference should be called at San Francisco in April to prepare the charter for a permanent organization. With British support, the Russians also secured votes in the General Assembly for Byelorussia and the Ukraine. Roosevelt attached great importance to the apparent Soviet willingness to collaborate in a structure of international order. He doubtless also supposed that the deliberations of the United Nations, especially among the great powers, would provide the means of remedying the omissions or errors of the various summit conferences.

Roosevelt and Churchill returned from Yalta well satisfied. Churchill told the House of Commons:

> The impression I brought back . . . is that Marshal Stalin and the Soviet leaders wish to live in honourable friendship and equality with the Western democracies. I feel also that their word is their bond. I know of no Government which stands to its obligations, even in its own despite, more solidly than the Russian Soviet Government.

During the war the Soviet government had discharged its military commitments with commendable promptitude. The Yalta agreements, however, represented the first experiment in postwar political collaboration. Here, as Churchill himself later wrote, "Our hopeful assumptions were soon to be falsified. Still, they were the only ones possible at the time."

After the war right-wing critics wrote that Roosevelt and Churchill had perpetrated a "betrayal" at Yalta, selling eastern Europe and China "down the river" in a vain effort to "appease" Stalin. The Yalta text makes it hard to sustain such charges. Had the agreements been kept, eastern Europe would have had freely elected democratic governments and Chiang Kai-shek would have been confirmed in control of China and Manchuria. Stalin later abandoned his Yalta pledges in order to achieve his purposes. The Soviet Union, moreover, gained no territory as a result of Yalta (except the Kurile Islands) that was not already, or about to be, under Soviet domination as a result of military operations—and such operations could have been checked only by countervailing force from the West.

In more recent years left-wing critics have made opposite charges: that Stalin conceded more at Yalta than did Roosevelt and Churchill, and that behind American policy was an aggressive determination to dominate the world, promote counterrevolution and, in particular, make eastern Europe and the Far East safe for American capitalism. Again the Yalta documents fail to sustain such charges. Roosevelt re-

marked at Yalta that "two years would be the limit" for keeping American troops in Europe; and the evidence suggests that the western Allies would have been wholly satisfied with an eastern Europe composed of nations friendly to Russia and (in the words of a State Department analysis) "in favor of far-reaching economic and social reforms, but not, however, in favor of a left-wing totalitarian regime to achieve these reforms."

All in all, military realities at the time set the terms of the agreements at Yalta. Roosevelt let those realities take precedence over political considerations. Short of preparing for a war against the Soviet Union, he had no other choice. And as he saw it, American interests then lay essentially in speeding victory in Europe and Asia. Like Churchill, he could depend only on hopeful assumptions about the future of eastern Europe.

Victory in Europe. For the Soviet Union, cooperation with noncommunists had been a response to the rise of Nazism. The Yalta Conference, taking place in the shadow of the Ardennes counteroffensive, reflected the still dangerous Nazi military threat. But the picture began to alter rapidly. A fortnight after Yalta, the United States Ninth Army had reached the Rhine at Düsseldorf. With the end of the war in sight, the Soviet need for wartime cooperation was disappearing: it was now time to begin the postwar struggle for Europe. Within a few weeks the Soviet Union took swift action in Romania and Poland to frustrate the Yalta pledges of political freedom. Stalin himself opened up a political offensive against the West, charging that the United States and Britain were engaged in separate peace negotiations with Germany. Roosevelt replied with indignation that he deeply resented these "vile misrepresentations."

At the end of March 1945 Roosevelt cabled Churchill that he was "watching with anxiety and concern the development of the Soviet attitude." This attitude portended danger not only for immediate issues, but for "future world cooperation." The President sent stern warnings to the Soviet leader and on April 6 told Churchill, "We must not permit anybody to entertain a false impression that we are afraid. Our Armies will in a very few days be in a position that will permit us to become 'tougher' than has heretofore appeared advantageous to the war effort." But Roosevelt, worn out by long years of terrible responsibility, was reaching the end. On April 12 he died of a massive cerebral hemorrhage, as truly a casualty of war as any man who died in battle.

These ominous political developments put military problems in a new context. As the Anglo-American armies plunged ahead into Germany, Churchill argued in March and April that they should race the

The world in flames

Americans and Russians, Torgau, Germany, April 1945

Russians to Berlin. "From a political standpoint," he said, "we should march as far east into Germany as possible." But General Eisenhower replied, "I regard it as militarily unsound . . . to make Berlin a major objective." The imperative consideration, in the view of the American Joint Chiefs, was the destruction of the German armed forces; and this, Eisenhower believed (incorrectly, as it turned out), required the pursuit of the remaining German troops to a supposed last stand in the south.

A month later, Churchill renewed his pleading, this time in connection with Prague. The Allied liberation of Prague, he said, might "make the whole difference to the postwar situation in Czechoslovakia." He went on to propose that Allied forces remain as far east as they could until Soviet Russia clarified its intentions with regard to Poland and Germany. Harry S Truman, who had succeeded to the American Presidency, hesitated at suggestions for deeper American involvement in central Europe, partly because of a fear of prejudicing future Soviet cooperation with the United Nations, partly because of the need for redeploying American troops to the Pacific. He accordingly treated the problem as a tactical one to be decided by the commander in the field. Eisenhower, for his part, declined to abandon strictly military criteria in the absence of orders from above. Though he could have put American troops into Prague far in advance of the Red Army, he refused to do so. It is by no means clear that Churchill's plan would have basically changed the postwar balance in Europe. But it seems evident that the American generals, as General Omar Bradley later wrote, "looked naïvely on this British inclination to complicate the war with political foresight and non-military objectives."

By now events in Europe were rushing to climax. Hitler's thousand-year *Reich*, racked by months of Allied bombing and now overrun by Allied armies from both west and east, was falling to pieces. The German dictator himself took refuge in his bunker in Berlin and on April 30 committed suicide. On May 3 the process of piecemeal German surrender began, culminating in a final ceremony of unconditional surrender at Eisenhower's headquarters in Rheims on May 7. As Churchill later wrote, the end of hostilities was "the signal for the greatest outburst of joy in the history of mankind." He added somberly that he himself moved amid cheering crowds "with an aching heart and a mind oppressed by forebodings."

Victory in the Far East. While the European war was coming to its troubled end, American forces continued to make steady progress in the Pacific. But Japanese resistance grew every day more fanatical. The use of kamikaze suicide planes and the last-ditch fighting in Iwo Jima and Okinawa seemed to confirm the horrendous American estimates of casualties to be expected in an invasion of the homeland. Within civilian Japan, though, sensible people recognized that the war was irretrievably lost.

In the meantime, an extraordinary new factor entered into American calculations. In 1939 the scientist Albert Einstein had called Roosevelt's attention to the possibility of using atomic energy for military purposes. In the next years the government sponsored a secret $2 billion operation known as the Manhattan Project to attempt the building of an atomic bomb. A brilliant group of physicists, working under the direction of J. Robert Oppenheimer in Los Alamos, New Mexico, steadily broke down the incredibly complex scientific and technological problems involved in the production of the weapon. On April 25, 1945, Secretary of War Stimson could tell President Truman, "Within four months we shall in all probability have completed the most terrible weapon ever known in human history, one bomb of which could destroy a whole city."

The next question was how and when this frightful weapon should be employed. Roosevelt seems never to have doubted that, once available, the bomb would be dropped. The momentum of wartime atomic policy militated to that conclusion. On June 1 a special committee recommended to Truman that the bomb be used against Japan as soon as possible. Many Manhattan Project scientists, intimately aware of the ghastly character of the weapon, opposed this recommendation, favoring a preliminary demonstration to the world in a desert or on a barren island. But this course was rejected, partly because of the fear

that the bomb might not go off, partly because only two bombs would be available by August and it seemed essential to reserve them for direct military use.

Within Japan, a new government was looking for a way out. In July it requested Soviet mediation to bring the war to an end, though it added, "So long as the enemy demands unconditional surrender, we will fight as one man." Moscow was cold to this request while Stalin departed for a new Big Three meeting at Potsdam, near Berlin. At the same time, the American government, following the Japanese peace explorations through decoded cable intercepts, came to the conclusion that the best way to hasten the end of the war would be to issue a solemn plea to the Japanese to surrender before it was too late. This warning was embodied somewhat cryptically in a declaration issued at Potsdam by Truman and Clement Attlee, who had succeeded Churchill as British prime minister, urging the Japanese to give up or face "the utter devastation of the Japanese homeland." The Japanese government was inclined to accept this ultimatum, but the military leaders angrily disagreed. On July 28 the Japanese prime minister, in a statement designed for domestic consumption, pronounced the Potsdam Declaration "unworthy of public notice."

Truman had already been informed while at Potsdam that the first bomb test in New Mexico on July 17 had been a triumphant success. The rejection

of the Potsdam Declaration now convinced him that the militarists were in control of Tokyo and that there was no point in delaying the use of the bomb against Japan. Some of the President's advisers, Secretary of State Byrnes particularly, believed that the use of the bomb would enhance the American position in negotiations with the Soviet Union. For Truman, that possibility was at most a secondary consideration, though he did decide neither to consult Stalin about the bomb nor to offer him, any more than Roosevelt had, any broad scientific information about the nature of the weapon. Primarily Truman was moved by his interpretation of Japanese political and military conditions. On his orders, on August 6, in a blinding flash of heat and horror, the first atomic bomb fell on Hiroshima, killing nearly one hundred thousand people, fatally injuring another hundred thousand through blast or radiation, and reducing the city to rubble.

Even after this appalling blow the Japanese military vetoed the civilian desire to accept the Potsdam Declaration. Two days after Hiroshima, the Red Army invaded Manchuria and, on the third day, with no word from Tokyo, the American air command, operating on earlier orders, dropped a second bomb on Nagasaki. In Tokyo the military still objected to unconditional surrender. It required the personal intervention of the emperor to overcome their opposition. With Japanese acceptance of Potsdam conditioned on the preservation of the imperial prerogatives, the act of surrender took place on September 2, 1945.

The decision to drop the atomic bomb was the most tragic in the long course of American history. Perhaps only so drastic a step would have achieved unconditional surrender so rapidly. On the other hand, thoughtful observers have wondered whether the American government, with Japan essentially beaten and on the verge of capitulation, had exhausted all the possible alternatives before at last having recourse to the bomb—whether there were not resources of negotiation or demonstration that, even at the cost of prolonging the war, should have been first attempted, with the bomb held in reserve as a weapon of last resort. Here perhaps prior atomic policy, and, still more, the doctrine of unconditional surrender had terrible consequences. Certainly, though the bomb terminated the war, it also placed the United States for many years in an ambiguous position before the world as the only nation to have employed so horrible a weapon.

Victory thus came—but in a way that converted triumph into tragedy. The Second World War ended. More than 25 million persons, soldiers and civilians, had died during the five years. Sixteen million Americans—more than 10 percent of the population—had been under arms; total casualties amounted to over a million, with nearly three hundred thousand deaths in battle. Now, in the autumn of 1945, the world stood on the threshold of a new epoch in human history—an epoch incalculably rich in hazards and potentialities. With apprehensive steps, mankind was entering the atomic age.

Suggestions for reading

THE SECOND WORLD WAR: THE HOME FRONT

R. E. Sherwood, *Roosevelt and Hopkins* (1948, rev. ed., 1950), remains the most vivid account of Roosevelt as a war-leader; it should be supplemented by J. M. Burns' valuable study, *Roosevelt: The Soldier of Freedom** (1970). For war mobilization, see the Bureau of the Budget, *The United States at War* (1946); Eliot Janeway, *The Struggle for Survival** (1951); and H. M. Somers, *Presidential Agency: OWMR* (1950); on price control, L. V. Chandler, *Inflation in the United States, 1940–1948* (1951); Chester Bowles, *Promises to Keep* (1971); and, for the penetrating reflections of a leading controller, J. K. Galbraith, *Theory of Price Control** (1952). The mobilization of science and technology is incisively depicted in J. P. Baxter, III, *Scientists Against Time** (1946); R. G. Hewlett and O. E. Anderson, Jr., *The New World* (1962), is authoritative on the development of the atomic bomb. Volume III of J. M. Blum, *From the Morgenthau Diaries: Years of War, 1941–1945* (1967), throws light on a variety of issues that concerned the Treasury.

For American society in wartime, see J. M. Blum, *V Was For Victory* (1976), which also deals with politics; Richard Polenberg, *War and Society: The United States, 1941–1945** (1972); Richard Polenberg, ed., *America at War: The Home Front, 1941–1945** (1968); and Richard Lingeman, *Don't You Know There's a War On* (1970). Francis Biddle provides thoughtful discussion of the civil-liberties problems he faced as Attorney General in *Democratic Thinking and the War* (1944) and in his distinguished memoir *In Brief Authority* (1962). On the Japanese-Americans, there are several good studies of which a recent and trenchant one is Roger Daniels, *Concentration Camps* (1971). L. S. Wittner, *Rebels Against War: The American Peace Movement, 1946–1960** (1969), is excellent on its subject. For black Americans, see Herbert Garfinkel, *When Negroes March** (1959); Louis Ruchames, *Race, Jobs and Politics: The Story of FEPC* (1953); R. M. Dalfiume, *Desegregation of the United States Armed Forces* (1969); August Meier and Elliott Rudwick, *CORE** (1973); and the magisterial study by Gunnar Myrdal, *An American Dilemma** (1944, rev. ed., 1962). On women, the best study is that of Chafe, previously cited. On wartime politics, besides various studies cited above, see the excellent study of the Republicans in Ellsworth Barnard, *Wendell Willkie: Fighter for Freedom** (1966), and the analysis of Democratic dissenters in J. M. Blum, ed., *The Price of Vision: The Diary of Henry A. Wallace, 1942–1946* (1973).

THE SECOND WORLD WAR: MILITARY OPERATIONS

A. R. Buchanan, *The United States and World War II*, 2 vols.* (1964), is a survey. For able analyses of American strategy, see S. E. Morison, *Strategy and Compromise** (1958); Louis Morton, *Strategy and Command* (1962); K. R. Greenfield, ed., *Command Decisions* (1959); and K. R. Greenfield, *American Strategy in World War II: A Reconsideration** (1963). The role of the American services is intensively portrayed in three multivolume series: Office of the Chief of Military History, *The United States Army in World War II*; S. E. Morison, *History of United States Naval Operations in World War II* (summarized in *The Two-Ocean War,* 1963); and W. F. Craven and J. L. Cate, *The Army Air Forces in World War II*, 7 vols. (1949–58). There is indispensable background in the six volumes of W. S. Churchill, *The Second World War** (1948–53); in two volumes on the Secretary of War: H. L. Stimson and McGeorge Bundy, *On Active Service in Peace and War* (1948), and E. E. Morison, *Turmoil and Tradition** (1960); and in the biography of the Chief of Staff, F. C. Pogue, *George C. Marshall,* 3 vols. (1963–73). Among the formidable number of American war memoirs, the most useful on the European theater are those of Dwight D. Eisenhower, Omar Bradley, H. H. Arnold, W. Bedell Smith, and Mark Clark; on the Pacific theater, those of Douglas MacArthur, Joseph Stilwell, Claire Chennault, Albert Wedemeyer, Courtney Whitney, Robert Eichelberger, W. F. Halsey, George C. Kenney, Walter Kreuger, and, as recounted by Walter Whitehill, Ernest J. King.

For the American military role in Europe, C. B. MacDonald, *The Mighty Endeavor: American Armed Forces in the European Theater in World War II* (1969), offers a comprehensive account. For strategic debates in Europe, see Chester Wilmot, *The Struggle for Europe** (1952); S. E. Ambrose, *The Supreme Commander: The War Years of General Dwight D. Eisenhower* (1970); Michael Howard, *The Mediterranean Strategy in the Second World War* (1968); and two volumes by Trumbull Higgins: *Winston*

*Available in a paperback edition.

708

The world in flames

Churchill and the Second Front, 1940–1943 (1957) and *Soft Underbelly: The Anglo-American Controversy Over the Italian Campaign, 1939–1945* (1968). John Toland, *The Last Hundred Days** (1966), and Cornelius Ryan, *The Last Battle** (1966), cover the fall of Germany. For the Pacific war, see John Toland, *The Rising Sun: The Decline and Fall of the Japanese Empire** (1970); Barbara Tuchman, *Stilwell and the American Experience in China, 1911–1945** (1971); T. H. White and Annalee Jacoby, *Thunder Out of China* (1946); John Hersey, *Hiroshima** (1946); W. S. Schoenberger, *Decisions of Destiny* (1970); and various volumes in the Army history, especially those by Louis Morton, C. F. Romanus, and Riley Sunderland.

The GI's view of the war is candidly portrayed in the gritty newspaper reporting of Ernie Pyle, *Here is Your War* (1943) and *Brave Men* (1944), and the sardonic cartoons of Bill Mauldin, *Up Front* (1945). See also the *New Yorker Book of War Pieces* (1947), and such novels as J. G. Cozzens, *Guard of Honor** (1949); Norman Mailer, *The Naked and the Dead** (1948); James Jones, *From Here to Eternity** (1951); William Styron, *The Long March** (1952); and Joseph Heller, *Catch-22** (1961). S. A. Stouffer, *et al., The American Soldier,* 2 vols.* (1949), contains important sociological data.

THE SECOND WORLD WAR: DIPLOMACY

J. L. Snell, *Illusion and Necessity: The Diplomacy of Global War** (1963), and Gaddis Smith, *American Diplomacy During the Second World War** (1965), are useful surveys. The volumes of Herbert Feis— *The China Tangle** (1953), *Churchill, Roosevelt, Stalin** (1957, 2nd ed., 1967), *The Atomic Bomb and the End of World War II** (rev. ed., 1966)—provide brilliant coverage of diplomatic questions. Two books by R. A. Divine, *Roosevelt and World War II** (1969) and *Second Chance: The Triumph of Internationalism in America** (1967), deal with war and postwar issues. For a left-revisionist view of American policy, see Gabriel Kolko, *The Politics of War: The World and United States Foreign Policy, 1943–1945** (1969). On Yalta, E. R. Stettinius, *Roosevelt and the Russians—The Yalta Conference* (1949), defends Administration policy, W. H. Chamberlin, *America's Second Crusade** (1950), attacks it from the right, and D. S. Clemens, *Yalta** (1970), questions it from the left. On relations with Russia, see W. H. McNeill, *America, Britain and Russia** (1953); J. L. Gaddis, *The United States and the Origins of the Cold War** (1972); Adam Ulam, *Expansion and Coexistence** (1968); J. R. Deane, *The Strange Alliance** (1953); P. E. Mosely, *The Kremlin and World Politics** (1960); Martin Herz, *Beginnings of the Cold War** (1966); G. C. Herring, *Aid to Russia, 1941–1946* (1973); and W. A. Harriman, *America and Russia in a Changing World* (1971). On relations with France, see W. L. Langer, *Our Vichy Gamble** (1947), and Milton Viorst, *Hostile Allies* (1965). On China, see Tang Tsou, *America's Failure in China, 1941–1950** (1963). On atomic diplomacy, see R. G. Hewlett and O. E. Anderson, *The New World* (1962), and M. J. Sherwin, *A World Destroyed: The Atomic Bomb and the Grand Alliance* (1975).

Particularly useful memoirs are Cordell Hull, *Memoirs,* 2 vols. (1948); W. D. Leahy, *I Was There* (1950); J. F. Byrnes, *Speaking Frankly* (1950) and *All in One Lifetime* (1958); Sumner Welles, *The Time for Decision* (1944) and *Seven Decisions That Shaped History* (1951); R. D. Murphy, *Diplomat Among Warriors* (1964); J. C. Grew, *Turbulent Era: A Diplomatic Record of Forty Years,* 2 vols. (1952); G. F. Kennan, *Memoirs, 1925–1950* (1967). Indispensable glimpses of American policy from foreign perspectives can be found in the memoirs or diaries of Winston Churchill, Charles de Gaulle, Joseph Goebbels, Albert Speer, Galeazzo Ciano, Milovan Djilas, Ivan Maisky, Lord Avon (Anthony Eden), Lord Halifax, Lord Montgomery, Harold Macmillan, Lord Alexander, Lord Tedder, Sir Frederick Morgan, Sir John Slessor, Sir Alexander Cadogan, Harold Nicolson, Lord Casey, and Sir Robert Menzies.

*Available in a paperback edition.

Suggestions for reading

CHAPTER **30** *The Cold War*

Retreat in Korea

The United States emerged from the Second World War a relatively unified, powerful, and confident nation, restored from the demoralization of the Great Depression, ready to take an active part in the affairs of the greater world. Victory gave Americans an uncritical pride in the productivity of their economy, in the prowess of their armed forces, in the rectitude of their motives, and in the strength of their liberal ideals.

The Americans of 1945 did not suppose, as so many had in 1918, that victory relieved them of further international responsibility. Many saw America's world role as a historic opportunity. Motives were varied. Some hoped to use American power to build a

lasting structure of world peace and to advance the cause of liberal democracy. Some, like former Vice President Henry Wallace, called for "the century of the common man." Some, like the magazine publisher Henry R. Luce, dreamed imperially of "the American Century." Others were less enthusiastic about the departure from ancient ways but stoically accepted the end of traditional isolationism. Problems remained at home: in particular, to prevent a repetition of the economic depression, the political hysteria, and the social complacency that followed the First World War.

Truman takes over

The new President.　The nation entered the postwar world under a new and inexperienced leader. "I feel as though the moon and all the stars and all the planets have fallen on me," Harry S Truman told newspapermen on the April day in 1945 when he heard the report of Roosevelt's death. "Please, boys, give me your prayers. I need them very much." A back-bencher from Missouri who had barely retained his own seat in the Senate four and a half years before, he had to fill the mighty place of the man who had dominated the affairs of the United States and the world for a dozen years.

On the record Truman seemed a Missouri courthouse politician of a familiar sort, a beneficiary of the notorious Pendergast machine in Kansas City, a Democratic wheel horse in the Senate, an old-time political pro whose chief attribute was loyalty to his organization and his President. On the other hand, those who knew him valued the spontaneous sense of decency that had led him to fight the Ku Klux Klan at the height of its power in Missouri, the courage in adversity that had enabled him to hold his Senate seat in 1940, and the concern for popular welfare he had displayed throughout his public career. Even back in Kansas City, for all his machine associations, his personal record was spotless. As wartime chairman of the Senate Committee to Investigate the National Defense Program, he had discharged a delicate job with intelligence and responsibility. He kept on his desk a motto from Mark Twain: "Always do right. This will gratify some people, & astonish the rest." No one could tell what the chemistry of the Presidency would do with this strange mixture of human elements.

Initial impressions were not encouraging. In his fourth week as President, Truman casually signed an order that abruptly stopped the delivery of goods under the lend-lease program. During the war, the United States had sent abroad over $50 billion worth of goods under that program, of which 60 percent had gone to Great Britain and 22 percent to the Soviet Union. The sudden termination of these deliveries caused resentment abroad and some real hardship. "This experience brought home to me," Truman subsequently wrote, "not only that I had to know exactly where I was going but also that I had to know that my basic policies were being carried out. If I had read that order, as I should have, the incident would not have occurred. But the best time to learn that lesson was right at the beginning of my duties as President."

The candor, the humility, and the cockiness were all characteristic. Though he never totally divested himself of a tendency to shoot from the hip, Truman gradually developed authority in his new role. His wide knowledge of history gave him a vigorous sense of the dignity and power of the Presidency. He worked hard. He accepted responsibility: he used to say of the presidential desk, "The buck stops here." He reconstructed the Cabinet, gradually transforming a Roosevelt Administration into a Truman Administration. Winston Churchill, meeting him at Potsdam in July 1945, was impressed by "his gay, precise, sparkling manner and obvious power of decision."

Experiment in world order

The postwar atmosphere.　This power of decision was almost immediately put to the test. For war had left the international order in a condition of acute derangement. With the Axis states vanquished, the European Allies battered and exhausted, the colonial empires in dissolution, and the underdeveloped world in tumult, great gaping holes appeared in the structure of world power. And war had also left only two states—the United States and the Soviet Union—with the political dynamism, ideological confidence, and military force to flow into these vacuums of power. The war had accustomed both states, moreover, to thinking and acting on a world scale.

The war's end thus saw a geopolitical rivalry between America and Russia as well as a clear-cut difference over the principles on which the peace should be organized—whether in terms of great-power spheres-of-influence or United Nations universalism (see pp. 699–700). And the factor that transformed this structural conflict into something akin to a religious war and began to give it apocalyptic overtones was the apparently irreconcilable ideological disagreement between the two superpowers. With the prewar world in pieces, America and Russia appeared in 1945 as the first truly global powers in the history of man, exerting their influence everywhere around the planet, encountering no serious opposition anywhere, except from each other—each, as Tocqueville had prophesied in *Democracy in America* a century earlier, seemingly "marked out by the will of Heaven to sway the destinies of half the globe."

Launching the United Nations.

Nevertheless war had bound the victors together in coalition, and the Dumbarton Oaks conference of 1944 had laid down the main lines for a postwar structure. On April 29, 1945, representatives of fifty nations met at San Francisco to adopt a United Nations Charter and create a permanent UN organization.

The charter, essentially an American product, was in the direct line of descent from the Covenant of the League of Nations. It was dominated by the belief that the best way to keep peace was through conciliation, backed up when necessary by collective military strength. Of the UN organs, the General Assembly and the Security Council had the widest authority. The Assembly was the legislative body, though its powers were limited to discussion and recommendation. The Security Council was the action agency; it was to this body that the architects of the UN assigned, in the language of the charter, "the primary responsibility for the maintenance of international peace and security."

The Security Council consisted of five permanent members—the United States, Britain, Russia, France, and China—with six further members (after 1966, ten) elected each year by the General Assembly. The charter gave the Council authority to settle international disputes by peaceful means—through investigation or mediation or whatever method seemed suitable. If such methods failed, Chapter 7 of the charter authorized the Council to take appropriate measures against any state that broke the peace. If necessary, it might use armed force supplied by the member states. However, the charter also limited the Council's authority to invoke these powers—especially by giving each permanent member a veto. Neither the United States nor the Soviet Union would have joined the UN without this means of protecting its interests. By 1976 the Soviet Union had used its veto 110 times, the United States 12 times.

Collective effort.

Surrounding the UN was a constellation of subsidiary agencies, among which the United Nations Relief and Rehabilitation Administration had particularly urgent responsibilities. Established in 1943 to bring food, clothing, medicine, and other supplies to liberated countries, UNRRA disbursed $2.7 billion over the next five years combating hunger and other ravages of war. Its director and many of its workers were American, and the United States contributed nearly three-quarters of its financial support.

While UNRRA tackled the immediate crisis, the

western Allies, meeting in July 1944 at Bretton Woods, New Hampshire, planned a long-term international economic framework. Bretton Woods led to the establishment of two institutions: the International Monetary Fund, designed to create a world monetary system based on fixed exchange rates; and the International Bank for Reconstruction and Development (better known as the World Bank), designed to supply capital for investment and trade in underdeveloped areas. The Soviet Union, regarding these institutions as the instruments of international capitalism, declined to participate.

It did, however, join other specialized UN agencies—the Food and Agricultural Organization, the International Trade Organization, the World Health Organization, and the International Labor Organization (taken over from the League). In addition, the newly organized United Nations Educational, Scientific, and Cultural Organization (UNESCO) fostered international efforts to raise cultural standards and promote intellectual exchange.

The unleashed power of the atom confronted the UN with its most fateful challenge. In June 1946 Bernard Baruch, the American delegate to the UN Atomic Energy Commission, presented an imaginative plan for the international control of atomic energy. The plan called for an International Atomic Development Authority empowered to own and operate the materials and facilities involved in the pro-

PEACE TODAY

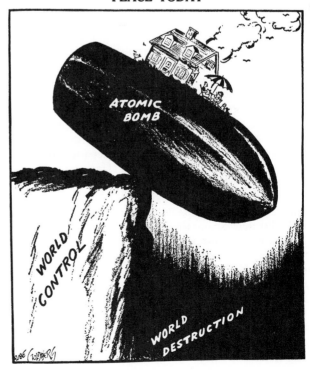

Experiment in world order

duction of atomic energy. The proposed agency was to have power to punish violations of its rules, and it was to be exempt from the great-power veto.

The Russians, however, regarded the veto as their basic protection in an international organization dominated by the United States, nor would they tolerate the idea of inspection within the Soviet Union. Their counterproposal called for the cessation of production and the destruction of stockpiles *before* the imposition of controls. It also retained the veto. These provisions were unacceptable to the United States. Though the United Nations Commission adopted the American plan, the threat of Soviet veto prevented further action.

The Cold War begins

The coalition in trouble. The United Nations could only register the realities of international life. It could not abolish profound disagreements in interest and ideology. These disagreements, held in check during the war by common opposition to Hitler, found new nourishment in postwar difficulties.

For Stalin the overriding concern remained the security of the Soviet Union. Determined to safeguard the Soviet frontiers by keeping eastern Europe under Soviet control, he doubtless construed the Yalta agreement in terms of the sphere-of-influence deal he had made with Churchill at Moscow four months before. In addition, he probably believed at first that the free elections promised at Yalta would produce reliably pro-Soviet regimes. But events soon made it clear that he had overestimated Soviet popularity in eastern Europe and underestimated western concern over the extension of Soviet power into central Europe. When after Yalta Stalin moved to fasten a procommunist regime on Poland, the new American President, only a few weeks in office, conveyed his disapproval in salty language to V. M. Molotov, the Soviet foreign minister. In May 1945 Truman sent Harry Hopkins to Moscow to make it clear that Truman was carrying forward Roosevelt's policies, to emphasize that Poland had become the "symbol" of the ability of Russia and the West to work out their problems, and to warn that "if present trends continued unchecked the entire structure of world cooperation . . . would be destroyed." As Churchill later described the mood in the summer of 1945, "The agreements and understandings at Yalta, such as they were, had already been broken or brushed aside by the triumphant Kremlin. New perils, perhaps as terrible as those we had surmounted, loomed and glared upon the torn and harassed world."

The partition of Germany and Austria

It was in this atmosphere that Truman, Stalin, and Churchill met at Potsdam outside Berlin at the end of July to consider the peace settlement with Germany and its satellites as well as the war with Japan. The western powers acquiesced in a temporary Polish occupation of Germany up to the Oder-Neisse line, with the final territorial decision to be reserved for the peace conference. The task of drawing up peace treaties with the minor Axis powers was assigned to a Council of Foreign Ministers. The talks on Japan led to the Anglo-American Potsdam Declaration.

Occupation of Germany. Of all the power vacuums created by the war, the most vital was in the heart of Europe. Not trusting the Germans to fill this vacuum themselves, the three powers proposed a joint occupation by the United States, Britain, Russia, and France. Each nation was to supervise its own zone of occupation, but each was also to participate in an Allied Control Council responsible for matters affecting Germany as a whole. The objectives of the occupation included disarmament, demilitarization, de-Nazification, and the encouragement of libertarian ideals.

Though the Potsdam Conference marked a retreat from the punitive proposals considered a year earlier at Quebec, the American occupation authorities at first imposed severe political and economic measures on Germany. American troops were forbidden to "fraternize" with Germans. An International Military Tribunal established at American instigation

tried twenty-two top Nazis in Nürnberg from November 1945 to October 1946; nineteen were convicted, of whom twelve were sentenced to death. Restrictions on the economy kept German living standards low.

The curtain falls. Potsdam was the last meeting between Stalin and the western leaders. When the Communist party received only 17 percent of the vote in the Hungarian elections of November 1945, Stalin decided to consolidate the communist position in eastern Europe without further regard for local or western sensibilities. There followed in the next years extermination of political dissent through staged trials, forced confessions, and executions. At first the Soviet purge concentrated on noncommunist leaders—Bela Kovacs in Hungary, Nikola Petkov in Bulgaria, Julius Maniu in Romania—but by 1949 it began to sweep through the Communist parties themselves, liquidating leaders suspected of inadequate loyalty to Stalinism, such as Laszlo Rajk in Hungary, Traicho Kostov in Bulgaria, and Rudolf Slansky in Czechoslovakia. Though Tito, the Communist leader of Yugoslavia, was beyond the reach of Stalin's power, his independent course led to his expulsion in 1948 from the Cominform, which Stalin had set up to replace the prewar Comintern as the means by which the Soviet Union controlled foreign Communist parties.

As the Russians hardened their grip on eastern Europe, the expectation arose in the West that they would use their zone, not just to secure their own frontiers, but as a springboard from which to dominate central and western Europe, now lying economically prostrate and politically vulnerable before them. The Soviet threat to democratic Europe was not seen at this point in military terms. Stalin's instrumentality, it was supposed, would be the obedient Communist parties of France, Italy, and Germany through which he might, without Russian military action, promote the Stalinization of the continent and thereby succeed where Hitler had failed in wielding the whole force of Europe by a single hand.

In Asia, moreover, the Soviet Union declined at the end of 1945 to carry out its promise (as Great Britain and America already had done) to withdraw its troops from Iran six months after the end of the war. In December pro-Soviet Iranians established a revolutionary regime in the northern province of Azerbaijan. In January 1946 Iran charged before the UN Security Council that Russia was interfering in its internal affairs. The Soviet Union rejected these charges and a new deadline for troop withdrawal as well. A protest from Truman finally brought a change in Soviet policy, and the troops left in May.

To American eyes, the Russian movement into Europe and Asia, along with the brutal extinction of civil freedoms in areas already under Russian control, seemed to portend a new phase in the world struggle between democracy and totalitarianism, with communism inheriting the mantle just relinquished by fascism. Communism in the forties did not, save in China, imply—as it might in later years—popular movements determined to reclaim political and economic independence for their nations. For most Americans, communism meant Stalinism, the system

715

that ruled Soviet Russia, a system correctly seen as not only extraordinarily cruel and repressive at home but in secure command of most Communist parties through the world. Stalinism was also seen, perhaps less correctly, as inherently aggressive and insatiable. This impression was understandable, however, when a Soviet official like Maxim Litvinov, foreign commissar in the 1930s and later ambassador to Washington, well known to the West as a champion of collective security, privately warned western friends against appeasement. If the West acceded to current Soviet demands, he said in 1946, "it would be faced, after a more or less short time, with the next series of demands."

In an important speech on February 9, 1946, Stalin was understood to be saying that the capitalist system rendered war inevitable. On March 5, Churchill, speaking at Fulton, Missouri, with Truman beside him on the platform, responded by warning against the "expansive tendencies" of the Soviet Union. "From Stettin in the Baltic to Trieste in the Adriatic," he said, "an iron curtain has descended across the Continent." What should the West do to meet the Russian challenge? "I am convinced that there is nothing they admire so much as strength, and there is nothing for which they have less respect than weakness, especially military weakness."

Why the Cold War?

The historical controversy. Churchill's speech set forth the official Anglo-American thesis: that the postwar antagonism, known by 1947 as the Cold War, was the necessary western response to an unprovoked course of expansion by Soviet communism. In later years this thesis fell under attack, especially in the United States. The "revisionist" critique took many forms, but predominant arguments were that America was more the postwar aggressor than Russia; that the American government systematically played on anticommunist emotions in order to cloak its real intentions, which were to establish economic hegemony throughout the world; and that (in the view, at least, of the more extreme revisionists) Washington had no choice but to seek an "open door" for American trade and investment because American capitalism had to expand in order to survive.

While this controversy continues thirty years later, one part of the revisionist critique has had lasting influence—that is, its insistence on looking at the postwar situation from the Soviet as well as the western viewpoint. From this perspective the western

effort to affect the future of eastern Europe could have been honestly perceived in Moscow as a threat to the security of the Soviet Union. In retrospect, it seems probable that Moscow was not intent on military aggression or dedicated, as a practical goal, to "world conquest." Stalin carefully refrained from committing the Red Army outside his own sphere of vital interest. While not forgoing the pleasures and benefits of intrigue and subversion in other parts of the world, he was prepared, in exchange for a free hand in the Soviet sphere, to concede America and Britain free hands in their spheres, including the freedom to suppress communist movements. He was even perhaps prepared to place China and Greece within the western sphere.

The "open door" interpretation of American policy has stood up less well. It is hard, for example, to explain American interest in eastern Europe by a supposed quest for markets, investment outlets, and raw materials. While Washington certainly worked for a freely trading world—against, among other things, the opposition of much of American business—it was not this desire that prompted objections to Soviet policy in eastern Europe, where the American economic stake was negligible. The democratic socialist leaders in western Europe—Clement Attlee and Ernest Bevin in England, Leon Blum in France, Ernst Reuter and Willy Brandt in West Germany—were in the forefront of opposition to the spread of Stalinism. These men had no interest in an open door for American capitalism; they had a profound interest in the future of democratic socialism. Observing the dismal fate of democratic socialists in eastern Europe, they concluded that they would meet the same fate if postwar chaos brought communism to power in their own countries. For a time, indeed, they regarded Washington's response to the Stalinist threat as naively slow. Moreover, the American leader who talked most about the importance of the open door, Henry Wallace, favored accommodation with Stalin, which suggests that preoccupation with the open door could lead equally to resistance or appeasement.

The postwar American military posture was hardly that of a nation bent on world empire. No government in modern history had conducted so swift a demobilization of its conventional military force; nor had any electorate so unitedly demanded it. Nor was Congress prepared to compensate by accepting Truman's recommendation for universal military training, though it agreed to continue selective service. Even as relations grew worse, the United States cut back its armed forces until they were reduced to almost an eighth of their wartime size. Though revisionist historians subsequently argued that American policy-makers had seen the atomic bomb as the means of controlling the postwar world, Washington made no attempt to practice nuclear diplomacy against the Soviet Union, ignoring the counsel of those, like the British philosopher Bertrand Russell, who urged the use of the bomb to compel the Russians to good behavior.

Nor were American leaders in the forties obsessively anticommunist. In China, for example, Truman worked for a coalition between Chiang Kai-shek and Mao Tse-tung. Nor did Washington dismiss the Soviet point about "friendly" regimes along the Russian border. The western powers would have been satisfied had the Russians settled for the Finnish pattern throughout eastern Europe—that is, permitting internal freedoms so long as foreign policy was acceptable to Moscow. Nor was Washington in these years hostile to anticolonialism. The United States supported the independence of India and Indonesia and nationalist revolutions in Egypt and elsewhere. Acquiescence in the French return to Indochina was a lamentable and fateful exception. The fundamental issue, as the Truman administration saw it, lay not between capitalism and revolution but between democracy and Stalinism.

The Cold War thus became an intricate, interlocking, reciprocal process, involving authentic differences in principle, real and supposed clashes of interest, and a wide range of misunderstanding and misperception. Each superpower believed with passion that its own safety as well as world peace depended on the success of its peculiar conception of world order. Each superpower, in pursuing its own clearly expressed and ardently cherished principles, only confirmed the fear of the other that it was bent on aggression. Soviet behavior in eastern Europe, Iran, and Berlin and the activity of Communist parties elsewhere seemed to confirm the western notion of an expansive Soviet Union. American postwar policy, especially in its expressions of concern about eastern Europe, assumed a threatening aspect for the Russians. Each superpower persevered in corroborating the fears of the other. Together they proceeded to deepen the Cold War.

The Axis states. The interacting process of suspicion and countersuspicion, action and counteraction, gathered speed. The first casualty was any hope of close collaboration in the postwar settlement. Germany remained a crucial issue. Each side came to feel that, if it did not fill the power vacuum, the other would, and that this would constitute an unacceptable threat; so each began to sponsor German revival in its own zone. By 1949 the German Federal Republic was established in the west; the German Democratic Republic in the east.

Potsdam had assigned to the Council of Foreign Ministers the task of drawing up peace treaties with Axis satellites. In December 1946 James F. Byrnes, now Truman's Secretary of State, finally came to an agreement with Moscow on treaties with Italy, Bulgaria, Hungary, Finland, and Romania. Though the eastern European treaties all contained solemn pledges to preserve political and intellectual freedom, in effect they turned the countries (except for Italy and Finland) over to Soviet dominated governments. No agreement was reached on Austria until 1955, when the superpowers agreed on Austrian neutralization.

By these treaties the western powers acquiesced in Soviet control of eastern Europe. In tacit exchange, the Soviet Union now acquiesced in American control of occupied Japan. There, as in Germany, the American occupation began in severity and, as circumstances changed, became progressively more benign.

At first General Douglas MacArthur, as supreme Allied commander, instituted a series of political and economic purges, culminating in the trial and punishment of leading officials in previous Japanese governments under standards more stringent than at Nürnberg. At the same time he imposed reforms designed to transform the defeated country into a model western democracy. A new constitution, adopted under American direction in 1946, renounced war as a sovereign right, adding that "land, sea and air forces, as well as other war potential, will never be maintained." The *zaibatsu*, the great family trusts, were threatened with dissolution; trade unions were encouraged, women were given the vote, land was redistributed among the peasants, the educational system was reorganized, and Shinto was abolished as the state religion.

After 1947 American policy began to change. As in the case of Germany, the United States began to look with favor on the idea of permitting an increase in Japanese production in order to reduce the burden on American taxpayers. Increasing apprehension about the Soviet Union soon raised the question whether a disarmed Japan would not leave a dangerous power vacuum in the Far East. A peace treaty with Japan, finally negotiated in 1951, registered the altered American attitude. The treaty terminated the occupation, conceded to Japan as a sovereign nation "the inherent right of individual or collective self-defense," and opened the way for American troops to remain in Japan through bilateral agreement.

The experience of military occupation in general, and especially the supposed success of MacArthur's reconstruction of Japan, increased the confidence of Americans in their capacity to build and rebuild nations around the world.

Truman assumes the initiative

The Truman Doctrine. At the end of 1946, Secretary of State James F. Byrnes resigned because of ill health, and Truman appointed General George C. Marshall to take his place. Marshall's unique national eminence helped remove the discussion of foreign policy from a partisan context. So too did the collaboration in a "bipartisan" foreign policy of Arthur H. Vandenberg, a Republican senator from Michigan, whose prewar record as an isolationist gave his views special weight among conservatives.

In the meantime communist pressure was mounting against Greece and Turkey; and early in 1947, Great Britain, in acute economic straits itself, notified Washington that in five weeks it must end financial support to a Greek government besieged by communist guerrillas receiving support from Yugoslavia and other Soviet satellites. Though Stalin had not in fact instigated the Greek uprising, this was not known in the West, which supposed that the collapse of Greece would embolden Moscow to press an offensive against Italy and France. Truman accordingly decided that America must take up the burden. Recalling the hard fight for a loan to Britain itself a year before, Truman feared that a conventional request for aid to Greece and Turkey would not pass the Congress. Accepting Vandenberg's judgment that he had to scare the hell out of the country, he went to Capitol Hill in person to urge what soon became known as the Truman Doctrine. "I believe," Truman said, "that it

must be the policy of the United States to support free peoples who are resisting attempted subjugation by armed minorities or outside pressures." Some, within the Administration and without, flinched at the sweeping language. But Congress responded to presidential evangelism and in May 1947 passed a bill granting $400 million in aid to Greece and Turkey over the next fifteen months. Though the subsequent collapse of the Greek insurgency was due as much to Tito's break with Stalin as to American assistance, the apparent efficacy of the Truman Doctrine in its initial application strengthened America's belief in both its ability and its responsibility to serve as guardian of freedom in the world.

The containment policy. The American return to Europe under the Truman Doctrine was the first application of a philosophy that had been evolving for some time in the minds of American policy-makers. The most extended statement was made by George F. Kennan, a member of the foreign service with long experience of the Soviet Union. Writing anonymously in *Foreign Affairs* in July 1947, Kennan argued that Soviet communism was like "a fluid stream which moves constantly, wherever it is permitted to move, toward a given goal." American policy, Kennan proposed, must be that of "the firm and vigilant containment of Russian expansive tendencies." The purpose of containment was not to enter the Russian sphere or overthrow the Soviet regime but rather to block the Soviet effort to flow into "every nook and cranny available to it in the basin of the world." In time this would force a measure of circumspection on the

Soviet-American relations: a dissenting view

Kremlin and "promote tendencies which must eventually find their outlet in either the break-up or the gradual mellowing of Soviet power."

The containment idea provoked heated debate in the United States. On the right, traditional isolationists, led by Senator Robert A. Taft of Ohio, doubted America's financial or moral capacity to sustain an activist international policy. In the center, commentators like Walter Lippmann feared that the containment psychology might lead people to see the Soviet Union as primarily a military threat to be met by military means and might involve the United States beyond its sphere of direct and vital interest. On the left, Americans unwilling to surrender the idea of the innocence or moderation of Stalin denounced the policy as aggressive and provocative. This group, which had some strength within the labor movement and the liberal community, found a spokesman in Henry Wallace, who resigned from Truman's Cabinet in protest against the hardening of policy toward the Soviet Union.

The Marshall Plan. The Truman Doctrine was an emergency effort to shore up crumbling positions in Greece and Turkey. It had been made necessary by a larger economic problem—the hard-pressed condition of Britain, confronted by a staggering deficit in its international balance of payments, as well as by acute shortages in food and power. Britain's plight was symptomatic of the plight of all western Europe. With UNRRA coming to an end, with crops damaged or destroyed over millions of acres by severe winter

weather, with little evidence of industrial recovery, with Communist parties and the Soviet Union threatening political and economic action, western Europe faced a frightening crisis. European city dwellers were living on less than 2,000 calories a day. The cradle of Western civilization seemed to Winston Churchill in 1947 "a rubble heap, a charnel house, a breeding ground for pestilence and hate." "The patient is sinking," said Secretary Marshall, "while the doctors deliberate."

In 1946 Congress had voted Britain a $3.75 billion loan, but it appeared likely to balk at more foreign credits along conventional lines. In an address at the Harvard commencement on June 5, 1947, Marshall accordingly set forth a revolutionary new proposal. After describing the European crisis, he called on the European countries themselves to draw up a plan for European recovery. "This is the business of the Europeans. . . . The role of this country should consist of friendly aid in the drafting of a European program and of later support. . . . The program should be a joint one, agreed to by a number, if not all, of European nations." Marshall added, significantly, "Our policy is directed not against any country or doctrine but against hunger, poverty, desperation, and chaos."

This was the proposal that, as British Foreign Secretary Ernest Bevin later told Parliament, he "grabbed . . . with both hands." Within three weeks, representatives of European states, west and east, met in Paris to discuss the Marshall offer. The prospect of Soviet and east European participation, however, was quickly disappointed when the Russians denounced the plan as American economic imperialism and

pulled out of the meeting, taking their satellites with them. A pro-Soviet coup in Czechoslovakia in February 1948—itself conceivably an overreaction to the Marshall Plan—completed the division of Europe. It also smoothed the way for the passage of the plan by the American Congress in March.

The sixteen remaining states (including Turkey) now formed the Organization for European Economic Cooperation to begin integrated economic planning. With generous contributions by the United States—$12.5 billion in four years—the west European economy was restored in a strikingly short time. By 1951 the Marshall Plan countries had raised their industrial output 40 percent over 1938. The stimulus provided by the Marshall Plan and the OEEC led both to continued economic expansion and to further experiments in European integration—especially the European Coal and Steel Community (1952) and the European Economic Community, better known as the Common Market, established by the Rome Treaties in 1957. The dramatic economic recovery both reduced the immediate threat of communism to western Europe and gave that region a more independent voice in world affairs.

The first Berlin crisis. The Marshall Plan checked the Soviet hope that economic disintegration might strengthen communism in western Europe. In response Moscow in 1949 organized the Council for Mutual Economic Assistance (COMECON) in eastern Europe. And in the spring of 1948 the Soviet Union presented the West with a new challenge when it cut off West Berlin by blockading all highway, river, and rail traffic into the former German capital. The evident purpose was to force the western powers out of Berlin.

The West now had several choices, all unattractive. If it retreated, it would encourage the Soviet Union to believe that it could win its objectives through a show of force. If it tried to break the blockade by sending armed convoys to Berlin, it ran the risk of a third world war. General Lucius Clay, the American commander in Germany, proposed a third course—the supply of West Berlin through an airlift. Truman adopted Clay's suggestion. On June 26, 1948, the airlift went into operation. When it became apparent that even winter weather could not halt the airlift and that the western counterblockade was hurting East Germany, Moscow developed second thoughts. On May 12, 1949—321 days after the start of the airlift—the Russians ended the blockade.

The Berlin crisis, following so closely on the communist coup in Czechoslovakia, convinced many western Europeans of the need for a regional defense agreement against possible Soviet aggression. Truman agreed that only "an inclusive security system" could dispel the fear that communism might overrun western Europe. By October 1948 the North Atlantic nations agreed on an alliance in which (in the language of Article 5 of the final pact) "an armed attack against one or more of them in Europe or North America shall be considered an attack against them all." Article 11, however, provided that the treaty was to be carried out by the signatories "in accordance with their respective constitutional processes," which presumably meant, in the American case, that Congress would have to authorize an American response. The treaty, creating the North Atlantic Treaty Organization (NATO), was signed in Washington on April 4, 1949, by the United States, Britain, France, Italy, Belgium, the Netherlands, Denmark, Norway, Portugal, Luxembourg, Iceland, and Canada.

The spring of 1948 also saw the prompt American recognition of the new Republic of Israel, proclaimed on May 14 when the British mandate in Palestine came to an end. Truman's action, though unpopular in the national-security bureaucracy, won general acclaim.

Confusion on the home front

The process of reconversion. Truman's course in domestic policy had run far less smoothly. He had decided, as soon as the war ended, to dissipate any doubt about where he stood on domestic issues. His

Berlin airlift:
it broke the blockade

message to Congress on September 6, 1945, was his answer to the question (as he later wrote) of whether "the progress of the New Deal [was] to be halted in the aftermath of war as decisively as the progress of Woodrow Wilson's New Freedom had been halted after the first World War." In this document and in six additional messages in the next three months, Truman laid out the main elements of what was called after 1948 the Fair Deal—full-employment legislation, public housing, farm-price supports, the nationalization of atomic energy, health insurance, a permanent Fair Employment Practices Commission, and an updating of New Deal legislation on conservation, social security, and minimum wages. Truman evidently saw himself as both the continuator and the consolidator of Roosevelt's brilliant improvisations. A man of orderly administrative habits, he tried to systematize the Presidency and to rationalize the recently expanded government.

At the same time, he was faced with the problem of reconverting the nation's economy from war to peace without creating depression. Predictions of 8 or 10 million unemployed had been common in 1945. But the American economy showed far more resilience than anyone expected. Between 1945 and 1946 government purchases of goods and services declined by a sum equal to almost one-quarter of the gross national product. This decline, according to theorists, should have brought in its wake a disastrous fall in the national output and a rise in unemployment. But the gross national product declined only slightly in the same period, and employment actually increased by 3 million.

This extraordinary achievement was due in great part to the pent-up demand for consumer goods after the deprivations of the war years. It was also due to sensible government policy. The Servicemen's Readjustment Act of 1944, known popularly as the G.I. Bill of Rights, assisted veterans in a variety of ways to find employment, education, and medical care; between 1945 and 1952 the government provided veterans with $13.5 billion for education and training alone. In addition, Congress considered in the winter of 1945–46 a so-called full-employment bill, committing the government to use federal investment and expenditure to assure "a full employment volume of production." Though conservative opposition succeeded in diluting the Murray-Wagner bill, the Employment Act of 1946, enacted in February, established the Council of Economic Advisers and charged the federal government with responsibility for maintaining a high level of economic activity.

Inflation rather than depression was the greater threat. With the war over, the nation was chafing more than ever under price and wage controls. Businessmen evaded the system through black markets; labor, seeking wage increases after years of wartime denial, went out on strike. When a railroad strike paralyzed the economy in the spring of 1946, Truman asked Congress for power to draft strikers into the army—a request that even conservatives deemed intemperate and that the Senate rejected. Congress subsequently extended the OPA but so weakened its authority that Truman vetoed the bill. There followed an interval in July 1946 with no controls at all, during which time prices shot up almost 25 percent. When Congress passed another bill a few weeks later, it was too late to put back the lid. The assault on OPA was, in the end, responsible for the largest price rise in a single year in American history. Wholesale prices increased more from 1946 to 1947 than they had during the entire Second World War.

The Eightieth Congress at home

The election of 1946. As the midterm congressional election approached, Truman seemed to have lost control of the economic and political situation. Labor resented his violent reaction to the railroad strike, farmers his attempt to roll back meat prices. Conservatives disliked his professions of liberalism; liberals distrusted his faltering performance and were dismayed by the elimination of New Deal personalities, like Harold Ickes and Henry Wallace, from the Administration. Republicans asked with penetrating effect, "Had enough?" "To err is Truman" became a popular joke.

To no one's surprise, the Republicans carried both houses of Congress for the first time since 1928

and won governorships in twenty-five states. The new Eightieth Congress proved a bulwark of conservatism. Its dominant figure was Robert A. Taft of Ohio, son of the former President and a senator of inexhaustible energy, knowledge, and self-confidence. His admirers regarded him as the epitome of old-fashioned American wisdom; his critics said he had the best mind in Washington until he made it up.

Taft had long been concerned with ending what he regarded as the privileged position created for organized labor by the Wagner Act of 1935. The Taft-Hartley bill as amended outlawed the closed shop but permitted a measure of union security through the "union shop" (that is, a contract requiring workers to join the union after being hired—as distinct from the closed shop, which demands that they join before being hired). However, its Section 14B legalized so-called right-to-work laws by which states could forbid the requirement of union membership as a condition of employment. It also provided for a cooling-off period before resort to strikes. Labor leaders denounced the law extravagantly as a "slave-labor" measure, and Truman vetoed it. But in early 1947 Congress passed the Taft-Hartley Act over his veto.

The conservatives also passed in 1947 a constitutional amendment forbidding presidential third terms—a belated act of vengeance against Franklin D. Roosevelt. The Twenty-second Amendment was ratified by the required thirty-six states in February 1951. In other areas the Eightieth Congress ignored Truman's legislative recommendations and passed more bills, including a major tax reduction in 1948, over his veto.

Truman fights back. As the 1948 presidential election approached, Truman's advisers, especially his White House counsel, Clark Clifford, concluded that his only hope for reelection lay in the militant advocacy of a liberal program. The President agreed and in early 1948 bombarded Congress with a series of reform proposals. Much of this was a reaffirmation of New Deal objectives, but in the field of racial justice he broke new ground.

Though he had grown up according to the Southern customs of a border state, Truman was a man of humane instinct. He was also aware of the considerable change in the position of black America wrought by the New Deal and the war. Recognizing the validity of black aspirations, he had appointed in 1946 a President's Committee on Civil Rights. A year later the committee recommended a permanent commission on civil rights, a mandatory FEPC, antilynching and anti-poll-tax laws, and a strengthening of civil-rights statutes and enforcement machinery. In an eloquent message on February 2, 1948, Truman made these proposals part of his executive program. This

To strengthen the right to equality of opportunity, the President's Committee recommends:

1. In general:

The elimination of segregation, based on race, color, creed, or national origin, from American life.

The separate but equal doctrine has failed in three important respects. First, it is inconsistent with the fundamental equalitarianism of the American way of life in that it marks groups with the brand of inferior status. Secondly, where it has been followed, the results have been separate and unequal facilities for minority peoples. Finally, it has kept people apart despite incontrovertible evidence that an environment favorable to civil rights is fostered whenever groups are permitted to live and work together. There is no adequate defense of segregation.... We believe that federal funds, supplied by taxpayers all over the nation, must not be used to support or perpetuate the pattern of segregation in education, public housing, public health services, or other public services and facilities.... A federal Fair Employment Practice Act prohibiting discrimination in private employment should provide both educational machinery and legal sanctions for enforcement purposes.

**From the President's Committee on Civil Rights,
To Secure These Rights, 1947.**

attempt to realize the promises of the Declaration of Independence for all Americans, regardless of race or color, represented Truman's boldest initiative in the domestic field.

The civil-rights proposals alienated the conservative Democrats of the South. In the meantime, the Truman Doctrine and the Marshall Plan outraged communist sympathizers in the North, as well as liberals like Henry A. Wallace, whose concern for world peace led them to overlook the implications of Stalinism. A new anticommunist liberal group, Americans for Democratic Action, while deeply opposed to Wallace, was skeptical of Truman. Old-line Democratic bosses shared this skepticism. As the Democratic convention drew near, a "dump-Truman" movement gained momentum.

The anti-Truman forces were unable to agree on an alternative, however, and in the end Truman won renomination with little difficulty. The choice of Senator Alben Barkley of Kentucky for the Vice Presidency was exceptionally popular. Truman's acceptance of a strong civil-rights plank after a floor fight brought the ticket the enthusiastic support of Northern liberals.

The 1948 campaign. The Republicans had once again nominated Governor Thomas E. Dewey of New York. Governor Earl Warren of California received the vice-presidential nomination. Dewey campaigned with the quiet confidence of a man who could not lose. Republican optimism swelled even further when

a communist-dominated Progressive party nominated Wallace for the Presidency and when the die-hard Southern Democrats formed the States Rights Democratic party (better known as the Dixiecrats) and nominated Strom Thurmond of South Carolina.

Only Truman thought he could win. He began a lively "give 'em hell" campaign across the country, telling audiences at every whistlestop that the record of the "do-nothing, good-for-nothing" Republican Eightieth Congress proved the worthlessness of Republican campaign promises. A fall in the price of corn and hogs alarmed the farmers. The Dixiecrat revolt confirmed the blacks in their Democratic allegiance, while the Wallace movement eliminated communism as an issue between the major parties and kept Catholics in the Democratic camp. Neither Dewey's personality nor his campaign roused much enthusiasm, even among his supporters. Truman, on the other hand, emerged as a pungent orator, an indomitable fighter, and—in contrast to his opponent—an intensely *human* being. By late October, shouting crowds greeted Truman's appearances with the joyful cry, "Pour it on, Harry." By election day he had traveled 31,700 miles and had delivered 356 speeches.

Public-opinion polls forecast a sure Republican victory. The Chicago *Tribune* put out an election extra announcing Dewey as the next President. But Truman received 24.1 million popular votes against 22 million for Dewey, and 303 electoral votes against 189. Thurmond carried four states (South Carolina, Mis-

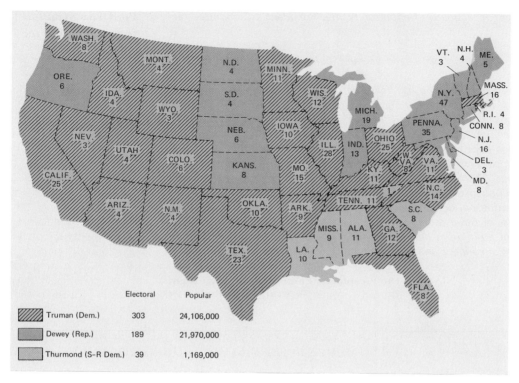

The election of 1948

sissippi, Alabama, and Louisiana) and polled 1.2 million voltes. Wallace also polled 1.2 million votes but carried no states. In addition, the Democrats captured both houses of Congress. Truman had at last established himself as President in his own right. As for the pollsters, one wit observed, "Public opinion polls reach everyone in America, from the farmer in his field right up to the President of the United States, Thomas E. Dewey."

The Fair Deal

Return to frustration. Truman regarded his victory as a mandate for liberalism. "We have rejected the discredited theory that the fortunes of the nation should be in the hands of a privileged few," he said in January 1949. "Instead, we believe that our economic system should rest on a democratic foundation and that wealth should be created for the benefit of all. The recent election shows that the American people are in favor of this kind of society and want to go on improving it." His state-of-the-union message was a ringing summons to a new era of social reform. "Every segment of our population and every individual," he concluded, "has a right to expect from his government a fair deal."

But his Fair Deal roused fierce opposition. Secretary of Agriculture Charles F. Brannan's plan to support farm income rather than prices and Federal Security Administrator Oscar Ewing's proposal for national health insurance were condemned as "socialistic." Congress refused to repeal the Taft-Hartley Act and rejected Truman's requests for federal aid to education and for middle-income housing. A Senate filibuster killed the FEPC. On the other hand, though thwarted in his legislative program for civil rights, Truman was able through executive action to combat segregation within the government and the armed services.

The year 1949 was marked by the first serious economic troubles since the war. Unemployment reached 4.6 million, or 7 percent of the labor force. By the middle of the year, however, the tide had begun to turn. Though the Eightieth Congress had not reduced taxes in 1948 for Keynesian reasons, the effect was to release funds for consumer spending. With this fiscal stimulus, reinforced by increased government expenditures, the economy began to right itself before the downturn could develop momentum.

The Fair Deal abroad. Truman did not see the Fair Deal as merely a domestic policy. In a listing of points in his inaugural address, he placed particular emphasis on Point Four—"a bold new program for making the benefits of our scientific advances and industrial progress available for the improvement and growth of underdeveloped areas." With western Europe presumably secure against communism, the next priority was to prevent the uncommitted third of the world from falling into communist hands.

The Point Four program of technical assistance to underdeveloped countries was a first response to what was evolving as a major challenge to the West—the "revolution of rising expectations" sweeping through Asia, Africa, and Latin America and producing an intense desire for political independence, economic growth, and social modernization. The war against poverty, Truman said, "is the only war we seek."

Revolution in China. The most conspicuous communist gain in the Third World was not the result of premeditated Soviet design. Stalin seems to have believed nearly as firmly as the United States in the capacity of the Nationalist regime of Chiang Kai-shek to organize China. If he had not, he would hardly have stripped Manchuria of nearly a billion dollars' worth of industrial equipment in 1945. Both superpowers underestimated the revolutionary possibilities in China—the ancient resentments against foreign domination, the pent-up demand for agrarian reform, the growing revulsion against the corruption and autocracy of the Kuomintang, and the skill and tenacity with which the Chinese Communists under Mao Tsetung exploited these discontents.

After the war Washington began by favoring a coalition between the Nationalists and the Communists. As so resolute an anticommunist as General Claire Chennault put it, "There is only one way out. . . . That is for us to sponsor thorough political reconstruction at Chungking, followed by true unifi-

cation between Chungking and Yenan." Generals Wedemeyer and MacArthur joined in a similar recommendation in December 1945. The new American ambassador to China, General Patrick J. Hurley, took enthusiastic personal charge of this effort. When a disenchanted Hurley resigned in November 1945, Truman appointed General George C. Marshall to continue his work. But the Nationalists believed that they could win a civil war; the communists were committed by ideology to domination. In January 1947 Marshall abandoned his mission, blaming its failure on both the reactionaries in the Kuomintang and the communists.

Though the Nationalists scored early military successes, they soon began to overextend themselves. The communists, welded by quasi-religious conviction and helped by the increasing popular hatred of the Nationalist government, now started to win victories. With each victory they captured more arms and attracted more deserters. In 1947 Truman sent Wedemeyer to China on a fact-finding tour. "The only basis on which national Chinese resistance to Soviet aims can be revitalized," Wedemeyer reported, "is through the presently corrupt, reactionary and

Mao and comrades:
spirited, efficient, incorruptible

725

inefficient Chinese National government." Therefore the United States should aid that government. But "until drastic political and economic reforms are undertaken United States aid cannot accomplish its purpose."

Chiang made no serious attempt at reform. Washington resolutely opposed proposals that would have entangled the United States in the fighting. By January 1949 the Nationalist armies had abandoned Peking and Tientsin. Shanghai fell in May, Canton in October. By the end of the year, the Nationalist regime had fled to the island of Formosa (Taiwan).

The collapse of Chiang provoked a bitter political debate in the United States. Some contended that anti-Nationalist prejudice—if not outright treason—in the State Department caused the "loss of China." But, as Wedemeyer explained the Nationalist defeat, it was "lack of spirit, primarily lack of spirit. It was not lack of equipment. In my judgment they could have defended the Yangtze with broomsticks if they had the will to do it." It was Chiang's failure to retain the support of his own people that brought about his defeat—this plus the efficiency, incorruptibility, and fanaticism of Mao Tse-tung and the Chinese communists. The American government accepted the result without undue surprise, put out a white paper placing the blame on Chiang, pronounced Taiwan in January 1950 a part of mainland China, declared American neutrality even if the communists sought to take the island by force, and adopted a general policy of "letting the dust settle."

Limited war

The dilemma of deterrence.
If the rhetoric of the Truman Doctrine seemed to call for a worldwide program of containing the communists, Truman himself did not construe the doctrine in any such crusading way, applying it neither to China nor to eastern Europe as it was applied to Greece and Turkey. Even with regard to Russia, he could make amiable public reference to Stalin in 1948 as "Uncle Joe." In 1949 he seemed to view the contest with the Soviet Union without alarm. The forward drive of communism in Europe had been stopped, in Berlin as well as in western Europe. The dust was settling in China. All this encouraged the President to continue to clamp down on the defense budget.

The National Security Act of 1947 established a unified defense establishment, creating a Secretary of Defense, a permanent Joint Chiefs of Staff, a National Security Council, and a Central Intelligence Agency. But Truman kept national-security expenditures under tight control; in 1947–50, they averaged only

$13 billion a year. By 1949 the army was down to ten active divisions. The capacity to fight small wars had dwindled. Deterrence rested on the idea of a retaliatory air-atomic strike against the Soviet Union. If war broke out, it seemed that Washington faced the choice either of doing nothing or of blowing up the world. Observers feared that this situation might invite communist aggression in some marginal area where the United States would not wish to respond by atomic war and lacked the means to respond otherwise.

The end of the atomic monopoly.
Then in September 1949 evidence reached Washington that an atomic explosion had occurred in the Soviet Union. With one stroke the Russians had not only broken the atomic monopoly but had proved to the world their own technological capacity. The era of American invincibility had come to an end.

In response, Truman concluded a bitter argument among his scientific advisers by directing the Atomic Energy Commission to proceed with the construction of a hydrogen bomb, a weapon even more fearful than the atomic bomb. At the same time, he instructed the National Security Council to undertake a basic reappraisal of America's strategic position. The result was a document known as NSC 68, which called for an increase in military expenditures from 5 to, if necessary, 20 percent of the gross national product and more ample capacity to deal with conventional and local wars. But, before NSC 68 could be translated into concrete policy, a new development reinforced the thesis that air-atomic power by itself would not assure American security.

War in Korea.
When American and Soviet troops entered Korea after the collapse of Japan in 1945, they had accepted the thirty-eighth parallel as a military dividing line. Time and the Cold War converted the military demarcation into a political frontier. In 1948 the Russians set up a People's Democratic Republic in North Korea, while the Americans recognized the Republic of South Korea. In June 1949 the bulk of the American army of occupation withdrew from South Korea. The position of the new republic in the American security system was not altogether clear. Both General Douglas MacArthur and Dean Acheson, who had now succeeded Marshall as Secretary of State, declared that South Korea lay outside the American defense perimeter in the Pacific. Should an attack occur, Acheson said, "The initial reliance must be on the people attacked to resist it and then upon the commitments of the entire civilized world under the Charter of the United Nations."

At just this time Kim Il-sung, the communist dictator of North Korea, came to Moscow to seek

Stalin's support for a North Korean invasion of South Korea. Misled perhaps by the MacArthur and Acheson statements, misled too perhaps by Kim's confidence that the South Koreans would welcome the North Koreans as liberators, Stalin gave Kim a green light. On June 25, 1950, North Korean troops crossed the thirty-eighth parallel in a surprise invasion.

Truman was confronted with what he later recalled as his toughest decision. In retrospect it appears that Stalin may well have acquiesced in a project that Kim wished for his own reasons and that seemed to involve minimal risks for the Soviet Union. But Truman was convinced that the invasion was a premeditated Soviet effort to test the American will. If the United States did not react in Korea, he believed, the Russians would sponsor similar thrusts elsewhere; and the result might be a third world war. And indeed, even if Stalin had not instigated the invasion, no one can tell how he would have interpreted an American failure to respond. Without hesitation, Truman committed American forces under General MacArthur to the defense of South Korea. At the same time he brought the matter before the United Nations Security Council. The absence of the Soviet delegate, who was boycotting the Security Council in pique over its refusal to seat a delegate from Communist China, made it possible for the US to condemn North Korean aggression without a Soviet veto. Truman, however, rejected proposals that he ask Congress for a joint resolution authorizing the commitment of

South Korea: to the front for limited objectives

the American troops to combat. His reliance instead on dubious theories of inherent presidential power dangerously enlarged the freedom of future Presidents to take the nation into war.

The original UN intention in South Korea was simply to repel the North Korean invasion. At first the communists drove the UN troops—made up of ROK (Republic of Korea) forces and American troops, soon to be reinforced by a smattering of units from other nations, especially Great Britain and Turkey—back to the southeastern corner of the peninsula. But on September 15, in a daring move, MacArthur landed an amphibious force at Inchon behind the enemy lines. By September 27 the UN forces were in Seoul, and by October 1 they had recovered almost all of Korea below the thirty-eighth parallel.

Crossing the thirty-eighth parallel. MacArthur's brilliant generalship now raised the question whether the UN forces should pursue the enemy into North Korea. Despite warnings from Peking that crossing the thirty-eighth parallel might provoke Chinese intervention, the UN General Assembly, "recalling that the essential objective was the establishment of a unified, independent, and democratic Korea," authorized UN forces on October 7 to move north.

On October 15, 1950, Truman and MacArthur met at Wake Island. When the President asked the General about the chances of Chinese or Soviet intervention in Korea, MacArthur replied, "Very little. . . . If the Chinese tried to get down to Pyongyang there would be the greatest slaughter." He added that he

The shifting front in Korea

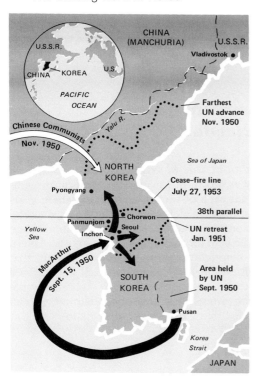

727

Limited war

believed all enemy resistance would end by Thanksgiving. Superbly confident, MacArthur ignored cautions from Washington and deployed his forces in a thin line across North Korea. On November 24 he declared that his final drive to end the war was "now approaching its decisive effort." Two days later, a Chinese communist army drove a wedge through the central sector. The UN forces retreated in disarray two-thirds of the way down the peninsula.

Relations between MacArthur and Washington, not easy in victory, became prickly in defeat. Years of proconsulship had charged a naturally proud and flamboyant personality with a conviction of independent authority. In a barrage of public statements after his November defeat MacArthur suggested that the blame lay, not in his own faulty intelligence or tactics, but in the Washington decision to limit the war to Korea and to forbid attack on Chinese bases in Manchuria. This "privileged sanctuary," he said in one message, was "an enormous handicap, without precedent in military history." On December 6 Truman ordered MacArthur to clear all subsequent statements with Washington.

No substitute for victory? The tension between MacArthur and Truman reflected fundamental disagreement over the purpose of the war. MacArthur believed that the United States must pursue the Korean conflict to a victorious conclusion. If this required an escalation of the war—the bombing of Manchurian bases, the blockade and nuclear bombing of China, the entry of the Nationalist Chinese—then so be it. "In war there is no substitute for victory."

The Administration, on the other hand, saw the conflict as a limited war for limited objectives. If Manchuria was a privileged sanctuary, so were Okinawa and Japan. To commit American military strength to the mainland of Asia might abandon Europe to Soviet aggression. To transform a limited war into a general war against Communist China would be, in General Omar Bradley's phrase, to fight "the wrong war, at the wrong place, at the wrong time, and with the wrong enemy."

The Administration was content to achieve the original objective of its intervention—the integrity of South Korea. A reversal of military fortunes now gave hope that this limited goal could be won. General Matthew B. Ridgway, who had taken command of the Eighth Army in December, began to recover the initiative. By March most of South Korea was once again free of communists, and Ridgway's troops were pressing on the thirty-eighth parallel. The Administration called for a diplomatic settlement. But a defiant MacArthur statement demanding enemy surrender killed the President's move toward negotiation. "By this act," Truman later said, "MacArthur left me no

choice—I could no longer tolerate his insubordination." When on April 5, Congressman Joseph Martin of Massachusetts, the Republican leader in the House, produced a new and provocative MacArthur letter, Truman relieved MacArthur of his command.

Truman's decision caused an outburst of public indignation. Senator Joseph McCarthy of Wisconsin ascribed MacArthur's recall to the machinations of a White House clique besotted by "bourbon and benedictine." Senator William Jenner of Indiana declared, "This country today is in the hands of a secret inner coterie which is directed by agents of the Soviet Union." The fever reached its pitch on April 19 when MacArthur, returning to the United States for the first time in fourteen years, addressed a joint session of Congress. He concluded with a reference to a barracks-room ballad popular in his youth "which proclaimed most proudly that 'old soldiers never die; they just fade away.' And like the old soldier of that ballad," he went on, "I now close my military career and just fade away, an old soldier who tried to do his duty as God gave him the light to see that duty."

There followed an extraordinary inquiry by the Senate Foreign Relations and Armed Services committees into the circumstances of MacArthur's dismissal. Beginning on May 3, MacArthur, Acheson, Marshall, Bradley, and other military and civilian leaders underwent a congressional interrogation that, in time, canvassed the most basic problems of global strategy. When the hearings ended on June 25, over 2 million words had been transcribed. This ventilation of the issues dispelled much of the turbulence. The Administration persuaded the country that the President and the Joint Chiefs, having the global interests of the country in view, might have been justified in overruling MacArthur's local recommendations. In a short time, Truman rode out the storm; and MacArthur in due course began to fade away.

The Korean War: repercussions

Could the Cold War have been avoided? By now the Cold War was in full swing. In retrospect it seems probable that each of the superpowers in these years was acting more on defensive grounds and on local considerations than the other realized. Neither nation had a master plan for world dominion. Yet the American government could hardly have been certain that Soviet aims would have remained local and limited had counterpolicies not developed. Acheson wrote twenty years after, "A school of academic criticism has concluded that we overreacted to Stalin, which in turn caused him to overreact to policies of the United States. This may be true. Fortunately, perhaps, these authors were not called upon to analyze a situation in which the United States had not taken the action which it did take."

In retrospect hard questions remain. His closest collaborators later described the Soviet dictator as a man with marked psychopathic traits, especially vengefulness, morbid suspicion, and an obsession with conspiracies. Could the democracies really have relied on the self-restraint of an increasingly paranoid Stalin if there had been no western resistance—no Truman Doctrine, no Marshall Plan, no NATO, no rearmament, no response to the Berlin blockade or to the invasion of South Korea? Had the democracies not rallied, would not Moscow have had an irresistible temptation to keep moving, always on the pretext of rendering its own borders even more secure? There thus seems even in retrospect an awful inevitability about the Cold War. Even without Stalin would not the Marxist-Leninist analysis have required Soviet leaders to believe that the mere existence of a capitalist power was by definition a threat to survival?

The globalization of containment. Though the limitations imposed on the Korean War showed that the defense of western Europe remained the top American priority, the fact that the war was fought at all expressed the growing American belief that Soviet expansion, if blocked in the main theater, would break out in secondary theaters. Korea thereby resulted in the transformation of containment from a selective European policy into a general global policy. Interpreting the North Korean invasion as part of a worldwide communist offensive, Truman proceeded to batten down hatches all around the world.

The image of an aggressive Russia commanding a highly centralized world communist movement—an image neither new, nor, in the age of Stalin, altogether false—now fastened itself dogmatically on the American mind. The new China, for example, began to be perceived simply as an extension of Soviet power. Three days after the North Korean attack, Truman canceled the policy of neutrality in the Chinese civil war, declared that the seizure of Taiwan by "communist forces" would threaten American security in the Pacific, and ordered the Seventh Fleet to prevent a mainland attack on the island (and also to prevent a Nationalist attack on the mainland). By 1951 Assistant Secretary of State Dean Rusk could speak of the Mao regime as a "colonial Russian government—a Slavic Manchukuo."

The nationalist uprising against French control in Indochina was incorporated into the larger pattern. During the Second World War Roosevelt had opposed the restoration of Indochina to French rule, favoring instead an international trusteeship to prepare Indochina for independence. This wise suggestion was forgotten after his death, and the return of the French colonial government produced dogged resistance on the part of Ho Chi Minh and the so-called Viet Minh. Though Ho had served the Comintern for twenty years, he was a nationalist as well as a communist; and the Viet Minh were seen by most Indochinese as a movement for national independence. Washington had paid little attention to the fighting in Indochina until the fall of mainland China roused anxieties about wholesale communist expansion in Asia. When the French government made token concessions to a client regime in Saigon, the Truman Administration began to give the French military and economic assistance. After Korea the State Department, condemning Ho as "an agent of world communism," pronounced the French role in Indochina "an integral part of the world-wide resistance by the Free Nations to Communist attempts at conquest."

In the United States, the Korean War brought about a quick reversal of the policy of military retrenchment. Major national-security expenditures rapidly increased; from 4 percent of the gross national product in 1948, national-defense expenditures rose above 13 percent by 1953. Two years after the attack on South Korea, the nation had 3.6 million men under arms—an increase of nearly 2.2 million. The Soviet problem was seen more and more in military terms. With American financial backing, Britain and France launched rearmament programs, and in September 1950 Acheson persuaded his European allies to go along with a measure of rearmament in Germany. In 1951 NATO forces were integrated under the command of General Eisenhower. Truman's decision to send four additional American divisions in Europe set off an impassioned but inconclusive "Great Debate" in which conservative legislators, led by Taft, challenged Truman's conviction that he had the power to take that step without congressional authorization.

Domestic repercussions. The Korean War had widespread domestic impact. Unlike Franklin Roosevelt, who except in wartime had sought when possible to act on the basis of congressional statute, Truman embraced an enlarged view of independent presidential prerogative. Fearing in April 1952 that a nationwide steel strike would stop the flow of military material to the troops in Korea, he directed the government to seize and operate the steel mills, defending this action as an exercise of the emergency powers of the President. But the Supreme Court, in the notable case of *Youngstown Steel & Tube Co.* v. *Sawyer*, rejected the presidential thesis, at least in its immediate application. Truman promptly complied with the decision.

729

Military spending stimulated the economy, increasing both the gross national product and inflation. Between the outbreak of war and the imposition of price and wage controls in January 1951, the cost of living rose at an annual rate of nearly 12 percent in retail prices and 24 percent in wholesale prices. Thereafter the controls and tax increases stabilized price levels.

It was easier to contain the economic than the psychological consequences of Korea. With the intensification of the Cold War, many Americans demanded to know why the nation they deemed so powerful and so safe in 1945 should now, five years later, appear in deadly peril. Some, resenting the complexity of history, found a satisfactory answer by tracing all troubles to the workings of the communist conspiracy—unsleeping, omnipresent, and diabolically cunning. Unquestionably there had been communist penetration of the American government, the labor movement, and the intellectual community, and there were now multiplying disclosures of communist espionage in Canada and other countries. Recognizing the reality of the problem and at the same time hoping to keep public reaction under control, Truman in 1947 had set up a federal loyalty program. "Disloyal and subversive elements must be removed from the employ of government." Truman said. "We must not, however, permit employees of the Federal government to be labelled as disloyal . . . when no valid basis exists for arriving at such a conclusion."

Despite these injunctions, the loyalty program—as a consequence of overzealous investigators, ignorant or malicious informers, and apprehensive loyalty boards—began to assume a drastic and promiscuous character. By December 1952, 6.6 million people had been checked for security. Of the 25,750 who received full FBI field investigations, 5,900 withdrew before or during adjudication and 490 were dismissed as ineligible on loyalty grounds. No cases of espionage were uncovered by the investigations. The outcome was an impressive testimonial to the public service, but it was purchased in many cases at a pitiful human cost. "It was not realized at first," Acheson later wrote, "how dangerous was the practice of secret evidence and secret informers, how alien to all our conceptions of justice and the rights of the citizen. . . . Experience proved again how soon good men become callous in the use of bad practices."

The government also initiated prosecutions against top communist leaders under the Smith Act of 1940, which prohibited groups from conspiring to advocate the violent overthrow of the government. Throughout the country, citizens anxious to protect their communities against the dread infection sometimes, in ardor or panic, failed to distinguish between disloyalty and traditional American radicalism or mere dissent.

The denunciation in 1948 of Alger Hiss, a former State Department official, as a communist spy and his conviction for perjury in January 1950 increased popular apprehension. If Hiss, a man of apparently unimpeachable respectability, was a communist agent, who might not be? The Administration compounded its troubles when Truman called the Hiss affair a "red herring" and Acheson, after Hiss' conviction, said, "I do not intend to turn my back on Alger Hiss." Then in February a little-known senator from Wisconsin, Joseph R. McCarthy, gave a speech in Wheeling, West Virginia. "I have here in my hand a list," he said—a list of communists in the State Department; whether he said there were 205 or 81 or 57 or "a lot" of communists (and this was a question around which much controversy would revolve) was in the end less important than his insistence that these communists were "known to the Secretary of State" and were "still working and making policy." With this speech, a remarkable figure began a brief but lurid career on the national stage.

The rise of McCarthyism. McCarthy's charges prompted an astonished Senate to appoint a subcommittee under Senator Millard Tydings of Maryland to look into his allegations. After weeks of hearings, the Tydings Committee declared that McCarthy had worked a "fraud and a hoax." Yet, for all the apparent failure of McCarthy's charges, the hearings also revealed the facility, agility, and lack of scruple with which he operated. His most characteristic weapon was what the journalist Richard Rovere called the "multiple untruth"—a statement so complicated, flexible, and grandiose in its mendacity as almost to defy rational refutation. To this McCarthy added unlimited impudence, an instinct for demagoguery, and an unmatched skill in alley-fighting. If the Tydings Committee thought it had disciplined McCarthy, it was wrong. In the election of 1950, McCarthy's intervention in Maryland, marked by a broad hint that Tydings, a conservative Democrat whom Roosevelt had tried in vain to purge in 1938, was procommunist, brought about Tydings' defeat. From that moment, the Wisconsin senator became a formidable figure in the Senate.

The Korean War meanwhile wrought a significant change in the public atmosphere. It created a climate that transformed McCarthy's crusade from an eccentric sideshow, like that of Martin Dies, into a popular movement. If communists were killing American boys in Korea, why should communists be given the benefit of the doubt in the United States? For a moment membership in any liberal or internationalist organization seemed to provide grounds for indicting a man's loyalty to his country. Politicians who knew better quailed, especially when they noted the fate of Tydings in 1950 and of William Benton of Connecticut, McCarthy's next major senatorial opponent, in 1952.

Though Truman's loyalty program had in some respects overridden traditional safeguards of civil freedom, it did not go nearly far enough for McCarthy and his followers. In September 1950, Congress passed the McCarran Internal Security Act, establishing a Subversive Activities Control Board to follow communist activities in the United States and setting up bars against the admission to the country of anyone who had once been a member of a totalitarian organization.* Truman vetoed the bill: "We need not fear the expression of ideas—we do need to fear their suppression. . . . Let us not, in cowering and foolish fear, throw away the ideals which are the fundamental basis of our free society." But Congress passed the bill over his veto.

The spectacle of McCarthyism infuriated the President. He told the American Legion:

> Slander, lies, character assassination—these things are a threat to every single citizen everywhere in this country. When even one American—who has done nothing wrong—is forced by fear to shut his mind and close his mouth, then all Americans are in peril. It is the job of all of us—of every American who loves his country and his freedom—to rise up and put a stop to this terrible business.

The 1952 election

Truman in retreat. But the backwash of the Korean War gave McCarthy an eager audience. The Administration and its leading officials—especially Secretary of State Acheson—fell under unsparing attack as communist sympathizers. The Republicans scored impressive gains in the congressional elections of 1950 and looked forward with increasing confidence to 1952.

---

*A second McCarran Act, also passed over Truman's veto, was the Immigration and Nationality Act of 1952. While this bill finally abolished the Asian-exclusion provisions of 1924, it retained the national-origins quota system, which discriminated in favor of immigrants from northern and western Europe and which critics condemned as a form of racism built into federal law. It also required that foreigners visiting the United States go through so complicated a system of loyalty checks that many came to feel that the United States regarded them as potential criminals.

Their confidence grew with revelations of corruption within the Administration. A congressional investigation of the Reconstruction Finance Corporation in 1951 exposed collusion and payoffs—mink coats and deep freezes—in RFC loans. Soon the phrase "five percenter" became the colloquialism for the fixer who arranged profitable transactions with the government for a 5 percent fee. In a few months, further exposures revealed extensive corruption in the Bureau of Internal Revenue and in the tax division of the Department of Justice. In addition, the Senate Crime Investigation Committee, under the chairmanship of Estes Kefauver of Tennessee, set forth before rapt television audiences the connections between politics and organized crime in big cities.

"There are two Trumans," the mordant commentator Elmer Davis once said, "—the White House Truman and the courthouse Truman. He does the big things right, and the little things wrong." The disclosures of 1951–52 called attention to the decline that had taken place in the governmental service from the relatively incorruptible thirties—a decline brought about in part because Truman's scorn for the "professional liberal" had driven many of the old New Dealers from government to be replaced by party hacks. When the facts got out, moreover, Truman, constrained by loyalty to old political associates, seemed grudging in his response; and, though the necessary house-cleaning finally took place, it took place too late for him to recapture public confidence. All this strengthened the idea of a "mess in Washington" and helped substantiate a growing national conviction that the Democratic party had been in power too long.

The campaign of 1952. Robert A. Taft's triumphant reelection to the Senate in 1950 over determined liberal and labor opposition made him the leading contender for the Republican nomination in 1952. But the powerful eastern wing of the party, fearing that the Ohio senator was too strong, too isolationist, and too conservative, turned to General Dwight D. Eisenhower. At the Chicago convention in July the Eisenhower supporters outmaneuvered their opposition in a battle over contested delegates. Eisenhower was nominated on the first ballot. Senator Richard M. Nixon of California, who had played an important part in the exposure of Alger Hiss, became his running mate.

Truman had meanwhile withdrawn from the Democratic contest. Though his choice for the Democratic nomination—Governor Adlai E. Stevenson of Illinois—at first demurred, the Democratic convention in Chicago drafted Stevenson for the top place on the ticket. Little known to voters outside Illinois, Stevenson in the next three months established him-

self as a brilliant, literate, and eloquent candidate. His campaign pledge was to "talk sense to the American people." He explained in a series of remarkable speeches that the problems of the age had no easy solution and called for restraint and sacrifice. Labor backed him, and he won particular support among intellectuals.

The Republican campaign was based on the themes of "Korea, communism, and corruption." Nixon, a more experienced campaigner than Eisenhower, developed these themes with particular relish, referring to the Democratic candidate, for example, as "Adlai the appeaser . . . who got a Ph.D. from Dean Acheson's College of Cowardly Communist Contain-

The victors: Chicago, 1952

Stevenson: a new day

ment." "I further charge," Nixon added, "that Mr. Truman, Dean Acheson and other administration officials for political reasons covered up this Communist Conspiracy and attempted to halt its exposure." Intellectual supporters of Stevenson were dismissed as "eggheads."

The campaign was interrupted by a revelation that Nixon had been a beneficiary of a fund collected on his behalf by California businessmen. For a moment, Eisenhower considered asking Nixon to retire from the ticket. But a histrionic television speech in an autobiographical vein saved the vice-presidential candidate. When Eisenhower, late in the campaign, declared his intention to go to Korea if elected, he clinched his victory. The popular vote showed 33.9 million for Eisenhower, 27.3 million for Stevenson; the margin in the Electoral College was 442 to 89. Though Eisenhower's election was more a personal than a party triumph, twenty years of Democratic rule had come to an end.

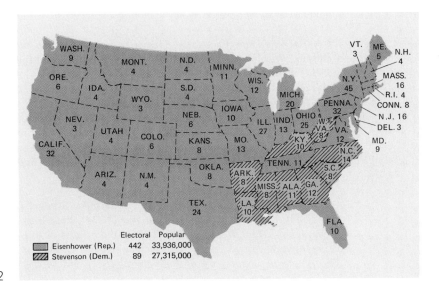

The election of 1952

Suggestions for reading

GENERAL

Truman's *Memoirs,* 2 vols. (1955–56), are pungent and controversial; his *Mr. President* (1952), William Hillman, ed., offers more informal glimpses of his Presidency. Jonathan Daniels, *The Man from Independence* (1950), is perceptive on Truman's formative years. Margaret Truman's affectionate *Harry S Truman** (1973) contains material not found elsewhere. Merle Miller, *Plain Speaking** (1974), conveys an authentic sense of personality but is unreliable in detail. B. J. Bernstein and A. J. Matusow, *The Truman Administration: A Documentary History** (1966), is a useful compilation. A. L. Hamby, *Beyond the New Deal: Harry S Truman and American Liberalism* (1973), is the best study of the Truman Administration; for dissent from the left, see B. J. Bernstein, ed., *Politics and Policies of the Truman Administration** (1970). Two volumes edited by R. S. Kirkendall—*The Truman Period as a Research Field* (1967, 1974)—are suggestive.

FOREIGN POLICY

For general foreign policy, Seyom Brown, *The Faces of Power** (1968), gives a cogent middle-of-the-road analysis. A. L. George and Richard Smoke, *Deterrence in American Foreign Policy: Theory and Practice** (1975), contain valuable case studies of postwar crises. Stanley Hoffmann, *Gulliver's Troubles* (1968), and Franz Schurmann, *The Logic of World Power* (1974), are idiosyncratic and instructive. R. J. Barnett, *Roots of War** (1972), offers a view from the moderate left. For the Cold War, W. H. McNeill, *America, Britain and Russia* (1953), and Herbert Feis, *Churchill, Roosevelt and Stalin** (1957), remain fundamental works. L. A. Rose, *Dubious Victory* (1973), portrays the situation in 1945. Feis, *From Trust to Terror** (1970), L. J. Halle, *The Cold War as History** (1967), and André Fontaine, *History of the Cold War,* 2 vols. (1968–69), carry the story forward. A brilliant contemporaneous critique is Walter Lippmann, *The Cold War** (1947). J. L. Gaddis, *The United States and the Origins of the Cold War** (1972), is intelligent and dispassionate. John Wheeler-Bennett and Anthony Nichols, *The Semblance of Peace** (1972), is an impressive restatement of orthodox views. The revisionist argument is made with moderation in Walter La Feber, *America, Russia and the Cold War, 1945–1966** (1967); with impassioned detail in Joyce and Gabriel Kolko, *The Limits of Power** (1971); see also L. C. Gardner, *Architects of Illusion** (1970), and T. G. Paterson, ed., *Cold War Critics* (1971). For a bracing counterattack, see R. J. Maddox, *The New Left and the Origins of the Cold War* (1973). Two compilations—L. C. Gardner, Arthur Schlesinger, Jr., and Hans Morgenthau, *The Origins of the Cold War** (1970), and J. V. Compton, ed., *America and the Origins of the Cold War** (1972)—give some flavor of the historiographical controversy.

On Soviet policy, R. A. Medvedev, *Let History Judge: The Origins and Consequences of Stalinism** (1972), is by an anti-Stalinist Soviet scholar. Strobe Talbott, ed., *Khrushchev Remembers,* 2 vols. (1970–74), is fascinating. For interpretations by American scholars, see Adam Ulam, *Expansion and Coexistence** (1968) and *The Rivals: America and Russia Since World War II** (1971); and M. D. Shulman, *Stalin's Foreign Policy Reappraised** (1963).

W. A. Harriman (and Elie Abel), *Special Envoy to Churchill and Stalin, 1941–1946* (1975), and Dean Acheson, *Present at the Creation* (1969), are indispensable memoirs. Other significant books by policy-makers include J. F. Byrnes, *Speaking Frankly* (1947) and *All in One Lifetime* (1958); Walter Millis and E. S. Duffield, eds., *The Forrestal Diaries* (1951); A. H. Vandenberg, Jr., and J. A. Morris, eds., *The Private Papers of Senator Vandenberg* (1952); G. F. Kennan, *Memoirs, 1925–1950* (1967); C. E. Bohlen, *Witness to History, 1929–1969* (1973); and J. M. Blum, ed., *The Price of Victory: The Diary of Henry A. Wallace, 1942–1946* (1973). For contemporaneous Republican views, consult J. F. Dulles, *War or Peace* (1950), and R. A. Taft, *A Foreign Policy for Americans* (1951). See also Gaddis Smith, *Dean Acheson* (1972), and J. T. Patterson, *Mr. Republican: A Biography of Robert A. Taft* (1972).

On economic relations with Britain, R. N. Gardner, *Sterling-Dollar Diplomacy* (1956), is the standard work. R. J. Kaiser, *Cold Winter, Cold War* (1974), describes the background of the Truman Doctrine; J. M. Jones, *The Fifteen Weeks** (1955), the origins of the Truman Doctrine and the Marshall Plan. Germany is discussed from various viewpoints in L. D. Clay, *Decision in Germany* (1950); John Gimbel, *The American Occupation of Germany* (1968); and W. P. Davidson, *The Berlin Blockade* (1958).

*Available in a paperback edition.

Akira Iriye, *The Cold War in Asia** (1974), is a good introduction. E. J. Kahn, Jr., *The China Hands* (1975), tells the shaming tale of the State Department's Far Eastern experts. For the Japanese settlement and occupation, see Herbert Feis, *Contest Over Japan** (1967), and E. O. Reischauer, *The United States and Japan* (3rd ed., 1965). Tang Tsou, *America's Failure in China, 1941–1950** (1963), and J. K. Fairbank, *The United States and China** (rev. 3rd ed., 1971), are two excellent works. G. D. Paige, *The Korean Decision: June 24–30, 1950** (1968), is meticulous. R. R. Simmons, *The Strained Alliance* (1975), argues that Kim Il Sung invaded South Korea for his own reasons, not for Moscow's. David Rees, *Korea: The Limited War* (1964), is a good summary; see, in addition, useful works by two generals, M. B. Ridgway, *The Korean War* (1967), and J. L. Collins, *War in Peacetime* (1969); and also Allen Whiting, *China Crosses the Yalu** (1960). MacArthur is discussed adoringly in Courtney Whitney, *MacArthur* (1956), and in Douglas MacArthur, *Reminiscences* (1964), and coolly in R. H. Rovere and Arthur Schlesinger, Jr., *The General and the President* (1951; reissued as *The MacArthur Controversy,* 1965).

For the beginnings of the Indochina imbroglio, see R. H. Fifield, *Americans in Southeast Asia* (1973); J. T. McAlister, *Vietnam: The Origins of Revolution* (1969); G. M. Kahin and J. W. Lewis, *The United States in Vietnam** (1967); and Ellen Hammer, *The Struggle for Indochina** (1954). Edward Friedman and Mark Selden, eds., *America's Asia: Dissenting Essays on Asian-American Relations** (1971), offers a revisionist critique of American Far Eastern policies.

For atomic energy, the authorized but judicious studies by R. G. Hewlett and O. E. Anderson, Jr., *The New World* (1962) and *Atomic Shield* (1969), are indispensable. For more personal views, consult B. M. Baruch, *Baruch, The Public Years* (1960), and the second volume of D. E. Lilienthal, *Journals: The Atomic Energy Years* (1964). On the United Nations, see Trygve Lie, *In the Cause of Peace* (1954), and J. G. Stoessinger, *The United Nations and the Superpowers* (1965).

DOMESTIC AFFAIRS
Samuel Lubell, *The Future of American Politics** (1952), is a penetrating analysis of the political currents of the Truman years; and John Gunther, *Inside U.S.A.* (1951), gives a vivid rendition of political and regional dramatics. S. K. Bailey, *Congress Makes a Law* (1950), deals with the origins of the Employment Act of 1946, while E. S. Flash, Jr., *Economic Advice and Presidential Leadership* (1965), reports on the Council of Economic Advisers in action. Specific aspects of Truman's domestic policy are considered in R. A. Lee, *Truman and Taft-Hartley* (1967); A. F. McClure, *The Truman Administration and the Problems of Postwar Labor* (1969); A. J. Matusow, *Farm Policies and Politics of the Truman Administration* (1967); R. O. Davies, *Housing Reform During the Truman Administration* (1966); P. H. Douglas, *Ethics in Government* (1952); and Estes Kefauver, *Crime in America* (1951). For the 1948 election, see Irwin Ross, *The Loneliest Campaign* (1968), and Allen Yarnell's uncritical *Democrats and Progressives* (1974); for the 1952 election, A. E. Stevenson, *Speeches* (1952), and J. B. Martin's authoritative *Adlai Stevenson of Illinois* (1976).

Diverging estimates of Truman and civil rights may be found in Richard Dalfiume, *Desegregation of the U.S. Armed Forces* (1969), and W. C. Berman, *The Politics of Civil Rights in the Truman Administration* (1970). D. R. McCoy and R. T. Ruetten, *Quest and Response* (1973), strikes a balance.

For the communist problem, Earl Latham, *The Communist Conspiracy in Washington* (1966), is a sober guide. R. H. Rovere, *Senator Joe McCarthy** (1959), is brilliantly critical; W. F. Buckley, Jr., *McCarthy and His Enemies* (1954), is admiring; M. P. Rogin, *The Intellectuals and McCarthy** (1967), gives the most solid explanation of McCarthy's grassroots strength; and Daniel Bell, ed., *The Radical Right** (1963), strives, not altogether persuasively, for sociological illumination. A. D. Harper, *The Politics of Loyalty* (1969), discusses Truman and the communist issue. Thoughtful contemporaneous discussions are to be found in Francis Biddle, *The Fear of Freedom* (1951), and Alan Barth, *The Loyalty of Free Men* (1951). Whittaker Chambers, *Witness* (1952), and Alger Hiss, *In the Court of Public Opinion* (1957), present contrasting views. For anti-Stalinist liberalism, see Reinhold Niebuhr, *The Children of Light and the Children of Darkness** (1944) and *The Irony of American History** (1952), and Arthur Schlesinger, Jr., *The Vital Center** (1949); for a critique of this position, Christopher Lasch, *The New Radicalism in America** (1965).

*Available in a paperback edition.

CHAPTER 31

Years of repose

In the years since 1929 the American people had experienced the worst depression in their history, the worst hot war, the worst Cold War, the worst limited war. Since 1933 they had followed Presidents who believed strongly in affirmative government and vigorous action. But a nation's capacity for crisis and crusades is limited. Just as the first two decades of the twentieth century—the activist decades dominated by Theodore Roosevelt and Woodrow Wilson—left the people with a yearning for normalcy, so the high-tension thirties and forties produced a fresh desire for respite. The new pursuit of normalcy, though, took place in stormier times and within the frameworks established by depression and war. Communist challenge and revolutionary ferment abroad, minority aspirations and population growth at home, confronted the nation with problems it could not easily ignore.

The Eisenhower mood

The new President. President Dwight D. Eisenhower embodied the popular mood. Sixty-two years old on his inauguration, he was already a national hero, beloved by his countrymen. After quiet years in the peacetime army, Eisenhower had been one of that group of remarkable military men who emerged during the Second World War. His service as supreme commander of the Allied Forces in Europe was followed by a postwar tour of duty as Chief of Staff. President of Columbia University in 1948, he returned to Europe as supreme commander of NATO in 1950. He resigned this post to seek the Republican nomination in 1952.

The appearance of being "above" politics was an important source of Eisenhower's popular strength. People weary of the "mess in Washington" and wanting an end to the controversies of the New Deal era saw him as the man to heal the nation's wounds. His appointed role, wrote the influential columnist Walter Lippmann, was "that of the restorer of order and peace after an age of violence and faction." His affable personality and accommodating temperament qualified him as national conciliator. Actually his surface geniality and imprecision concealed much political cunning, an instinct for self-protection, and considerable ability, not always employed, to enforce his will.

Eisenhower and the Presidency. He had been the candidate of what would later be termed the Eastern establishment against the Midwestern, small-town, isolationist Republicans who had favored Robert A. Taft; and he was expected to lead his long-embattled party to accept both the international policies and the social reforms of the Roosevelt-Truman epoch. In foreign policy this anticipation was sound. But the new President had little interest in domestic matters, assigned them low priority, and, though he had no hope of dismantling the New Deal, was in some respects more conservative than Taft.

An exponent of the Whig theory of the Presidency, Eisenhower rejected the idea of strong presidential leadership. Roosevelt and Truman, he felt, had aggrandized the executive branch at the expense of the other branches of government. It was his duty now to "restore" the constitutional balance. In dealing with Congress, he believed that his responsibility was simply to propose policies; thereafter members of Congress could "vote their own consciences." Even within his official family, he did not, save in rare

"Hillside Burrows": Daly City, California

Under the Constitution the President of the United States is alone responsible for the "faithful execution of the laws." Our government is fixed on the basis that the President is the only person in the executive branch who has the final authority. Everyone else in the executive branch is an agent of the President. There are some people, and sometimes members of Congress and the press, who get mixed up in their thinking about the powers of the President. The important fact to remember is that the President is the only person in the executive branch who has final authority, and if he does not exercise it, we may be in trouble. If he exercises his authority wisely, that is good for the country. If he does not exercise it wisely, that is too bad, but it is better than not exercising it at all.

Yet our government is so vast that branches of the administrative machinery do not always tie in smoothly with the White House. The Cabinet represents the principal medium through which the President controls his administration. I made it a point always to listen to Cabinet officers at length and with care, especially when their points of view differed from mine.

I never allowed myself to forget that the final authority was mine. I would ask the Cabinet to share their counsel with me, even encouraging disagreement and argument to sharpen up the different points of view. On major issues I would frequently ask them to vote, and I expected the Cabinet officers to be frank and candid in expressing their opinions to me. At the same time, I insisted that they keep me informed of the major activities of their departments in order to make certain that they supported the policy once I had made a decision.

From Harry S Truman, *Memoirs*, Vol. I, *Year of Decisions*, 1955

cases, insist on his own views. He once said of his Cabinet, "I have given way on a number of personal opinions to this gang." He was not, he liked to remark, the desk-pounding sort of President. Though disposed to complain about the Republican party in private, he realized that he was far more popular than the party and therefore did not propose to risk his public standing by acting as a party-leader. "In the general derogatory sense," he observed in 1955, "you can say that, of course, that I do not like politics."

In running the Presidency, Eisenhower rejected the informal methods of his civilian predecessors in favor of the military staff system. Former Governor Sherman Adams of New Hampshire, as chief of the executive staff, controlled the domestic flow to the President. In foreign affairs, Secretary of State John Foster Dulles had a similar monopoly. "I don't want people springing things on me!" the President often said. Commitment to the staff system confined Eisenhower's knowledge of public matters. He seldom read the daily newspapers and drew on fewer sources of information and ideas than his predecessors.

Some observers welcomed what they regarded as a necessary institutionalization of the Presidency. Others were more skeptical. Sam Rayburn, House Democratic leader, once said of Eisenhower as President: "No, won't do. Good man, but wrong business."

Modern Republicanism at home

Eisenhower's domestic purposes. Eisenhower came to the Presidency at a time of unexpected population growth. The fall in the birth rate during the Depression had led demographers to predict that the nation's population would soon level off. Instead, the return to prosperity in the war years produced a swing to earlier marriages and larger families. At the same time, medical advances—the introduction of penicillin and other antibiotics, of antipolio vaccines, and of new surgical techniques—brought about a steady drop in the death rate. Between 1935 and 1957 the birth rate rose from 16.9 to 25 per thousand, the death rate fell from 10.9 to 9.6, and life expectancy rose toward 70. Furthermore, about 2.25 million immigrants entered the country in the fifties—more than in any decade since the twenties. The nation's population had grown only about 9 million in the thirties; it grew 19 million in the forties and 28 million in the fifties. The increase in the fifties alone was almost equal to the total population of the country a century earlier.

To cope with the consequent strain on the institutions and facilities of American society, Eisenhower offered what he called "modern Republicanism" or "dynamic conservatism." This meant in practice an acceptance of the social and economic framework of the New Deal tempered by a determination to reduce public spending and cut back the activity of the federal government.

Inexperienced in domestic problems, Eisenhower tended to defer to those whose superior wisdom, in his view, was certified by their financial success. His Cabinet was dominated by Secretary of the Treasury George M. Humphrey, an Ohio businessman who reinforced deeply conservative views with a strong personality. When the new Secretary of Defense, Charles E. Wilson of General Motors, was asked whether he foresaw a conflict between his business and official commitments, he replied, "I cannot conceive of one because for years I thought what was good for our country was good for General Motors, and *vice versa.*" The Secretary of the Interior, Douglas McKay of Oregon, summed up the general attitude when he said, "We're here in the saddle as an Administration representing business and industry." The conspicuous exception was the Secretary of Labor, Martin Durkin of the Plumbers Union, whose appointment prompted the remark that the Cabinet consisted of "eight millionaires and a plumber." His presence displeased prominent Republicans like Taft (who termed the appointment "incredible"); and after eight months of vain effort to persuade the Administration to go along on Taft-Hartley revision, Durkin resigned.

Eisenhower economics: inflation. The death in July 1953 of Senator Taft, who was in his way a Tory reformer, removed what might have been a constructive influence on Eisenhower's domestic policy. Thereafter the administration stalled on social questions, concentrating instead on the pursuit of price stability.

One consequence was a feeling within the Administration that, if recession set in, the government should let events take their course, even at the cost of unemployment, rather than risk inflation through a reduction of the interest rate or an increase in public spending. Indeed, the influential Secretary of the Treasury actually believed that cutting government spending was the best way to offset decline.

This fear of stimulative measures was no doubt a factor in the fall in the rate of economic growth from 4.3 percent in the years 1947–52 to 2.5 percent in the years 1953–60. A good deal of this slowdown resulted from recessions in 1953–54, 1957–58, and 1960–61. The 1953–54 recession was occasioned by an $11-billion drop in government spending at the end of the Korean War. The 1957–58 recession was both sharper and shorter. Unemployment rose to 7 percent of the labor force. The federal deficit for the fiscal year 1958–59, which pumped $12.4 billion into the economy, was probably responsible for bringing this setback to a quick end.

The demands on government proved hard to control. For all its concern with budget-balancing, the Eisenhower Administration achieved a budgetary surplus less than half the time and piled up an overall deficit of $18.2 billion as well as the largest peacetime deficit (in 1959) thus far in American history. This record disturbed the more conservative members of the Administration. When Eisenhower sent Congress a $72-billion budget in 1957, Secretary of the Treasury Humphrey said that, if the "terrific" tax burden were not reduced, "I will predict that you will have a depression that will curl your hair."

Despite the Administration's conservative inclinations, prices mounted through the decade. Though the inflation caused by the Korean War was followed by comparative price stability in 1952–55, prices rose in 1955–58 by 8 percent. The climb persisted—contrary to the expectations of orthodox economic theory—even through the recession of 1957–58. Moreover, the true extent of inflation was disguised by a drop in farm prices. If farm prices had risen along with other prices, the price index would have been about eight points higher by 1960.

Economists concluded that changes in the structure of the market had removed key industrial prices from the play of market forces. "Administered" prices—that is, prices and wages set in concentrated industries by decisions independent of the market—could not be effectively controlled by policies designed to repress aggregate demand, like raising the interest rate, controlling the money supply, or cutting public spending. Given its faith in "free enterprise," the Eisenhower Administration was unwilling to in-

terfere with business decisions through wage-price guidelines or other forms of federal intervention.

Eisenhower economics: big government. Eisenhower had a fear of "statism" and cited such projects as the Tennessee Valley Authority as examples of "creeping socialism." He promised what he called a "revolution" in the federal government, "trying to make it smaller rather than bigger and finding things it can stop doing instead of seeking new things to do." The intention was to cut the federal role in every direction—spending, taxation, regulation—and stimulate local and private enterprise.

In power development, the Administration thus favored corporate over public activity. The great power site at Hell's Canyon on the Snake River went to the Idaho Power Company, a Maine corporation, for the construction of three low dams in place of the high multipurpose federal dam urged by public-power advocates. In an evident effort to check the expansion of TVA, the Administration arranged with the newly formed Dixon-Yates syndicate to erect a steam-power plant in Arkansas to provide electricity for TVA customers. The circumstances in which the Dixon-Yates contract was negotiated were so disreputable, however, that the Administration was finally forced to repudiate it. Off-shore oil lands were turned over to the adjacent states. The most prodigal of Eisenhower's domestic programs was the Interstate Highway Act of 1956, which committed the federal government to pay 90 percent of the construction costs of interstate highways and which advocates of other modes of transportation regarded as a subsidy to the automotive industry. Regulatory commissions were now staffed more largely by men sympathetic to the industries they were supposed to regulate.

Particularly close to the President's heart was the vision of transferring countless functions from the federal government to the states. When his Commission on Intergovernmental Relations failed to come up with a comprehensive program for such transfers, Eisenhower in 1957 appealed personally to the Governors' Conference for action. After working for a year, the resulting committee of governors and federal officials could find only two minor programs, costing $80 million, to recommend for transfer from federal to state hands. The notion of a sweeping shift of federal functions either to state and local governments or to private business seemed doomed to frustration. In 1960 the size and structure of the federal government were much what they had been in 1952.

McCarthy: zenith and decline. Some voters had supported Eisenhower in the belief that a Republican President would be able to contain McCarthyism. Eisenhower's campaign, however, had not been reas-

suring on this point. In 1951 McCarthy denounced General Marshall as part of "a conspiracy so immense and an infamy so black as to dwarf any previous venture in the history of man." Later Eisenhower, to avoid offending McCarthy, deleted a paragraph of praise for Marshall from a campaign speech in Wisconsin. This action foreshadowed the President's reluctance to engage himself personally in the McCarthy issue. As he later put it, "I will not get in the gutter with *that* guy."

For over a year, President Eisenhower tried to get along with McCarthy. The Wisconsin senator, agile and unscrupulous as ever, took full advantage of the Administration's indulgence. Before 1953 only the bully of the Senate, he now began, as chairman of the Senate Committee on Government Operations, to swagger without challenge through the executive branch in pursuit of alleged communists and fellow travelers.

A main target was the State Department. He began with an investigation of the Voice of America, the government agency for foreign broadcasts. Next he moved in on the International Information Administration and for a few months exerted direct control over its appointments and policies. His chief counsel, Roy Cohn, accompanied by a committee colleague, G. David Schine, made a whirlwind tour of United States information offices in Europe, plucking offending books from the shelves and terrorizing employees.

Determined to propitiate the right wing, John Foster Dulles was ready to collaborate with McCarthy and even to anticipate his demands. Veteran foreign-service officers whose political reporting had aroused McCarthy's ire were drummed from the service. A McCarthy disciple, W. Scott McLeod, was appointed chief of State Department personnel. The Secretary ordered State Department libraries to remove books by "authors who obviously follow the Communist line or participate in Communist front organizations." Such books as the thrillers of Dashiell Hammett, *The Selected Works of Tom Paine*, and even Whittaker Chambers' *Witness* were banned; a number of the proscribed books were actually burned. By June 1953 the panic had spread so widely that the President himself intervened to arrest it. "Don't join the book burners," he said. "Don't think you are going to conceal faults by concealing evidence that they ever existed."

Meanwhile posses of road-company McCarthys sprang up across the land. What was conceived as an effort to guard the national security became a heresy hunt employing techniques traditionally used to ferret out nonconformists—guilt by association, loyalty oaths, testimony of secret informers, blacklists, suppressions of speech and assembly, interrogation and intimidation by legislative committees. In the 1954 campaign Vice President Nixon boasted of the number of "security risks" who had been driven from government. One notable victim was the great physicist Dr. J. Robert Oppenheimer, the father of the atomic bomb but subsequently an opponent of the hydrogen bomb. Oppenheimer's security clearance was withdrawn in 1953 because of ancient left-wing associations well known to security officers a decade before when Oppenheimer was heading the Manhattan Project. A review board declared that the Oppenheimer case "demonstrated that the Government can search . . . the soul of an individual whose relationship to his Government is in question." It added that national security "in times of peril must be absolute."

Thoughtful people began to wonder whether such ideas as these might not be the most subversive of all. George Kennan said that "absolute security" was an unattainable and self-devouring end—that its frenzied pursuit would lead only to absolute tyranny. Judge Learned Hand summed up the feelings of many Americans:

> I believe that that community is already in process of dissolution where each man begins to eye his neighbor as a possible enemy, where nonconformity with the accepted creed, political as well as religious, is a mark of disaffection; where denunciation, without specification or backing, takes the place of evidence.

If the Korean War had given McCarthy his opportunity for influence, the end of that war in July 1953 brought about his decline. As war frustrations receded, McCarthyism began to lose its emotional base. By now, in his increasingly erratic course, McCarthy had become embroiled with the army, launching a sensational, if unproductive, search for communists and spies at Fort Monmouth, New Jersey. The matter was further complicated by the efforts of Roy Cohn to obtain favored treatment for his sidekick Schine, who had recently been drafted. For a time Vice President Nixon tried to reconcile McCarthy and Secretary of the Army Robert Stevens. But, goaded beyond endurance, the army finally fought back. The denouement took place in a series of televised hearings from April 22 to June 17, 1954.

The Army-McCarthy hearings were a compelling spectacle, marked by vivid and sharply etched personalities and passages of passion and conflict. They commanded a fascinated audience, amounting at times to 20 million people. Viewers trained through long exposure to TV westerns to distinguish between good and bad guys had little trouble deciding to which category McCarthy belonged. After thirty-five days of the grating voice, the sarcastic condescension, the irrelevant interruption ("point of order, Mr. Chairman, point of order"), and the unsupported accusation, McCarthy effectively achieved his own destruction. The spell was at last broken. On December 2, 1954, the Senate censured McCarthy by a sixty-seven to twenty-two vote. The Wisconsin senator was finished. His death in 1957 merely ratified his political demise.

He left, however, a heritage—not only in the broken lives of those he attacked but, paradoxically, in a greatly enhanced conception of presidential prerogative. When McCarthy demanded access to Department of Defense files, Eisenhower in May 1954 claimed "an uncontrolled discretion" to refuse information anywhere in the executive branch. This was the most absolute assertion of the presidential right to withhold information from Congress ever uttered to that point. Because of the detestation of McCarthy, right-minded people generally applauded the Eisenhower theory. But this theory, which acquired in 1957 the name of "executive privilege," ushered in an extraordinary time of executive denial. In its remaining years, the Eisenhower administration rejected more congressional requests, often entirely reasonable, for information than Presidents had done in the first century of American history.

The battle of desegregation. The gravest domestic issue lay in the field of race relations. The struggle to assure blacks their full rights as American citizens had resumed, after a long quiescence, during the New Deal and had gathered momentum during and after the Second World War. Though most of President Truman's civil-rights program was rejected by Congress, his fight for that program established civil rights as a national issue.

Thwarted in Congress, the champions of civil rights now turned to the courts. The Supreme Court, once chary of taking on cases involving Negro rights, started doing so after the war. The early decisions reflected the Fabian tactics of the Court under Chief

Little Rock, 1957:
separate but equal had no place

Justice Fred M. Vinson of Kentucky (1946–53). The Vinson Court sought to work toward equal rights within the inherited legal framework—that is, by accepting the *Plessy* v. *Ferguson* doctrine (see p. 386) of "separate but equal," construing it literally, and rejecting separate facilities when they were not in full and exact fact equal.

Beginning in 1952, attorneys for the National Association for the Advancement of Colored People (NAACP) argued before the Supreme Court against state laws requiring the segregation of children in public education. On May 17, 1954, in the case of *Brown* v. *Board of Education of Topeka*, the Court, speaking through Earl Warren, the new Chief Justice, responded with a unanimous decision reversing *Plessy* v. *Ferguson* and interpreting the Fourteenth Amendment as outlawing racial discrimination in public schools. "We conclude," the Court said, "that in the field of public education, the doctrine of 'separate but equal' has no place. Separate educational facilities are inherently unequal." A year later, the Court called on school authorities to submit plans for desegregation and gave local federal courts the responsibility of deciding whether the plans constituted "good faith compliance." The Court concluded by ordering action "with all deliberate speed."

The border states moved toward compliance. But in South Carolina, Georgia, Alabama, and Mississippi, resistance began to harden, especially after the spread in 1955–56 of the militantly segregationist White Citizens' Councils and a 1956 manifesto by Southern members of Congress, condemning the decision. Some Southern states passed laws to frustrate the Supreme Court ruling. A favorite device was to divert state funds to what might be passed off technically as a private school system. Extreme segregationists revived the pre-Civil War doctrine of nullification under the more mellifluous name of "interposition." Fanatics incited violence, as in Clinton, Tennessee, in 1956.

The crisis of Little Rock. The strategy of resistance came to a climax in 1957 in Little Rock, Arkansas. Governor Orval Faubus, contending that integration would threaten public order, mobilized the Arkansas national guard in an effort to deny nine black students enrollment in the Central High School. Eisenhower had been skeptical about what the government could do to promote equal rights: "It is difficult through law and through force to change a man's heart." But Faubus' open challenge compelled the President to defend the Supreme Court. After a face-to-face discussion with Eisenhower, Faubus withdrew the national guard. When the black boys and girls then entered Central High School, they were mobbed by crowds of angry whites. On September 24,

The assertion of black rights:
Martin Luther King, Jr., and friends,
Montgomery, 1956

1957, Eisenhower sent federal troops into Little Rock. Order was restored, and black children entered the school.

In the meantime, Congress was finally taking action on behalf of racial justice. The Civil Rights Act of 1957, the first of its kind since Reconstruction, authorized the Department of Justice to seek injunctions on behalf of black voting rights. A second act, in 1960, provided for the appointment of federal referees to safeguard voting rights. For its part, the Warren Court extended the principle of the *Brown* case to new fields, striking down segregation over the next years in interstate commerce, in public buildings, in airports and interstate bus terminals, in parks and other public recreational facilities. Both Congress and the Court, by concentrating on segregation as embodied in law, left untouched the wide and bitter realm of *de facto* discrimination; but at the same time, by accepting and, in the Court's case, declaring the moral necessity of equality, they were changing the values of American society.

Blacks themselves were increasingly taking the lead in the struggle. Lawyers like Thurgood Marshall of the NAACP argued the constitutional cases. In the South new leaders emerged to urge the assertion of black rights through nonviolent resistance. Beginning in December 1955, the blacks of Montgomery, Alabama, under the inspiration of a young minister, Dr. Martin Luther King, Jr., boycotted the city's segregated bus system. King, who was strongly influenced by Thoreau and Gandhi, counseled his followers to avoid provocation and to confront "physical force with an even stronger force, namely, soul force." The boycott, reinforced by suits in the federal courts, achieved the desegregation of the bus system in a year. Passive resistance was widely used in the winter of 1959–60 to challenge the refusal to serve blacks at Southern lunch counters. The rapid spread of "sit-in" demonstrations through the South and the support

743

they evoked in the North and among moderate Southern whites testified to the rising moral force of the protest against segregation.

By 1960 blacks were still far from the goal of integration. But, if only limited progress had been made in school desegregation and in assuring the right to vote, vast progress had been made in gaining acceptance for the moral case against discrimination. The rather pallid Southern filibuster against a civil-rights bill in 1960 was marked by the fact that, with one or two exceptions, no one tried any longer to argue the philosophy of white supremacy.

The Warren Court.

When Eisenhower appointed Earl Warren, he did not realize what sort of Chief Justice he was getting. The former Republican governor of California turned out to have a spacious view of the Constitution; and his humane approach received support and elaboration from three other Eisenhower appointees—John M. Harlan, Potter Stewart, and, most consistently, William J. Brennan—as well as from distinguished hold-overs from the Roosevelt Court, Hugo Black, Felix Frankfurter, and William O. Douglas.

In addition to its initiatives in the field of racial justice, the Warren Court, especially in the 1956–57 term, sought to mend the holes McCarthyism had made in the fabric of civil freedom. The *Watkins* and *Sweezy* cases, with their condemnation of exposure "for the sake of exposure," restricted legislative investigations to questions deemed pertinent to a legislative objective. The *Yates* case, reversing one count in the conviction of a group of California communists, construed the Smith Act of 1940 as distinguishing between "the statement of an idea which may prompt its hearers to take unlawful action, and advocacy that such action be taken." The *Jencks* case required that Federal Bureau of Investigation reports, if used by the prosecution in a criminal trial, be made available to the defense.

These decisions stirred up passing furor and led to congressional rage at the Court. In the longer run their impact was less drastic than civil libertarians hoped or than the heirs of McCarthy feared. Indeed, the Court itself sharply qualified the *Watkins* and *Sweezy* rulings by the *Barenblatt* and *Uphaus* decisions in 1959 and 1960, affirming a wide scope for federal and state legislative investigations in the area of communism.

Thoughtful critics felt at times that the activism of the Warren Court was carrying the judiciary into decisions that properly belonged to legislative or executive processes. Defenders replied that legislative and executive inertia had created a vacuum of power, which, if not filled by the Supreme Court, would have severely strained the bonds of social order.

The second term.

As a national hero, above politics, Eisenhower enjoyed a popularity far exceeding that of his party. In 1954, the Democrats took control of both the House and the Senate. In spite of a coronary thrombosis in 1955 and ileitis in 1956, Eisenhower decided to run for reelection. "Some of my medical advisers," he said, "believe that adverse effects on my health will be less in the Presidency than in any other position I might hold." Most voters accepted with sympathy his need for a more carefully regulated life, made affectionate jokes about his long hours on the golf course, and accorded him undiminished confidence. Though Eisenhower several times suggested to Nixon that he might prefer a Cabinet post, his Vice President declined the hint and secured renomination.

The Democrats, over the brief opposition of Harry Truman, renominated Adlai Stevenson, whose penetrating comment on national issues had kept him in the forefront among the party leaders. Estes Kefauver of Tennessee, who had been Stevenson's chief rival till shortly before the convention, received the vice-presidential nomination over John F. Kennedy of Massachusetts. Eisenhower won decisively, carrying the popular vote by 35.6 to 26 million and the Electoral College by 457 to 73. The Democrats, who had regained control of Congress in 1954, slightly increased their majorities in both houses.

If Eisenhower's first term had seen the end of both the Korean War and McCarthyism—if, indeed, only a Republican could perhaps have presided so tranquilly over the liquidation of those angry issues—his second term proved less successful. The Administration's reluctance to move swiftly against the recession of 1957–58 damaged confidence, and its claim to moral rectitude was tarnished in a series of scandals. These scandals forced the resignation of the Secretary of the Air Force, the chairman of the Republican National Committee, the chairman of the Interstate Commerce Commission, the General Services Administrator, the Public Buildings Administrator, a number of lesser officials, and, finally, in September 1958, Sherman Adams, the Assistant to the President.

The 1958 elections brought a Democratic landslide. The Democratic majority in the House—282 to 153—was the largest since 1936. In addition, the Democrats gained a 62 to 34 majority in the Senate. But the Democratic sweep had little effect on the President's conservative policies. The departure of the moderate Adams, ironically, gave Eisenhower's more conservative inclinations free play. His posture in domestic affairs remained to the end one of dogged defense of the budget. In what a later decade would regard as wasted years, little was done to tackle the problem of the cities, of the environment, of racial relations, and of social order at a time when these problems were still relatively manageable.

The American people in the fifties

A homogenized society? The quiescence of government expressed the national mood. People did not want to be bothered by public issues. They sought security rather than adventure, comfort rather than challenge. Society seemed to reward those who lacked rough edges, eschewed eccentricity, excited no suspicion, and played the company game. In a training film circulated by a leading chemical firm, the sound track said, as the camera panned over men in white coats at a Monsanto laboratory, "No geniuses here; just a bunch of average Americans working together." More and more people were spending their whole lives in organizations—their days in great corporations, their nights in great suburban enclaves. By 1960 the suburban population had increased nearly 50 percent in a decade and almost equaled that of the central cities. Both corporation and suburb appeared to foster a pervasive, benign, and invincible conformity. America had become, it was said, a case of the bland leading the bland.

The compelling medium of television advanced the process of homogenization. Originally developed in the 1930s, television went on the market in the late forties. In 1950, 3.2 million Americans owned sets; in 1960, 50 million. By 1960 more households had television than had running water or indoor toilets. It was estimated that these families spent five hours a day watching the tiny screen. "The strongest sustained

Moving day: benign conformity

attention of Americans," said Dr. Frank Stanton, president of the Columbia Broadcasting System, "is now, daily and nightly, bestowed on television as it is bestowed on nothing else." Programming was dominated by three large networks and a collection of advertising agencies. The result dismayed thoughtful viewers. Edward R. Murrow, who himself did much to elevate the medium, wrote, "Television in the main is being used to distract, delude, amuse and insulate."

Most striking of all was the hold the mood of quiescence seemed to have on the young. Older generations, recalling their springtimes of revolt—cultural in the twenties, political in the thirties—looked with incredulity on this "uncommitted generation" composed of prudent young men and women who shunned risk and subordinated everything to a steady job, a house in the surburbs, and a company retirement plan—a generation apparently fearful of politics, mistrustful of ideas, incurious about society, desperate about personal security.

Even the church threatened to become an instrument of the new acquiescence. Though religious statistics are notoriously unreliable, it appears that in the second quarter of the century church membership grew twice as fast as population. This religiosity was conspicuously indifferent, however, to historical religion. According to one public opinion poll, 80 percent of those responding claimed they regarded the Bible as the revealed word of God but only 35 percent could name the four Gospels and over half could not name one. Belief was deemed good in general. As Eisenhower said, "Our government makes no sense unless it is founded in a deeply felt religious faith—and I don't care what it is." Religion became a part of "belonging," a convenient way to establish social identity.

In place of the austere intellectual structure of the traditional faiths, the best-selling religious books of the period purveyed a "cult of reassurance"—Rabbi Joshua Loth Liebman's *Peace of Mind* (1946), Bishop Fulton J. Sheen's *Peace of Soul* (1949), the Reverend Norman Vincent Peale's *The Power of Positive Thinking* (1952). These and other books portrayed God as the man upstairs, someone up there watching over me, the everlasting source of protection and comfort. The nondoctrinal faith seemed designed to dispel anxiety, to induce self-confidence, to guarantee success for the individual in his professional career and victory for the nation in its struggle against atheistic communism.

Stirrings under the surface. Yet the break between decades is never sharp, and under the complacent surface of the fifties other tendencies were at work. The religious community, for example, did not watch the outburst of popular religiosity with un-

745

qualified enthusiasm. The "neo-orthodoxy" of Reinhold Niebuhr, especially as formulated in *The Nature and Destiny of Man* (1941, 1943), had profound influence among believers and nonbelievers alike as a majestic restatement of traditional Christian insights. Where the Niebuhrians insisted on the independence of Christian faith from the official culture, the popularizers identified faith with the values of middle-class society. Where one urged the church to re-establish transcendent norms, the other wanted faith to sanction the status quo. Niebuhr himself sharply criticized the notion that public avowals constituted authentic belief. "The greatest corruption of all," he wrote, "is a corrupt religion." He agreed that religion could produce peace of soul, but not the peace of positive thoughts or of self-congratulation; true religion aimed rather at the "peace of God which passeth all understanding." "That peace passes understanding," added Niebuhr, "precisely because it is a peace with pain in it." The object of faith was to induce not contentment but contrition, not complacency but repentance.

The intellectual community in general weighed the decade and found it smug and torpid. Novelists and social critics portrayed American conformism in such books as David Riesman's *The Lonely Crowd* (1950), Sloan Wilson's *The Man in the Gray Flannel Suit* (1955), and W. H. Whyte, Jr.'s *The Organization Man* (1956). In *The Affluent Society* (1958), J. K. Galbraith persuasively questioned the "conventional wisdom" that put forward the maximization of economic growth as the answer to all problems, pointing out that in America this had produced a combination of private opulence and public squalor and had notably failed to eradicate poverty.

As the rise of the "lost generation" had expressed a rejection of Babbittry by the youth of the 1920s, so the rise of the "beat generation" expressed a dissent by the youth of the fifties from the ethos of affluence. The rebels of the fifties were more chaotic and pitiful than their lighthearted and talented predecessors. Hipsters and beatniks congregated in San Francisco and New Orleans, shared a special vocabulary, admired "cool cats" like James Dean and Marlon Brando, and lost no opportunity to exhibit their biting contempt for the "squares" of the world. Sympathetic observers saw in these "antiheroes" a brave attempt to reject the suffocating embrace of a conformist society. Others saw in them a tiresome conformity of their own and dismissed them as "rebels without a cause," dedicated to an aimless flight from responsibility. As the beat novelist Jack Kerouac put it in an exchange between two characters in *On The Road* (1957), "We gotta go and never stop going till we get there." "Where we going, man?" "I don't know, but we gotta go."

Republican foreign policy

Ending the Korean War. Eisenhower's preference for inaction served him better abroad than at home. Fulfilling his 1952 campaign pledge, he had visited Korea in the interval between his election and the inauguration. Though this trip produced no miracles, it expressed the theme of conciliation that would be the President's personal contribution to the conduct of foreign affairs. Cease-fire negotiations, initiated in July 1951, continued to drag on, however, as did hostilities; indeed, some of the heaviest fighting of the war took place around Porkchop Hill in the Chorwon area in July 1953.

The sticking-point was whether, and how, prisoners of war should be repatriated. Many of the 173,000 North Koreans in United Nations hands had made clear that they did not want to return to North Korea. United Nations negotiators accordingly rejected communist insistence on compulsory repatriation. In the spring of 1953, exasperated by the deadlock, Eisenhower decided to signal the communists "that, in the absence of satisfactory progress, we intended to move decisively without inhibition in our use of weapons, and would no longer be responsible for confining hostilities to the Korean Peninsula." Whether because of this threat of nuclear war, or because Moscow had tired of paying the costs of the war and the death of Stalin in March 1953 had given new flexibility to Soviet policy, the North Koreans now accepted voluntary repatriation. An armistice was concluded at Panmunjom on July 27, 1953.

The armistice provided for a demilitarized zone, established a Neutral Nations Supervisory Commission to carry out the armistice terms, and called for a political conference to settle remaining questions, including the future of Korea. But the conference was never held, and in subsequent years each side repeatedly charged the other with violations of the armistice. The United States signed a mutual-defense treaty with South Korea in 1954 and kept an uncertain hand in South Korean affairs. The increasingly capricious actions of the aging Syngman Rhee caused widespread protest both in South Korea and in Washington, culminating in his overthrow in April 1960 and the establishment in 1961 of a new—and eventually, more dictatorial—government under General Park Chung Hee.

The Korean War had lasted three years and one month. During that time 33,629 Americans had lost their lives in battle, along with about 3,000 from other UN countries and about 50,000 South Koreans. Total communist battle casualties were estimated at 1.5 million. For all the bitterness and frustration the war produced at home, it had stopped aggression in Korea, briefly strengthened the authority of the United Na-

tions, and shown the communist world that the democratic nations were prepared to meet military challenge. It had also accustomed the nation to the idea of war on presidential initiative and to the belief that American military force was effective on the Asian mainland.

Eisenhower and Dulles.

Ending the Korean War marked a first success for Eisenhower as a man of peace. His pacific instincts and pragmatic temper, however, were somewhat at odds with the ideological militancy of his party and especially of his Secretary of State. The differences should not be exaggerated. Eisenhower fully accepted the premises of the Cold War (as, indeed, did Adlai Stevenson), reposed complete confidence in John Foster Dulles, and granted him exceptional authority over the day-to-day conduct of foreign policy, reserving only the right to intervene in extreme cases. Nevertheless, as Sherman Adams later wrote, "The hard and uncompromising line that the United States government took toward Soviet Russia and Red China between 1953 and the early months of 1959 was more a Dulles line than an Eisenhower one."

The grandson of one Secretary of State (John Foster) and nephew of another (Robert Lansing), Dulles had begun his diplomatic career as his grandfather's secretary at the Hague Conference of 1907. He had been at Versailles in 1919; and, though an isolationist in the thirties, he had emerged by 1944 as the leading Republican spokesman on foreign affairs. By profession a lawyer and by avocation a Presbyterian layman, Dulles united a talent for close legal argument with a penchant for righteous moralism. Critics found him legalistic and sanctimonious. One British foreign secretary, Herbert Morrison, spoke of his "du-

plicity," and another, Harold Macmillan, questioned his "intellectual integrity."

Though identified with many aspects of the Truman-Acheson foreign policy, Dulles had turned against that policy as the 1952 election drew near. Containment, he now said, was "negative, futile and immoral." It would commit the United States to a policy of indefinite coexistence, whereas the proper goal, in his view, was not to coexist with the communist threat but to end it. "We will abandon the policy of containment," Dulles said, "and will actively develop hope and resistance spirit within the captive peoples." The mere statement by the United States "that it wants and expects liberation to occur would change, in an electrifying way, the mood of the captive peoples." By such means the Cold War could be brought to an end; moreover, the cost would be far less than the cost of containment. In short, the infusion of "dynamism" into American foreign policy would both push back communism and balance the budget.

Thus Eisenhower in his first state-of-the-union message canceled Truman's 1950 order to neutralize the Straits of Formosa, thereby "unleashing" Chiang Kai-shek and his Nationalist forces for presumed reconquest of the mainland. He also reaffirmed the Republican platform pledge to repudiate "all commitments contained in secret understandings such as those of Yalta which aid Communist enslavement." However, Chiang's forces were, in effect, "re-leashed" by the mutual-security pact of 1955 with Nationalist China; the publication of the Yalta documents revealed no secret agreements; and American inaction in face of anti-Soviet upheavals in East Germany in 1953 and Hungary in 1956 ended talk of "liberation."

The Dulles foreign policy rested on the atomic

Europe, North Africa, and the Middle East

bomb as the center of American strategy. Fearing that an attempt to provide limited-war forces would unbalance the budget, Eisenhower rejected the idea that the United States should diversify its military establishment. "My feeling was then," he wrote in 1963, "and still remains, that it would be impossible for the United States to maintain the military commitments which it now sustains around the world (without turning into a garrison state) did we not possess atomic weapons and the will to use them."

As Dulles defined the "new look" in 1954, it "was to depend primarily upon a great capacity to retaliate, instantly, by means and at places of our choosing." He explained that this meant rejecting the policy of "meeting aggression by direct and local opposition" in favor of "more reliance on deterrent power and less dependence on local defensive power." In other words, local aggression was presumably to be countered in the future, not by limited war, but by a threat to retaliate directly against the Soviet Union or Communist China. The threat by itself, Dulles apparently thought, would be sufficient to stop aggression. As he put it on another occasion, the "necessary art" was "the ability to get to the verge without getting into the war. . . . If you are scared to go to the brink, you are lost." The doctrine of "massive retaliation" would lower the cost of national defense, bringing "more bang for the buck."

The institutionalization of the Cold War.
Seeing the godless communist conspiracy as both evil in itself and the source of all the world's troubles, Dulles absolutized the philosophy of the Cold War. His rigid views took root in a group of government

agencies—the State Department (which he purged of active dissenters), the Defense Department, the National Security Council, the Central Intelligence Agency—all of which developed vested institutional interests in the idea of a militarily expansionist Soviet Union. The Cold War conferred power, appropriations, and public influence on these agencies; and, by the natural law of bureaucracies, their stake in the conflict steadily increased.

Denied limited-war capability by the massive-retaliation strategy, restrained as well by Eisenhower's own circumspection, the Eisenhower Administration turned from conventional armed force to the CIA as the routine instrument of American intervention abroad. In earlier years the CIA had concentrated on sending agents, equipped with radios, into the Soviet Union and eastern Europe. During Marshall Plan days the CIA had quietly helped democratic (including socialist) parties, trade unions, and newspapers in western Europe in an attempt to counteract Soviet subsidies to procommunist organizations. Now the absolutist philosophy freed the CIA from normal moral restraints; and the fact that its director, Allen W. Dulles, was the Secretary of State's brother gave it unusual freedom of initiative. In the 1950s CIA covert action grew ambitious and aggressive. The CIA set itself not just to support friends but to subvert foes—helping to overthrow governments regarded as procommunist in Iran (1953) and Guatemala (1954), failing to do so in Indonesia (1958), helping to install supposedly prowestern governments in Egypt (1954) and Laos (1959), organizing an expedition of Cuban refugees against the Fidel Castro regime (1960), even plotting the assassination of Castro (with the collabo-

The CIA on its own

ration, incredibly, of American gangsters) and of the procommunist Congolese leader Patrice Lumumba (1960). Such activity fed the American government's conviction both of its ability and its right to decide the destiny of other nations. It also led to secret invasions of American liberties: thus for twenty years after 1953 the CIA ran a mail-intercept program of massive scope and indisputable illegality without briefing any President as to what it was doing.

The Cold War had long since been institutionalized in the Soviet Union, where the Russians were already equipped with a dogma of inevitable conflict and, through its network of communist parties, with the means of local intervention. This meant on both sides by the 1950s a propensity to perceive local conflicts in global terms, political conflicts in moral terms, and relative differences in absolute terms. Each side saw mankind as divided between forces of light and forces of darkness. Each assumed that the opposing bloc was under the organized and unified control of the other. Washington supposed that what was then called the free world should reshape itself on the American model; Moscow that the communist world should reshape itself on the Russian model.

Crisis in Southeast Asia. The rising American concern with the Third World responded to modifications in Soviet foreign policy, forecast by Stalin in a statement to the Nineteenth Party Congress in 1952. Stalin's death on March 5, 1953, was followed by harsh and obscure feuds among Soviet leaders, resulting in the victory of N. S. Khrushchev by 1957–58. During these years, the communists steadily carried forward Stalin's injunction to pick up "the banner of nationalism where it had been dropped by the bourgeoisie." They launched major campaigns to win over the developing nations. The Soviet claim that communism offered the best road to modernization acquired some plausibility in the fifties because of both the Russian rate of industrial growth, averaging about three times that of the United States, and unexpected Soviet technical breakthroughs—the hydrogen bomb (1953), the first intercontinental ballistic missile and Sputnik, the first earth satellite (1957), the first moon satellite (1959), and the first man in space (1961).

Especially striking was the emergence of China, the most populous nation in the world, as a communist state. Washington assumed Communist China to be a Soviet subsidiary and therefore a new instrument in the monolithic communist plan of world conquest. Apprehension over China heightened American interest in Indochina. Here, Eisenhower later wrote, the conflict "began gradually, with Chinese intervention, to assume its true complexion of a struggle between Communism and non-Communist forces rather than one between a colonial power and colonists who were intent on attaining independence." While there was no evidence of Chinese intervention in what remained essentially a nationalist uprising, the United States by 1954 was paying nearly 80 percent of the cost of the war against Ho Chi Minh and the Viet Minh. The French position, however, had grown desperate. The war was bitterly unpopular in the homeland, while in Indochina the guerrillas were spreading across the country. In March 1954, with substantial French forces under siege in the valley of Dienbienphu in western Tonkin, Paris asked Washington for armed intervention.

In the preceding August the National Security Council had said, "The loss of Indochina would be critical to the security of the United States." Eisenhower himself remarked in a press conference that Indochina was of "transcendent" concern; "you have a row of dominoes set up, you knock over the first one. . . . You could have the beginning of a disintegration that would have the most profound influences." Dulles now advocated the use of the atomic bomb to raise the siege of Dienbienphu. Vice President Nixon suggested to a convention of newspaper editors the possibility of "putting American boys in." The Administration made preparations for a strike on April 28. But leading senators, among them Lyndon B. Johnson and John F. Kennedy, were highly skeptical. Then Winston Churchill, once again British prime minister, rejected the plan. "What we are being asked to do," Churchill said, "is assist in misleading the Congress into approving a military operation which would be in itself ineffective, and might well bring the world to the verge of major war." Finding no support in Congress or in London, Eisenhower decided against military intervention.

Dienbienphu fell, after fifty-six days, on May 7. Four days later Eisenhower informed Paris that he would seek authority from Congress to send troops to Indochina if the French would make political concessions to anticommunist nationalists. Soon, however, Pierre Mendès-France came to power in Paris pledged to end the war in a month. In the next weeks negotiations at Geneva, from which the United States stood aside, produced a provisional settlement. Under pressure from their respective large-power patrons, both Vietnamese factions reluctantly accepted the temporary partition of their nation at the seventeenth parallel—this to be a "military demarcation line" and "not in any way [to] be interpreted as constituting a political or territorial boundary"—with reunification to come through general elections scheduled for July 1956.

Washington had watched the negotiations with grim disapproval, and the National Security Council pronounced the result a "disaster . . . a major forward stride of Communism which may lead to the loss of Southeast Asia." The American response was to set up

Ngo Dinh Diem: stubborn nationalist

the Southeast Asia Treaty Organization (SEATO), bringing three Asian states (Thailand, Pakistan, and the Philippines) together with the United States, Britain, France, Australia, and New Zealand. A special protocol extended the organization's protection to South Vietnam, Laos, and Cambodia. SEATO's provisions were, however, less stringent than those of NATO, calling only for consultation among the signatories in case of communist subversion and for action by each state "in accordance with its constitutional processes" in case of armed attack.

The Administration now gave special assistance to South Vietnam and its new premier Ngo Dinh Diem, a devout Catholic and stubborn nationalist whose strength of purpose had impressed many Americans, liberal and conservative, during his American stay in 1950–53. In 1955 Diem rejected the elections provided for in the Geneva accords. Soon he deposed Emperor Bao Dai, the French puppet, and, as president of the new Republic of Vietnam, moved to revive the economy, suppress political opposition, abolish village self-government, and confirm his personal control. American aid continued, and a fatal involvement deepened.

In the meantime, the mutual-security pact with Nationalist China enlarged Dulles' ring of alliances. Once unleashed, Chiang Kai-shek had put troops on the Pescadores islands in the Straits of Formosa, notably Quemoy and Matsu. When the Chinese communists started bombing Quemoy in September 1954, Eisenhower supplemented the mutual-security pact by persuading Congress in January 1955 to pass the Formosa Resolution authorizing the President to use armed force "as he deems necessary" to defend Formosa and the Pescadores.

In the Middle East Dulles induced the British to create a regional defense organization under the Baghdad Pact of 1955 (later known as CENTO—the Central Treaty Organization). American aid programs to underdeveloped countries were integrated with the alliance system. The aid itself was predominantly military—the Point Four idea receded, the very name being dropped—and it went in the main to such embattled states as South Korea, South Vietnam, and Formosa. Condemning neutralism as "immoral," Dulles hoped to force all nations to choose sides in the Cold War. Some observers felt that he had undue faith in the capacity of military pacts to stabilize underdeveloped areas. Critics referred acidly to his "pactomania."

Nationalism and the superpowers

Nationalism versus the Cold War. The Administration continued to insist it was reversing the Truman-Acheson policies. "Isn't it wonderful," said Vice President Nixon in 1954, "finally to have a Secretary of State who isn't taken in by the Communists, who stands up to them?" But observers were more impressed by continuities than by reversals. Though the Dulles tone was more moralistic and ideological than that of his predecessors and his proposals more bellicose, his militancy was offset by the President's caution and optimism; and the actual results were essentially an extension and elaboration of the Truman-Acheson idea of containment.

The containment policy had begun, however, in Europe, where it was a reasonable response to the struggle between democracy and Stalinism. In its extended form after Korea, it now presupposed a world consumed, as Europe had been, by this struggle. And indeed, for a decade after 1945, America and Russia managed to bestride the globe as superpowers, working to consolidate their positions around the planet—America through its pacts, Russia through its parties. But the concepts of the Cold War did not apply in the European sense to regions increasingly convulsed by the demands for political and economic independence on the part of peoples long subject to colonial or neocolonial control.

Nationalism was the Third World's dominating emotion. In most cases the new nationalist states had no great interest in the conflict between America and Russia except as they could exploit it for their own purposes. As the superpowers tried to enlist the developing countries on one side or the other in their Cold War, the new states tended to respond by playing off one superpower against the other and using the Cold War as a means of getting aid for themselves. Despite pretenses and alliances, the new states—even, it developed, those that pronounced themselves communist—responded in the end to their own national interests.

Nationalism in Southeast Asia. Nationalism continued to thrive in Southeast Asia. In Vietnam, though President Diem in Saigon had been a consistent opponent of French rule, he could not compete with Ho Chi Minh in Hanoi as a nationalist leader. Moreover, the discontent aroused by Diem's increasingly arbitrary regime now gave the Vietnamese communists a new chance to seize power. In 1958 a communist-nationalist movement soon called the National Liberation Front or, more popularly, the Viet Cong, began guerrilla warfare against Diem. This development alarmed Washington. "The loss of South Vietnam," said Eisenhower on April 4, 1959, "would set in motion a crumbling process that could, as it progressed, have grave consequences for us. . . . We reach the inescapable conclusion that our own national interests demand some help from us in sustaining in Vietnam the morale, the economic progress, and the military strength necessary to its continued existence in freedom." From 1955 to 1961 military aid to South Vietnam averaged $200 million annually.

It was in Laos, however, that the military crisis was more acute and American intervention more active. The Pathet Lao, a communist-led guerrilla movement, was roaming the countryside; and the

Ho Chi Minh

United States in 1958 vetoed the effort of Prince Souvanna Phouma to establish a neutral Laos under a coalition government with Pathet Lao participation. Regarding the upper Mekong Valley as the gateway to Southeast Asia, the United States put nearly $300 million into Laos between the period of the Geneva Accords and the end of 1960—more aid per capita than it sent to any other country.

In 1959 the CIA installed General Phoumi Nosavan as head of a prowestern government in Vientiane. When Phoumi was overthrown by a nationalist revolt in 1960, Souvanna regained power and, rebuffed by the Americans, established relations with Russia. At the end of the year, Phoumi, with American support, put an army into the field. American policy now forced Souvanna, the neutralist, into reluctant collaboration with the Pathet Lao.

In the meantime, the Chinese communists, who had not abandoned their hope of annexing Formosa to mainland China, began heavy bombardment of the islands of Quemoy and Matsu, now occupied by a hundred thousand Nationalist soldiers, in August 1958. Though Eisenhower was irritated by Chiang Kai-shek's increased troop commitment to the offshore islands, he saw no alternative but to convince Peking that the United States would intervene, "perhaps using nuclear weapons," if the communists attempted an invasion. After three months the shelling tapered off. Under American pressure Chiang eventually reduced the size of his forces on the islands.

Though this crisis passed, problems in Indochina remained troubling at the end of the decade.

Nationalism in the Middle East.

In the Middle East, Arab nationalism, now surging in unprecedented force, posed problems in a part of the world where Britain and France had traditional interests and which Russia had long coveted. The United States watched this area with growing concern. This was partly because of extensive American oil investments and even more because of the Republic of Israel, which had shown its tough capacity for survival when it defeated the assault of neighboring Arab states in 1948–49 and which, with the fervent support not only of the American Jewish community but of many other Americans, had come to seem a particular American charge.

The center of Arab nationalism was the new regime in Egypt, installed by revolution in 1952 and, after 1954, under the purposeful leadership of Colonel Gamal Abdel Nasser. When the Baghdad Pact exalted Egypt's chief Arab rival, Iraq, and portended Egypt's diplomatic isolation, Moscow established relations with Nasser, sent Egypt arms, and proposed to subsidize the construction of a great dam at Aswan on the Nile. Washington responded by offering to arrange western financing for the dam. Nasser already dominated Syria; he was stepping up Egyptian raids across the Israeli border; in March 1956 he incited a revolution in Jordan. Then in July 1956 Dulles withdrew the American offer just as Egypt was about to accept it. Nasser retaliated by nationalizing the Suez Canal.

Britain and France regarded Nasser's seizure of the canal as a threat to western Europe's vital supplies of oil. Moreover, Sir Anthony Eden, now British prime minister, saw Nasser in the image of Hitler and believed that appeasement would only inflame his ambitions and invite the spread of Soviet influence. France felt that Nasser's support was helping to prolong a nationalist revolt in Algeria. Together, Britain and France determined to overthrow Nasser.

Eden understood Dulles to agree with him that Nasser must be made to "disgorge what he has swallowed." But despite shows of private indignation, Dulles really felt that the use of western force against Nasser would only alienate the new nations of Asia and Africa. By October, communication between London and Washington had pretty well broken down.

In the meantime, another element in a complicated drama was approaching its climax—Israel's fear that Egyptian rearmament would permanently alter the balance of power in the Middle East. In October, British and French officials met secretly with Israeli leaders in France. On October 29, Israel attacked Egypt. Two days later Britain and France entered the war against Egypt on the patently spurious excuse of trying to localize the conflict. Ironically, one of the effects of the Anglo-French intervention was to save the Egyptian forces from probable defeat by the Israelis.

The situation was further complicated by a nationalist uprising against Soviet domination in Hungary beginning on October 24. Though deeply involved in the brutal suppression of this revolution, the Soviet Union threatened to use force—including the hint of long-range missiles against western Europe—to "crush the aggressors" in Egypt. This threat, along with the fear of estranging the ex-colonial world, led Eisenhower to bring intense personal pressure on Eden to call off the Suez expedition. At the same time, a run on Britain's gold reserves threatened the pound, and Secretary of the Treasury Humphrey informed London that Britain could expect no financial aid from the United States until a statement on withdrawal had been made. On November 6 Eden ordered a cease-fire.

The American government now initiated immediate action in the United Nations—backed by the Soviet Union and opposed by Britain and France—to condemn Israel as the aggressor. While the rigid American line in the UN resulted in the rescue and

Uprising in Hungary, October 1956

reinstatement of Nasser without rebuke for past Egyptian harassment of Israel, the Anglo-French adventure was nonetheless ill-conceived and ill-prepared, and Dulles was right in supposing that gunboat imperialism was obsolescent.

Still, despite the power of Arab nationalism, Dulles persisted in regarding Soviet penetration as the essential Middle Eastern problem. "The existing vacuum in the Middle East," Eisenhower told Congress in January 1957, "must be filled by the United States before it is filled by Russia. . . . Considering Russia's announced purpose of dominating the world, it is easy to understand its hope of dominating the Middle East." Eisenhower asked Congress to declare a vital American interest in preventing such domination and to authorize the commitment of American forces to aid Middle Eastern nations "requesting such aid, against overt armed aggression from any nation controlled by International Communism." Congress by joint resolution passed the so-called Eisenhower Doctrine in March 1957. In April Eisenhower sent the Sixth Fleet to Jordan when King Hussein was threatened by a pro-Nasser movement and in July 1958 landed fourteen thousand troops to protect a pro-western government in Lebanon. In neither case did the American military presence lead to hostilities.

Nationalism in Latin America. In Latin America nationalist aspirations struck at the political and economic domination of the United States. In the years after the Second World War, the Good Neighbor policy of the thirties had suffered neglect. In the 1940s, Latin America was swept by nationalist ferment. The resulting revolutions sometimes (as in Argentina) took authoritarian, sometimes (as in Venezuela) democratic, forms. Then toward the end of the forties a counterrevolutionary reaction set in. By 1954 thirteen Latin American presidents were military men. Now a new surge of protest arose against dictatorships, bringing the overthrow of, among others, Perón of Argentina in 1955, Pérez Jiménez of Venezuela in 1958, Batista of Cuba in 1959, and Trujillo of the Dominican Republic in 1961.

All through this ebb and flow, Washington, insofar as it thought about the hemisphere at all, tried to fit it into the framework of the Cold War. The Truman Administration concentrated on a program of inter-American military cooperation—a program that was expanded under the Eisenhower Administration. The Eisenhower Administration also placed great reliance on foreign private investment, a policy that led it to favor authoritarian regimes in Latin America. Vice President Nixon, visiting Cuba, praised the "competence and stability" of the Batista dictatorship. Eisenhower himself presented the Legion of Merit to two Latin American dictators—Pérez Jiménez of Venezuela (for his "sound foreign-investment policies") and Manuel Odría of Peru. When Nixon visited these two countries in May 1958, after the dictators had been thrown out, the people's resentment against United States identification with the hated regimes led to mob violence. The fact that the Vice President of the United States should be stoned and spat upon in Latin America strikingly revealed the deterioration of relations since the Good Neighbor policy.

The course of the Cuban revolution of 1958–59 seemed even more ominous. The hemisphere hailed the overthrow of the Batista regime and welcomed the advent of a revolutionary government led by Fidel Castro. In Cuba Castro initiated a long-needed program of social and agrarian reform. But he combined this program with a terrorism that, if less than that of his predecessor, still showed a callous disregard for the processes of justice. A romantic Marxist nationalist rather than a disciplined communist, Castro needed the United States as his enemy and therefore rebuffed conciliatory American gestures. For its part, Washington grew obsessed with the expropriation of American property in Cuba.

For all his excesses, Castro became for a moment a hero through much of Latin America. The rapid spread of the *fidelista* enthusiasm suggested the magnitude of the problem the United States faced in

Fidel Castro:
a turbulent personality

coming to terms with the Latin American demand for economic development, social reform, and national self-assertion. When President Kubitschek of Brazil proposed "Operation Pan America" and an Inter-American Development Bank in 1957, Washington had shown no interest; but by 1960 Under Secretary of State Douglas Dillon and Milton Eisenhower, the President's brother, persuaded the Administration to offer "a broad new social development program for Latin America" based on the Inter-American Development Bank. The Organization of American States endorsed the Dillon program in the Act of Bogotá in September 1960.

In time, surrounded increasingly by communists and lashed by the intensities of his own turbulent personality, Castro led Cuba into the Soviet camp. Fearful of a Soviet satellite in the Western Hemisphere, Eisenhower in March 1960 agreed to a CIA proposal to arm and train a force of Cuban exiles for possible use against Castro. When Castro ordered the United States to cut its embassy to eleven persons, the Eisenhower Administration broke relations in January 1961.

Vicissitudes of the Cold War. Eisenhower had a genuine desire for conciliation and peace. Though he never questioned the premises of the Cold War, he strove in his circuitous and intermittent way to mitigate its intensity. The death of Stalin in 1953 had given new opportunity to western diplomacy as well as new outlet both to energies of normalization stir-

ring within Russia and to energies of nationalism spreading elsewhere in the communist empire. Hoping for a less rigid Soviet leadership, Churchill wanted a summit meeting at once. But Dulles, forever fearful that a reduction in tension would relax the western guard, successfully opposed the idea. In 1953–54 the West may well have lost a chance to test significant new Soviet proposals, especially regarding the neutralization of Germany.

By early 1955 Churchill finally persuaded Dulles to drop his opposition to a summit conference. When the Soviet Union, after a decade's stalemate, agreed to sign an Austrian peace treaty in May, omens for the Big Four meeting seemed auspicious. The meeting itself, taking place at Geneva in July, produced no substantive results. But, as the first of its sort since Potsdam, it did restore personal contact among the heads of the powers, and the "spirit of Geneva" diminished for a moment the ideological ferocity of the Cold War.

Other currents seemed to be carrying the Cold War into a season of thaw. At the Twentieth Party Congress in 1956, Khrushchev gave his famous "secret speech" denouncing the crimes of Stalin. He also amended the Leninist doctrine of the inevitability of war; in the nuclear age, he said, the conflict between capitalism and communism would be decided by peaceful competition between social systems. Soviet as well as western leaders were increasingly impressed by the incalculable perils presented by nuclear weapons—by the fact, for example, that a single plane could deliver more destructive power than all the planes in all the air forces delivered during the Second World War. Also the problem of radioactive fallout had come sharply to the world's attention in 1954, when both the United States and the Soviet Union tested large-yield nuclear weapons in the atmosphere. As scientists analyzed the long-term effects of radioactive contamination on the bones, blood, and germ plasm of humans, concern mounted over the continuation of nuclear testing. In March 1958 the Soviet Union suspended testing, and the United States and Britain followed suit in October (while Russia briefly resumed).

Khrushchev's dilemma. If Khrushchev was determined to limit the risk of nuclear war between the superpowers, he also seems to have felt he could not admit this determination without revealing a sense of Soviet weakness that might increase western intransigence. He therefore evidently hoped to obtain the risk-limiting measures, such as the denial of nuclear weapons to West Germany, by threats rather than by persuasion. Moreover, he was under increasing secret pressure from Communist China, which regarded his policy of "peaceful coexistence" as a betrayal of

Marxism-Leninism and which might soon challenge Russia for the leadership of the international communist movement. And Khrushchev himself was temperamentally something of a plunger, fond of the spectacular and the audacious, unable to resist targets of opportunity created by western confusion or disarray.

All these factors led him to transform the defensive Cold War of Stalin into what the West perceived as a more far-flung and aggressive contest. "While Stalin conducted a Cold War of position," Hans Morgenthau later wrote, "Khrushchev conducted a Cold War of movement." His speeches were boastful and truculent, and the launching of Sputnik seemed to verify his horrendous claims about Soviet superiority in intercontinental ballistic missiles. He liked to tell small countries how many bombs would be required to destroy them, and he did not hesitate (as in 1956 against England and France over Suez and later against the United States in Cuba) to threaten war against great powers. He greatly increased Soviet activity in the Middle East, Southeast Asia, Latin America, and Africa and appeared eager to exploit every western vulnerability. Confronted by inflammatory rhetoric and worldwide intrusion, the West did not appreciate his more pacific purposes. Moreover, if Khrushchev could secure "peaceful coexistence" (from which he always rigorously excluded ideological coexistence), he confidently predicted the withering away of capitalism and the triumph of communism by peaceful means. This is what he meant when he told the western democracies, "We will bury you"—not that the communists would kill their adversaries but that they would outlive them.

His policy thus bounded back and forth between belligerence and conciliation. Hoping perhaps to end up with a denuclearized Germany, Khrushchev reopened the Berlin question in October–November 1958. But early in 1959 Khrushchev grew conciliatory again; and, on the strong recommendation of Prime Minister Macmillan after a visit to Moscow in February, the West in March accepted a summit meeting in principle. Even Secretary of State Dulles, now ravaged by cancer, acquiesced in the drift toward negotiation. In April Dulles resigned, to be replaced by Christian A. Herter; five weeks later Dulles was dead. Though a foreign ministers' meeting in Geneva in May resulted in a deadlock over Berlin, the movement toward the summit continued. In the summer of 1959 Nixon visited Russia, and Anastas Mikoyan, a veteran Soviet leader, the United States. This exchange paved the way for an extraordinary visit to the United States by Khrushchev. The Khrushchev tour, marked by a series of picturesque incidents, reached its climax in private talks between Khrushchev and Eisenhower at Camp David, in Maryland. Following these talks, the United States agreed to a summit meeting, and Khru-

An extraordinary visit: Khrushchev on tour

shchev agreed to drop his deadline on Berlin. For a moment the "spirit of Camp David" seemed to renew the "spirit of Geneva."

The dark year. The summit meeting was scheduled for Paris on May 16, 1960. Then on May 5 Khrushchev announced the shooting down of an American plane over the Soviet Union. Washington promptly said that the plane had innocently strayed from course on a meteorological flight. On May 7 Khrushchev gleefully sprang his trap. The pilot was alive, he said, and had confessed that he was engaged in espionage. Khrushchev added, "I am quite willing to grant that the President knew nothing about the plane."

The story was indeed true. At irregular intervals for about four years, the CIA had been sending the U-2, an aircraft capable of flying at exceptional heights, on photographic missions over the Soviet Union. At this point the Administration owned up to the act of espionage. Secretary Herter went on to argue that the United States was morally entitled to conduct such flights in order to protect the "free world" from surprise attack. Herter and, soon, Nixon implied that the flights would continue. Eisenhower, rejecting Khrushchev's proffered escape clause, accepted full responsibility. Khrushchev now came to Paris demanding that Eisenhower apologize for the flights and punish those responsible. Eisenhower rejected these demands, and the summit collapsed.

It is not clear whether sharpening Chinese criticism had already persuaded Khrushchev before the U-2 incident that he had better refurbish his revolutionary image, or whether the Eisenhower Administration, with its addiction to clandestine methods, had unexpectedly undercut his policy. In any case Khrushchev, while continuing to defend peaceful coexistence within the communist world (as at a meeting of eighty-one Communist parties in Moscow in October–November 1960), made it clear that he would have no serious dealings with Washington until there was a new American President.

End of the Eisenhower era

The election of 1960. The electorate faced the election of 1960 in a troubled state of mind. After the U-2 fiasco, the request of the Japanese government that, in view of anti-American riots in Tokyo, Eisenhower cancel a scheduled presidential visit provided further evidence of a decline in American influence. The fact that since 1958 the United States balance of payments had been in deficit and that gold was flowing out of the country deepened anxiety. Within the United States, the persistence of economic stagnation and the rise of unemployment toward 6 percent of the labor force caused further problems for the Republicans.

Nevertheless a confident Republican convention gave the presidential nomination to Vice President Nixon with Henry Cabot Lodge of Massachusetts as his running mate. The Democrats turned to Senator John F. Kennedy of Massachusetts, who had established himself as the most popular candidate in the primaries. The Democratic Senate leader, Lyndon B. Johnson, who had run second to Kennedy in the convention balloting, accepted the vice-presidential nomination.

The 1960 campaign was marked by an innovation in American politics—a series of television debates in which the two candidates responded to questions put to them by newspaper reporters. Observers believed that Kennedy's poise and command in these confrontations destroyed the Republican argument that he was too young and inexperienced for the Presidency. The campaign itself revolved around the question of America's condition as a nation. The United States, Kennedy contended, was falling behind both in the world competition with communism and in meeting

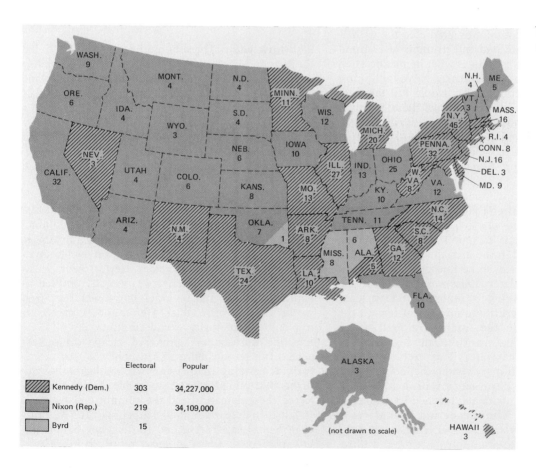

The election of 1960

	Electoral	Popular
Kennedy (Dem.)	303	34,227,000
Nixon (Rep.)	219	34,109,000
Byrd	15	

(not drawn to scale)

The conjunction of an immense military establishment and a large arms industry is new in the American experience. The total influence—economic, political, even spiritual—is felt in every city, every State house, every office of the Federal government. We recognize the imperative need for this development. Yet we must not fail to comprehend its grave implications. Our toil, resources and livelihood are all involved; so is the very structure of our society.

In the councils of government, we must guard against the acquisition of unwarranted influence, whether sought or unsought, by the military-industrial complex. The potential for the disastrous rise of misplaced power exists and will persist. We must never let the weight of this combination endanger our liberties or democratic processes. We should take nothing for granted....

Akin to, and largely responsible for the sweeping changes in our industrial-military posture, has been the technological revolution during recent decades.... The prospect of domination of the nation's scholars by Federal employment, project allocations, and the power of money is ever present—and is gravely to be regarded. Yet, in holding scientific research and discovery in respect, as we should, we must also be alert to the equal and opposite danger that public policy could itself become the captive of a scientific-technological élite.

From Dwight D. Eisenhower, Farewell Address, January 17, 1961.

its own goals of economic growth and social progress. The process of decline could be reversed only by a "supreme national effort" under strong presidential leadership to "get the country moving again"—a "New Frontier."

The popular vote was the closest since 1888. With the admission of Alaska (January 3, 1959) and Hawaii (August 21, 1959), there were now fifty states in the Union. Kennedy's popular margin was only 119,057 out of 68.3 million votes; taking into account the votes for splinter-party candidates, he was a minority victor. The margin in the Electoral College was more

decisive—303 for Kennedy to 219 for Nixon (with 15 Southern votes for Senator Harry F. Byrd of Virginia).

The Eisenhower record. Like Washington and Jackson, Eisenhower left behind a testament for the American people in the form of a farewell address. Speaking with unaccustomed directness, he said that public policy could become "the captive of a scientific-technological élite" and warned against "the acquisition of unwarranted influence, whether sought or unsought, by the military-industrial complex." Though these had not been themes of his own Ad-

New states, 1959

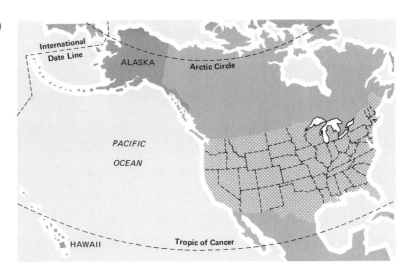

ministration, they identified salient problems of the future.

As he left the White House, Eisenhower told his young successor that, if the United States could not persuade others to join in saving Laos, which he described as the key to all Southeast Asia, then it should be willing "as a last desperate hope, to intervene unilaterally." Mentioning the Cuban refugees under training by the CIA in Guatemala, he recommended that "this effort be continued and accelerated," saying it was "the policy of this government" to aid anti-Castro forces "to the utmost." Yet, for all the bellicosity of this valedictory counsel, his own Administration had been a rare interlude of peace in an age of continous war. Whether through good luck or good management or a combination of both, the American government concluded one war and began no others during the Eisenhower Presidency. The people would remember the man of war as a man of peace. Whether passivity served the nation as well at home as it may have abroad was a question that the next decade would have to decide.

Suggestions for reading

GENERAL

Dwight D. Eisenhower's two volumes of memoirs—*Mandate for Change* (1963) and *Waging Peace* (1965)—are valuable if predictable. Herbert Parmet, *Eisenhower: The Necessary President* (1972), is the best historical survey; see also C. C. Alexander, *Holding the Line* (1975). R. L. Branyan and L. H. Larsen, eds., *The Eisenhower Administration, 1953–1961: A Documentary History,* 2 vols. (1972), is a useful compilation. Revealing accounts by participants in the Eisenhower Administration include Sherman Adams, *Firsthand Report* (1961); E. J. Hughes, *The Ordeal of Power** (1963); and Arthur Larson, *Eisenhower: The President Nobody Knew* (1968). See also R. M. Nixon, *Six Crises* (1962); L. L. Strauss, *Men and Decisions* (1962); and E. T. Benson, *Cross Fire* (1962). K. S. Davis, *Soldier of Democracy* (1952), is a good biography of Eisenhower up to his election. R. J. Donovan, *Eisenhower: The Inside Story* (1956), and R. H. Rovere, *Affairs of State: The Eisenhower Years* (1956), offer illuminating sidelights on the first term. For not unfavorable comments from the left, see I. F. Stone, *The Haunted Fifties* (1964).

FOREIGN AND MILITARY POLICY

W. W. Rostow, *The United States in the World Arena** (1960), sums up the conventional wisdom of the fifties; Seyom Brown, *The Faces of Power** (1968), is a trenchant discussion of the main issues. For contemporaneous views by participants, see M. B. Ridgway and H. H. Martin, *Soldier: Memoirs of Matthew B. Ridgway* (1956); J. M. Gavin, *War and Peace in the Space Age* (1958); and Maxwell Taylor, *Uncertain Trumpet* (1959); and for commentaries by "defense intellectuals," H. A. Kissinger, *Nuclear Weapons and Foreign Policy** (1956) and *The Necessity for Choice* (1961); S. P. Huntington, *The Common Defense** (1961), and ed., *Changing Patterns of Military Politics* (1962); and R. E. Osgood, *Limited War* (1957). On Dulles, see Townsend Hoopes, *The Devil and John Foster Dulles** (1973).

Hugh Thomas, *Suez* (1967) and *Cuba* (1971), provide invaluable background. R. E. Neustadt, *Alliance Politics** (1967), has an incisive analysis of the Suez affair in the context of Anglo-American relations. P. W. Bonsal, American ambassador to Cuba in 1959–60, gives an objective and authoritative account of the evolution of Castro's relations with the United States in *Cuba, Castro, and the United States* (1971); his predecessor E. E. T. Smith is less objective in *The Fourth Floor* (1962). See also Theodore Draper, *Castroism: Theory and Practice* (1965). Milton Eisenhower, *The Wine Is Bitter* (1963), describes the awakening of the Eisenhower Administration to the problem of Latin America.

The best analysis of the American experience in Vietnam is Frances FitzGerald, *Fire in the Lake** (1972). See also in addition to books cited in Chapter 30: Victor Bator, *Vietnam: A Diplomatic Tragedy* (1965); Melvin Gurtov, *The First Vietnam Crisis** (1967); Robert Shaplen, *The Lost Revolution* (1965); and Jean Lacouture, *Vietnam: Between Two Truces* (1966). On Laos, see Arthur Dommen, *Conflict in Laos* (1964, rev. ed., 1971). Useful documentary collections are M. G. Raskin and B. B. Fall, eds., *The*

*Available in a paperback edition.

Viet-Nam Reader (1965); Marvin Gettelman, ed., *Vietnam: History, Documents and Opinions* (2nd ed., 1970); and Marvin and Susan Gettleman, Lawrence and Carol Kaplan, *Conflict in Indochina* (1970). A selection from the Pentagon history of the American involvement in Vietnam is to be found in Neil Sheehan, *et al., The Pentagon Papers** (1971).

DOMESTIC ISSUES

On McCarthyism at high noon and at twilight, see, in addition to the books mentioned in Chapter 30, Michael Straight, *Trial by Television* (1954); J. A. Wechsler, *The Age of Suspicion* (1953); P. M. Stern, *The Oppenheimer Case* (1969); and Samuel Stouffer, *Communism, Conformity and Civil Liberties** (1955).

On economic issues, J. K. Galbraith, *The Affluent Society** (1958), is a penetrating critique of prevailing conceptions. Three useful works on the Eisenhower economic policy are E. L. Dale, *Conservatives in Power: A Study of Frustration* (1960); A. H. Hansen, *Economic Issues of the 1960's* (1960); and S. E. Harris, *The Economics of the Political Parties* (1962). J. B. Rae, *The Road and the Car in American Life* (1971), considers the impact of the highway program.

P. L. Murphy, *The Constitution in Crisis Times: 1918–1969** (1972), provides a general conspectus. R. H. Saylor, B. B. Boyer, and R. E. Gooding, Jr., eds., *The Warren Court: A Critical Analysis* (1969), is informed and sympathetic; A. M. Bickel, *The Supreme Court and the Idea of Progress** (1970), and P. B. Kurland, *Politics, the Constitution and the Warren Court** (1970), enter thoughtful dissents. Richard Kluger, *Simple Justice* (1975), is a rich account of the school desegregation decision of 1954; J. B. Martin, *The Deep South Says Never* (1957), describes the immediate impact of the decision and Anthony Lewis, *Portrait of a Decade* (1964), the aftermath. M. L. King, Jr., *Stride Toward Freedom* (1958), is a central document in the black revolution; August Meier, Elliott Rudwick, and F. L. Broderick, eds., *Black Protest Thought in the 20th Century** (2nd ed., 1971), is a valuable anthology; Harold Cruse, *The Crisis of the Negro Intellectual** (1967), is a perceptive if uneven historical essay; L. E. Lomax, *The Negro Revolt** (1963), is an astute journalistic account; and Talcott Parsons and K. B. Clark, eds., *The Negro American** (1966), is a useful collection of analytical essays.

On politics, Samuel Lubell, *The Revolt of the Moderates* (1956), is a searching contemporaneous statement. For Adlai Stevenson, see, in addition to the J. B. Martin biography cited in Chapter 30, his own book, *The New America* (1957); for Kefauver, J. B. Gorman, *Kefauver* (1971). T. H. White gives a memorable picture of the 1960 election in *The Making of the President, 1960** (1961).

For appraisals of American society in general, Eric Larrabee, *The Self-Conscious Society* (1960), is a useful review. The more enduring works include J. K. Galbraith, *American Capitalism: The Concept of Countervailing Power** (1952) and *The Affluent Society** (1958) (both reissued in revised editions); David Riesman, *et. al., The Lonely Crowd** (1952); F. L. Allen, *The Big Change: America Transforms Itself* (1952); W. H. Whyte, Jr., *The Organization Man** (1956); David Potter, *People of Plenty* (1954); and, for an eclectic and thoughtful synoptic view, Max Lerner, *America As a Civilization* (1957). The values of the business community are discussed in F. X. Sutton, *et al., The American Business Creed* (1956). C. W. Mills offers a radical analysis in *White Collar** (1951) and *The Power Elite** (1956). For the impact of the mass media, see D. J. Boorstin, *The Image** (1962). On the religious boom, see Will Herberg, *Protestant-Catholic-Jew* (2nd ed., 1960), and W. L. Miller, *Piety Along the Potomac: Notes on Politics and Morals in the Fifties* (1964). Bruce Cook, *The Beat Generation** (1971), is an effective account.

*Available in a paperback edition.

CHAPTER 32

Years of revolt

John F. Kennedy, forty-three years old in 1960, was the youngest man and the first Roman Catholic elected to the American Presidency as well as the first President born in the twentieth century. Scion of a numerous, spirited, and wealthy Irish-American family, a Harvard graduate and war hero, he was elected after the war to the House of Representatives and in 1952 to the Senate. His book *Profiles in Courage* received the Pulitzer Prize for biography in 1957. Handsome in appearance and graceful in manner, cool, lucid, and ironic in play of mind—he once described himself as an "idealist without illusions"—activist in temperament and purpose, he had an affirmative view of the Presidency and a high sense of America's national and world responsibilities. He was proficient in the game of politics, but he also hoped, in the manner of Wilson and Roosevelt, to tap resources of idealism he felt had been too long repressed in American society. He attracted and sought out men and women of ideas; intellectuals and academics now entered government in unprecedented numbers.

The Thousand Days

Kennedy and the Cold War. The new administration faced tricky problems abroad. Kennedy's Secretary of State, Dean Rusk, was experienced in foreign affairs and held tenacious Cold War views. Adlai Stevenson, who was moving beyond his Cold War positions of the fifties, became ambassador to the United Nations. Often frustrated in his dealings with the State Department, Kennedy relied increasingly on his White House staff and especially on McGeorge Bundy, a Harvard intellectual who served as his Special Assistant for National Security.

The new President lacked the ideological passions of the preceding Administration. Though a child of the Cold War, he saw it not as a religious but as a power conflict. Still, in power terms, the Cold War seemed active enough, especially after a militant speech delivered by Khrushchev on January 6, 1961, two weeks before Kennedy's inauguration. The Soviet leader exultantly predicted the irresistible triumph of communism, especially—in passages that alarmed Washington—through Soviet support for "national liberation wars" in the Third World. Citing Vietnam, Algeria, and Cuba as promising examples, Khrushchev called Asia, Africa, and Latin America "the most important centers of revolutionary struggle against imperialism."

In retrospect it is possible to surmise that Khrushchev's bellicosity was intended less as a provocation to the United States than as part of a complex maneuver involving China. For he also took occasion to reaffirm his rejection of nuclear war and his belief in "peaceful coexistence"—views that Communist China continued to oppose. By insisting on them in an otherwise truculent context, Khrushchev may have been trying to show the communist movement that nuclear coexistence was not incompatible with revo-

Vietnam

lution in the Third World. Perhaps he thought militancy would bemuse the Chinese while softer words would gratify the West. Inevitably Peking and Washington each believed only the passages written for the other.

Reading Khrushchev's speech as a declaration of hostility, Kennedy responded somewhat grandiloquently in his inaugural address: "Let every nation know, whether it wishes us well or ill, that we shall pay any price, bear any burden, meet any hardship, support any friend, oppose any foe, in order to assure the survival and the success of liberty." The irony was that both leaders wanted to escape from the arms race. While Khrushchev was twisting and turning in his hope of diminishing the risk of nuclear catastrophe without losing ground to China, Kennedy felt equally that a third world war would mean the end of civilization. His inaugural address went on to condemn the arms race, asked to "bring the absolute power to destroy other nations under the absolute control of all nations," emphasized that "civility is not a sign of weakness," and declared: "Let us never negotiate out of fear. But let us never fear to negotiate."

The world of diversity. The mingling of themes suggests the ways in which Kennedy was a transitional figure in American foreign policy. Despite his inaugural extravagance, he had an acute sense of the limitations of American power. Nine months after his inauguration, he asked the American people to "face the fact that the United States is neither omnipotent or omniscient—that we are only 6 percent of the world's population—that we cannot impose our will upon the other 94 percent of mankind—that we cannot right every wrong or reverse each adversity—and that therefore there cannot be an American solution to every world problem."

Kennedy thus had no illusions about the feasibility of a *pax Americana*. But, if he did not think there could be an American solution to every world problem, he did not think there could be a Russian solution either. His broad idea, which he set forth to Khrushchev in a meeting in Vienna in June 1961, was that each superpower should abstain from initiatives that, by upsetting the rough balance into which the postwar world had settled, might invite miscalculation and compel reaction by the other. In the longer run, his vision was of what he called a "world of diversity"—a world of nations various in institutions and creeds, "where, within a framework of international cooperation, every country can solve its own problems according to its own traditions and ideals."

In his view, the "revolution of national independence" was the source and guarantee of the world of diversity. Communism could be one element in this pluralistic world, but diversity, he argued, was ultimately incompatible with the communist belief that all societies went through the same stages and all roads had a single destination. "The great currents of

Khrushchev and Kennedy, Vienna, 1961: a "world of diversity"

American University speech

history," he said, "are carrying the world away from the monolithic and toward the pluralist idea—away from communism and toward national independence and freedom." In a speech at the American University in June 1963 he summed up his policy in a conscious revision of Wilson's famous line: "If we cannot now end our differences, at least we can help make the world safe for diversity."

Struggle for the Third World. Given the nuclear stalemate, Kennedy agreed with Khrushchev that the Third World had become the immediate battleground between democracy and communism. Abandoning the "for-us-or-against-us" policy of the Eisenhower years, he repudiated Dulles' aphorism that neutralism was "immoral" and made clear the new Administration's sympathy with states struggling for nationhood outside the framework of the Cold War.

Kennedy's purpose was to encourage the developing countries of Africa, Asia, and Latin America to turn to democratic methods in their quest for independence and growth. An increasing share of American foreign aid now went to modernize economies rather than to build armies. The Peace Corps—an undertaking especially close to Kennedy's heart—channeled the idealism of individual Americans into face-to-face cooperation in the developing countries. An expanded Food for Peace program under George S. McGovern used American agricultural abundance to foster development in emergent nations.

There remained the problem of protecting the fragile democratization process against communist disruption and overthrow—the problem spotlighted by Khrushchev's fervent espousal of national-liberation wars. The American view was that, the nuclear standoff having reduced the threat of general war, the great danger to world peace would come if local crises in the Third World led on to Soviet-American confrontation. To prevent this, it seemed necessary to persuade Moscow to abandon the national-liberation-war strategy. The search for ways of frustrating Soviet attempts to exploit insurgencies in the Third World became a Washington obsession.

The answer was thought to lie in teaching countries under attack the techniques of "counterinsurgency." On Kennedy's personal insistence, counterinsurgency doctrine was invented and propounded, counterinsurgency schools were established, and elite

763

A Peace Corps worker in Ghana

counterinsurgency units, like the Green Berets, were formed. The theory was that counterinsurgency would operate within a context of social reform. But the political component did not take root, and the counterinsurgency mystique primarily nourished the American belief in the capacity and right to intervene in foreign lands. It brought out the worst in the overconfident activism of the New Frontier: the faith that American energy and technology could solve everything; the "when in doubt, do something" approach to policy; the officious pragmatism that could quickly degenerate into cynical manipulation.

Latin America: crisis and hope. It also provided a new outlet for the energies of the CIA. The potential conflict between the constructive and aggressive sides of Kennedy's Third World policy became manifest early in the new Administration. Kennedy had inherited from Eisenhower the force of anti-Castro Cubans trained and equipped by the CIA in Guatemala. Confronted with the choice of disbanding this group or permitting it to try an invasion of their homeland, Kennedy accepted the recommendation of the Joint Chiefs of Staff and the Secretaries of State and Defense and let the CIA expedition go ahead.

On April 17, 1961, about twelve hundred Cubans landed at the Bahia de Cochinas (Bay of Pigs), on the southern coast of Cuba. After three days the invasion collapsed. To the world, and to many Americans, the Bay of Pigs was an indefensible exercise in intervention, and for a moment the bright promise of the new Administration seemed blighted. Refusing escalation, Kennedy spurned proposals that he send in the marines and took full responsibility for the fiasco, remarking wryly that victory had a hundred fathers but defeat was an orphan.

In the longer run, he pursued a policy directed toward Cuba's economic and diplomatic isolation. The CIA developed an ambitious program of covert action designed to encourage resistance and sabotage within Cuba. It even continued to plot the assassination of Castro, though those in charge of this project

did not disclose it to John McCone, who became CIA director after the Bay of Pigs, nor, so far as is known, to Kennedy himself. The CIA activities had little effect, except to irritate Castro, who avowed his dedication to Marxism-Leninism and continued to organize guerrilla action against democratic regimes in Latin America, especially Venezuela.

Kennedy's main reliance, however, was on the use of American economic assistance to advance democratic reform in Latin America—a program set forth in the Alliance for Progress in March 1961. Building upon Latin American proposals, like Kubitschek's Operation Pan America, and greatly extending last-minute efforts within the Eisenhower Administration, Kennedy called for a concerted, hemisphere-wide effort over the next decade to accelerate economic growth and raise living standards. Most novel was the emphasis—against the wishes both of North American business and Latin American oligarchies—on the necessity for economic planning and structural change within a democratic framework. "Those who make peaceful revolution impossible," he told the Latin American diplomatic corps, "will make violent revolution inevitable." At an inter-American conference at Punta del Este, Uruguay, in August 1961 the Latin American states (except for Cuba) subscribed to the goals of the Alliance.

The Alliance was accompanied by a determined effort to support progressive democratic forces in Latin America and to oppose military dictatorship. When an army coup nullified the results of a presidential election in Peru in 1962, Kennedy suspended diplomatic and economic relations until the military junta restored political freedom and pledged new elections. His dramatically successful visits to Venezuela, Colombia, Mexico, and Central America enabled the United States for a moment to recover its popularity of Good Neighbor days. No President since Roosevelt had shown such interest in the hemisphere.

Trouble in Southeast Asia. Another troubling inheritance was the crisis in Laos. Kennedy, who felt in general that the United States was "overcommitted" in Southeast Asia, felt in particular that neither superpower had enough at stake in Laos to justify armed confrontation. He consequently rejected Eisenhower's counsel of unilateral American military intervention—a decision facilitated by his disenchantment with the military advice of the Joint Chiefs of Staff after the Bay of Pigs—and reversed the Eisenhower effort to build a bastion of the West in the Laotian jungle. Instead he sought neutralization under the leadership of Prince Souvanna Phouma.

Protracted negotiations conducted by the veteran diplomat Averell Harriman in Geneva in 1961–62 finally resulted in Soviet-American agreement on a neutralist regime including representatives of the prowestern faction and of the communist Pathet Lao. The neutralization proclaimed at Geneva was not, however, achieved. North Vietnam continued to send men and supplies to the Viet Cong in South Vietnam via the Ho Chi Minh trails in southeastern Laos and maintained a military presence in Laos to protect the infiltration effort. In response, a CIA mission aided the coalition government. When Pathet Lao ministers withdrew from the government in 1963, the Pathet Lao insurgency resumed in the northeast. The result was *de facto* partition of the country.

In South Vietnam, the situation appeared militarily more manageable than in Laos. In the spring of 1961 Vice President Johnson, on a visit to Saigon, pronounced Diem the Churchill of South Asia; and on his return, while recommending against American combat involvement, he said, "We must decide whether to help these countries to the best of our ability or throw in the towel in the area and pull back our defenses to San Francisco." In the meantime, Kennedy sent a small force of Green Berets to instruct the South Vietnamese army in the black arts of counterinsurgency and authorized minor CIA operations against North Vietnam. But despite the great numerical superiority of the South Vietnamese forces—250,000 in November 1961 against 15,000 Viet Cong—the situation of the Saigon government was growing worse. That same month a presidential mission, headed by General Maxwell Taylor, recommended the dispatch of an American task force—perhaps 10,000 men—and urged the consideration of air strikes against the "ultimate source of aggression" in North Vietnam.

Kennedy rejected these recommendations. Sending in troops, he remarked, was "like taking a drink. The effect wears off, and you have to take another." Nevertheless, while declining to commit American combat units, he accepted the theory that the assignment of American military "advisers" to South Vietnamese units would improve their tactics and stiffen their resistance. In early 1962 the advisers began to arrive, and soon American helicopters and personnel were taking a part in the fighting. At the same time, aware that lack of popular support was a central cause of Diem's difficulties, Kennedy urged the regime to enlarge its base by political and economic reform. Diem, profoundly authoritarian by temperament, disdained such advice.

Two clashing views arose within the government over Vietnam policy. One group, led by Harriman, now Assistant Secretary of State for Far Eastern Affairs, saw the issue as primarily political and local; the crisis had resulted, this group believed, from Diem's reactionary policies in face of a communist-managed peasant insurrection. The other group, centered in the Pentagon, conceived the situation as one not of civil war but of external aggression, attributing the crisis to the instigation and support of the Viet Cong by Hanoi and, beyond this, by China and Russia. This group, supported by the American ambassador and the general in charge of the military advisory group in Saigon, agreed with General Earle Wheeler, the Army Chief of Staff, who said in November 1962, "The essence of the problem in Vietnam is military." Kennedy, endorsing the military optimism, told Congress in January 1963, "The spearpoint of aggression has been blunted in South Vietnam."

Deeper into the quagmire. Optimism was unwarranted. The Viet Cong continued to gain, and Buddhist protests against the Saigon government in the spring demonstrated Diem's failure to unite his people. Diem's brother Ngo Dinh Nhu urged him on to further repression. Belatedly perceiving that Vietnam was as much a political as a military problem, Kennedy intensified pressure on Diem to get rid of his brother and reform his regime. Belief that stopping national-liberation wars was the key to peace, and also fear that the "loss" of Indochina would have adverse political consequences at home, thus drew the Kennedy administration further into the morass.

Henry Cabot Lodge, sent to Saigon in August as American ambassador to carry out this policy, was confronted by new outrages against the Buddhists. Dissident Vietnamese generals soon received his assurance that, if there was a coup, a new regime would receive American support. In October, with Lodge's knowledge, the generals prepared for a coup. On November 1 they overthrew and murdered Diem and Nhu—whom Lodge had arranged to fly out of the country—and South Vietnam moved into a new phase of turmoil.

Kennedy never fully clarified his views on Vietnam. On the one hand, he accepted the domino theory; "for us to withdraw," he said in July 1963, ". . . would mean a collapse not only of South Vietnam but of Southeast Asia." On the other hand, he laid down in July 1962 a plan for the phased withdrawal of American forces by the end of 1965—a plan that remained in effect until March 1964. Though he gradually increased the number of American "advisers"—there were 16,300 American troops in Vietnam at the end of 1963—less than 100 Americans were killed in combat during his Presidency.

While regarding the United States as overcommitted in Southeast Asia, Kennedy felt that, the commitment having been made, America could not let South Vietnam fall cheaply to the communists. How far he would have gone to prevent this outcome no one can know. His memory of the French predicament a decade before had persuaded him that too

765

large an infusion of white soldiers would only unite Vietnamese nationalism against the alien presence; and he had shown at the Bay of Pigs and elsewhere his capacity to refuse escalation. "In the final analysis," he said of the people of South Vietnam in September 1963, "it is their war. They are the ones who have to win it or lose it. We can help them, we can give them equipment, we can send our men out there as advisers, but they have to win it, the people of Vietnam." Still, by enlarging the American role, Kennedy greatly complicated the problems of subsequent disengagement.

The revival of limited war.
The Soviet relationship remained the overriding question for American policy. Confronted by Khrushchev's Cold War of movement, Kennedy felt that the strategy of relying on nuclear weapons to deter local as well as general war increased the risk of nuclear holocaust. Secretary of Defense Robert S. McNamara, a professor turned industrial manager, therefore began the diversification of American military force so that the level of reaction could be graduated to meet the level of threat—a shift in strategic doctrine from "massive retaliation" to "flexible response." This shift implied a rapid increase in the American capability for conventional war. It was designed primarily to enable the West to respond to Soviet aggression in Europe without immediate resort to nuclear weapons. A fateful side-effect was to create forces that could be used in limited "brush-fire" wars elsewhere in the world.

However, Kennedy was imprisoned by a fallacious "missile gap" notion he had himself expounded during his campaign. He was also reluctant to antagonize the Joint Chiefs of Staff at a time when McNamara was struggling to gain control of the military establishment. He therefore yielded to Pentagon pressure and in the spring of 1961 requested not only more conventional force but more long-range nuclear missiles.

The missile buildup of 1961, as some in the Administration felt at the time and most felt later, was an overreaction to the Khrushchev speech. It was more than American security demanded; it ended any hope of freezing the rival missile forces at relatively low levels; and it sent the wrong message to Moscow, no doubt leading Khrushchev to feel that, for his own security and prestige, he had to increase Soviet missile strength. The Soviet Union—the first state to do so since 1958—began in September 1961 an extensive series of tests in the atmosphere, exploding in October a device nearly three thousand times more powerful than the bomb dropped on Hiroshima.

For the longer run, Kennedy, with McNamara's strong backing, wanted to stop the arms race. Speaking before the United Nations in September, he presented a plan for general and complete disarmament. This goal, he said, was "no longer a dream—it is a practical matter of life or death. The risks inherent in disarmament pale in comparison to the risks inherent in an unlimited arms race. . . . Mankind must put an end to war—or war will put an end to mankind." But the appeal fell on deaf ears; and, with reluctance, Kennedy himself resumed atmospheric testing in April 1962. So the two superpowers, still in the lockstep of the Cold War, proceeded to intensify the arms race.

Kennedy and Khrushchev.
The Vienna meeting in June 1961 had not been a success. Perhaps misled by the Bay of Pigs into seeing Kennedy as irresolute, Khrushchev brusquely rejected Kennedy's proposal of a global standstill and adopted an intransigent, even bullying attitude on most questions.

For Moscow, Germany remained a critical issue, the more so because of the rising flow of refugees—now thirty thousand a month—from East Germany into West Berlin. Khrushchev told Kennedy that by the end of the year he would conclude with East Germany a peace treaty that would extinguish western occupation-and-access rights in West Berlin. Kennedy replied that so drastic an alteration in the world balance of power was unacceptable; Khrushchev himself would not accept a comparable shift in favor of the West. Khrushchev said, if America wanted war over Berlin, there was nothing the Soviet Union could do about it; he was going to sign the treaty by December 31. When the two men parted, Kennedy commented, "It will be a cold winter."

Returning to the United States, Kennedy in July 1961 requested a further increase in the defense budget, called out 150,000 reservists, and announced a program, which set off an ugly outburst of near-panic and which he soon regretted, of fallout shelters for protection against nuclear attack. Though these measures, especially the last, soon came to seem an overreaction, all of them, including the last, may have persuaded Khrushchev that he could not solve the Berlin question by intimidation. In addition, Kennedy, acknowledging Russia's security interests in central and eastern Europe, declared his readiness to work out arrangements "to meet these concerns." On August 13 the East Germans erected the Berlin Wall, thereby stopping the refugee flow. Khrushchev postponed his treaty deadline in October; and the Berlin crisis, for a moment so frightening to the world, subsided.

In western Europe, Kennedy hoped for steady movement toward unification, particularly through the admission of Great Britain to the European Economic Community (see p. 720). To this end, he secured the passage in September 1962 of the Trade

Expansion Act, creating authority to negotiate tariff reductions up to 50 percent for the purpose of bargaining with an enlarged Common Market. But Kennedy's so-called grand design for Europe was frustrated by President de Gaulle's veto in January 1963 of British membership—an action precipitated by the French president's resentment of what he considered the British effort at the Nassau Conference of December 1962 to maintain its "special relationship" with the United States and caused more generally by de Gaulle's unrelenting opposition to what he saw as an American attempt to dominate the military and economic arrangements of the new Europe.

The missile crisis. Khrushchev by no means abandoned his goal of driving the West out of Berlin. In the summer of 1962, carrying his Cold War of movement to its ultimate audacity, he decided to establish in Cuba bases for nuclear missiles targeted against the United States—an unprecedented step for the Russians, who had never before placed their missiles in any other country. If successful, the operation would not only protect Cuba from American invasion—the objective later alleged by Khrushchev (though this could have been more simply achieved by stationing Soviet troops on the island)—but would give Russia a potent bargaining counter when it chose to reopen the Berlin question. Moreover, by making shorter-range missiles effective against American targets, it would double Soviet nuclear first-strike capacity and do so without additional strain on the Soviet budget. It would deal America a shattering political blow by showing the Soviet capacity to penetrate the American sphere of influence. And it would strengthen the Russian hand against the militant Chinese by proving Moscow capable of bold action in support of communist revolution.

Washington had not objected to Russian supply of defensive weapons to Cuba; but Kennedy warned in September 1962 that, if there was evidence of "significant offensive capability either in Cuban hands or under Soviet direction . . . the gravest issues would arise." Khrushchev repeatedly denied publicly and privately that he had any such intention. Nor did Washington consider such recklessness likely. Then, on October 14, a U-2 overflight found conclusive evidence that Khrushchev had lied.

Kennedy's first decision was that, one way or another, the Soviet nuclear missiles had to be removed from Cuba. Later critics have suggested that he should have accepted them without protest. After all the Americans had their Jupiter missiles in Turkey (though this was because the State Department had delayed in executing Kennedy's order that they be withdrawn). Moreover, the United States would still retain nuclear superiority even after the Cuban buildup. But Kennedy regarded the attempted nuclearization of Cuba as "a deliberately provocative and unjustified change in the status quo." If the United States were to accept so gross an intrusion into what the Russians, always themselves so preternaturally sensitive to spheres of interest, had previously respected as the American zone, this would, he feared, persuade both Moscow and the western allies that the Soviet Union could get away with almost anything. It might well embolden Khrushchev to further acts that would make the third world war inescapable.

For six days Kennedy and a small group of advisers debated behind locked doors how best to get the missiles out. One faction, led by Dean Acheson and the Joint Chiefs of Staff, advocated the destruction of the bases by surprise air attack. The other, led by Attorney General Robert F. Kennedy, the President's brother, and Secretary of Defense McNamara, sharply opposed this course on moral grounds—as a Pearl Harbor in reverse against a small country—and on practical grounds—because it might kill Russians at the missile sites and force the Soviet Union into drastic retaliation. Naval blockade, this group argued, would both show the American determination to get the missiles out and allow Moscow time and room to pull back without undue humiliation. President Kennedy announced his course in the first public disclosure of the crisis on October 22—to establish a naval quarantine against further shipments; to demand the dismantling of the bases and the removal of the missiles; and to warn that any nuclear attack launched from Cuba would be regarded "as an attack by the Soviet Union on the United States, requiring a full retaliatory response upon the Soviet Union."

The days that followed were more tense than any since the Second World War. Moscow continued to deny the presence of nuclear weapons until, in a dramatic moment before the United Nations, Ambassador Adlai Stevenson confronted the Soviet delegate with blown-up aerial photographs of the nuclear installations. Meanwhile work was continuing day and night to make the bases operational. An American invasion force was massing in Florida. Soviet ships, presumably carrying more missiles, were drawing near the island; Kennedy kept the interception line close to Cuba to give Khrushchev maximum time for reflection. Finally, after indescribable suspense, Soviet ships began to turn back. "We're eyeball to eyeball," said Dean Rusk, "and I think the other fellow just blinked."

It remained for negotiation to complete the resolution of the crisis. On October 26 Kennedy received a long, passionate letter from Khrushchev dilating on the horror of nuclear war and offering to remove the missiles and send no more if the United States would end the quarantine and agree not to invade Cuba. But on the following morning there arrived a second letter from Khrushchev, harder in tone and proposing an entirely different trade: the Soviet missiles in Cuba for the American missiles in Turkey; a Soviet guarantee of Turkish integrity for an American guarantee of Cuban integrity. Robert Kennedy now recommended that his brother ignore the second letter and respond to the first. The President followed this advice. Robert Kennedy took the American restatement of the first Khrushchev proposal to the Soviet ambassador, who then asked him about the Turkish missiles. The Attorney General replied that, while this could be no *quid pro quo*, his brother had ordered their removal some time back, "and it was our judgment that, within a short time after this crisis was over, those missiles would be gone." The next day, October 28, a favorable reply came from Khrushchev.

Khrushchev's bluff had failed. In short order the bases were dismantled and the missiles on their way home. Castro's resistance, however, made it impossible to establish the UN inspection to which Khrushchev had agreed, and the United States never formally completed the reciprocal pledge not to invade Cuba. But in substance the deal went into effect anyway. U-2 overflights, which the Russian antiaircraft batteries made no attempt to stop, took the place of UN inspection; the Jupiter missiles left Turkey; and the United States, which had no intention of invading Cuba in any case, now ended hit-and-run raids by Cuban refugees from American territory. In the autumn of 1963 Kennedy began secret explorations through the United Nations looking toward a normalization of relations with Cuba.

Détente: 1963. The American success—Kennedy forbade gloating and refused to claim a triumph—was the result of Kennedy's combination of toughness and restraint and of his careful deployment of power. He now hoped he had made to Khrushchev the point he had tried to make in Vienna—that neither side dare tamper carelessly with the complex and explosive international equilibrium.

In this hope he renewed his quest for a test-ban treaty. "I am haunted," he said in March 1963, "by the feeling that by 1970, unless we are successful, there may be ten nuclear powers instead of four, and by 1975 fifteen or twenty." Negotiations bogged down during the spring. In an effort to break the deadlock, Kennedy, in his notable speech at American University in June 1963, called on Americans as well as Russians to rethink the Cold War: "We must reexamine our own attitude—as individuals and as a Nation—for our attitude is as essential as theirs." He rejected the "holy war" idea: "No government or social system is so evil that its people must be consid-

ered as lacking in virtue." Both sides, he said, were "caught up in a vicious and dangerous cycle in which suspicion on one side breeds suspicion on the other, and new weapons beget counterweapons." He specified a nuclear test ban as a first means of breaking this cycle.

Khrushchev, who later described the American University address as "the greatest speech by any American President since Roosevelt," came back with proposal of a limited ban designed to outlaw tests in the atmosphere, in outer space, and under water—in environments, in other words, where violations could be detected without physical inspection. Kennedy sent Harriman to Moscow; and, after arduous negotiations, Washington, London, and Moscow agreed in July on the text of the treaty. In September it was ratified by the Senate. Though France and China declined to sign it, the test-ban treaty represented the most significant formal step toward peace since the onset of the Cold War. And the warm reception given in his own country to the American University speech, with its quiet rejection of clichés of the Cold War, signified the change Kennedy's reliance on reason had wrought in national attitudes toward foreign policy.

Space. The competition between the superpowers produced at least one benign by-product. In April 1961 the Russians put the first man, Yuri Gagarin, into space orbit. Ten months before the Gagarin flight, a government scientific committee had proposed that the United States send a manned expedition to the moon before 1970; but Eisenhower had little sympathy with space exploration. On May 25, 1961, Kennedy took up the proposal, declaring that the United States "should commit itself to achieving the goal, before this decade is out, of landing a man on the moon and returning him safely to earth." The idea was greeted with disapproval by those who thought the money should be spent in meeting human needs on earth and with skepticism by those who doubted whether the project was feasible.

Nonetheless, Kennedy pushed ahead. In February 1962 John Glenn became the first American to enter space orbit; and National Aeronautic and Space Administration (NASA) scientists in the Apollo program were already hard at work breaking down the technical problems of a moonshot. Six months before the deadline, on July 16, 1969, the moonship Apollo 11 was launched from Cape Kennedy, Florida. On July 20 Captain Neil A. Armstrong became the first man to walk on the moon.

Beating Russia to the moon was not Kennedy's main interest. Indeed, he suggested at Vienna in 1961 and again at the UN in 1963 that the Americans and the Russians go to the moon together. He was re-

Years of revolt

A giant step for mankind

sponding rather to the newest of new frontiers, to the ultimate challenge and mystery of space itself. "Why, some say, the moon? . . . The great British explorer George Mallory, who was to die on Mount Everest, was asked why did he want to climb it, and he said, 'Because it is there.' Well, space is there, and . . . the moon and planets are there, and new hopes for knowledge and peace are there." Kennedy's sense of history was surely right. When all else about the twentieth century is forgotten, it may still be remembered as the century when man first burst his terrestrial bonds and began the endless voyage, beyond planet and galaxy, into the illimitable dark.

The New Frontier. In domestic policy, Kennedy, elected by an exceptionally narrow popular margin and confronted by the powerful coalition of Republicans and Southern Democrats that had dominated domestic policy since 1938, proceeded with circumspection. The 1962 congressional election—the most successful for any incumbent Administration since 1943—strengthened his popular mandate but did not significantly improve his parliamentary situation.

Nonetheless, Kennedy strove perseveringly to achieve his aim of getting the country moving again. In economic policy he relied heavily on Walter Heller, an economist who served as chairman of the Council of Economic Advisers, as well as on Douglas Dillon, the liberal Republican whom he appointed Secretary of the Treasury. In February 1961 8.1 percent of the labor force, 5½ million people, were unemployed. Though conditions improved by the end of 1961, largely because of the increase in government cash contributions to the economy, the first months of 1962 saw business investment again fall off. Worried

by this relapse, by the inflationary bias produced by concentrated corporate and labor power, and by the continuing problem of the nation's balance of payments, the Council of Economic Advisers urged business and labor to keep wage increases within the limit of advances in productivity.

This standard, later the basis of the "wage-price guideposts," was urged with particular force in the case of the steel industry, which exerted a bellwether effect on industrial costs. The Steelworkers Union accepted a noninflationary contract on the tacit assumption that the steel companies would forgo a price increase. When the companies, led by United States Steel, announced without warning a major price rise in the spring of 1962, Kennedy reacted with anger and, through a variety of pressures, forced the companies to retract their action. The episode—especially Kennedy's off-the-record remark, "My father always told me that all businessmen were sons-of-bitches, but I never believed it till now"—provoked a wave of business criticism of Washington reminiscent of the Roosevelt years.

A stock-market slump in May 1962 aggravated the economic situation. But, despite business clamor, Kennedy, the first Keynesian President, steadily pursued expansionist policies: in 1962, liberalized depreciation allowances and the investment credit; in 1963, the proposal of general tax reduction, enacted in 1964. These Keynesian measures fostered the longest peacetime expansion of the American economy in history, with an average annual increase in the gross national product of 5.6 percent in the Kennedy years. By 1964 unemployment had declined to 5.2 percent. Prices remained stable.

While fiscal stimulation increased output and employment, it did not solve the question of localized and structural poverty. The contemporary poor, unlike the ambitious immigrants of the nineties or the angry unemployed of the thirties, were largely a demoralized and inarticulate minority who in many cases had inherited their poverty and accepted it as a permanent condition. In 1962 Michael Harrington's *The Other America* provided a powerful account of the distress of the invisible poor. Kennedy had already begun to attack the "culture of poverty" through the Area Development Act of 1961 and through programs directed at Appalachia, an eleven-state region stretching from Pennsylvania to Alabama and centering in eastern Kentucky and West Virginia; and in 1963 he reached the conclusion that, if the forgotten Americans were to be helped, tax reduction required a counterpart in the form of a comprehensive war against poverty.

The black revolution. In the urgent area of civil rights, Kennedy concentrated at first on executive rather than legislative action. Challenged by "freedom riders" defying Jim Crow in interstate bus terminals, Attorney General Robert F. Kennedy found ways to end segregation in interstate transportation. In October 1962 the President sent federal troops into Oxford, Mississippi, in order to protect James Meredith, a black student, in the right, assured him by the courts, to attend the University of Mississippi. The Administration worked to secure blacks the right to vote and appointed an unprecedented number to higher office.

But these actions fell behind the pace of the black revolution. "This Administration," said Martin Luther King, Jr., "has outstripped all previous ones in the breadth of its civil rights activity. Yet the movement, instead of breaking out into the open plains of progress, remains constricted and confined. A sweeping revolutionary force is pressed into a narrow tunnel." To the left of King's Southern Christian Leadership Conference rose more militant organizations —the Congress of Racial Equality (CORE) and the Student Nonviolent Coordinating Committee (SNCC). As black discontent grew, so too did Southern resistance. In April 1963, when King began a campaign to end discrimination in shops, restaurants, and employment in Birmingham, Alabama, Police Commissioner Eugene "Bull" Connor harassed King's marchers with firehoses, electric cattle prods, and growling police dogs.

The Birmingham episode caused a surge of indignation throughout the nation. Then, in June, Governor George Wallace of Alabama personally tried to block the admission of two black students to the state university, but he folded under federal pressure. That night Kennedy went on television to pronounce the civil-rights question "a moral issue . . . as old as the scriptures and . . . as clear as the American Constitution," and to commit the nation to the proposition "that race has no place in American life or law." With this speech he launched a fight for new and more sweeping civil-rights legislation.

Later that same night, Medgar Evers, the head of the Mississippi NAACP, was shot down by a white killer. Despite such incidents, the civil-rights movement clung to the faith that the righteousness of their cause made success inevitable. In August Dr. King led a quarter of a million people, black and white, on a great march in front of the Lincoln Memorial in Washington, where they listened to King's moving eloquence ("I have a dream") and sang the old Baptist hymn the civil-rights movement had made its own, "We Shall Overcome."

The movement for equal rights, in which whites and blacks had long worked together, had concentrated on Congress and the courts. Now it was becoming a mass movement, increasingly black in membership and leadership and employing tactics of direct action. Television, as in the Birmingham case, instantaneously transformed local troubles into national issues. Emotional intensity was growing. "In the process of gaining our rightful place," King said at the Lincoln Memorial, "we must not be guilty of wrongful deeds. Let us not seek to satisfy our thirst for freedom

Washington, 1963: "We shall overcome"

by drinking from the cup of bitterness and hatred." But in the same year the black novelist James Baldwin, in his bitter warning to white America, *The Fire Next Time*, wrote that the Negro "no longer believes in the good faith of white Americans."

Kennedy and America. On November 22, 1963, while riding with his wife in an open car through Dallas, Texas, Kennedy was shot and killed. His murder sent a wave of incredulity, shame, and grief across the United States and around the planet.

In the next decade his place in history became a subject of contention. Revisionists portrayed him as a rigid and embattled Cold Warrior; others found this unpersuasive in the light of his policies after the missile crisis. Some dismissed his leadership in domestic affairs as too much style and too little substance; others noted his narrow margins in Congress and valued the educational impact of the intelligence and perseverance with which he addressed major issues. Some charged that in general he promised too much through politics and excited hopes that could not be satisfied. Others felt that this point overestimated the extent to which voters saw promises as pledges of delivery rather than of direction and that it underestimated the need for hope if anything at all was to be accomplished.

On balance it may be said that Kennedy inherited tough problems at home and abroad and had little enough time and parliamentary leverage to do as much about them as he keenly wished. None the less his directness and openness of mind, his faith in reason, and his generous vision of American life helped break the intellectual as well as the political crust that had settled over American society in the fifties. He communicated a skepticism about ideas and institutions that most Americans in the preceding decade had regarded with self-satisfaction. Kennedy's message was that abroad the old Cold War was played out, that at home the American way of life was in bad shape, that the nation was neglectful of its young and its old, callous toward its poor and its minorities, that its cities and schools and landscapes were a mess, and that national motives were tending toward meanness and materialism. He was greatly admired and trusted in the black community, and he was the first President since Roosevelt who had anything to say to the young. With his more radical younger brother, Robert Kennedy, the intimate partner in the great decisions of his Administration, he produced an image of concern and courage.

Kennedy's words and actions encouraged a great release of critical energy throughout American society. A new literature of protest examined hitherto sacrosanct or shadowed corners of American life, casting a harsh light on suppressed issues like poverty

Kennedy's funeral: a wave of grief and shame

and racial injustice and freely assailing such national ikons as television, the cigarette, the pesticide, billboards, the funeral parlor, the automobile, and the brand-name drug. The outpouring of social criticism was comparable to that of the progressive period and the New Deal.

In the United States Kennedy renewed the belief that government could play an affirmative role and that public policy must be determined by reasoned discussion. Abroad he was widely perceived, like Roosevelt and Wilson before him, as a carrier of American idealism and a friend of mankind. For a moment he made politics seem in truth (in a phrase he cherished from John Buchan's *Pilgrim's Way*) "the greatest and most honorable adventure."

The Johnson years

The Great Society. The Presidency now descended to a political leader of an older generation, Lyndon Baines Johnson. A Texan, fifty-five years old, Johnson had come to the Vice Presidency from twenty-three years in Congress as representative and then senator, ending as Democratic leader of the Senate. No President since Polk had had such impressive legislative experience. He was also the first President from a Southern state since Andrew Johnson a century before. A fervent New Dealer who had become more conservative in his middle years, he retained an authentic concern for the poor and, though a Southerner, for black America. His admirers rejoiced in the power of his formidable personality, the sincerity of his social concern, and the resourcefulness with which he pursued his purposes; others found him egotistical, histrionic, secretive, devious, and vindictive.

In the national shock after Dallas the new President took over his responsibilities with firmness and strength. He soon appointed a commission under Chief Justice Warren to investigate his predecessor's assassination. The commission reported in 1964 that the murderer was a rootless and embittered former communist named Lee Harvey Oswald. Critics later challenged both the commission's procedures and its conclusions.

In other respects, Johnson made clear his determination to continue his predecessor's policies and (unlike Truman in 1945) his predecessor's Cabinet. His experience and inclination led him toward the field of domestic affairs. Both tax-reduction and civil-rights bills were on their way to enactment at the time of Kennedy's death, and the rush of national remorse assured them quick passage. The tax cut, injecting $11.5 billion into the economy, speeded economic growth. The Civil Rights Act of 1964 prohibited discrimination in the use of federal funds and in places of public accommodation and established an Equal Employment Opportunity Commission. Another far-reaching law, the Voting Rights Act of 1965, eliminated illegal barriers to the right to vote and empowered the national government to register those whom the states refused to put on the voting list.

Seeking a distinctive name for his domestic program, Johnson in May 1964 called for a Great Society—"a place where the city of man serves not only the needs of the body and the demands of commerce but the desire for beauty and the hunger for community." The Great Society, he said in his annual message of 1965, "asks not only how much, but how good; not only how to create wealth, but how to use it; not only how fast we are going, but where we are headed. It proposes as the first test for a nation: the quality of its people." The Great Society incorporated and soon extended Kennedy's New Frontier, especially with the passage of the Economic Opportunity Act of 1964, which carried into legislation Kennedy's vision of a war on poverty.

The Great Society provided the central issue of the 1964 presidential campaign. Johnson selected the veteran liberal Senator Hubert Humphrey of Minnesota as his running mate. The Republicans nominated Senator Barry Goldwater of Arizona, a likable businessman with inflexibly conservative views. Convinced that the danger to freedom came from the activity of government, Goldwater had proposed in his book *The Conscience of a Conservative* (1960) that the graduated income tax be abolished and that the federal government withdraw from the bulk of its public programs at a rate of 10 percent a year. He also urged the sale of the TVA, questioned the social-security system, and advocated the bombing of North Vietnam. Though Goldwater's personal dash and his

Victory, 1964: L.B.J. and H.H.H.

campaign slogan—"In your heart you know he's right"—evoked ardent enthusiasm among his followers, the bulk of the voters were disturbed by the spirit that led him, in accepting the Republican nomination, to proclaim: "Extremism in the defense of liberty is no vice."

The Johnson-Humphrey ticket won 61.1 percent of the popular vote and carried all but six states—the most decisive presidential triumph since 1936. Victory brought Johnson nearly forty Northern Democratic congressmen—enough to assure, for the first time since 1938, a working progressive majority in the House of Representatives. This enabled him in 1965–66 to compile the most impressive record of domestic legislation in a single session for thirty years. Long-sought bills for federal aid to education and for medical care to the old through the social-security system (popularly known as Medicare) were at last enacted. In addition, Congress, responding belatedly to the crisis of the cities, authorized the establishment of a new federal department, the Department of Housing and Urban Development (to which Johnson appointed Robert C. Weaver, the first black to serve in the Cabinet); it liberalized the immigration laws, abolishing the national origins quotas of 1924; and it institutionalized Kennedy's experiments in federal support for the arts in the National Foundation on the Arts and Humanities Act. In 1966, though it rejected a civil-rights bill banning discrimination in the sale or rental of housing, Congress passed Johnson's rent-subsidy and model-cities programs and gave the government authority to set safety standards for automobiles and highways.

Among Great Society programs the most original was the war on poverty, conducted by the Office of Economic Opportunity. Headed by Sargent Shriver, Kennedy's brother-in-law and former head of the Peace Corps, OEO included a Job Corps for dropouts from the educational system; a Neighborhood Youth

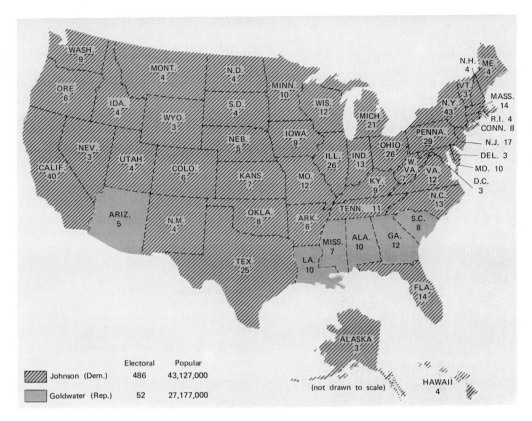

The election of 1964

	Electoral	Popular
Johnson (Dem.)	486	43,127,000
Goldwater (Rep.)	52	27,177,000

Corps for unemployed teenagers; the Volunteers in Service to America (VISTA), in effect a domestic Peace Corps; a Head Start program for young children; an Upward Bound program to send bright children to college; and, in its most controversial feature, a Community Action program designed to secure the "maximum feasible participation" of the poor in planning and running the antipoverty effort. A venture so unprecedented could not avoid experiment and confusion. Local politicians particularly saw Community Action as a threat to their own prerogatives, and other critics felt that OEO gave professionals in the social-welfare field undue opportunity to impose their own ideas on the helpless poor.

Between 1965 and 1970 nearly $10 billion was committed to OEO programs. The number of Americans below the poverty line declined by nearly half in the ten years after 1959, though much of this probably resulted from the general rise in the level of economic activity. While the OEO disappeared in the early seventies, it left an important legacy in techniques designed to help the poor meet their problems: neighborhood-oriented health and legal services, job training, compensatory education, and self-help institutions in the slums.

Between 1964 and 1970 federal spending for health, education, welfare services, and income maintenance tripled. Much of this, however, went to meet the income and medical needs of people over sixty-five, especially through social security and Medicare.

Only a small share went to the innovative Great Society programs that, oversold and underfunded, were perhaps too readily dismissed as failures. Still these years gave the city, the poor, the old, the blacks, the consumers, and the environment new claims on national resources. One significant result was to alter the composition of the federal budget. The "defense shift" of 1948–53 had created a pattern by which government spending held at about 28 to 29 percent of the gross national product, nondefense spending at about 15 percent, and defense spending at about 9 to 10 percent. With the "welfare shift" of the sixties total government spending rose to about 33 percent of the gross national product, with nondefense spending rising to about 25 percent and defense spending declining to about 6 to 7 percent.

Foreign policy: Latin America. As time went on, however, Johnson's increasing absorption in foreign affairs diverted his attention from domestic problems. Abroad as at home Johnson initially proposed to continue Kennedy's policies. But in foreign policy he quickly introduced significant modifications of his own. Latin American policy was soon reshaped to make it more acceptable both to North American business and to right-wing governments south of the border. While continuing economic assistance, Johnson liquidated the two distinctive goals of the Alliance for Progress—structural change and political democratization. Thus Washington welcomed the military coup that established authoritarian government in Brazil in 1964.

The reversion to older ways in dealing with Latin America received its most spectacular expression in Johnson's response to civil war in the Dominican Republic in 1965. Claiming that a popular revolution against a conservative regime had been taken over by "a band of communist conspirators," Johnson, without consulting the Organization of American States, sent 22,289 Marines to the Dominican Republic. The size, the unilateral character, and the impetuosity of American intervention caused deep concern throughout Latin America, reviving the mistrust that Roosevelt's Good Neighbor policy and Kennedy's Alliance for Progress had striven to dispel. The intervention also began to break up the consensus Johnson had laboriously forged in the United States. Liberals, including some associated with the Kennedy Administration, saw the action as the expression of a tendency to use American power not with precision but with extravagance—a foreign policy, it was believed, of overkill.

Central and South America, 1952–76

Vietnam: the war Americanized. These same apprehensions became crucial in the controversies over the most intractable item in Johnson's inheritance—the war in Indochina. For the public, Vietnam still seemed a marginal issue. Johnson barely mentioned it in his January 1964 state-of-the-union address and gave it little more than a hundred words a year later. This lack of public emphasis, however, was perhaps due less to presidential indifference than to a desire to minimize debate and manage the situation without congressional interference.

For the overthrow of Diem had failed to bring stability. Neither General Minh, who led the coup and was himself ousted in January 1964, nor his successor General Khanh proved capable of rallying the South Vietnamese people behind the war. Concerned over the growing strength of the Viet Cong, now presumed to number nearly one hundred thousand, Johnson laid on in February the "A-34" program of clandestine hit-and-run military operations against North Vietnam, organized but not conducted by American personnel. The Joint Chiefs of Staff had meanwhile been urging American bombing strikes against North Vietnam, and in May Johnson's advisers drafted but did not submit a congressional resolution authorizing American military action.

When South Vietnamese commandoes under A-34 raided two islands in the Gulf of Tonkin at the end of July, North Vietnamese PT boats, pursuing the raiders, encountered the destroyer *Maddox* on electronic intelligence patrol and fired on it on August 2. Two days later another American destroyer was reported under attack in the gulf. Though subsequent investigations raised the greatest doubt about the second report, the Administration without full attempts at verification seized on the pretext, claimed two unprovoked attacks, ordered retaliatory air strikes against North Vietnamese targets, and sent Congress the Southeast Asia resolution authorizing the President to "take all necessary steps, including the use of armed force" to assist South Vietnam and prevent aggression. To popular applause the Senate passed the Tonkin Gulf resolution, as it was promptly known, by a vote of 88 to 2, the House by 416 to 0.

Two days after signing the resolution, Johnson, now turning his attention to Senator Goldwater, who had been urging escalation in Vietnam, said, "Others are eager to enlarge the conflict. They call upon us to supply American boys to do the job that Asian boys should do. They ask us to take reckless action which might risk the lives of millions and engulf much of Asia." Through the campaign he continued to condemn those who "say that we ought to go north and drop bombs." Johnson undoubtedly hoped to avoid direct American intervention. But early in 1965 Washington was persuaded that the army of South Vietnam, though it still outnumbered the Viet Cong by at least six to one, was on the verge of collapse. Something, it was felt, had to be done to save the situation; and a Viet Cong mortar attack killing American advisers at Pleiku on February 7 provided a new pretext. Johnson instantly ordered reprisal bombing against northern targets. This in March swelled into the Rolling Thunder campaign of systematic and gradually escalating air war against North Vietnam. In April he decided to increase American forces in South Vietnam and, for the first time, use American combat units in offensive action.

Up to this point, Hanoi's role in the war had been to infiltrate men into South Vietnam—4,400 to 7,400 in 1964, according to American estimates, and mostly native southerners. Now, evidently in response to American escalation, units of the North Vietnamese regular army began for the first time to appear in South Vietnam. In June General William C. Westmoreland, the American commander in Saigon, requested the dispatch of 200,000 American troops and their commitment to ground war in South Vietnam. Despite some dissent in the Administration, notably from Under Secretary of State George W. Ball, Johnson in July announced his response to Westmoreland: "We will meet his needs." With the sending of American bombers into North Vietnam and American combat units into South Vietnam, the Indochina War entered a new and fatal phase. By the end of 1965 there were 184,300 American troops in Vietnam.

The Johnson rationale. The immediate reason for the Americanization of the war was to revive morale in Saigon by offering assurance of the American determination to stay the course. In February 1965 General Khanh gave way to General Nguyen Van Thieu; after June 1965, Thieu as chief of state shared power with his prime minister, the flamboyant Air Marshal Nguyen Cao Ky. Following an election in September 1967 (which Ky later denounced as "a farce"), Thieu and Ky served in uneasy tandem as president and vice president.

A second reason was the hope that bombing would break the will of the North Vietnamese and induce them to order the National Liberation Front (who were thought to be under their control) to call off the war. Though the experience of the Second World War and of Korea had demonstrated the limitations of strategic bombing, and though these limitations would presumably be even greater in the case of guerrilla warfare, Johnson simply could not conceive that, if pounded long enough, North Vietnam would not have a breaking-point; that, if American power were applied, the problem could not be solved. As W. W. Rostow, who succeeded Bundy as Special Assistant for National Security, put it, American influence on the outcome "flows from the simple fact that we are the greatest power in the world—if we behave like it."

At the same time it was believed that bombing, if it could not altogether stop the infiltration of men and supplies into South Vietnam, would at least make the cost of infiltration prohibitive. Since most infiltration took place along the Ho Chi Minh trail network, American planes began in 1964 to carry out bombing missions against North Vietnamese units in Laos, while the CIA had already organized an army of Meo tribesmen to prevent the Pathet Lao and the North Vietnamese from overrunning the Plaine des Jarres. A secret war in Laos thus developed alongside the open war in Vietnam.

The Americanization of the war, it was supposed, would quickly force Hanoi into a negotiated settlement. For the next years negotiating efforts punctuated the process of escalation, most notably during the thirty-seven-day bombing pause of December 1964–January 1965. Unfortunately, acts of escalation repeatedly undercut the attempts at negotiation. In any case, American proposals always included the preservation of the Saigon regime and the withdrawal of North Vietnamese forces prior to American withdrawal. From the viewpoint of Hanoi and the National Liberation Front, such terms would amount to unconditional surrender.

The larger reason for the Americanization of the war lay in the assumption, inherited from previous Administrations and not reexamined now, that the defense of South Vietnam from communist takeover was vital to the security of the United States. Johnson accepted the universalized Dulles version of the Truman Doctrine and felt that concessions to communism in Indochina would encourage communist aggression first in South Asia and eventually all along the frontiers of freedom. "Ike has made a promise," he would say. "I have to keep it." Keeping American commitments in Vietnam thus became a test of American will and credibility everywhere. "We learned from Hitler at Munich," said Johnson, "that success only feeds the appetite of aggression. . . . To withdraw from one battlefield means only to prepare for the next."

Since it was hard to see in Ho Chi Minh and North Vietnam a threat comparable to that presented by Hitler at Munich, the Administration contended that the "free world" was confronted by a premeditated plan of Chinese expansion, of which the NLF and North Vietnam were only the spearhead. "Over this war, and all Asia," said Johnson, "is another reality: the deepening shadow of Communist China. . . . The contest in Vietnam is part of a wider pattern of aggressive purpose." In 1967 Secretary of State Rusk invoked the specter of "a billion Chinese

on the mainland, armed with nuclear weapons," and Vice President Humphrey said, "The threat to world peace is militant, aggressive Asian communism, with its headquarters in Peking, China."

The American effort also had a positive goal. The experience of military occupation after the Second World War had given Americans undue faith in their talent for "nation-building." Johnson, the old New Dealer, talked about TVAs on the Mekong and compared Marshal Ky to Rexford G. Tugwell; similarly, Humphrey saw "a tremendous opening here for realizing the dream of the Great Society in the great area of Asia, not just here at home." Social evangelism provided a further reason to justify the American adventure.

Nor did Johnson see the war as reason for hostility toward the Soviet Union; rather, he believed that, if the problem of national-liberation wars could be solved in Vietnam, relations with the Soviet Union would be stabilized. In October 1964 Khrushchev had been replaced by the collective leadership of L. I. Brezhnev (who in time became the dominant partner) and A. N. Kosygin. Johnson, seeking to thaw the Cold War, announced a policy of "bridge-building" to eastern Europe. In 1966 he joined with the Soviet Union in supporting a UN treaty providing for the internationalization and demilitarization of space. In 1967 he secured the ratification of a consular convention with Russia and met with Kosygin in Glassboro, New Jersey. In 1968 he concluded with Russia and fifty other nations a treaty on the nonproliferation of nuclear weapons.

"Hawks" and "doves." Vietnam remained Johnson's most urgent problem. Despite an endless series of optimistic assurances from General Westmoreland, the Americanization of the war did not produce the expected results. The number of American troops steadily grew—385,300 by the end of 1966; 485,600 by the end of 1967; 536,100 by the end of 1968—but Westmoreland's "meatgrinder" strategy of victory through "attrition" made no progress against the capacity of the NLF and the North Vietnamese, benefiting from the 10 to 1 ratio of guerrilla war, to replenish their losses and match every escalation. In the meantime, American casualties also grew: deaths in combat rose from 1,130 in 1965 to 4,179 in 1966, 7,482 in 1967, and 12,588 in 1968.

The bombing increased too. By the end of 1968 American planes had dropped 3.2 million tons of explosives on this hapless land (as against a total of 2 million tons on all fronts in the Second World War and 635,000 tons in the Korean War). The result was a country gutted and devastated by bombs, burned by napalm, turned into a wasteland by chemical defoliation, a land of ruin and wreck. "It became necessary

Haiphong, North Vietnam: gutted by bombs

Robert F. Kennedy, now senator from New York, added a powerful voice. In February 1966 Kennedy proposed that the NLF be admitted "to a share of power and responsibility" in a coalition government as the only way to end the war. Vice President Humphrey replied that this would be like putting "a fox in the chicken coop; soon there wouldn't be any chickens left"; and the debate sharpened. As dove senators, joined by foreign-policy experts like Walter Lippmann, George F. Kennan, and Hans Morgenthau, enlarged the attack on the war, Johnson denounced the opposition as "nervous Nellies" ready to "turn on their own leaders, and their country, and on our fighting men."

In the spring of 1967 Lippmann wrote that the Indochina War had become "the most unpopular war in American history." Antiwar protests exploded in major cities, culminating on October 21, 1967, when 200,000 people led by noted literary figures like Norman Mailer and Robert Lowell marched on the Pentagon. Martin Luther King, attributing the waning of civil-rights enthusiasm to preoccupation with Vietnam, joined the peace movement. Though the campuses had generally supported escalation, the restriction of educational deferments early in 1968 confronted college students with the reality of the war. "L.B.J., L.B.J.," students chanted, "how many kids did you kill today?" Never before in American history were so many young men declaring conscientious objection, burning draft cards, or fleeing abroad to avoid military service. Many more, accepting what they saw as their democratic obligation, brought their antiwar convictions with them into the army. Middle-class parents, oblivious as long as the war had swept up only poor whites and poor blacks, began to wonder whether Vietnam was worth the sacrifice of their own sons. This widened the national opposition.

In the meantime, Vietnam had been affecting American life in other ways. Johnson's domestic policy was an early casualty. The Republican comeback

to destroy the town to save it," said an American major standing in the rubble of Ben Tre; and for more and more Americans this summed up the ghastly logic of the American intervention. The technological war was too gross to cope with guerrilla warfare: it was like trying to weed a garden with a bulldozer. Bombing failed to stop the movement of troops and supplies; instead of breaking the spirit of the enemy, it succeeded, if anything, in hardening Hanoi's will. In August 1967, McNamara, who had developed grave doubts about the war and had become the main proponent of negotiation within the Administration, told the Senate Armed Services Committee that air power had failed.

Johnson nevertheless escalated the bombing, though never enough to suit the Joint Chiefs of Staff, always the tireless advocates of further escalation. Insisting that military means had not yet received a fair try, the Chiefs wanted to bomb the centers of Hanoi and Haiphong, to mine Haiphong harbor, to invade Cambodia, Laos, and even North Vietnam. But Johnson, fearing that too drastic escalation would bring China into the war, maintained political restrictions over military action. Within the United States escalation received enthusiastic support from "hawks" in Congress and the country. But, as the national debate intensified, the "doves," who called for disengagement and a negotiated solution, spoke out with increasing passion.

Though sizable majorities backed escalation in public-opinion polls until 1968, the protest movement against the war, arising in universities with the "teach-ins" of the spring of 1965, grew steadily in strength. In the Senate, where Ernest Gruening of Alaska and Wayne Morse of Oregon had been alone in their opposition to the Tonkin Gulf resolution, doubts about the war now began to find effective lodgment, especially in the Foreign Relations Committee, whose chairman, J. William Fulbright, became a caustic and increasingly influential critic. Soon

Passionate "Dove," Washington, 1967

Despite the long years of support and vast expenditure of lives and funds, the United States in the end abandoned South Vietnam. There is no other true way to put it.... After introduction of American combat troops into South Vietnam in 1965, the war still might have been ended within a few years, except for the ill-considered policy of graduated response against North Vietnam. Bomb a little, stop it a while to give the enemy a chance to cry uncle, then bomb a little bit more but never enough to really hurt. That was no way to win. Yet even with the handicap of graduated response, the war still could have been brought to a favorable end following defeat of the enemy's Tet offensive in 1968. The United States had in South Vietnam at that time the finest military force—though not the largest—ever assembled. Had President Johnson provided reinforcements, and had he authorized the operations I had planned in Laos and Cambodia and north of the DMZ, along with intensified bombing and the mining of Haiphong Harbor, the North Vietnamese would have broken. But that was not to be. Press and television had created an aura not of victory but of defeat, and timid officials in Washington listened more to the media than to their own representatives on the scene.

From General William C. Westmoreland, *A Soldier Reports,* 1976.

There may be a limit beyond which many Americans and much of the world will not permit the United States to go. The picture of the world's greatest super-power killing or seriously injuring 1,000 noncombatants a week, while trying to pound a tiny backward nation into submission on an issue whose merits are hotly disputed, is not a pretty one. It could conceivably produce a costly distortion in the American national consciousness and in the world image of the United States—especially if the damage to North Vietnam is complete enough to be 'successful.'

From Secretary of Defense Robert S. McNamara, Memorandum to President Johnson, May 19, 1967.

in the 1966 elections lost him his working majority in the House of Representatives; and the mounting cost of the war—over $20 billion a year by 1967—argued against the expansion of domestic programs. He even stopped using the phrase Great Society. War spending soon produced inflation at home—in 1968 the consumer price index, after a decade of relative stability, rose by 4.2 percent—and balance-of-payments strains abroad.

The 1968 election. The Administration continued to profess optimism about the war and to discern light at the end of the tunnel. "I see progress as I travel all over Vietnam," said General Westmoreland in November 1967. ". . . The enemy's hopes are bankrupt." And on January 1, 1968: "We should expect our gains of 1967 to be increased manyfold in 1968." Four weeks later, during the Tet holiday, the lunar New Year, a massive enemy offensive took American and South Vietnamese forces by surprise, convulsed thirty provincial capitals, and even penetrated the American Embassy in Saigon. While the North Vietnamese failed to achieve their maximum objectives and suffered grievous losses in the process, the Tet offensive destroyed what remained of the Johnson Administration's credibility on Vietnam and gave potent support to the dove argument that escalation had failed.

Westmoreland's reaction was to escalate further; and his February request for 206,000 additional troops produced a showdown within the Administration. Johnson, exasperated by McNamara's opposition to escalation, shifted him to the World Bank; but the new Secretary of Defense, Clark Clifford, though earlier a hawk, had begun to question the war when a mission he undertook in 1967 had disclosed to him that pro-American Asian states, though much nearer Indochina than the Americans, saw much less at stake in the Indochina War than Washington did. Now in the Pentagon and confronted by the Westmoreland request, Clifford concluded that further escalation was futile and disengagement the proper course.

The Tet offensive intensified domestic criticism of the war. "Are we like the God of the Old Testament," Robert Kennedy asked, "that can decide, in Washington, D.C., what cities, what towns, what hamlets in Vietnam are going to be destroyed?" The approach of the 1968 presidential election consolidated protest within Johnson's own party. The antiwar activists, having failed to persuade Kennedy to oppose Johnson, turned to another senatorial dove, Eugene McCarthy of Minnesota. A man of enigmatic and mischievous intelligence, McCarthy, followed by a virtual "children's crusade," campaigned effectively against Johnson and the war in the New Hampshire primary in March. The Tet offensive, McCarthy's success in New Hampshire, and Kennedy's entry into the contest for Democratic nomination increased the pressure on Johnson. In Washington not only Clifford and civilian officials in the Defense Department but Dean Acheson, McGeorge Bundy, and other former hawks urged him to abandon the war. On March 31, 1968, Johnson announced the cessation of bombing in North Vietnam except in the area below the twentieth parallel. Also, faced by defeat in the impending Wisconsin primary, he withdrew from the presidential contest. In a few weeks, negotiations began in Paris between the North Vietnamese and an American delegation led by Averell Harriman.

With Johnson's withdrawal Humphrey became the Administration candidate. Once a liberal leader, Humphrey was now identified with Johnson and the war and did nothing to diminish this identification. Kennedy and McCarthy, on the other hand, generated crusading enthusiasm among their followers— Kennedy among the poor, the blacks, the Mexican-Americans, McCarthy among suburbanites and independent voters, both among the young and the intellectuals. Their combined vote in a succession of primaries expressed a widespread repudiation of the Johnson Administration within his own party. However, on June 6, the night of his victory in the California primary, Kennedy was murdered by a Palestinian Arab who resented the senator's sympathy for Israel. The nation, appalled at the assassination of a second Kennedy within five years, mourned the death of a man many believed the most brilliant and creative among the national leaders.

After Kennedy's death Humphrey had no serious opposition. Protest against the war policy erupted, however, in shocking scenes at the Democratic convention in Chicago in August, when local police in a frenzy of violence clubbed hundreds of antiwar agitators. Senator Edmund Muskie of Maine received the vice-presidential nomination. In the meantime, Richard M. Nixon, completing an astonishing political comeback, won the Republican nomination and picked Governor Spiro T. Agnew of Maryland, the first suburban politician to rise to national prominence, as his running mate.

The campaign itself was desultory and unenlightening. Nixon, who in past years had been more hawkish than the Administration, now pledged that "new leadership will end the war" and hinted that he had a secret plan to produce that result. Humphrey came out from under the shadow of the unpopular Johnson Presidency too slowly to rouse the enthusiasm of the Kennedy-McCarthy wing of the party. Agnew attracted attention by careless comment about "fat Japs" and "Polacks" and by suggesting that "if you've seen one city slum you've seen them all." The most picturesque candidate, running on the American Independent party ticket, was former Governor George Wallace of Alabama. Attacking "pointy-headed" intellectuals and invoking local values against federally enforced equal rights. Wallace

Robert F. Kennedy: enthusiasm in California, 1968

Richard M. Nixon, 1968:
an astonishing comeback

vagueness of his campaigning, frittered away his commanding lead of September.

Much depended on the progress of negotiations in Paris. Hanoi wanted a total cessation of the bombing of North Vietnam and the presence of the National Liberation Front at the conference table. Washington thought it had persuaded Saigon to come to the table too; and on October 31 Johnson announced a bombing halt. But the next day Thieu, perhaps fearing that diplomatic success might elect the Democrats and expecting more sympathy from a Republican administration, reneged. The campaign ended in confusion.

The vote cast—73.2 million—was the largest in American history, but it included only 61 percent of the eligible electorate (as against 62 percent in 1964 and 63.8 in 1960). Nixon received 31.8 million votes as against 31.3 million for Humphrey and 9.9 million for Wallace. With only 43.4 percent of the total, he became a minority President. The margins were greater in the Electoral College: 301 for Nixon, 191 for Humphrey, and 46, all in the Deep South, for Wallace. The Democrats carried both houses of Congress, which made Nixon the first President since Zachary Taylor whose party on his election did not control at least one chamber.

Lyndon Johnson left the White House an unpopular and unlamented President. Yet history may see in the Great Society a serious effort to overcome the

threatened for a time to do well not only in the South but among blue-collar workers in the North. In October, however, when organized labor threw itself into the contest, the working-class vote moved back to the Democrats. In the meantime, Nixon, through the

The election
of 1968

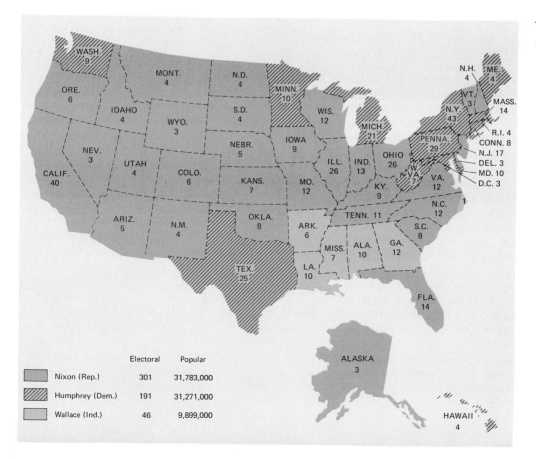

		Electoral	Popular
	Nixon (Rep.)	301	31,783,000
	Humphrey (Dem.)	191	31,271,000
	Wallace (Ind.)	46	9,899,000

tensions and inequities produced by social and technological change. The irony of his Presidency was that he sacrificed domestic policy, a field in which his knowledge was great and his instinct sure, to foreign policy, where his knowledge was scant and his instinct simplistic.

A decade of violence

The social fabric unravels. The decade that had begun in exhilaration and hope was dissolving into bitterness and hate. "Before my term is ended," Kennedy had said in 1961, "we shall have to test anew whether a nation organized and governed such as ours can endure. The outcome is by no means certain." Convinced that the inequalities in American society were a source of danger to American life, Kennedy tried to get America moving toward his New Frontier, carrying the poor and nonwhites with him. He was murdered. After his death his brother Robert made himself the peculiar champion of the outcasts and victims of American life. He was murdered. Martin Luther King was the eloquent advocate of nonviolence in the pursuit of racial justice. In April 1968 an assassin killed him. Some Americans regarded these murders as isolated aberrations. Others began to lose faith in a society that destroyed the three men of the decade who seemed most to embody American idealism.

The panorama of American life, especially after 1963, became one of epithets, demonstrations, sit-ins, marches, burnings, riots, shootings, bombings. Frustrated minorities, feeling the "system" hopelessly rigged against them, turned to violence, if only because they could see no other way to get a hearing for just grievances. Political philosophers offered rationales for violent action. The experience of a generation of war doubtless habituated people to killing; and the war in Vietnam, by legitimizing violent methods in a dubious cause abroad, justified for some the use of violence in better causes at home. Television transmitted the techniques of protest, encouraging habits of instant reaction and hopes of instant results.

The black revolution turns left. In the black community the center of agitation was shifting from the South to the North. Dr. King, though still the preeminent leader, appealed particularly to Southern blacks responsive to religious traditions and accustomed to daily relations with whites. But, whereas in 1910 only 9 percent of blacks lived outside the South and only 27 percent in urban areas, by 1970, 47 percent lived outside the South and 70 percent in urban areas. Washington was now 71 percent nonwhite,

Newark 54 percent, Detroit 44 percent; and the proportion in Northern cities tended to grow as the last wave of white immigrants, moving out to the suburbs, abandoned the decaying central city to the newcomers.

The civil-rights legislation of the sixties was addressed primarily to the removal of legal and political disabilities and therefore applied most particularly to the South. Even here progress was slow. In 1967, thirteen years after the Supreme Court decision, only 16 percent of the 3 million black students in the South were attending desegregated schools. Improvement in voter registration was more impressive; and race barriers fell in restaurants, hotels, and other places of public resort.

Northern blacks faced different problems. The rights provided by the new laws were those they nominally possessed already. Their concern was less with the abolition of legal and political barriers than with the achievement of equal social and economic opportunity, an objective that seemed to require radical social action and one that roused more white resistance. Black housing and black schools were inferior; black unemployment was greater; and the rise in politics of the "white backlash," astutely encouraged by racist politicians like George Wallace, increased the black sense of grievance and frustration. Northern blacks were less involved in the old-time religion and, shut off in ghettos, were more hostile toward whites. Despair thus grew in the ghettos and produced challenges to King's ideals of nonviolence and an integrated society.

A movement founded in 1930 under the name Nation of Islam and now known as the Black Muslims gathered strength. Its leader was Elijah Muhammad, its most eloquent voice Malcolm X, and its program one of black separatism, self-discipline, and self-defense. Breaking with the Muslims in 1964, Malcolm X called for "a working unity among all peoples, black as well as white." He had hardly embarked in new directions, however, before he was murdered in February 1965, apparently as an aftermath of the feud with the Muslims. His powerful *Autobiography* (1965) became a central document of black nationalism.

Events strengthened the nationalist mood. In August 1965 riots in Watts, California, eventually suppressed by the National Guard, resulted in thirty-four deaths and property damage of $35 million. In 1966 National Guardsmen put down riots in Chicago. In 1967 riots swept through the black sections of Tampa, Cincinnati, Atlanta, and New Brunswick, New Jersey, and broke out with desperate force in Detroit and Newark. These developments both encouraged and expressed a growing radicalization of the urban black—a radicalization symbolized in the summer of

The case for violence

There has always existed in the Black colony of Afro-America a fundamental difference over which tactics from the broad spectrum of alternatives Black people should employ in their struggle for national liberation. One side of this difference contends that Black people ... must employ no tactic that will anger the oppressor whites. This view holds that Black people constitute a hopeless minority and that salvation for Black people lies in developing brotherly relations....

On the other side of the difference, we find that the point of departure is the principle that the oppressor has no rights that the oppressed is bound to respect. Kill the slavemaster, destroy him utterly, move against him with implacable fortitude. Break his oppressive power by any means necessary.... The heirs of Malcolm have picked up the gun and, taking first things first, are moving to expose the endorsed leaders for the Black masses to see them for what they are and always have been. The choice offered by the heirs of Malcolm is to repudiate the oppressor ... or face a merciless, speedy and most timely execution for treason.

From Huey P. Newton, "In Defense of Self Defense," The Black Panther, July 3, 1967.

1966 when Stokely Carmichael of SNCC and Floyd McKissick of CORE raised the standard of "black power."

Black power. The idea of black power could imply simply a demand for black regrouping and self-reliance as part of the transition to eventual integration on an equal basis; integration on any other basis, it was contended, would mean surrender to white values. In this sense black power was an affirmation of racial and cultural pride. Black became beautiful; blacks threw away hair-straighteners and rejoiced in the Afro; soul music and soul food became badges not of shame but of identity. Black power, said Dr. King, was a "call to manhood."

But, as expounded by black nationalists, it meant permanent racial separation, even retaliatory vengeance against the "honky"; the blacks, Carmichael said in 1968, must become "the executioners of our executioners." In this more drastic mood, slogans of the King period—"We Shall Overcome" and "Freedom Now"—gave way to more bitter phrases—"Burn, Baby, Burn" and "Violence Is as American as Cherry Pie." The most militant black-power group, the Black

Stokely Carmichael, Berkeley, 1966

Panther party, was organized on military lines in 1966 with Bobby Seale as chairman, Huey P. Newton as Minister of Defense, and Eldridge Cleaver as Minister of Information. Cleaver's *Soul on Ice* (1967), with its disturbing fusion of sensitivity and savagery, was a strong statement of the Black Panther ethos.

Cleaver and Carmichael agreed in rejecting the older black leadership—Roy Wilkins and the NAACP, Whitney Young, Jr., and the Urban League, even Dr. King and his Southern Christian Leadership Conference. Those leaders for their part condemned separatism and violence as self-defeating. As King wrote of the new militancy, "In advocating violence it is imitating the worst, the most brutal, and the most uncivilized value of American life." He added, "There is no salvation for the Negro through isolation. . . . The black man needs the white man and the white man needs the black man."

For white America the emergence of black power constituted an unmistakable warning that the national society would have to move with greater speed and effect if it was convincingly to redress the injustices it had so long perpetrated against its black citizens. Lyndon Johnson, appropriating for himself the equal rights slogan "We Shall Overcome," pressed the fight for civil-rights legislation, securing the passage of an open-housing law in 1968. He appointed Thurgood Marshall as the first black Justice to the Supreme Court. A presidential Commission on Civil Disorders, set up during the riots of 1967 under the chairmanship of Governor Otto Kerner of Illinois, concluded somberly: "Our nation is moving toward two societies, one black, one white—separate but unequal."

A few weeks later Martin Luther King was assassinated in Memphis. As the nation underwent a spasm of shock and grief, riots exploded in ghetto after ghetto across the land, resulting in forty-three deaths, thirty-five hundred injuries, and twenty-seven thousand arrests. The subsequent murder of Robert Kennedy, the one white leader in whom black Americans believed, intensified a mood of alienation and hopelessness. But this mood was still more a warning than a broad reality. Polls in 1969 showed that the majority of black Americans continued to feel that they could win equality without violence and to accept the ideal of a multiracial society.

Revolt on the campus. The campuses, silent during the fifties, were stirred into purposeful activity by the New Frontier gospel of challenge and hope. The Peace Corps, VISTA, and civil-rights projects like "Freedom Summer" in Mississippi in 1964 were only the most dramatic form of the new commitment. But after Kennedy's murder in 1963 and the Americanization of the Indochina War in 1965 youthful idealism took a new turn. These events confirmed the younger generation's worst suspicions about the absurdity and even wickedness of contemporary American society.

Tension between generations was hardly novel, but it now assumed unprecedentedly doctrinaire forms, as in the motto popularized in demonstrations at the University of California in 1964: "You can't trust anyone over thirty." The militant young saw the older generation as the instrumentality of a corrupt society controlled by great bureaucracies of government and business. In its influential Port Huron statement (1962), Students for a Democratic Society denounced élitism and centralization and raised the standard of "participatory democracy." Against adult hypocrisy the young radicals advanced a politics of personal authenticity. Against dehumanizing organization they cried: "Don't bend, fold, spindle or mutilate!" Against Vietnam: "Make love, not war."

Since the university was the first large organization the young encountered, it became a prime target in their revolt against the world of structures. More young men and women were going to college than ever before; total enrollment more than doubled in the decade, rising from 3.8 million in 1960 to 8.5 million in 1970. What university presidents hailed as the "multiversity," many students saw as a callously impersonal assembly line of higher education. As the war continued to escalate, radical students, with mounting rage, assailed academic collaboration with military effort—the Reserve Officers Training Corps, recruiting on campuses by CIA or by companies manufacturing tools of war like napalm, research financed by the Pentagon or CIA. As changes in the draft reduced student immunity, the number of disaffected young multiplied. As undergraduate defiance and provocation increased, university authorities began to call in the local police. In 1968–69 four thousand students were arrested. Where police violence went out of control—as at Columbia University and the Democratic convention in 1968 and at Harvard in 1969—student radicalization intensified.

The New Left. Violence thus begot violence. As early as 1967, the SDS national secretary announced, "We are working to build a guerrilla force in an urban environment. . . . Che's message is applicable to urban America." Che Guevara, the Argentinian revo-

lutionary who had worked with Castro and was to die in Bolivia, became for the militant young the ideal of the incorruptible revolutionary. The example of the Black Panthers was also influential, as was the analysis of the Algerian revolution by the black psychiatrist Frantz Fanon. Characteristic of the new mood was the SDS's Weatherman faction (so-called because of the Bob Dylan lyric, "You don't need a weatherman to know which way the wind is blowing"). Seeing American (or, as they preferred to put it, Amerikan) society as irretrievably corrupt, they concluded that the only way to deal with an inherently destructive apparatus was to destroy it.

Soon an ideology emerged to justify violence. In his book *One Dimensional Man* (1964), the philosopher Herbert Marcuse joined insights from Marx and Freud to argue that the welfare state had integrated the working class into capitalism and disqualified it as an agency of revolutionary change. The hope for a transformation that would restore the wholeness of man lay, he said, in "the substratum of the outcasts and outsiders, the exploited and persecuted of other races." Though Marcuse was not himself a man of violence, he argued for the suppression of ideas he considered antisocial and affirmed "a 'natural right' of resistance for oppressed and overpowered minorities. . . . If they use violence, they do not start a new chain of violence but try to break an established one. . . . No third person, and least of all the educator and intellectual, has the right to preach them abstention."

One function of violence in New Left ideology was to "unmask" the "Establishment" by provoking it into acts of violent retaliation. Some of the time, however, the Establishment, whether because of bad conscience or Machiavellian ingenuity, employed a subtler tactic denounced by the militants as "cooptation"—the tactic of disarming dissent by absorbing it. Thus revolutionaries appeared on television talk shows and commanded large lecture fees. But government also showed itself capable of more drastic action. Policemen beat up long-haired demonstrators, often on meager pretexts; the FBI sent agents, who also sometimes turned out to be *provocateurs*, into New Left groups; and the Department of Justice made recurrent efforts to indict and imprison New Left leaders. This produced a series of celebrated trials: in 1968, the trial of Dr. Benjamin Spock and three others for conspiring to encourage draft resistants to violate the Selective Service Act; in 1969–70, the prolonged and often raucous trial of seven New Left leaders for crossing state lines with the intent to incite violence at the 1968 Democratic convention; and a number of trials of Black Panthers and other Negro militants, one of which, involving an escape attempt and a courtroom shoot-up, led to the subsequent arrest and trial of Angela Davis, a black teacher and communist, for allegedly supplying guns used in the episode.

The hippie scene. Not all those estranged by the high-technology society took the path of political activism. Some responded rather by dropping out of society. These defectors followed trails marked out by the beatniks of the fifties. But the "hippies" of the sixties were generally less educated, less verbal, younger, and of lower social class. Where the beats were a literary movement, the hippies were, in the phrase of the decade, a "life-style." As the beat poet Gregory Corso put it, "The hippies are acting out what the beats wrote."

Disdaining ties, jackets, and socks, affecting long hair, beards, and beads, hating the adult world as "uptight" and "plastic," they congregated in the middle sixties in the Haight-Ashbury district of San Francisco or the Sunset Strip of Los Angeles or New York's East Village. They called themselves "flower children," in part because of their custom of offering flowers to cops and other persecutors, and celebrated their rites, not in the teach-ins or sit-ins of the activists, but in "be-ins" or "love-ins." Some found solace in religion, which they regarded more as a means to experience than as a guide to morality—from the "Jesus freaks" through the Pentecostalists speaking in tongues to the witch covens and the satanists, not to mention the devotees of astrology, Zen Buddhism, and I Ching. Some joined together in "communes" weirdly reminiscent of the communitarian enthusiasm in nineteenth-century America. Though the communes had a dizzying variety of customs, creeds, and diets, they were characteristically based on the idea of the "extended family," with collective property, love, and children. Living was often hard and

sometimes squalid. By 1970 over two hundred communes scattered across the land involved perhaps forty thousand people, mostly under the age of thirty.

Do your own thing, drop out, turn on—these were the principles of the hippie ethos. Above all, the hippie mystique was founded on the use of drugs. During the nineteenth century in America, narcotics had been sold freely; before the Pure Food and Drug Act of 1906 (see p. 525), popular patent medicines often had a narcotic base. In 1914 the Federal Narcotics bureau estimated that one in every four hundred Americans was an addict. The Harrison Act of that year was the first of a series of federal laws and regulations designed to control the use of narcotics, one result of which was to transfer the narcotics traffic to the underworld.

By the thirties the use of drugs was pretty well confined to nonwhite ghettos and to the jazz world. The increase in drug use after the Second World War produced a tough Narcotics Control Act in 1956. This act drew no distinction between soft and nonaddictive drugs like marijuana and hard drugs like heroin and imposed severe mandatory sentences for sale or possession. The law had little effect, however, and by the sixties the hippies, followed by college students and later by high-school students, were increasingly into drugs.

For those trying to blow their minds and open wide what Aldous Huxley called in an influential book *The Doors of Perception* (1954), marijuana ("pot" or "grass") was the most common drug. Some, wishing something more intense than the mild euphoria they enjoyed when "stoned" on pot, turned to stronger hallucinogens, notably lysergic acid diethylamide (LSD or "acid") and mescaline; others to amphetamines, especially methedrine ("pep pills" or "speed"). LSD "highs" sometimes produced "good trips," with extraordinary heightening of perceptions of sound, color, and motion; they also very often produced "bad trips" and chemical changes leading to panic, prolonged depression, psychosis, and suicide. For some, notably Dr. Timothy Leary and his followers, LSD became a "sacrament" and psychedelic ecstasy a new form of religious revelation. By the conservative estimate of the director of the Institute of Mental Health, there were in 1969 more than 100,000 "active narcotic abusers" in the United States, and 8 to 12 million who had used marijuana at least once.

As the decade came to an end, the idyl—the Age of Aquarius—was turning sour. In the cities the flower people gave way to a new, tough breed, the "street people," priding themselves on "ripping off" (stealing), "trashing" (vandalism), "gang bangs" (mass rape), and promiscuous violence. Even worse were the roving motorcycle gangs, like the sadistic Hell's Angels in California. Throughout the scene were the pushers of hard drugs. In August 1969 the atrocious murder of the actress Sharon Tate and six others at the order of Charles Manson by three women members of Manson's hippie "family," though it was briefly glorified by the Weathermen and by some in the drug culture, forced many in the new generation to confront, as one put it, "the pig in ourselves, the childish, egotistical, selfish irresponsibility."

Rise of the counterculture. Out of the varieties of revolt, out of New Left activism, the hippie movement, the communes, the drug trips, the rock music, there emerged the outline of what came to be known from within as "the Movement" and from without as the "counterculture."

Music played a vital role in the formation of the counterculture. English groups, especially the Beatles and later the Rolling Stones, registered the trajectory of the young—from the communal "We All Live in a Yellow Submarine" through the psychedelic "Lucy in the Sky with Diamonds" to Mick Jagger's sinister "Sympathy for the Devil." Bob Dylan was the generation's American bard, singing his poignant and evocative songs—first social conscience and then folk rock—about drugs, race, sex, life, and memory. As Hollywood, already against the wall economically, sought out a new market, films reflected the generation's moods, from the derisive satire of *The Graduate* (1967) through the romantic pessimism of *Easy Rider* (1969) to the celebration of violence in *Bonnie and Clyde* (1967) and *The Wild Bunch* (1969).

If Marcuse was the approved ideologist for the political rebellion, Norman Mailer was, initially at least, the most eloquent exponent of the cultural rebellion. A gifted writer and bravura personality, Mailer had first won attention with his novel on the Second World War, *The Naked and the Dead* (1948). His 1957 essay "The White Negro" mythologized the "hipster" (from which the word "hippie" subsequently came) as an existential sub-hero, surviving in a death-haunted society by setting out on "that uncharted journey with the rebellious imperatives of the self." Mailer foresaw the "underground revolution" of the sixties; but by the time it arrived and hipsters surfaced *en masse* in the form of the street people, Mailer had moved on to other things. Too many aspects of "straight" society, from the Kennedys to the Apollo project, fascinated him; and, as a man who relished audiences and influence, he became almost a member of the Establishment himself.

Other prophets fell by the wayside. Next to Mailer, Paul Goodman best articulated the first impulses of the cultural rebellion. His *Growing Up Absurd* (1960) sharply defined the predicament of the young in an irrational society. But the cultural revolt, as it gathered momentum, moved toward an irration-

Bob Dylan: poignant bard

alism of its own that left Goodman behind. Ideas gave way to feelings; and the goal became increasingly the achievement of a mystical consciousness that would transcend the mind-body dualism and end the alienation of self from the organic world around it. Allen Ginsberg, the only poet who survived from the beats as an influence among the hippies and whose *Howl* (1955) became a manifesto for the new generation, and Alan Watts propagated the gospel of Zen Buddhism. Timothy Leary and the novelist Ken Kesey (*One Flew Over the Cuckoo's Nest*, 1962) argued for drugs as the means to transcendence.

The counterculture was more unified in mood than in ideas. But the unity of mood seemed to portend for a moment the creation of a new consciousness—a consciousness that Charles Reich described in his briefly popular book *The Greening of America* (1970) as Consciousness III, superseding the entrepreneurial consciousness of the nineteenth century and the managerial consciousness of the earlier twentieth century. Consciousness III rejected the achievement society, the "Corporate State," and all structural and institutional solutions; mistrusted logic, analysis, and rationality; and, against materialism, consumerism, militarism, technology, and nationalism, affirmed ideals of community, selfhood, and existential experience.

The emerging consciousness, it was believed, would be the basis for a new American revolution. But the revolution never arrived. After an astonishingly short period, the anguished alienation, the private and political despair, the millennial hope of young Americans in the late sixties and early seventies simply evaporated. It came to seem, even to veterans of the Movement, an exotic historical memory. Sociologists and historians were hard put to account for this short and sharp season of unrest. While the end of the Indochina War and the rise of unemployment in the early seventies hastened its decline, some explanations placed particular emphasis on the demographic curve—on the extraordinary population bulge in the sixties among persons between the ages of fourteen and twenty-four. In the seventy years between 1890 and 1960 that age group had increased by only 12.5 million. In the single decade of the 1960s, it grew by a fantastic 13.8 million.

So unexpected and unprecedented an enlargement in the youth population created for a giddy moment a vivid youth consciousness, a separate youth culture, even perhaps, as the young felt themselves increasingly numerous, influential, and op-pressed, a youth class. The demographic abnormality had other effects. The flood of young people swamped existing facilities for what sociologists called "socialization"—for the absorption of the newcomers into the life of the community. This generated resentment and frustration, encouraging a drift into political extremism, dropping-out, communes, drugs, violence, and even crime. The youth explosion coincided, moreover, with genuine and profound social conflicts, especially over war and race, giving added intensity and volatility to what would have been in any case highly divisive issues.

The young people of the sixties were products of the postwar baby boom. As the rate of population growth slowed after the mid-fifties, and as the means of social integration expanded, the fourteen to twenty-four group became a smaller and more manageable injection into society. Youth soon subsided as a distinct and rebellious social class. None the less, the revolt left its mark. It compelled many people over thirty to acknowledge the gap between their professed ideals and the lives they actually lived. It helped force issues to the top of the national agenda—not only war and race but the role of women, the protection of the environment, the functions of education, the implications of a runaway technology, the significance of community and selfhood. For all its transience, extravagance, and excess, the youth rebellion of the sixties contributed to a fundamental reappraisal of American values.

Suggestions for reading

DOMESTIC POLICY

W. L. O'Neill, *Coming Apart: An Informal History of America in the 1960's* (1971), is penetrating but uneven. J. L. Sundquist, *Politics and Policy* (1968), is a solid and valuable survey. Jim Heath, *Decade of Disillusionment* (1975), is sober and dispassionate. For the Kennedy Administration, L. J. Paper, *The Promise and the Performance: The Leadership of John F. Kennedy* (1975), provides a political scientist's analysis. Henry Fairlie, *The Kennedy Promise* (1973), is a thoughtful polemic. A. M. Schlesinger, Jr., *A Thousand Days* (1965), and T. C. Sorensen, *Kennedy* (1965), are comprehensive accounts by participants; see also K. P. O'Donnell and D. F. Powers with Joe McCarthy, *"Johnny, We Hardly Knew Ye"* (1972), Pierre Salinger, *With Kennedy* (1966), and R. E. Neustadt, *Presidential Power* (rev. ed., 1969, with afterword on Kennedy). J. M. Burns, *John Kennedy* (1959), is an admirable biography written on the eve of the 1960 election. On economic questions, Seymour Harris, *The Economics of the Kennedy Years* (1964), and Walter Heller, *New Dimensions of Political Economy* (1966), are essential. J. K. Galbraith's brilliant books, *The New Industrial State* (1967) and *Economics and the Public Purpose* (1973), open up wider questions. For the Kennedy assassination, see the Warren Commission *Report* (1964), and a thoughtful critique by E. J. Epstein, *Inquest* (1966). William Manchester, *Death of a President* (1967), provides a sometimes powerful, sometimes lurid, account of the tragedy.

*Available in a paperback edition.

787

For Johnson, Doris Kearns, *Lyndon Johnson and the American Dream* (1976), is a fascinating biographical study. Johnson's own book, *The Vantage Point** (1971), is formal but useful. George Reedy, *The Twilight of the Presidency** (1970), Harry McPherson, *A Political Education* (1972), and Jack Valenti, *A Very Human President* (1975), are illuminating works by Johnson staffers. E. F. Goldman, an historian who served briefly in the White House, has written about *The Tragedy of Lyndon Johnson** (1969). Eli Ginzberg and R. M. Solow, eds., *The Great Society** (1974), is a balanced assessment; for contemporaneous doubts from the left, see M. E. Gettleman and David Mermelstein, eds., *The Great Society Reader* (1967). On the war against poverty, Michael Harrington, *The Other America** (1963), provided initial stimulus; H. P. Miller, *Rich Man, Poor Man** (1964), is a valuable statistical analysis; H. M. Caudill, *Night Comes to the Cumberlands** (1963), is a graphic portrayal of conditions in Appalachia; D. P. Moynihan, *Maximum Feasible Misunderstanding** (1969), is a toughtful critique. M. I. Gelfand, *A Nation of Cities* (1975), and B. J. Frieden and Marshall Kaplan, *The Politics of Neglect* (1975), focus on the urban crisis.

For the politics of the period, H. S. Parmet, *The Democrats: The Years After FDR* (1976), is enlightening. T. H. White's two volumes, *The Making of the President, 1964**, *1968** (1965, 1969), recount the presidential elections in vivid style. Norman Mailer, *Miami and the Siege of Chicago** (1968), evokes the atmosphere of the two conventions of that year. For the impact of Robert F. Kennedy, see Jack Newfield, *Robert Kennedy* (1969), A. M. Schlesinger, Jr., *Robert Kennedy and His Times* (1977), and George Plimpton and Jean Stein, *American Journey* (1970). Eugene McCarthy writes on the 1968 campaign in *Year of the People* (1969); see also Jeremy Larner, *Nobody Knows: Reflections on the McCarthy Campaign of 1968* (1970).

FOREIGN AND MILITARY POLICY

For the Kennedy Administration, in addition to the Schlesinger and Sorensen books, there is valuable material in Roger Hilsman, *To Move a Nation** (1967), Chester Bowles, *Promises to Keep** (1971), and W. W. Rostow, *The Diffusion of Power* (1972). Louise FitzSimons, *The Kennedy Doctrine* (1972), and R. J. Walton, *Cold War and Counter-Revolution** (1972), are revisionist critiques. On defense policy, see R. S. McNamara, *The Essence of Security* (1968); H. L. Trewhitt, *McNamara* (1971); A. C. Enthoven and K. W. Smith, *How Much Is Enough? Shaping the Defense Program, 1961–1969** (1971); and J. H. Kaplan, *Security in the Nuclear Age* (1975).

On the Bay of Pigs, see H. B. Johnson, *The Bay of Pigs* (1964). On the missile crisis, R. F. Kennedy, *Thirteen Days* (1971 ed., with an afterword by R. E. Neustadt and G. T. Allison), is an indispensable account by a participant; Elie Abel, *The Missile Crisis* (1966), is an effective journalistic recapitulation; G. T. Allison, *Essence of Decision** (1971), is a rigorous analysis; R. A. Divine, ed., *The Cuban Missile Crisis** (1971), is a collection of essays from varying viewpoints. For the Alliance for Progress, see W. D. Rogers, *The Twilight Struggle* (1967), a useful account by a participant, and Jerome Levinson and Juan de Onis, *The Alliance That Lost Its Way** (1970).

For the Johnson foreign policy, P. L. Geyelin, *Lyndon B. Johnson and the World* (1966), is perceptive; Theodore Draper, *Abuse of Power** (1967), and J. W. Fulbright, *The Arrogance of Power** (1967), are sharply and convincingly critical. On the Dominican affair, see Jerome Slater, *Intervention and Negotiation* (1970), A. F. Lowenthal, *The Dominican Intervention* (1972), and, for a memoir by a participant, J. B. Martin, *Overtaken by Events* (1966).

On Vietnam, in addition to works cited in Chapters 30 and 31, see the following accounts by participants: Townsend Hoopes, *The Limits of Intervention** (1969); Chester Cooper, *The Lost Crusade* (1970); Maxwell Taylor, *Swords and Ploughshares* (1972), W. C. Westmoreland, *A Soldier Reports* (1976); and Nguyen Cao Ky, *Twenty Years and Twenty Days* (1976).

Specific episodes are well described in E. G. Windchy, *Tonkin Gulf* (1971); Anthony Austin, *The President's War* (1971); and Don Oberdorfer, *Tet* (1971). David Halberstam, *The Best and the Brightest** (1972), is a lively journalistic account. Aspects of domestic criticism are reflected in A. M.

---

*Available in a paperback edition.

Schlesinger, Jr., *The Bitter Heritage** (1966); Louis Menashe and Ronald Radosh, eds., *Teach-Ins: U.S.A.* (1967); Norman Mailer, *The Armies of the Night** (1968); and Noam Chomsky, *American Power and the New Mandarins** (1969). W. W. Rostow defends the war in *The Diffusion of Power* (1972). Thomas Powers describes the home front in *The War At Home* (1973).

A SOCIETY IN FERMENT

The course of the black revolution may be followed in these works by black leaders: James Baldwin, *The Fire Next Time** (1963); Malcolm X, *Autobiography** (1965); Eldridge Cleaver, *Soul on Ice** (1967); Stokely Carmichael and C. V. Hamilton, *Black Power** (1967); M. L. King, Jr., *Where Do We Go from Here: Chaos or Community?** (1967); Julius Lester, *Look Out, Whitey!** (1968); and H. P. Newton, *To Die for the People** (1972). C. E. Lincoln, ed., *Martin Luther King, Jr.,** (1970), is a valuable collection of pieces. For black nationalism, see J. H. Bracey, Jr., *et al., Black Nationalism in America** (1969). J. W. Silver, *Mississippi: The Closed Society** (rev. ed., 1966), is an excellent portrayal by a white historian of conditions in the Deep South. C. E. Silberman, *Crisis in Black and White** (1964), is a sensitive contemporaneous report. August Meier and Elliott Rudwick, *CORE** (1973), and Howard Zinn, *SNCC* (1965), study two leading black organizations.

On the stirrings among the young, Alexander Klein, ed., *Natural Enemies: Youth and the Clash of Generations* (1970), is a useful collection of documents; Kenneth Keniston, *The Uncommitted** (1965), *Young Radicals** (1968), and *Youth and Dissent** (1971), contain perceptive and sympathetic diagnoses; and Margaret Mead, *Culture and Commitment** (1970), is a sagacious analysis.

Irwin Unger, *The Movement** (1974), is an account of the New Left by a professional historian. Jack Newfield, *A Prophetic Minority* (new introduction, 1970), and Paul Jacobs and Saul Landau, eds., *The New Radicals* (1966), are indispensable. Kirkpatrick Sale, *SDS** (1973), describes the most militant student organization. Jerry Rubin, *Do It!** (1970), and Tom Hayden, *Trial* (1970), are declarations by New Left leaders. For ideology, see Herbert Marcuse, *One Dimensional Man** (1964), and Carl Oglesby, ed., *The New Left Reader** (1969); for critique, Irving Howe, ed., *Beyond the New Left** (1970), and Maurice Cranston, ed., *The New Left* (1971).

Ronald Berman, *America in the Sixties** (1968), is a thoughtful survey from a conservative viewpoint. On the counterculture, Norman Mailer, *Advertisements for Myself* (1959) and *The Presidential Papers** (1963), and Paul Goodman, *Growing Up Absurd** (1960), are essential introductions. Theodore Roszak, *The Making of a Counter-Culture** (1969), C. A. Reich, *The Greening of America** (1970), and Philip Slater, *The Pursuit of Loneliness** (1970), evoke the contemporaneous mood. The counterculture testifies about itself in Henry Gross, *The Flower People* (1968); Jerry Hopkins, ed., *The Hippie Papers* (1968); Jonathan Eisen, ed., *Altamont: Death of Innocence in the Woodstock Nation* (1970); R. S. Gold, ed., *The Rebel Culture** (1970); the editors of *Rolling Stone, The Age of Paranoia: How the Sixties Ended* (1972); and, for a massive and invaluable collection of documents, Mitchell Goodman, ed., *The Movement Toward a New America* (1970). For drugs, David Musto, *The American Disease* (1973), supplies indispensable background. In Helen Perry, *The Human Be-In* (1970), an attempt is made to relate communes to earlier American communitarian experience; see also Keith Melville, *Communes in the Counter Culture** (1972).

On social disorder, the *Reports* of three presidential commissions are indispensable: the Kerner Commission on Civil Disorders (1968); the Scranton Commission on Campus Unrest (1970); and the Eisenhower Commission on the Causes and Prevention of Violence (1970). See also H. D. Graham and T. R. Gurr, *Violence in America* (1969); Thomas Rose, ed., *Violence in America* (1970); and R. H. Connery, ed., *Urban Riots* (1969).

---

*Available in a paperback edition.

CHAPTER 33

The Presidency in crisis

The man who became President in January 1969 was the antithesis of the rebel mood of the sixties. Fifty-six years old on his inauguration, Richard Milhous Nixon came from a lower-middle-class Quaker family in California, where a frugal upbringing had instilled traditional virtues of work, discipline, and ambition. Receiving a law degree in 1937, he served in the navy during the Second World War and entered politics thereafter, gaining election to the House of Representatives in 1946 and to the Senate in 1950. His diligence as a member of a House investigating committee helped break the case of Alger Hiss, and anticommunism was the issue with which he was most identified in his early career. His alacrity in dispensing accusations of disloyalty outraged his political opponents, who denounced him as Tricky Dick, but Republicans admired him as an intelligent lawyer and a good party man.

Elected Vice President in 1952, Nixon did not enjoy easy relations with Eisenhower but served him faithfully. After being defeated by Kennedy in 1960, Nixon was defeated again in 1962 for the governorship of California; and his career was supposed over. But, with dogged perseverance, he rebuilt his position until he won nomination and election in 1968. Lonely and solemn as a young man, he appeared fluent and affable in middle age. Sympathizers saw him as the embodiment of middle-class values in a degenerate time; critics found him defensive, righteous, and shifty.

From confrontation to negotiation

Once more into the quagmire. Foreign affairs were Nixon's consuming interest and, in his view of himself, his field of main expertise. His first Secretary of State, William P. Rogers, had been Attorney General during the Eisenhower Administration; but his principal adviser was Henry A. Kissinger, a Harvard intellectual who had come to the United States from Germany as a boy in 1938 and was an accomplished diplomatic historian as well as an astute analyst of strategic problems. Serving as Nixon's Special Assistant for National Security, Kissinger carried to extreme lengths the process already well advanced in earlier administrations of centralizing control over foreign policy in the White House.

The Indochina War remained the nation's most anguishing international problem. In November 1968 the North Vietnamese had responded to the start of negotiations in Paris by withdrawing troops from the northern two provinces of South Vietnam. But Johnson, as lame-duck President, decided to keep up the military pressure, and withdrawals ceased. President Thieu delayed five weeks before sending representatives to Paris. Once there, the Saigon delegates stalled further by raising inane objections to the shape of the negotiating table. This momentous question was finally settled four days before Nixon's inauguration. Nixon promptly recalled Averell Harriman as chief negotiator, and the meetings thereafter produced little except propaganda and recrimination.

The new Administration shared Johnson's preconceptions about the war. "Our defeat and humiliation in South Vietnam," Nixon said in November 1969, "without question would promote recklessness in the councils of those great powers who have not yet abandoned their goals of world conquest." The world's hope for the survival of freedom, he added, "will be determined by whether the American people have the moral stamina and the courage to meet the challenge of free-world leadership." He also feared that "precipitous withdrawal" from Vietnam would produce a right-wing reaction within the United States.

Instead Nixon proposed to "wind down" the war through a policy of Vietnamization. Vietnamization meant the replacement of American troops by South Vietnamese until South Vietnamese forces could "assume the full responsibility for the security of South Vietnam." The withdrawal policy was pursued with some steadiness, reducing the number of American ground troops in Vietnam from the high point of 543,400 in April 1969 to 60,000 by September 1972. This withdrawal, accompanied by a cutback in Amer-

Nixon and Kissinger: central control of foreign policy

ican ground offensives, resulted in the lowering of American casualties. At the same time, the proportion of draftees in the American forces in Vietnam fell sharply. All this diminished the domestic political impact of the war and bought time for the Vietnamization policy to produce results, though it was not always clear whether the intended result of Vietnamization was negotiation or victory.

The serious negotiating effort was conducted in great secrecy by Kissinger, who made thirteen clandestine trips to France between 1969 and 1971 for this purpose. Ho Chi Minh died in September 1969; but neither his successors in Hanoi nor the National Liberation Front in South Vietnam were prepared to abandon the objective of thirty years: the control of South Vietnam. The American proposals, varying in detail, all called for the concurrent withdrawal of American and North Vietnamese forces from South Vietnam, and all involved a favored position for the Thieu regime in Saigon. Indeed, at times, the American proposals appeared subject to Thieu's veto. The objectives remained irreconcilable.

Widening the war. Nixon retained the hope that Vietnamization, if it would not produce negotiation, might produce victory, which he defined as the survival of an anticommunist regime in Saigon. He hailed Thieu as one of the four or five greatest political leaders of the world; and Washington supported Thieu in South Vietnam's presidential election of 1971, though with some embarrassment after his opponents, denouncing the contest as rigged, bowed out of the race. Further strengthening of the Thieu regime soon demanded, in Nixon's judgment, extraordinary military measures—measures long urged by the Joint Chiefs of Staff, rejected by Johnson, and designed to destroy the North Vietnamese buildup in the presumably neutral countries of Cambodia and Laos.

For nearly twenty years the wily Prince Sihanouk had managed through artful dodging to preserve the neutrality of Cambodia. In the middle sixties Hanoi had begun to set up staging areas in Cambodia for attacks on South Vietnam. Early in 1969 Nixon initiated secret B-52 raids over Cambodia—thirty-five hundred in the next fourteen months, concealed from Congress by a system of false bombing reports. In March 1970 Sihanouk was overthrown by a prowestern coup headed by General Lon Nol. On April 30 Nixon, after two visits to the bracing movie *Patton*, announced an American incursion into Cambodia to "clean out major enemy sanctuaries." If, said Nixon, "the world's most powerful nation . . . acts like a pitiful, helpless giant . . . all other nations will be on notice that despite its overwhelming power the United States when a real crisis comes will be found wanting. . . . We will not be humiliated. We will not be defeated."

For much of 1969 the American antiwar movement had been in abeyance, its leaders wishing to give the new President a chance to end the war. Then on October 15 the Vietnam Moratorium Committee brought hundreds of thousands of citizens to Washington in an impressive demonstration against the war. Vice President Agnew promptly said that the protest had been "encouraged by an effete corps of impudent snobs who characterize themselves as intellectuals." Six months later, the invasion of Cambodia set off the most widespread and intense college protests in American history, involving 1.5 million students and half of America's twenty-five hundred campuses. On May 4, 1970, four students were killed and ten wounded by National Guardsmen at Kent State University in Ohio; Nixon who a few days before had described student agitators as "bums," observed sententiously, "When dissent turns to violence, it invites tragedy." On May 14 police killed two black youths and wounded twelve at Jackson State College in Mississippi.

The Cambodian episode also produced strong reactions on Capitol Hill. For some time legislators had been growing restive over what seemed to some the loss to the executive of the constitutional power to declare war; the dispatch of American troops into Cambodia now raised the constitutional issue in acute form. Many found this an employment of presidential power without precedent in American history—a military invasion of another country undertaken without statutory or treaty basis, without authorization by or even consultation with the American Congress, without the excuse of emergency, the sanctuaries having been there for several years, or of the need to repel sudden attack. The Administration replied that the President was exercising authority to protect American troops inherent in his role as commander in chief—a principle that, critics felt, would not be persuasive if invoked by the Soviet Union as a justification for similar action by the Red Army. Congress, hoping to reclaim lost powers, now repealed the Tonkin Gulf resolution (see p. 775) and debated a variety of proposals to cut off funds for the further prosecution of the war. The publication by the *New York Times* and other journals in June 1971 of the so-called Pentagon Papers, made available by a former Pentagon official named Daniel Ellsberg, strengthened the antiwar mood by documenting the concealments and deceptions that had accompanied earlier stages of the war.

At the same time, television was bringing the savagery of the "living-room war" into millions of American homes every night. People watched with growing discomfort as the tiny screen showed Vietnamese children horribly burned by American napalm or Americans systematically setting fire to Vietnamese villages. The disclosure that American soldiers had massacred more than a hundred unarmed Vietnamese civilians at My Lai in March 1968

Kent State, May 4, 1970

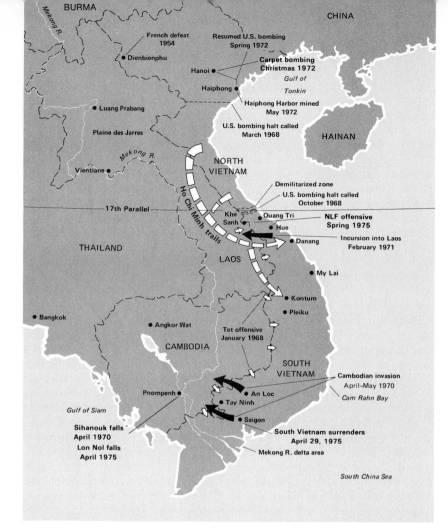

Map labels:
BURMA
CHINA
French defeat 1954
• Dienbienphu
Resumed U.S. bombing Spring 1972
Carpet bombing Christmas 1972
Hanoi •
Gulf of Tonkin
Haiphong •
Haiphong Harbor mined May 1972
• Luang Prabang
HAINAN
Plaine des Jarres
U.S. bombing halt called March 1968
Mekong R.
Vientiane •
NORTH VIETNAM
Ho Chi Minh trails
Demilitarized zone
U.S. bombing halt called October 1968
17th Parallel
Khe Sanh •
• Quang Tri
NLF offensive Spring 1975
• Hue
THAILAND
• Danang
Incursion into Laos February 1971
LAOS
• My Lai
• Bangkok
• Kontum
• Angkor Wat
• Pleiku
Tet offensive January 1968
CAMBODIA
SOUTH VIETNAM
Cambodian invasion April–May 1970
Pnompenh •
• An Loc
Cam Rahn Bay
• Tay Ninh
Gulf of Siam
• Saigon
Sihanouk falls April 1970
Lon Nol falls April 1975
South Vietnam surrenders April 29, 1975
Mekong R. delta area
South China Sea

made war atrocities a national issue. The subsequent arrest and conviction of Lieutenant William F. Calley, Jr., produced strong if confused reactions. Some defended Calley; Nixon interceded sympathetically on his behalf. Some thought it unfair that Calley should be the only man convicted for the massacre. Some demanded the prosecution of top military and civilian leaders as war criminals. Whatever else, My Lai forced many Americans suddenly to see the war from an appalled new perspective, to wonder whether the United States had not brutalized itself in Vietnam, and to conclude that the means employed and the destruction wrought had grown out of all proportion to the interests involved and the goals sought. In 1971 public opinion polls reported that 65 percent of respondents believed it "morally wrong" for Americans to be fighting in Vietnam. By this time an estimated thirty to forty thousand young American war resisters were in exile abroad, most of them in Canada.

Disgust with the war was seeping into the army itself. By 1970 soldiers in Vietnam were wearing peace symbols and refusing to go into combat. The use of marijuana was general; and, according to estimates, 10 to 15 percent of the troops were addicted to heroin. "Fragging"—the use of fragmentation grenades to kill unpopular officers—was not uncommon. In the United States underground newspapers and antiwar coffee houses ventilated G.I. discontent. Amnesty for draft dodgers and deserters became an increasingly popular issue. Military morale and discipline were probably worse than at any point in American history. The incipient demoralization of the army strengthened the spreading determination to get out of the war.

Indochina dénouement. But the war went on. As American ground strength declined, Nixon relied increasingly on air and naval power. By the end of 1971 his Administration had dropped 3.3 million tons of bombs on South Vietnam, Laos, Cambodia, and, toward the end, North Vietnam—more in three years than the Johnson Administration had dropped in five (and the bombing rate mounted in Nixon's fourth year). But aerial terror accomplished no more than it had in the past. When a strong North Vietnamese offensive in the spring of 1972 set back South Viet-

The Presidency in crisis

namese forces, Nixon, fearing loss of "respect for the office of the President of the United States" on the eve of a scheduled trip to Moscow, retaliated by ordering the air force to widen the bombing of North Vietnam and the navy to mine North Vietnamese harbors. This would be, he said, the "decisive military action to end the war"; and it was required because "an American defeat in Vietnam would encourage this kind of aggression all over the world . . . in the Mid-East, in Europe, and other areas." Some supposed that intensification of the war would cause the Russians to cancel the summit; but Moscow, fearing that cancellation might throw Washington into the embrace of Peking, swallowed hard and digested the new escalation. The war went on.

As the 1972 election approached, the Nixon Administration, determined to neutralize the war as a campaign issue, made a change of decisive significance in the American negotiating position. In April it finally abandoned its longtime insistence that the withdrawal of American troops from South Vietnam be accompanied by the simultaneous withdrawal of North Vietnamese troops. In August the withdrawal of American ground combat troops was completed. Nixon also soon offered reconstruction assistance to North Vietnam. For its part, Hanoi dropped its demands for a political settlement in advance of a cease-fire and for the immediate elimination of Thieu. "Peace is at hand," Kissinger announced on October 26. But Thieu, repeating his performance of four years earlier, declined to come aboard. He thought, not unreasonably, that an agreement that removed American troops while leaving 145,000 North Vietnamese in place in South Vietnam did not bode well for his own future.

After the election Kissinger tried to reshape the agreement to meet some of Thieu's objections. Hanoi resisted the proposed changes. In December the talks broke down. Over Christmas, in one of the most savage acts of a savage war, Nixon ordered the saturation bombing of Hanoi and Haiphong, with B-52s smashing the North Vietnamese cities for twelve days. The ostensible reason was to force essential concessions from Hanoi. It seems probable that the real purpose was to persuade Thieu to accept the agreement by improving his relative military position and by reminding him of the damage American air power had the capacity to inflict. On January 5, 1973, Nixon secretly promised Thieu that "we will respond with full force should the settlement be violated by North Vietnam." A billion dollars' worth of planes, tanks, and other weapons was rushed to South Vietnam. Thieu remained dubious. But continued American pressure obliged him to accede. The agreement, as signed in Paris on January 23, differed little from the one originally reached in October.

The Paris Accords established a cease-fire and proposed complicated machinery to bring about a political settlement. Given the irreconcilable differences between the two regimes, the machinery was plainly unworkable. Skeptics discerned a cynical policy designed to provide a "decent interval" between American withdrawal and Thieu's collapse. The last American troops, along with American prisoners-of-war, went at the end of March 1973. Both Vietnamese governments violated the Paris Accords from the start. Saigon, without objection from Washington, denied the Viet Cong the political role pledged at Paris. Hanoi sent fresh troops and weapons south. The "cease-fire war" began. More South Vietnamese soldiers died in 1974 than in 1965, 1966, or 1967. The fighting remained at a low level until Hanoi launched a major offensive in March 1975. The American government claimed that emergency military assistance from the United States would enable Thieu to "stabilize" the military situation. It proclaimed that failure to go the last mile with Thieu would cause the world to look on the United States as a feeble and perfidious nation. Congress had heard such talk before and was unmoved. At the end of April 1975 Thieu fell in South Vietnam and Lon Nol in Cambodia.

The Indochina War was at last at an end. Ho Chi Minh's dream was on the verge of fulfillment. The future would tell whether the reality of a communist Indochina would turn out to be so fatal to the West as to justify thirty years of war against the dream.

Indochina inquest. The war killed at least 1.5 million Indochinese and turned a third of the population into refugees. The 6.7 million tons of bombs dropped

Prisoner of war: home at last, April 1973

by American planes left the landscape scarred with craters. Defoliation, undertaken to deprive the Viet Cong of forest cover, affected one-third of the forest area of South Vietnam and destroyed perhaps half the country's mangrove forests. The indiscriminate use of chemical herbicides and giant bulldozers led to talk of "ecocide"—the crime of destroying the natural environment. President Marcos of the Philippines spoke for many Asians when he said in 1971, "Heaven forbid that the U.S. should duplicate what it has done in South Vietnam if the war should come to our country."

For the United States the Indochina War had lasted longer than any war in its history. It left more American dead—fifty-seven thousand—than any war except the Civil War and the two World Wars, and cost more money than any war except the Second World War. Direct war costs amounted to $150 billion. The ultimate cost was impossible to determine; estimates ranged from $350 to $676 billion.

The more serious costs were not quantifiable. The war devastated an American generation. There were no parades for returning veterans. The country that had carelessly sent soldiers to Vietnam treated them with cruel indifference when they came home. On the other extreme were the young men who had acted early on the conviction that so many came to in the end: that the war was immoral. The debate whether two hundred thousand draft evaders and deserters should receive amnesty, conditional or unconditional, carried the divisions of war into the aftermath. As for the 60 percent of the generation who neither fought nor fled, the war had gravely weakened their faith in the judgment and the word of their government.

America's myth of itself as a benevolent, wise, and invincibly powerful nation perished in the jungles of Indochina. The bitter experience corroded finally the spirit of self-confidence that had characterized America in 1945. By the early seventies the American people were divided, the economy was in trouble, the armed forces were in discredit, national motives were in doubt, and liberal ideals themselves seemed implicated in the disaster. One result was an intensive examination of the bases of American foreign policy to account for the ghastly consequence.

Most Americans believed that America had extended its power around the planet in order to protect free nations from communist aggression. But the shock of Vietnam put the situation in a chilling new light. In the course of twenty-five years, it now seemed, America had established an empire of its own. It had military commitments to 47 nations; 375 major bases and 3,000 minor facilities in foreign lands; 1 million troops stationed abroad; 2.5 million more troops under arms at home. It had spent more

than $1 trillion for its own military programs and $150 billion for foreign aid. American business also controlled more than half of all direct foreign private investment, produced more than half of the world's manufactured products, and consumed a disproportionate quantity of the world's raw materials.

How had this empire arisen? On the left, Vietnam confirmed the tendency to ascribe everything—not only the Indochina War but the Cold War and even American participation in the Second World War—to the supposed quest of American capitalism for world hegemony. It was true that American overseas investments had grown strikingly in the postwar period—from $8.4 billion in 1945 to more than $100 billion by 1973. Though it was hard to argue that America went into Vietnam to gain markets or protect investments, sophisticated exponents of the Open Door thesis contended that, because defeat in Vietnam would jeopardize American markets and investments throughout the Third World, economic interest compelled Washington to a course of ruthless counterrevolution.

Close analysis of the figures showed, however, that the dependence of American capitalism on the underdeveloped world was limited. Two-thirds of American exports went to industrialized rather than to developing countries, and sales to the Third World amounted to about 3 percent of the annual national output. Investment in the Third World represented a declining fraction of total foreign investment—35 percent in 1960 and only 26 percent in 1973. Of Third World investment, 40 percent was in petroleum; with that excluded, only about one-sixth of American overseas investment was in the developing nations, and few American businessmen seemed interested in increasing that proportion. In so far as American capitalism depended on the world outside, it depended on markets and investments in developed and not in underdeveloped countries. Nor had American business been, for example, notably eager for escalation in Vietnam.

If not American capitalism, what? No single explanation of the imperial impulse seemed satisfactory. A number of factors converged to lead Americans to appoint themselves custodians of freedom, entitled to intervene freely and righteously around the planet. The American empire, such as it was, resulted from the distortion of initially honorable beliefs: the belief in the necessity of creating an international structure of peace; the belief in America's mission to uplift and save suffering mankind; the belief in America's capacity to instruct and rebuild other nations. The perversion of these beliefs was strengthened by the national reaction to the real problem of Stalinist communism and then by the rigid and absolute form taken by the counterideology of anticommunism.

A special pressure encouraging interventionist policies, above all in Vietnam, was the military establishment. The armed forces had emerged from the Second World War with unprecedented power and status. When the wartime military leaders, most of whom were sober and responsible men, departed the scene, a new group took over, more in the school of MacArthur than of Marshall, professionally persuaded that political problems had military solutions, professionally committed to multiplying threats, appropriations, and weapons, professionally adept at playing upon national desires to appear virile and patriotic. This was not quite Eisenhower's "military-industrial complex." The military establishment was an independent force in its own right, operating according to its institutional aspirations and not at the bidding of business, which by the late sixties had turned predominantly against escalation in Vietnam.

A look at other nations corroborated the proposition that the imperial impulse was not rooted in a specific system of ownership. Every great power, whatever its ideology, had its military machine. Every military machine supposed that national security required the domination of "strategic" weaker states, if only to prevent their domination by some rival power. If, for example, the invasion by the Red Army to overthrow a national-communist regime in Czechoslovakia in 1968 was not imperialism, then the term had no meaning. If it was imperialism, then imperialism was not uniquely rooted in capitalism, nor would the abolition of capitalism end it. It seemed likely that no change in the system of ownership would reduce the power of the professional military in a time of chronic international crisis.

The decline of the superpowers. After the Second World War, the United States and the Soviet Union, entering the vacuums of power left in the wake of war, had divided and dominated the planet. Each superpower had sought to extend its empire in order to protect itself from the other. But the reign of the superpowers was drawing to a close. Where American and Soviet power had flowed into the vacuums from without, the resurgence of nationalism—in Europe, within the communist world, and in the Third World—was now replenishing these vacuums from within. The reinvigoration of nationalism meant growing opposition to the United States in the western bloc, growing opposition to the Soviet Union in the communist bloc, and growing opposition to both in the Third World. The consequence was to place limits on the power of the two countries. Tocqueville's celebrated forecast—America and Russia, each "marked out by the will of Heaven to sway the destinies of half the globe"—had in the end an exceedingly short run.

In addition, the fragmentation of the communist world by nationalism altered the nature of the problem that communism presented to the United States. The intensifying quarrel between Russia and China meant the end of any single center of authority in the communist movement and hence the end of a unified communist ideology and discipline. In the age of Stalin communist parties everywhere had responded to the directives of Moscow; the rise of "polycentrism" set communist states free to pursue national policies. It could no longer be assumed that the extension of communism meant the automatic extension of Soviet, or Chinese, power.

Though Nixon himself had been a zealous Cold Warrior who had condemned Kennedy and Johnson as inadequately militant in their Cuba and Vietnam policies, he was also a realist who recognized, as he said in 1970, that "the postwar period in international relations had ended." This appeared to call for some diminution of the global role of the United States. In Guam in July 1969 Nixon promulgated what he thereafter termed the Nixon Doctrine. The "central thesis," Nixon said in 1970, was that "the United States will participate in the defense and development of allies and friends, but cannot—and will not—conceive *all* the plans, design *all* the programs, execute *all* the decisions and undertake *all* the defense of the free nations of the world. We will help where it will make a real difference and is considered in our interest." Even in such cases, he added, the nations directly threatened had the "primary responsibility" of providing the manpower for their own defense.

This retreat from overseas activity reflected the national mood. Economic assistance, so long a basic part of American foreign policy, also lost its popularity and suffered severe reductions. Even liberal senators now argued that foreign aid encouraged American military intervention in other nations, enriched native oligarchies, and undercut the internal discipline necessary for economic development.

But Nixon soon rejected the view that his doctrine portended a general contraction of American overseas obligations. By 1971 he was warning against the "danger" of "underinvolvement" and emphasizing that the Nixon Doctrine did not mean the "precipitate shrinking of the American role" or "the automatic reduction of the American presence everywhere." In the end it was not clear what the Nixon Doctrine meant beyond the withdrawal of American ground forces from exposed places, especially from Vietnam.

Rapprochement with communist powers. Nixon's broader task in the new era was to adjust American policy to changing international realities as well as to the mounting domestic revulsion against

From confrontation to negotiation

the war in Vietnam. His *beau idéal* of a statesman was de Gaulle, who had always supposed national interest more potent than ideology; Kissinger, the student of Metternich and Bismarck, reinforced this pragmatic view. As President, Nixon began to liberate himself from the ideological obsessions of the Dulles years. Security, as he saw it, demanded no longer the roll-back of communism but rather the reestablishment of the classical balance of power. "It will be a safer world and a better world," he said in 1971, "if we have a strong, healthy United States, Europe, Soviet Union, China, Japan—each balancing the other, not playing one against the other, an even balance."

His boldest step in the pursuit of the balance-of-power design was his reversal of American policy toward the Chinese People's Republic. After the Korean War domestic political pressures had frozen successive Administrations into a posture of grim non-recognition of the Peking regime. The excesses of the Cultural Revolution of 1966–68 seemed to verify the theory that Maoism represented the ultimate in communist fanaticism. However, China and the Soviet Union had each come to fear the rival communist state more than their mutual capitalist adversary. When Russia stationed nearly fifty divisions along its Chinese frontier, Mao Tse-tung and Chou En-lai evidently decided they must take steps to block a Soviet-American alliance against China. Washington was responsive, and a mission by Kissinger to Peking in July 1971 was followed by an extraordinary presidential trip to China in early 1972. Nixon stayed in China for nearly a week—a longer state visit than any President had ever made to a foreign nation. On February 27, he signed a declaration saying that Taiwan, where Chiang Kai-shek still ruled, was legally part of mainland China, that American forces would eventually withdraw from Taiwan, and that the island's future was to be settled by the Chinese themselves.

Nixon and Chou En-lai: a reversal of policy

The new China policy came as a notable shock to both Japan and India. During the India-Pakistan War of December 1971 Nixon, despite public avowals of neutrality, had instructed his government secretly to "tilt" American power in favor of Pakistan, thereby confirming India's inclination to strengthen ties to the Soviet Union. Critics wondered whether Nixon was putting too many Asian eggs in the Chinese basket and thereby undermining his own balance-of-power policy. But most Americans welcomed his courage in terminating the sterile pretense that Communist China did not exist. And under Kissinger's sophisticated guidance the American government resisted the temptation to push its luck too far by trying to incite the two communist powers against each other.

As for the relationship between the United States and the Soviet Union, this, Nixon said, was moving "from an era of confrontation to an era of negotiation." Progress was made toward defining the status quo in Europe. The ratification in May 1972 of treaties by West Germany with Russia and Poland opened the way to the territorial settlement the wartime coalition had failed to conclude after the Second World War. A quadripartite agreement on the status of West Berlin gave promise of ending what had been for twenty-five years a situation of danger between the Soviet Union and the West. A European Secuity Conference, long proposed by the Soviet Union and finally held in Helsinki in August 1975, ratified Europe's postwar borders.

The arms race remained the most urgent question. After the Cuban missile crisis, the Soviet Union had drastically enlarged its production of land-based intercontinental ballistic missiles (ICBMs). By 1972, it had 50 percent more missile-launchers than the United States, though the United States retained a more than two-to-one superiority in offensive nuclear warheads. And American security rested not only on ICBMs but on submarine-based missiles (the Polaris–Poseidon system) and on the strategic bombing force—three independent systems, each capable of inflicting deadly damage even after a Soviet first strike, and one at least—the sea-based deterrent—invulnerable to Soviet attack. With the Soviet Union now in a comparable state of assured retaliatory capacity, it seemed absurd for the two powers, each with the ability to incinerate the other, to continue piling overkill on overkill. Never the less in the late sixties both began the construction of antiballistic missile (ABM) systems, highly expensive and of doubtful effectiveness; worse, if effective, such systems would upset the existing stalemate, give the nation with the more extensive ABM defense a new advantage, and set off an even more costly phase in the arms race.

Beset by budgetary difficulties, each government was prepared to explore measures for arms control. The first series of Strategic Arms Limitations Talks (SALT-I) was concluded by Nixon and Brezhnev in Moscow in May 1972. An ABM treaty limited each country to two major ABM deployments and to two hundred ABM missiles and launchers. As for offensive weapons, a so-called Interim Agreement, worked out on the principle of "essential equivalence," provided that for five years the Soviet Union could keep its lead in delivery vehicles and aggregate megatonnage while the United States kept its lead in warheads. The fact that the restrictions were quantitative, however, encouraged the competition to take a qualitative form. SALT-I did not end the arms race; rather it rechanneled it. After 1972 each country rushed to build weapons systems not covered in the agreements—the United States its cruise missile, the Soviet Union its Backfire supersonic bomber.

The Interim Agreement thus failed in its effort to keep things in place until serious arms reduction could be achieved. The Vladivostok Accord of December 1974 was intended to lay the basis for SALT-II agreements. However, the "ceilings" imposed by both SALT-I and the Vladivostok Accord were so high that they became targets rather than limitations. After thirty years of talk between Moscow and Washington, no new offensive systems had been cut back, nor a single nuclear weapon dismantled or destroyed. The two countries had twice as many strategic weapons in 1975 as they had in 1970 when the SALT talks began. Moreover, the export, largely by the United States, of nuclear reactors capable of generating plutonium for bombs was defeating the purpose of the Non-Proliferation Treaty of 1969, which, in any case, forty countries, including China, France, and India, had declined to sign. The potential for nuclear proliferation led experts to the ghastly prediction that, unless the nuclear powers began to reduce their own stockpiles and establish effective mechanisms for international control, nuclear war would be likely by the end of the century.

Debate over détente. At first Nixon's policy of rapprochement with China and Russia encountered little resistance at home. His anticommunist credentials facilitated the process. Observers wryly noted the irony of the old Red-hunter exchanging unctuous toasts with Chou En-lai and Brezhnev. Even conservatives confined themselves to stoical warnings.

The idea of "détente" did indeed respond to concrete interests of both superpowers—the prevention of nuclear war; the containment of military budgets; Soviet apprehension about China and need for western technology; American acknowledgement of the disappearance of a monolithic communist threat; the intensifying claims in both countries of internal problems.

Détente also created problems. Where détente had reality, it was as the expression of a certain stability achieved in the equilibrium of power; it was the recognition of situations that had already come into existence. It was, in short, the consequence rather than the cause of stabilization. It therefore applied primarily to Europe. In parts of the world where power relationships were in a condition of flux, détente was at best a wistful hope. In the Middle East, Africa, East Asia, instability had deep roots of its own. It was far beyond the joint capacity of the Soviet Union and the United States to control even if they should agree on a policy.

The very concept of détente was amorphous. In Soviet eyes it meant a series of specific and limited agreements. "Ideological coexistence" was excluded. Nor did it imply a broad guarantee of the status quo. From the Soviet viewpoint the status quo was the world revolution; those who blocked the revolution were the disturbers of the status quo. Some Americans had a more naive view. When détente failed to live up to unrealistic expectations, disenchantment set in.

The détente debate cut across party lines. Henry Kissinger, who became Secretary of State in 1973, and Senator J. W. Fulbright, the Democratic chairman of the Senate Foreign Relations Committee until 1975, defended détente. James Schlesinger, Secretary of Defense from 1973 to 1975, and Senator Henry Jackson, a Democrat from Washington, were foremost critics. The debate was less fundamental than the vehemence of its rhetoric sometimes suggested. All agreed, in principle at least, on the goal of bringing the nuclear arms race under control; all agreed in principle on better trade relations; all agreed in principle on freer intellectual exchange; all agreed on the need for continued vigilance. The argument was essentially over the relative weight to be given to these various factors in the scales of negotiation.

On the arms race, the advocates of détente felt that the situation in which each power could absorb a nuclear attack and still destroy the other met the security requirements of both. As Kissinger cried, "What in the name of God is strategic superiority? What is the significance of it, politically, militarily, operationally, at these levels of numbers? What do you do with it?" As for human rights in the Soviet Union, the supporters of détente contended that the reduction of tension would do more than the restoration of a siege mentality to liberalize Soviet society. The Kissinger–Fulbright conclusion was that the United States should press forward with the SALT-II talks and even take certain risks in the effort to bring

From confrontation to negotiation

The détente debate

In looking back over my experiences of some fifty years with the Soviet Union, I find that my basic judgments remain little altered, although conditions have changed radically. I have been attacked for those judgments from both ends of the political spectrum. Some have called me a warmonger; others denounced me as too soft on Communism. I continue to maintain, as in 1945, that on ideology there is no prospect of compromise between the Kremlin and ourselves, but that we must find ways to settle as many areas of conflict as possible in order to live together on this small planet without war. I have constantly believed that internal pressures by the Russian people and the influence of world opinion would lead in time to some relaxation in the Soviet system, and that greater respect for human rights would gradually develop. This has certainly been happening, though unevenly and far too slowly. I heartily approve the policy of détente.... I decry those who contend that any relaxation of tensions must inevitably benefit the Russians, to our disadvantage. It seems to me we have no choice. In this nuclear age, war is unthinkable. Our interest is bound to be served by relieving tensions as much as we can, by working for what I have called 'competitive coexistence.' I for one do not fear the competition.

From W. Averell Harriman (with Elie Abel), *Special Envoy to Churchill and Stalin, 1941–1946*, 1975

We are told that détente is our best hope for a lasting peace. Hope it may offer, but only so long as we have no illusions about it.... When the stakes are war and peace, we can bargain successfully only if we are strong militarily and only if we are willing to defend ourselves if necessary. We must also have a sense of unity and a national purpose in our foreign policy.... For many years we remained the strongest nation on earth. Through the 1950s and on into the 1960s our national security was coupled with a sense of national unity and purpose. But that changed. The Soviet Union has now forged ahead in producing nuclear and conventional weapons.... Let us not be satisfied with a foreign policy whose principal accomplishment seems to be our acquisition of the right to sell Pepsi-Cola in Siberia. It is time that we, the people of the United States, demand a policy that puts our own nation's interests as the first priority.... Our foreign policy in recent years seems to be a matter of placating potential adversaries. Does our government fear that the American people lack willpower?

From Ronald Reagan, Speech at Phillips Exeter Academy, Exeter, New Hampshire, February 10, 1976.

---

the arms race under control; that the United States should actively promote commercial relations, give the Soviet Union most-favored-nation status, and encourage American exporters to sell to Russia; and that the United States should not harass the Soviet Union over internal questions, such as the treatment of intellectuals or Jewish emigration.

Critics of détente were deeply concerned by what they regarded as a dangerous decay in the American military position relative to the Soviet Union. They pointed to the steady decline of the military budget. By 1975 defense expenditures were less in constant dollars than they had been at any time since before the Korean War. Defense spending, which had accounted for 47 percent of federal outlays in 1960,

accounted for 25 percent in 1975. The budget for strategic forces was about one-third in real terms what it had been at the end of the Eisenhower Administration. For Schlesinger and Jackson, mutual assured destruction—MAD, as they called it—promised little security unless the United States matched or surpassed the Soviet Union at key numerical levels. If Russia were permitted to achieve a war-winning capability, they believed, this would demoralize the West and allow Soviet power to expand through nuclear blackmail and other forms of diplomatic and political pressure.

The conservative critics of détente therefore were skeptical about SALT and wanted to accelerate the American arms build-up even at the risk of provoking a counter build-up by the Soviet Union. On the issue of human rights they were joined by liberals who favored arms control but were outraged by the treatment accorded such Soviet dissenters as the physicist Andrei Sakharov and the novelist Aleksander Solzhenitsyn. Solzhenitsyn's visit to the United States in 1975 dramatized the problem of Soviet repression. Many Americans saw the presidential refusal to invite him to the White House lest it offend the Kremlin as a dismal preview of the costs of détente. Soviet restrictions on the migration of Soviet Jews led in 1973–74 to a congressional battle over the Jackson Amendment, an attempt to condition trading concessions on changes in Soviet migration policy. The persistence of congressional agitation over what the Kremlin regarded as an internal question eventually drove Moscow to cancel the Soviet–American Trade Agreement of 1972.

By 1976 the bloom had gone off détente. Soviet indifference to the so-called "Basket Three" of the Helsinki Agreement on European Security, with its pledges to increase the flow of people, ideas, and information across the Iron Curtain, along with the apparent Soviet renewal of the Cold War of movement in Portugal and Angola, was putting the supporters of détente on the defensive. Many people agreed when the French journalist André Fontaine defined détente as simply "the Cold War pursued by other means—and sometimes by the same." Nevertheless there appeared no alternative to détente if the term were construed with due regard for its inherent limitations. Although not an end to the Cold War, détente at least represented its modulation into a form less menacing to the future of mankind.

Middle Eastern cockpit. The limitations of détente were on vivid display in the Middle East. This region had been an historic target of Russian concern and ambition. The United States had a deep moral commitment to the survival of Israel and a strong—if conflicting—economic interest in Arab oil. But Russian and American concerns were superimposed on a part of the world torn by bitter indigenous hatreds endowed with a life and potency of their own.

The Arab states remained unreconciled to the existence of Israel. Nasser of Egypt was no more under the control of Moscow than Israeli leaders were under the control of Washington. In June 1967 Israel, responding to the Egyptian blockade of the port of Elath on the Gulf of Aqaba, launched a surprise attack on Egypt and won a smashing victory in the Six Days War. After the war Israel retained possession of territories deemed essential to defense against future Arab attack—the Sinai Peninsula against Egypt and the Golan Heights against Syria as well as the Gaza Strip and the West Bank of the Jordan River. In November

1967 the UN Security Council passed Resolution 242 calling for "withdrawal of Israeli forces from territories occupied in the recent conflict" (though not necessarily, it was noted, from *all* such territories) and for the general acknowledgment of the sovereignty and independence of all states in the area.

The package deal thus outlined was not achieved, the Arab states refusing to recognize Israel, Israel refusing to abandon the territory won in 1967. The bitterness of the Palestinian refugees—Arabs expelled from Israel—added another explosive element, especially after the formation of the Palestine Liberation Organization and even more extreme terrorist groups. In December 1969 Secretary of State Rogers presented a plan designed to revive the terms of Resolution 242. The death of Nasser in September 1970 brought Anwar el-Sadat into power in Cairo and resulted in more flexible Egyptian attitudes. A precarious peace, punctuated by Arab raids and Israeli reprisals, prevailed until October 5, 1973.

Then, on Yom Kippur, the Jewish holy day of atonement, Egypt and Syria struck at Israel. Caught by surprise, Israeli forces reeled under the blow. The Egyptians were fighting with advanced Soviet weapons, and the United States at once rushed further arms to Israel. After ten days of Israeli disarray, a counterattack cut off the Egyptian Third Army in the Sinai. There followed a series of still unfathomed events. On the night of October 24 Nixon put American nuclear forces on worldwide alert—a most unusual step. The ostensible reason was to counter an alleged Soviet threat to intervene militarily on behalf of Egypt, though it was later questioned both within and without the American government whether available intelligence supported such a Soviet intention. Israeli officials subsequently claimed that the alert was accompanied by warnings that, if Israel did not spare the Egyptian force and conclude the war, it would have to fight on alone. The American purpose, it was supposed, was to bring about a military stalemate and preserve the American position as Middle East mediator.

A powerful new factor, suddenly introduced into the Middle East equation, argued against the United States' taking a drastic anti-Arab position. In 1960 Venezuela had persuaded the oil-producing states of the Middle East to join in forming the Organization of Petroleum Exporting Countries (OPEC). The original point of OPEC was to concert policies in order to defend national economies against the manipulation of the world market by western oil companies. On October 19, 1973, OPEC, now controlled by an Arab majority, imposed a ban on oil exports to the United States and western Europe in retaliation for American support of Israel. The oil embargo represented a historic reversal in the balance of power between the industrialized world and the Third World. For centuries underdeveloped countries possessing vital raw materials had been a particular object of western empire. OPEC now showed that their ownership of raw materials, far from placing them at the mercy of the West, might place the West at their mercy.

The October War thus altered the situation in the Middle East in two salient respects: it shattered the belief in Israel's military invincibility, and it demonstrated western vulnerability in face of Arab use of oil as a political weapon. Both American interests—Israel and oil—called more urgently than ever for a political settlement. This became Kissinger's major objective in 1974–75. Relying on a strong personal relationship with Sadat as well as on the traditional American influence in Israel, he visited the Middle East on an average of one out of every six weeks. His "shuttle diplomacy" sought to bring Israel and Egypt step by step toward a resolution of outstanding issues. At the same time, he tried to reduce Soviet influence by systematically excluding Moscow from his Middle Eastern negotiations. For a season Kissinger's bilateral efforts had a measure of success. In September 1975 an interim agreement on the Sinai provided for partial Israeli troop withdrawal in exchange for an Egyptian pledge to resolve differences by peaceful means and an American commitment to send technicians to man an early warning system in a buffer zone created by the Israeli withdrawal. Washington also assured Israel that it would continue to supply the arms required to maintain a military balance in the Middle East.

By 1976 the step-by-step approach was under increasing attack. The hard question of the occupied territories seemed remote from resolution. Some mitigation of the Palestinian problem, perhaps through the formation of a Palestinian state, began to appear an unavoidable part of a final settlement. Critics called for an end to bilateral diplomacy in favor of a major effort, in association with other Arab states and with the Soviet Union, to settle underlying causes in the spirit of Resolution 242. The future of Israel—with 3.5 million Israelis surrounded by 100 million hostile Arabs endowed by oil with new international power—remained uncertain.

The Kissinger thesis. The Middle East displayed Kissinger's virtuoso qualities as a negotiator—his intelligence, resourcefulness, perseverance, and stamina—at their best. Some observers, however, saw limitations in his approach to diplomacy. He seemed to regard international relations as a chess game played by masters in a sealed room. Legislatures, newspapers, public opinion therefore became nuisances and irritations, distracting the mind and jogging the elbow of the master as he prepared his next move. Kissinger's style of diplomacy naturally found it easier to deal with authoritarian states—not because authoritarianism was regarded as philosophically superior but because authoritarian regimes could be relied upon to deliver their countries. Kissinger's greatest success lay in dealing with historic adversaries, especially Russia and China. He proved less successful in dealing with historic friends and allies.

In their faith in peace through the balancing of power, Nixon and Kissinger seemed to minimize the need for international institutions designed to accommodate the interests of the great powers and protect the interests of smaller states. No previous administration had displayed such skepticism about the United Nations or such disdain about America's UN obligations. Mistrust of the UN fed on the fact that, with the increase in membership from the Third World, the United States could no longer count on a majority in the General Assembly. The Third World nations, often expressing ancient resentments in shrill language, roused apprehensions that a "tyranny of the majority" was growing in the organization. The counteroffensive launched in 1975–76 by Daniel Patrick Moynihan in his brief tenure as U.S. ambassador to the UN brought American relations with the UN to a new low—a situation to which the General Assembly itself had significantly contributed by welcoming Yasir Arafat of the Palestine Liberation Organization, a pistol holster on his hip, to the rostrum in 1974 and by passing in 1975 a resolution equating Zionism with racism. Anti-Israel actions by subsidiary UN bodies, such as UNESCO, increased criticism in the United States and elsewhere. Plain speaking by American delegates was invigorating and useful. But broad denunciations of the UN as, in Moynihan's words, a "theater of the absurd" overlooked the extent to which the organization remained not only an indispensable point of contact with the Third World but the only place where global problems—food, population, energy, inflation, environment, development assistance, drugs—could be collectively considered and confronted.

The preference for authoritarian regimes infected United States policy throughout the world. In Europe Nixon so sedulously identified Washington with right-wing dictatorships in Greece and Portugal that, when the inevitable political upheavals took place, new and more democratic governments came to power with vigorous anti-American predispositions. In Africa the Nixon administration sought to enlarge contacts with white regimes—not only with South Africa and Rhodesia but with Portuguese colonial regimes in Angola and Mozambique. Washington's solicitude for white Africa alienated the Organization of African Unity and greatly reduced American influence in black Africa. The Nixon policy undermined the American position in 1975–76 when the United

States sought to counter the introduction by the Soviet Union of a Cuban expeditionary force in a bold attempt to decide the outcome of a civil war in newly independent Angola.

Events followed a similar pattern in Latin America. Commending the military dictatorship in Brazil, Nixon said, "As Brazil goes so will go the rest of that Latin American continent." In 1972 Nixon announced that it would be United States policy to retaliate against governments that nationalized American firms without assuring adequate compensation. This would be done not only by ending bilateral American aid but by trying to veto aid from the World Bank and other multilateral institutions. Such concern for private business did not increase American popularity in the Western Hemisphere.

The election of a Marxist regime headed by Salvador Allende in Chile in 1970 produced special excitement in Washington. Before the election Kissinger had directed the CIA to take covert action against Allende's candidacy. After the election, observing that Allende's victory presented "massive problems for us," he authorized the CIA to spend $8 million to "destabilize" the new government. Allende strove in the main to preserve constitutional processes; but he had received only 36 percent of the vote, and his economic policy was neither well managed nor perhaps acceptable to the Chilean majority. In the end his regime might have fallen anyway. But Washington, reinforcing the CIA by a credit squeeze and other economic measures, contributed to Allende's downfall and probable murder in a military coup in 1973. The succeeding military regime under General Augusto Pinochet shocked much of the world by its policies of repression and torture. Yet it remained a favorite of Washington, receiving more than twice as much bilateral economic assistance in 1975 as the next-largest Latin American recipient of United States aid.

Kissinger's theory was that détente could work only if the Soviet Union and the United States respected each other's spheres of influence. He saw the Soviet Union as a status quo power for which revolution beyond the Soviet zone was a temptation, not a necessity—a temptation from which the Kremlin would quickly recede when the United States showed the "will" to defend what Russia would accept as legitimate American interests. He therefore saw no incompatibility between seeking an accommodation with Moscow and reacting vigorously against communist gains in Indochina, Chile, and Angola; quite the contrary. In this view Pinochet, because less disturbing to Soviet-American relations, would be better for détente than Allende. This was the Soviet theory of détente too, as Moscow had shown in Czechoslovakia and elsewhere. Nor indeed could the fragile peace easily survive a Soviet Cold War of movement designed to upset the global balance of power.

But it was essential to distinguish between clear cases of Soviet intervention, as in Cuba in 1962 and evidently in Angola in 1976, and indigenous civil wars and revolutions, as in Indochina and Chile. By regarding every Marxist victory as an addition to Soviet power, the official doctrine denied the reality of polycentrism and made Washington the arsenal of counterrevolution. In a deeper sense, Washington's support of authoritarian regimes for short-run diplomatic purposes ignored the human values involved and damaged what had been historically America's most precious international asset—the bond that was felt to run between the United States and ordinary people around the world.

Recession of American power. For some years Kissinger enjoyed virtual immunity as the architect of American foreign policy. His wit, insouciance, and proficiency seized the national imagination. He beguiled Congress. Polls regularly reported him at the top of the list of most-admired Americans. By the mid-1970s public opinion had grown more skeptical. His addiction to ambiguity and secrecy had become self-defeating. In addition, his policy, despite its pursuit of détente, seemed to require a specific American response to domestic turmoil in countries that Americans increasingly regarded as outside the realm of direct and vital American interest.

There had been, indeed, a change in the priorities of American foreign policy. Political and strategic issues, at which Kissinger excelled, were giving way to economic issues. Economic issues called not for dramatic strokes but for persistence in undramatic policies, not for brilliant individuals but for enduring institutions. Nor did they give great scope to American power. While the United States remained the world's largest economy, its share of the world's gross national product had declined from 39 percent in 1950 to 27 percent in 1974; its share of world exports from 16 percent in 1950 to 12 percent in 1974; its share of international reserves from 50 percent in 1950 to 7 percent in 1974. All this, accompanied by the trauma of Indochina, by the rise of the Soviet Union to nuclear equality, and by the insistent claims of domestic problems, was producing a revulsion against postwar dreams of an American Century.

This revulsion did not mean a return to traditional isolationism. There were still four hundred thousand American troops stationed around the world. Nor were Americans prepared to abandon historic interests in Europe, Latin America, or the Pacific. But the illusions of globalism had yielded to a more selective and realistic internationalism. This new mood corresponded to a rhythm of activism and

From confrontation to negotiation

withdrawal in the history of American foreign policy. In 1952 Frank L. Klingberg, examining American history since 1776, had identified four "introvert" phases, averaging about twenty-one years in length, and three "extrovert" phases, averaging about twenty-seven years. The fourth phase of extroversion had begun about 1940 and, by the theory, would last to about 1967. Klingberg therefore predicted an American retreat from global involvement in the late 1960s, to last, presumably, till the late 1980s.

Whatever the merits of the cyclical scheme, Americans had predominantly resolved by the mid-1970s that the national capacity to decide the destiny of other nations was strictly limited. In the aftermath of Vietnam, Americans began to conclude that not everything that happened in the world was of equal concern to the United States; that in an age of local upheaval and savagery many terrible things would take place which the United States lacked the power to prevent or the wisdom to cure; that Washington could not be the permanent guarantor of stability on a turbulent planet; and that military force was not always the most effective means of national influence. In a sense, this mood was a return to fundamentals— to the view of the Founding Fathers that the new republic would regenerate the world not through its power but through its example.

Decline and fall

Nixon and the economy.
For Nixon domestic policy was admittedly secondary to foreign policy. "I've always thought this country could run itself domestically without a President," he said in 1968. "All you need is a competent cabinet to run the country at home." His disposition was to mistrust the national government, to relax federal regulation, and to give free rein to business enterprise.

His most urgent economic problem was the inflation generated by the Indochina War. In 1970 the consumer price index was 16 percent higher than in 1967 and prices were still rising. In the tradition of economic orthodoxy, Nixon at first supposed that a severe monetary policy would suffice to bring inflation under control. He denounced "jawboning" (official admonitions against price or wage increases) and price-wage guidelines, as developed in the Kennedy years. Instead he called for tight money and high interest rates.

The immediate effect of what he termed his "game plan" was to produce the first recession in a decade. Unemployment rose to 5.8 percent (4.6 million persons) in 1970. But inflation did not stop. From January 1969 to August 1971 the cost of living in-

creased by an astonishing 14.5 percent. Furthermore, inflation was overpricing American exports and weakening the dollar abroad. In 1971 the balance-of-payments deficit reached the record figure of $29.6 billion. There was, in addition, for the first time since 1893, a deficit in the balance of trade; imports exceeded exports by almost $3 billion.

Still confident that tight money could stop inflation, Nixon said in June 1970: "I will not take this nation down the road of wage and price controls, however politically expedient that may seem." But as "stagflation"—the combination of stagnation and inflation—persisted, Nixon finally was forced to jettison his game plan. Fortified by the appointment of a Texas Democrat, John B. Connally, as Secretary of the Treasury, Nixon declared himself a Keynesian in the summer of 1971 and on August 15 announced a startling reversal of economic course: a ninety-day price-wage freeze (Phase 1), to be followed in November by Phase 2, a system of wage and price controls. In his August announcement Nixon also suspended the convertibility of dollars into gold, thereby making American goods more competitive in world markets. This was followed in December by the formal devaluation of the dollar. These measures meant the end of the international monetary system based on gold-dollar convertibility set up at Bretton Woods (see p. 713).

The New Federalism.
In the longer term, Nixon hoped to reduce the role of the national government in American economic life. "After a third of a century of power flowing from the people and the States to Washington," he said in August 1969, "it is time for a New Federalism in which power, funds and responsibility will flow from Washington to the States and to the people." The New Federalism sought to distinguish between those governmental tasks that were inescapably national and those that, it was thought, could be better discharged locally. In order to strengthen the capacity of local government to assume federal functions, Nixon promoted the idea, originally brought forward during the Johnson Administration, of "revenue-sharing." In the end revenue-sharing was the most notable legislative achievement of the New Federalism. The State and Local Fiscal Assistance Act of 1972 provided for the distribution of $30 billion in unrestricted funds to states and localities over a period of five years. Special revenue-sharing programs for manpower and urban community development were enacted in 1973 and 1974.

Some critics doubted that state and local governments were more honest and efficient than the national government. Critics also contended that "no-strings" revenue-sharing discriminated against the cities, the poor, and the ethnic minorities—all particular

The time has now come in America to reverse the flow of power and resources from the States and communities in Washington, and start power and resources flowing back from Washington to the States and communities and, more important, to the people, all across America.... We have made the Federal Government so strong it grows muscle-bound and the States and localities so weak they approach impotence. If we put more power in more places, we can make government more creative in more places. That way we multiply the number of people with the ability to make things happen—and we can open the way to a new burst of creative energy throughout America.... The further away government is from the people, the stronger government becomes and the weaker people become. And a nation with a strong government and a weak people is an empty shell....

The idea that a bureaucratic élite in Washington knows best what is best for people everywhere and that you cannot trust local government is really a contention that you cannot trust people to govern themselves. This notion is completely foreign to the American experience. Local government is the government closest to the people and it is most responsive to the individual person; it is people's government in a far more intimate way than the government in Washington can ever be....

Giving up power is hard. But I would urge all of you, as leaders of this country, to remember that the truly revered leaders in world history are those who gave power to people, not those who took it away.... What this Congress can be remembered for is opening the way to a New American Revolution—a peaceful revolution in which power was turned back to the people.

From Richard M. Nixon, State of the Union Address, January 22, 1971.

beneficiaries of the now-diminished categorical grant-in-aid programs (that is, federal grants to special categories of the population). The "war on poverty" was abandoned as such, with the Office of Economic Opportunity undergoing reduction and dismantlement. Categorical grants were plainly better adapted than block grants to the carrying out of national social priorities. Still, general revenue-sharing won support, especially from financially hard-pressed local governments, because of its relative flexibility and lack of red tape; and it was widely applauded by citizens who felt the national government had grown too remote and unmanageable.

The welfare system, partly federal and partly local in character, posed especially difficult problems. There had been a disturbing expansion of relief rolls during the sixties, especially in the category of Aid to Families with Dependent Children (AFDC). Between 1961 and 1970 the AFDC caseload rose from 921,000 to 2.2 million families, with an increase of almost 30 percent in 1970 alone. The federal welfare bill grew from $2.1 billion in 1960 to nearly $18 billion in 1972, while the number of persons on welfare rolls increased from 7.3 million in 1961 to 14.9 million in 1972. Fifteen percent of the population of New York, a quarter of the population of Newark, and about 6 percent of all Americans were on welfare.

Though this welfare explosion was often attributed to the migration to Northern cities of black families forced by mechanization off Southern farms, in fact the rate of such migration did not increase during the sixties. What did increase was turmoil in the ghettos; historically, relief rolls have tended to expand in response to militancy among the poor. Moreover, the antipoverty officials of the Johnson Administration had taught the poor how to apply for relief and had presented welfare as a right. Then unemployment, induced by Nixon's anti-inflation program in 1969–71, decisively swelled the rolls. Of families on welfare, about 49 percent were white and 46 percent black. Of those receiving welfare in 1971, 55.5 percent were children, 15.6 percent old people, 9.4 percent blind and disabled. Less than 1 percent of welfare recipients were able-bodied unemployed males.

The existing welfare system buckled under the new burdens thrust upon it. It was widely condemned because it required employed fathers to leave the household in order that their families could qualify for public assistance, because its procedures were degrading, and because it helped only about a fourth of the poor. A presidential Commission on Income Maintenance, established by Johnson in 1964, recommended a minimum annual cash income of $2,400 for

805

families of four. In 1969 Nixon called for the replacement of AFDC by a Family Assistance Plan that would give every family of four on welfare with no outside income a basic federal payment of $1,600 a year. There was also a "work requirement" under which recipients with school-age children could be referred to work or training on penalty of forfeiting a part of their FAP payments. The FAP, with its provision for a guaranteed minimum income, was a path-breaking conception. Unfortunately it roused opposition from many Democrats, some for partisan reasons, some because they deemed the benefits too low and the work requirement too coercive, as well as from conservative Republicans and from the social-welfare establishment, which had a vested interest in the existing system. The White House itself blew hot and cold. After passing the House of Representatives in 1970, the FAP failed in the Senate. The Nixon Administration thereafter backed off from it, but the idea of a guaranteed income remained on the agenda of the future.

Daniel P. Moynihan, the architect of the FAP, conceived it as part of a general shift from a "services strategy"—the attempt to help the poor by supplying them with specialized service programs—to an "income strategy"—helping the poor by giving them cash or some cash equivalent, such as food stamps. The services strategy and its reliance on case-work were considered to imply that government and the welfare professionals knew best what was good for the poor. The income strategy supposedly gave the poor greater freedom to make their own choices. "The best judge of each family's priorities is the family itself," Nixon said in 1969. "The best way to ameliorate the hardships of poverty is to provide the family with additional income—to be spent as each family sees fit." Though critics felt that cash transfers to poor families would not do much to alleviate such structural problems of poverty as education, job training, housing, and transportation, none the less the underlying philosophy had wide appeal and was reflected in the rise of income-support programs to nearly one-third of the federal budget by 1975.

Concentration of presidential power. In pushing his policies, Nixon faced the fact of Democratic control in both houses of Congress. While the President could indicate his priorities by messages, the Democratic congressional majority both had priorities of its own and the capacity to forward them by legislation, especially through the appropriations power. Confronted by statutes that conflicted with his own conception of priorities, Nixon increasingly responded by refusing to spend funds voted by Congress.

Impoundment, as this practice was called, had a minor status in law and custom. Previous Presidents

had used it, however, to effect savings or to stretch out the spending of funds, not to set aside the expressed will of Congress. Nixon not only impounded far more money than any of his predecessors—by 1973, his impoundments affected more than a hundred federal programs and reached the level of $15 billion—but used impoundment to nullify laws passed by the legislative branch and even claimed this power as a constitutional right. The courts later rejected this claim and ordered the release of impounded funds.

Nixon also freely engaged in selective enforcement of statutes and attempted—in another action overruled in the courts—to use the pocket veto in the middle of congressional sessions. And he revived and expanded the unconditional theory of executive privilege set forth in the Eisenhower Administration. Kennedy and Johnson had returned to the traditional and restricted view of the President's power to withhold information from Congress. But Nixon claimed presidential denial as an inherent and unreviewable constitutional right. His Attorneys General asserted on his behalf that Congress had no power to compel testimony over presidential objection from any one of the 2.5 million employees in the executive branch.

In addition to concentrating power in the executive branch at the expense of Congress, he sought to concentrate power in the White House at the expense of the executive departments. Where Franklin D. Roosevelt had fought the Second World War with no more than a dozen special assistants, Nixon by 1972 had forty-eight—the largest White House staff in history. Nixon and his White House aides, especially H. R. Haldeman and John D. Ehrlichman, had not only a general determination, with which other Presidents could have sympathized, to make the executive bureaucracy responsive to presidential purpose but a specific mistrust of the civil service as Democratic and hostile. They soon began to fear that even members of the Cabinet were becoming the prisoners of their civil servants. Cabinet meetings became infrequent, and Cabinet members found it increasingly difficult to gain access to Nixon. In time the more independent-minded among them departed. The establishment in the White House in 1970 of the Domestic Council under Ehrlichman's direction represented an attempt to control domestic policy as effectively as Kissinger's national security staff controlled foreign policy.

The "great silent majority." Underlying Nixon's domestic policy was a conviction that small and loud minorities had had too much influence on national policy and that the time had come to govern in the interests of the middle class, the "great silent majority." The defense of traditional middle-class values—

Nixon and staff: one of the most corrupt in American history

work, economy, self-reliance, and, above all, law and order—became the particular theme of the Attorney General, John Mitchell, and the Vice President, Spiro T. Agnew. In their view, the solid average American, harassed by government, crime, inflation, taxes, riots, drugs, pornography, welfare chiselers, and uppity blacks, represented the heart of the Nixon constituency and the foundation of a future Republican majority. Republican political experts noted that, while Nixon's margin over Humphrey in 1968 had been exceedingly narrow, if George Wallace's 13.5 per cent could be added to Nixon's 43.4 per cent, Nixon would be unbeatable in 1972.

The great bulk of the electorate, it was pointed out, was unyoung, unpoor, and unblack. In particular, there seemed an unprecedented chance to make the South into a Republican stronghold. This led to the "Southern strategy"—a slowdown on civil rights under the standard of "benign neglect"; attacks on the busing of pupils as a means of achieving school integration; a rhetorical barrage against welfare, crime, the media of opinion, and the intellectual community. That strategy had the further advantage of prying away from the Democrats white blue-collar families in the North who felt threatened by racial adjustments demanded of them at a distance by upper-class liberals.

The reconstitution of the Supreme Court was an important element in the Southern strategy. Nixon, who during his campaign had blamed the Supreme Court for encouraging disorder and crime, now took advantage of vacancies to appoint justices more to his liking. The retirement of Earl Warren in 1968 enabled Nixon the next year to designate Warren Burger as the new Chief Justice. Nixon's next two appointments, both federal judges from the South, were turned down by the Senate, the first because of conflicts of interest, the second because of evident intellectual mediocrity. In a bitter statement Nixon attributed their rejection to "the fact that they had the misfortune of being born in the South." Subsequently, however, four less vulnerable but equally conservative nominees, one born in the South, were approved. By 1976 the Supreme Court had taken on a markedly more conservative complexion.

Vice President Agnew emerged as a particularly arresting spokesman for law and order. His gaudy rhetoric and addiction to alliteration ("the nattering nabobs of negativism") won him a devoted national audience. "It is time for the preponderant majority, the responsible citizens of this country, to assert their rights," Agnew said in 1969. "If, in challenging, we polarize the American people, I say it is time for a positive polarization." Agnew concentrated much of his own challenge against television and the press, questioning the fairness of the mass media and demanding in somewhat menacing terms that they be "made more responsive to the views of the nation."

The antiwar demonstrations of 1969–70, and especially the outbursts following the Kent State shootings, encouraged Nixon to pursue a strategy of confrontation, confident that the majority of voters were fed up with protest and violence. This policy roused doubts among his own appointees: Secretary of the Interior Walter J. Hickel wrote Nixon that his Administration appeared "to lack appropriate concern for the attitude of a great mass of Americans—our young people." Nevertheless Nixon made lawlessness the central theme of the 1970 midterm election. In a concluding speech, he denounced "creeping permissiveness," called for "new and strong laws that will give the peace forces new muscle to deal with the criminal forces," and said that "appeasement" of "thugs and hoodlums" in American society must end. This appeal failed. The Republicans lost nine seats in the House and eleven governorships but gained two seats in the Senate.

As the 1972 election approached, Democratic optimism was dissipated in a long and fatiguing series of primary contests. Senator George McGovern of South Dakota, beating back a late challenge from Hubert Humphrey, emerged as front-runner, though George Wallace drew an impressive number of primary votes. McGovern, a Second World War hero and former college professor who had served in the Kennedy Administration and was a long-time opponent of the Indochina War, succeeded in uniting the Robert Kennedy and Eugene McCarthy forces of 1968; and, benefiting by reforms in the delegate-selection process brought about by a Democratic party commission that he himself had chaired, he won first-ballot nomination at the Democratic convention in July. Senator Thomas Eagleton of Missouri, his choice as running mate, retired from the ticket after failing to disclose to McGovern a history of psychiatric treatment. His replacement was Sargent Shriver of Maryland, former head of Kennedy's Peace Corps and Johnson's war on poverty and later ambassador to Paris. In August the Republicans renominated Nixon and Agnew.

Thrown badly off stride by the Eagleton affair, McGovern never recovered momentum. In addition, his casual proposal during the primaries of his own

McGovern and Shriver: off stride

version of a guaranteed minimum income won him a reputation for radicalism. Republicans denounced him as the champion of "acid, abortion and amnesty." Continuing the effort to win over those who had voted for Wallace in 1968, Republican campaigners played astutely upon racial and cultural nerves. The success of the "Southern strategy" was guaranteed when Wallace, disabled in an assassination attempt in May, decided not to field a party of his own. Then Kissinger's claim twelve days before the election that peace was at hand in Vietnam neutralized McGovern's strongest issue. Nor did the Twenty-sixth Amendment, ratified in 1971 and lowering the voting age to eighteen, help the Democrats as much as they had expected.

Nixon sailed to an impressive victory, carrying every area except Massachusetts and the District of Columbia. In an election marked by ticket-splitting and voter indifference—the turnout of 55 percent was the lowest since 1948—he polled 46 million votes against 28.5 million for McGovern, winning the largest proportion (60.8 percent) of the popular vote since 1964 and the largest margin in the Electoral College (520 to 17) since 1936. However, the Democrats added two to their Senate majority and retained control of the House. As in the 1950s, the voters balanced a Republican President with a Democratic Congress.

Watergate. On the night of June 17, 1972, five men, equipped with cameras and electronic bugging devices, had been arrested in the offices of the Democratic National Committee in the Watergate building in Washington. The burglars gave false names, but one, James McCord, was soon identified as chief of security for the Committee to Re-elect the President. The Committee's chairman, John Mitchell, who had resigned as Attorney General to run Nixon's campaign, promptly denied any involvement on the part of his organization (soon known popularly as CREEP). The incident had little impact on the presidential election, even after the *Washington Post* suggested that the Watergate break-in was related to a larger campaign of political sabotage and after serious doubts had been raised about the methods by which the Nixon people had raised the unprecedentedly large campaign fund of $55 million. McGovern called the Nixon Administration "the most corrupt" in American history. Few voters listened.

It is not clear whether Nixon knew in advance about the break-in. There can be no doubt, however, that the atmosphere he created in the White House stimulated those around him to drastic and lawless action. Underneath his conventional exterior Nixon was a man of agitated and compulsive emotion. "There was another side to him," John Ehrlichman said later, "like the flat, dark side of the moon." He saw life as a battlefield and believed that the nation was swarming with personal enemies bent on his destruction. He was, wrote Jeb Stuart Magruder, CREEP's deputy director, "absolutely paranoid about criticism." The campus riots after Cambodia in 1970, along with the Weathermen and the Black Panthers, fed this paranoia. When John Dean became White House counsel in July 1970, he found, he later said, "a climate of excessive concern over the political impact of demonstrators, excessive concern over leaks, an insatiable appetite for political intelligence, all coupled with a do-it-yourself White House staff, regardless of the law." Nixon's hatred was directed especially at what his associates called the "eastern establishment" and perceived as a self-appointed élite that did not understand or represent the real America. Musing about his enemies, Nixon told the White House hatchet man, Charles Colson, "One day we'll get them—we'll get them on the ground where we want them. And we'll stick our heels in, step on them hard and twist, right, Chuck?"

That spirit generated the Enemies List, circulated by John Dean with the injunction that the point was to "use the available Federal machinery to screw our political enemies." In 1970 T. C. Huston, another young White House aide, drew up a plan, adopted by Nixon, authorizing, in the name of national security, burglary, electronic surveillance, mail interception, and other practices forbidden by law. J. Edgar Hoover's protest compelled Nixon to rescind his order; but in 1971 Nixon, unsettled by Daniel Ellsberg's release of the Pentagon Papers, set up a secret White House unit known as "the plumbers" to effectuate the Huston plan. The plumbers soon burgled the office of Ellsberg's psychiatrist, forged official cables in an effort to implicate John F. Kennedy in the assassination of Ngo Dinh Diem, wiretapped foreign embassies, and engaged in other edifying activities. This was again done in the name of "national security"—words that, as Egil Krogh, a top plumber, later said "served to block critical analysis. . . . Freedom of the President to pursue his planned course was the ultimate national security objective."

In the winter of 1971–72 polls showed Nixon trailing Senator Edmund Muskie and roused concern in the White House about the forthcoming election. The plumbers now moved into domestic politics and helped organize a campaign of "dirty tricks" designed to bring Muskie into disrepute. Early in 1972 G. Gordon Liddy, a plumber who became general counsel of CREEP, outlined larger plans of espionage and sabotage to Mitchell, who demurred at the cost but not at the illegality. Scaled down, the plans became acceptable. In May the Democratic headquar-

ters were entered for the first time; bugs were planted on telephones, and documents were copied. All was going well until the night of June 17.

The cover-up. Whether or not Nixon knew of the Watergate entry in advance, he knew about it immediately afterward. In February 1971 he had installed microphones in the White House to record all presidential conversations, and the tapes subsequently provided evidence of Nixon's response to Watergate. On June 20 he held a long conversation with Haldeman, of which eighteen and a half minutes were mysteriously erased from the tape. On June 23 Haldeman observed to him, "We're back in the problem area because the FBI is out of control." Nixon told him to tell the FBI, "Don't go any further into this case, period!" The reasons, he made clear, were political; the pretext would be national security.

The cover-up had begun. Incriminating documents were systematically destroyed. But there were problems. Neither the FBI—though Hoover, who had died in May, had been replaced by a complaisant political appointee—nor the CIA proved as pliable as the White House hoped. Moreover, Robert Woodward and Carl Bernstein, two young reporters on the *Washington Post*, began to dig quietly and implacably into the story. The cover-up strategy relied increasingly on two main elements—bribes and lies. Several hundred thousand dollars were raised to buy the silence of the Watergate defendants and the attendant plumbers. Everyone who knew the truth, from Nixon down, denied publicly and privately that Watergate was anything more than a personal adventure by those caught in the act. "Under my direction," Nixon told a press conference in August, "counsel to the President, Mr. Dean, has conducted an investigation. . . . I can say categorically that his investigation indicates that no one in the White House staff, no one in this Administration, presently employed, was involved in this very bizarre incident." Dean had made no such investigation or report.

In September a federal grand jury indicted the five Watergate burglars and two of the plumbers. Nixon congratulated Dean on the fact that the indictments had gone no further. He added, "I want the most comprehensive notes on all of those that had tried to do us in. . . . They are asking for it and they are going to get it. . . . We have not used the power in this first four years, as you know. We have never used it. We haven't used the Bureau and we haven't used the Justice Department, but things are going to change now."

Things indeed were going to change. In January 1973 the Watergate trial began before Judge John J. Sirica. On February 2 Sirica said he was "not satisfied"

Decline and fall

that the full story had been disclosed and called for further investigation. On February 7 the Senate voted to establish a select committee to inquire into charges of corruption in the 1972 election. The chairman was Senator Sam Ervin of North Carolina. Woodward and Bernstein were meanwhile beginning to uncover sources in the executive branch—FBI agents who resented the limitations put by the White House on their inquiries and soon a mysterious and knowledgeable figure who was identified only as Deep Throat.

Impeachment. "We have a cancer—within—close to the Presidency, that's growing," John Dean told Nixon on March 21. "It's growing daily. It's compounding." Two days later James McCord broke the ranks of the Watergate group, saying there had been perjury in the trial and political pressure on the defendants to plead guilty and remain silent. The conspiracy was unraveling. The problem now, as Nixon, Haldeman, and Ehrlichman saw it, was whom to throw to the wolves. One candidate was Jeb Stuart Magruder. Another was the acting director of the FBI; "let him twist slowly, slowly in the wind," said Ehrlichman. Another, so Dean came to believe, was Dean himself. Another was John Mitchell; "he's the big enchilada," said Ehrlichman. In April Dean and Magruder, fearing that they were being set up as fall guys, followed McCord's example and turned state's

evidence. On April 30 Haldeman and Ehrlichman were thrown to the wolves. As for Nixon, his resolve was still, in the language of the tapes, to "tough it out."

On May 17 the Ervin Committee began public hearings, carried by television to an enraptured nation. At the same time, Elliot Richardson, up for confirmation as Attorney General, agreed under senatorial pressure to appoint an independent special prosecutor. He named Professor Archibald Cox of the Harvard Law School, Kennedy's solicitor general. Both Ervin and Cox now pressed their somewhat competitive inquiries. Dean's testimony before the Ervin Committee in June was especially precise and effective. Then in July the committee learned for the first time of the existence of the tapes. There began a struggle—Nixon, on the one hand; Ervin and Cox, on the other—for access to the tapes. Nixon, in his own words, stonewalled, claiming executive privilege first for his staff, later for the tapes and himself. Privately he denied, as to Elliot Richardson and other Republican leaders, knowledge or complicity, while publicly he put out a succession of statements, each admitting a little more than the one before. The investigations pressed on.

In the meantime, another issue arose to assail the beleaguered Administration. Investigations by the federal attorney in Maryland concluded that Vice

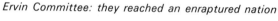
Ervin Committee: they reached an enraptured nation

President Agnew had received bribes as governor of Maryland and subsequently as Vice President. Though Nixon said in August, "My confidence in his integrity has not been shaken," the evidence was persuasive. In October, Attorney General Richardson negotiated a deal by which Agnew resigned his position and confessed to falsifying his income tax returns. He was fined $10,000 and put on probation for three years. In exchange, the other charges were dropped. Acting under the Twenty-fifth Amendment, which had been ratified in 1967, Nixon appointed a new Vice President, Gerald Ford, the minority leader of the House. After Agnew resigned, Nixon said to Richardson, "Now that that's over, we can get rid of Cox."

Cox, in his pursuit of the tapes, was pressing too close. When the Court of Appeals required that Nixon turn over nine tapes to Judge Sirica, Nixon refused to comply, offering a summary of the particular tapes and ordering Cox to seek no more. Cox rejected Nixon's proposal. Nixon then ordered Richardson to fire Cox. Richardson declined to do so and resigned, as did his Deputy Attorney General. The ranking official left in the Justice Department carried out Nixon's order. The "Saturday night massacre" produced a "firestorm" of national protest, with nearly half a million telegrams inundating the White House in the next week. Newspapers and magazines called for Nixon's resignation. Impeachment resolutions were introduced in the House of Representatives. Under the explosion of public indignation, Nixon yielded the nine tapes. Leon Jaworski of Texas was named to succeed Cox.

It was the beginning of the end. More and more of the lesser Watergate actors were indicted. New issues emerged. Nixon, it developed, had paid only $792 in federal income tax in 1970, $878 in 1971; his claim for tax deductions on his vice-presidential papers had been illegally backdated to escape the provisions of a new tax law, and he owed the government nearly half a million dollars. Millions of federal dollars had been dubiously spent on the improvement of his houses in San Clemente, California, and Key Biscayne, Florida. No previous chief executive, it seemed, had ever tried to make himself rich out of the Presidency.

In December the House Judiciary Committee, with Congressman Peter Rodino of New Jersey as chairman and John Doar as chief counsel, began an inquiry to determine whether there were grounds for impeachment. The committee immediately confronted a constitutional question. The Founding Fathers had regarded impeachment, in Madison's words, as a means of defending the community against "the incapacity, negligence or perfidy of the chief Magistrate." Impeachment in this view did not require the breaking of any particular law. Hamilton had written in *The Federalist* No. 65 that it applied to "those offences which proceed from the misconduct of public men, or, in other words, from the abuse or violation of some public trust. They are of a nature which may with peculiar propriety be denominated POLITICAL." However, officials confronted by the threat of impeachment had always argued for a much more restricted view, claiming that impeachment applied only to violations of specific criminal statutes.

Impeachment

Article I

In his conduct of the office of President of the United States, Richard M. Nixon, in violation of his constitutional oath faithfully to execute the office of President of the United States ... and in violation of his constitutional duty to take care that the laws be faithfully executed, has prevented, obstructed, and impeded the administration of justice.... Richard M. Nixon, using the powers of his high office, engaged personally and through his subordinates and agents in a course of conduct or plan designed to delay, impede, and obstruct the investigation of such unlawful entry; to cover up, conceal and protect those responsible; and to conceal the existence and scope of other unlawful covert activities.... In all of this, Richard M. Nixon has acted in a manner contrary to his trust as President and subversive of constitutional government, to the great prejudice of the cause of law and justice and to the manifest injury of the people of the United States.

Wherefore Richard M. Nixon, by such conduct, warrants impeachment and trial, and removal from office.

Article II

Using the powers of the office of President of the United States, Richard M. Nixon ... has repeatedly engaged in conduct violating the constitutional rights of citizens, impairing the due and proper administration of justice in the conduct of lawful inquiries, or contravening the laws governing agencies of the executive branch....

Wherefore, Richard M. Nixon, by such conduct, warrants impeachment and trial, and removal from office.

Article III

In his conduct of the office of President of the United States, Richard M. Nixon ... has failed without lawful cause or excuse to produce papers and things, as directed by duly authorized subpoenas ... and willfully disobeyed such subpoenas ... thereby assuming for himself functions and judgments necessary to the exercise of the sole power of impeachment vested by the Constitution in the House of Representatives....

Wherefore, Richard M. Nixon, by such conduct, warrants impeachment and trial, and removal from office.

From the House of Representatives Committee on the Judiciary, August 4, 1974.

Nixon, confident that no statutory crime could be proved against him, continued to stonewall. "I'm not a crook," he cried in November. There was more talk of executive privilege and of defending the institution of the Presidency. In March 1974 a federal grand jury indicted Mitchell, Haldeman, Ehrlichman, Colson, and three others. Nixon was named as a "co-conspirator," unindicted because of prosecutorial doubts whether a President could be brought to trial. As Jaworski subpoenaed more tapes, Nixon decided to anticipate the inevitable and release the tapes himself. It was a fatal miscalculation. The reaction was worse than to the Saturday night massacre. The tapes displayed Nixon as mean-spirited, indecisive, bigoted, amoral, and foul-mouthed. The demand for resignation, even among Republicans, rose to a new crescendo.

Nixon, playing upon his reputation in foreign policy, now visited the Middle East, then the Soviet Union. Ironically the old Red-hunter found his strongest support in Moscow and Peking. In Washington concern deepened about Nixon's psychological condition. He alarmed a group of congressmen by telling them, "I can pick up my phone and 70 million Russians can be killed in twenty minutes." Alexander Haig, a four-star general who succeeded Haldeman as Nixon's chief White House aide, asked the Pentagon to disregard any orders from the commander in chief. The Secretary of Defense instructed military commands to accept no orders from the White House without his own countersignature. Such precautions turned out to be unnecessary. But they registered the degree of official apprehension.

On Capitol Hill, the mills ground remorselessly on. In mid-July, after weeks of hearings, the House Judiciary Committee heard John Doar's analysis of the evidence against the President. Once again the nation turned on its television sets. In somber headcounts, the committee voted three articles of impeachment, charging Nixon with obstruction of justice in the Watergate case, with abuse of presidential power in a number of specified respects, and with unconstitutionally defying its subpoenas. Six Republicans joined with the Democratic majority in passing the first articles, seven on the second.

In the meantime, the Supreme Court had ruled that Nixon must turn over tapes that might contain evidence of crime. After a delay Nixon complied. Transcripts of his meetings with Haldeman six days after the break-in left no doubt that he had planned the cover-up. This was at last the "smoking pistol" required to still all doubts. Four Republicans on the Judiciary Committee who had voted against impeachment reversed their positions. Senator Goldwater said that Nixon could count on no more than fifteen votes

Resignation of an imperial President

in the Senate. Four days later, on August 9, Nixon resigned the Presidency.

The Imperial Presidency. Resignation left the exact degree of Nixon's guilt undetermined. It also failed to settle definitively the constitutional dispute about impeachment; for certain of the charges voted by the House Judiciary Committee were criminal in nature, and it was Nixon's persistent obstruction of justice, a criminal offense, that turned his own party against him. But the Watergate inquiries did prove that Nixon's Administration, for all its talk about law and order, was indeed the most corrupt in American history.

More than forty members of the Administration underwent criminal prosecution, led by those particular champions of law and order, Agnew and Mitchell. A Vice President, two Cabinet members, a dozen members of the White House staff, and nearly fifteen others scattered through the executive branch pleaded guilty or were convicted after trial. Officers of twenty large corporations were found guilty of making illegal contributions to Nixon's reelection campaign. Watergate seemed to have vindicated the processes of American democracy. Most Americans welcomed Nixon's resignation not alone with relief but with a measure of self-congratulation. In the end, it was said, the system had worked.

Others took less satisfaction in the outcome. If Nixon had kept no tapes, or if he had burned them, or if there had not been in the right place at the right time a senator like Ervin, a judge like Sirica, a newspaper like the *Washington Post*, Nixon and his associates might well have survived. It seemed a very near thing. A major consequence of Watergate was to increase popular cynicism about government, politics, and parties, strengthening well-established tendencies toward independent voting and intensifying the defection from the party system.

Yet, as Ervin subsequently reflected, "One of the great advantages of the three separate branches of government is that it's difficult to corrupt all three at the same time." A new interest developed in the problem of presidential power and accountability. The separation of powers had worked well enough through American history to restrain presidential aggrandizement in domestic affairs. But foreign affairs, as Vietnam had already demonstrated, constituted the grave weakness in the original system of accountability. Confronted by presidential initiatives abroad, Congress—along with the courts and the citizenry—had come to lack confidence in its information and judgment and was happy to abdicate responsibility to the executive. This was especially the case after the Second World War because the last period of sustained congressional intervention in foreign policy, from the rejection of the Treaty of Versailles to the rigid neutrality legislation of the 1930s, had given Congress itself a severe institutional inferiority complex. International crisis had thus opened the great breach in the system of accountability. Nixon's particular innovation was to take the powers that had flowed to the Presidency to meet foreign threats, real or imagined, and try to project them for his own purposes at home. The Imperial Presidency, as it came to be known, was in part an aberration but in part too a culmination.

Since the growth of presidential power had been in the longer run as much a consequence of congressional abdication as of presidential usurpation, Congress had a major role to play in containing the runaway Presidency and restoring the balance of the Constitution. The Vietnam experience had drawn attention to the virtual appropriation by the Presidency of the war-making power confided by the Constitution to Congress. In 1973 Congress passed a War Powers Act that, on the one hand, gave the President for the first time explicit authority to go to war in certain specified circumstances but on the other required the termination of hostilities within ninety days unless Congress explicitly authorized their continuation. The ambiguity of the statute left unresolved the question whether the act enlarged or restricted a President's power to go to war on his own.

In domestic affairs, Congress passed in 1974 the Congressional Budget and Impoundment Control Act.

This law instituted procedures to prevent the unlimited impoundment policies of the Nixon era. It also established a legislative budget process comparable to the one Congress had given the President in the Budget and Accounting Act of 1921 (see p. 584). In the same year Congress passed the Federal Election Campaign Act providing for partial federal financing of presidential campaigns and seeking to limit the role of private money in elections. A Supreme Court decision in 1976 sustained the public financing provisions but, by equating money with speech under the First Amendment, removed some of the restraints on personal contributions.

Watergate further stimulated a new determination to open up the workings of government. States passed "sunshine laws" designed to increase citizen access to governmental decisions. Political candidates were called on to disclose the sources of their income. A national Freedom of Information Act, passed by Congress in 1966, acquired new vitality. The spotlight even penetrated into what had been the most secretive and sacrosanct agencies of government—the CIA and the FBI. Congressional investigations in 1975–76 revealed extraordinary abuses of power by both agencies—not only the CIA assassination and covert action projects but the FBI's use of *agents provocateurs*, burglaries, wiretapping, mail intercepts, and even J. Edgar Hoover's incredible effort to drive Martin Luther King, Jr., to suicide. The public reaction to these revelations dethroned Hoover posthumously from his long reign as a national icon and produced strong demands for congressional oversight over the policies and actions of the intelligence community.

Dilemmas of the economic order

A Ford, not a Lincoln. Gerald R. Ford, the new President, was sixty-one years old. A Republican wheelhorse, he had served a quarter-century in the House without ever achieving consideration in any Republican convention as a candidate for President or even for Vice President. But he was liked on all sides in Washington as an honest, open, self-possessed politician of accommodating temperament and conservative inclination. The one defect in a general record of political decency was his misbegotten effort to impeach Justice William O. Douglas of the Supreme Court in 1970.

"I am a Ford, not a Lincoln," he had said disarmingly after being sworn in as Vice President; and, after being sworn in as President, "I am acutely aware that you have not elected me as your President by your ballots." Complying with the Twenty-fifth Amendment, he named Governor Nelson Rockefeller of New York as his Vice President. This meant that for the first time in American history both the President and the Vice President had come to office and power not, like all their predecessors, through election but through appointment—a result unintended by the drafters of the Twenty-fifth Amendment seven years before and disconcerting to those who favored the provision in the Constitution (Article II, Section 1) stipulating that the President and Vice President were to "be elected."

A people whose nerves had been worn ragged by Nixon's deceit and mystification found the new President's candor and accessibility initially reassuring. Then, thirty days after he took office, Ford stunned the nation by granting Nixon a "full, free and absolute pardon" for all crimes he committed against the United States during his Presidency. Ford's concern was that a public trial of the disgraced former President would have a divisive effect. His purpose, he explained, was "to heal the wounds throughout the United States."

The effect was the opposite. Most Americans were outraged by the double standard of justice that punished those who had executed Nixon's wishes but spared Nixon himself. Ford seemed to have espoused the principle, dubious in a democracy, that the greater the power the less the accountability. Some critics wondered, though Ford emphatically denied it,

Gerald R. Ford and Nelson Rockefeller, February 1974

whether the pardon had been agreed on in advance as the price of resignation. Even many who did not want to see a former President behind bars felt that pardon would have been more appropriate further down the road, after the evidence of Nixon's misdeeds had been clearly set forth in court and recorded for history. In one stroke Ford dissipated the confidence that had flowed to him on his accession and inflicted a wound on his Administration from which it never quite recovered.

Nevertheless the Presidency itself survived. During the Watergate crisis some had feared that the pursuit and exposure of Nixon would damage the Presidency as an institution. The fear was clearly unfounded. The aftermath showed the Presidency to be relatively indestructible. Ford was an old Capitol Hill man without particular appetite for power and adulation. Yet despite this, despite his stigma of illegitimacy as an unelected President, despite his shaky position in his own party and in the country, his Presidency drew strength from the continuing authority of the office and also from the continuing deference, in many areas, of Congress. When the Democrats greatly increased their congressional majorities in 1974, Ford responded by using the veto power with almost unprecedented freedom. In his first months he vetoed more bills than Nixon had vetoed in five and a half years; more public bills indeed than any President had vetoed in so short a period. Only a fraction of his vetoes were overridden.

Congressional deference was, as usual, especially marked in international affairs. While Ford, following the example of Truman (with whom he liked to compare himself) rather than that of Lyndon Johnson, reconstructed his Cabinet with some promptitude, he retained Kissinger as Secretary of State, thereby ensuring continuity in foreign policy. When Cambodian communists seized an unarmed American ship, the *Mayagüez*, in May 1975, Ford swiftly retaliated by ordering air strikes and sending in the marines. Congress joined in the general applause, though Ford had merely informed legislators of his action, rather than consulting them in the spirit of the War Powers Act. Skeptics regarded this show of American force against an inexperienced government in a weak country as unseemly and unnecessary. But the return of the ship and crew produced a temporary spurt in Ford's popularity. He also provided secret assistance to one side in the Angolan civil war, though, when this became public, the Senate denied him further funds to pursue an interventionist policy. His Pacific Doctrine of December 1975 asserted an American interest in a stable balance of power in the Pacific, to be attained in partnership with Japan and through a normalization of relations with China.

Dilemmas of the economic order

The 1976 election. Maintaining a precarious hold on his party, Ford beat back a strong challenge from Ronald Reagan of California, the favorite of the Republican right, to win nomination. His vice presidential candidate, selected to appease the Reaganites, was Senator Robert Dole of Kansas. For the Democrats, Jimmy Carter, a former governor of Georgia almost unknown to the nation, emerged as candidate from a series of arduous primaries. Carter, an indefatigable man of sharp intelligence but of enigmatic views, rested his case more on moralistic reassurance—"I'll never lie to you," he told his audiences—than on clarity in policy. He chose the liberal Senator Walter Mondale of Minnesota as his running mate.

The campaign was desultory and unenlightening. Neither Ford nor Carter distinguished himself in a series of three debates; nor did their speeches effectively define the issues between them. Carter took the electoral college by a vote of 297–241 and the popular vote by 40.3 million to 38.5 million. Voter turnout continued to decline—from 55.4 percent in 1972 to 53.3 percent in 1976.

The election revealed problems in the new campaign-finance law. Each major party candidate, in accepting $22 million of federal money for the fall campaign, renounced private fund-raising. But the removal by the Supreme Court of limits on personal spending opened the way to huge expenditures by rich candidates for other offices. The law, too, had the effect of "institutionalizing out" third parties, which historically had provided so valuable a means of getting new ideas on the national agenda. Two minor candidates—Eugene McCarthy and Lester Maddox, another former Georgia governor—received no federal funds and were denied participation in the debates.

The victor, a graduate of the Naval Academy and a southern Baptist of ostentatious piety, was fifty-two years old. He was the first President elected from the deep South since Zachary Taylor, the first fundamentalist to run for the Presidency since William Jennings Bryan, the first ex-governor since Franklin Roosevelt, and the first successful businessman (unless Herbert Hoover be so regarded) to occupy the White House in American history. His convincing record as governor on racial justice—he owed his election to black votes—portended progress on this most grievous of national issues; and his training as a nuclear engineer promised expert attention to the most overwhelming world problem—the control of nuclear weapons. His election appeared to mark the liquidation as a political issue not only of the Civil War but of the Indochina War, in view of his campaign pledge to pardon draft resisters, and of Watergate. His rise from outside the national political establishment created the expectation of fresh initiatives in public policy.

The energy crisis. One international development—the Arab oil embargo of October 1973—had extensive domestic repercussions. American economic growth had been based in large part on cheap energy. But significant changes had taken place in the pattern of energy production. In the 1870s 90 percent of American energy came from sustainable sources, like water power. A century later more than 90 percent came from nonrenewable mineral sources—44 percent from petroleum, 32 percent from natural gas, 18 percent from coal. Moreover, domestic coal production had begun to decline after 1947, domestic oil extraction after 1970, domestic natural gas production after 1974. Estimates of untapped domestic reserves of mineral fuels began to decline too.

In the meantime, demand continued to grow. By the 1970s the United States, with 6 percent of the world's population, was consuming one-third of the world's energy. The increased reliance on oil was accompanied by an increased reliance on imports. Though the United States remained the world's top oil producer, oil imports rose from 8 percent of demand in 1950 to 40 percent by 1974, nor did the proportion decline in the next two years. A steadily increasing proportion of imported oil came from the Middle East—about 30 percent by the early 1970s. Here seven great oil companies—"the Seven Sisters"—had long dominated the field. As OPEC became more aggressive on behalf of the producing countries, the major oil companies, which, despite the nationalization of their local interests, were still involved in the oil fields through long-term management contracts and guaranteed access to the oil, became the machinery for maintaining the OPEC cartel—once masters, now servants.

As early as 1952, the Materials Policy Commission, headed by William S. Paley, had warned the Truman Administration of the "extraordinarily rapid rate at which we are utilizing our materials and energy resources." Such warnings, repeated from time to time over a generation, had been ignored in the enthusiasm for economic growth. The oil embargo at last dramatized the resources issue. For a few months, pumps went empty at filling stations, cars queued up for gasoline, speed limits were reduced, conservation measures were encouraged. In retrospect the gasoline shortage of 1973–74 remains mysterious. No one knows how much oil leaked through the embargo or whether the oil companies exploited the crisis to make inordinate profits. The London *Economist* observed skeptically that every predicted materials shortage since the war had ended in a glut within five to ten years.

Nevertheless the energy issue was squarely on the national agenda—the more so when, after the embargo was lifted, the oil-exporting nations raised the

The Presidency in crisis

world price from \$3 to \$11 a barrel. In his last months Nixon had called for what he termed Operation Independence, designed to produce self-sufficiency in energy by 1980. Under his successor a vigorous debate erupted about the road to self-sufficiency. The Ford Administration favored "deregulation" on the theory that higher prices would reduce consumption and that higher profits would encourage the oil and natural gas corporations to develop new sources of energy. Many Democrats felt that government had to play the key role to prevent the corporations from ripping off the consumer. Some argued that the best way to loosen the grip of OPEC would be to break up the Seven Sisters, thereby denying the Arab states their means of controlling the world market and restoring competition to the production and distribution of oil.

Everyone agreed, however, on the need to lower domestic demand through measures of energy conservation. Everyone agreed too on the importance of developing alternative sources of energy. The Energy Policy and Conservation Act of 1975 affirmed these objectives but left other questions, including the extent of future dependence on imported oil, unresolved. And the whole effort to achieve energy independence encountered the competing claims of the environmental movement.

The growth debate. The accelerating rate of technological change, combined with population growth and the expanding demands of an affluent society,

During the oil embargo

had produced by the late sixties what many perceived as an incipient ecological crisis. The increasingly visible results of unbridled economic expansion were pollution of water and air, erosion of the soil, disturbance of the balance of nature, and disruption of the self-replenishing cycle that for eons had sustained life on earth. America the Beautiful was increasingly marked, not by alabaster cities and fruited plains, but by black oil slicks smearing the beaches; by rivers and lakes filled with sewage, industrial wastes, phosphates, and detergents; by towns enveloped in smog spewed forth by automobile exhausts, factory chimneys, and burning dumps; by the destruction through the use of pesticides of the relationship among plants, animals, and the natural environment. Most ludicrous of all was the possibility that fluorocarbon gases discharged from aerosol spray cans would breach the shield of ozone that protected the earth from ultraviolet radiation. If this prediction came true—much scientific evidence supported it—and if nothing were done about aerosol cans, then, someone observed, the world would perish neither with a bang nor a whimper but with a psssst.

In response there arose a popular movement determined to save the natural environment. This movement brought about the passage of a number of national clean air and water laws and the establishment in 1970 of the Environmental Protection Agency as well as environmental statutes in nearly half the states. As a result, fuming factory smokestacks disappeared from most American cities, and automobile exhausts were pouring 85 percent less carbon monoxide and hydrocarbons into the air than a decade earlier. The level of soot and dust dropped by 14 percent. Municipalities sought new methods of disposing of sewage, manufacturing wastes, and refuse. The recycling of used products came into vogue.

Those concerned with finding alternative sources of energy to supplement oil and natural gas began to charge, however, that the environmental movement was immobilizing energy production. Of the alternative sources, only solar energy raised no environmental problems; but massive research and investment were required before energy captured from the rays of the sun could become economic. Coal, still the largest energy resource in the United States, raised acute environmental problems. High-sulphur coal was a particularly noxious cause of air pollution. Moreover, the shift from the deep mining of coal to strip mining (44 percent of coal production in 1970) aggravated the ecological crisis. Ripping the surface off the soil produced landslides in the hills, sulphuric acid and sedimentation in the streams, and permanent damage to soil, foliage, and wildlife.

For a time it had been supposed that nuclear power could take care of future energy needs. Here

Dilemmas of the economic order

again environmental difficulties, of an even more dangerous sort, began to emerge. Nuclear reactors were costly to build, hazardous because of radiation, and mighty contributors to thermal pollution. By the mid-1970s neither the problem of the disposal of radioactive nuclear wastes nor that of the reactor cooling system had been satisfactorily met. Some engineers emphasized the catastrophic consequences of a nuclear accident and argued that existing safety precautions were inadequate. By 1976 there were fifty-eight licensed nuclear plants, supplying about 2 percent of total energy demand. Public resistance to the building of more plants was on the increase.

Looking to the farther future, some observers began to question the very gospel of growth without end. They spoke of the limits of growth, the finiteness of raw materials, the inevitability of a global age of scarcity. Reviving the pessimism of Malthus, they contended that world population—4 billion souls in the mid-seventies, perhaps six to 6 to 7 billion by 2000—was pressing inexorably on the planet's diminishing stock of resources. The more optimistic replied, in the words of the bacteriologist René Dubos, "Trend is not destiny." The very recognition of the problem, they contended, stimulated the search for remedy, and humankind's capacity for innovation was far from exhausted. Moreover, the cessation of growth, while relieving some social problems, would intensify others. Growth provided a means of enlarging the slices of the economic pie without altering the relationship among them and thereby of buying social peace. A no-growth society would force hard and politically explosive decisions on the distribution of income. The competition for limited resources, between classes and between nations, would become a "zero-sum game," in which what one won, another lost. The result would be either authoritarianism—the imposition of controls over technology, population, labor, wealth—or anarchy.

The challenge to the idea of growth was fundamental. It went to the heart of the western ethos, which had so long regarded expansion as the law of life; it particularly ran counter to the creed of the American people, for whom the maximization of growth had been a sacred ideal. Yet persistence in uncontrolled growth might mean the eventual extinction of life on the planet. If the no-growth argument was perhaps unduly drastic, even the pro-growth argument acknowledged the need for social controls over technology. Whatever the outcome, the debate was on.

Employment and inflation. The energy-versus-the-environment dilemma was matched by a comparable dilemma in economic policy: inflation versus unemployment. Two months after the 1972 election, Nixon had abandoned the Phase 2 program of wage and price control. During its fourteen months of existence the program had been loosely administered by people who did not believe in controls. Still, inflation slowed down. Once controls were removed in January 1973, prices shot up.

By 1974, the United States was experiencing its worst inflation since 1947. Using 1967 as 100, the consumer price index rose from 110 in Nixon's first year to 148 in 1974 and more than 161 in 1975. The rate of inflation in 1973 was nearly 9 percent; in 1974, over 12 percent (over 20 percent in the wholesale price index). All this was the culmination in the steady decline in the value of the dollar from $1 in 1940 to 50 cents by 1957 to 40 cents when Nixon came to office to about 25 cents in 1976. In other words, it took roughly four dollars in the bicentennial year to buy what one dollar had bought in 1940.

Confronted by soaring prices, the Ford Administration, ideologically opposed to controls, resorted to the orthodox panacea and slowed down the economy. The result in 1974–75 was the worst economic recession in nearly forty years. National output had its sharpest decline since the end of the war production in 1945–46. Unemployment rose from 3.5 percent of the labor force in 1969 to nearly 9 percent—8.25 million people—by mid-1975. Joblessness was cushioned, however, by unemployment compensation, by a

PURCHASING POWER OF THE CONSUMER DOLLAR: UNITED STATES CITY AVERAGE			
1967 = $1.00			
1913	$3.37	1948	$1.39
1918	$2.21	1953	$1.24
1923	$1.96	1958	$1.15
1928	$1.95	1963	$1.09
1933	$2.58	1968	$ .96
1938	$2.37	1973	$ .72
1943	$1.93	1975	$ .62

From Bureau of Labor Statistics, 1976.

food-stamp program that, after modest beginnings in 1962, grew to nearly $6 billion a year, by medicaid and other forms of federal cash payment. One unexpected result was to diminish agitation for welfare reform. Though state governors continued to call for the replacement of state and local welfare programs by a single, federally financed cash system of income maintenance, others felt that incremental changes—above all, the food-stamp program—along with an increase in public-service employment, foreshadowed

Lining up for unemployment compensation, 1975: still a painful therapy

by the passage in 1973 of a minimal Comprehensive Employment and Training Act based on the WPA experience of the thirties, reduced the urgency of comprehensive welfare reform.

None the less, though the human cost of depression was less than in the 1930s, unemployment was still painful therapy for millions of families. Moreover, it produced only a slight abatement of inflation. The 1975 figure of 7 percent would have been regarded as intolerable during the years between the Korean and Vietnam wars when the annual rate of inflation averaged 1.3 percent. In addition, the enormous federal deficits incurred in 1975–76 in order to counter recession threatened to rekindle inflation.

There was considerable controversy about the causes of the inflation of the 1970s. Some saw it as a temporary problem arising from fortuitous and transient circumstances—the Arab oil embargo, the world food shortage, the devaluations of the dollar. Others wondered whether the problem was not deeper, whether the postwar economy did not itself contain an inherent propensity toward inflation. That propensity, it was suggested, derived in part from the post-New Deal commitment to high employment, in part from the power of concentrated industries to put up prices and wages by administrative decision. Whatever form inflation took, it was pointed out, whether it was commodity-based or price-based or wage-based or Arab-based, it appeared beyond all question the malady to which the postwar economic organism most readily and habitually succumbed.

By this view, just as depression expressed a structural crisis in the economic order in the 1930s, so inflation expressed a structural crisis in the economic order in the 1970s. To continue the stop-and-go cycle of combating inflation by unemployment and then combating unemployment by inflation seemed intolerable. Those who did not think that inflation would fade away therefore called for the stabilization of prices through some form of "incomes policy"—more particularly by establishing a public interest in price and wage decisions in areas of economic concentration where prices and wages did not respond to the play of market forces.

The corporate economy. The central unit of the American economy was more than ever the corporation. During the sixties the great corporations tightened their control over American industry; the top eighty-seven corporations, with assets of more than $1 billion, increased their share of the total assets of industrial corporations from 26 to 46 percent. By 1972 corporations with more than $100 million in assets constituted 3.3 percent of the total but controlled 70 percent of corporate assets and made 75 percent of corporate profits.

Oligopoly or shared monopoly—control of a market by a small number of firms—characterized widening areas of the economy. The rise of the conglomerate—a single corporation extending its operations into many varied markets—enlarged the zones of concentration and domination. By 1970 the two hundred largest industrial corporations were active in more than ten times that number of product markets. The largest merger wave in American history took place in the late sixties, and four-fifths of all mergers resulted in conglomeration.

As part of this process, corporations took advantage of the technological revolution in agriculture to establish bridgeheads in the countryside. Mechanization, increasing man-hour productivity twice as fast on the farm as in industry, reduced the number of farm workers from 7.4 million in 1950 to 3.2 million in 1975 and the number of farms from 5.6 million to 2.8 million while total output steadily increased. A single farm worker produced food for sixteen people in 1951 and for fifty-one two decades later. The American farmer not only heaped food on his own country's tables but produced a surplus that constituted about a fifth of all exports during the sixties.

At the same time the average size of farms increased from 167 to 384 acres; and the largest forty thousand farms—less than 2 percent of the total—accounted for one-third of all farm sales. Government subsidies went primarily to large- and medium-size agricultural enterprises. The corporate invasion of farming began as a result of investment in land for speculation and for tax shelters, but increasingly it aimed to control every stage of food production and distribution. The goal, as Tenneco (formerly Tennessee Gas and Transmission) put it, was "integration from the seedling to the supermarket." Corporate farming—"agribusiness"—made its first strides in the South and West; cattle, poultry, fruits, cotton, and lettuce were early conquests. By 1970 nearly half the agricultural land in California was owned by forty-five corporate farms. Enjoying the competitive advantages of vertical integration as well as superior access to capital, credit, and government subsidies, corporate farming intensified the pressure on small farmers. The family farm held its own mainly in the corn and wheat regions of the Middle West. Observers doubted the economic advantages to the consumer of agribusiness—certainly the insistence on machine harvesting in corporate farms lowered the quality of food—and questioned the social costs as more than 20 million Americans, 4 million of them black, were forced off the land and into the cities in the years after 1940.

Corporate expansion overseas entered into a dramatic new phase. The American-based multinational corporation carried increasing quantities of American capital, technology, plants, and jobs to foreign coun-

The Presidency in crisis

tries. In the decade after 1958 domestic manufacturing capacity increased 72 percent while the foreign capacity of American firms increased 471 percent. The multinationals went predominantly into the industrialized world; and the French editor Jean-Jacques Servan-Schreiber wrote persuasively in 1968 of "the American challenge," forecasting the American economic takeover of western Europe. In 1970 the American firm of General Motors had gross annual sales larger than the gross national product of all but twenty-two of the world's states. In 1975 the fifteen largest privately owned industrial corporations on the planet were multinationals, all but four owned and managed in the United States.

American corporations had been doing business abroad for a long time. But never before had corporate managers striven so purposefully to integrate production and distribution on an international scale. Admirers saw the multinational corporation as a farsighted recognition of planetary realities, moving beyond the increasingly irrelevant and obsolescent world of nation states. Critics denounced the multi-

American corporation overseas

821

The great corporation: roll it back

The authors pile up the evidence toward one searing conclusion—that corporate economic, product and environmental crimes ... are part of a raging corporate radicalism which generates technological violence, undermines the integrity of government, breaks laws, blocks needed reforms, and repudiates a quality-competitive system with substantial consumer sovereignty....

The central question, then, is what changes are necessary to direct corporate resources toward respecting the values and pleas that are beyond the balance sheet's morality? And what are the instruments to achieve these changes?... A deconcentration of corporate power in two principal ways—through antitrust action and the federal chartering of corporations to rewrite the contract between the corporation and its creator—the state.... The charter can make the grant of corporate status conditional on a responsiveness to well-defined public interests and a social accounting of corporate performance. The charter can establish structural receptiveness to official accountability, detailed disclosure, and rights of access by the various constituencies including victims.... But even solid structural changes have a way of concentrating old powers in new forms sooner or later unless there is a continual assertion and defense of individual rights and responsibilities within the corporate institution itself.... The entire range of legal sanctions against both the corporate structure and its officials has to be reconsidered ... beyond just simple civil-criminal fines toward a more flexible array of civil-criminal sanctions tailored to maximum deterrence.... Together with such internal changes, the emergence of full-time, independent corporate monitors, staffed by lawyers and other skilled professionals in Washington and state capitals, would have lasting effect.... The modern corporation is the engine of the world's largest production machine. If it is to be more than a mindless, parochial juggernaut, the hands of diverse human values and trusteeships for future generations must be exerted on the steering wheel.

From Ralph Nader, Introduction to *America, Inc.: Who Owns and Operates the United States?*, by Morton Mintz and Jerry S. Cohen, 1971.

national corporation as the ultimate instrument of world capitalist hegemony.

By the mid-1970s, however, American multinationals were beginning to encounter problems. The international recession of 1973–74 had dispelled the illusion of endless foreign profits. Governments around the world were whittling away the advantages of transnational operation by taxation. Within the United Nations there was increasing interest in matching international operation by international regulation. Within the United States the disclosure of the role of International Telephone and Telegraph in prodding Washington to overthrow the Allende regime in Chile was followed by revelations in 1975–76 of an international system of bribery operated by American oil and aircraft firms and extending to Japan, the Netherlands, and Italy as well as to the Third World. Though this system reflected on the bribed as well as on the bribers, the result was to strengthen suspicion of the multinationals and to reinforce the movement to bring them under control.

Plan or no plan. The phenomenon of the great corporation continued to baffle its critics. Nationalization, the traditional solution of the Old Left, was not politically feasible; in any case, the example of the Soviet Union gave little hope that a change in the system of ownership would significantly alter the social impact of large-scale organizations. The New Left, contending that "small is beautiful," tended to favor the dismantlement of the corporate system, even at the cost of a reduction in living standards. Liberals continued to debate the old question of the inevitability of economic concentration—the argument that had divided the New Nationalism of Theodore Roosevelt and the New Freedom of Woodrow Wilson.

Some analysts, like Adolf Berle, J. K. Galbraith, and David Lilienthal, contended that sophisticated technology created needs for capital, research, development, and long-range planning that could only be met by the great corporation. And the great corporation could be made safe for democracy, they believed,

The great corporation: here to stay

From J. K. Galbraith, *The New Industrial State*, 1967.

through a combination of external pressure—the countervailing powers of government, labor, consumers, and other firms—with a growing sense of inner responsibility, produced by what Berle saw as the emergence of a corporate conscience. This sense would be strengthened, in Galbraith's view, by the rising purpose and power of the "technostructure," those scientists, engineers, and economists without whom the great corporation could not survive, and of their colleagues in the "educational and scientific estate."

Others, including members of Congress most concerned with the questions, inclined toward the classical antitrust theories of the Sherman Act. They explained economic concentration not as a natural growth but as the artificial creation of greedy entrepreneurs in alliance with high finance and, more recently, with government. They denied that concentration promoted efficiency or innovation, claimed it as the leading cause of stagflation, pointed to the undemocratic pressures and powers exerted by large corporations, and called for policies of "deconcentration"—the breakup of great enterprises into small and competitive units.

An influential spokesman for this view was Ralph Nader, a practitioner in the new field of "public service law." Under Nader's leadership, teams of lawyers and economists, known popularly as "Nader's Raiders," documented cases of corporate inefficiency and graft and of corporate domination of government regulatory commissions. Nader's own book *Unsafe at Any Speed* (1965) started the movement for auto safety and led in the course of the decade to the recall by manufacturers of thousands of defective cars. Subsequent Nader investigations uncovered conditions ranging from filth in meatpacking plants to air and water pollution to industrial price-fixing. Nader's example inspired a revival of the consumers' movement, moribund since New Deal days, resulting in truth-in-packaging, truth-in-lending, and auto-safety legislation; labeling of drugs by generic names; health warnings on cigarette packages; restrictions on cigarette advertising; and the establishment of the National Commission on Product Safety. Nader accompanied his brilliant guerrilla warfare against corporate iniquity with proposals for the democratization, decentralization, and federal chartering of corporations as well as "creative regulation" by strengthening the capacity of the "public citizen" to act against the corporation. In his insistence on high ethical standards and citizen responsibility as well as in his muckraking methods, Nader represented in some respects a throwback to the progressive era at the start of the century; by embodying the notion of one man taking on the giant monopolies, he gave hope to many individuals in a new age dominated by the idea of powerlessness.

The corporation posed in acute form the larger problem of the control of economic society. In the mid-seventies the word "planning," hardly heard in respectable circles since the New Deal, began to be uttered once again in public discussion. As some analyzed the situation, Americans had three economic objectives—high employment, stable prices, and an unregulated economy. But experience appeared to have shown that only two of these could be achieved at the same time. With high employment and an unregulated economy, prices would be unstable. With stable prices and an unregulated economy, employment would be uncertain. And the goal of high employment and stable prices required a measure of national planning.

The proponents of planning did not advocate mandatory or comprehensive state planning. They sought flexible, "indicative" planning under which government would work with industry and labor in estimating resources and requirements, coordinating policies and formulating long-range goals. Support for this conception of national planning cut across party lines, enlisting progressive businessleaders as well as legislators in the New Deal tradition like Hubert Humphrey, liberal economists like J. K. Galbraith, and the labor movement.

Opposition to national planning also extended from left to right. Radicals denounced the idea as "corporate socialism" and called for policies of dispersion and decentralization. Some Democratic governors, like Edmund G. Brown, Jr., of California, believing that government had tried to do too much and must contract its aims and operations, preached retrenchment and austerity. Conservatives denounced the planning idea as leading to an "economic police state" and argued that ambitious government programs on the Great Society model inevitably produced excessive spending, bureaucracy, waste, and corruption. Gerald Ford, inveighing against "regulatory bondage," proposed "deregulation" as the primary goal of national policy. Advocates of planning rejoined that the unregulated market place had manifestly failed to solve the problems of unemployment, inflation, and urban decay and to meet the nation's needs for health care, education, welfare, and environmental protection. The "new minimalism," as one critic termed the recoil against affirmative government, would only institutionalize intolerable living conditions for the poor and the black. Here too a debate had begun that would extend far into the future.

Suggestions for reading

THE NIXON AND FORD ADMINISTRATIONS

For Nixon, see the campaign biography by Earl Mazo and Stephen Hess, *Nixon, A Political Portrait* (1968); the description of his political comeback by Jules Witcover, *The Resurrection of Richard Nixon* (1970); and the critical analysis by Garry Wills, *Nixon Agonistes** (1970). Rowland Evans, Jr., and R. D. Novak, *Nixon in the White House: A Critical Portrait** (1971), provide an excellent account of the Nixon Administration in midstream. D. P. Moynihan, *The Politics of a Guaranteed Income** (1973) and *Coping* (1973), R. P. Nathan, *The Plot That Failed** (1975), V. J. Burke, *Nixon's Good Deed: Welfare Reform* (1976), and R. P. Nathan, *et al., Monitoring Revenue Sharing** (1975), set forth the hopes and problems of the New Federalism. Former Nixon associates offer testimony in Walter Hickel, *Who Owns America?** (1971), R. J. Whalen, *Catch the Falling Flag* (1972), William Safire, *Before the Fall* (1975), and Clark Mollenhoff, *Game Plan for Disaster* (1976). Jules Witcover and R. M. Cohen describe Agnew's fall in *Heartbeat Away** (1974).

The domestic political situation is perceived as in a condition of crisis by Samuel Lubell, *The Hidden Crisis in American Politics** (1970), F. G. Dutton, *Changing Sources of Power** (1971), and David Broder, *The Party's Over** (1972). R. M. Scammon and B. J. Wattenberg take a more conventional view in *The Real Majority** (1970). Stephen Schlesinger, *The New Reformers* (1975), discusses forces for change in American politics. H. E. Alexander, *Money in Politics* (1972), is the standard work on this troubling and pervasive question. Walter De Vries and V. L. Tarrance portray the decline of party loyalties in *The Ticket-Splitters** (1972). W. D. Burnham, *Critical Elections and the Mainsprings of American Politics** (1970), is a searching study by a political scientist. R. S. Anson, *McGovern* (1972), is a superior campaign biography. T. H. White, *The Making of the President, 1972* (1973), covers the

*Available in a paperback edition.

campaign. J. F. ter Horst, *Gerald Ford and the Future of the Presidency* (1974), is enlightening; see also Clark Mollenhoff, *The Man Who Pardoned Nixon* (1976). For Jimmy Carter, see his memoir *Why Not the Best?* (1975).

FOREIGN AFFAIRS

Alastair Buchan, *The End of the Postwar Era* (1975), gives a trenchant English view of the new international situation. Bernard and Marvin Kalb, *Kissinger* (1974), is favorable; G. W. Ball, *Diplomacy for a Crowded World: An American Foreign Policy* (1976), critical. George Schwab and Henry Friedlander, eds., *Detente in Historical Perspective* (1975), present a diversity of viewpoints. R. W. Tucker, *A New Isolationism** (1972), argues the case for the recession of American power.

For Vietnam, Gareth Porter, *A Peace Denied* (1975), discusses the Paris armistice and ensuing developments. R. A. Falk, Gabriel Kolko, and R. J. Lifton, eds., *Crimes of War* (1971), review atrocities in Indochina; and Telford Taylor, *Nuremberg and Vietnam** (1970), is a trenchant analysis. For the influence of the military establishment, consult Adam Yarmolinsky, *The Military Establishment** (1971); J. A. Donovan, *Militarism, U.S.A.* (1970); and J. W. Fulbright, *The Pentagon Propaganda Machine* (1970). R. J. Barnet, *Roots of War** (1972), offers a radical view of American foreign policy; and in *The Age of Imperialism** (1969), Harry Magdoff gives a Marxist interpretation. R. W. Tucker, *The Radical Left and American Foreign Policy** (1971), is a thoughtful commentary.

CRISIS OF THE PRESIDENCY

A. M. Schlesinger, Jr., *The Imperial Presidency* (1973), portrays the growth of presidential power. T. E. Cronin, *The State of the Presidency** (1975), provides an excellent analysis of recent thought about the Presidency. T. H. White, *Breach of Faith* (1975), Anthony Lukas, *Nightmare* (1976), and Jonathan Schell, *The Time of Illusion* (1976), are vivid surveys of the Watergate affair and its aftermath. W. E. Porter discusses Nixon and the press in *Assault on the Media* (1975). Watergate confessionals have thus far come from Jeb Stuart Magruder, Charles Colson, E. H. Hunt, and James McCord. Carl Bernstein and Robert Woodward pursue the Watergate story in *All the President's Men** (1974) and Nixon's last days in the White House in *The Final Days* (1976). John Ehrlichman, *The Company* (1976), is an insider's novel about a Nixonesque White House. An authoritative account by the special prosecutor is Leon Jaworski, *The Right and the Power* (1976).

ECONOMIC PROBLEMS

Two useful introductions to the ecological crises are Garrett De Bell, ed., *The Environmental Handbook* (1970), and R. M. Linton, *Terracide* (1970). Barbara Ward and Rene Dubos place the problem in its world setting in *Only One Earth* (1972). Rachel Carson, *Silent Spring** (1962), helped awaken American concern over environmental problems. Barry Commoner, *The Closing Circle** (1971), lays particular stress on the destructive impact of technology, while Paul Ehrlich, *The Population Bomb** (1968), focuses on population growth.

The energy crisis is considered from various viewpoints in S. D. Freeman, *Energy: The New Era** (1974), R. B. Mancke, *The Failure of U.S. Energy Policy** (1974), and Michael Tanzer, *The Energy Crisis** (1975). Anthony Sampson, *The Seven Sisters* (1975), is a colorful account of the oil multinationals. The Club of Rome reports—D. H. Meadows, *et al.*, *The Limits to Growth** (1972), and Mihajlo Mesarovic and Eduard Pestel, *Mankind at the Turning Point* (1974)—draw apocalyptic conclusions. R. L. Heilbroner provides a measured and equally gloomy statement in *Inquiry into the Human Prospect* (1974). John Maddox replies to the Club of Rome in *The Doomsday Syndrome** (1972). Andrew Weinraub, *et al.*, *The Economic Growth Controversy** (1973), is a useful introduction. Peter Passell and Leonard Ross defend growth against all comers in *The Retreat from Riches** (1973). For the multinational corporation, see Raymond Vernon, *Sovereignty at Bay* (1971), and R. J. Barnet and R. E. Muller, *Global Reach* (1974). J. M. Blair, ed., *The Roots of Inflation* (1975), is an illuminating discussion.

*Available in a paperback edition.

EPILOGUE

Into the third century

In the bicentennial year the population of the United States passed 215 million. This would have disappointed Abraham Lincoln, who in 1862 had forecast 251 million by 1930. Still the total had nearly quintupled since the centennial year and more than doubled since 1920. The rate of increase had more recently slowed down. The postwar baby boom tapered off after 1957, ushering in a time of declining growth. By 1974 the fertility rate had fallen to 1.86 children per couple, the lowest in the history of the United States; it was still lower in 1975. If it thereafter returned to the replacement level of 2.1, the American population would increase a meager 30 percent in the next seventy years. If it remained below that level, the republic would enter a stage of zero population growth (ZPG), except for immigration.

The assertive society

Profile of a population. No one knows why Americans suddenly decided to bring fewer children into the world. Doubtless the economic discouragements created by inflation and recession were compounded by apprehensions about the future of children in an age of local and nuclear violence. Also women were marrying later: only 28 percent of females between twenty and twenty-four were unmarried in 1960 as against 40 percent in 1975. And more had jobs: by 1975, for the first time, more than half of school-age children had mothers who worked outside the home. The invention of birth control pills and the spread of vasectomies and other sterilization procedures gave couples new control over the size of their families. So too did the legalization of abortion; with the adoption of a liberal abortion law by New York in 1970 and a Supreme Court decision in 1973 curtailing the power of states to ban abortion, legal abortions rose from eighteen thousand in 1968 (though no one could say how many illegal abortions were taking place) to a million in 1975. In any case, the large family of the fifties fell out of fashion. The two-children family became the new ideal.

The new family was markedly less stable. Beginning with California in 1970, 45 states passed some form of "no-fault" divorce statute enabling either spouse to get a divorce without having to offer traditional grounds or win the other's consent. There were more than a million divorces in 1975—twice as many as a decade earlier. This meant that a third of American marriages now ended in divorce. A growing num-

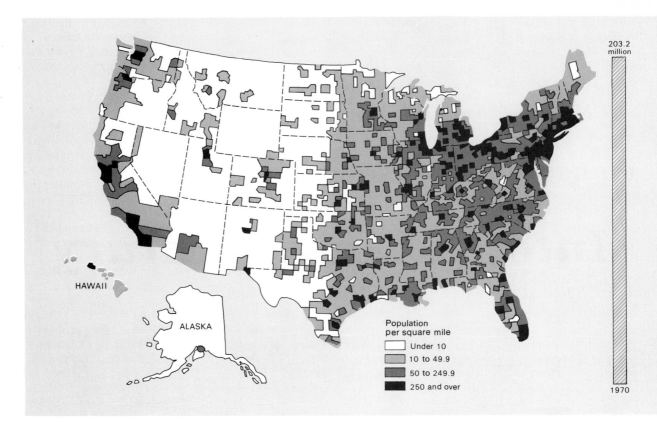

Population 1970

ber of households, especially among the young, were formed and dissolved without legal ceremony. By the early seventies one out of every eight families was headed by a woman, and single-parent families were growing almost three times as fast as two-parent families.

The decline in the birth rate also affected the age composition of the people. The number of Americans between fourteen and twenty-four increased by nearly 14 million in the sixties, would increase by less than a million in the seventies, and would decline in the eighties. The generation of the baby boom would continue as a disproportionate bulge in the population curve. But, after having supplied the basis for the youthful unrest of the sixties, it might have very different social impact when its members became middle-aged, even more different when they became a claimant group of old folks.

The proportion of old folks was expected to grow. Life expectancy, as a result of new medical discoveries, continued to rise: by 1975 it reached 76.7 for white women and 68.9 for white men, an increase of 2.1 years and 1.2 years respectively in a decade. For nonwhites the figure lagged behind: 71.3 for women and 62.9 for men. In 1974 the United States had the lowest death rate since records were started in 1900. While the number of Americans under the age of five declined by more than a million from 1970 to 1975, the number over sixty-five grew by 2.5 million. In 1900 one out of every twenty-four Americans had been sixty-five or older; by 1975 the figure was nearly one out of every nine; by 2000 it was forecast as one in eight. The growth in the elderly population, many poor and infirm, would inevitably affect politics and economic policy.

Immigration meanwhile increased from an annual average of about one hundred thousand in the 1940s to nearly four hundred thousand in the early 1970s. The composition of the new arrivals changed dramatically as a result of the Immigration and Nationality Act of 1965. That act abolished the discriminatory national origins quota system (see p. 596) and established needed skills and the reuniting of families as the criteria for admission. One unexpected consequence was a rapid increase in the number of Asian immigrants from about 7 percent of the total in 1965 to one-third a decade later. The proportion admitted from Latin America and southern and eastern Europe also increased; the proportion from western Europe and Canada declined precipitately. In

Into the third century

1965 Canada, Mexico, and Great Britain had been the leading sources; a decade later Mexico, the Philippines, and Korea headed the list.

In addition to those legally admitted, a new and large influx of "illegals" began in the late sixties. By 1975 the Immigration and Naturalization Service estimated that there were more than 7 million illegal aliens in the country. The "wetbacks," crossing from Mexico to provide cheap agricultural labor in Texas and California (and so called because they waded the Rio Grande to avoid immigration barriers), were an old and limited problem; but the new wave of illegals came predominantly from the Caribbean area or from South America, often entered on a temporary visa, and then disappeared into the urban crowd. Though it was often charged that the "illegals" were taking jobs away from Americans, evidence suggested that they performed rough and menial tasks rejected by native American workers and thereby filled a vacuum in the labor market. Their illegal status, however, intensified social problems by causing them to shun public facilities designed to support and educate the poor.

The increase in immigration, in conjunction with the drop in the birth rate, meant that immigration accounted for a larger share of population growth—nearly one-quarter by the bicentennial year. In the fifties one out of every nine new Americans had been an immigrant, in the sixties one out of six, in the seventies more than one out of five. Obviously, should the nation ever attain ZPG, immigration would account for 100 percent of population increase. For the first time in half a century immigration was emerging again as a significant factor in life—and at a time when the traditional mechanisms of assimilation and acculturation were under increasing attack.

Where the people lived. Americans continued a wandering folk. Nearly one-fifth moved each year from one residence to another. The most striking geographical growth after the Second World War came in the so-called "sunbelt"—the states below the thirty-seventh parallel from Virginia across to southern California. Between 1950 and 1975 the sunbelt population grew by nearly 60 percent—almost twice as fast as the rest of the nation. In 1964 California passed New York to become the most populous state. 85 percent of the growth between 1970 and 1975 took place in the South and West.

Money was also moving from the apprehensive and turbulent Northeast into the booming "southern rim" with its advantages in energy sources, raw materials, ports, waterways, highways, lower taxes and wages, bracing air, temperate climate, and wide-open spaces. As wealth grew in the sunbelt, some analysts anticipated an all-out war in the business community

between "Yankees" and "cowboys"—on the one hand, the traditional financial élite of the East, with patrician values and cosmopolitan experience; on the other, the raw sunbelt plutocracy, its money drawn from oil and defense, its politics (presumably) from the primitivism of Texas millionaires. Others, however, had more confidence in the capacity of the eastern establishment to defer the showdown by absorbing, if not the millionaires, at least their children.

In the shorter run, the shift of population and income had evident political implications. Between the Civil War and the Second World War only two men born outside the Northeast (including Ohio) made the White House. After 1945 only one man from the same area even achieved a presidential nomination. If the shift continued, the Southern and Western states would have increasing strength in national elections and probably a majority in the House of Representatives after the 1980 census. Whether the sunbelt would operate as a political unit remained unclear. Despite the antigovernment rhetoric favored by politicians of the region, Southern economic growth depended heavily on federal funds. In 1974 the southern rim collected $13 billion more from Washington than it contributed in federal taxes; nine Northern states showed a net loss of more than $20 billion in the same exchange. This reliance on the federal government, along with the pluralizing effects of industrial growth, might give politics along the southern rim patterns little different from the rest of the country.

An equally significant redistribution of population was taking place between city and suburb. By 1970 37.6 percent of Americans lived in suburbs as against 31.4 percent in cities. In the next years, suburban population increased, and even the countryside began to grow at a faster rate than the cities. In the early seventies, the five largest metropolitan areas—New York, Los Angeles, Chicago, Philadelphia, Detroit—experienced a sharp decline in the rate at which people moved into them. Urban growth was confined largely to the sunbelt.

The idea of suburbia—ranch houses, green lawns, station wagons, swimming pools, shopping centers—exerted continuing appeal. But in fact suburban homogeneity began to crumble under the migration from the cities. There were soon working-class as well as middle-class suburbs. Sociologists in the seventies wrote of "the urbanization of the suburbs." The sharp demarcation between urban and suburban problems began to fade away.

Ordeal of the city. The disorders of industrial society were meanwhile rising to climax in the city. Poverty, racial tension, unequal and inadequate education, air and water pollution, the deterioration of

Emblem of suburbia

municipal services, the choking of transportation, the swamping of the welfare system, the decay of public housing, the upsurge of crime, the spread of congestion, filth, drugs, alienation, and anger, the erosion of the sense of community—all these made the city a central battlefield in the future of the nation.

Populated more and more by the poor, the brown, and the black, cities had fewer resources on which to draw at the very time that the need for public facilities became more urgent. The property tax was both overburdened and regressive; municipal taxing powers were limited; the removal of business to the suburbs contracted the tax base; state legislatures, dominated by rural counties, were often indifferent. Education consumed nearly a fifth of municipal budgets and remained the most helpful means of social conciliation and improvement. But inner-city schools tended to be overcrowded and under-equipped. *De facto* segregation and chaotic family life in the ghettos undermined educational motivation. The drop-out rate was three times as high among black high-school students as among white. Many schools were demoralized by defeatism and paralyzed by drug addiction and random violence.

"Crime in the streets" became an issue in the 1964 presidential campaign; and, though many who invoked the phrase used it as a code word with which to incite emotion against blacks, the rise in crime was sharp and disquieting. In 1960 violent crimes had been committed in cities over 250,000 at the rate of less than 300 per 100,000 people; the rate increased to over 1,000 by 1973. Crimes were characteristically committed by males between eighteen and twenty-four, generally poor, often drug addicts. The rate was naturally highest where poverty, drugs, discrimination, and unemployment converged: the ghetto. And, though some tried to suggest that violent crime was a form of race war committed by blacks against whites, the victims themselves, except in robberies, were typically young, poor, and black.

Beyond street crime there lay the murky underworld of organized crime. Whether or not the Mafia existed as the closely organized, centrally controlled criminal secret society sentimentally portrayed in the popular film *The Godfather* (1972), no one could doubt the existence of interstate criminal syndicates, sometimes working together in loose confederation, sometimes waging savage war against each other, spreading corruption and fear into the business community, the labor movement, and local government. The annual net income of organized crime was estimated in 1967 as $6–7 billion by President Johnson's Commission on Law Enforcement and Administration of Justice.

Criminals, organized or unorganized, indulged themselves increasingly in murders, two-thirds of which in the early seventies were committed with guns. More than 90 million firearms were in American households, of which 25 million were handguns, easily concealed in hip pockets. Two hundred fifteen million Americans comfortably outstripped all other modern democratic peoples in rates of homicide, assault, rape, and robbery, providing about fifty times as many gun murders each year as did England, Japan, and West Germany with their combined population of 214 million. Pressure for effective federal gun control, arising after the assassinations of the sixties, was regularly frustrated by the impassioned lobbying of the National Rifle Association.

In 1969 the Commission on the Causes and Prevention of Violence predicted that, unless the nation awoke to the crisis of the cities, within a few years

> . . . central business districts . . . will be largely deserted except for police patrols during nighttime hours. High rise apartment buildings and residential compounds protected by private guards and security devices will be fortified cells for upper-middle and high-income populations. . . . Ownership of guns will be almost universal in the suburbs; homes will be fortified by an array of devices from window grills to electronic surveillance equipment, armed citizen volunteers in cars will supplement inadequate police patrols. . . . Residential neighborhoods in the central city will be unsafe in differing degrees, and the ghetto slum neighborhoods will be places of terror with widespread crime, perhaps entirely out of police control during night-time hours.

In 1972 Stanley Kubrick's film *A Clockwork Orange* offered a horrific rendition of this vision of the urban future.

Crime was the ultimate expression of urban disorganization. And the troubles of Metropolis were compounded by the fact that it had begun to give way to Megalopolis. Cities wandered aimlessly into the surrounding countryside, generating suburbs and then exurbs, sprawling across municipal and even state frontiers, creating vast untaxable urban regions, stretching from Boston to Washington, from Pittsburgh through Chicago to Milwaukee, from San Diego to San Francisco. With more than two out of every three Americans living in metropolitan regions, the government of cities had become the greatest challenge to the American political system.

The urban crisis of the sixties had been one of riot and upheaval. Though this subsided in the seventies, it was quickly replaced by a new crisis—the crisis of municipal finance. The fiscal plight of the cities was dramatized in 1975 when the greatest of them all, New York City, came very close to financial default. New York's problems arose partly from local circumstance—an improvident borrowing policy, heavy pension commitments to city employees, and an inordinately heavy welfare burden. This last, which devoured one-third of New York's current spending, resulted in part from New York state welfare requirements; Chicago with the same percentage of its population on welfare rolls, had almost no welfare-related charges on its city budget. The crisis resulted too from the fact that New York was a national city, taking in poor citizens from other parts of the United States, thereby reducing tensions and taxes in Southern states and in Puerto Rico.

But New York also presented in more acute form problems common to most large cities: in particular, the flight of the tax producers, leaving the city to the tax consumers—the poor, the elderly and the nonwhite minorities; and the accumulating claims of education, housing, and medical care against a shrinking tax base. Though grudging federal action at almost the last hour saved New York from bankruptcy

Ordeal of the city

in 1975, the need for a comprehensive urban strategy had become manifest. The Supreme Court decision on legislative apportionment in *Baker* v. *Carr* (1962) facilitated urban representation in state legislatures. But states were financially strapped too. In the end it was a national problem. The establishment in 1965 of the Department of Housing and Urban Development created a base for national action. Vital elements in a national urban strategy included the federalization of welfare, a revision of revenue-sharing to recognize the particular needs of cities, and federal guarantees for municipal bonds. Such a strategy confronted, however, the mistrust of cities that, since the time of Jefferson, had been an abiding prejudice of the American mind.

The people at work. Of a civilian labor force of 93 million in 1975, 81.5 million were employed in industry and services, 3.2 million in agriculture; 8 million were unemployed. Manufacturing capacity had almost tripled between 1950 and 1975. Output per worker-hour had almost doubled. The increase in productivity came in part from the techniques summed up in the word "automation." The basis of automation was the electronic computer. The first electric digital computer was built in 1946; and scientists and engineers rapidly developed the dazzling potentialities of what Norbert Wiener called "cybernetics," the science devoted to the study of communication and control mechanisms. The distinctive element in the industrial application of the computer was the introduction into the manufacturing sequence of self-regulating devices based on the "feedback" principle. The computer, once programmed, absorbed information that enabled it to continue, vary, or correct automatic operations. The computer promised to revolutionize every aspect of industry from research through production to marketing and to affect the methods of everyone from the engineer to the economist.

The specialized requirements of the new technology contributed to an unprecedented expansion of higher education. Enrollment in colleges and universities increased from less than 2 million students in 1940 to 3.6 million in 1960 and 8.8 million in 1974. In 1940 only one-quarter of adults had had a high-school education and only one-tenth had attended college; by the 1970s, over half were high-school graduates and over a fifth had attended college. Some institutions, however, overreacted to the educational boom of the sixties and, with the drop in the birth rate, faced the prospect of surplus faculty and plant in the seventies and a grim economic future.

Automation also contributed to changes in the composition of the labor force. In the fifties white-collar workers began for the first time to outnumber blue-collar workers. By 1975 there were 27 million blue-collar workers, predominantly employed in the production of goods, as against 42 million white-collar workers, predominantly employed in the production of services. Some observers concluded from the statistics that the working class had become a minority and that rising incomes and suburbanization were eroding the distinction between working-class and middle-class culture. But in fact not all white-collar workers were removed from the blue-collar culture. Many had manual jobs (mail-carriers, janitors, garbage-collectors, shoeshine boys); some were wives of blue-collar workers. This fact permitted writers to continue to speak of "the working class majority."

Nevertheless the fastest-growing occupational categories were professional and technical workers, managers, and administrators. By 1975 these groups constituted more than a quarter of the labor force. Because organized labor could not keep up with the expansion of the service sector, membership in labor unions slowly declined as a proportion of nonfarm employment from 31.4 percent in 1960 to 27.2 percent in 1972. Four out of every five members of the labor force did not belong to unions at all.

The distribution of income appeared hardly to have changed since the Second World War. In 1947 the poorest 20 percent of families received 5 percent of cash income and the richest 5 percent 17.5 percent. In the 1970s the bottom group still received 5 percent and the top group 16 percent. If noncash income were included, the share going to the rich greatly increased. On the other hand, some analysts argued that if discounts were made for demographic peculiarities—the increasing incidence of old age, youthful marriage, and divorce—the result would show a trend toward greater equality of income, at least among stable families.

In 1973 the top 1 percent of families was estimated to own about one-quarter of the wealth in the country. While the number of those classified as poor had dropped from about 40 million in 1961 to about 24 million in 1969, the poor increased in the seventies, partly as a result of the recession, partly as a result of the rising proportion of old folks in the population. A tax system riddled with loopholes had become ineffectual as a mechanism for redistribution. Public sector spending, which some saw as the means of transferring income to the poor, did indeed help the very poor, but it also built facilities used preponderantly by the middle class. If the United States were to become a more equalitarian society, a new attack was evidently required on the distribution of income.

Women in revolt. The goal of equality was pursued with greater passion in the social than in the economic field. In the sixties and seventies a diversity of social groups rebelled against the roles in which they felt American society had cast them, roles that, they believed, demeaned their status and falsified their identity. Students, blue-collar workers, convicts, homosexuals—all began to organize against what they conceived as the psychic aggression of the social order. Most powerful of all was the revolt of the only minority that, in fact, constituted a majority of Americans—women—who, outnumbered by men in 1940, exceeded male population by 5.5 million thirty-five years later.

To males the idea that the American woman saw herself in a position of inferiority came as a surprise. Foreigners had long told them that America was a matriarchy. In comic strips Maggie was always chasing Jiggs with a rolling-pin. Philip Wylie's popular polemic *Generation of Vipers* (1942) had contended that the American male was systematically castrated by his women from mother to teacher to wife to daughter and that "momism" was the curse of American life. In some sense this may have been true, but the power of the American woman was exercised by stealth and subterfuge from a position of weakness.

Earlier feminist agitations had gained women a measure of legal identity and, in due course, the right to vote. But all indexes showed them remaining in secure social and economic inferiority. Women were the weaker sex, their place was the home, their destiny to serve their husband and children. When they struck out on their own, most professions (except for elementary-school teaching, nursing, librarianships, and prostitution) resisted them. Shirley Chisholm, the first black congresswoman, said she was subjected to more discrimination as a woman than as a black. Women constituted more than 51 percent of the population in 1970 but only 9 percent of the full professors on university faculties, 7.6 percent of the doctors, and 2.8 percent of the lawyers. The average earnings of a woman college graduate were about the same as those of a man with an eighth-grade education. Seven percent of working-women earned more than $10,000, as against 40 percent of working-men.

And in some respects the position of women had been getting worse. The early feminist movement had stimulated able women to seek careers. The example of Eleanor Roosevelt and Frances Perkins in the thirties, the participation of women in the Second World War as WACs and WAVEs and as workers in munitions plants—all this had strengthened the image of the self-reliant woman. But in the forties and fifties the tide had turned, as the tide turned against the Negro after Reconstruction. By 1960 women were receiving a smaller proportion of university degrees than in 1930; their median earnings relative to similarly employed men were declining; in 1971 the percentage of women in managerial and proprietorial jobs was lower than in 1960.

It was against this background that Betty Friedan in her influential book *The Feminine Mystique* (1963) called on women to recognize what society was doing to them and to demand equal rights and opportunities. Finding even the civil-rights groups and the New Left dominated by "male chauvinism"—"the only position for women in SNCC," said Stokeley Carmichael in 1964, "is prone"—Friedan and others established the National Organization for Women (NOW) in 1966. The chief recruiting instrument for women's liberation was the "consciousness-raising" group, where women in towns across the land met in "rap sessions" to reflect on their lives. This activity raised the consciousness of many men too, startled to discover the manifold ways in which male condescension and female subordination were built into the structure and language of society.

NOW, which claimed about sixty thousand members in 1976, concentrated initially on economic and social issues: an equal-rights amendment, equal pay for equal work, the abolition of sexual discrimination in employment; child-care centers; equal access to education and the professions; and birth control and abortion. Beginning in 1971, the National Women's Political Caucus ("Women! Make policy not coffee") worked with some success to enlarge female participation in politics. NOW and NWPC stayed within the system, and their goals commanded support from most Americans. Men were increasingly prepared to take a larger share in child-rearing and household tasks; some, noting that "Mr." as a title did not reveal whether or not a man was married, were even willing to acquiesce in "Ms." as a substitute for both "Miss" and "Mrs."

Women's liberation also generated various forms of revolutionary feminism based on the idea that through history men, as the master class, were propelled by *machismo* to war and tyranny and that racism and imperialism were the consequences of male supremacy. In this more drastic mood militants saw marriage as a condition where the husband was a rapist, the wife a prostitute, and family responsibility an enslavement. As an interim measure, they proposed "marriage contracts" spelling out household roles and obligations. Some moved on to attack the "nuclear family" itself, hoping to replace it by an extended family structure with the collective raising of children. Others advocated lesbianism. Some observers believed that revolutionary feminism was essentially an enthusiasm of young, educated, middle-class women and that its failure to find a convincing place for the rearing of children doomed it to futility. None the less, by 1976 the radical feminists caused a split within NOW itself. According to polls, however,

Women on the march

We, men and women who hereby constitute ourselves as the National Organization for Women, believe that the time has come for a new movement toward true equality for all women in America, and toward a fully equal partnership of the sexes, as part of the world-wide revolution of human rights now taking place within and beyond our national borders....

WE REJECT the current assumption that a man must carry the sole burden of supporting himself, his wife, and family, and that a woman is automatically entitled to lifelong support by a man upon her marriage, or that marriage, home and family are primarily woman's world and responsibility—hers, to dominate— his to support. We believe that a true partnership between the sexes demands a different concept of marriage, an equitable sharing of the responsibilities of home and children and of the economic burdens of their support....

IN THE INTERESTS OF THE HUMAN DIGNITY OF WOMEN, we will protest, and endeavor to change, the false image of women now prevalent in the mass media, and in the texts, ceremonies, laws, and practices of the major social institutions. Such images perpetuate contempt for women by society and by women for themselves.... WE BELIEVE THAT women will do most to create a new image of women by acting *now, and by speaking out in behalf of their own equality, freedom, and human dignity—not in pleas for special privilege, nor in enmity toward men, who are also victims of the current, half-equality between the sexes—but in an active, self-respecting partnership with men.*

From the National Organization for Women, Statement of Purpose, 1966.

most women continued to think that taking care of family was more rewarding than having a career.

By the early seventies barriers to women were falling throughout American society. In 1950 a third of the female population was in the labor force; by 1975 nearly a half, though women continued to hold the low-paying jobs and, whatever the job, earned less than men. The proportion of women in higher education and the professions was growing, in part because of government "affirmative action" guidelines. Few male sanctuaries remained. Even West Point and Annapolis surrendered. So did so unlikely a field as

Majority rights

crime. Female arrests for "serious" crimes increased 52 percent between 1968 and 1973.

In 1972 the Senate approved the Equal Rights Amendment, first submitted by Alice Paul's National Woman's Party in 1923. This amendment proposed to write into the Constitution the rule that "equality of rights under the law shall not be denied or abridged by the United States or by any state on account of sex." Thirty-four states had ratified it by mid-1975. But women's liberation and the ERA campaign produced a backlash in the form of movements led by female dissenters who wished to reaffirm woman's subordinate role under such slogans as "total woman." None the less the women's liberation movement had indeed altered the consciousness of American society, had greatly increased male sensitivity to female frustrations and humiliations, and had encouraged in women themselves new purposes of self-reliance and self-assertion.

The rise of ethnicity. Women's liberation was only one expression of a broad drive of submerged groups for identity and justice. Other movements followed ethnic rather than sex lines. The old theory had been of the United States as a "melting-pot" where many nationalities fused into one: *e pluribus unum*. But after the Second World War spokesmen for so-called "ethnic" groups began to see the melting-pot as a symbol of cultural imperialism, designed to force a diverse and polyglot society into a white Anglo-Saxon Protestant (WASP) mold. (The word "ethnic" applied in fact to any group whose members claimed a common origin but came by the 1970s to refer particularly to immigrants from southern and eastern Europe, especially Poles, Italians, Greeks, and Slavs.)

Some social scientists thought that ethnicity provided a category as vital for understanding modern industrial society as class had been for understanding the first impact of industrialization; others, however, saw it precisely as a means of distracting attention from class. In practice, ethnicity implied a reassertion of ancestral traditions and values against the dominant WASP culture. Where an older generation had discarded nationality traits in the quest for Americanization, the new generation formed "antidefamation" leagues to combat anti-Semitism, Polish jokes, or the idea that all Italians were members of the Mafia. Writers, saluting the "unmeltable ethnics," drew the portrait of neighborhoods based on nationality, populated by hard-working, unassuming, patriotic people. Social scientists measured "antiethnic" discrimination in American institutions. Thus one study showed that, while Italians, Poles, blacks, and Latins made up over one-third of Chicago's population, they constituted less than one–twenty-fifth of the directors

and officers in Chicago's major corporations and banks.

Politics, along with athletics and crime, had provided historic means for ethnic advance. However, the ethnic role in politics was diffused by conflicts between each established group and the next wave: the Anglo-Saxons versus the Irish; the Irish versus the Italians; the Italians versus the east Europeans; the other white ethnics versus the Jews; all white ethnics versus the browns and the blacks.

The last tension became especially acute as a result of the civil-rights programs of the sixties. Low-income whites were not against equal rights in principle; but they were against equal rights at the expense of their children, their neighborhoods, their jobs, and their safety in the streets. Many felt that the national government was intervening on behalf of blacks as it had never done for them and that black gains were taking place at their own expense. Politicians like Nixon, Agnew, and Wallace played astutely on this tension. It also to some degree divided the old New Deal coalition. Low-income whites talked bitterly about "limousine liberals" who fled to the suburbs and left them to face the day-to-day consequences of racial change.

Black America. Though the black birth rate was also declining somewhat, black population increased in the mid-seventies at a rate about double that of whites. In 1974 24 million blacks made up 11.4 percent of the American people. The position of black Americans had improved in notable respects in the sixties. By 1971 the median family income of blacks had increased from 53 to 63 percent of that of white families, and a majority of blacks were living in families with incomes of at least $8,000 a year. Enrollment of blacks in colleges nearly quadrupled between 1964 and 1974; by the later date, 18 percent of blacks of college age were in college as against 25 percent of whites. Between 1970 and 1974 black population in the suburbs grew by nearly one-fifth. Throughout the land blacks freely entered places of resort and accommodation where black faces had never been seen before except as servants.

But the economic troubles of the seventies showed the extreme vulnerability of the black position. The old precept "last hired, first fired" still prevailed. The jobless rate for blacks was at least twice as high as for whites; among teenage blacks, the rate was four or five times as high. The gap between black and white income began to widen; by 1974 black income was down to 58.5 percent of white. Black jobs were still predominantly at the bottom of the employment scale; less than 3 percent of managers, administrators, and proprietors were black. Progress in reducing black poverty ground to a halt. Though blacks did move to the suburbs, they often encountered resistance and sometimes violence. Black gains, it appeared, had come in the main from increasing the size of the pie, not from altering the relationship of the slices, and therefore now shrank as economic growth slowed down. All this suggested that blacks were still victims of an institutionalized discrimination so deeply imbedded in society that it eluded both national legislation and individual good will.

The one area where black progress was incontestable was in politics. The Voting Rights Act of 1965—which Edward Brooke of Massachusetts, the first black senator since Reconstruction, called "the most significant victory for blacks"—began a transformation of American politics. By the bicentennial year, though blacks still made up less than 1 percent of elected officials, there were more than thirty-five hundred in office, including eighteen in Congress, nearly three hundred in state legislatures, and mayors in Washington, Los Angeles, Newark, Gary, Atlanta, and a number of Southern towns. Gains were especially striking in the ex-Confederate states, which had seventy-two black elected officials in 1965 and more than fifteen hundred a decade later.

The issue for blacks in the fifties and sixties, Brooke and others believed, had been legal equality. The issue in the seventies was "real equality," and political action was the key. "Anyone looking for the civil rights movement in the streets," said the mayor of Atlanta, "is fooling himself. Politics is the civil rights movement of the seventies." The Congressional Black Caucus, formed in 1970, used traditional means to exert pressure for black interests; and the National Conference on Black Politics, founded in 1972, tried to influence both parties by organizing at the grass roots. Though black registration and voting continued to fall below the expectations of the leadership, blacks nevertheless gained sufficient power to persuade even a onetime militant segregationist like George Wallace to cultivate black mayors and to crown a black homecoming queen at the very university that, a decade earlier, he had sworn to deny to black students.

Political debates in the early seventies focused on the question of achieving racial balance in schools through the busing of pupils. Striking progress had been made since *Brown* v. *Board of Education* (see p. 743) in school desegregation, especially in the South, which was by a large margin in 1974 the most integrated region in the country. However, the Brown decision was applied in different ways, depending on local circumstances and courts. Northern cities, where residential patterns created *de facto* segregation, proved especially resistant to desegregation policies.

The schoolbus took over 40 percent of American students to school in any case. Busing for racial balance worked well in many medium-sized communities. Reasonable busing had been sustained in 1971 by a unanimous Supreme Court in *Swann* v. *Charlotte-Mecklenburg Board of Education* as a means of dismantling dual school systems. In many communities the courts found busing to be the only means to overcome segregation. To abandon busing, many believed, would be to abandon the national commitment to an integrated society.

But busing against residential patterns violated deep feelings, especially in districts to which parents may have moved to assure better schooling for their children and in homogeneous neighborhoods, like South Boston. Sociologists claimed—though this was disputed—that court-ordered busing increased the white flight to the suburbs. Nor was it clear that mixed schooling significantly improved the quality of education for blacks or eliminated differences in achievement between black and white children. Some observers thought that the busing dilemma placed too heavy a burden on the judiciary and that educational integration was too narrow a weapon to overcome a broad social problem. In extreme cases busing might take children from good and safe school districts into inferior and hazardous schools far from their homes.

Politicians seized upon the problem. Nixon denounced mandatory busing; Ford stood aside when antibusing groups rioted against court orders; Democrats like Henry Jackson and Wallace made busing a major issue in 1976. Outbreaks of violence in Boston and Louisville in the mid-seventies testified to the explosiveness of the question. Enthusiasts sought to outlaw busing by a constitutional amendment. In 1975 polls showed that, while white majorities in every section of the country approved of educational integration, over 70 percent of whites opposed busing at the means of achieving it.

Even among blacks nearly half opposed busing, with about 40 percent in favor. While the national NAACP kept up the fight for desegregation through busing, its Atlanta branch abandoned a desegregation suit in 1973 in exchange for more jobs and power for blacks within the system. Black separationists, like Roy Innis of CORE, opposed busing. Some blacks resented the implication that black children could not be properly educated except in the company of white children. Busing, said the black political scientist Charles Hamilton, was "a subtle way of maintaining black dependency on whites." Many believed that the troubles attendant upon forced integration were a damaging experience for black pupils.

It appeared that busing, while a useful and sometimes necessary instrument, was a limited remedy. It also appeared that the analogy, frequently invoked, between black immigrants to the cities and their European predecessors was invalid. White immigrants

Busing in South Boston: deep feelings

had survived squalid ghetto conditions because with time and success they knew they could move into better neighborhoods. Racial prejudice denied blacks the escape-valve of outward mobility. The policies that absorbed white immigrants into metropolitan America did not work for blacks. The long-run hope, the urban historian Richard Wade and others argued, lay in new policies—the stipulation, for example, that public subsidies for multi-unit dwellings provide for 10 to 15 percent low- and moderate-income families—that would break entrenched residential patterns and open up the outer areas to black residents. This too conformed with the demand of the black political leadership for "real equality."

Hispanic Americans. By the mid-seventies the Census Bureau reported over 11 million persons of Spanish origin in the United States; in addition, most of the 7 million "illegals" were Hispanic. Sixty percent were Mexican, 15 percent Puerto Rican, 7 percent Cuban; the rest came mostly from Central and South America. The Mexicans lived in the main in the Southwest, the Puerto Ricans in the Northeast, the Cubans in Florida. Their income levels varied considerably but in general surpassed those of black Americans while falling substantially behind those of whites. Most were employed in lower-paying occupations or as craftsmen.

Spanish-speaking enclaves had survived in New Mexico for nearly five centuries, and for many decades Mexicans had entered the United States to satisfy the need for cheap agricultural labor. But it was not till after the Second World War that the Mexican-Americans, who in the sixties called themselves proudly "Chicanos," began to act as a conscious minority.

Pride in their history and traditions facilitated the quest for identity. In California, Cesar Chavez and his United Farm Workers improved the wages and working conditions of migrant farm-laborers. In New Mexico, Reies Lopez Tijerina tried to reclaim land grants that "Anglos" had long since wangled from the original owners. In Texas, Jose Angel Gutierrez formed a political party, *La Raza Unida*. John F. Kennedy was the first President to recognize the Chicanos, and his brother Robert, a friend of Chavez, received their impassioned support. In 1974 Arizona and New Mexico elected governors of Spanish descent.

The Puerto Rican population on the mainland rose by 55 percent in the sixties, with more than three-fifths living in New York City. The brilliant musical show *West Side Story* (1957), adapting the Romeo and Juliet theme to "rumbles" among Puerto Rican street gangs, won a sympathetic hearing for problems in the larger community. Hardworking and religious, the Puerto Ricans showed considerable aptitude for acculturation. In 1970 New York elected its first Puerto Rican congressman, Herman Badillo.

The Puerto Ricans of New York had political rivalries with the blacks as well as problems among themselves. With recession in the United States, the tide of migration began to flow back to Puerto Rico; but returning natives encountered economic difficulties there. They also encountered contention between the Puerto Rican majority, who wished to remain part of the United States as a commonwealth or even to acquire statehood, and a passionate minority that demanded Puerto Rican independence. In 1950 Puerto Rican nationalists had tried to kill President Truman. In later years they carried out intermittent terrorist activities on the mainland.

837

Cesar Chavez

The Hispanic community in general identified its interests with those seeking wider economic and political opportunity. Its more specific interest was in promoting bilingualism in education, manpower training, and on the ballot. One by-product was the replacement of French by Spanish as the language most commonly taught in American high schools.

Indians. The oldest and truest Americans, the Indians, no longer were the vanishing Americans. As a result of public-health improvements, Indian birth rates were about double those of the nation as a whole. Indian population had grown from 334,000 in 1940 to about 850,000 in 1976. Half lived in the West and a quarter in the South. Over half lived on 266 reservations; most of the rest lived in cities. Wherever they lived, they tended to be the poorest of the poor, at the end of the line in employment, income, education, health, and life expectancy. The suicide rate among Indians was twice that of the rest of the population.

National policy toward the Indians continued to vacillate between the goals of autonomy and assimilation. The effort begun under the New Deal by John Collier to encourage "a self-governing self-determination" and to revitalize tribal government was rejected by Congress after the Second World War. The new policy, crystallized in a congressional resolution of 1953, had the ultimate goal of "termination"—that is, liquidating the reservation system, dismantling the tribes, removing special federal protection and services, and hoping that Indians could somehow fend for themselves as individuals in white society. The Bureau of Indian Affairs in Washington continued to be a white agency governing reservation Indians according to highly paternalistic principles.

The Kennedy Administration arrested the termination process and began to move toward self-deter-

mination. But a great deal was at stake—55 million acres of Indian lands with water, timber, grass, and minerals—and white interests, working through the congressional Interior Committees and the Bureau of Indian Affairs, were determined to deny Indians control of their territory. Then in 1970 the Nixon Administration, in one of its notable actions, asked Congress to repeal the termination resolution of 1953 and proclaimed "self-determination without termination" as the new national policy. The Indians were to assume control of their own affairs, and the national government, acting as their trustee, would protect their land and resources. Nixon followed this by setting in process the Indianization of the Indian Bureau; by 1974 more than 60 percent of the Bureau's employees had Indian forebears.

However, Congress failed to pass enabling legislation; and, in so far as the executive branch executed the new policy, the effect was to give power to tribal governments dominated in some cases by leaders who were in collusion with white interests and unresponsive to their own people. Indian activists, inspired in part by the black example, meanwhile formed nationalist organizations and denounced the reservation leaders as "Uncle Tomahawks." The National Congress of American Indians (NCAI), founded during the Second World War (in which twenty-five thousand Indians had served in the armed forces), became more aggressive; and the American Indian Movement (AIM), formed by urban Indians in 1968, raised the standard of "red power." A number of books—notably *Custer Died for Your Sins* (1969) by Vine Deloria, Jr., a Standing Rock Sioux and former executive director of the NCAI; and Dee Brown's *Bury My Heart at Wounded Knee* (1971)—brought the Indian case to the large public. Films like *Little Big Man* (1970) showed Indians as the victims rather than the villains of the West, often cruelly massacred by whites rather in the manner of My Lai. *Billy Jack* (1971), the tale of a proud halfbreed who returned to his tribal grounds, began as a vogue enthusiasm in the counterculture and ended as one of the all-time moneymakers, grossing over $30 million.

In November 1972 militant Indians, led by the AIM, occupied the Indian Bureau in Washington and left it in a shambles. The next February an AIM group, returning to the scene of the Indian massacre at Wounded Knee, South Dakota (see p. 404), seized the small village and held it for seventy-one days, again wreaking great destruction. Such episodes alienated the Nixon Administration, which abandoned the reform effort begun so promisingly in 1970. Random AIM terrorism also antagonized many Indians, not only tribal leaders whose power was threatened by the militants but men like Deloria, who wrote, "When the media collide with a social movement its chief

We, the first Americans, come to the Congress of the United States that you give us the chance to try to solve what you call the Indian problem. You have had two hundred years and you have not succeeded by your standards. It is clear that you have not succeeded in ours.... We ask you, as the representatives of the people of the United States, to serve as our representatives too—to help us see that assurances do not become empty promises. And, if necessary, to enact legislation which will create such a process where Indians can really shape government policy and control their own lives and destinies....

The present [congressional] committees have pushed for termination, and have fostered on Congress seemingly neutral and technical legislation, under the guise of Indian expertise, which has taken away our land, our water rights, our mineral resources and handed them over to the white man. You have been duped—as we have been duped. These committees have created a monstrous bureaucracy insensitive to Indians which trembles and cringes before them.... We know you are highly conscious of your national obligations when you deliberate on such problems as the war in Viet Nam. We know that you have even taken those obligations seriously enough to go to Viet Nam in order to personally inform yourself on how the Executive carries out the commitments of the United States. We ask that you do no less at home—for the United States has made older and more sacred commitments to the people who have occupied these shores for twenty-five thousand years.... In essence, we ask the restoration of what you claimed at the founding of your nation—the inalienable right to pursue happiness.

From the American Indian Task Force, Statement to Congress, November 12, 1969.

contribution seems to be the simplification of issues and the creation of instant personalities." George McGovern called the AIM leaders "a group of rip-off artists who are exploiting the Indian problem for their own selfish needs." By 1975, the AIM, with its urban orientation and violent tactics, had failed to win support on the reservations and was in decline. Nevertheless the predicament of the Indian was on the white conscience as never before in American history.

The permissive society. Sexual and ethnic self-assertion were part of a larger revolt against custom and authority. The American cultural revolution had begun in the sixties. The New Leftists then conceived life in political and ideological terms and were prepared to use violence to attain their objectives. That mood faded in the seventies. A minuscule group like the Symbionese Liberation Army, which murdered a black superintendent of schools in California in 1973 and in 1974 kidnaped Patricia Hearst, a granddaughter of the populist-radical-reactionary newspaper publisher (see p. 497), seemed an anachronism, as did the two demented California women who tried to kill Gerald Ford in 1975; all were working in isolation.

The rebelliousness of the seventies, more in the mood of the hippies than of the New Left, sought its revolution in individual lives. Demonstrations became infrequent, campuses quieted down, the great urban riots were a memory. Most of the young revolutionaries, at last over the fatal age of thirty, quietly dropped back into the system. A few retired to the psychiatrist's couch or continued aimless experimentation. Between 1970 and 1975 Jerry Rubin went through *est*, gestalt therapy, bioenergetics, rolfing,

Wounded Knee, 1973

The New Left grows older

When in doubt, burn. *Fire is the revolutionary's god. Fire is instant theater. No words can match fire.*

Politicians only notice poverty when the ghettos burn.

The burning of the first draft card caused earth tremors under the Pentagon. Burn the flag. Burn churches.

Burn, burn, burn....

Amerika is falling apart: the alternative is revolution or catastrophe.

The revolution has replaced the church as the country's moral authority.

From Jerry Rubin, Do It!, 1970.

I saw us move out of youth-oriented yippie consciousness to think of ourselves as parents, adults, mature men. I had always feared aging ... But I actually enjoy getting older. I have become happier. At 37 I feel better than I have at any other time in my life. I want to be politically active again—but not at the expense of my happiness and health. I do not want to be in a crazy movement that psychologically drains its people. I know that many ex-political people feel this way. We want to be active again, but in a new way. We remember how the movement used and destroyed personal relationships. We hate imperialism as much as before, but we are not into martyrdom.... We always have to fight the self-destructive urge within ourselves.

From Jerry Rubin, Growing (Up) at 37, 1976.

massage, jogging, health foods, tai chi, Esalen, hypnotism, modern dance, Silva Mind Control, Arica, acupuncture, sex therapy, Reichian therapy . . . in any case, the gospel of "burn, burn, burn" was far behind. Eldridge Cleaver, who had fled to Algeria as a black-power extremist, returned an American patriot.

Some activists were undone by a sense of fatigue and futility. Some were frightened by what excursions into violence had revealed of their own capacity for destructiveness. The Indochina War came to an end. Recession turned the worries of the young toward jobs. And, in a sense, the rebel sixties had won some of their points. By the seventies, so far as people's dress, appearance, conduct, and perception of sexual identity were concerned, there never had been a time when individual variations were more pronounced or individual choice was more unfettered. Men, so long the sober species, blossomed out in mustaches, beards, sideburns, and flowing hair. Casting aside the traditional suit, they wore anything from blue jeans and work shirts to cowboy boots and embroidered jackets. For their part, women (and men too) reveled for a season in the miniskirt and, by rejecting the attempt of Paris designers in 1971 to order them into calf-length midiskirts, declared their independence of *haute couture*. Slacks, regrettably, became the casual wear of everyone from dowagers to hookers.

The new tolerance extended to what had been historically the most sensitive of all problems for Americans—sex. The objective study of sexuality had gained new impetus from two works by the biologist Alfred Kinsey: *Sexual Behavior in the Human Male* (1948) and *Sexual Behavior of the Human Female* (1953). The sexual act itself received unrelenting scrutiny from William Masters and Virginia Johnson in *Human Sexual Response* (1968). While sociologists doubted that changes in American sexual practices had been all that great, there was plainly a vast change in public attitudes in the sixties and seventies. The old inhibitions and reticences disappeared. Ninety-five percent of males and over 80 percent of females between eighteen and twenty-four acknowledged premarital intercourse. Married couples sometimes indulged in "swinging"—group intercourse with other couples. Oral sex and other less conventional forms of sexual expression became common.

Homosexuals, male and female, came "out of the closet" to declare their identity. Appropriating the word "gay," they organized in defense of their civil rights, even persuading the American Psychiatric Association in 1973 to stop listing homosexuality as a psychiatric disorder. Homosexual themes became so aggressive in the arts that one observer complained, "The love that dare not speak its name just won't shut up these days."

The candid recognition of sexuality as part of life transformed society's ideas of what was acceptable in books, on the stage, in films, and even, though more

840

Into the third century

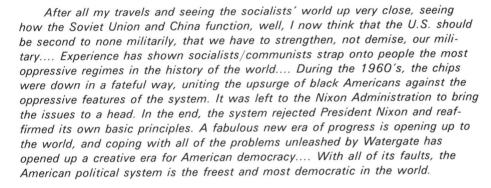

The New Left comes home

America's support of colonialism must be shattered before the resources and administrative machinery of the nation can be freed for the task of creating a truly free and humanistic society here at home. It is at this point, at the juncture of foreign policy and domestic policy, that the Negro revolution becomes one with the world revolution.... In their rage against the police, against police brutality, the blacks lose sight of the fundamental reality: that the police are only an instrument for the implementation of the policies of those who make the decisions. Police brutality is only one facet of the crystal of terror and oppression.... [Blacks] are asked to die for the System in Vietnam. In Watts they are killed by it. Now—NOW!—they are asking each other, in dead earnest: Why not die right here in Babylon fighting for a better life, like the Viet Cong? If those little cats can do it, what's wrong with big studs like us?

A mood sets in spreads across America, across the face of Babylon, jells in black hearts everywhere.

From Eldridge Cleaver, *Soul on Ice*, 1968.

After all my travels and seeing the socialists' world up very close, seeing how the Soviet Union and China function, well, I now think that the U.S. should be second to none militarily, that we have to strengthen, not demise, our military.... Experience has shown socialists/communists strap onto people the most oppressive regimes in the history of the world.... During the 1960's, the chips were down in a fateful way, uniting the upsurge of black Americans against the oppressive features of the system. It was left to the Nixon Administration to bring the issues to a head. In the end, the system rejected President Nixon and reaffirmed its own basic principles. A fabulous new era of progress is opening up to the world, and coping with all of the problems unleashed by Watergate has opened up a creative era for American democracy.... With all of its faults, the American political system is the freest and most democratic in the world.

From Eldridge Cleaver, Interview, *Rolling Stone*, September 11, 1975, "Why I Left the U.S. and Why I Am Returning," *New York Times*, November 18, 1975.

slowly, in television. The barriers of censorship crumbled away, at least in the large cities. The question of "hard-core" pornography, for which no social or artistic defense could be offered, remained in suspense as a result of an erratic series of Supreme Court decisions. "Soft-core" pornography flourished in the cinemas. Insensate violence, which some found more objectionable than sex, was unconstrained in movies and hardly constrained on television (and television sets, by the mid-seventies, were in 99 percent of American homes).

Drugs were another inheritance from the sixties. The Department of Health, Education and Welfare reported in 1976 that, of Americans between eighteen and twenty-five, over half had smoked marijuana at least once. Increasing prices were causing some of the young to turn to liquor in the fashion of their parents. Half a dozen states removed criminal penalties for the private use of marijuana, and more prepared to follow. Hard drugs, especially heroin and cocaine, presented continuing and more dangerous problems.

Some observers regarded the dissolution of old taboos as evidence of progress toward more healthy and authentic human relations. Others saw the "permissive society" as proof of moral collapse. Religion itself, in the eyes of stern moralists, was infected by the new laxity. Even in the Roman Catholic Church the release of liberal energy brought about by Pope John XXIII and the Second Vatican Council had wrought striking changes in what had long seemed an indestructibly conservative institution. Masses were of a sudden conducted in English; meat was eaten on Friday; nuns doffed their habits; priests questioned the rules on celibacy and birth control and left the priesthood in unprecedented numbers. The Catholic left, once embraced in Dorothy Day's doughty but tiny Catholic Worker Movement, now pervaded the Catholic community and, rallied by radical priests like Philip and Daniel Berrigan, defied the political state. Protestant churches, with their female ministers, rock services, and, on occasion, homosexual marriages, seemed even worse.

841

The assertive society

Certainly the old Calvinist ethic, based on work, discipline, achievement, and social duty, appeared to be giving way to a new hedonism, based on individual fulfillment through individual gratification and drawing its energy from consumer capitalism, with its commitment to the manufacture of wants, as well as from the counterculture, with its commitment to the priority of the self. The organization man and the hippie did not seem in the end too far apart. Whether this hedonistic ethos, so plainly the product of an age of abundance, could long survive the harsh demands of an age of incipient scarcities was a problem for the future.

Literature and art. America of the seventies, a more highly educated society than ever before, consumed more books than ever before. Fifteen thousand had been issued in 1960; more than forty thousand in 1974. Nearly 60 percent of the books published in the seventies were educational and professional. Novels made up less than 20 percent. The continuing expansion of the paperback market, with half a billion sold each year in the mid-seventies, brought books within everyone's reach.

As usual, writing reflected the preoccupations of the people. On lower literary levels, romantic tales ("gothics") vied with science fiction and sex melodrama for the attention of escapists. Serious writers in the years after the Second World War, moving beyond the social art of the depression years, tended to be private, somewhat withdrawn from the problems of society, deeply involved in individual quests for personal identity and meaning. These quests often took place in strongly rendered regional or ethnic contexts. Thus the tradition of Southern writing, intensified and elaborated by Faulkner in the twenties and thirties, was continued in the postwar years by Robert Penn Warren of Tennessee, notably in *All the King's Men* (1946), his novel about Huey Long's Louisiana, and by writers of the next generation—William Styron of Virginia, whose *Confessions of Nat Turner* (1967) was the attempt of a Southern white to come to a reckoning with the historical fact of slavery; Walker Percy of Mississippi; and the exquisite women writers Eudora Welty of Mississippi and Flannery O'Connor of Georgia.

In the North the WASP novel of manners, perfected by James and Howells, exemplified in the prewar generation by the astute satire of J. P. Marquand and the sardonic realism of James Gould Cozzens, was still alive. But the age of Anglo-Saxon dominance was receding; brilliant younger writers—John Cheever, John Updike, and, more in the older school, Louis Auchincloss—portrayed the WASP at bay in an increasingly heterogeneous and bewildering society. The stories and novels of Joyce Carol Oates caught with eerie intensity the hysteria under the surface of middle-class American life.

Ethnicity became as potent a theme in fiction as in sociology. Following the path broken by James T. Farrell in the thirties, Edwin O'Connor (*The Last Hurrah*, 1956) and J. F. Powers recorded further phases in the assimilation of the Irish into American life. Mario Puzo dealt with the Italian-Americans in *The Dark Arena* (1955) and in his best seller *The Godfather* (1969). Richard Wright's *Native Son* (1940) was a powerful portrayal of the fate of the American black; and Ralph Ellison's *Invisible Man* (1952), one of the distinguished novels of the period, displayed in forceful terms the struggle of the Negro for visibility in American society. James Baldwin in a series of books played upon the agony of two minorities—blacks and homosexuals.

Most striking of all was the emergence of a gifted generation of Jewish novelists. Coming from a rich traditional culture, afflicted by historical and contemporary woes, the best writers in this school not only offered vivid annotations of Jewish-American life but spoke in some sense for all minorities in the quest for self-understanding. Philip Roth in *Goodbye, Columbus* (1959) and *Portnoy's Complaint* (1969) combined a merciless novelist's eye with sharp comic and mimetic instincts. Bernard Malamud fabulized Jewish urban life in a series of piquant fantasies. J. D. Salinger's tales about the Glass family, especially in *Franny and Zooey* (1961), explored the possibilities of mysticism and sainthood in an affluent society. In *The Catcher in the Rye* (1951) Salinger also portrayed an adolescent crisis of identity—Huck Finn at an Eastern prep school—in terms that spoke arrestingly to a whole generation. And two other Jewish writers, Saul Bellow and Norman Mailer, transcended their cultural base to deal in large terms with the incoherence and anguish of contemporary life.

No American novelist dealt more searchingly with contemporary man than Bellow in such novels as *The Adventures of Augie March* (1953), *Seize the Day* (1954), *Herzog* (1964), and *Humboldt's Gift* (1975). He was the artist of the dialectic between inner consciousness and external society—the predicament of "civilized people" of whom his character Herzog said, "What they love is an imaginary human situation invented by their own genius and which they believe is the only true and the only human reality." But, where Bellow looked on the ravages of modernity with increasing distaste, his younger and less finished contemporary Mailer plunged truculently into the swirl around him.

War veteran, novelist, poet, journalist, film director and actor, political aspirant, pugilist, male chauvinist, showman, public personality, the spoiled and symptomatic talent of his time, Mailer saw art as, above all, the precipitate of minority experience. "What characterizes the sensations of being a member of a minority group," he wrote,

> is that one's emotions are forever locked in the chains of ambivalence—the expression of an emotion forever releasing its opposite—the ego in perpetual transit from the tower to the dungeon and back again. By this definition nearly everyone in America is a member of a minority group, alienated from the self by a double sense of identity and so at the mercy of a self which demands action and more action to define the most rudimentary borders of identity.

Though by the sixties some critics believed Mailer more comfortable in his nonfiction, like *The Armies of the Night* (1968) and *Of a Fire on the Moon* (1970), his highly charged reporting was of a piece with the vision of the American experience conveyed brilliantly in his novel *Why Are We in Vietnam?* (1967). The tension between rationality and irrationality, between the public act and the underground emotion, fascinated him; and though he himself wondered whether his "vision, for lack of some cultivation in the middle, was not too compulsively ready for the apocalyptic," no writer took on more cheerfully the existential risks of American art.

For some writers the key to chaos lay in disconnection and parody, as in the satiric fantasies of Kurt Vonnegut, Jr., who became especially popular among the young, or the cabalistic hallucinations of Donald Barthelme. The parallel development of "black humor" moved into a phase of exuberant if savage anarchism, well typified in Joseph Heller's war novel, *Catch-22* (1961), and concluded in nihilism with the sadistic "sick joke" and deliberate attempts, in the manner of Lennie Bruce, to become as wounding to as many people and groups as possible, exercises redeemed only by an evident component of self-loathing.

The cultural vibrations ran through poetry, where Robert Lowell in *Life Studies* (1959) and *For the Union Dead* (1964) registered the impact of an incoherent age on a Puritan sensibility, and where Sylvia Plath expressed the terror of women in a world of treacherous men. The best drama of the period, Eugene O'Neill's *A Long Day's Journey into Night*, was produced in 1956 but written fifteen years before. Arthur Miller revived the social drama in strong and somber plays like *Death of a Salesman* (1949); and such dramas as Tennessee Williams' *A Streetcar Named Desire* (1947) and Edward Albee's *Who's Afraid of Virginia Woolf?* (1962) concentrated with brilliant if cold effect on the pathology of modern life. In due course new currents struck the drama when the "theater of the absurd" of Ionesco and the "theater of cruelty" of Artaud came from Europe to stimulate American playwrights off Broadway, if not on.

Other arts were affected by the tendencies toward anarchy and nihilism. In painting, abstract expressionism superseded for a season the representational art of an earlier time. Jackson Pollock, who had died little known in 1956, was now taken up as the forerunner of an attempt to give the tensions of contemporary culture their objective correlative in color and design. In the sixties "pop art" sought to discover

Jackson Pollock, Autumn Rhythm, *oil on canvas, 105" x 207"*
George A. Hearn Fund, Metropolitan Museum of Art

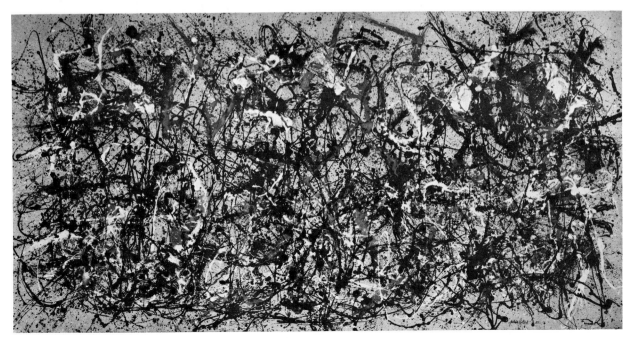

artistic significance in the commercial artifacts of contemporary civilization. Meantime John Cage and other composers explored the possibilities of experiment in music.

The velocity of history

The electronic society. The artistic sensibility itself seemed to be in a stage of profound dissociation. The Canadian Marshall McLuhan, a professional literary critic and amateur anthropologist, ascribed this condition to the basic shift that, in his view, western civilization was undergoing as it moved from a typographical to an electronic culture. Where Marx had located the motive force of history in changes in the means of production, McLuhan located it in changes in the means of communication.

The sensibility created by the print media, he argued, had given experience a frame and viewed it in sequence and from a distance. The print culture's qualities were logic, precision, specialization, individualism. But the world, and America first of all, was moving from the mechanical to the electronic age—the fantastic new epoch of electronic mechanisms of information, feedback and control, foreshadowed by movies, television, the computer, the space satellite. "Everything descends upon us from everywhere all at once," McLuhan wrote. "The contained, the distinct, the separate—our western legacy—are being replaced by the flowing, the unified, the fused." The new modes of communication, founded on instantaneity, simultaneity, and collectivity, promised to alter the very reflexes of psychological reaction and expectation. Where the print culture had programmed the mind in a one-at-a-time, step-by-step way, the electronic culture undermined linear processes of thought, replacing one-at-a-time by all-at-once. Though the terms of McLuhan's argument were extravagant and McLuhan himself soon fell out of fashion, there remained the possibility that, beneath the hyperbole and the showmanship, he was onto a significant and fertile truth.

Certainly the movement into the electronic age accentuated the gap between generations. Those born after 1950 were the first generation to grow up in the electronic environment. They may well have differed more from their parents than the older generation differed from its great-grandparents; all previous generations in the United States had been conditioned by the same linear culture. Indeed, as the pace of change intensified, the experience of parents became less relevant to the needs of children. Parents therefore were decreasingly effective as models and authorities.

Some observers even saw the old condemned by the whirl of history to become strangers in the land of the young.

The electronic age also contributed to the increasing instability of American politics. For a century a cluster of agencies—the political machine, the farm organization, the trade union, the chamber of commerce, the ethnic federation—had mediated between the politician and the voter, interceding for each on behalf of the other and providing the links that held the party system together. Electronic innovations were now severing those links and bypassing the traditional political structure. Television presented the politicians directly to the voter; public opinion polls presented the voter directly to the politician; and the mediating agencies were withering away.

As voters increasingly made their own judgments on the basis of what they themselves saw on the tiny screen, party loyalties, once as sacred as religious affiliations, lost their grip. Beginning in the fifties, voters began to use both parties for their own purposes, thus balancing off a Republican President with a Democratic Congress. Not only ticket-splitting but nonvoting increased. The proportion of voters describing themselves as "independent" grew strikingly. By the mid-seventies the "independent" party was twice as large as the Republican party (37 to 18 percent) and almost as large as the Democrats (42 percent). Among young voters independents outnumbered Democrats. The political analyst Samuel Lubell saw "a war of the voters against the party system." Some observers expected a trend toward multiple parties and minority victors; others even began to speculate about a "politics without parties." Whether or not the two-party system was in dissolution, no one could deny that it was in crisis.

The law of acceleration. The salient fact of the modern age was the increasing instability generated by the cumulative momentum of science and technology. Henry Adams had been the first American historian to note the ever-quickening acceleration in the velocity of history. "The world did not [just] double or treble its movement between 1800 and 1900," he wrote in "The Rule of Phase Applied to History" (1909), "but, measured by any standard known to science—by horsepower, calories, volts, mass in any shape—the tension and vibration and volume and so-called progression of society were fully a thousand times greater in 1900 than in 1800." And the pace of change, urged ever onward by the self-accelerating internal processes of scientific inquiry, increased exponentially in the twentieth century when, it was noted, of all the scientists who had ever lived in the history of the planet, 90 percent were alive and active.

844

Science, as it pushed back the frontiers of knowledge, was thrusting forward into the very bases of human life. The discovery in 1953 of the double-helical shape of deoxyribonucleic acid (DNA), for which the American James D. Watson and the Englishmen F. H. C. Crick and Maurice Wilkins received the Nobel Prize (1962), gave extraordinary new impetus to the field of molecular biology. The unveiling of the genetic code provided new insight into basic life processes and held out possibilities not only for the cure of genetic diseases but for genetic transplantation, test-tube babies, and "cloning"—that is, the production of genetically identical copies of individual human beings. In addition, scientists might soon develop the capacity through genetic surgery to alter man's genetic makeup. Scientists also saw the possibility of remolding not only the body but the mind, if not through genetic engineering, then through drugs, psychosurgery (operation on the brain in order to modify behavior), electrochemical controls, or the system of behavioral conditioning and reinforcements set forth by the psychologist B. F. Skinner.

Within a generation science had begun to devise the means to transform reproduction, consciousness, intellect, behavior, and the very genetic nature of human beings. These developments, opening frightening vistas of manipulation by white-coated Dr. Strangeloves, increased public suspicion of science. Scientists themselves recoiled from some of the consequences of their work. James D. Watson, reflecting on his clarification of the genetic code, called in 1971 for an end to experimentation with human cell fusion and embryos: "If we do not think about the matter now, the possibility of our having a free choice will one day suddenly be gone." In 1974 a group of prominent molecular biologists called for a moratorium on certain gene-transplant experiments.

Watson added that the idea science always moves forward "represents a form of laissez-faire nonsense dismally reminiscent of the creed that American business, if left to itself, will solve everybody's problems." If science and technology could not be left to themselves, they had to be brought under forms of social control. Leading scientists now helped found the Institute of Society, Ethics and Life to consider the moral problems raised by scientific success. Congress, which had established an Office of Technology Assessment in 1972, began in the mid-seventies to discuss the possibility of more comprehensive government supervision of scientific research. Some scientists, wishing to forestall government control, proposed "science courts" through which the scientific community itself could evaluate the social implications of research. Other scientists rejected this idea as the reintroduction of authoritarianism into science.

The last frontier. The most spectacular expression of the onward drive of science and technology came in humanity's leap into space. By the end of 1974 the United States and the Soviet Union had made over 1,600 successful spacecraft launchings (of which 783 were American). Kennedy's old idea of joint American-Russian orbital flights reached fruition in the Apollo-Soyuz mission in 1975. In the bicentennial year unmanned American spacecraft—Viking 1 and 2—successfully landed complex instrument packages on the surface of Mars and transmitted photographs and scientific data back to Earth. Two Pioneer spacecraft were flying past Jupiter through the asteroid belt toward Uranus and Saturn, where they were due to arrive in 1979. The development of the Space Shuttle, a reusable manned rocket, would make space flights routine; the system was scheduled to become operational by the end of the decade. The next years were expected to produce "skylabs" and other space stations and, in due course, a permanent manned base on the moon—all this bringing closer the world portrayed by Stanley Kubrick and Arthur C. Clarke in their haunting film *2001, A Space Odyssey* (1969). Though some Americans seemed almost blasé after half a dozen landings on the moon, the adventure of space and above all the possibility of life elsewhere in the galaxy were seizing the public imagination, as shown by the new popularity of science fiction and by the tremendous vogue in the mid-seventies of the television series *Star Trek*.

As the space probes went forward, the question was ever more insistently raised whether earthlings were alone in the universe. Finding evidence that the chemical elements basic to life existed beyond the earth's solar system, scientists worked on means to communicate with other intelligences in the universe. In 1971 American radio astronomers, physicists, biologists, and cryptographers joined colleagues from the Soviet Union and other nations at Byurakan Astro-

Apollo-Soyuz, 1975:
another spectacular expression

If extraterrestrial civilizations are ever discovered, the affect on human scientific and technological capabilities will be immense, and the discovery can positively influence the whole future of Man.... Why should an advanced society wish to expend the effort to communicate such information to a backward, emerging, novice civilization like our own? I can imagine that they are motivated by benevolence; that during their emerging phases, they were themselves helped along by such messages and that this is a tradition worthy of continuance.... I do not believe that there is any significant danger from the receipt of such a message, providing the most elementary cautions are adhered to.

From Carl Sagan, *The Cosmic Connection*, 1973.

A thousand, or ten thousand, years of evolutionary difference is just nothing on cosmic scales; and the chances that we could come across another civilization in the Universe at approximately the same level of development—and with which we could effect some kind of intellectual understanding—are, therefore, vanishingly small. And such being the case, what gain ... could we hope to derive from contacts with hypothetical civilisations which are likely to be removed, not thousands, but millions or hundred millions of years from our level? Certainly the risks entailed in such an encounter would vastly exceed any possible interest—let alone benefit; and could easily prove fatal. Therefore, should we ever hear that "space-phone" ringing in the form of observational evidence which may admit of no other explanation, for God's sake let us not answer; but rather make ourselves as inconspicuous as we can to avoid attracting attention.

**From Professor Zdenek Kopal, University of Manchester,
quoted in the London *Telegraph*, March 3, 1972.**

physical Observatory in Soviet Armenia for the world's first Conference on Communication with Extra-Terrestrial Intelligence. With every passing year, scientists around the world watched ever more urgently for signals from the sky, wondering what nature of being might be on similar watch in remote and unknown planets, what forms of intelligence, perhaps immeasurably superior forms, might exist in the cold reaches of galactic space.

After two centuries. July 4, 1976, marked the two hundredth anniversary of the Declaration of Independence. America was still a youngish nation. If one counted American history by generations, eight would span the entire national experience; if by lifetimes, three would nearly do it. Justice Oliver Wendell Holmes, who died just before his ninety-fourth birthday in 1935, told his last secretary: "Always remember that you have spoken to a man who once spoke to a veteran of the American Revolution." In 1976 there were still 166 widows receiving Civil War pensions.

As the republic faced its third century, many Americans found themselves in moods of unaccustomed foreboding. The feeling of immunity from world troubles, conferred at first by two great oceans, later by the brief monopoly of nuclear weapons, had slipped away. Americans now had a sense, new to their experience, of being on the defensive—of being shoved and harried by peremptory and hostile historical forces, at home as well as abroad. Polls reported an alarming increase in a sense of alienation from American society, a decline of confidence in institutions and leadership, even a fear of a breakdown in the country.

Still it was not necessary to accept the idea of irreversible decline. No one could doubt that the republic had its troubles. But, if the American crisis seemed acute, it was perhaps not the result of a peculiar depravity in the economic system or the national character. It may well have been because the revolution wrought of science and technology had gone farther in America than anywhere else. The world was changing faster than ever before, and changing fastest of all in America. As the nation on the farthest frontier of technological development, America had been the first to experience the shattering impact of the acceleration in the velocity of history. The crises were not uniquely American: they were the crises of modernity. Every nation, whatever its system of ide-

Into the third century

ology or ownership, would undergo comparable crises as it began to attain a comparable stage of technological development. The American turmoil might well be less the proof of decay than the price of progress.

As the processes of change gathered momentum, the immediate results had been—were almost bound to be—social and moral confusion, frustration, fear, violence. The challenge might well be insoluble within the existing value system. Could values change? Gunnar Myrdal, the Swedish social scientist, once remarked that a good thing about America's Calvinist tradition was the possibility of conversions: "I know of no nation in the world that can change its fundamental attitudes so rapidly as Americans." Certainly in half a century America had undergone notable conversions: from economic laissez faire to government intervention and regulation; from commitment to white supremacy to commitment to a multiracial society; from isolationism to globalism and then back toward a more selective internationalism; from the puritanical to the permissive society; from the idea that national morality required the prohibition of alcoholic beverages to the idea that drinking is a private habit; from male supremacy to sexual equality; from the exaltation to the questioning of economic growth. Such shifts displayed the national capacity to alter value systems. At the bicen-tennial, American values were again in flux. The turmoil, the confusion, even the violence could be the birth pangs of a new epoch in the history of man.

If Americans developed the intelligence, will, and leadership to control the law of acceleration, the United States could still avoid internal demoralization and disintegration. As Americans did this, they could begin to recover influence in the world by offering an example to other nations destined soon to struggle themselves with the problems created by the ever-quickening velocity of history.

So, entering their third century, facing new trials and opportunities, Americans found themselves somewhat in the situation of Scott Fitzgerald's Gatsby, who had come so long a way and whose "dream must have seemed so close that he could hardly fail to grasp it. He did not know that it was already behind him, somewhere back in that vast obscurity beyond the city, where the dark fields of the republic rolled on under the night.

"Gatsby believed in the green light, the orgastic future that year by year recedes before us. It eluded us then, but that's no matter—to-morrow we will run faster, stretch out our arms farther. . . . And one fine morning—

"So we beat on, boats against the current, borne back ceaselessly into the past."

Suggestions for reading

THE PEOPLE

Current apprehensions about the city are well summed up in the Report of the Commission on the Cities in the '70s, F. R. Harris and J. V. Lindsay, cochairmen, *The State of the Cities** (1972). R. C. Wood, *The Necessary Majority: Middle America and the Urban Crisis* (1972), records the conclusions of a former Secretary of Housing and Urban Development. E. C. Banfield, *The Unheavenly City* (1970), takes a more relaxed view. Jean Gottman, *Megalopolis** (1961), remains a valuable study. F. F. Piven and R. A. Cloward, *Regulating the Poor** (1971), provide a provocative analysis of the welfare system. Ramsey Clark, *Crime in America** (1970), is a humane survey. V. R. Fuchs and I. F. Leveson, *The Service Economy** (1968), describe the shift of labor from goods to services. The rise of the Southern rim is somewhat melodramatically portrayed in Kirkpatrick Sale, *Power Shift* (1975).

For the women's liberation movement, W. H. Chafe, *The American Woman, Her Changing Social, Economic and Political Roles, 1920–1970** (1974), and G. G. Yates, *What Women Want: The Ideas of the Movement* (1975), offer historical assessments. For documentation, see Betty Friedan, *The Feminine Mystique** (1963); Robin Morgan, ed., *Sisterhood is Powerful** (1970), and Judith Hole and Ellen Levine, *Rebirth of Feminism** (1972), two useful anthologies; and two perceptive discussions, Elizabeth Janeway, *Man's World, Women's Place: A Study in Social Mythology** (1971), and Juliet Mitchell, *Women's Estate* (1972). Midget Decter is critical in *The New Chastity** (1972). Michael Gordon, ed., *The Nuclear Family in Crisis** (1972), provides diverse views on the future of the family. Morton Hunt, *Sexual Behavior in the 1970s* (1974), brings Kinsey up to date. See also Paul Robinson, *The Modernization of Sex* (1976).

*Available in a paperback edition.

The problems of ethnicity are canvassed in Nathan Glazer and D. P. Moynihan, *Beyond the Melting Pot* (1963), and Glazer and Moynihan, eds., *Ethnicity: Theory and Experience* (1975). In *Affirmative Discrimination* (1975), Glazer questions government affirmative action policies. E. D. Baltzell, *The Protestant Establishment** (1964), describes the WASP at bay. Michael Novak, *The Rise of the Unmeltable Ethnics** (1972), hails the east European revolt. L. H. Fuchs, ed., *American Ethnic Politics* (1968), and Edgar Lilt, *Ethnic Politics in America* (1970), consider political implications.

Blue-collar workers are discussed in S. A. Levitan, ed., *Blue-Collar Workers* (1972), and Andrew Levison, *The Working Class Majority** (1974). S. A. Levitan, *et al., Still a Dream: The Changing Status of Blacks Since 1960* (1975), is a useful statistical survey. For the Mexican-Americans, see M. S. Meier and Feliciano Rivera, *The Chicanos** (1972), Hundley Norris, ed., *The Chicano* (1975), and F. C. Garcia, ed., *La Causa Politica: A Chicano Political Reader* (1975); Cesar Chavez is well portrayed in Peter Matthiessen, *Sal Si Puedes* (1969), and Jacques Levy, *Cesar Chavez* (1975). Piri Thomas records Puerto Rican life in the city in *Down These Mean Streets** (1967). Valuable works on the Indian are A. M. Josephy, ed., *Red Power** (1971); Stuart Levine and N. O. Lurie, eds., *The American Indian Today** (rev. ed., 1968); S. A. Levitan and Barbara Hetrick, *Big Brother's Indian Programs* (1972); and Margaret Szasz, *Education and the American Indian* (1974).

THE CULTURE

For diagnoses of the national condition, see A. M. Schlesinger, Jr., *The Crisis of Confidence* (1969), R. N. Goodwin, *The American Condition** (1974), and Daniel Bell, *The Cultural Contradictions of Capitalism* (1976). Marshall McLuhan's eccentric but suggestive views can be traced in *The Gutenberg Galaxy* (1962), *Understanding Media* (1964), and *The Medium Is the Massage* (1967). V. C. Ferkiss, *Technological Man** (1969), and Alvin Toffler, *Future Shock** (1970), speculate about the consequences for man and society of the increased velocity of history.

For contemporary developments in religion, see A. M. Greeley, *Come Blow Your Mind with Me* (1971), J. C. Cooper, *Religion in the Age of Aquarius** (1971), and D. E. Harrell, Jr., *All Things are Possible* (1975). Educational problems are considered in Charles Silberman, *Crisis in the Classroom* (1970); Jonathan Kozol, *Death at an Early Age** (1967); Paul Goodman, *Growing Up Absurd** (1960); Arthur Bestor, *The Restoration of Learning* (1955); and Christopher Jencks and David Riesman, *The Academic Revolution* (2nd ed., 1969).

The impact of movies is discussed in Amos Vogel, *Film As a Subversive Art* (1974), and Robert Sklar, *Movie-Made America* (1975). A series by Erik Barnouw describes the history of broadcasting in the United States; the impact of television is evaluated in N. N. Minow, *et al., Presidential Television* (1973), and Edwin Diamond, *The Tin Kazoo* (1975).

Norbert Wiener considers the impact of the electronic computer in *The Human Use of Human Beings: Cybernetics and Society** (1954); see also Martin Greenberger, ed., *Computers, Communications, and the Public Interest* (1972).

The case for the existence of other beings in the universe is analyzed in Carl Sagan and I. S. Shklovsky, *Intelligent Life in the Universe** (1968), and Sagan, *The Cosmic Connection** (1973). For the moonshot, see Henry Cooper, *Apollo on the Moon* (1969), and Norman Mailer, *Of a Fire on the Moon** (1971). B. W. Aldiss supplies a history of science fiction in *Billion Year Spree** (1973).

*Available in a paperback edition.

Into the third century

Appendix

The Declaration of Independence*

THE UNANIMOUS DECLARATION OF THE THIRTEEN UNITED STATES OF AMERICA,

WHEN in the Course of human events it becomes necessary for one people to dissolve the political bands which have connected them with another, and to assume among the Powers of the earth, the separate and equal station to which the Laws of Nature and of Nature's God entitle them, a decent respect to the opinions of mankind requires that they should declare the causes which impel them to the separation.

We hold these truths to be self-evident, that all men are created equal, that they are endowed by their Creator with certain unalienable Rights, that among these are Life, Liberty and the pursuit of Happiness. That to secure these rights, Governments are instituted among Men, deriving their just Powers from the consent of the governed. That whenever any Form of Government becomes destructive of these ends, it is the Right of the People to alter or to abolish it, and to institute new Government, laying its foundation on such principles and organizing its Powers in such form, as to them shall seem most likely to effect their Safety and Happiness. Prudence, indeed, will dictate that Governments long established should not be changed for light and transient causes; and accordingly all experience hath shewn, that mankind are more disposed to suffer, while evils are sufferable, than to right themselves by abolishing the forms to which they are accustomed. But when a long train of abuses and usurpations, pursuing invariably the same Object evinces a design to reduce them under absolute Despotism, it is their right, it is their duty, to throw off such Government, and to provide new Guards for their future security. Such has been the patient sufferance of these Colonies; and such is now the necessity which constrains them to alter their former Systems of Government. The history of the present King of Great Britain is a history of repeated injuries and usurpations, all having in direct object the establishment of an absolute

Tyranny over these States. To prove this, let Facts be submitted to a candid world.

He has refused his Assent to Laws, the most wholesome and necessary for the public good.

He has forbidden his Governors to pass Laws of immediate and pressing importance, unless suspended in their operation till his Assent should be obtained; and when so suspended, he has utterly neglected to attend to them.

He has refused to pass other Laws for the accommodation of large districts of people, unless those people would relinquish the right of Representation in the Legislature, a right inestimable to them and formidable to tyrants only.

He has called together legislative bodies at places unusual, uncomfortable, and distant from the depository of their Public Records, for the sole Purpose of fatiguing them into compliance with his measures.

He has dissolved Representative Houses repeatedly, for opposing with manly firmness his invasions on the rights of the People.

He has refused for a long time, after such dissolutions, to cause others to be elected; whereby the Legislative Powers, incapable of Annihilation, have returned to the People at large for their exercise; the State remaining in the mean time exposed to all the dangers of invasion from without, and convulsions within.

He has endeavoured to prevent the Population of these States; for that purpose obstructing the Laws for Naturalization of Foreigners; refusing to pass others to encourage their migrations hither, and raising the conditions of new Appropriations of Lands.

He has obstructed the Administration of Justice, by refusing his Assent to Laws for establishing Judiciary Powers.

He has made Judges dependent on his Will alone, for the tenure of their offices, and the amount and payment of their salaries.

He has erected a multitude of New Offices, and sent

*Reprinted from the facsimile of the engrossed copy in the National Archives. The original spelling, capitalization, and punctuation have been retained. Paragraphing has been added.

hither swarms of Officers to harrass our People, and eat out their substance.

He has kept among us, in times of peace, Standing Armies without the Consent of our legislatures.

He has affected to render the Military independent of and superior to the Civil Power.

He has combined with others to subject us to a jurisdiction foreign to our constitution, and unacknowledged by our laws; giving his Assent to their Acts of pretended Legislation:

For Quartering large bodies of armed troops among us:

For protecting them, by a mock Trial, from Punishment for any Murders which they should commit on the Inhabitants of these States:

For cutting off our Trade with all parts of the world:

For imposing Taxes on us without our Consent:

For depriving us in many cases, of the benefits of Trial by Jury:

For transporting us beyond Seas to be tried for pretended offences:

For abolishing the free System of English Laws in a neighbouring Province, establishing therein an Arbitrary government, and enlarging its Boundaries so as to render it at once an example and fit instrument for introducing the same absolute rule into these Colonies:

For taking away our Charters, abolishing our most valuable Laws, and altering fundamentally the Forms of our Governments:

For suspending our own Legislatures, and declaring themselves invested with Power to legislate for us in all cases whatsoever.

He has abdicated Government here, by declaring us out of his Protection, and waging War against us.

He has plundered our seas, ravaged our Coasts, burnt our towns, and destroyed the lives of our people.

He is at this time transporting large Armies of foreign Mercenaries to compleat the works of death, desolation and tyranny, already begun with circumstances of Cruelty and perfidy scarcely paralleled in the most barbarous ages, and totally unworthy the Head of a civilized nation.

He has constrained our fellow Citizens taken Captive on the high Seas to bear Arms against their Country, to become the executioners of their friends and Brethren, or to fall themselves by their Hands.

He has excited domestic insurrections amongst us, and has endeavoured to bring on the inhabitants of our frontiers, the merciless Indian Savages, whose known rule of warfare, is an undistinguished destruction of all ages, sexes and conditions.

In every stage of these Oppressions We have Petitioned for Redress in the most humble terms: Our repeated Petitions have been answered only by repeated injury. A Prince, whose character is thus marked by every act which may define a Tyrant, is unfit to be the ruler of a free People.

Nor have We been wanting in attentions to our Brittish brethren. We have warned them from time to time of attempts by their legislature to extend an unwarrantable jurisdiction over us. We have reminded them of the circumstances of our emigration and settlement here. We have appealed to their native justice and magnanimity, and we have conjured them by the ties of our common kindred to disavow these usurpations, which, would inevitably interrupt our connections and correspondence. They too have been deaf to the voice of justice and of consanguinity. We must, therefore, acquiesce in the necessity, which denounces our Separation, and hold them, as we hold the rest of mankind, Enemies in War, in Peace Friends.

WE, THEREFORE, the Representatives of the UNITED STATES OF AMERICA, in General Congress, Assembled, appealing to the Supreme Judge of the world for the rectitude of our intentions, do, in the Name, and by Authority of the good People of these Colonies, solemnly publish and declare, That these United Colonies are, and of Right ought to be FREE AND INDEPENDENT STATES; that they are Absolved from all Allegiance to the British Crown, and that all political connection between them and the State of Great Britain, is and ought to be totally dissolved; and that, as Free and Independent States, they have full Power to levy War, conclude Peace, contract Alliances, establish Commerce, and to do all other Acts and Things which Independent States may of right do. And for the support of this Declaration, with a firm reliance on the protection of divine Providence, we mutually pledge to each other our Lives, our Fortunes and our sacred Honor.

The Constitution
of the United States of America*

We the People of the United States, in Order to form a more perfect Union, establish Justice, insure domestic Tranquility, provide for the common defence, promote the general Welfare, and secure the Blessings of Liberty to ourselves and our Posterity, do ordain and establish this Constitution for the United States of America.

Article. I.

Section. 1. All legislative Powers herein granted shall be vested in a Congress of the United States, which shall consist of a Senate and House of Representatives.

Section. 2. The House of Representatives shall be composed of Members chosen every second Year by the People of the several States, and the Electors in each State shall have the Qualifications requisite for Electors of the most numerous Branch of the State Legislature.

No Person shall be a Representative who shall not have attained to the Age of twenty five Years, and been seven Years a Citizen of the United States, and who shall not, when elected, be an Inhabitant of that State in which he shall be chosen.

Representatives and direct Taxes† shall be apportioned among the several States which may be included within this Union, according to their respective Numbers, which shall be determined by adding to the whole Number of free Persons, including those bound to Service for a Term of Years, and excluding Indians not taxed, three fifths of all other Persons.‡ The actual Enumeration shall be made within three Years after the first Meeting of the Congress of the United States, and within every subsequent Term of ten Years, in such Manner as they shall by Law direct. The Number of Representatives shall not exceed one for every thirty Thousand, but each State shall have at Least one Representative; and until such enumeration shall be made, the State of New Hampshire shall be entitled to chuse three; Massachusetts eight; Rhode Island and Providence Plantations one; Connecticut five; New York six; New Jersey four; Pennsylvania eight; Delaware one; Maryland six; Virginia ten; North Carolina five; South Carolina five; and Georgia three.

When vacancies happen in the Representation from any State, the Executive Authority thereof shall issue Writs of Election to fill such Vacancies.

The House of Representatives shall chuse their Speaker and other Officers; and shall have the sole Power of Impeachment.

Section. 3. The Senate of the United States shall be composed of two Senators from each State, chosen by the Legislature thereof, for six Years; and each Senator shall have one Vote.*

Immediately after they shall be assembled in Consequence of the first Election, they shall be divided as equally as may be into three Classes. The Seats of the Senators of the first Class shall be vacated at the Expiration of the second Year, of the second Class at the Expiration of the fourth Year, and of the third Class at the Expiration of the sixth Year, so that one third may be chosen every second Year; and if Vacancies happen by Resignation, or otherwise, during the Recess of the Legislature of any State, the Executive thereof may make temporary Appointments until the next Meeting of the Legislature, which shall then fill such Vacancies.†

No Person shall be a Senator who shall not have attained to the Age of thirty Years, and been nine Years a Citizen of the United States, and who shall not, when elected, be an Inhabitant of that State for which he shall be chosen.

The Vice President of the United States shall be President of the Senate, but shall have no Vote, unless they be equally divided.

The Senate shall chuse their other Officers, and also a

---

*From the engrossed copy in the National Archives. Original spelling, capitalization, and punctuation have been retained.
† Modified by the Sixteenth Amendment.
‡ Replaced by the Fourteenth Amendment.

*Superseded by the Seventeenth Amendment.
† Modified by the Seventeenth Amendment.

President pro tempore, in the Absence of the Vice President, or when he shall exercise the Office of President of the United States.

The Senate shall have the sole Power to try all Impeachments. When sitting for that Purpose, they shall be on Oath or Affirmation. When the President of the United States is tried, the Chief Justice shall preside: And no Person shall be convicted without the Concurrence of two thirds of the Members present.

Judgment in Cases of Impeachment shall not extend further than to removal from Office, and disqualification to hold and enjoy any Office of honor, Trust or Profit under the United States: but the Party convicted shall nevertheless be liable and subject to Indictment, Trial, Judgment and Punishment, according to Law.

Section. 4. The Times, Places and Manner of holding Elections for Senators and Representatives, shall be prescribed in each State by the Legislature thereof, but the Congress may at any time by Law make or alter such Regulation, except as to the Places of chusing Senators.

The Congress shall assemble at least once in every Year, and such Meeting shall be on the first Monday in December, unless they shall by Law appoint a different Day.*

Section. 5. Each House shall be the Judge of the Elections, Returns and Qualifications of its own Members, and a Majority of each shall constitute a Quorum to do Business; but a smaller Number may adjourn from day to day, and may be authorized to compel the Attendance of absent Members, in such Manner, and under such Penalties as each House may provide.

Each House may determine the Rules of its Proceedings, punish its Members for disorderly Behaviour, and, with the Concurrence of two thirds, expel a Member.

Each House shall keep a Journal of its Proceedings, and from time to time publish the same, excepting such Parts as may in their Judgment require Secrecy; and the Yeas and Nays of the Members of either House on any question shall, at the Desire of one fifth of those Present, be entered on the Journal.

Neither House, during the Session of Congress, shall, without the Consent of the other, adjourn for more than three days, nor to any other Place than that in which the two Houses shall be sitting.

Section. 6. The Senators and Representatives shall receive a Compensation for their Services, to be ascertained by Law, and paid out of the Treasury of the United States. They shall in all Cases, except Treason, Felony and Breach of the Peace, be privileged from Arrest during their Attendance at the Session of their respective Houses, and in going to and returning from the same; and for any Speech or Debate in either House, they shall not be questioned in any other Place.

No Senator or Representative shall, during the Time for which he was elected, be appointed to any civil Office under the Authority of the United States, which shall have been created, or the Emoluments whereof shall have been encreased during such time; and no Person holding any Office under the United States, shall be a Member of either House during his Continuance in Office.

Section. 7. All Bills for raising Revenue shall originate in the House of Representatives; but the Senate may propose or concur with Amendments as on other Bills.

Every Bill which shall have passed the House of Representatives and the Senate shall, before it become a Law, be presented to the President of the United States; If he approve he shall sign it, but if not he shall return it, with his Objections to that House in which it shall have originated, who shall enter the Objections at large on their Journal, and proceed to reconsider it. If after such Reconsideration two thirds of that House shall agree to pass the Bill, it shall be sent, together with the Objections, to the other House, by which it shall likewise be reconsidered, and if approved by two thirds of that House, it shall become a Law. But in all such Cases the Votes of both Houses shall be determined by yeas and Nays, and the Names of the Persons voting for and against the Bill shall be entered on the Journal of each House respectively. If any Bill shall not be returned by the President within ten Days (Sundays excepted) after it shall have been presented to him, the Same shall be a Law, in like Manner as if he had signed it, unless the Congress by their Adjournment prevent its Return, in which Case it shall not be a Law.

Every Order, Resolution, or Vote to which the Concurrence of the Senate and House of Representatives may be necessary (except on a question of Adjournment) shall be presented to the President of the United States; and before the Same shall take Effect, shall be approved by him, or being disapproved by him shall be repassed by two thirds of the Senate and House of Representatives, according to the Rules and Limitations prescribed in the Case of a Bill.

Section. 8. The Congress shall have Power To lay and collect Taxes, Duties, Imposts and Excises, to pay the Debts and provide for the common Defence and general Welfare of the United States; but all Duties, Imposts and Excises shall be uniform throughout the United States;

To borrow Money on the credit of the United States;

To regulate Commerce with foreign Nations, and among the several States, and with the Indian Tribes;

To establish an uniform Rule of Naturalization, and uniform Laws on the subject of Bankruptcies throughout the United States;

To coin Money, regulate the Value thereof, and of foreign Coin, and fix the Standard of Weights and Measures;

To provide for the Punishment of counterfeiting the Securities and current Coin of the United States;

To establish Post Offices and post Roads;

To promote the Progress of Science and useful Arts, by securing for limited Times to Authors and Inventors the exclusive Right to their respective Writings and Discoveries;

*Superseded by the Twentieth Amendment.

To constitute Tribunals inferior to the supreme Court;

To define and punish Piracies and Felonies committed on the high Seas, and Offences against the Law of Nations;

To declare War, grant Letters of Marque and Reprisal, and make Rules concerning Captures on Land and Water;

To raise and support Armies, but no Appropriation of Money to that Use shall be for a longer Term than two Years;

To provide and maintain a Navy;

To make Rules for the Government and Regulation of the land and naval Forces;

To provide for calling forth the Militia to execute the Laws of the Union, suppress Insurrections and repel Invasions;

To provide for organizing, arming, and disciplining, the Militia, and for governing such Part of them as may be employed in the Service of the United States, reserving to the States respectively, the Appointment of the Officers, and the Authority of training the Militia according to the discipline prescribed by Congress;

To exercise exclusive Legislation in all Cases whatsoever, over such District (not exceeding ten Miles square) as may, by Cession of particular States, and the Acceptance of Congress, become the Seat of the Government of the United States, and to exercise like Authority over all Places purchased by the Consent of the Legislature of the State in which the Same shall be, for the Erection of Forts, Magazines, Arsenals, dock-Yards, and other needful Buildings;—And

To make all Laws which shall be necessary and proper for carrying into Execution the foregoing Powers, and all other Powers vested by this Constitution in the Government of the United States, or in any Department or Officer thereof.

Section. 9. The Migration or Importation of such Persons as any of the States now existing shall think proper to admit, shall not be prohibited by the Congress prior to the Year one thousand eight hundred and eight, but a Tax or duty may be imposed on such Importation, not exceeding ten dollars for each Person.

The Privilege of the Writ of Habeas Corpus shall not be suspended, unless when in Cases of Rebellion or Invasion the public Safety may require it.

No Bill of Attainder or ex post facto Law shall be passed.

No Capitation, or other direct, Tax shall be laid, unless in Proportion to the Census or Enumeration herein before directed to be taken.

No Tax or Duty shall be laid on Articles exported from any State.

No Preference shall be given by any Regulation of Commerce or Revenue to the Ports of one State over those of another: nor shall Vessels bound to, or from, one State, be obliged to enter, clear, or pay Duties in another.

No Money shall be drawn from the Treasury, but in Consequence of Appropriations made by Law, and a regular Statement and Account of the Receipts and Expenditures of all public Money shall be published from time to time.

No Title of Nobility shall be granted by the United States: And no Person holding any Office of Profit or Trust under them, shall, without the Consent of the Congress, accept of any present, Emolument, Office, or Title, of any kind whatever, from any King, Prince, or foreign State. Section. 10. No State shall enter into any Treaty, Alliance, or Confederation; grant Letters of Marque and Reprisal; coin Money; emit Bills of Credit; make any Thing but gold and silver Coin a Tender in Payment of Debts; pass any Bill of Attainder, ex post facto Law, or Law impairing the Obligation of Contracts, or grant any Title of Nobility.

No State shall, without the Consent of the Congress, lay any Imposts or Duties on Imports or Exports, except what may be absolutely necessary for executing its inspection Laws: and the net Produce of all Duties and Imposts, laid by any State on Imports or Exports, shall be for the Use of the Treasury of the United States; and all such Laws shall be subject to the Revision and Controul of the Congress.

No State shall, without the Consent of Congress, lay any Duty of Tonnage, keep Troops, or Ships of War in time of Peace, enter into any Agreement or Compact with another State, or with a foreign Power, or engage in War, unless actually invaded, or in such imminent Danger as will not admit of delay.

Article. II.

Section. 1. The executive Power shall be vested in a President of the United States of America. He shall hold his Office during the Term of four Years, and, together with the Vice President, chosen for the same Term, be elected, as follows:

Each State shall appoint, in such Manner as the Legislature thereof may direct, a Number of Electors, equal to the whole Number of Senators and Representatives to which the State may be entitled in the Congress: but no Senator or Representative, or Person holding an Office of Trust or Profit under the United States, shall be appointed an Elector.

The Electors shall meet in their respective States, and vote by Ballot for two Persons, of whom one at least shall not be an Inhabitant of the same State with themselves. And they shall make a List of all the Persons voted for, and of the Number of Votes for each; which List they shall sign and certify, and transmit sealed to the Seat of the Government of the United States, directed to the President of the Senate. The President of the Senate shall, in the Presence of the Senate and House of Representatives, open all the Certificates, and the Votes shall then be counted. The Person having the greatest Number of Votes shall be the President, if such Number be a Majority of the whole Number of Electors appointed; and if there be more than one who have such Majority, and have an equal Number of Votes, then the House of Representatives shall immediately chuse by Ballot one of them for President; and if no Person have a Majority, then from the five highest on the List the said House shall in like Manner chuse the President. But in chusing the President, the Votes shall be taken by States, the Representation from each State having one Vote; A quorum for this Purpose shall consist of a Member or Members from two thirds of the States, and a Majority of all the States shall be necessary to a Choice. In every Case, after the Choice of the President, the Person having the greatest Number of Votes of the Electors shall be the Vice President. But if there should remain two or more who have equal Votes, the Senate shall chuse from them by Ballot the Vice President.*

The Congress may determine the Time of chusing the Electors, and the Day on which they shall give their Votes; which Day shall be the same throughout the United States.

No Person except a natural born Citizen, or a Citizen of the United States, at the time of the Adoption of this Constitution, shall be eligible to the Office of President; neither shall any Person be eligible to that Office who shall not have attained to the Age of thirty five Years, and been fourteen Years a Resident within the United States.

In Case of the Removal of the President from Office, or of his Death, Resignation, or Inability to discharge the Powers and Duties of the said Office, the Same shall devolve on the Vice President, and the Congress may by Law provide for the Case of Removal, Death, Resignation or Inability, both of the President and Vice President, declaring what Officer shall then act as President, and such Officer shall act accordingly, until the Disability be removed, or a President shall be elected.†

The President shall, at stated Times, receive for his Services, a Compensation, which shall neither be encreased nor diminished during the Period for which he shall have been elected, and he shall not receive within that Period any other Emolument from the United States, or any of them.

Before he enter on the Execution of his Office, he shall take the following Oath or Affirmation:—''I do solemnly swear (or affirm) that I will faithfully execute the Office of President of the United States, and will to the best of my Ability, preserve, protect and defend the Constitution of the United States.''

Section. 2. The President shall be Commander in Chief of the Army and Navy of the United States, and of the Militia of the several States, when called into the actual Service of the United States; he may require the Opinion, in writing, of the principal Officer in each of the executive Departments, upon any Subject relating to the Duties of their respective Offices, and he shall have Power to grant Reprieves and Pardons for Offences against the United States, except in Cases of Impeachment.

He shall have Power, by and with the Advice and Consent of the Senate, to make Treaties, provided two thirds of the Senators present concur; and he shall nominate, and by and with the Advice and Consent of the Senate, shall appoint Ambassadors, other public Ministers and Consuls, Judges of the supreme Court, and all other Officers of the United States, whose Appointments are not herein otherwise provided for, and which shall be established by Law; but the Congress may by Law vest the Appointment of such inferior Officers, as they think proper, in the President alone, in the Courts of Law, or in the Heads of Departments.

The President shall have Power to fill up all Vacancies that may happen during the Recess of the Senate, by granting Commissions which shall expire at the End of their next Session.

Section. 3. He shall from time to time give to the Congress Information of the State of the Union, and recommend to their Consideration such Measures as he shall judge necessary and expedient; he may, on extraordinary Occasions, convene both Houses, or either of them, and in Case of Disagreement between them, with Respect to the Time of Adjournment, he may adjourn them to such Time as he shall think proper; he shall receive Ambassadors and other public Ministers; he shall take Care that the Laws be faithfully executed, and shall Commission all the Officers of the United States.

Section. 4. The President, Vice President and all civil Officers of the United States, shall be removed from Office on Impeachment for, and Conviction of, Treason, Bribery, or other high Crimes and Misdemeanors.

Article. III.

Section. 1. The judicial Power of the United States, shall be vested in one supreme Court, and in such inferior Courts as the Congress may from time to time ordain and establish. The Judges, both of the supreme and inferior Courts, shall hold their Offices during good Behaviour, and shall, at stated Times, receive for their Services, a Compensation, which shall not be diminished during their Continuance in Office.

Section. 2. The judicial Power shall extend to all Cases, in Law and Equity, arising under this Constitution, the Laws of the United States, and Treaties made, or which shall be made, under their Authority;—to all Cases affecting Ambassadors, other public Ministers and Consuls;—to all Cases of admiralty and maritime Jurisdiction;—to Controversies to which the United States shall be a Party;—to Controversies between two or more States;—between a State and Citizens of another State;*—between Citizens of different States,—between Citizens of the same State

*Superseded by the Twelfth Amendment.
†Modified by the Twenty-fifth Amendment.

*Modified by the Eleventh Amendment.

claiming Lands under Grants of different States, and between a State, or the Citizens thereof, and foreign States, Citizens or Subjects.

In all Cases affecting Ambassadors, other public Ministers and Consuls, and those in which a State shall be Party, the supreme Court shall have original Jurisdiction. In all the other Cases before mentioned, the supreme Court shall have appellate Jurisdiction, both as to Law and Fact, with such Exceptions, and under such Regulations as the Congress shall make.

The Trial of all Crimes, except in Cases of Impeachment, shall be by Jury; and such Trial shall be held in the State where the said Crimes shall have been committed; but when not committed within any State, the Trial shall be at such Place or Places as the Congress may by Law have directed.

Section. 3. Treason against the United States, shall consist only in levying War against them, or in adhering to their Enemies, giving them Aid and Comfort. No Person shall be convicted of Treason unless on the Testimony of two Witnesses to the same overt Act, or on Confession in open Court.

The Congress shall have Power to declare the Punishment of Treason, but no Attainder of Treason shall work Corruption of Blood, or Forfeiture except during the Life of the Person attainted.

Article. IV.

Section. 1. Full Faith and Credit shall be given in each State to the public Acts, Records, and judicial Proceedings of every other State. And the Congress may by general Laws prescribe the Manner in which such Acts, Records and Proceedings shall be proved, and the Effect thereof.

Section. 2. The Citizens of each State shall be entitled to all Privileges and Immunities of Citizens in the several States.

A Person charged in any State with Treason, Felony, or other Crime, who shall flee from Justice, and be found in another State, shall on Demand of the executive Authority of the State from which he fled, be delivered up, to be removed to the State having Jurisdiction of the Crime.

No Person held to Service or Labour in one State, under the Laws thereof, escaping into another, shall, in Consequence of any Law or Regulation therein, be discharged from such Service or Labour, but shall be delivered up on Claim of the Party to whom such Service or Labour may be due.

Section. 3. New States may be admitted by the Congress into this Union; but no new State shall be formed or erected within the Jurisdiction of any other State, nor any State be formed by the Junction of two or more States, or Parts of States, without the Consent of the Legislatures of the States concerned as well as of the Congress.

The Congress shall have Power to dispose of and make all needful Rules and Regulations respecting the Territory or other Property belonging to the United States; and nothing in this Constitution shall be so construed as to Prejudice any Claims of the United States, or of any particular State.

Section. 4. The United States shall guarantee to every State in this Union a Republican Form of Government, and shall protect each of them against Invasion; and on Application of the Legislature, or of the Executive (when the Legislature cannot be convened) against domestic Violence.

Article. V.

The Congress, whenever two thirds of both Houses shall deem it necessary, shall propose Amendments to this Constitution, or, on the Application of the Legislatures of two thirds of the several States, shall call a Convention for proposing Amendments, which, in either Case, shall be valid to all Intents and Purposes, as Part of this Constitution, when ratified by the Legislatures of three fourths of the several States, or by Conventions in three fourths thereof, as the one or the other Mode of Ratification may be proposed by the Congress; Provided that no Amendment which may be made prior to the Year One thousand eight hundred and eight shall in any Manner affect the first and fourth Clauses in the Ninth Section of the first Article; and that no State, without its Consent, shall be deprived of its equal Suffrage in the Senate.

Article. VI.

All Debts contracted and Engagements entered into, before the Adoption of this Constitution, shall be as valid against the United States under this Constitution, as under the Confederation.

This Constitution, and the Laws of the United States which shall be made in Pursuance thereof; and all Treaties made, or which shall be made, under the Authority of the United States, shall be the supreme Law of the Land; and the Judges in every State shall be bound thereby, any Thing in the Constitution or Laws of any State to the Contrary notwithstanding.

The Senators and Representatives before mentioned, and the Members of the several State Legislatures, and all executive and judicial Officers, both of the United States and of the several States, shall be bound by Oath or Affirmation, to support this Constitution; but no religious Test shall ever be required as a Qualification to any Office or public Trust under the United States.

Article. VII.

The Ratification of the Conventions of nine States, shall be sufficient for the Establishment of this Constitution between the States so ratifying the Same.

done in Convention by the Unanimous Consent of the States present the Seventeenth Day of September in the Year of our Lord one thousand seven hundred and Eighty seven and of the Independence of the United States of America the Twelfth. *In witness* whereof We have hereunto subscribed our Names,

Articles in Addition to, and Amendment of, the Constitution of the United States of America, Proposed by Congress, and Ratified by the Legislatures of the Several States, Pursuant to the Fifth Article of the Original Constitution.

Amendment I*

Congress shall make no law respecting an establishment of religion, or prohibiting the free exercise thereof; or abridging the freedom of speech, or of the press; or the right of the people peaceably to assemble, and to petition the Government for a redress of grievances.

Amendment II

A well regulated Militia, being necessary to the security of a free State, the right of the people to keep and bear Arms shall not be infringed.

Amendment III

No Soldier shall, in time of peace, be quartered in any house, without the consent of the Owner, nor in time of war, but in a manner to be prescribed by law.

Amendment IV

The right of the people to be secure in their persons, houses, papers, and effects, against unreasonable searches and seizures, shall not be violated, and no Warrants shall issue, but upon probable cause, supported by Oath or affirmation, and particularly describing the place to be searched, and the persons or things to be seized.

Amendment V

No person shall be held to answer for a capital or otherwise infamous crime, unless on a presentment or indictment of a Grand Jury, except in cases arising in the land or naval forces, or in the Militia, when in actual service in time of War or public danger; nor shall any person be subject for the same offence to be twice put in jeopardy of life or limb; nor shall be compelled in any criminal case to be a witness against himself, nor be deprived of life, liberty, or property, without due process of law; nor shall

private property be taken for public use, without just compensation.

Amendment VI

In all criminal prosecutions, the accused shall enjoy the right to a speedy and public trial, by an impartial jury of the State and district wherein the crime shall have been committed, which district shall have been previously ascertained by law, and to be informed of the nature and cause of the accusation; to be confronted with the witnesses against him; to have compulsory process for obtaining witnesses in his favor, and to have the Assistance of Counsel for his defence.

Amendment VII

In suits at common law, where the value in controversy shall exceed twenty dollars, the right of trial by jury shall be preserved, and no fact tried by a jury, shall be otherwise reexamined in any Court of the United States, than according to the rules of the common law.

Amendment VIII

Excessive bail shall not be required, nor excessive fines imposed, nor cruel and unusual punishments inflicted.

Amendment IX

The enumeration in the Constitution, of certain rights, shall not be construed to deny or disparage others retained by the people.

Amendment X

The powers not delegated to the United States by the Constitution; nor prohibited by it to the States, are reserved to the States respectively, or to the people.

Amendment XI*

The Judicial power of the United States shall not be construed to extend to any suit in law or equity, commenced or prosecuted against one of the United States by Citizens of another State, or by Citizens or Subjects of any Foreign State.

Amendment XII†

The Electors shall meet in their respective States and vote by ballot for President and Vice-President, one of whom, at least, shall not be an inhabitant of the same

*The first ten amendments were passed by Congress September 25, 1789. They were ratified by three-fourths of the states December 15, 1791.

*Passed March 4, 1794. Ratified January 23, 1795.
†Passed December 9, 1803. Ratified June 15, 1804.

State with themselves; they shall name in their ballots the person voted for as President, and in distinct ballots the person voted for as Vice-President, and they shall make distinct lists of all persons voted for as President, and of all persons voted for as Vice-President, and of the number of votes for each, which lists they shall sign and certify, and transmit sealed to the seat of the government of the United States, directed to the President of the Senate;—The President of the Senate shall, in the presence of the Senate and House of Representatives, open all the certificates and the votes shall then be counted;—The person having the greatest number of votes for President, shall be the President, if such number be a majority of the whole number of Electors appointed; and if no person have such majority, then from the persons having the highest numbers not exceeding three on the list of those voted for as President, the House of Representatives shall choose immediately, by ballot, the President. But in choosing the President, the votes shall be taken by states, the representation from each state having one vote; a quorum for this purpose shall consist of a member or members from two-thirds of the states, and a majority of all the states shall be necessary to a choice. And if the House of Representatives shall not choose a President whenever the right of choice shall devolve upon them, before the fourth day of March next following, then the Vice-President shall act as President, as in the case of the death or other constitutional disability of the President.—The person having the greatest number of votes as Vice-President, shall be the Vice-President, if such number be a majority of the whole number of Electors appointed, and if no person have a majority, then from the two highest numbers on the list, the Senate shall choose the Vice-President; a quorum for the purpose shall consist of two-thirds of the whole number of Senators, and a majority of the whole number shall be necessary to a choice. But no person constitutionally ineligible to the office of President shall be eligible to that of Vice-President of the United States.

Amendment XIII*

SECTION 1. Neither slavery nor involuntary servitude, except as a punishment for crime whereof the party shall have been duly convicted, shall exist within the United States, or any place subject to their jurisdiction.

SECTION 2. Congress shall have power to enforce this article by appropriate legislation.

Amendment XIV†

SECTION 1. All persons born or naturalized in the United States, and subject to the jurisdiction thereof, are citizens of the United States and of the State wherein they reside.

*Passed January 31, 1865. Ratified December 6, 1865.
†Passed June 13, 1866. Ratified July 9, 1868.

No State shall make or enforce any law which shall abridge the privileges or immunities of citizens of the United States; nor shall any State deprive any person of life, liberty, or property, without due process of law; nor deny to any person within its jurisdiction the equal protection of the laws.

SECTION 2. Representatives shall be apportioned among the several States according to their respective numbers, counting the whole number of persons in each State, excluding Indians not taxed. But when the right to vote at any election for the choice of electors for President and Vice-President of the United States, Representatives in Congress, the Executive and Judicial officers of a State, or the members of the Legislature thereof, is denied to any of the male inhabitants of such State, being twenty-one years of age, and citizens of the United States, or in any way abridged, except for participation in rebellion, or other crime, the basis of representation therein shall be reduced in the proportion which the number of such male citizens shall bear to the whole number of male citizens twenty-one years of age in such State.

SECTION 3. No person shall be a Senator or Representative in Congress, or elector of President and Vice-President, or hold any office, civil or military, under the United States, or under any State, who, having previously taken an oath, as a member of Congress, or as an officer of the United States, or as a member of any State legislature, or as an executive or judicial officer of any State, to support the Constitution of the United States, shall have engaged in insurrection or rebellion against the same, or given aid or comfort to the enemies thereof. But Congress may by a vote of two-thirds of each House, remove such disability.

SECTION 4. The validity of the public debt of the United States, authorized by law, including debts incurred for payment of pensions and bounties for services in suppressing insurrection or rebellion, shall not be questioned. But neither the United States nor any State shall assume or pay any debt or obligation incurred in aid of insurrection or rebellion against the United States, or any claim for the loss or emancipation of any slave; but all such debts, obligations, and claims shall be held illegal and void.

SECTION 5. The Congress shall have the power to enforce, by appropriate legislation, the provisions of this article.

Amendment XV*

SECTION 1. The right of citizens of the United States to vote shall not be denied or abridged by the United States or by any State on account of race, color, or previous condition of servitude—

SECTION 2. The Congress shall have power to enforce this article by appropriate legislation.

*Passed February 26, 1869. Ratified February 2, 1870.

Amendment XVI*

The Congress shall have power to lay and collect taxes on incomes, from whatever source derived, without apportionment among the several States, and without regard to any census or enumeration.

Amendment XVII†

The Senate of the United States shall be composed of two Senators from each State, elected by the people thereof, for six years; and each Senator shall have one vote. The electors in each State shall have the qualifications requisite for electors of the most numerous branch of the State legislatures.

When vacancies happen in the representation of any State in the Senate, the executive authority of such State shall issue writs of election to fill such vacancies: *Provided,* That the legislature of any State may empower the executive thereof to make temporary appointments until the people fill the vacancies by election as the legislature may direct.

This amendment shall not be so construed as to affect the election or term of any Senator chosen before it becomes valid as part of the Constitution.

Amendment XVIII‡

SECTION 1. After one year from the ratification of this article the manufacture, sale, or transportation of intoxicating liquors within, the importation thereof into, or the exportation thereof from the United States and all territory subject to the jurisdiction thereof for beverage purposes is hereby prohibited.

SECTION 2. The Congress and the several States shall have concurrent power to enforce this article by appropriate legislation.

SECTION 3. This article shall be inoperative unless it shall have been ratified as an amendment to the Constitution by the legislatures of the several States, as provided in the Constitution, within seven years from the date of the submission hereof to the States by the Congress.

Amendment XIX§

The right of citizens of the United States to vote shall not be denied or abridged by the United States or by any State on account of sex.

Congress shall have power to enforce this article by appropriate legislation.

*Passed July 12, 1909. Ratified February 3, 1913.
†Passed May 13, 1912. Ratified April 8, 1913.
‡Passed December 18, 1917. Ratified January 16, 1919.
§Passed June 4, 1919. Ratified August 18, 1920.

Amendment XX*

SECTION 1. The terms of the President and Vice-President shall end at noon on the 20th day of January, and the terms of Senators and Representatives at noon on the 3d day of January, of the years in which such terms would have ended if this article had not been ratified; and the terms of their successors shall then begin.

SECTION 2. The Congress shall assemble at least once in every year, and such meeting shall begin at noon on the 3d day of January, unless they shall by law appoint a different day.

SECTION 3. If, at the time fixed for the beginning of the term of the President, the President elect shall have died, the Vice-President elect shall become President. If a President shall not have been chosen before the time fixed for the beginning of his term, or if the President elect shall have failed to qualify, then the Vice-President elect shall act as President until a President shall have qualified; and the Congress may by law provide for the case wherein neither a President elect nor a Vice-President elect shall have qualified, declaring who shall then act as President, or the manner in which one who is to act shall be selected, and such person shall act accordingly until a President or Vice-President shall have qualified.

SECTION 4. The Congress may by law provide for the case of the death of any of the persons from whom the House of Representatives may choose a President whenever the right of choice shall have devolved upon them, and for the case of the death of any of the persons from whom the Senate may choose a Vice-President whenever the right of choice shall have devolved upon them.

SECTION 5. Sections 1 and 2 shall take effect on the 15th day of October following the ratification of this article.

SECTION 6. This article shall be inoperative unless it shall have been ratified as an amendment to the Constitution by the legislatures of three-fourths of the several States within seven years from the date of its submission.

Amendment XXI†

SECTION 1. The eighteenth article of amendment to the Constitution of the United States is hereby repealed.

SECTION 2. The transportation or importation into any State, Territory, or possession of the United States for delivery or use therein of intoxicating liquors, in violation of the laws thereof, is hereby prohibited.

SECTION 3. This article shall be inoperative unless it shall have been ratified as an amendment to the Constitution by conventions in the several States, as provided in the Constitution, within seven years from the date of the submission hereof to the States by the Congress.

*Passed March 2, 1932. Ratified January 23, 1933.
†Passed February 20, 1933. Ratified December 5, 1933.

Amendment XXII[*]

No person shall be elected to the office of the President more than twice, and no person who has held the office of President, or acted as President, for more than two years of a term to which some other person was elected President shall be elected to the office of the President more than once.

But this Article shall not apply to any person holding the office of President when this Article was proposed by the Congress, and shall not prevent any person who may be holding the office of President, or acting as President, during the term within which this Article becomes operative from holding the office of President or acting as President during the remainder of such term.

Amendment XXIII[†]

SECTION 1. The District constituting the seat of Government of the United States shall appoint in such manner as the Congress may direct:

A number of electors of President and Vice President equal to the whole number of Senators and Representatives in Congress to which the District would be entitled if it were a State, but in no event more than the least populous State; they shall be in addition to those appointed by the States, but they shall be considered, for the purposes of the election of President and Vice President, to be electors appointed by the State; and they shall meet in the District and perform such duties as provided by the twelfth article of amendment.

SECTION 2. The Congress shall have power to enforce this article by appropriate legislation.

Amendment XXIV[‡]

SECTION 1. The right of citizens of the United States to vote in any primary or other election for President or Vice President, or for Senator or Representative in Congress, shall not be denied or abridged by the United States or any State by reason of failure to pay any poll tax or other tax.

SECTION 2. The Congress shall have power to enforce this article by appropriate legislation.

Amendment XXV[§]

SECTION 1. In case of the removal of the President from office or of his death or resignation, the Vice President shall become President.

*Passed March 12, 1947. Ratified March 1, 1951.
† Passed June 16, 1960. Ratified April 3, 1961.
‡ Passed August 27, 1962. Ratified January 23, 1964.
§ Passed July 6, 1965. Ratified February 11, 1967.

SECTION 2. Whenever there is a vacancy in the office of the Vice President, the President shall nominate a Vice President who shall take office upon confirmation by a majority vote of both Houses of Congress.

SECTION 3. Whenever the President transmits to the President pro tempore of the Senate and the Speaker of the House of Representatives his written declaration that he is unable to discharge the powers and duties of his office, and until he transmits to them a written declaration to the contrary, such powers and duties shall be discharged by the Vice President as Acting President.

SECTION 4. Whenever the Vice President and a majority of either the principal officers of the executive department or of such other body as Congress may by law provide, transmit to the President pro tempore of the Senate and the Speaker of the House of Representatives their written declaration that the President is unable to discharge the powers and duties of his office, the Vice President shall immediately assume the powers and duties of the office of Acting President.

Thereafter, when the President transmits to the President pro tempore of the Senate and the Speaker of the House of Representatives his written declaration that no inability exists, he shall resume the powers and duties of his office unless the Vice President and a majority of either the principal officers of the executive department or of such other body as Congress may by law provide, transmit within four days to the President pro tempore of the Senate and the Speaker of the House of Representatives their written declaration that the President is unable to discharge the powers and duties of his office. Thereupon Congress shall decide the issue, assembling within forty-eight hours for that purpose if not in session. If the Congress, within twenty-one days after receipt of the latter written declaration, or, if Congress is not in session, within twenty-one days after Congress is required to assemble, determines by two-thirds vote of both Houses that the President is unable to discharge the powers and duties of his office, the Vice President shall continue to discharge the same as Acting President; otherwise, the President shall resume the powers and duties of his office.

Amendment XXVI[*]

SECTION 1. The right of citizens of the United States, who are eighteen years of age or older, to vote shall not be denied or abridged by the United States or by any State on account of age.

SECTION 2. The Congress shall have power to enforce this article by appropriate legislation.

*Passed March 23, 1971. Ratified July 5, 1971.

Presidential elections (1789–1840)

Year	Number of states	Candidates	Parties	Popular vote	Electoral vote	Percentage of popular vote
1789	11	GEORGE WASHINGTON	No party designations		69	
		John Adams			34	
		Minor Candidates			35	
1792	15	GEORGE WASHINGTON	No party designations		132	
		John Adams			77	
		George Clinton			50	
		Minor Candidates			5	
1796	16	JOHN ADAMS	Federalist		71	
		Thomas Jefferson	Democratic-Republican		68	
		Thomas Pinckney	Federalist		59	
		Aaron Burr	Democratic-Republican		30	
		Minor Candiates			48	
1800	16	THOMAS JEFFERSON	Democratic-Republican		73	
		Aaron Burr	Democratic-Republican		73	
		John Adams	Federalist		65	
		Charles C. Pinckney	Federalist		64	
		John Jay	Federalist		1	
1804	17	THOMAS JEFFERSON	Democratic-Republican		162	
		Charles C. Pinckney	Federalist		14	
1808	17	JAMES MADISON	Democratic-Republican		122	
		Charles C. Pinckney	Federalist		47	
		George Clinton	Democratic-Republican		6	
1812	18	JAMES MADISON	Democratic-Republican		128	
		DeWitt Clinton	Federalist		89	
1816	19	JAMES MONROE	Democratic-Republican		183	
		Rufus King	Federalist		34	
1820	24	JAMES MONROE	Democratic-Republican		231	
		John Quincy Adams	Independent Republican		1	
1824	24	JOHN QUINCY ADAMS	Democratic-Republican	108,740	84	30.5
		Andrew Jackson	Democratic-Republican	153,544	99	43.1
		William H. Crawford	Democratic-Republican	46,618	41	13.1
		Henry Clay	Democratic-Republican	47,136	37	13.2
1828	24	ANDREW JACKSON	Democratic	647,286	178	56.0
		John Quincy Adams	National Republican	508,064	83	44.0
1832	24	ANDREW JACKSON	Democratic	687,502	219	55.0
		Henry Clay	National Republican	530,189	49	42.4
		William Wirt	Anti-Masonic	33,108	7	2.6
		John Floyd	National Republican		11	
1836	26	MARTIN VAN BUREN	Democratic	765,483	170	50.9
		William H. Harrison	Whig	739,795	73	49.1
		Hugh L. White	Whig		26	
		Daniel Webster	Whig		14	
		W. P. Mangum	Whig		11	
1840	26	WILLIAM H. HARRISON	Whig	1,274,624	234	53.1
		Martin Van Buren	Democratic	1,127,781	60	46.9

Candidates receiving less than 1 percent of the popular vote have been omitted. For that reason the percentage of popular vote given for any election year may not total 100 percent.

Before the passage of the Twelfth Amendment in 1804, the Electoral College voted for two presidential candidates; the runner-up became Vice President. Figures are from *Historical Statistics of the United States, Colonial Times to 1957* (1961), pp. 682–83; and the U.S. Department of Justice.

Presidential elections (1844–1900)

Year	Number of states	Candidates	Parties	Popular vote	Electoral vote	Percentage of popular vote
1844	26	JAMES K. POLK	Democratic	1,338,464	170	49.6
		Henry Clay	Whig	1,300,097	105	48.1
		James G. Birney	Liberty	62,300		2.3
1848	30	ZACHARY TAYLOR	Whig	1,360,967	163	47.4
		Lewis Cass	Democratic	1,222,342	127	42.5
		Martin Van Buren	Free Soil	291,263		10.1
1852	31	FRANKLIN PIERCE	Democratic	1,601,117	254	50.9
		Winfield Scott	Whig	1,385,453	42	44.1
		John P. Hale	Free Soil	155,825		5.0
1856	31	JAMES BUCHANAN	Democratic	1,832,955	174	45.3
		John C. Frémont	Republican	1,339,932	114	33.1
		Millard Fillmore	American	871,731	8	21.6
1860	33	ABRAHAM LINCOLN	Republican	1,865,593	180	39.8
		Stephen A. Douglas	Democratic	1,382,713	12	29.5
		John C. Breckinridge	Democratic	848,356	72	18.1
		John Bell	Constitutional Union	592,906	39	12.6
1864	36	ABRAHAM LINCOLN	Republican	2,206,938	212	55.0
		George B. McClellan	Democratic	1,803,787	21	45.0
1868	37	ULYSSES S. GRANT	Republican	3,013,421	214	52.7
		Horatio Seymour	Democratic	2,706,829	80	47.3
1872	37	ULYSSES S. GRANT	Republican	3,596,745	286	55.6
		Horace Greeley	Democratic	2,843,446	*	43.9
1876	38	RUTHERFORD B. HAYES	Republican	4,036,572	185	48.0
		Samuel J. Tilden	Democratic	4,284,020	184	51.0
1880	38	JAMES A. GARFIELD	Republican	4,453,295	214	48.5
		Winfield S. Hancock	Democratic	4,414,082	155	48.1
		James B. Weaver	Greenback-Labor	308,578		3.4
1884	38	GROVER CLEVELAND	Democratic	4,879,507	219	48.5
		James G. Blaine	Republican	4,850,293	182	48.2
		Benjamin F. Butler	Greenback-Labor	175,370		1.8
		John P. St. John	Prohibition	150,369		1.5
1888	38	BENJAMIN HARRISON	Republican	5,477,129	233	47.9
		Grover Cleveland	Democratic	5,537,857	168	48.6
		Clinton B. Fisk	Prohibition	249,506		2.2
		Anson J. Streeter	Union Labor	146,935		1.3
1892	44	GROVER CLEVELAND	Democratic	5,555,426	277	46.1
		Benjamin Harrison	Republican	5,182,690	145	43.0
		James B. Weaver	People's	1,029,846	22	8.5
		John Bidwell	Prohibition	264,133		2.2
1896	45	WILLIAM McKINLEY	Republican	7,102,246	271	51.1
		William J. Bryan	Democratic	6,492,559	176	47.7
1900	45	WILLIAM McKINLEY	Republican	7,218,491	292	51.7
		William J. Bryan	Democratic; Populist	6,356,734	155	45.5
		John C. Wooley	Prohibition	208,914		1.5

*Greeley died shortly after the election; the electors supporting him then divided their votes among minor candidates.
Candidates receiving less than 1 percent of the popular vote have been omitted. For that reason the percentage of popular vote given for any election year may not total 100 percent.

Presidential elections (1904–1956)

Year	Number of states	Candidates	Parties	Popular vote	Electoral vote	Percentage of popular vote
1904	45	THEODORE ROOSEVELT	Republican	7,628,461	336	57.4
		Alton B. Parker	Democratic	5,084,223	140	37.6
		Eugene V. Debs	Socialist	402,283		3.0
		Silas C. Swallow	Prohibition	258,536		1.9
1908	46	WILLIAM H. TAFT	Republican	7,675,320	321	51.6
		William J. Bryan	Democratic	6,412,294	162	43.1
		Eugene V. Debs	Socialist	420,793		2.8
		Eugene W. Chafin	Prohibition	253,840		1.7
1912	48	WOODROW WILSON	Democratic	6,296,547	435	41.9
		Theodore Roosevelt	Progressive	4,118,571	88	27.4
		William H. Taft	Republican	3,486,720	8	23.2
		Eugene V. Debs	Socialist	900,672		6.0
		Eugene W. Chafin	Prohibition	206,275		1.4
1916	48	WOODROW WILSON	Democratic	9,127,695	277	49.4
		Charles E. Hughes	Republican	8,533,507	254	46.2
		A. L. Benson	Socialist	585,113		3.2
		J. Frank Hanly	Prohibition	220,506		1.2
1920	48	WARREN G. HARDING	Republican	16,143,407	404	60.4
		James N. Cox	Democratic	9,130,328	127	34.2
		Eugene V. Debs	Socialist	919,799		3.4
		P. P. Christensen	Farmer-Labor	265,411		1.0
1924	48	CALVIN COOLIDGE	Republican	15,718,211	382	54.0
		John W. Davis	Democratic	8,385,283	136	28.8
		Robert M. La Follette	Progressive	4,831,289	13	16.6
1928	48	HERBERT C. HOOVER	Republican	21,391,993	444	58.2
		Alfred E. Smith	Democratic	15,016,169	87	40.9
1932	48	FRANKLIN D. ROOSEVELT	Democratic	22,809,638	472	57.4
		Herbert C. Hoover	Republican	15,758,901	59	39.7
		Norman Thomas	Socialist	881,951		2.2
1936	48	FRANKLIN D. ROOSEVELT	Democratic	27,752,869	523	60.8
		Alfred M. Landon	Republican	16,674,665	8	36.5
		William Lemke	Union	882,479		1.9
1940	48	FRANKLIN D. ROOSEVELT	Democratic	27,307,819	449	54.8
		Wendell L. Willkie	Republican	22,321,018	82	44.8
1944	48	FRANKLIN D. ROOSEVELT	Democratic	25,606,585	432	53.5
		Thomas E. Dewey	Republican	22,014,745	99	46.0
1948	48	HARRY S TRUMAN	Democratic	24,105,812	303	49.5
		Thomas E. Dewey	Republican	21,970,065	189	45.1
		J. Strom Thurmond	States' Rights	1,169,063	39	2.4
		Henry A. Wallace	Progressive	1,157,172		2.4
1952	48	DWIGHT D. EISENHOWER	Republican	33,936,234	442	55.1
		Adlai E. Stevenson	Democratic	27,314,992	89	44.4
1956	48	DWIGHT D. EISENHOWER	Republican	35,590,472	457	57.6
		Adlai E. Stevenson	Democratic	26,022,752	73	42.1

Candidates receiving less than 1 percent of the popular vote have been omitted. For that reason the percentage of popular vote given for any election year may not total 100 percent.

Presidential elections (1960–1976)

Year	Number of states	Candidates	Parties	Popular vote	Electoral vote	Percentage of popular vote
1960	50	JOHN F. KENNEDY	Democratic	34,227,096	303	49.9
		Richard M. Nixon	Republican	34,108,546	219	49.6
1964	50	LYNDON B. JOHNSON	Democratic	43,126,506	486	61.1
		Barry M. Goldwater	Republican	27,176,799	52	38.5
1968	50	RICHARD M. NIXON	Republican	31,785,480	301	43.4
		Hubert H. Humphrey	Democratic	31,275,165	191	42.7
		George C. Wallace	American Independent	9,906,473	46	13.5
1972	50	RICHARD M. NIXON	Republican	47,169,911	520	60.7
		George S. McGovern	Democratic	29,170,383	17	37.5
1976	50	JIMMY CARTER	Democratic	40,827,394	297	50.0
		Gerald R. Ford	Republican	39,145,977	240	47.9

Candidates receiving less than 1 percent of the popular vote have been omitted. For that reason the percentage of popular vote given for any election year may not total 100 percent.

Admission of states

Order of admission	State	Date of admission	Order of admission	State	Date of admission
1	Delaware	December 7, 1787	26	Michigan	January 26, 1837
2	Pennsylvania	December 12, 1787	27	Florida	March 3, 1845
3	New Jersey	December 18, 1787	28	Texas	December 29, 1845
4	Georgia	January 2, 1788	29	Iowa	December 28, 1846
5	Connecticut	January 9, 1788	30	Wisconsin	May 29, 1848
6	Massachusetts	February 7, 1788	31	California	September 9, 1850
7	Maryland	April 28, 1788	32	Minnesota	May 11, 1858
8	South Carolina	May 23, 1788	33	Oregon	February 14, 1859
9	New Hampshire	June 21, 1788	34	Kansas	January 29, 1861
10	Virginia	June 25, 1788	35	West Virginia	June 30, 1863
11	New York	July 26, 1788	36	Nevada	October 31, 1864
12	North Carolina	November 21, 1789	37	Nebraska	March 1, 1867
13	Rhode Island	May 29, 1790	38	Colorado	August 1, 1876
14	Vermont	March 4, 1791	39	North Dakota	November 2, 1889
15	Kentucky	June 1, 1792	40	South Dakota	November 2, 1889
16	Tennessee	June 1, 1796	41	Montana	November 8, 1889
17	Ohio	March 1, 1803	42	Washington	November 11, 1889
18	Louisiana	April 30, 1812	43	Idaho	July 3, 1890
19	Indiana	December 11, 1816	44	Wyoming	July 10, 1890
20	Mississippi	December 10, 1817	45	Utah	January 4, 1896
21	Illinois	December 3, 1818	46	Oklahoma	November 16, 1907
22	Alabama	December 14, 1819	47	New Mexico	January 6, 1912
23	Maine	March 15, 1820	48	Arizona	February 14, 1912
24	Missouri	August 10, 1821	49	Alaska	January 3, 1959
25	Arkansas	June 15, 1836	50	Hawaii	August 21, 1959

Population of the United States (1790–1975)

Year	Total population (in thousands)	Number per square mile of land area (continental United States)	Year	Total population (in thousands)	Number per square mile of land area (continental United States)
1790	3,929	4.5	1837	15,843	
1791	4,056		1838	16,264	
1792	4,194		1839	16,684	
1793	4,332		1840	17,120	9.8
1794	4,469		1841	17,733	
1795	4,607		1842	18,345	
1796	4,745		1843	18,957	
1797	4,883		1844	19,569	
1798	5,021		1845	20,182	
1799	5,159		1846	20,794	
1800	5,297	6.1	1847	21,406	
1801	5,486		1848	22,018	
1802	5,679		1849	22,631	
1803	5,872		1850	23,261	7.9
1804	5,065		1851	24,086	
1805	6,258		1852	24,911	
1806	6,451		1853	25,736	
1807	6,644		1854	26,561	
1808	6,838		1855	27,386	
1809	7,031		1856	28,212	
1810	7,224	4.3	1857	29,037	
1811	7,460		1858	29,862	
1812	7,700		1859	30,687	
1813	7,939		1860	31,513	10.6
1814	8,179		1861	32,351	
1815	8,419		1862	33,188	
1816	8,659		1863	34,026	
1817	8,899		1864	34,863	
1818	9,139		1865	35,701	
1819	9,379		1866	36,538	
1820	9,618	5.6	1867	37,376	
1821	9,939		1868	38,213	
1822	10,268		1869	39,051	
1823	10,596		1870	39,905	13.4
1824	10,924		1871	40,938	
1825	11,252		1872	41,972	
1826	11,580		1873	43,006	
1827	11,909		1874	44,040	
1828	12,237		1875	45,073	
1829	12,565		1876	46,107	
1830	12,901	7.4	1877	47,141	
1831	13,321		1878	48,174	
1832	13,742		1879	49,208	
1833	14,162		1880	50,262	16.9
1834	14,582		1881	51,542	
1835	15,003		1882	52,821	
1836	15,423		1883	54,100	

Figures are from *Historical Statistics of the United States, Colonial Times to 1957* (1961), pp. 7, 8; *Statistical Abstract of the United States: 1974*, p. 5; Census Bureau for 1974 and 1975.

Appendix

Year	Total population (in thousands)	Number per square mile of land area (continental United States)	Year	Total population (in thousands)*	Number per square mile of land area (continental United States)
1884	55,379		1930	122,775	41.2
1885	56,658		1931	124,040	
1886	57,938		1932	124,840	
1887	59,217		1933	125,579	
1888	60,496		1934	126,374	
1889	61,775		1935	127,250	
1890	63,056	21.2	1936	128,053	
1891	64,361		1937	128,825	
1892	65,666		1938	129,825	
1893	66,970		1939	130,880	
1894	68,275		1940	131,669	44.2
1895	69,580		1941	133,894	
1896	70,885		1942	135,361	
1897	72,189		1943	137,250	
1898	73,494		1944	138,916	
1899	74,799		1945	140,468	
1900	76,094	25.6	1946	141,936	
1901	77,585		1947	144,698	
1902	79,160		1948	147,208	
1903	80,632		1949	149,767	
1904	82,165		1950	150,697	50.7
1905	83,820		1951	154,878	
1906	85,437		1952	157,553	
1907	87,000		1953	160,184	
1908	88,709		1954	163,026	
1909	90,492		1955	165,931	
1910	92,407	31.0	1956	168,903	
1911	93,868		1957	171,984	
1912	95,331		1958	174,882	
1913	97,227		1959	177,830	
1914	99,118		1960	178,464	60.1
1915	100,549		1961	183,672	
1916	101,966		1962	186,504	
1917	103,414		1963	189,197	
1918	104,550		1964	191,833	
1919	105,063		1965	194,237	
1920	106,466	35.6	1966	196,485	
1921	108,541		1967	198,629	
1922	110,055		1968	200,619	
1923	111,950		1969	202,599	
1924	114,113		1970	203,875	57.5†
1925	115,832		1971	207,045	
1926	117,399		1972	208,842	
1927	119,038		1973	210,396	
1928	120,501		1974	211,894	
1929	121,770		1975	213,631	

*Figures after 1940 represent total population including Armed Forces abroad, except in official census years.
† Figure includes Alaska and Hawaii.

Presidents, Vice Presidents, and Cabinet members (1789–1841)

President	Vice President	Secretary of State	Secretary of Treasury	Secretary of War
George Washington 1789–97	John Adams 1789–97	Thomas Jefferson 1789–94 Edmund Randolph 1794–95 Timothy Pickering 1795–97	Alexander Hamilton 1789–95 Oliver Wolcott 1795–97	Henry Knox 1789–95 Timothy Pickering 1795–96 James McHenry 1796–97
John Adams 1797–1801	Thomas Jefferson 1797–1801	Timothy Pickering 1797–1800 John Marshall 1800–01	Oliver Wolcott 1797–1801 Samuel Dexter 1801	James McHenry 1797–1800 Samuel Dexter 1800–01
Thomas Jefferson 1801–09	Aaron Burr 1801–05 George Clinton 1805–09	James Madison 1801–09	Samuel Dexter 1801 Albert Gallatin 1801–09	Henry Dearborn 1801–09
James Madison 1809–17	George Clinton 1809–13 Elbridge Gerry 1813–17	Robert Smith 1809–11 James Monroe 1811–17	Albert Gallatin 1809–14 George Campbell 1814 Alexander Dallas 1814–16 William Crawford 1816–17	William Eustis 1809–13 John Armstrong 1813–14 James Monroe 1814–15 William Crawford 1815–17
James Monroe 1817–25	Daniel D. Tompkins 1817–25	John Quincy Adams 1817–25	William Crawford 1817–25	George Graham 1817 John C. Calhoun 1817–25
John Quincy Adams 1825–29	John C. Calhoun 1825–29	Henry Clay 1825–29	Richard Rush 1825–29	James Barbour 1825–28 Peter B. Porter 1828–29
Andrew Jackson 1829–37	John C. Calhoun 1829–33 Martin Van Buren 1833–37	Martin Van Buren 1829–31 Edward Livingston 1831–33 Louis McLane 1833–34 John Forsyth 1834–37	Samuel Ingham 1829–31 Louis McLane 1831–33 William Duane 1833 Roger B. Taney 1833–34 Levi Woodbury 1834–37	John H. Eaton 1829–31 Lewis Cass 1831–37 Benjamin Butler 1837
Martin Van Buren 1837–41	Richard M. Johnson 1837–41	John Forsyth 1837–41	Levi Woodbury 1837–41	Joel R. Poinsett 1837–41

Appendix

Secretary of Navy	Postmaster General	Attorney General
	Samuel Osgood 1789–91 Timothy Pickering 1791–95 Joseph Habersham 1795–97	Edmund Randolph 1789–94 William Bradford 1794–95 Charles Lee 1795–97
Benjamin Stoddert 1798–1801	Joseph Habersham 1797–1801	Charles Lee 1797–1801
Benjamin Stoddert 1801 Robert Smith 1801–09	Joseph Habersham 1801 Gideon Granger 1801–09	Levi Lincoln 1801–05 John Breckinridge 1805-07 Caesar Rodney 1807–09
Paul Hamilton 1809–13 William Jones 1813–14 Benjamin Crowninshield 1814–17	Gideon Granger 1809–14 Return Meigs 1814–17	Caesar Rodney 1809–11 William Pinkney 1811–14 Richard Rush 1814–17
Benjamin Crowninshield 1817–18 Smith Thompson 1818–23 Samuel Southard 1823–25	Return Meigs 1817–23 John McLean 1823–25	Richard Rush 1817 William Wirt 1817–25
Samuel Southard 1825–29	John McLean 1825–29	William Wirt 1825–29
John Branch 1829–31 Levi Woodbury 1831–34 Mahlon Dickerson 1834–37	William Barry 1829–35 Amos Kendall 1835–37	John M. Berrien 1829–31 Roger B. Taney 1831–33 Benjamin Butler 1833–37
Mahlon Dickerson 1837–38 James K. Paulding 1838–41	Amos Kendall 1837–40 John M. Niles 1840–41	Benjamin Butler 1837–38 Felix Grundy 1838–40 Henry D. Gilpin 1840–41

Presidents, Vice Presidents, and Cabinet members (1841–77)

President	Vice President	Secretary of State	Secretary of Treasury	Secretary of War
William H. Harrison 1841	John Tyler 1841	Daniel Webster 1841	Thomas Ewing 1841	John Bell 1841
John Tyler 1841–45		Daniel Webster 1841–43 Hugh S. Legaré 1843 Abel P. Upshur 1843–44 John C. Calhoun 1844–45	Thomas Ewing 1841 Walter Forward 1841–43 John C. Spencer 1843–44 George M. Bibb 1844–45	John Bell 1841 John C. Spencer 1841–43 James M. Porter 1843–44 William Wilkins 1844–45
James K. Polk 1845–49	George M. Dallas 1845–49	James Buchanan 1845–49	Robert J. Walker 1845–49	William L. Marcy 1845–49
Zachary Taylor 1849–50	Millard Fillmore 1849–50	John M. Clayton 1849–50	William M. Meredith 1849–50	George W. Crawford 1849–50
Millard Fillmore 1850–53		Daniel Webster 1850–52 Edward Everett 1852–53	Thomas Corwin 1850–53	Charles M. Conrad 1850–53
Franklin Pierce 1853–57	William R. King 1853–57	William L. Marcy 1853–57	James Guthrie 1853–57	Jefferson Davis 1853–57
James Buchanan 1857–61	John C. Breckinridge 1857–61	Lewis Cass 1857–60 Jeremiah S. Black 1860–61	Howell Cobb 1857–60 Philip F. Thomas 1860–61 John A. Dix 1861	John B. Floyd 1857–61 Joseph Holt 1861
Abraham Lincoln 1861–65	Hannibal Hamlin 1861–65 Andrew Johnson 1865	William H. Seward 1861–65	Salmon P. Chase 1861–64 William P. Fessenden 1864–65 Hugh McCulloch 1865	Simon Cameron 1861–62 Edwin M. Stanton 1862–65
Andrew Johnson 1865–69		William H. Seward 1865–69	Hugh McCulloch 1865–69	Edwin M. Stanton 1865–67 Ulysses S. Grant 1867–68 John M. Schofield 1868–69
Ulysses S. Grant 1869–77	Schuyler Colfax 1869–73 Henry Wilson 1873–77	Elihu B. Washburne 1869 Hamilton Fish 1869–77	George S. Boutwell 1869–73 William A. Richardson 1873–74 Benjamin H. Bristow 1874–76 Lot M. Morrill 1876–77	John A. Rawlins 1869 William T. Sherman 1869 William W. Belknap 1869–76 Alphonso Taft 1876 James D. Cameron 1876–77

Secretary of Navy	Postmaster General	Attorney General	Secretary of Interior
George E. Badger 1841	Francis Granger 1841	John J. Crittenden 1841	
George E. Badger 1841 Abel P. Upshur 1841–43 David Henshaw 1843–44 Thomas Gilmer 1844 John Y. Mason 1844–45	Francis Granger 1841 Charles A. Wickliffe 1841–45	John J. Crittenden 1841 Hugh S. Legaré 1841–43 John Nelson 1843–45	
George Bancroft 1845–46 John Y. Mason 1846–49	Cave Johnson 1845–49	John Y. Mason 1845–46 Nathan Clifford 1846–48 Isaac Toucey 1848–49	
William B. Preston 1849–50	Jacob Collamer 1849–50	Reverdy Johnson 1849–50	Thomas Ewing 1849–50
William A. Graham 1850–52 John P. Kennedy 1852–53	Nathan K. Hall 1850–52 Sam D. Hubbard 1852–53	John J. Crittenden 1850–53	Thomas McKennan 1850 A. H. H. Stuart 1850–53
James C. Dobbin 1853–57	James Campbell 1853–57	Caleb Cushing 1853–57	Robert McClelland 1853–57
Isaac Toucey 1857–61	Aaron V. Brown 1857–59 Joseph Holt 1859–61 Horatio King 1861	Jeremiah S. Black 1857–60 Edwin M. Stanton 1860–61	Jacob Thompson 1857–61
Gideon Welles 1861–65	Horatio King 1861 Montgomery Blair 1861–64 William Dennison 1864–65	Edward Bates 1861–64 James Speed 1864–65	Caleb B. Smith 1861–63 John P. Usher 1863–65
Gideon Welles 1865–69	William Dennison 1865–66 Alexander Randall 1866–69	James Speed 1865–66 Henry Stanbery 1866–68 William M. Evarts 1868–69	John P. Usher 1865 James Harlan 1865–66 O. H. Browning 1866–69
Adolph E. Borie 1869 George M. Robeson 1869–77	John A. J. Creswell 1869–74 James W. Marshall 1874 Marshall Jewell 1874–76 James N. Tyner 1876–77	Ebenezer R. Hoar 1869–70 Amos T. Akerman 1870–71 G. H. Williams 1871–75 Edwards Pierrepont 1875–76 Alphonso Taft 1876–77	Jacob D. Cox 1869–70 Columbus Delano 1870–75 Zachariah Chandler 1875–77

Presidents, Vice Presidents, and Cabinet members (1877–1923)

President	Vice President	Secretary of State	Secretary of Treasury	Secretary of War	Secretary of Navy
Rutherford B. Hayes 1877–81	William A. Wheeler 1877–81	William M. Evarts 1877–81	John Sherman 1877–81	George W. McCrary 1877–79 Alexander Ramsey 1879–81	R. W. Thompson 1877–81 Nathan Goff, Jr. 1881
James A. Garfield 1881	Chester A. Arthur 1881	James G. Blaine 1881	William Windom 1881	Robert T. Lincoln 1881	William H. Hunt 1881
Chester A. Arthur 1881–85		F. T. Frelinghuysen 1881–85	Charles J. Folger 1881–84 Walter Q. Gresham 1884 Hugh McCulloch 1884–85	Robert T. Lincoln 1881–85	William E. Chandler 1881–85
Grover Cleveland 1885–89	T. A. Hendricks 1885	Thomas F. Bayard 1885–89	Daniel Manning 1885–87 Charles S. Fairchild 1887–89	William C. Endicott 1885–89	William C. Whitney 1885–89
Benjamin Harrison 1889–93	Levi P. Morton 1889–93	James G. Blaine 1889–92 John W. Foster 1892–93	William Windom 1889–91 Charles Foster 1891–93	Redfield Procter 1889–91 Stephen B. Elkins 1891–93	Benjamin F. Tracy 1889–93
Grover Cleveland 1893–97	Adlai E. Stevenson 1893–97	Walter Q. Gresham 1893–95 Richard Olney 1895–97	John G. Carlisle 1893–97	Daniel S. Lamont 1893–97	Hilary A. Herbert 1893–97
William McKinley 1897–1901	Garret A. Hobart 1897–1901 Theodore Roosevelt 1901	John Sherman 1897–98 William R. Day 1898 John Hay 1898–1901	Lyman J. Gage 1897–1901	Russell A. Alger 1897–99 Elihu Root 1899–1901	John D. Long 1897–1901
Theodore Roosevelt 1901–09	Charles Fairbanks 1905–09	John Hay 1901–05 Elihu Root 1905–09 Robert Bacon 1909	Lyman J. Gage 1901–02 Leslie M. Shaw 1902–07 George B. Cortelyou 1907–09	Elihu Root 1901–04 William H. Taft 1904–08 Luke E. Wright 1908–09	John D. Long 1901–02 William H. Moody 1902–04 Paul Morton 1904–05 Charles J. Bonaparte 1905–06 Victor H. Metcalf 1906–08 T. H. Newberry 1908–09
William H. Taft 1909–13	James S. Sherman 1909–13	Philander C. Knox 1909–13	Franklin MacVeagh 1909–13	Jacob M. Dickinson 1909–11 Henry L. Stimson 1911–13	George von L. Meyer 1909–13
Woodrow Wilson 1913–21	Thomas R. Marshall 1913–21	William J. Bryan 1913–15 Robert Lansing 1915–20 Bainbridge Colby 1920–21	William G. McAdoo 1913–18 Carter Glass 1918–20 David F. Houston 1920–21	Lindley M. Garrison 1913–16 Newton D. Baker 1916–21	Josephus Daniels 1913–21
Warren G. Harding 1921–23	Calvin Coolidge 1921–23	Charles E. Hughes 1921–23	Andrew W. Mellon 1921–23	John W. Weeks 1921–23	Edwin Denby 1921–23

Postmaster General	Attorney General	Secretary of Interior	Secretary of Agriculture	Secretary of Commerce and Labor	
David M. Key 1877–80 Horace Maynard 1880–81	Charles Devens 1877–81	Carl Schurz 1877–81			
Thomas L. James 1881	Wayne MacVeagh 1881	S. J. Kirkwood 1881			
Thomas L. James 1881 Timothy O. Howe 1881–83 Walter Q. Gresham 1883–84 Frank Hatton 1884–85	B. H. Brewster 1881–85	Henry M. Teller 1881–85			
William F. Vilas 1885–88 Don M. Dickinson 1888–89	A. H. Garland 1885–89	L. Q. C. Lamar 1885–88 William F. Vilas 1888–89	Norman J. Colman 1889		
John Wanamaker 1889–93	W. H. H. Miller 1889–93	John W. Noble 1889–93	Jeremiah M. Rusk 1889–93		
Wilson S. Bissel 1893–95 William L. Wilson 1895–97	Richard Olney 1893–95 Judson Harmon 1895–97	Hoke Smith 1893–96 David R. Francis 1896–97	J. Sterling Morton 1893–97		
James A. Gary 1897–98 Charles E. Smith 1898–1901	Joseph McKenna 1897–98 John W. Griggs 1898–1901 Philander C. Knox 1901	Cornelius N. Bliss 1897–98 E. A. Hitchcock 1898–1901	James Wilson 1897–1901		
Charles E. Smith 1901–02 Henry C. Payne 1902–04 Robert J. Wynne 1904–05 George B. Cortelyou 1905–07 George von L. Meyer 1907–09	Philander C. Knox 1901–04 William H. Moody 1904–06 Charles J. Bonaparte 1906–09	E. A. Hitchcock 1901–07 James R. Garfield 1907–09	James Wilson 1901–09	George B. Cortelyou 1903–04 Victor H. Metcalf 1904–06 Oscar S. Straus 1906–09	
Frank H. Hitchcock 1909–13	G. W. Wickersham 1909–13	R. A. Ballinger 1909–11 Walter L. Fisher 1911–13	James Wilson 1909–13	Charles Nagel 1909–13	
				Secretary of Commerce	**Secretary of Labor**
Albert S. Burleson 1913–21	J. C. McReynolds 1913–14 T. W. Gregory 1914–19 A. Mitchell Palmer 1919–21	Franklin K. Lane 1913–20 John B. Payne 1920–21	David F. Houston 1913–20 E. T. Meredith 1920–21	W. C. Redfield 1913–19 J. W. Alexander 1919–21	William B. Wilson 1913–21
Will H. Hays 1921–22 Hubert Work 1922–23 Harry S. New 1923	H. M. Daugherty 1921–23	Albert B. Fall 1921–23 Hubert Work 1923	Henry C. Wallace 1921–23	Herbert C. Hoover 1921–23	James J. Davis 1921–23

Presidents, Vice Presidents, and Cabinet members (1923–63)

President	Vice President	Secretary of State	Secretary of Treasury	Secretary of War	Secretary of Navy
Calvin Coolidge 1923–29	Charles G. Dawes 1925–29	Charles E. Hughes 1923–25 Frank B. Kellogg 1925–29	Andrew W. Mellon 1923–29	John W. Weeks 1923–25 Dwight F. Davis 1925–29	Edwin Denby 1923–24 Curtis D. Wilbur 1924–29
Herbert C. Hoover 1929–33	Charles Curtis 1929–33	Henry L. Stimson 1929–33	Andrew W. Mellon 1929–32 Ogden L. Mills 1932–33	James W. Good 1929 Patrick J. Hurley 1929–33	Charles F. Adams 1929–33
Franklin Delano Roosevelt 1933–45	John Nance Garner 1933–41 Henry A. Wallace 1941–45 Harry S Truman 1945	Cordell Hull 1933–44 E. R. Stettinius, Jr. 1944–45	William H. Woodin 1933–34 Henry Morgenthau, Jr. 1934–45	George H. Dern 1933–36 Harry H. Woodring 1936–40 Henry L. Stimson 1940–45	Claude A. Swanson 1933–40 Charles Edison 1940 Frank Knox 1940–44 James V. Forrestal 1944–45
Harry S Truman 1945–53	Alben W. Barkley 1949–53	James F. Byrnes 1945–47 George C. Marshall 1947–49 Dean G. Acheson 1949–53	Fred M. Vinson 1945–46 John W. Snyder 1946–53	Robert P. Patterson 1945–47 Kenneth C. Royall 1947	James V. Forrestal 1945–47
				Secretary of Defense James V. Forrestal 1947–49 Louis A. Johnson 1949–50 George C. Marshall 1950–51 Robert A. Lovett 1951–53	
Dwight D. Eisenhower 1953–61	Richard M. Nixon 1953–61	John Foster Dulles 1953–59 Christian A. Herter 1959–61	George M. Humphrey 1953–57 Robert B. Anderson 1957–61	Charles E. Wilson 1953–57 Neil H. McElroy 1957–61 Thomas S. Gates 1959–61	
John F. Kennedy 1961–63	Lyndon B. Johnson 1961–63	Dean Rusk 1961–63	C. Douglas Dillon 1961–63	Robert S. McNamara 1961–63	

Postmaster General	Attorney General	Secretary of Interior	Secretary of Agriculture	Secretary of Commerce	Secretary of Labor	Secretary of Health, Education and Welfare
Harry S. New 1923–29	H. M. Daugherty 1923–24 Harlan F. Stone 1924–25 John G. Sargent 1925–29	Hubert Work 1923–28 Roy O. West 1928–29	Henry C. Wallace 1923–24 Howard M. Gore 1924–25 W. M. Jardine 1925–29	Herbert C. Hoover 1923–28 William F. Whiting 1928–29	James J. Davis 1923–29	
Walter F. Brown 1929–33	J. D. Mitchell 1929–33	Ray L. Wilbur 1929–33	Arthur M. Hyde 1929–33	Robert P. Lamont 1929–32 Roy D. Chapin 1932–33	James J. Davis 1929–30 William N. Doak 1930–33	
James A. Farley 1933–40 Frank C. Walker 1940–45	H. S. Cummings 1933–39 Frank Murphy 1939–40 Robert Jackson 1940–41 Francis Biddle 1941–45	Harold L. Ickes 1933–45	Henry A. Wallace 1933–40 Claude R. Wickard 1940–45	Daniel C. Roper 1933–39 Harry L. Hopkins 1939–40 Jesse Jones 1940–45 Henry A. Wallace 1945	Frances Perkins 1933–45	
R. E. Hannegan 1945–47 Jesse M. Donaldson 1947–53	Tom C. Clark 1945–49 J. H. McGrath 1949–52 James P. McGranery 1952–53	Harold L. Ickes 1945–46 Julius A. Krug 1946–49 Oscar L. Chapman 1949–53	C. P. Anderson 1945–48 C. F. Brannan 1948–53	W. A. Harriman 1946–48 Charles Sawyer 1948–53	L. B. Schwellenbach 1945–48 Maurice J. Tobin 1948–53	
A. E. Summerfield 1953–61	H. Brownell, Jr. 1953–57 William P. Rogers 1957–61	Douglas McKay 1953–56 Fred Seaton 1956–61	Ezra T. Benson 1953–61	Sinclair Weeks 1953–58 Lewis L. Strauss 1958–61	Martin P. Durkin 1953 James P. Mitchell 1953–61	Oveta Culp Hobby 1953–55 Marion B. Folsom 1955–58 Arthur S. Flemming 1958–61
J. Edward Day 1961–63 John A. Gronouski 1963	Robert F. Kennedy 1961–63	Stewart L. Udall 1961–63	Orville L. Freeman 1961–63	Luther H. Hodges 1961–63	Arthur J. Goldberg 1961–62 W. Willard Wirtz 1962–63	A. H. Ribicoff 1961–62 Anthony J. Celebrezze 1962–63

Presidents, Vice Presidents, and Cabinet members, (1963–   )

President	Vice President	Secretary of State	Secretary of Treasury	Secretary of Defense	Postmaster General*	Attorney General
Lyndon B. Johnson 1963–69	Hubert H. Humphrey 1965–69	Dean Rusk 1963–69	C. Douglas Dillon 1963–65 Henry H. Fowler 1965–68 Joseph W. Barr 1968–69	Robert S. McNamara 1963–68 Clark M. Clifford 1968–69	John A. Gronouski 1963–65 Lawrence F. O'Brien 1965–68 W. Marvin Watson 1968–69	Robert F. Kennedy 1963–65 N. deB. Katzenbach 1965–67 Ramsey Clark 1967–69
Richard M. Nixon 1969–74	Spiro T. Agnew 1969–73 Gerald R. Ford 1973–74	William P. Rogers 1969–73 Henry A. Kissinger 1973–74	David M. Kennedy 1969–70 John B. Connally 1970–72 George P. Shultz 1972–74 William E. Simon 1974	Melvin R. Laird 1969–73 Elliot L. Richardson 1973 James R. Schlesinger 1973–74	Winton M. Blount 1969–71	John M. Mitchell 1969–72 Richard G. Kleindienst 1972–73 Elliot L. Richardson 1973 William B. Saxbe 1974
Gerald R. Ford 1974–77	Nelson A. Rockefeller 1974–77	Henry A. Kissinger 1974–77	William E. Simon 1974–77	James R. Schlesinger 1974–75 Donald H. Rumsfeld 1975–77		William B. Saxbe 1974–75 Edward H. Levi 1975–77
Jimmy Carter 1977–	Walter F. Mondale 1977–	Cyrus R. Vance 1977–	W. Michael Blumenthal 1977–	Harold Brown 1977–		Griffin Bell 1977–

*On July 1, 1971, the Post Office became an independent agency. After that date, the Postmaster General was no longer a member of the Cabinet.

Secretary of Interior	Secretary of Agriculture	Secretary of Commerce	Secretary of Labor	Secretary of Health, Education and Welfare	Secretary of Housing and Urban Development	Secretary of Transportation
Stewart L. Udall 1963–69	Orville L. Freeman 1963–69	Luther H. Hodges 1963–65 John T. Connor 1965–67 Alexander B. Trowbridge 1967–68 C. R. Smith 1968–69	W. Willard Wirtz 1963–69	Anthony J. Celebrezze 1963–65 John W. Gardner 1965–68 Wilbur J. Cohen 1968–69	Robert C. Weaver 1966–68 Robert C. Wood 1968–69	Alan S. Boyd 1966–69
Walter J. Hickel 1969–71 Rogers C. B. Morton 1971–74	Clifford M. Hardin 1969–71 Earl L. Butz 1971–74	Maurice H. Stans 1969–72 Peter G. Peterson 1972 Frederick B. Dent 1972–74	George P. Shultz 1969–70 James D. Hodgson 1970–73 Peter J. Brennan 1973–74	Robert H. Finch 1969–70 Elliot L. Richardson 1970–73 Caspar W. Weinberger 1973–74	George W. Romney 1969–73 James T. Lynn 1973–74	John A. Volpe 1969–73 Claude S. Brinegar 1973–74
Rogers C. B. Morton 1974–75 Stanley K. Hathaway 1975 Thomas D. Kleppe 1975–77	Earl L. Butz 1974–76	Frederick B. Dent 1974–75 Rogers C. B. Morton 1975 Elliot L. Richardson 1975–77	Peter J. Brennan 1974–75 John T. Dunlop 1975–76 W. J. Usery 1976–77	Caspar W. Weinberger 1974–75 Forrest D. Mathews 1975–77	James T. Lynn 1974–75 Carla A. Hills 1975–77	Claude S. Brinegar 1974–75 William T. Coleman 1975–77
Cecil D. Andrus 1977–	Robert Bergland 1977–	Juanita Kreps 1977–	F. Ray Marshall 1977–	Joseph Califano 1977–	Patricia Roberts Harris 1977–	Brock Adams 1977–

Source of illustrations

Source of illustrations

590: Brown Brothers
592: Culver Pictures
593: Culver Pictures
594: (*top*) Ford Archive, Henry Ford Museum; (*bottom*) Brown Brothers
595: Photoworld
597: (*both*) Brown Brothers
598: Historical Pictures Service, Inc.
600: United Press International
601: (*both*) Culver Pictures
602: The New-York Historical Society
605: Library of Congress
606: Brown Brothers
607: International News Photo
609: The Bettmann Archive
611: Museum of the City of New York
614: Courtesy, Estate of Walker Evans
616: © 1929 by The New York Times Company, reprinted by permission
617: Culver Pictures
618: Library of Congress
620: Culver Pictures
621: Culver Pictures
623: (*top*) Freelance Photographers Guild; (*bottom*) Wide World Photos
627: Wide World Photos
628: Brown Brothers
629: (*top*) Wide World Photos; (*bottom*) United Press International
630: United Press International
632: Tennessee Valley Authority
635: United Press International
636: United Press International
638: Culver Pictures
640: Culver Pictures
642: Freelance Photographers Guild
643: The Franklin D. Roosevelt Library
645: Freelance Photographers Guild
646: Library of Congress
647: Wide World Photos
649: Wide World Photos
650: Wide World Photos
651: Granger Collection
654: Brown Brothers
658: Wide World Photos
660: Brown Brothers
663: Zeitgeschichtliches Bildarchiv Heinrich Hoffmann
667: Imperial War Museum, London
668: Brown Brothers
669: Wide World Photos
671: United Press International
672: Fox Photo, Ltd.

673: Wide World Photos
674: Brown Brothers
675: The Bettmann Archive
677: Imperial War Museum, London
678: United Press International
679: Navy Department, The National Archives
682: U.S. Army Photo
684: United Press International
685: Brown Brothers
686: Culver Pictures
687: Wide World Photos
690: Culver Pictures
691: (*top*) Imperial War Museum, London; (*bottom*) U.S. Coast Guard Photo, The National Archives
695: (*top*) U.S. Navy Photo; (*bottom*) U.S. Coast Guard Photo
702: U.S. Army Photo
705: U.S. Army Photo
706: U.S. Air Force Photo
707: Cornell Capa, Magnum Photos
710: John Dominis, Time-Life Picture Agency
713: Goldberg, World Journal Tribune
715: United Press International
718: Wide World Photos
719: (*top*) United Press International; (*bottom*) Crown Copyright. Victoria and Albert Museum. Photo by John R. Freeman.
720: United Press International
721: Walter Saunders, Time-Life Picture Agency
724: United Press International
725: Wide World Photos
727: United Press International
732: United Press International
733: United Press International
736: Robert A. Isaacs
741: Eve Arnold, Magnum Photos
742: Burt Glinn, Magnum Photos
743: Wide World Photos
745: J. R. Eyerman, Time-Life Picture Agency
747: Henri Dauman, Magnum Photos
750: Nicolas Tikhomiroff, Magnum Photos
751: United Press International
753: Erick Lessing, Magnum Photos
754: Andrew St. George, Magnum Photos
755: Elliott Erwitt, Magnum Photos

757: Burt Glinn, Magnum Photos
760: Donald McCullin, Magnum Photos
762: Wide World Photos
763: Wide World Photos
764: United Press International
769: United Press International
770: United Press International
771: Henri Dauman, Magnum Photos
772: Wide World Photos
777: (*top*) United Press International; (*bottom*) Marc Riboud, Magnum Photos
778: (*both*) Wide World Photos
779: Burt Glinn, Magnum Photos
780: Official White House Photo
782: (*both*) Wide World Photos
783: Wide World Photos
786: Elliott Landy, Magnum Photos
790: Dennis Brack, Black Star
792: United Press International
793: United Press International
795: Charles Gatewood, Magnum Photos
798: Wide World Photos
800: (*top*) United Press International; (*bottom*) Wide World Photos
805: Wide World Photos
807: New York Times Pictures
808: Wide World Photos
810: Mark Godfrey, Magnum Photos
811: Mark Godfrey, Magnum Photos
812: United Press International
813: Wide World Photos
815: United Press International
817: Sepp Seitz, Magnum Photos
819: Alex Webb, Magnum Photos
821: Arthur Tress, Magnum Photos
822: Wide World Photos
823: Wide World Photos
826: Salvatore C. DiMarco, Jr.
830: Charles Gatewood, Magnum Photos
831: Sepp Seitz, Magnum Photos
834: Wide World Photos
837: United Press International
838: Paul Fusco, Magnum Photos
839: United Press International
840: (*both*) Wide World Photos
841: (*top*) United Press International; (*bottom*) Wide World Photos
843: The Metropolitan Museum of Art, George A. Hearn Fund, 1957
845: United Press International

880

Source of illustrations

Index

Boldface numbers refer to maps, charts, or illustrations. When an entry is mentioned both in the text and in the artwork of a single page, the page number is set lightface.

phy, 652, 656; and progressive reforms, 526–27; and speculation, 224, 343, 605–07, 616. *See also* Business; Industry; Laissez-faire policy; Trusts
Capone, Al, 598
Cardozo, Benjamin N., 648
Cardozo, Francis L., 372
Caribbean, 3, 32, 81, 140, 269, 284, 491, 492, 495, 502, 540, 549; and international interests, 530; naval bases in, 674. *See also* Latin America
Carlisle, Lord, 107, 108
Carlyle, Thomas, 235
Carmichael, Stokely, 782, 833
Carnegie, Andrew, 428–29, 434, 455, 503
Caroline, 229
Carpetbaggers, 366, 367, 372, 378, 383, 389, 390
Carranza, Venustiano, 549, 550, 551
Carter, James C., 484
Carter, Jimmy, 816
Carteret, Sir George, 35, 36
Cartier, Jacques, 7–8
Carver, John, 20
Casablanca Conference (*1943*), 700
Cass, Lewis, 270, 276
Castle Garden, 289
Castro, Cipriano, 530
Castro, Fidel, 748, 753, 754, 768, 784
Catchings, Waddill, 609
Cathay Company, 10
Catherine of Aragon, 9
Catholic Worker Movement, 841
Catholics. *See* Roman Catholic Church
Catt, Carrie Chapman, 452, 514
Cattle-raising, 408–11, 526
Caucus, 207
Cavelier, Robert (Sieur de la Salle), 70
Cavendish, Thomas, 12
Censorship, 567, 571, 841
Central America. *See* Caribbean; Latin America
Central Intelligence Agency (CIA), 726, 748, 752, 754, 755, 757, 764, 765, 784, 803, 809, 814
Central Pacific Railroad, 358, **421,** 422
Central Treaty Organization (CENTO), **748,** 951
Cerro Gordo, Battle of, 266, **268**
Cervera, Pascual, 500, 501
Chamberlain, Neville, 663, 668, 669, 670, 671
Chambers, Whittaker, 741
Champlain, Samuel de, 8, 70
Chancellorsville, Battle of, 345, **347**
Chandler, Zach, 467, 468
Channing, William Ellery, 235, 239, 282
Chaplin, Charlie, 601
Charity Organization Society, 450
Charles I (king of England), 18, 21, 23, 25, 30–31, 36, 42, 86
Charles II (king of England), 31, 32, 33, 36, 37, 40, 41, 42, 43, 44
Charles River Bridge v. *Warren Bridge,* 227–28
Charleston, S.C., **356–57**
Charlestown, 21; bombardment of, 97, 105
Charter of Liberties (*1701*), 35, 41
Chase, Salmon P., 271, 303, 305, 318,

330, 331, 332, 341, 361, 368–69, 374
Chase, Samuel, 158
Chattanooga, Battle of, 348
Chauncey, Charles, 65
Chautauqua movement, 455
Chavez, Cesar, 837, 838
Cheever, John, 842
Chemical defoliation, 796
Chennault, Claire, 725
Cherokee Indians, 71, 92, 215
Cherokee Outlet, 414
Chesapeake & Ohio Railroad, 326
Cheves, Langdon, 167
Cheyenne Indians, 402, 403
Chiang Kai-shek, 623, 667, 668, 697, 698, 701, 703, 704, 717, 725, 726, 747, 750, 752, 798
Chicago anarchists, 439
Chicanos, 837
Chickamauga, Battle of, 348
Chief Joseph's Rebellion, 402
Child Labor Act (*1916*), 547
Chile, 495, 550, 803, 822
China, 469, 494, 502, 504–05, 532, 533, 540, 548, 574, 657, 679, 697–98; alliance with Russia, 503; Japanese imperialism in, 623–24, 666, 678; revolution in, 725–26; and Second World War, 687, 694–97; and U.S. trade, 286–87, 369, 666; and Washington Conference, 583. *See also* China, Communist; China, Nationalist
China, Communist, 697, 725–26, 749, 761, 794–97; and Formosan Straits, 747, 752; and Korean War, 728; and peaceful coexistence, 754, 762; and Vietnam, 749–50
China, Nationalist, 697, 699, 701, 703, 704, 715, 717, 725, 726, 728, 747, 750, 752, 798
Chinese Eastern Railway, 623
Chisholm, Shirley, 833
Chisholm v. *Georgia,* 150
Chisum, John, 410
Chivington, John M., 402
Chivington massacre, **402**
Choate, Joseph H., 485
Chou En-lai, 798, 799
Chouart, Médart (Sieur de Groseilliers), 71
Christian Science. *See* Church of Christ, Scientist
Christian Socialists, 487
Church, 63–66, 745, 841; and reform, 234, 452–54; and state, 113. *See also* Religion; *individual denominations*
Church of Christ, Scientist, 453
Church of England, 9, 10, 19, 21, 454. *See also* Anglican Church; Episcopal Church
Church of Jesus Christ of Latter Day Saints, 238
Churchill, Winston, 668, 671, 672, 673, 674, 679, 688–89, 690, 691, 697, 701, 705, 712, 714, 716, 720; and Atlantic Charter, 677–78, 699–700; and Yalta Conference, 702–04
Cincinnati, 178–79
Cities, 829–32; black ghettos in, 781, 783, 837; disorders in, 781, 783, 805; economic origins of, 60–62; growth of,

191, 289, 291, 357, 443–48, 511; and machine politics, 371–72, 448, 449–50; population in, 781, 829; and schools, 454, 832; and slums, 447–48, 773. *See also* Government, municipal
Citizenship, 306, 307, 363
Civil liberties, 149–50, 375, 567, 568, 580, 685; and Supreme Court, 744; and Truman, 730, 731
Civil rights, 362, 363, 375, 742–43, 772, 781, 783, 833, 835; and L. B. Johnson, 772, 783; and Kennedy, 770–71; and Truman, 722–23
Civil Rights Act: (*1866*), 363, 364, 384; (*1875*), 375, 384; (*1957*), 743; (*1964*), 772
Civil Rights Cases, 384
Civil service, 207, 212, 380, 450, 468. *See also* Spoils system
Civil Service Commission, 471, 472, 473
Civil Service Act (*1883*), 467, 471–72
Civil War, 277, 300, 320, 322–52, 378, 495; alignment of states, **324;** campaigns of, 332–43, 345–53; casualties during, 796; demobilization after, 358; economic consequences of, 357–58, 418, 419–20; and Emancipation Proclamation, 340–42; and England, 332, 337–38; financing of, 331–32; and Mexico, 369; mobilization for, 326–32; naval operations of, 335–36; and re-election of Lincoln, 351–52; and slavery issue, 338–39. *See also* Confederacy; Secession; Union
Civilian Conservation Corps (CCC), 653
Clark, Champ, 543
Clark, George Rogers, 162
Clark, J. Reuben, 621
Clark, James Freeman, 235
Clark, William, 162, 259
Clarke, Arthur C., 845
Classes, social, 200, 205, 251; and distribution of wealth, 433–36; divisions among, 200, 458; middle class, 450, 520, 521, 655, 806–07; mobility of, 68–69, 113, 205, **206;** and progressivism, 518, 521
Clay, Henry, 167, 212, 214, 216, 219, 223, 371; "American System" of, 179–80, 181, 184, 186, 208, 209, 210, 216, 222, 228, 263; and Compromise of *1850*, 273, 274; and compromise tariff, 219; and election of *1844*, 262; and Latin American revolutions, 185; and Missouri Compromise, 197; and National Republicans, 205; and Treaty of Ghent, 174; and War of *1812*, 168, 174, 175
Clay, Lucius, 721
Clayton, John M. 285, 286
Clayton Act (*1914*), 547, 586
Clayton-Bulwer Treaty (*1850*), 285
Cleaver, Eldridge, 783, 840, 841
Clemenceau, Georges, 571, 573
Clemens, Samuel L., 407, 460–61, 503, 712
Cleveland, Grover, 472–73, 503; Administration of, 425, 440, 464, 473–74, 481–84, 485–86, 492, 495–96, 496–97, 498
Clifford, Clark, 722, 777, 779

Clinton, De Witt, 169, 190
Clinton, George, 163
Clinton, Henry, 97, 105, 108–09, 110,111
Clipper ships, 287–88
Cloning, 845
Coal mining, 358, 523–24, 578, 585, 684, 817
Cochran, Thomas C., 420
Coexistence, 718–19, 729, 747–48, 751, 755, 761
Cohens v. *Virginia,* 184
Cohn, Roy, 741, 742
Cold Harbor, Battle of, 349
Cold War, 710–33, 747, 748–49, 751, 754–56, 768; absolutist policy of, 748–49; beginnings of, 714–16; and detente, 768, 799–801, 803; and Kennedy, 761–62; and Moscow Summit, 754–55; and nationalism, 749; and nuclear-test-ban treaty, 768
Cole, Nathan, 64
Coleridge, Samuel Taylor, 235
Colfax, Schuyler, 370, 371
Collective bargaining, 438, 512, 637, 650
Colleges and universities, 66, 113, 200, 242, 244, 452, 456–57, 777, 783–84, 832, 835; women on faculties of, 833. *See also* Campus revolt; Draft
Colleton, Sir John, 36
Collier, John, 404, 838
Colombia, 285, 530, 531, 549, 582–83, 764
Colonial life: and education, 66–68; and government, 57–58, 62–63; on plantation and farm, 51–56, 58–60; and religion, 62–66; in towns and cities, 56–58, 60–62
Colonies, early American, 10–25; assemblies in, 56, 62–63, 114, 116; corporate, 47; county government in, 56, 59–60; and Declaration of Independence, 99, 100; earliest European settlements in, 7–8; East-West split in, 83–84; governors in, 47, 82, 94, 95; imperial authority over, 82–83; life in, 51–62; political strife in, 41–48; post-Revolutionary governments of, 114–15; private property in, 113–14; proprietary, 24–25, 34, 57; religion as factor in proliferation of, 18–21; during Restoration, 34–41; royal, 35, 36, 47; towns in, 56, 58; unity of, 88, 98, 100. *See also individual colonies*
Colorado, 402; statehood of, **406,** 452
Colored Farmers' National Alliance and Co-operative Union, 478
Colson, Charles, 809
Columbia Broadcasting System, 745
Columbian Exposition (*1893*), 433, 459–60, 483
Columbus, Christopher, 4–5, 7
Comanche Indians, 401, 402
Cominform, 715
Comintern, 701, 715
Commission on the Causes and Prevention of Violence, 831
Commission on Civil Disorders, 783
Commission on Income Maintenance, 805
Commission on Intergovernmental Relations, 740

Committee on Government Operations (Senate), 741
Committee on Public Information (CPI), 567
Committee on Un-American Activities, 651
Committee to Defend America by Aiding the Allies, 676
Committee to Re-Elect the President (CREEP), 808
Committees of Correspondence, 92, 93, 94
Commodity Credit Corporation, 479*n*
Common law, 201*n*
Common Market, 720, 766–67
Commons, John R., 518, 599, 609, 610
Commonwealth v. *Hunt,* 296
Communes, 785
Communism, 579, 626, 715, 718, 726, 757; and capitalism, 700, 716, 755; containment of vs. coexistence with, 718–19, 729, 747–48, 751, 755, 761; and Red scare, 579–81, 730–31, 740–41; resistance to, 714, 715, 716, 729; and uncommitted nations, 749; and Yalta Conference, 402–04. *See also* Cold War; Soviet Union
Communist Labor party, 579
Communist Party of America, 579, 600, 626, 631, 652, 671
Communist party congresses: Nineteenth, 749; Twentieth, 754
Communitarianism, 245, 785
Community Action program, 773
Comprehensive Employment and Training Act, 820
Compromise of *1850,* 272–75, 276, 277, 300
Comstock, Henry, 406
Concord, Battle of, 96–97
Confederacy, 296, 300, 316, 346; and amnesty, 360, 373–74; and border states, 324–26; Congress of, 325, 343; and conscription, 328–29; Constitution of, 327; and England, 332, 337–38; preparation for war, 328–29; and readmission of states, 350, 357, 360–61, **365;** and secession, 272, 274, 277, 313, 315, 316, 317, 324–26, 358; and surrender, 353. *See also* Civil War
Confederation of Industrial Organizations, 479
Conference on Communication with Extra-Terrestrial Intelligence, 846
Conference for Progressive Political Action, 599
Confiscation Act (*1862*), 339
Conglomerates, 820
Congo, 749
Congregationalists, 19, 21, 63, 92, 234, 237, 452
Congress, U.S., 116, 119, 125, 126, 183, 247, 269, 313, 359–60, 361–62, 363, 364, 369, 467, 475, 476, 644, 645, 722–23, 725, 806, 814, 815
Congress of Industrial Organizations (CIO), 516, 649, 650, 652, 653
Congress of Racial Equality (CORE), 606, 770, 782, 836
Congressional Black Caucus (*1970*), 836
Congressional Budget and Impounding Control Act (*1974*), 814

Congressional Unions, 515
Conkling, Roscoe, 371, 380, 466, 467, 468, 469, 470, 471
Connally, John B., 804
Connecticut, colony of, 24, 41, 42, 46, 47, 76, 114, 116, 121; charter of, 41; dispute with Pennsylvania, 92; in Dominion of New England, 44–46; settling of, 24
Connor, Eugene, 770
Conquistadors, 5–6
Conscience Whigs, 266, 271, 274
Consciousness III, 786
Conscription Act: Confederate (*1862*), 328; Union (*1863*), 331
Conservation, 526, 640
Conservatism: in government, 468–76, 592, 722; and laissez-faire doctrine, 433–36, 469; and New Deal, 655
Conservative party, Southern Democratic, 373, 383–84, 385, 389–90, 393, 466, 651
Constitution, English, 115
Constitution, state, 114–15; in post-Civil War South, 366
Constitution, U.S., 115–16, 124–28, 150, 247, 269, 435; amending of, 126; and Congress, 126, 814; and executive, 125, 126; and federal and state powers, 126; and judicial review, 227; liberal construction of, 227, 744; opposition to, 127–28; ratification of, 127–28. *See also* Amendments, constitutional; Articles of Confederation; Bill of Rights
Constitutional Convention (*1787*), 122, 124–28, 134, 183, 196
Constitutional Union party, 314
Consumers, 823
Continental Army: enlistment of, 103; establishment of, 98; in Revolutionary War, 103–12
Continental Congress, First, 94–96, 98; final resolutions of, 95; moderates at, 95; radical contingency of, 95
Continental Congress, Second, 98–100, 115, 121; and Continental Army, 98; and French alliance, 107–08, 111–12; and independence, 99; and peace negotiations, 112; in Revolution, 118; voting in, 124-25
Conventions, national nominating, 207, 222
Cook, James, 259
Cooke, Jay, 331–32, 374, 423
Coolidge, Calvin, 578, 581; Administration of, 591–606, 610–12; and business, 591–92, 594–95, 605–07, 610–11; and internationalism, 603–04; and Latin American affairs, 602–03
Coolidge, Grace, 591
Cooper, Anthony Ashley, 36, 37
Cooper, James Fenimore, 200, 282
Copernicus, Nicolaus, 67
Copperheads, 360, 364
Coral Sea, Battle of the, 695, **697**
Cornell, Alonzo B., 469
Corning, Erastus, 292
Cornwallis, Lord Charles, 105, 110, 111
Coronado, Vasquez, 7
Corporations, 199, 200, 227, 295, 435, 745, 820–23

902

Index

E 9 0
F 1
G 2
H 3
I 4
J 5